Quantum Computing for Computer Scientists

The multidisciplinary field of quantum computing strives to exploit some of the uncanny aspects of quantum mechanics to expand our computational horizons. *Quantum Computing for Computer Scientists* takes readers on a tour of this fascinating area of cutting-edge research. Written in an accessible yet rigorous fashion, this book employs ideas and techniques familiar to every student of computer science. The reader is not expected to have any advanced mathematics or physics background. After presenting the necessary prerequisites, the material is organized to look at different aspects of quantum computing from the specific standpoint of computer science. There are chapters on computer architecture, algorithms, programming languages, theoretical computer science, cryptography, information theory, and hardware. The text has step-by-step examples, more than two hundred exercises with solutions, and programming drills that bring the ideas of quantum computing alive for today's computer science students and researchers.

Noson S. Yanofsky, PhD, is an Associate Professor in the Department of Computer and Information Science at Brooklyn College, City University of New York and at the PhD Program in Computer Science at The Graduate Center of CUNY.

Mirco A. Mannucci, PhD, is the founder and CEO of HoloMathics, LLC, a research and development company with a focus on innovative mathematical modeling. He also serves as Adjunct Professor of Computer Science at George Mason University and the University of Maryland.

QUANTUM COMPUTING FOR
COMPUTER SCIENTISTS

Noson S. Yanofsky
Brooklyn College, City University of New York

and

Mirco A. Mannucci
HoloMathics, LLC

CAMBRIDGE
UNIVERSITY PRESS

CAMBRIDGE
UNIVERSITY PRESS

32 Avenue of the Americas, New York NY 10013-2473, USA

Cambridge University Press is part of the University of Cambridge.

It furthers the University's mission by disseminating knowledge in the pursuit of education, learning, and research at the highest international levels of excellence.

www.cambridge.org
Information on this title: www.cambridge.org/9780521879965

First published 2008
Reprinted with corrections 2013

A catalog record for this publication is available from the British Library.

Library of Congress Cataloging in Publication data
Yanofsky, Noson S., 1967–
Quantum computing for computer scientists / Noson S. Yanofsky and Mirco A. Mannucci.
    p. cm.
Includes bibliographical references and index.
ISBN 978-0-521-87996-5 (hardback)
1. Quantum computers. I. Mannucci, Mirco A., 1960– II. Title.
QA76.889.Y35 2008
004.1–dc22   2008020507

ISBN 978-0-521-87996-5 Hardback

Dedicated to
Moishe and Sharon Yanofsky
and
to the memory of
Luigi and Antonietta Mannucci

*Wisdom is one thing: to know the thought by which
all things are directed through all things.*

ἓν τὸ σοφόν, ἐπίστασθαι γνώμην,
ὅκη κυβερνᾶται πάντα διὰ πάντων.

Heraclitus of Ephesus (535–475 BCE)
as quoted in Diogenes Laertius's
Lives and Opinions of Eminent Philosophers
Book IX, 1.

Contents

Preface

Quantum computing is a fascinating new field at the intersection of computer science, mathematics, and physics, which strives to harness some of the uncanny aspects of quantum mechanics to broaden our computational horizons. This book presents some of the most exciting and interesting topics in quantum computing. Along the way, there will be some amazing facts about the universe in which we live and about the very notions of information and computation.

The text you hold in your hands has a distinct flavor from most of the other currently available books on quantum computing. First and foremost, we do not assume that our reader has much of a mathematics or physics background. This book should be readable by anyone who is in or beyond their second year in a computer science program. We have written this book specifically with computer scientists in mind, and tailored it accordingly: we assume a bare minimum of mathematical sophistication, a first course in discrete structures, and a healthy level of curiosity. Because this text was written specifically for computer people, in addition to the many exercises throughout the text, we added many programming drills. These are a hands-on, fun way of learning the material presented and getting a real feel for the subject.

The calculus-phobic reader will be happy to learn that derivatives and integrals are virtually absent from our text. Quite simply, we avoid differentiation, integration, and all higher mathematics by carefully selecting only those topics that are critical to a basic introduction to quantum computing. Because we are focusing on the fundamentals of quantum computing, we can restrict ourselves to the finite-dimensional mathematics that is required. This turns out to be not much more than manipulating vectors and matrices with complex entries. Surprisingly enough, the lion's share of quantum computing can be done without the intricacies of advanced mathematics.

Nevertheless, we hasten to stress that this is a technical textbook. We are not writing a popular science book, nor do we substitute hand waving for rigor or mathematical precision.

Most other texts in the field present a primer on quantum mechanics in all its glory. Many assume some knowledge of classical mechanics. We do not make these assumptions. We only discuss what is needed for a basic understanding of quantum computing *as a field of research in its own right,* although we cite sources for learning more about advanced topics.

There are some who consider quantum computing to be solely within the domain of physics. Others think of the subject as purely mathematical. We stress the computer science aspect of quantum computing.

It is not our intention for this book to be the definitive treatment of quantum computing. There are a few topics that we do not even touch, and there are several others that we approach briefly, not exhaustively. As of this writing, the bible of quantum computing is Nielsen and Chuang's magnificent *Quantum Computing and Quantum Information* (2000). Their book contains almost everything known about quantum computing at the time of its publication. We would like to think of our book as a useful first step that can prepare the reader for that text.

FEATURES

This book is almost entirely self-contained. We do not demand that the reader come armed with a large toolbox of skills. Even the subject of complex numbers, which is taught in high school, is given a fairly comprehensive review.

The book contains many solved problems and easy-to-understand descriptions. We do not merely present the theory; rather, we explain it and go through several examples. The book also contains many exercises, which we strongly recommend the serious reader should attempt to solve. There is no substitute for rolling up one's sleeves and doing some work!

We have also incorporated plenty of programming drills throughout our text. These are hands-on exercises that can be carried out on your laptop to gain a better understanding of the concepts presented here (they are also a great way of having fun). We hasten to point out that we are entirely language-agnostic. The student should write the programs in the language that feels most comfortable. We are also paradigm-agnostic. If declarative programming is your favorite method, go for it. If object-oriented programming is your game, use that. The programming drills build on one another. Functions created in one programming drill will be used and modified in later drills. Furthermore, in Appendix C, we show how to make little quantum computing emulators with MATLAB or how to use a ready-made one. (Our choice of MATLAB was dictated by the fact that it makes very easy-to-build, quick-and-dirty prototypes, thanks to its vast amount of built-in mathematical tools.)

This text appears to be the first to handle quantum programming languages in a significant way. Until now, there have been only research papers and a few surveys on the topic. Chapter 7 describes the basics of this expanding field: perhaps some of our readers will be inspired to contribute to quantum programming!

This book also contains several appendices that are important for further study:

■ Appendix A takes readers on a tour of major papers in quantum computing. This bibliographical essay was written by Jill Cirasella, Computational Sciences Specialist at the Brooklyn College Library. In addition to having a master's degree in library and information science, Jill has a master's degree in logic, for which she wrote a thesis on classical and quantum graph algorithms. This dual background uniquely qualifies her to suggest and describe further readings.

- Appendix B contains the answers to some of the exercises in the text. Other solutions will also be found on the book's Web page. We strongly urge students to do the exercises on their own and then check their answers against ours.
- Appendix C uses MATLAB, the popular mathematical environment and an established industry standard, to show how to carry out most of the mathematical operations described in this book. MATLAB has scores of routines for manipulating complex matrices: we briefly review the most useful ones and show how the reader can quickly perform a few quantum computing experiments with almost no effort, using the freely available MATLAB quantum emulator Quack.
- Appendix D, also by Jill Cirasella, describes how to use online resources to keep up with developments in quantum computing. Quantum computing is a fast-moving field, and this appendix offers guidelines and tips for finding relevant articles and announcements.
- Appendix E is a list of possible topics for student presentations. We give brief descriptions of different topics that a student might present before a class of his peers. We also provide some hints about where to start looking for materials to present.

ORGANIZATION

The book begins with two chapters of mathematical preliminaries. Chapter 1 contains the basics of complex numbers, and Chapter 2 deals with complex vector spaces. Although much of Chapter 1 is currently taught in high school, we feel that a review is in order. Much of Chapter 2 will be known by students who have had a course in linear algebra. We deliberately did not relegate these chapters to an appendix at the end of the book because the mathematics is necessary to understand what is really going on. A reader who knows the material can safely skip the first two chapters. She might want to skim over these chapters and then return to them as a reference, using the index and the table of contents to find specific topics.

Chapter 3 is a gentle introduction to some of the ideas that will be encountered throughout the rest of the text. Using simple models and simple matrix multiplication, we demonstrate some of the fundamental concepts of quantum mechanics, which are then formally developed in Chapter 4. From there, Chapter 5 presents some of the basic architecture of quantum computing. Here one will find the notions of a qubit (a quantum generalization of a bit) and the quantum analog of logic gates.

Once Chapter 5 is understood, readers can safely proceed to their choice of Chapters 6 through 11. Each chapter takes its title from a typical course offered in a computer science department. The chapters look at that subfield of quantum computing from the perspective of the given course. These chapters are almost totally independent of one another. We urge the readers to study the particular chapter that corresponds to their favorite course. Learn topics that you like first. From there proceed to other chapters.

Figure 0.1 summarizes the dependencies of the chapters.

One of the hardest topics tackled in this text is that of considering two quantum systems and combining them, or "entangled" quantum systems. This is done mathematically in Section 2.7. It is further motivated in Section 3.4 and formally presented in Section 4.5. The reader might want to look at these sections together.

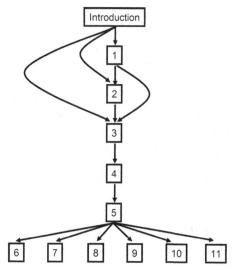

Figure 0.1. Chapter dependencies.

There are many ways this book can be used as a text for a course. We urge instructors to find their own way. May we humbly suggest the following three plans of action:

(1) A class that provides some depth might involve the following: Go through Chapters 1, 2, 3, 4, and 5. Armed with that background, study the entirety of Chapter 6 ("Algorithms") in depth. One can spend at least a third of a semester on that chapter. After wrestling a bit with quantum algorithms, the student will get a good feel for the entire enterprise.

(2) If breadth is preferred, pick and choose one or two sections from each of the advanced chapters. Such a course might look like this: (1), 2, 3, 4.1, 4.4, 5, 6.1, 7.1, 9.1, 10.1, 10.2, and 11. This will permit the student to see the broad outline of quantum computing and then pursue his or her own path.

(3) For a more advanced class (a class in which linear algebra and some mathematical sophistication is assumed), we recommend that students be told to read Chapters 1, 2, and 3 on their own. A nice course can then commence with Chapter 4 and plow through most of the remainder of the book.

If this is being used as a text in a classroom setting, we strongly recommend that the students make presentations. There are selected topics mentioned in Appendix E. There is no substitute for student participation!

Although we have tried to include many topics in this text, inevitably some others had to be left out. Here are a few that we omitted because of space considerations:

- many of the more complicated proofs in Chapter 8,
- results about oracle computation,
- the details of the (quantum) Fourier transforms, and
- the latest hardware implementations.

We give references for further study on these, as well as other subjects, throughout the text.

ANCILLARIES

We are going to maintain a Web page for the text at

www.sci.brooklyn.cuny.edu/∼noson/qctext.html/

The Web page will contain

- ▓ periodic updates to the book,
- ▓ links to interesting books and articles on quantum computing,
- ▓ some answers to certain exercises not solved in Appendix B, and
- ▓ errata.

The reader is encouraged to send any and all corrections to

noson@sci.brooklyn.cuny.edu

Help us make this textbook better!

ACKNOLWEDGMENTS

Both of us had the great privilege of writing our doctoral theses under the gentle guidance of the recently deceased Alex Heller. Professor Heller wrote the following[1] about his teacher Samuel "Sammy" Eilenberg and Sammy's mathematics:

> As I perceived it, then, Sammy considered that the highest value in mathematics was to be found, not in specious depth nor in the overcoming of overwhelming difficulty, but rather in providing the definitive clarity that would illuminate its underlying order.

This never-ending struggle to bring out the underlying order of mathematical structures was always Professor Heller's everlasting goal, and he did his best to pass it on to his students. We have gained greatly from his clarity of vision and his view of mathematics, but we also saw, embodied in a man, the classical and sober ideal of contemplative life at its very best. We both remain eternally grateful to him.

While at the City University of New York, we also had the privilege of interacting with one of the world's foremost logicians, Professor Rohit Parikh, a man whose seminal contributions to the field are only matched by his enduring commitment to promote younger researchers' work. Besides opening fascinating vistas to us, Professor Parikh encouraged us more than once to follow new directions of thought. His continued professional and personal guidance are greatly appreciated.

We both received our Ph.D.'s from the Department of Mathematics in The Graduate Center of the City University of New York. We thank them for providing us with a warm and friendly environment in which to study and learn real mathematics. The first author also thanks the entire Brooklyn College family and, in particular, the Computer and Information Science Department for being supportive and very helpful in this endeavor.

---

[1] See page 1349 of Bass et al. (1998).

Several faculty members of Brooklyn College and The Graduate Center were kind enough to read and comment on parts of this book: Michael Anshel, David Arnow, Jill Cirasella, Dayton Clark, Eva Cogan, Jim Cox, Scott Dexter, Edgar Feldman, Fred Gardiner, Murray Gross, Chaya Gurwitz, Keith Harrow, Jun Hu, Yedidyah Langsam, Peter Lesser, Philipp Rothmaler, Chris Steinsvold, Alex Sverdlov, Aaron Tenenbaum, Micha Tomkiewicz, Al Vasquez, Gerald Weiss, and Paula Whitlock. Their comments have made this a better text. Thank you all!

We were fortunate to have had many students of Brooklyn College and The Graduate Center read and comment on earlier drafts: Shira Abraham, Rachel Adler, Ali Assarpour, Aleksander Barkan, Sayeef Bazli, Cheuk Man Chan, Wei Chen, Evgenia Dandurova, Phillip Dreizen, C. S. Fahie, Miriam Gutherc, Rave Harpaz, David Herzog, Alex Hoffnung, Matthew P. Johnson, Joel Kammet, Serdar Kara, Karen Kletter, Janusz Kusyk, Tiziana Ligorio, Matt Meyer, James Ng, Severin Ngnosse, Eric Pacuit, Jason Schanker, Roman Shenderovsky, Aleksandr Shnayderman, Rose B. Sigler, Shai Silver, Justin Stallard, Justin Tojeira, John Ma Sang Tsang, Sadia Zahoor, Mark Zelcer, and Xiaowen Zhang. We are indebted to them.

Many other people looked over parts or all of the text: Scott Aaronson, Stefano Bettelli, Adam Brandenburger, Juan B. Climent, Anita Colvard, Leon Ehrenpreis, Michael Greenebaum, Miriam Klein, Eli Kravits, Raphael Magarik, John Maiorana, Domenico Napoletani, Vaughan Pratt, Suri Raber, Peter Selinger, Evan Siegel, Thomas Tradler, and Jennifer Whitehead. Their criticism and helpful ideas are deeply appreciated.

Thanks to Peter Rohde for creating and making available to everyone his MATLAB q-emulator Quack and also for letting us use it in our appendix. We had a good deal of fun playing with it, and we hope our readers will too.

Besides writing two wonderful appendices, our friendly neighborhood librarian, Jill Cirasella, was always just an e-mail away with helpful advice and support. Thanks, Jill!

A very special thanks goes to our editor at Cambridge University Press, Heather Bergman, for believing in our project right from the start, for guiding us through this book, and for providing endless support in all matters. This book would not exist without her. Thanks, Heather!

We had the good fortune to have a truly stellar editor check much of the text many times. Karen Kletter is a great friend and did a magnificent job. We also appreciate that she refrained from killing us every time we handed her altered drafts that she had previously edited.

But, of course, all errors are our own!

This book could not have been written without the help of my daughter, Hadassah. She added meaning, purpose, and joy.

N.S.Y.

My dear wife, Rose, and our two wondrous and tireless cats, Ursula and Buster, contributed in no small measure to melting my stress away during the long and painful hours of writing and editing: to them my gratitude and love. (Ursula is a scientist cat and will read this book. Buster will just shred it with his powerful claws.)

M.A.M.

Introduction

THE FEATURES OF THE QUANTUM WORLD

In order to learn quantum computing, it is first necessary to become familiar with some basic facts about the quantum world. In this introduction, some unique features of quantum mechanics are introduced, as well as the way they influence the tale we are about to tell.[2]

From Real Numbers to Complex Numbers

Quantum mechanics is different from most other branches of science in that it uses complex numbers in a fundamental way. Complex numbers were originally created as a mathematical curiosity: $i = \sqrt{-1}$ was the asserted "imaginary" solution to the polynomial equation $x^2 = -1$. As time went on, an entire mathematical edifice was constructed with these "imaginary" numbers. Complex numbers have kept lonely mathematicians busy for centuries, while physicists successfully ignored these abstract creations. However, things changed with the systematic study of wave mechanics. After the introduction of Fourier analysis, researchers learned that a compact way to represent a wave was by using functions of complex numbers. As it turns out, this was an important step on the road to using complex numbers in quantum theory. Early quantum mechanics was largely based on wave mechanics.

At first glance, we do not seem to experience complex numbers in the "real world." The length of a rod is a real number, not a complex number. The temperature outside today is $73°$, not $(32 - 14i)°$. The amount of time a chemical process takes is 32.543 seconds, not $-14.65i$ seconds. One might wonder what possible role complex numbers can have in any discussion of the physical world. It will soon become apparent that they play an important, indeed an essential, role in quantum mechanics. We shall explore complex numbers in Chapters 1 and 2 of the text.

---

[2] This Introduction is not the proper place for technical details. Some of the concepts are covered in the text and some of them can be found only in quantum mechanics textbooks. See the end of Chapter 4 for some recommendations of easy, yet detailed, introductions to quantum physics.

From Single States to Superpositions of States

In order to survive in this world, human beings, as infants, must learn that every object exists in a unique place and in a well-defined state, even when we are not looking at it. Although this is true for large objects, quantum mechanics tells us that it is false for objects that are very small. A microscopic object can "hazily" be in more than one place at one time. Rather than an object's being in one position or another, we say that it is in a "superposition," i.e., in some sense, it is simultaneously in more than one location at the same time. Not only is spatial position subject to such "haziness" but so are other familiar physical properties, like energy, momentum, and certain properties that are unique to the quantum world, such as "spin."

We do not actually see superposition of states. Every time we look, or more properly, "measure," a superposition of states, it "collapses" to a single well-defined state. Nevertheless, before we measure it, it is in many states at the same time.

One is justified in greeting these claims with skepticism. After all, how can one believe something different from what every infant knows? However, we will describe certain experiments that show that this is exactly what happens.

From Locality to Nonlocality

Central to modern science is the notion that objects are directly affected only by nearby objects or forces. In order to determine why a phenomenon occurs at a certain place, one must examine all the phenomena and forces near[3] that place. This is called "locality," i.e., the laws of physics work in a local way. One of the most remarkable aspects of quantum mechanics is that its laws predict certain effects that work in a nonlocal manner. Two particles can be connected or "entangled" in such a way that an action performed on one of them can have an immediate effect on the other particle light-years away. This "spooky action at a distance," to use Einstein's colorful expression, was one of the most shocking discoveries of quantum mechanics.

From Deterministic Laws to Probabilistic Laws

To which specific state will a superposition of states collapse when it is measured? Whereas in other branches of physics the laws are deterministic,[4] i.e., there is a unique outcome to every experiment, the laws of quantum mechanics state that we can only know the probability of the outcome. This, again, might seem dubious. It was doubted by the leading researchers of the time. Einstein himself was skeptical and coined the colorful expression "God does not play dice with the Universe" to express this. However, because of repeated experimental confirmations, the probabilistic nature of quantum mechanics is no longer in question.

---

[3] By "near" we mean anything close enough to affect the object. In physics jargon, anything in the past light cone of the object.

[4] Statistical mechanics being one major exception.

From Certainty to Uncertainty

The laws of quantum mechanics also inform us that there are inherent limitations to the amount of knowledge that one can ascertain about a physical system. The primary example of such a limitation is the famous "Heisenberg's uncertainty principle."

There are other important features of the quantum world that we shall not explore here. These different features were all motivating forces behind the advent of quantum computing. Rather than an historical review of how these features affected quantum computing, let us look at several areas in computer science and see how the aforementioned features affected each of those areas.[5]

THE IMPLICATIONS OF THE QUANTUM WORLD ON COMPUTER SCIENCE

Architecture

The concept of superposition will be used to generalize the notion of bit to its quantum analog, the qubit. Whereas a bit can be in either one of two states, superposition will allow a qubit to be both states simultaneously. Putting many qubits together gives us quantum registers. It is this superposition that is the basis for quantum computing's real power. Rather than being in one state at a time, a quantum computer can be in many states simultaneously.

After generalizing the notion of bit, the notion of a gate that manipulates bits will be extended to the quantum setting. We shall have quantum gates that manipulate qubits. Quantum gates will have to follow the dynamics of quantum operations. In particular, certain quantum operations are reversible, and hence certain quantum gates will have to be reversible.[6]

Algorithms

The field of quantum algorithms uses superposition in a fundamental way. Rather than having a computer in one state at a time, one employs that aspect of the quantum world to place a quantum computer in many states simultaneously. One might think of this as massive parallelism. This needs special care: we cannot measure the computer while it is in this superposition because measuring it would collapse it to a single position. Our algorithms will start with the quantum computer in a single position. We shall then delicately place it in a superposition of many states. From there, we manipulate the qubits in a specified way. Finally, (some of) the qubits are measured. The measurement will collapse the qubits to the desired bits, which will be our output.

---

[5] For an historical view of quantum computing as seen through the major papers that launched the subject, see Appendix A.

[6] It so happens that reversible computation has a long history predating quantum computing. This history will be reviewed in due course.

Entanglement will also play a role in quantum computing, as the qubits can be entangled. By measuring some of them, others automatically reach the desired position.

Consider searching for a particular object in an unordered array. A classical algorithm examines the first entry in the array, then the second entry, and so on. The algorithm stops when either the object is found or the end of the array is reached. So for an array with n elements, in the worst-case scenario, an algorithm would have to look at n entries of the array.

Now imagine a computer that uses superposition. Rather than having the machine look at this entry or that entry, let it look at *all* entries simultaneously. This will result in a fantastic speedup. It turns out that such a quantum computer will be able to find the object in $\sqrt{n}$ queries to the array. This is one of the first quantum algorithms and is called "Grover's algorithm."

Another algorithm that demonstrates the power and usefulness of quantum computing is Shor's algorithm for factoring numbers. The usual algorithm to factor a number involves looking at many possible factors of the number until a true factor is found. Shor's algorithm uses superposition (and a touch of number theory) to look at many possible factors simultaneously.

Shor's algorithm is partially based on earlier quantum algorithms that were created to solve slightly contrived problems. Although these earlier algorithms (Deutch, Deutch-Joza, and Simon's periodicity algorithm) solve artificial problems, we shall study them so that we can learn different techniques of quantum software design.

Programming Languages

Algorithms must eventually develop into concrete software if they are to be useful in real-life applications. The bridge that makes this step possible is programming. Quantum computing is no exception: researchers in the field have started designing quantum programming languages that will enable future generations of programmers to take control of quantum hardware and implement new quantum algorithms. We shall introduce a brief survey of programming languages (for the first time, to our knowledge, in a quantum computing textbook), starting with quantum assembler and progressing to high-level quantum programming, in particular quantum functional programming.

Theoretical Computer Science

The goal of theoretical computer science is to formalize what engineers have done, and more important, to formalize what the engineers *cannot* do. Such an analysis is carried out by describing and classifying theoretical models of computation. The superposition of quantum mechanics has a vague feel of nondeterminism that theoretical computer scientists have used (of course, nondeterminism is a purely fictional concept and superposition is an established fact of the physical world). The indeterminacy of which state the superposition will collapse to is related to a probabilistic computation. We will be led to generalize the definition of a Turing machine to that of a quantum Turing machine. With a clear definition in place, we will be able to classify and relate all these different ideas.

We shall not only be interested in what a quantum Turing machine can do. We are also interested in the question of efficiency. This brings us to quantum complexity theory. Definitions of quantum complexity classes will be given and will be related to other well-known complexity classes.

Cryptography

Indeterminacy and superposition will be used in quantum versions of public key distribution protocols. The fact that a measurement disturbs a quantum state shall be used to detect the presence of an eavesdropper listening in on (measuring) a communication channel. Such detection is not easily achievable in classical cryptography. Whereas classical public key distribution protocols rely on the fact that certain inverse functions are computationally hard to calculate, quantum key distribution protocols are based on the fact that certain laws of quantum physics are true. It is this strength that makes quantum cryptography so interesting and powerful.

There is also a public key protocol that uses entanglement in a fundamental way. Related to cryptography is teleportation. In teleportation, a state of a system is transported as opposed to a message. The teleportation protocol uses entangled particles that can be separated across the universe.

The most amazing part of quantum cryptography is that it is not only a theoretical curiosity. There are, in fact, actual commercially available quantum cryptography devices currently in use.

Information Theory

It is impossible to discuss topics such as compression, transmission, and storage, without mentioning information. Information theory, now an established field, was introduced by Claude Shannon in the forties, and has developed a vast array of techniques and ideas that find their use in computer science and engineering. As this book deals with quantum computation, it is imperative that we ask: is there a satisfactory notion of quantum information? What is the information content encoded by a stream of qubits? It turns out that such notions exist. Just as classical information is related to measures of order (the so-called entropy of a source of signals), quantum information is paired with the notion of quantum entropy. We shall explore, chiefly through examples, how order and information in the quantum realm differ from familiar notions, and how these differences can be exploited to achieve new results in data storage, transmission, and compression.

Hardware

There is no future for quantum computing without quantum computers. We are going to spell out the challenges behind the implementation of quantum machines, especially one that is embedded in the very nature of the quantum world: decoherence.

We shall also describe the desirable features that a prospective quantum machine must exhibit in order to be useful.

A few proposals for quantum hardware will be showcased. The emphasis here is not on technical details (this is a book for computer scientists, not a quantum engineering handbook!). Instead, our goal is to convey the gist of these proposals and their chances of success as they are currently assessed.

1

Complex Numbers

You, have you really understood all that stuff?
What?
The story of imaginary numbers?

Robert Musil, *The Confusions of Young*
Törless (1907)[1]

Complex numbers lie at the very core of quantum mechanics and are therefore absolutely essential to a basic understanding of quantum computation. In this chapter we present this important system of numbers from both the algebraic and the geometric standpoints. Section 1.1 presents some motivation and the basic definitions. The algebraic structure and operations on complex numbers are given in Section 1.2. The chapter concludes with Section 1.3, where complex numbers are presented from a geometric point of view and advanced topics are discussed. Our hope is that this chapter will help you get a little closer to what Sir Roger Penrose has very aptly called the "magic of complex numbers" (Penrose, 2005).

· ·

Reader Tip. Many readers will find that they are already familiar with some of the material presented in this chapter. The reader who feels confident in her comprehension of the fundamental knowledge of complex numbers, the basic operations, and their properties can safely move on to later chapters. We suggest, though, that you at least skim through the following pages to see what topics are covered. Return to Chapter 1 as a reference when needed (using the index to find specific topics). ♡

· ·

---

[1] For the German-speaking reader, here is the original text (the translation at the beginning is ours):

Du, hast du das vorhin ganz verstanden?
Was?
Die Geschichte mit den imaginären Zahlen?

Musil's *Törless* is a remarkable book. A substantial part is dedicated to the struggle of young Törless to come to grips with mathematics, as well as with his own life. Definitely recommended!

1.1 BASIC DEFINITIONS

The original motivation for the introduction of complex numbers was the theory of algebraic equations, the part of algebra that seeks solutions of polynomial equations. It became readily apparent that there are plenty of cases in which no solution among familiar numbers can be found. Here is the simplest example:

$$x^2 + 1 = 0. \tag{1.1}$$

Indeed, any possible x^2 would be positive or zero. Adding 1 ends up with some quantity to the left that is strictly positive; hence, no solution exists.

Exercise 1.1.1 Verify that the equation $x^4 + 2x^2 + 1 = 0$ has no solution among the real numbers. (Hint: Factor the polynomial.) ∎

The aforementioned argument seems to dash any hope of solving Equation (1.1). But does it?

Before building any new number system, it pays to remind ourselves of other sets of numbers that we usually work with

- positive numbers, $\mathbb{P} = \{1, 2, 3, \ldots\}$;
- natural numbers, $\mathbb{N} = \{0, 1, 2, 3, \ldots\}$;
- integers (or whole numbers), $\mathbb{Z} = \{\ldots, -3, -2, -1, 0, 1, 2, 3, \ldots\}$;
- rational numbers, $\mathbb{Q} = \left\{ \frac{m}{n} | m \in \mathbb{Z}, n \in \mathbb{P} \right\}$;
- real numbers, $\mathbb{R} = \mathbb{Q} \bigcup \{\ldots, \sqrt{2}, \ldots, e, \ldots, \pi, \ldots, \frac{e}{\pi} \ldots\}$;

In none of these familiar number systems can a valid solution to Equation (1.1) be found. Mathematics often works around difficulties by simply *postulating* that such a solution, albeit unknown, is available somewhere. Let us thus boldly assume that this enigmatic solution does indeed exist and determine what it looks like: Equation (1.1) is equivalent to

$$x^2 = -1. \tag{1.2}$$

What does this state? That the solution of Equation (1.1) is a number such that its square is -1, i.e., a number i such that

$$i^2 = -1 \quad \text{or} \quad i = \sqrt{-1}. \tag{1.3}$$

Of course we know that no such number exists among known (i.e., real) numbers, but we have already stated that this is not going to deter us. We will simply allow this new creature into the realm of well-established numbers and use it as it pleases us. Because it is *imaginary*, it is denoted i. We will impose on ourselves an important restriction: aside from its weird behavior when squared, i will behave just like an ordinary number.

Example 1.1.1 What is the value of i^3? We shall treat i as a legitimate number, so

$$i^3 = i \times i \times i = (i^2) \times i = -1 \times i = -i. \tag{1.4}$$

□

Exercise 1.1.2 Find the value of i^{15}. (Hint: Calculate i, i^2, i^3, i^4, and i^5. Find a pattern.) ■

In opening the door to our new friend i, we are now flooded with an entire universe of new numbers: to begin with, all the multiples of i by a real number, like $2 \times i$. These fellows, being akin to i, are known as **imaginary numbers**. But there is more: add a real number and an imaginary number, for instance, $3 + 5 \times i$, and you get a number that is neither a real nor an imaginary. Such a number, being a hybrid entity, is rightfully called a **complex number**.

Definition 1.1.1 *A complex number is an expression*

$$c = a + b \times i = a + bi, \tag{1.5}$$

where a, b are two real numbers; a is called the real part of c, whereas b is its imaginary part. The set of all complex numbers will be denoted as $\mathbb{C}$. When the $\times$ is understood, we shall omit it.

Complex numbers can be added and multiplied, as shown next.

Example 1.1.2 Let $c_1 = 3 - i$ and $c_2 = 1 + 4i$. We want to compute $c_1 + c_2$ and $c_1 \times c_2$.

$$c_1 + c_2 = 3 - i + 1 + 4i = (3 + 1) + (-1 + 4)i = 4 + 3i. \tag{1.6}$$

Multiplying is not as easy. We must remember to multiply each term of the first complex number with each term of the second complex number. Also, remember that $i^2 = -1$.

$$c_1 \times c_2 = (3 - i) \times (1 + 4i) = (3 \times 1) + (3 \times 4i) + (-i \times 1) + (-i \times 4i)$$
$$= (3 + 4) + (-1 + 12)i = 7 + 11i. \tag{1.7}$$

□

Exercise 1.1.3 Let $c_1 = -3 + i$ and $c_2 = 2 - 4i$. Calculate $c_1 + c_2$ and $c_1 \times c_2$. ■

With addition and multiplication we can get all polynomials. We set out to find a solution for Equation (1.1); it turns out that complex numbers are enough to provide solutions for *all* polynomial equations.

Proposition 1.1.1 (Fundamental Theorem of Algebra). Every polynomial equation of one variable with complex coefficients has a complex solution.

Exercise 1.1.4 Verify that the complex number $-1 + i$ is a solution for the polynomial equation $x^2 + 2x + 2 = 0$. ■

This nontrivial result shows that complex numbers are well worth our attention. In the next two sections, we explore the complex kingdom a little further.

Programming Drill 1.1.1 *Write a program that accepts two complex numbers and outputs their sum and their product.*

1.2 THE ALGEBRA OF COMPLEX NUMBERS

Admittedly, the fact that we know how to handle them does not explain away the oddity of complex numbers. What *are* they? What does it mean that i squared is equal to -1?

In the next section, we see that the geometrical viewpoint greatly aids our intuition. Meanwhile, we would like to convert complex numbers into more familiar objects by carefully looking at how they are built.

Definition 1.1.1 tells us *two* real numbers correspond to each complex number: its real and imaginary parts. A complex number is thus a two-pronged entity, carrying its two components along. How about *defining* a complex number as an ordered pair of reals?

$$c \longmapsto (a, b). \tag{1.8}$$

Ordinary real numbers can be identified with pairs $(a, 0)$

$$a \longmapsto (a, 0), \tag{1.9}$$

whereas imaginary numbers will be pairs $(0, b)$. In particular,

$$i \longmapsto (0, 1). \tag{1.10}$$

Addition is rather obvious – it adds pairs componentwise:

$$(a_1, b_1) + (a_2, b_2) = (a_1 + a_2, b_1 + b_2). \tag{1.11}$$

Multiplication is a little trickier:

$$(a_1, b_1) \times (a_2, b_2) = (a_1, b_1)(a_2, b_2) = (a_1 a_2 - b_1 b_2, a_1 b_2 + a_2 b_1). \tag{1.12}$$

Does this work? Multiplying i by itself gives

$$i \times i = (0, 1) \times (0, 1) = (0 - 1, 0 + 0) = (-1, 0), \tag{1.13}$$

which is what we wanted.

Using addition and multiplication, we can write any complex number in the usual form:

$$c = (a, b) = (a, 0) + (0, b) = (a, 0) + (b, 0) \times (0, 1) = a + bi. \tag{1.14}$$

We have traded one oddity for another: i was previously quite mysterious, whereas now it is just $(0, 1)$. A complex number is nothing more than an ordered pair of ordinary real numbers. Multiplication, though, is rather strange: perhaps the reader would have expected a componentwise multiplication, just like addition. We shall see later that by viewing complex numbers through yet another looking glass the strangeness linked to their multiplication rule will fade away.

Example 1.2.1 Let $c_1 = (3, -2)$ and $c_2 = (1, 2)$. Let us multiply them using the aforementioned rule:

$$c_1 \times c_2 = (3 \times 1 - (-2) \times 2, -2 \times 1 + 2 \times 3)$$

$$= (3 + 4, -2 + 6) = (7, 4) = 7 + 4i. \tag{1.15}$$

$\square$

Exercise 1.2.1 Let $c_1 = (-3, -1)$ and $c_2 = (1, -2)$. Calculate their product. ■

So far, we have a set of numbers and two operations: addition and multiplication. Both operations are **commutative**, meaning that for arbitrary complex numbers c_1 and c_2,

$$c_1 + c_2 = c_2 + c_1 \tag{1.16}$$

and

$$c_1 \times c_2 = c_2 \times c_1. \tag{1.17}$$

Both operations are also **associative**:

$$(c_1 + c_2) + c_3 = c_1 + (c_2 + c_3) \tag{1.18}$$

and

$$(c_1 \times c_2) \times c_3 = c_1 \times (c_2 \times c_3). \tag{1.19}$$

Exercise 1.2.2 Verify that multiplication of complex numbers is associative. ■

Moreover, multiplication **distributes** over addition: for all c_1, c_2, c_3, we have

$$c_1 \times (c_2 + c_3) = (c_1 \times c_2) + (c_1 \times c_3). \tag{1.20}$$

Let us verify this property: first we write the complex numbers as pairs $c_1 = (a_1, b_1)$, $c_2 = (a_2, b_2)$, and $c_3 = (a_3, b_3)$. Now, let us expand the left side

$$
\begin{aligned}
c_1 \times (c_2 + c_3) &= (a_1, b_1) \times ((a_2, b_2) + (a_3, b_3)) \\
&= (a_1, b_1) \times (a_2 + a_3, b_2 + b_3) \\
&= (a_1 \times (a_2 + a_3) - b_1 \times (b_2 + b_3), \\
&\quad\, a_1 \times (b_2 + b_3) + b_1 \times (a_2 + a_3)) \\
&= (a_1 \times a_2 + a_1 \times a_3 - b_1 \times b_2 - b_1 \times b_3, \\
&\quad\, a_1 \times b_2 + a_1 \times b_3 + b_1 \times a_2 + b_1 \times a_3).
\end{aligned}
\tag{1.21}
$$

Turning to the right side of Equation (1.20) one piece at a time gives

$$c_1 \times c_2 = (a_1 \times a_2 - b_1 \times b_2, a_1 \times b_2 + a_2 \times b_1) \tag{1.22}$$

$$c_1 \times c_3 = (a_1 \times a_3 - b_1 \times b_3, a_1 \times b_3 + a_3 \times b_1); \tag{1.23}$$

summing them up we obtain

$$
\begin{aligned}
c_1 \times c_2 + c_1 \times c_3 = (a_1 \times a_2 - b_1 \times b_2 + a_1 \times a_3 - b_1 \times b_3, \\
a_1 \times b_2 + a_2 \times b_1 + a_1 \times b_3 + a_3 \times b_1),
\end{aligned}
\tag{1.24}
$$

which is precisely what we got in Equation (1.21).

Having addition and multiplication, we need their complementary operations: subtraction and division.

Subtraction is straightforward:

$$c_1 - c_2 = (a_1, b_1) - (a_2, b_2) = (a_1 - a_2, b_1 - b_2); \tag{1.25}$$

in other words, subtraction is defined componentwise, as expected.

As for division, we have to work a little: If

$$(x, y) = \frac{(a_1, b_1)}{(a_2, b_2)}, \tag{1.26}$$

then by definition of division as the inverse of multiplication

$$(a_1, b_1) = (x, y) \times (a_2, b_2) \tag{1.27}$$

or

$$(a_1, b_1) = (a_2 x - b_2 y, a_2 y + b_2 x). \tag{1.28}$$

So we end up with

$$(1) \qquad a_1 = a_2 x - b_2 y, \tag{1.29}$$

$$(2) \qquad b_1 = a_2 y + b_2 x. \tag{1.30}$$

To determine the answer, we must solve this pair of equations for x and y. Multiply both sides of (1) by a_2 and both sides of (2) by b_2. We end up with

$$(1') \qquad a_1 a_2 = a_2^2 x - b_2 a_2 y, \tag{1.31}$$

$$(2') \qquad b_1 b_2 = a_2 b_2 y + b_2^2 x. \tag{1.32}$$

Now, let us add (1') and (2') to get

$$a_1 a_2 + b_1 b_2 = (a_2^2 + b_2^2)x. \tag{1.33}$$

Solving for x gives us

$$x = \frac{a_1 a_2 + b_1 b_2}{a_2^2 + b_2^2}. \tag{1.34}$$

We can perform the same trick for y by multiplying (1) and (2) by b_2 and $-a_2$, respectively, and then summing. We obtain

$$y = \frac{a_2 b_1 - a_1 b_2}{a_2^2 + b_2^2}. \tag{1.35}$$

In more compact notation, we can express this equation as

$$\frac{a_1 + b_1 i}{a_2 + b_2 i} = \frac{a_1 a_2 + b_1 b_2}{a_2^2 + b_2^2} + \frac{a_2 b_1 - a_1 b_2}{a_2^2 + b_2^2} i. \tag{1.36}$$

Notice that both x and y are calculated using the same denominator, namely, $a_2^2 + b_2^2$. We are going to see what this quantity means presently. In the meantime, here is a concrete example.

Example 1.2.2   Let $c_1 = -2 + i$ and $c_2 = 1 + 2i$. We will compute $\frac{c_1}{c_2}$. In this case, $a_1 = -2$, $b_1 = 1$, $a_2 = 1$, and $b_2 = 2$. Therefore,

$$a_2^2 + b_2^2 = 1^2 + 2^2 = 5, \tag{1.37}$$

$$a_1a_2 + b_1b_2 = -2 \times 1 + 1 \times 2 = 0, \tag{1.38}$$

$$a_2b_1 - a_1b_2 = 1 \times 1 - (-2) \times 2 = 1 + 4 = 5. \tag{1.39}$$

The answer is thus $\left(\frac{0}{5}, \frac{5}{5}\right) = (0, 1) = i$. $\square$

Exercise 1.2.3   Let $c_1 = 3i$ and $c_2 = -1 - i$. Calculate $\dfrac{c_1}{c_2}$.   ■

Now, let us go back to the mysterious denominator in the quotient formula in Equation (1.36). Real numbers have a unary operation, the absolute value, given by

$$|a| = +\sqrt{a^2}. \tag{1.40}$$

We can define a generalization of this operation[2] to the complex domain by letting

$$|c| = |a + bi| = +\sqrt{a^2 + b^2}. \tag{1.41}$$

This quantity is known as the **modulus** of a complex number.

Example 1.2.3   What is the modulus of $c = 1 - i$?

$$|c| = |1 - i| = +\sqrt{1^2 + (-1)^2} = \sqrt{2}. \tag{1.42}$$

$\square$

The geometric meaning of the modulus is discussed in the next section. For now, we remark that the quantity in the denominator of the quotient of two complex numbers is nothing more than the modulus squared of the divisor:

$$|c|^2 = a^2 + b^2. \tag{1.43}$$

This modulus must be different from zero, which always happens unless the divisor is itself zero.

Exercise 1.2.4   Calculate the modulus of $c = 4 - 3i$.   ■

Exercise 1.2.5   Verify that given two arbitrary complex numbers c_1 and c_2, the following equality always holds:

$$|c_1||c_2| = |c_1c_2|. \tag{1.44}$$

■

Exercise 1.2.6   Prove that

$$|c_1 + c_2| \le |c_1| + |c_2|. \tag{1.45}$$

When are they, in fact, equal? (Hint: Square both sides.)   ■

Exercise 1.2.7   Show that for all $c \in \mathbb{C}$, we have $c + (0, 0) = (0, 0) + c = c$. That is, $(0, 0)$ is an additive identity.   ■

---

[2] The definition given in Equation (1.40) is entirely equivalent to the more familiar one: $|a| = a$ if $a \ge 0$, and $|a| = -a$ if $a < 0$.

Exercise 1.2.8   Show that for all $c \in \mathbb{C}$ we have $c \times (1, 0) = (1, 0) \times c = c$. That is, $(1, 0)$ is a multiplicative identity.   ∎

In summation, we have defined a new set of numbers, $\mathbb{C}$, endowed with four operations, verifying the following properties:

(i) Addition is commutative and associative.
(ii) Multiplication is commutative and associative.
(iii) Addition has an identity: $(0, 0)$.
(iv) Multiplication has an identity: $(1, 0)$.
(v) Multiplication distributes with respect to addition.
(vi) Subtraction (i.e., the inverse of addition) is defined everywhere.
(vii) Division (i.e., the inverse of multiplication) is defined everywhere except when the divisor is zero.

A set with operations satisfying all these properties is called a **field**. $\mathbb{C}$ is a field, just like $\mathbb{R}$, the field of real numbers. In fact, via the identification that associates a real number to a complex number with 0 as the imaginary component, we can think of $\mathbb{R}$ as a subset[3] of $\mathbb{C}$. $\mathbb{R}$ sits inside $\mathbb{C}$; but $\mathbb{C}$ is a vast field, so vast, indeed, that all polynomial equations with coefficients in $\mathbb{C}$ have a solution in $\mathbb{C}$ itself. $\mathbb{R}$ is also a roomy field, but not enough to enjoy this last property (remember Equation (1.1)). A field that contains all solutions for any of its polynomial equations is said to be **algebraically complete**. $\mathbb{C}$ is an algebraically complete field, whereas $\mathbb{R}$ is not.

There is a unary operation that plays a crucial role in the complex domain. The reader is familiar with "changing signs" of real numbers. Here, however, there are *two* real numbers attached to a complex number. Therefore, there are *three* ways of changing sign: either change the sign of the real part or change the sign of the imaginary part, or both. Let us analyze them one by one.

Changing both signs of the complex number is done by multiplying by the number $-1 = (-1, 0)$.

Exercise 1.2.9   Verify that multiplication by $(-1, 0)$ changes the sign of the real and imaginary components of a complex number.   ∎

Changing the sign of the imaginary part only is known as **conjugation**.[4] If $c = a + bi$ is an arbitrary complex number, then the conjugate of c is $\bar{c} = a - bi$. Two numbers related by conjugation are said to be **complex conjugates** of each other.

Changing the sign of the real part ($c \longmapsto -\bar{c}$) has no particular name, at least in the algebraic context.[5]

The following exercises will guide you through conjugation's most important properties.

---

[3] A subset of a field that is a field in its own right is called a **subfield**: $\mathbb{R}$ is a subfield of $\mathbb{C}$.
[4] Its "geometric" name is **real-axis reflection**. The name becomes obvious in the next section.
[5] In the geometric viewpoint, it is known as **imaginary-axis reflection**. After reading Section 1.3, we invite you to investigate this operation a bit further.

Exercise 1.2.10   Show that conjugation respects addition, i.e.,

$$\overline{c_1} + \overline{c_2} = \overline{c_1 + c_2}. \tag{1.46}$$

∎

Exercise 1.2.11   Show that conjugation respects multiplication, i.e.,

$$\overline{c_1} \times \overline{c_2} = \overline{c_1 \times c_2}. \tag{1.47}$$

∎

Notice that the function

$$c \longmapsto \overline{c} \tag{1.48}$$

given by conjugation is **bijective**, i.e., is one-to-one and onto. Indeed, two different complex numbers are never sent to the same number by conjugation. Moreover, every number is the complex conjugate of some number. A function from a field to a field that is bijective and that respects addition and multiplication is known as a **field isomorphism**. Conjugation is thus a field isomorphism of $\mathbb{C}$ to $\mathbb{C}$.

Exercise 1.2.12   Consider the operation given by flipping the sign of the real part. Is this a field isomorphism of $\mathbb{C}$? If yes, prove it. Otherwise, show where it fails.   ∎

We cannot continue without mentioning another property of conjugation:

$$c \times \overline{c} = |c|^2. \tag{1.49}$$

In words, the modulus squared of a complex number is obtained by multiplying the number with its conjugate. For example,

$$(3 + 2i) \times (3 - 2i) = 3^2 + 2^2 = 13 = |3 + 2i|^2. \tag{1.50}$$

We have covered what we need from the algebraic perspective. We see in the next section that the geometric approach sheds some light on virtually all topics touched on here.

Programming Drill 1.2.1   *Take the program that you wrote in the last programming drill and make it also perform subtraction and division of complex numbers. In addition, let the user enter a complex number and have the computer return its modulus and conjugate.*

1.3 THE GEOMETRY OF COMPLEX NUMBERS

As far as algebra is concerned, complex numbers are an algebraically complete field, as we have described them in Section 1.2. That alone would render them invaluable as a mathematical tool. It turns out that their significance extends far beyond the algebraic domain and makes them equally useful in geometry and hence in physics. To see why this is so, we need to look at a complex number in yet another way. At the beginning of Section 1.2, we learned that a complex number is a pair of real

Imaginary

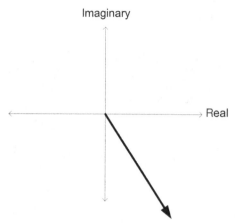

Real

Figure 1.1. Complex plane.

numbers. This suggests a natural means of representation: real numbers are placed on the line, so pairs of reals correspond to points on the plane, or, equivalently, correspond to **vectors** starting from the origin and pointing to that point (as shown in Figure 1.1).

In this representation, real numbers (i.e., complex numbers with no imaginary part) sit on the horizontal axis and imaginary numbers sit on the vertical axis. This plane is known as the **complex plane** or the **Argand plane**.

Through this representation, the algebraic properties of the complex numbers can be seen in a new light. Let us start with the modulus: it is nothing more than the **length** of the vector. Indeed, the length of a vector, via Pythagoras' theorem, is the square root of the sum of the squares of its edges, which is precisely the modulus, as defined in the previous section.

Example 1.3.1   Consider the complex numbers $c = 3 + 4i$ depicted in Figure 1.2. The length of the vector is the hypotenuse of the right triangle whose edges have length 3 and 4, respectively. Pythagoras' theorem gives us the length as

$$length(c) = \sqrt{4^2 + 3^2} = \sqrt{16 + 9} = \sqrt{25} = 5. \tag{1.51}$$

This is exactly the modulus of c.   □

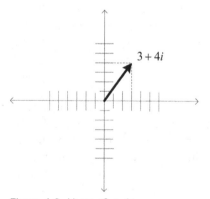

$3 + 4i$

Figure 1.2. Vector $3 + 4i$.

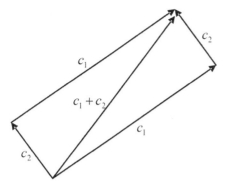

Figure 1.3. Parallelogram rule.

Next comes addition: vectors can be added using the so-called **parallelogram rule** illustrated by Figure 1.3. In words, draw the parallelogram whose parallel edges are the two vectors to be added; their sum is the diagonal.

Exercise 1.3.1 Draw the complex numbers $c_1 = 2 - i$ and $c_2 = 1 + i$ in the complex plane, and add them using the parallelogram rule. Verify that you would get the same result as adding them algebraically (the way we learned in Section 1.2). ∎

Subtraction too has a clear geometric meaning: subtracting c_2 from c_1 is the same as adding the negation of c_2, i.e., $-c_2$, to c_1. But what is the negation of a vector? It is just the vector of the same length pointed in the opposite direction (see Figure 1.4).

Exercise 1.3.2 Let $c_1 = 2 - i$ and $c_2 = 1 + i$. Subtract c_2 from c_1 by first drawing $-c_2$ and then adding it to c_1 using the parallelogram rule. ∎

To give a simple geometrical meaning to multiplication, we need to develop yet another characterization of complex numbers. We saw a moment ago that for every complex number we can draw a right triangle, whose edges' lengths are the real and imaginary parts of the number and whose hypotenuse's length is the modulus. Now, suppose someone tells us the modulus of the number what else do we need to know to draw the triangle? The answer is the angle at the origin.

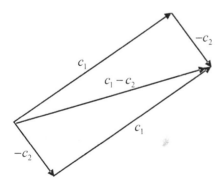

Figure 1.4. Subtraction.

The modulus ρ *and* the angle θ (notice: two real numbers, as before) are enough to uniquely determine the complex number.

$$(a, b) \longmapsto (\rho, \theta). \tag{1.52}$$

We know how to compute ρ from a, b:

$$\rho = \sqrt{(a^2 + b^2)}. \tag{1.53}$$

θ is also easy, via trigonometry:

$$\theta = \tan^{-1}\left(\frac{b}{a}\right). \tag{1.54}$$

The (a, b) representation is known as the **Cartesian representation** of a complex number, whereas (ρ, θ) is the **polar representation**.

We can go back from polar to Cartesian representation, again using trigonometry:

$$a = \rho \cos(\theta), \qquad b = \rho \sin(\theta). \tag{1.55}$$

Example 1.3.2   Let $c = 1 + i$. What is its polar representation?

$$\rho = \sqrt{1^2 + 1^2} = \sqrt{2} \tag{1.56}$$

$$\theta = \tan^{-1}\left(\frac{1}{1}\right) = \tan^{-1}(1) = \frac{\pi}{4} \tag{1.57}$$

c is the vector of length $\sqrt{2}$ from the origin at an angle of $\frac{\pi}{4}$ radians, or $45°$. $\square$

Exercise 1.3.3   Draw the complex number given by the polar coordinates $\rho = 3$ and $\theta = \frac{\pi}{3}$. Compute its Cartesian coordinates.   ∎

Programming Drill 1.3.1   *Write a program that converts a complex number from its Cartesian representation to its polar representation and vice versa.*

Before moving on, let us meditate a little: what kind of insight does the polar representation give us? Instead of providing a ready-made answer, let us begin with a question: how many complex numbers share exactly the same modulus? A moment's thought will tell us that for a *fixed* modulus, say, $\rho = 1$, there is an entire circle centered at the origin (as shown in Figure 1.5).

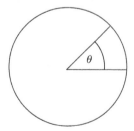

Figure 1.5. Phase θ.

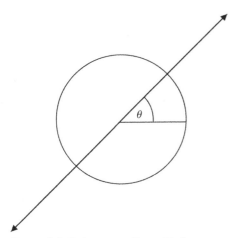

Figure 1.6. Points on a line with the same phase.

So, here comes the angle: imagine the circle as your watch, and the complex number as the needle. Angle θ tells us the "time." The "time" is known in physics and engineering as the **phase**, whereas the length of the "needle" (i.e., the modulus) is the **magnitude** of the number.

Definition 1.3.1 *A complex number is a magnitude and a phase.*

The ordinary positive reals are just complex numbers such that their phase is zero. The negative reals have phase π. By the same token, imaginary numbers are numbers with constant phase equal to $\frac{\pi}{2}$ (positive imaginary) or $\frac{3\pi}{2}$ (negative imaginary).

Given a constant phase, there is an entire line of complex numbers having that phase as depicted in Figure 1.6.

Observe that a complex number has a unique polar representation only if we confine the phase between 0 and 2π:

$$0 \le \theta < 2\pi \tag{1.58}$$

(and the $\rho \ge 0$). If we restrict θ in this fashion, though, we cannot in general add angles (the sum may be bigger than 2π). A better course is to let the angle be anything and *reduce* it modulo 2π:

$$\theta_1 = \theta_2 \quad \text{if and only if } \theta_2 = \theta_1 + 2\pi k, \text{ for some integer } k. \tag{1.59}$$

Two complex numbers in polar representations will be identical if their magnitude is the same and if the angles are the same modulo 2π, as shown by the following example.

Example 1.3.3 Are the numbers $(3, -\pi)$ and $(3, \pi)$ the same? Indeed they are: their magnitude is the same and their phases differ by $(-\pi) - \pi = -2\pi = (-1)2\pi$. $\qquad\square$

We are now ready for multiplication: given two complex numbers in polar coordinates, (ρ_1, θ_1) and (ρ_2, θ_2), their product can be obtained by simply multiplying their magnitude and *adding* their phase:

$$(\rho_1, \theta_1) \times (\rho_2, \theta_2) = (\rho_1 \rho_2, \theta_1 + \theta_2). \tag{1.60}$$

Example 1.3.4 Let $c_1 = 1 + i$ and $c_2 = -1 + i$. Their product, according to the algebraic rule, is

$$c_1 c_2 = (1 + i)(-1 + i) = -2 + 0i = -2. \tag{1.61}$$

Now, let us take their polar representation

$$c_1 = \left(\sqrt{2}, \frac{\pi}{4}\right), \qquad c_2 = \left(\sqrt{2}, \frac{3\pi}{4}\right). \tag{1.62}$$

(Carry out the calculations!) Therefore, their product using the rule described earlier is

$$c_1 c_2 = \left(\sqrt{2} \times \sqrt{2}, \frac{\pi}{4} + \frac{3\pi}{4}\right) = (2, \pi). \tag{1.63}$$

If we revert to its Cartesian coordinates, we get

$$(2 \times \cos(\pi), 2 \times \sin(\pi)) = (-2, 0), \tag{1.64}$$

which is precisely the answer we arrived at with the algebraic calculation in Equation (1.61).

Figure 1.7 is the graphical representation of the two numbers and their product.

As you can see, we simply rotated the first vector by an angle equal to the phase of the second vector and multiplied its length by the length of the second vector. $\square$

Exercise 1.3.4 Multiply $c_1 = -2 - i$ and $c_2 = -1 - 2i$ using both the algebraic and the geometric method; verify that the results are identical. $\blacksquare$

. . . .

Reader Tip. Most of the rest of this chapter are basic ideas in complex numbers; however, they will not really be used in the text. The part on roots of unity will arise in our discussion of Shor's algorithm (Section 6.5). The rest is included for the sake

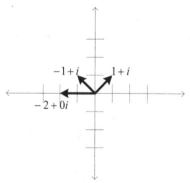

Figure 1.7. Two complex numbers and their product.

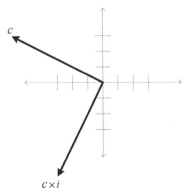

Figure 1.8. Multiplication by i.

of completeness. The restless reader can safely skim the rest of this chapter on the first reading. ♡
....

We have implicitly learned an important fact: multiplication in the complex domain has something to do with *rotations* of the complex plane. Indeed, observe just what happens by left or right multiplication by i:

$$c \longmapsto c \times i. \tag{1.65}$$

i has modulus 1, so the magnitude of the result is exactly equal to that of the starting point. The phase of i is $\frac{\pi}{2}$, so multiplying by i has the net result of rotating the original complex number by 90°, a right angle. The same happens when we multiply any complex number; so we can safely conclude that multiplication by i is a right-angle counterclockwise rotation of the complex plane, as shown in Figure 1.8.

Exercise 1.3.5 Describe the geometric effect on the plane obtained by multiplying by a real number, i.e., the function

$$c \longmapsto c \times r_0, \tag{1.66}$$

where r_0 is a fixed real number. ∎

Exercise 1.3.6 Describe the geometric effect on the plane obtained by multiplying by a generic complex number, i.e., the function

$$c \longmapsto c \times c_0, \tag{1.67}$$

where c_0 is a fixed complex number. ∎

Programming Drill 1.3.2 *If you like graphics, write a program that accepts a small drawing around the origin of the complex plane and a complex number. The program should change the drawing by multiplying every point of the diagram by a complex number.*

Now that we are armed with a geometric way of looking at multiplication, we can tackle division as well. After all, division is nothing more than the inverse operation of multiplication. Assume that

$$c_1 = (\rho_1, \theta_1) \quad \text{and} \quad c_2 = (\rho_2, \theta_2), \tag{1.68}$$

are two complex numbers in polar form; what is the polar form of $\frac{c_1}{c_2}$? A moment's thought tells us that it is the number

$$\frac{c_1}{c_2} = \left(\frac{\rho_1}{\rho_2}, \theta_1 - \theta_2 \right). \tag{1.69}$$

In words, we divide the magnitudes and subtract the angles.

Example 1.3.5 Let $c_1 = -1 + 3i$ and $c_2 = -1 - 4i$. Let us calculate their polar co-ordinates first:

$$c_1 = \left(\sqrt{(-1)^2 + 3^2}, \tan^{-1} \left(\frac{3}{-1} \right) \right) = (\sqrt{10}, \tan^{-1}(-3)) = (3.1623, 1.8925),$$
$$\tag{1.70}$$

$$c_2 = \left(\sqrt{(-1)^2 + (-4)^2}, \tan^{-1} \left(\frac{-4}{-1} \right) \right) = (\sqrt{17}, \tan^{-1}(4)) = (4.1231, -1.8158),$$
$$\tag{1.71}$$

therefore, in polar coordinates the quotient is

$$\frac{c_1}{c_2} = \left(\frac{3.1623}{4.1231}, 1.8925 - (-1.8158) \right) = (0.7670, 3.7083). \tag{1.72}$$

$\square$

Exercise 1.3.7 Divide $2 + 2i$ by $1 - i$ using both the algebraic and the geometrical method and verify that the results are the same. ∎

You may have noticed that in Section 1.2, we have left out two important operations: powers and roots. The reason was that it is much easier to deal with them in the present geometric setting than from the algebraic viewpoint.

Let us begin with powers. If $c = (\rho, \theta)$ is a complex number in polar form and n a positive integer, its nth power is just

$$c^n = (\rho^n, n\theta), \tag{1.73}$$

because raising to the nth power is multiplying n times. Figure 1.9 shows a complex number and its first, second, and third powers.

Exercise 1.3.8 Let $c = 1 - i$. Convert it to polar coordinates, calculate its fifth power, and revert the answers to Cartesian coordinates. ∎

What happens when the base is a number of magnitude 1? Its powers will also have magnitude 1; thus, they will stay on the same unit circle. You can think of the various powers $1, 2, \ldots$ as time units, and a needle moving counterclockwise at

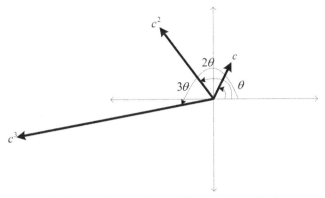

Figure 1.9. A complex number and its square and cube.

constant speed (it covers exactly θ radians per time unit, where θ is the phase of the base).

Let us move on to roots. As you know already from high-school algebra, a root is a fractional power. For instance, the square root means raising the base to the power of one-half; the cube root is raising to the power of one-third; and so forth. The same holds true here, so we may take roots of complex numbers: if $c = (\rho, \theta)$ is a complex in polar form, its nth root is

$$c^{\frac{1}{n}} = \left(\rho^{\frac{1}{n}}, \frac{1}{n}\theta \right). \tag{1.74}$$

However, things get a bit more complicated. Remember, the phase is defined only up to multiples of 2π. Therefore, we must rewrite Equation (1.74) as

$$c^{\frac{1}{n}} = \left(\sqrt[n]{\rho}, \frac{1}{n}(\theta + k2\pi) \right). \tag{1.75}$$

It appears that there are *several* roots of the same number. This fact should not surprise us: in fact, even among real numbers, roots are not always unique. Take, for instance, the number 2 and notice that there are two square roots, $\sqrt{2}$ and $-\sqrt{2}$.

How many nth roots are there? There are precisely n nth roots for a complex number. Why? Let us go back to Equation (1.75).

$$\frac{1}{n}(\theta + 2k\pi) = \frac{1}{n}\theta + \frac{k}{n}2\pi. \tag{1.76}$$

How many different solutions can we generate by varying k? Here they are:

$k = 0$	$\frac{1}{n}\theta$
$k = 1$	$\frac{1}{n}\theta + \frac{1}{n}2\pi$
$\vdots$	$\vdots$
$k = n - 1$	$\frac{1}{n}\theta + \frac{n-1}{n}2\pi$

$$(1.77)$$

That is all: when $k = n$, we obtain the first solution; when $k = n + 1$, we obtain the second solution; and so forth. (Verify this statement!)

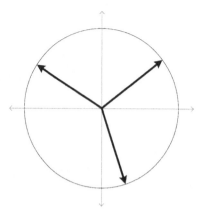

Figure 1.10. The three cube roots of unity.

To see what is happening, let us assume that $\rho = 1$; in other words, let us find nth roots of a complex number $c = (1, \theta)$ on the unit circle. The n solutions in Equation (1.77) can be interpreted in the following way: Draw the unit circle, and the vectors whose phase is $\frac{1}{n}\theta$, $\frac{1}{n}\theta$ plus an angle equal to $\frac{k}{n}$ of the entire circle, where $k = 1, \ldots, n$. We get precisely the vertices of a regular polygon with n edges. Figure 1.10 is an example when $n = 3$.

Exercise 1.3.9   Find all the cube roots of $c = 1 + i$.   ∎

By now we should feel pretty comfortable with the polar representation: we know that any complex number, via the polar-to-Cartesian function, can be written as

$$c = \rho(\cos(\theta) + i \sin(\theta)). \tag{1.78}$$

Let us introduce yet another notation that will prove to be very handy in many situations. The starting point is the following formula, known as **Euler's formula**:

$$e^{i\theta} = \cos(\theta) + i \sin(\theta). \tag{1.79}$$

The full justification of the remarkable formula of Euler lies outside the scope of this book.[6] However, we can at least provide some evidence that substantiates its

---

[6] For the calculus-savvy reader: Use the well-known Taylor expansions.

$$e^x = 1 + x + \frac{x^2}{2} + \cdots + \frac{x^n}{n!} + \cdots, \tag{1.80}$$

$$\sin(x) = x - \frac{x^3}{3!} + \cdots + \frac{(-1)^n}{(2n+1)!}x^{2n+1} + \cdots, \tag{1.81}$$

$$\cos(x) = 1 - \frac{x^2}{2} + \cdots + \frac{(-1)^n}{(2n)!}x^{2n} + \cdots. \tag{1.82}$$

Assume that they hold for complex values of x. Now, formally multiply $\sin(x)$ by i and add componentwise $\cos(x)$ to obtain Euler's formula.

validity. First of all, if $\theta = 0$, we get what we expected, namely, 1. Secondly,

$$
\begin{aligned}
e^{i(\theta_1 + \theta_2)} &= \cos(\theta_1 + \theta_2) + i \sin(\theta_1 + \theta_2) \\
&= \cos(\theta_1) \cos(\theta_2) - \sin(\theta_1) \sin(\theta_2) \\
&\quad + i((\sin(\theta_1) \cos(\theta_2) + \sin(\theta_2) \cos(\theta_1))) \qquad (1.83) \\
&= (\cos(\theta_1) + i \sin(\theta_1))((\cos(\theta_2) + i \sin(\theta_2)) \\
&= e^{i\theta_1} \times e^{i\theta_2}.
\end{aligned}
$$

In other words, the exponential function takes sums into products as it does in the real case.

Exercise 1.3.10 Prove **De Moivre's formula**:

$$
(e^{\theta i})^n = \cos(n\theta) + i \sin(n\theta). \qquad (1.84)
$$

(Hint: The trigonometric identities used earlier, with induction on n, will do the work.) ■

Now that we know how to take the exponential of an imaginary number, there is no problem in defining the exponential of an arbitrary complex number:

$$
e^{a+bi} = e^a \times e^{bi} = e^a(\cos(b) + i \sin(b)). \qquad (1.85)
$$

Euler's formula enables us to rewrite Equation (1.78) in a more compact form:

$$
c = \rho \, e^{i\theta}. \qquad (1.86)
$$

We shall refer to Equation (1.86) as the **exponential form** of a complex number.

Exercise 1.3.11 Write the number $c = 3 - 4i$ in exponential form. ■

The exponential notation simplifies matters when we perform multiplication:

$$
c_1 c_2 = \rho_1 \, e^{i\theta_1} \rho_2 \, e^{i\theta_2} = \rho_1 \rho_2 \, e^{i(\theta_1 + \theta_2)}. \qquad (1.87)
$$

Exercise 1.3.12 Rewrite the law for dividing complex numbers in exponential form.

■

With this notation, we can look at the roots of the complex number $1 = (1, 0) = 1 + 0i$. Let n be a fixed number. There are n different **roots of unity**. Setting $c = (1, 0)$ in Equation (1.75), we get

$$
c^{\frac{1}{n}} = (1, 0)^{\frac{1}{n}} = \left(\sqrt[n]{1}, \frac{1}{n}(0 + 2k\pi) \right) = \left(1, \frac{2k\pi}{n} \right). \qquad (1.88)
$$

By permitting $k = 0, 1, 2, \ldots, n-1$, we get n different roots of unity. Notice that if we set $k = n$, we get back to the first one. The kth root of unity in exponential form is $e^{2\pi i k/n}$. We denote these n different roots of unity by

$$
\omega_n^0 = 1, \omega_n^1, \omega_n^2, \ldots, \omega_n^{n-1}. \qquad (1.89)
$$

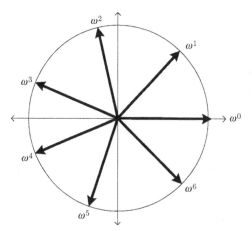

Figure 1.11. The seventh root of unity and its powers.

Geometrically these n roots of unity correspond to splitting up the unit circle into n parts where the first partition is $(1, 0)$. Figure 1.11 is a picture of the seventh root of unity and all its powers.

If we multiply two roots of unity, we get

$$\omega_n^j \omega_n^k = e^{2\pi i j/n} e^{2\pi i k/n} = e^{2\pi i (j+k)/n} = \omega_n^{j+k}. \tag{1.90}$$

Notice also that

$$\omega_n^j \omega_n^{n-j} = \omega_n^n = 1, \tag{1.91}$$

and hence

$$\overline{\omega_n^j} = \omega_n^{n-j}. \tag{1.92}$$

Exercise 1.3.13   Draw all the fifth roots of unity.   ■

We are now in a position to characterize geometrically any function on complex numbers. The simplest functions one can think of beyond the elementary operations are **polynomials**. An arbitrary polynomial with complex coefficients looks like

$$P(x) = c_n x^n + c_{n-1} x^{n-1} + \cdots + c_0, \tag{1.93}$$

where $c_0, c_1, \ldots, c_{n-1}$ are in $\mathbb{C}$. $P(x)$ can be seen as a function from $\mathbb{C}$ to $\mathbb{C}$

$$P(x) : \mathbb{C} \longrightarrow \mathbb{C}. \tag{1.94}$$

To build some geometric intuition on polynomials, you can try your hand at the following two exercises.

Exercise 1.3.14   Describe the geometric meaning of the function

$$c \longmapsto c^n \tag{1.95}$$

from $\mathbb{C}$ to $\mathbb{C}$.   ■

Exercise 1.3.15   Describe the geometric meaning of the function

$$c \longmapsto c + c_0 \tag{1.96}$$

from $\mathbb{C}$ to $\mathbb{C}$.   ■

After polynomials, the next set of functions are **rational functions**, or quotients of polynomials:

$$R(x) = \frac{P_0(x)}{P_1(x)} = \frac{c_n x^n + c_{n-1} x^{n-1} + \cdots + c_0}{d_m x^m + d_{m-1} x^{m-1} + \cdots + d_0}. \tag{1.97}$$

In general, describing the action on the plane provided by a rational function is no simple matter. The simplest case, though, is relatively easy and a very important one:

$$R_{a,b,c,d}(x) = \frac{ax + b}{cx + d}, \tag{1.98}$$

where a, b, c, d are in $\mathbb{C}$ and $ad - bc \neq 0$ is known as the **Möbius transformation**. The following set of exercises introduce some of the basic properties of Möbius transformations. (In particular, we show that the set of Möbius transformations form a group.)[7]

Exercise 1.3.16   When $a = d = 0$ and $b = c = 1$, we get $R(x) = \frac{1}{x}$. Describe the geometrical effect of this transformation. (Hint: See what happens to the points inside and outside the circle of radius 1.)   ■

Exercise 1.3.17   Prove that the composition of two Möbius transformations is a Möbius transformation. In other words, if $R_{a,b,c,d}$ and $R_{a',b',c',d'}$ are two Möbius transformations, the transformation $R_{a',b',c',d'} \circ R_{a,b,c,d}$ given by

$$R_{a',b',c',d'} \circ R_{a,b,c,d}(x) = R_{a',b',c',d'}(R_{a,b,c,d}(x)) \tag{1.99}$$

is also a Möbius transformation.   ■

Exercise 1.3.18   Show that the identity transformation, i.e., the transformation that leaves every point fixed, is a Möbius transformation.   ■

Exercise 1.3.19   Show that each Möbius transformation has an inverse that is also a Möbius transformation, i.e., for each $R_{a,b,c,d}$ you can find $R_{a',b',c',d'}$ such that

$$R_{a',b',c',d'} \circ R_{a,b,c,d}(x) = x. \tag{1.100}$$

■

There are many more functions in the complex domain, but to introduce them one needs tools from **complex analysis**, i.e., calculus over the complex numbers. The main idea is quite simple: replace polynomials with a power series, i.e., polynomials

---

[7] Möbius transformations are a truly fascinating topic, and perhaps the best entrance door to the geometry of complex numbers. We invite you to find out more about them in Schwerdtfeger (1980).

with an infinite number of terms. The functions one studies are the so-called **analytic functions**, which are functions that can be coherently pieced together from small parts, each of which is represented by a series.

Programming Drill 1.3.3 *Expand your program. Add functions for multiplication, division, and returning the polar coordinates of a number.*

We have covered the basic language of complex numbers. Before we embark on our quantum journey, we need another tool: vector spaces over the complex field.

....

References: Most of the material found in this chapter can be found in any calculus or linear algebra textbook. References for some of the more advanced material presented at the end of the chapter can be found in, e.g., Bak and Newman (1996), Needham (1999), Schwerdtfeger (1980), and Silverman (1984).

The history of complex numbers goes back to the mid-sixteenth century during the Italian Renaissance. The story of Tartaglia, Cardano, Bombelli and their effort to solve algebraic equations is well worth reading. Some of this fascinating tale is in Nahin (1998), Mazur (2002), and several wonderful sections in Penrose (1994).

2

Complex Vector Spaces

> *Philosophy is written in that great book which continually lies open before us (I mean the Universe). But one cannot understand this book until one has learned to understand the language and to know the letters in which it is written. It is written in the language of mathematics, and the letters are triangles, circles and other geometric figures. Without these means it is impossible for mankind to understand a single word; without these means there is only vain stumbling in a dark labyrinth.*[1]
>
> Galileo Galilei

Quantum theory is cast in the language of complex vector spaces. These are mathematical structures that are based on complex numbers. We learned all that we need about such numbers in Chapter 1. Armed with this knowledge, we can now tackle complex vector spaces themselves.

Section 2.1 goes through the main example of a (finite-dimensional) complex vector space at tutorial pace. Section 2.2 provides formal definitions, basic properties, and more examples. Each of Section 2.3 through Section 2.7 discusses an advanced topic.

. . . .

Reader Tip. The reader might find some of this chapter to be "just boring math." If you are eager to leap into the quantum world, we suggest reading the first two or three sections before moving on to Chapter 3. Return to Chapter 2 as a reference when needed (using the index and the table of contents to find specific topics). ♡

. . . .

[1] *... La filosofia é scritta in questo grandissimo libro che continuamente ci sta aperto innanzi a gli occhi (io dico l'universo), ma non si puo intendere se prima non s'impara a intender la lingua, e conoscer i caratteri, ne' quali é scritto. Egli é scritto in lingua matematica, e i caratteri sono triangoli, cerchi, ed altre figure geometriche, senza i quali mezi e impossibile a intenderne umanamente parola; senza questi e un aggirarsi vanamente per un'oscuro laberinto...* (Opere Il Saggiatore p. 171).

A small disclaimer is in order. The theory of complex vector spaces is a vast and beautiful subject. Lengthy textbooks have been written on this important area of mathematics. It is impossible to provide anything more than a small glimpse into the beauty and profundity of this topic in one chapter. Rather than "teaching" our reader complex vector spaces, we aim to cover the bare minimum of concepts, terminology, and notation needed in order to start quantum computing. It is our sincere hope that reading this chapter will inspire further investigation into this remarkable subject.

2.1 $\mathbb{C}^n$ AS THE PRIMARY EXAMPLE

The primary example of a complex vector space is the set of vectors (one-dimensional arrays) of a fixed length with complex entries. These vectors will describe the states of quantum systems and quantum computers. In order to fix our ideas and to see clearly what type of structure this set has, let us carefully examine one concrete example: the set of vectors of length 4. We shall denote this set as $\mathbb{C}^4 = \mathbb{C} \times \mathbb{C} \times \mathbb{C} \times \mathbb{C}$, which reminds us that each vector is an ordered list of four complex numbers.

A typical element of $\mathbb{C}^4$ looks like this:

$$\begin{bmatrix} 6 - 4i \\ 7 + 3i \\ 4.2 - 8.1i \\ -3i \end{bmatrix}. \tag{2.1}$$

We might call this vector V. We denote the jth element of V as $V[j]$. The top row is row number 0 (not 1);[2] hence, $V[1] = 7 + 3i$.

What types of operations can we carry out with such vectors? One operation that seems obvious is to form the **addition** of two vectors. For example, given two vectors of $\mathbb{C}^4$

$$V = \begin{bmatrix} 6 - 4i \\ 7 + 3i \\ 4.2 - 8.1i \\ -3i \end{bmatrix} \quad \text{and} \quad W = \begin{bmatrix} 16 + 2.3i \\ -7i \\ 6 \\ -4i \end{bmatrix}, \tag{2.2}$$

---

[2] Computer scientists generally start indexing their rows and columns at 0. In contrast, mathematicians and physicists tend to start indexing at 1. The difference is irrelevant. We shall generally follow the computer science convention (after all, this is a computer science text).

we can add them to form $V + W \in \mathbb{C}^4$ by adding their respective entries:

$$
\begin{bmatrix} 6 - 4i \\ 7 + 3i \\ 4.2 - 8.1i \\ -3i \end{bmatrix}
+
\begin{bmatrix} 16 + 2.3i \\ -7i \\ 6 \\ -4i \end{bmatrix}
=
\begin{bmatrix} (6 - 4i) + (16 + 2.3i) \\ (7 + 3i) + (-7i) \\ (4.2 - 8.1i) + (6) \\ (-3i) + (-4i) \end{bmatrix}
=
\begin{bmatrix} 22 - 1.7i \\ 7 - 4i \\ 10.2 - 8.1i \\ -7i \end{bmatrix}.
$$

(2.3)

Formally, this operation amounts to

$$(V + W)[j] = V[j] + W[j].$$

(2.4)

Exercise 2.1.1   Add the following two vectors:

$$
\begin{bmatrix} 5 + 13i \\ 6 + 2i \\ 0.53 - 6i \\ 12 \end{bmatrix}
+
\begin{bmatrix} 7 - 8i \\ 4i \\ 2 \\ 9.4 + 3i \end{bmatrix}.
$$

(2.5)

■

The addition operation satisfies certain properties. For example, because the addition of complex numbers is commutative, addition of complex vectors is also **commutative**:

$$
V + W =
\begin{bmatrix} (6 - 4i) + (16 + 2.3i) \\ (7 + 3i) + (-7i) \\ (4.2 - 8.1i) + (6) \\ (-3i) + (-4i) \end{bmatrix}
=
\begin{bmatrix} 22 - 1.7i \\ 7 - 4i \\ 10.2 - 8.1i \\ -7i \end{bmatrix}
$$

$$
=
\begin{bmatrix} (16 + 2.3i) + (6 - 4i) \\ (-7i) + (7 + 3i) \\ (6) + (4.2 - 8.1i) \\ (-4i) + (-3i) \end{bmatrix}
= W + V.
$$

(2.6)

Similarly, addition of complex vectors is also **associative**, i.e., given three vectors V, W, and X, we may add them as $(V + W) + X$ or as $V + (W + X)$. Associativity states that the resulting sums are the same:

$$(V + W) + X = V + (W + X).$$

(2.7)

Exercise 2.1.2   Formally prove the associativity property.   ■

There is also a distinguished vector called **zero**:

$$\mathbf{0} = \begin{bmatrix} 0 \\ 0 \\ 0 \\ 0 \end{bmatrix}, \tag{2.8}$$

which satisfies the following property: for all vectors $V \in \mathbb{C}^4$, we have

$$V + \mathbf{0} = V = \mathbf{0} + V. \tag{2.9}$$

Formally, $\mathbf{0}$ is defined as $\mathbf{0}[j] = 0$.

Every vector also has an **(additive) inverse** (or **negative**). Consider

$$V = \begin{bmatrix} 6 - 4i \\ 7 + 3i \\ 4.2 - 8.1i \\ -3i \end{bmatrix}. \tag{2.10}$$

There exists in $\mathbb{C}^4$ another vector

$$-V = \begin{bmatrix} -6 + 4i \\ -7 - 3i \\ -4.2 + 8.1i \\ 3i \end{bmatrix} \in \mathbb{C}^4 \tag{2.11}$$

such that

$$V + (-V) = \begin{bmatrix} 6 - 4i \\ 7 + 3i \\ 4.2 - 8.1i \\ -3i \end{bmatrix} + \begin{bmatrix} -6 + 4i \\ -7 - 3i \\ -4.2 + 8.1i \\ 3i \end{bmatrix} = \begin{bmatrix} 0 \\ 0 \\ 0 \\ 0 \end{bmatrix} = \mathbf{0}. \tag{2.12}$$

In general, for every vector $W \in \mathbb{C}^4$, there exists a vector $-W \in C^4$ such that $W + (-W) = (-W) + W = \mathbf{0}$. $-W$ is called the **inverse** of W. Formally,

$$(-W)[j] = -(W[j]). \tag{2.13}$$

The set $\mathbb{C}^4$ with the addition, inverse operations, and zero such that the addition is associative and commutative, form something called an **Abelian group**.

What other structure does our set $\mathbb{C}^4$ have? Take an arbitrary complex number, say, $c = 3 + 2i$. Call this number a **scalar**. Take a vector

$$
V = \begin{bmatrix} 6 + 3i \\ 0 + 0i \\ 5 + 1i \\ 4 \end{bmatrix}. \tag{2.14}
$$

We can **multiply an element by a scalar** by multiplying the scalar with each entry of the vector; i.e.,

$$
(3 + 2i) \cdot \begin{bmatrix} 6 + 3i \\ 0 + 0i \\ 5 + 1i \\ 4 \end{bmatrix} = \begin{bmatrix} 12 + 21i \\ 0 + 0i \\ 13 + 13i \\ 12 + 8i \end{bmatrix}. \tag{2.15}
$$

Formally, for a complex number c and a vector V, we form $c \cdot V$, which is defined as

$$
(c \cdot V)[j] = c \times V[j], \tag{2.16}
$$

where the $\times$ is complex multiplication. We shall omit the $\cdot$ when the scalar multiplication is understood.

Exercise 2.1.3 Scalar multiply $8 - 2i$ with $\begin{bmatrix} 16 + 2.3i \\ -7i \\ 6 \\ 5 - 4i \end{bmatrix}$. ∎

Scalar multiplication satisfies the following properties: for all $c, c_1, c_2 \in \mathbb{C}$ and for all $V, W \in \mathbb{C}^4$,

- $1 \cdot V = V$,
- $c_1 \cdot (c_2 \cdot V) = (c_1 \times c_2) \cdot V$,
- $c \cdot (V + W) = c \cdot V + c \cdot W$,
- $(c_1 + c_2) \cdot V = c_1 \cdot V + c_2 \cdot V$.

Exercise 2.1.4 Formally prove that $(c_1 + c_2) \cdot V = c_1 \cdot V + c_2 \cdot V$. ∎

An Abelian group with a scalar multiplication that satisfies these properties is called a **complex vector space**.

Notice that we have been working with vectors of size 4. However, everything that we have stated about vectors of size 4 is also true for vectors of arbitrary size. So the set $\mathbb{C}^n$ for a fixed but arbitrary n also has the structure of a complex vector space. In fact, these vector spaces will be the primary examples we will be working with for the rest of the book.

Programming Drill 2.1.1 *Write three functions that perform the addition, inverse, and scalar multiplication operations for $\mathbb{C}^n$, i.e., write a function that accepts the appropriate input for each of the operations and outputs the vector.*

2.2 DEFINITIONS, PROPERTIES, AND EXAMPLES

There are many other examples of complex vector spaces. We shall need to broaden our horizon and present a formal definition of a complex vector space.

Definition 2.2.1 *A **complex vector space** is a nonempty set $\mathbb{V}$, whose elements we shall call vectors, with three operations*

- *Addition:* $+ : \mathbb{V} \times \mathbb{V} \longrightarrow \mathbb{V}$
- *Negation:* $- : \mathbb{V} \longrightarrow \mathbb{V}$
- *Scalar multiplication:* $\cdot : \mathbb{C} \times \mathbb{V} \longrightarrow \mathbb{V}$

*and a distinguished element called the **zero vector** $\mathbf{0} \in \mathbb{V}$ in the set. These operations and zero must satisfy the following properties: for all V, W, $X \in \mathbb{V}$ and for all $c, c_1, c_2 \in \mathbb{C}$,*

   (i) *Commutativity of addition:* $V + W = W + V$,
  (ii) *Associativity of addition:* $(V + W) + X = V + (W + X)$,
 (iii) *Zero is an additive identity:* $V + \mathbf{0} = V = \mathbf{0} + V$,
  (iv) *Every vector has an inverse:* $V + (-V) = \mathbf{0} = (-V) + V$,
   (v) *Scalar multiplication has a unit:* $1 \cdot V = V$,
  (vi) *Scalar multiplication respects complex multiplication:*

$$c_1 \cdot (c_2 \cdot V) = (c_1 \times c_2) \cdot V, \tag{2.17}$$

 (vii) *Scalar multiplication distributes over addition:*

$$c \cdot (V + W) = c \cdot V + c \cdot W, \tag{2.18}$$

(viii) *Scalar multiplication distributes over complex addition:*

$$(c_1 + c_2) \cdot V = c_1 \cdot V + c_2 \cdot V. \tag{2.19}$$

To recap, any set that has an addition operation, an inverse operation, and a zero element that satisfies Properties (i), (ii), (iii), and (iv) is called an **Abelian group**. If, furthermore, there is a scalar multiplication operation that satisfies all the properties, then the set with the operations is called a **complex vector space**.

Although our main concern is complex vector spaces, we can gain much intuition from real vector spaces.

Definition 2.2.2 *A **real vector space** is a nonempty set $\mathbb{V}$ (whose elements we shall call vectors), along with an addition operation and a negation operation. Most important, there is a scalar multiplication that uses $\mathbb{R}$ and not $\mathbb{C}$, i.e.,*

$$\cdot : \mathbb{R} \times \mathbb{V} \longrightarrow \mathbb{V}. \tag{2.20}$$

This set and these operations must satisfy the analogous properties of a complex vector space.

In plain words, a real vector space is like a complex vector space except that we only require the scalar multiplication to be defined for scalars in $\mathbb{R} \subset \mathbb{C}$. From the fact that $\mathbb{R} \subset \mathbb{C}$, it is easy to see that for every $\mathbb{V}$ we have $\mathbb{R} \times \mathbb{V} \subset \mathbb{C} \times \mathbb{V}$. If we have a given

$$\cdot : \mathbb{C} \times \mathbb{V} \longrightarrow \mathbb{V}, \tag{2.21}$$

then we can write

$$\mathbb{R} \times \mathbb{V} \hookrightarrow \mathbb{C} \times \mathbb{V} \longrightarrow \mathbb{V}. \tag{2.22}$$

We conclude that every complex vector space can automatically be given a real vector space structure.

Let us descend from the abstract highlands and look at some concrete examples.

Example 2.2.1 $\mathbb{C}^n$, the set of vectors of length n with complex entries, is a complex vector space that serves as our primary example for the rest of the book. In Section 2.1, we exhibited the operations and described the properties that are satisfied. □

Example 2.2.2 $\mathbb{C}^n$, the set of vectors of length n with complex entries, is also a real vector space because every complex vector space is also a real vector space. The operations are the same as those in Example 2.2.1. □

Example 2.2.3 $\mathbb{R}^n$, the set of vectors of length n with real number entries, is a real vector space. Notice that there is no obvious way to make this into a complex vector space. What would the scalar multiplication of a complex number with a real vector be? □

In Chapter 1, we discussed the geometry of $\mathbb{C} = \mathbb{C}^1$. We showed how every complex number can be thought of as a point in a two-dimensional plane. Things get more complicated for $\mathbb{C}^2$. Every element of $\mathbb{C}^2$ involves two complex numbers or four real numbers. One could visualize this as an element of four-dimensional space. However, the human brain is not equipped to visualize four-dimensional space. The most we can deal with is three dimensions. Many times throughout this text, we shall discuss $\mathbb{C}^n$ and then revert to $\mathbb{R}^3$ in order to develop an intuition for what is going on.

It pays to pause for a moment to take an in-depth look at the geometry of $\mathbb{R}^3$. Every vector of $\mathbb{R}^3$ can be thought of as a point in three-dimensional space or equivalently, as an arrow from the origin of $\mathbb{R}^3$ to that point. So the vector $\begin{bmatrix} 5 \\ -7 \\ 6.3 \end{bmatrix}$ shown in Figure 2.1 is 5 units in the x direction, -7 units in the y direction, and 6.3 units in the z direction.

Given two vectors $V = \begin{bmatrix} r_0 \\ r_1 \\ r_2 \end{bmatrix}$ and $V' = \begin{bmatrix} r'_0 \\ r'_1 \\ r'_2 \end{bmatrix}$ of $\mathbb{R}^3$, we may add them to form $\begin{bmatrix} r_0 + r'_0 \\ r_1 + r'_1 \\ r_2 + r'_2 \end{bmatrix}$. Addition can be seen as making a parallelogram in $\mathbb{R}^3$ where you attach the beginning of one arrow to the end of the other one. The result of the addition is

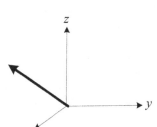

Figure 2.1. A vector in three dimensional space.

the composition of the arrows (see Figure 2.2). The reason that we can be ambiguous about which arrow comes first demonstrates the commutativity property of addition.

Given a vector $V = \begin{bmatrix} r_0 \\ r_1 \\ r_2 \end{bmatrix}$ in $\mathbb{R}^3$, we form the inverse $-V = \begin{bmatrix} -r_0 \\ -r_1 \\ -r_2 \end{bmatrix}$ by looking at

the arrow in the opposite direction with respect to all dimensions (as in Figure 2.3).

And finally, the scalar multiplication of a real number r and a vector $V = \begin{bmatrix} r_0 \\ r_1 \\ r_2 \end{bmatrix}$

is $r \cdot V = \begin{bmatrix} rr_0 \\ rr_1 \\ rr_2 \end{bmatrix}$, which is simply the vector V stretched or shrunk by r (as in Fig-

ure 2.4).

It is useful to look at some of the properties of a vector space from the geometric point of view. For example, consider the property $r \cdot (V + W) = r \cdot V + r \cdot W$. This corresponds to Figure 2.5.

Exercise 2.2.1   Let $r_1 = 2$, $r_2 = 3$, and $V = \begin{bmatrix} 2 \\ -4 \\ 1 \end{bmatrix}$. Verify Property (vi), i.e., calculate $r_1 \cdot (r_2 \cdot V)$ and $(r_1 \times r_2) \cdot V$ and show that they coincide.   ∎

Exercise 2.2.2   Draw pictures in $\mathbb{R}^3$ that explain Properties (vi) and (viii) of the definition of a real vector space.   ∎

Let us continue our list of examples.

Example 2.2.4 $\mathbb{C}^{m \times n}$, the set of all m-by-n matrices (two-dimensional arrays) with complex entries, is a complex vector space.   □

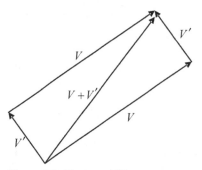

Figure 2.2. Vector addition.

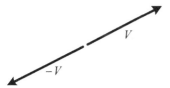

Figure 2.3. Inverse of a vector.

For a given $A \in \mathbb{C}^{m \times n}$, we denote the complex entry in the jth row and the kth column as $A[j, k]$ or $c_{j,k}$. We shall denote the jth row as $A[j, -]$ and the kth column as $A[-, k]$. Several times throughout the text we shall show the row and column numbers explicitly to the left and top of the square brackets:

$$A = \begin{array}{c} \\ \mathbf{0} \\ \mathbf{1} \\ \vdots \\ \mathbf{m-1} \end{array} \overset{\begin{array}{cccc} \mathbf{0} & \mathbf{1} & \cdots & \mathbf{n-1} \end{array}}{\begin{bmatrix} c_{0,0} & c_{0,1} & \cdots & c_{0,n-1} \\ c_{1,0} & c_{1,1} & \cdots & c_{1,n-1} \\ \vdots & \vdots & \ddots & \vdots \\ c_{m-1,0} & c_{m-1,1} & \cdots & c_{m-1,n-1} \end{bmatrix}}. \tag{2.23}$$

The operations for $\mathbb{C}^{m \times n}$ are given as follows: Addition is

$$\begin{bmatrix} c_{0,0} & c_{0,1} & \cdots & c_{0,n-1} \\ c_{1,0} & c_{1,1} & \cdots & c_{1,n-1} \\ \vdots & \vdots & \ddots & \vdots \\ c_{m-1,0} & c_{m-1,1} & \cdots & c_{m-1,n-1} \end{bmatrix} + \begin{bmatrix} d_{0,0} & d_{0,1} & \cdots & d_{0,n-1} \\ d_{1,0} & d_{1,1} & \cdots & d_{1,n-1} \\ \vdots & \vdots & \ddots & \vdots \\ d_{m-1,0} & d_{m-1,1} & \cdots & d_{m-1,n-1} \end{bmatrix}$$

$$= \begin{bmatrix} c_{0,0} + d_{0,0} & c_{0,1} + d_{0,1} & \cdots & c_{0,n-1} + d_{0,n-1} \\ c_{1,0} + d_{1,0} & c_{1,1} + d_{1,1} & \cdots & c_{1,n-1} + d_{1,n-1} \\ \vdots & \vdots & \ddots & \vdots \\ c_{m-1,0} + d_{m-1,0} & c_{m-1,1} + d_{m-1,1} & \cdots & c_{m-1,n-1} + d_{m-1,n-1} \end{bmatrix}. \tag{2.24}$$

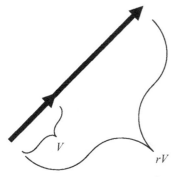

Figure 2.4. A real multiple of a vector.

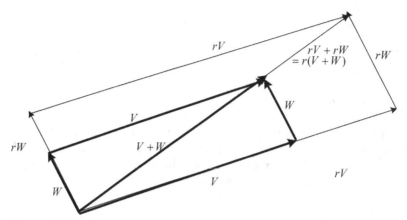

Figure 2.5. Scalar multiplication distributes over addition.

The inverse operation is given as

$$-\begin{bmatrix} c_{0,0} & c_{0,1} & \cdots & c_{0,n-1} \\ c_{1,0} & c_{1,1} & \cdots & c_{1,n-1} \\ \vdots & \vdots & \ddots & \vdots \\ c_{m-1,0} & c_{m-1,1} & \cdots & c_{m-1,n-1} \end{bmatrix} = \begin{bmatrix} -c_{0,0} & -c_{0,1} & \cdots & -c_{0,n-1} \\ -c_{1,0} & -c_{1,1} & \cdots & -c_{1,n-1} \\ \vdots & \vdots & \ddots & \vdots \\ -c_{m-1,0} & -c_{m-1,1} & \cdots & -c_{m-1,n-1} \end{bmatrix}.$$

(2.25)

Scalar multiplication is given as

$$c \cdot \begin{bmatrix} c_{0,0} & c_{0,1} & \cdots & c_{0,n-1} \\ c_{1,0} & c_{1,1} & \cdots & c_{1,n-1} \\ \vdots & \vdots & \ddots & \vdots \\ c_{m-1,0} & c_{m-1,1} & \cdots & c_{m-1,n-1} \end{bmatrix}$$

$$= \begin{bmatrix} c \times c_{0,0} & c \times c_{0,1} & \cdots & c \times c_{0,n-1} \\ c \times c_{1,0} & c \times c_{1,1} & \cdots & c \times c_{1,n-1} \\ \vdots & \vdots & \ddots & \vdots \\ c \times c_{m-1,0} & c \times c_{m-1,1} & \cdots & c \times c_{m-1,n-1} \end{bmatrix}.$$

(2.26)

Formally, these operations can be described by the following formulas:

For two matrices, $A, B \in \mathbb{C}^{m \times n}$, we add them as

$$(A + B)[j, k] = A[j, k] + B[j, k].$$

(2.27)

The inverse of A is

$$(-A)[j, k] = -(A[j, k]).$$

(2.28)

The scalar multiplication of A with a complex number $c \in \mathbb{C}$ is

$$(c \cdot A)[j, k] = c \times A[j, k]. \tag{2.29}$$

Exercise 2.2.3 Let $c_1 = 2i$, $c_2 = 1 + 2i$, and $A = \begin{bmatrix} 1-i & 3 \\ 2+2i & 4+i \end{bmatrix}$. Verify Properties (vi) and (viii) in showing $\mathbb{C}^{2 \times 2}$ is a complex vector space. ■

Exercise 2.2.4 Show that these operations on $\mathbb{C}^{m \times n}$ satisfy Properties (v), (vi), and (viii) of being a complex vector space. ■

Programming Drill 2.2.1 *Convert your functions from the last programming drill so that instead of accepting elements of $\mathbb{C}^n$, they accept elements of $\mathbb{C}^{m \times n}$.*

When $n = 1$, the matrices $\mathbb{C}^{m \times n} = \mathbb{C}^{m \times 1} = \mathbb{C}^m$, which we dealt with in Section 2.1. Thus, we can think of vectors as special types of matrices.

When $m = n$, the vector space $\mathbb{C}^{n \times n}$ has more operations and more structure than just a complex vector space. Here are three operations that one can perform on an $A \in \mathbb{C}^{n \times n}$:

■ The **transpose** of A, denoted A^T, is defined as

$$A^T[j, k] = A[k, j]. \tag{2.30}$$

■ The **conjugate** of A, denoted $\overline{A}$, is the matrix in which each element is the complex conjugate of the corresponding element of the original matrix,[3] i.e., $\overline{A}[j, k] = \overline{A[j, k]}$.

■ The transpose operation and the conjugate operation are combined to form the **adjoint** or **dagger** operation. The adjoint of A, denoted as $A^\dagger$, is defined as $A^\dagger = (\overline{A})^T = \overline{(A^T)}$ or $A^\dagger[j, k] = \overline{A[k, j]}$.

Exercise 2.2.5 Find the transpose, conjugate, and adjoint of

$$\begin{bmatrix} 6-3i & 2+12i & -19i \\ 0 & 5+2.1i & 17 \\ 1 & 2+5i & 3-4.5i \end{bmatrix}. \tag{2.31}$$

■

These three operations are defined even when $m \neq n$. The transpose and adjoint are both functions from $\mathbb{C}^{m \times n}$ to $\mathbb{C}^{n \times m}$.

These operations satisfy the following properties for all $c \in \mathbb{C}$ and for all A, $B \in \mathbb{C}^{m \times n}$:

(i) Transpose is idempotent: $(A^T)^T = A$.
(ii) Transpose respects addition: $(A + B)^T = A^T + B^T$.
(iii) Transpose respects scalar multiplication: $(c \cdot A)^T = c \cdot A^T$.

---

[3] This notation is overloaded. It is an operation on complex numbers and complex matrices.

(iv) Conjugate is idempotent: $\overline{\overline{A}} = A$.
(v) Conjugate respects addition: $\overline{A + B} = \overline{A} + \overline{B}$.
(vi) Conjugate respects scalar multiplication: $\overline{c \cdot A} = \overline{c} \cdot \overline{A}$.
(vii) Adjoint is idempotent: $(A^\dagger)^\dagger = A$.
(viii) Adjoint respects addition: $(A + B)^\dagger = A^\dagger + B^\dagger$.
(ix) Adjoint relates to scalar multiplication: $(c \cdot A)^\dagger = \overline{c} \cdot A^\dagger$.

Exercise 2.2.6 Prove that conjugation respects scalar multiplication, i.e., $\overline{c \cdot A} = \overline{c} \cdot \overline{A}$. ∎

Exercise 2.2.7 Prove Properties (vii), (viii), and (ix) using Properties (i) – (vi). ∎

The transpose shall be used often in the text to save space. Rather than writing

$$
\begin{bmatrix}
c_0 \\
c_1 \\
\vdots \\
c_{n-1}
\end{bmatrix}
\tag{2.32}
$$

which requires more space, we write $[c_0, c_1, \cdots, c_{n-1}]^T$.

When $m = n$, there is another binary operation that is used: **matrix multiplication**. Consider the following two 3-by-3 matrices:

$$
A = \begin{bmatrix}
3 + 2i & 0 & 5 - 6i \\
1 & 4 + 2i & i \\
4 - i & 0 & 4
\end{bmatrix}, \quad
B = \begin{bmatrix}
5 & 2 - i & 6 - 4i \\
0 & 4 + 5i & 2 \\
7 - 4i & 2 + 7i & 0
\end{bmatrix}.
\tag{2.33}
$$

We form the matrix product of A and B, denoted $A \star B$. $A \star B$ will also be a 3-by-3 matrix. $(A \star B)[0, 0]$ will be found by multiplying each element of the 0th row of A with the corresponding element of the 0th column of B. We then sum the results:

$$
(A \star B)[0, 0] = ((3 + 2i) \times 5) + (0 \times 0) + ((5 - 6i) \times (7 - 4i))
$$
$$
= (15 + 10i) + (0) + (11 - 62i) = 26 - 52i.
\tag{2.34}
$$

The $(A \star B)[j, k]$ entry can be found by multiplying each element of $A[j, -]$ with the appropriate element of $B[-, k]$ and summing the results. So,

$$
(A \star B) = \begin{bmatrix}
26 - 52i & 60 + 24i & 26 \\
9 + 7i & 1 + 29i & 14 \\
48 - 21i & 15 + 22i & 20 - 22i
\end{bmatrix}.
\tag{2.35}
$$

Exercise 2.2.8 Find $B \star A$. Does it equal $A \star B$? ∎

Matrix multiplication is defined in a more general setting. The matrices do not have to be square. Rather, the number of columns in the first matrix must be the same as the number of rows in the second one. Matrix multiplication is a binary operation

$$\star : \mathbb{C}^{m \times n} \times \mathbb{C}^{n \times p} \longrightarrow \mathbb{C}^{m \times p}. \tag{2.36}$$

Formally, given A in $\mathbb{C}^{m \times n}$ and B in $\mathbb{C}^{n \times p}$, we construct $A \star B$ in $\mathbb{C}^{m \times p}$ as

$$(A \star B)[j, k] = \sum_{h=0}^{n-1} (A[j, h] \times B[h, k]). \tag{2.37}$$

When the multiplication is understood, we shall omit the $\star$.

For every n, there is a special n-by-n matrix called the **identity matrix**,

$$I_n = \begin{bmatrix} 1 & 0 & \cdots & 0 \\ 0 & 1 & \cdots & 0 \\ \vdots & \vdots & \ddots & \vdots \\ 0 & 0 & \cdots & 1 \end{bmatrix}, \tag{2.38}$$

that plays the role of a unit of matrix multiplication. When n is understood, we shall omit it.

Matrix multiplication satisfies the following properties: For all A, B, and C in $\mathbb{C}^{n \times n}$,

(i) Matrix multiplication is associative: $(A \star B) \star C = A \star (B \star C)$.
(ii) Matrix multiplication has I_n as a unit: $I_n \star A = A = A \star I_n$.
(iii) Matrix multiplication distributes over addition:

$$A \star (B + C) = (A \star B) + (A \star C), \tag{2.39}$$

$$(B + C) \star A = (B \star A) + (C \star A). \tag{2.40}$$

(iv) Matrix multiplication respects scalar multiplication:

$$c \cdot (A \star B) = (c \cdot A) \star B = A \star (c \cdot B). \tag{2.41}$$

(v) Matrix multiplication relates to the transpose:

$$(A \star B)^T = B^T \star A^T. \tag{2.42}$$

(vi) Matrix multiplication respects the conjugate:

$$\overline{A \star B} = \overline{A} \star \overline{B}. \tag{2.43}$$

(vii) Matrix multiplication relates to the adjoint:

$$(A \star B)^\dagger = B^\dagger \star A^\dagger. \tag{2.44}$$

Notice that commutativity is *not* a basic property of matrix multiplication. This fact will be very important in quantum mechanics.

Exercise 2.2.9 Prove Property (v) in the above list. ■

Exercise 2.2.10 Use A and B from Equation (2.33) and show that $(A \star B)^\dagger = B^\dagger \star A^\dagger$. ∎

Exercise 2.2.11 Prove Property (vii) from Properties (v) and (vi). ∎

Definition 2.2.3 *A complex vector space $\mathbb{V}$ with a multiplication $\star$ that satisfies the first four properties is called a* **complex algebra***.*

Programming Drill 2.2.2 *Write a function that accepts two complex matrices of the appropriate size. The function should do matrix multiplication and return the result.*

Let A be any element in $\mathbb{C}^{n \times n}$. Then for any element $B \in \mathbb{C}^n$, we have that $A \star B$ is in $\mathbb{C}^n$. In other words, multiplication by A gives one a function from $\mathbb{C}^n$ to $\mathbb{C}^n$. From Equations (2.39) and (2.41), we see that this function preserves addition and scalar multiplication. We will write this map as $A : \mathbb{C}^n \longrightarrow \mathbb{C}^n$.

Let us look ahead for a moment and see what relevance this abstract mathematics has for quantum computing. Just as $\mathbb{C}^n$ has a major role, the complex algebra $\mathbb{C}^{n \times n}$ shall also be in our cast of characters. The elements of $\mathbb{C}^n$ are the ways of describing the states of a quantum system. Some suitable elements of $\mathbb{C}^{n \times n}$ will correspond to the changes that occur to the states of a quantum system. Given a state $X \in \mathbb{C}^n$ and a matrix $A \in \mathbb{C}^{n \times n}$, we shall form another state of the system $A \star X$ which is an element of $\mathbb{C}^n$.[4] Formally, $\star$ in this case is a function $\star : \mathbb{C}^{n \times n} \times \mathbb{C}^n \longrightarrow \mathbb{C}^n$. We say that the algebra of matrices "**acts**" on the vectors to yield new vectors. We shall see this **action** again and again in the following chapters.

Programming Drill 2.2.3 *Write a function that accepts a vector and a matrix and outputs the vector resulting from the "action."*

We return to our list of examples.

Example 2.2.5 $\mathbb{C}^{m \times n}$, the set of all m-by-n matrices (two-dimensional arrays) with complex entries, is a real vector space. (Remember: Every complex vector space is also a real vector space.) □

Example 2.2.6 $\mathbb{R}^{m \times n}$, the set of all m-by-n matrices (two-dimensional arrays) with real entries, is a real vector space. □

Definition 2.2.4 *Given two complex vector spaces $\mathbb{V}$ and $\mathbb{V}'$, we say that $\mathbb{V}$ is a* **complex subspace** *of $\mathbb{V}'$ if $\mathbb{V}$ is a subset of $\mathbb{V}'$ and the operations of $\mathbb{V}$ are restrictions of operations of $\mathbb{V}'$.*

Equivalently, $\mathbb{V}$ is a complex subspace of $\mathbb{V}'$ if $\mathbb{V}$ is a subset of the set $\mathbb{V}'$ and

  (i) $\mathbb{V}$ is closed under addition: For all V_1 and V_2 in $\mathbb{V}$, $V_1 + V_2 \in \mathbb{V}$.
  (ii) $\mathbb{V}$ is closed under scalar multiplication: For all $c \in \mathbb{C}$ and $V \in \mathbb{V}$, $c \cdot V \in \mathbb{V}$.

---

[4] This might seem reminiscent of computer graphics. In fact, there is a vague relationship that we shall see when we discuss the Bloch sphere (in Chapter 5) and unitary matrices.

It turns out that being closed under addition and multiplication implies that $\mathbb{V}$ is also closed under inverse and that $\mathbf{0} \in \mathbb{V}$.

Example 2.2.7 Consider the set of all vectors of $\mathbb{C}^9$ with the second, fifth, and eighth position elements being 0:

$$[c_0, c_1, 0, c_3, c_4, 0, c_6, c_7, 0]^T. \tag{2.45}$$

It is not hard to see that this is a complex subspace of $\mathbb{C}^9$. We shall see in a few moments that this subspace is the "same" as $\mathbb{C}^6$. $\square$

Example 2.2.8 Consider the set $Poly_n$ of polynomials of degree n or less in one variable with coefficients in $\mathbb{C}$.

$$P(x) = c_0 + c_1 x + c_2 x^2 + \cdots + c_n x^n. \tag{2.46}$$

$Poly_n$ forms a complex vector space. $\square$

For completeness, let us go through the operations. Addition is given as

$$P(x) + Q(x) = (c_0 + c_1 x + c_2 x^2 + \cdots + c_n x^n) + (d_0 + d_1 x + d_2 x^2 + \cdots + d_n x^n)$$
$$= (c_0 + d_0) + (c_1 + d_1)x + (c_2 + d_2)x^2 + \cdots + (c_n + d_n)x^n. \tag{2.47}$$

Negation is given as

$$-P(x) = -c_0 - c_1 x - c_2 x^2 - \cdots - c_n x^n. \tag{2.48}$$

Scalar multiplication by $c \in \mathbb{C}$ is given as

$$c \cdot P(x) = c \times c_0 + c \times c_1 x + c \times c_2 x^2 + \cdots + c \times c_n x^n. \tag{2.49}$$

Exercise 2.2.12 Show that $Poly_n$ with these operations satisfies the properties of being a complex vector space. ∎

Exercise 2.2.13 Show that $Poly_5$ is a complex subspace of $Poly_7$. ∎

Example 2.2.9 Polynomials in one variable of degree n or less with coefficients in $\mathbb{C}$ also form a real vector space. $\square$

Example 2.2.10 Polynomials in one variable of degree n or less with coefficients in $\mathbb{R}$

$$P(x) = r_0 + r_1 x + r_2 x^2 + \cdots + r_n x^n \tag{2.50}$$

form a real vector space. $\square$

Definition 2.2.5 *Let $\mathbb{V}$ and $\mathbb{V}'$ be two complex vector spaces. A* **linear map** *from $\mathbb{V}$ to $\mathbb{V}'$ is a function $f : \mathbb{V} \longrightarrow \mathbb{V}'$ such that for all V, V_1, $V_2 \in \mathbb{V}$, and $c \in \mathbb{C}$,*

   (i) *f respects the addition: $f(V_1 + V_2) = f(V_1) + f(V_2)$,*
   (ii) *f respects the scalar multiplication: $f(c \cdot V) = c \cdot f(V)$.*

Almost all the maps that we shall deal with in this text are linear maps. We have already seen that when a matrix acts on a vector space, it is a linear map. We shall call any linear map from a complex vector space to itself an **operator**. If $F : \mathbb{C}^n \longrightarrow \mathbb{C}^n$ is an operator on $\mathbb{C}^n$ and A is an n-by-n matrix such that for all V we have $F(V) = A \star V$, then we say that F is **represented** by A. Several different matrices might represent the same operator.

Computer scientists usually store a polynomial as the array of its coefficients, i.e., a polynomial with $n + 1$ complex coefficients is stored as an $n + 1$ vector. So it is not surprising that $Poly_n$ is the "same" as $\mathbb{C}^{n+1}$. We will now formulate what it means for two vector spaces to be the "same."

Definition 2.2.6   *Two complex vector spaces* $\mathbb{V}$ *and* $\mathbb{V}'$ *are* **isomorphic** *if there is a one-to-one onto linear map* $f : \mathbb{V} \longrightarrow \mathbb{V}'$. *Such a map is called an* **isomorphism**. *When two vector spaces are isomorphic, it means that the names of the elements of the vector spaces are renamed but the structure of the two vector spaces are the same. Two such vector spaces are "essentially the same" or "the same up to isomorphism."*

Exercise 2.2.14   Show that all real matrices of the form

$$
\begin{bmatrix} x & y \\ -y & x \end{bmatrix}
\tag{2.51}
$$

comprise a real subspace of $\mathbb{R}^{2 \times 2}$. Then show that this subspace is isomorphic to $\mathbb{C}$ via the map $f : \mathbb{C} \longrightarrow \mathbb{R}^{2 \times 2}$ that is defined as

$$
f(x + iy) = \begin{bmatrix} x & y \\ -y & x \end{bmatrix}.
\tag{2.52}
$$

■

Example 2.2.11   Consider the set $Func(\mathbb{N}, \mathbb{C})$ of functions from the natural numbers $\mathbb{N}$ to the complex numbers $\mathbb{C}$. Given two functions $f : \mathbb{N} \longrightarrow \mathbb{C}$ and $g : \mathbb{N} \longrightarrow \mathbb{C}$, we may add them to form

$$
(f + g)(n) = f(n) + g(n).
\tag{2.53}
$$

The additive inverse of f is

$$
(-f)(n) = -(f(n)).
\tag{2.54}
$$

The scalar multiple of $c \in \mathbb{C}$ and f is the function

$$
(c \cdot f)(n) = c \times f(n).
\tag{2.55}
$$

Because the operations are determined by their values at each of their "points" in the input, the constructed functions are said to be constructed **pointwise**.   □

Exercise 2.2.15 Show that $Func(\mathbb{N}, \mathbb{C})$ with these operations forms a complex vector space. ∎

Example 2.2.12 We can generalize $Func(\mathbb{N}, \mathbb{C})$ to other sets of functions. For any $a < b$ in $\mathbb{R}$, the set of functions from the interval $[a, b] \subseteq \mathbb{R}$ to $\mathbb{C}$ denoted $Func([a, b], \mathbb{C})$ is a complex vector space. □

Exercise 2.2.16 Show that $Func(\mathbb{N}, \mathbb{R})$ and $Func([a, b], \mathbb{R})$ are real vector spaces. ∎

Example 2.2.13 There are several ways of constructing new vector spaces from existing ones. Here we see one method and Section 2.7 describes another. Let $(\mathbb{V}, +, -, \mathbf{0}, \cdot)$ and $(\mathbb{V}', +', -', \mathbf{0}', \cdot')$ be two complex vector spaces. We construct a new complex vector space $(\mathbb{V} \times \mathbb{V}', +'', -'', \mathbf{0}'', \cdot'')$ called the **Cartesian product**[5] or the **direct sum** of $\mathbb{V}$ and $\mathbb{V}'$. The vectors are ordered pairs of vectors $(V, V') \in \mathbb{V} \times \mathbb{V}'$. Operations are performed pointwise:

$$(V_1, V_1') +'' (V_2, V_2') = (V_1 + V_2, V_1' +' V_2'), \tag{2.56}$$

$$-''(V, V') = (-V, -'V'), \tag{2.57}$$

$$\mathbf{0}'' = (\mathbf{0}, \mathbf{0}'), \tag{2.58}$$

$$c \cdot'' (V, V') = (c \cdot V, c \cdot' V'). \tag{2.59}$$

□

Exercise 2.2.17 Show that $\mathbb{C}^m \times \mathbb{C}^n$ is isomorphic to $\mathbb{C}^{m+n}$. ∎

Exercise 2.2.18 Show that $\mathbb{C}^m$ and $\mathbb{C}^n$ are each a complex subspace of $\mathbb{C}^m \times \mathbb{C}^n$. ∎

2.3 BASIS AND DIMENSION

A basis of a vector space is a set of vectors of that vector space that is special in the sense that all other vectors can be uniquely written in terms of these basis vectors.

Definition 2.3.1 *Let $\mathbb{V}$ be a complex (real) vector space. $V \in \mathbb{V}$ is a* **linear combination** *of the vectors $V_0, V_1, \ldots, V_{n-1}$ in $\mathbb{V}$ if V can be written as*

$$V = c_0 \cdot V_0 + c_1 \cdot V_1 + \cdots + c_{n-1} \cdot V_{n-1} \tag{2.60}$$

for some $c_0, c_1, \ldots, c_{n-1}$ in $\mathbb{C}$ ($\mathbb{R}$).

Let us return to $\mathbb{R}^3$ for examples.

---

[5] A note to the meticulous reader: Although we used $\times$ for the product of two complex numbers, here we use it for the Cartesian product of sets and the Cartesian product of vector spaces. We feel it is better to overload known symbols than to introduce a plethora of new ones.

Example 2.3.1   As

$$
3 \begin{bmatrix} 5 \\ -2 \\ 3 \end{bmatrix} + 5 \begin{bmatrix} 0 \\ 1 \\ 4 \end{bmatrix} - 4 \begin{bmatrix} -6 \\ 1 \\ 0 \end{bmatrix} + 2.1 \begin{bmatrix} 3 \\ 1 \\ 1 \end{bmatrix} = \begin{bmatrix} 45.3 \\ -2.9 \\ 31.1 \end{bmatrix}, \tag{2.61}
$$

we say that

$$
[45.3, -2.9, 31.1]^T \tag{2.62}
$$

is a linear combination of

$$
\begin{bmatrix} 5 \\ -2 \\ 3 \end{bmatrix}, \begin{bmatrix} 0 \\ 1 \\ 4 \end{bmatrix}, \begin{bmatrix} -6 \\ 1 \\ 0 \end{bmatrix}, \quad \text{and} \quad \begin{bmatrix} 3 \\ 1 \\ 1 \end{bmatrix}. \tag{2.63}
$$

$\square$

Definition 2.3.2   *A set $\{V_0, V_1, \ldots, V_{n-1}\}$ of vectors in $\mathbb{V}$ is called **linearly independent** if*

$$
\mathbf{0} = c_0 \cdot V_0 + c_1 \cdot V_1 + \cdots + c_{n-1} \cdot V_{n-1} \tag{2.64}
$$

implies that $c_0 = c_1 = \cdots = c_{n-1} = 0$. This means that the only way that a linear combination of the vectors can be the zero vector is if all the c_j are zero.

It can be shown that this definition is equivalent to saying that for any nonzero $V \in \mathbb{V}$, there are *unique* coefficients $c_0, c_1, \ldots, c_{n-1}$ in $\mathbb{C}$ such that

$$
V = c_0 \cdot V_0 + c_1 \cdot V_1 + \cdots + c_{n-1} \cdot V_{n-1}. \tag{2.65}
$$

The set of vectors are called linearly independent because each of the vectors in the set $\{V_0, V_1, \ldots, V_{n-1}\}$ cannot be written as a combination of the others in the set.

Example 2.3.2   The set of vectors

$$
\left\{ \begin{bmatrix} 1 \\ 1 \\ 1 \end{bmatrix}, \begin{bmatrix} 0 \\ 1 \\ 1 \end{bmatrix}, \begin{bmatrix} 0 \\ 0 \\ 1 \end{bmatrix} \right\} \tag{2.66}
$$

is linearly independent because the only way that

$$
\mathbf{0} = \begin{bmatrix} 0 \\ 0 \\ 0 \end{bmatrix} = x \begin{bmatrix} 1 \\ 1 \\ 1 \end{bmatrix} + y \begin{bmatrix} 0 \\ 1 \\ 1 \end{bmatrix} + z \begin{bmatrix} 0 \\ 0 \\ 1 \end{bmatrix} \tag{2.67}
$$

can occur is if $0 = x$, $0 = x + y$, and $0 = x + y + z$. By substitution, we see that $x = y = z = 0$. $\square$

Example 2.3.3 The set of vectors

$$\left\{ \begin{bmatrix} 1 \\ 1 \\ 1 \end{bmatrix}, \begin{bmatrix} 0 \\ 1 \\ 1 \end{bmatrix}, \begin{bmatrix} 2 \\ -1 \\ -1 \end{bmatrix} \right\} \tag{2.68}$$

is not linearly independent (called **linearly dependent**) because

$$\mathbf{0} = \begin{bmatrix} 0 \\ 0 \\ 0 \end{bmatrix} = x \begin{bmatrix} 1 \\ 1 \\ 1 \end{bmatrix} + y \begin{bmatrix} 0 \\ 1 \\ 1 \end{bmatrix} + z \begin{bmatrix} 2 \\ -1 \\ -1 \end{bmatrix} \tag{2.69}$$

can happen when $x = 2$, $y = -3$, and $z = -1$. □

Exercise 2.3.1 Show that the set of vectors

$$\left\{ \begin{bmatrix} 1 \\ 2 \\ 3 \end{bmatrix}, \begin{bmatrix} 3 \\ 0 \\ 2 \end{bmatrix}, \begin{bmatrix} 1 \\ -4 \\ -4 \end{bmatrix} \right\} \tag{2.70}$$

is not linearly independent. ■

Definition 2.3.3 *A set $\mathcal{B} = \{V_0, V_1, \ldots, V_{n-1}\} \subseteq \mathbb{V}$ of vectors is called a **basis** of a (complex) vector space $\mathbb{V}$ if both*

 (i) *every, $V \in \mathbb{V}$ can be written as a linear combination of vectors from $\mathcal{B}$ and*
 (ii) *$\mathcal{B}$ is linearly independent.*

Example 2.3.4 $\mathbb{R}^3$ has a basis

$$\left\{ \begin{bmatrix} 1 \\ 1 \\ 1 \end{bmatrix}, \begin{bmatrix} 0 \\ 1 \\ 1 \end{bmatrix}, \begin{bmatrix} 0 \\ 0 \\ 1 \end{bmatrix} \right\}. \tag{2.71}$$

□

Exercise 2.3.2 Verify that the preceding three vectors are in fact a basis of $\mathbb{R}^3$. ■

There may be many sets that each form a basis of a particular vector space but there is also a basis that is easier to work with called the **canonical basis** or the **standard basis**. Many of the examples that we will deal with have canonical basis. Let us look at some examples of canonical basis.

■ $\mathbb{R}^3$:

$$\left\{ \begin{bmatrix} 1 \\ 0 \\ 0 \end{bmatrix}, \begin{bmatrix} 0 \\ 1 \\ 0 \end{bmatrix}, \begin{bmatrix} 0 \\ 0 \\ 1 \end{bmatrix} \right\}. \tag{2.72}$$

■ $\mathbb{C}^n$ (and $\mathbb{R}^n$):

$$E_0 = \begin{bmatrix} 1 \\ 0 \\ \vdots \\ 0 \end{bmatrix}, \quad E_1 = \begin{bmatrix} 0 \\ 1 \\ \vdots \\ 0 \end{bmatrix}, \ \dots, \ E_i = \begin{bmatrix} 0 \\ \vdots \\ 1 \\ 0 \end{bmatrix}, \ \dots, \ E_{n-1} = \begin{bmatrix} 0 \\ 0 \\ \vdots \\ 1 \end{bmatrix}. \tag{2.73}$$

Every vector $[c_0, c_1, \dots, c_{n-1}]^T$ can be written as

$$\sum_{j=0}^{n-1} (c_j \cdot E_j). \tag{2.74}$$

■ $\mathbb{C}^{m \times n}$: The canonical basis for this vector space consists of matrices of the form

$$E_{j,k} = \begin{array}{c} \\ \mathbf{0} \\ \mathbf{1} \\ \vdots \\ \mathbf{j} \\ \vdots \\ \mathbf{m-1} \end{array} \begin{array}{cccccc} \mathbf{0} & \mathbf{1} & \cdots & \mathbf{k} & \cdots & \mathbf{n-1} \\ \begin{bmatrix} 0 & 0 & \cdots & 0 & \cdots & 0 \\ 0 & 0 & \cdots & 0 & \cdots & 0 \\ \vdots & \vdots & \cdots & & \cdots & \vdots \\ 0 & 0 & \cdots & 1 & \cdots & 0 \\ \vdots & \vdots & \cdots & & \cdots & \vdots \\ 0 & 0 & \cdots & 0 & \cdots & 0 \end{bmatrix} \end{array}, \tag{2.75}$$

where $E_{j,k}$ has a 1 in row j, column k, and 0's everywhere else. There is an $E_{j,k}$ for $j = 0, 1, \dots, m-1$ and $k = 0, 1, \dots, n-1$. It is not hard to see that for every m-by-n matrix, A can be written as the sum:

$$A = \sum_{j=0}^{m-1} \sum_{k=0}^{n-1} A[j, k] \cdot E_{j,k}. \tag{2.76}$$

■ $Poly_n$: The canonical basis is formed by the following set of monomials:

$$1, x, x^2, \dots, x^n. \tag{2.77}$$

■ *Func*($\mathbb{N}, \mathbb{C}$): The canonical basis is composed of a countably infinite[6] number of functions f_j ($j = 0, 1, 2, \dots$), where f_j is defined as

$$f_j(n) = \begin{cases} 1, & \text{if } j = n, \\ 0, & \text{otherwise.} \end{cases} \tag{2.78}$$

The definition previously given of a finite linear combination can easily be generalized to an infinite linear combination. It is not hard to see that any function $f \in Func(\mathbb{N}, \mathbb{C})$ can be written as the infinite sum

$$f = \sum_{j=0}^{\infty} c_j \cdot f_j, \tag{2.79}$$

where $c_j = f(j)$. It is also not hard to see that these functions are linearly independent. Hence they form a basis for $Func(\mathbb{N}, \mathbb{C})$.

■ (For the calculus-savvy reader.) $Func([a, b], \mathbb{C})$: The canonical basis is composed of an uncountably infinite number of functions f_r for $r \in [a, b] \subseteq \mathbb{R}$, which is defined as

$$f_r(x) = \begin{cases} 1, & \text{if } r = x, \\ 0, & \text{otherwise.} \end{cases} \tag{2.80}$$

These functions are linearly independent. Analogous to the last countable discrete summation given in Equation (2.79), we may write any function $f \in Func([a, b], \mathbb{C})$ as an integral:

$$f = \int_a^b c_r \cdot f_r, \tag{2.81}$$

where $c_r = f(r)$. Hence the f_r form a basis for $Func([a, b], \mathbb{C})$.

It is easy to construct a basis for a Cartesian product of two vector spaces. If $\mathcal{B} = \{V_0, V_1, \dots, V_{m-1}\}$ is a basis for $\mathbb{V}$ and $\mathcal{B}' = \{V_0', V_1', \dots, V_{m-1}'\}$ is a basis for $\mathbb{V}'$, then $\mathcal{B} \bigcup \mathcal{B}' = \{V_0, V_1, \dots, V_{m-1}, V_0', V_1', \dots, V_{m-1}'\}$ is a basis of $\mathbb{V} \times \mathbb{V}'$.

Let us look at $\mathbb{R}^3$ carefully. There is the canonical basis:

$$\mathcal{B} = \left\{ \begin{bmatrix} 1 \\ 0 \\ 0 \end{bmatrix}, \begin{bmatrix} 0 \\ 1 \\ 0 \end{bmatrix}, \begin{bmatrix} 0 \\ 0 \\ 1 \end{bmatrix} \right\}. \tag{2.82}$$

---

[6] If the reader does not know the difference between "countably" and "uncountably" infinite, fear not. These notions do not play a major role in the tale we are telling. We shall mostly stay within the finite world. Suffice it to state that an infinite set is countable if the set can be put in a one-to-one correspondence with the set of natural numbers $\mathbb{N}$. A set is uncountably infinite if it is infinite and cannot be put into such a correspondence.

There are, however, many other bases of $\mathbb{R}^3$, e.g.,

$$\mathcal{B}_1 = \left\{ \begin{bmatrix} 1 \\ 1 \\ 1 \end{bmatrix}, \begin{bmatrix} 0 \\ 1 \\ 1 \end{bmatrix}, \begin{bmatrix} 0 \\ 0 \\ 1 \end{bmatrix} \right\}, \tag{2.83}$$

$$\mathcal{B}_2 = \left\{ \begin{bmatrix} 1 \\ 0 \\ -1 \end{bmatrix}, \begin{bmatrix} 2 \\ 1 \\ 2 \end{bmatrix}, \begin{bmatrix} 3 \\ -2 \\ 0 \end{bmatrix} \right\}. \tag{2.84}$$

It is no coincidence that all these bases have the same number of vectors.

Proposition 2.3.1 For every vector space, every basis has the same number of vectors.

Definition 2.3.4 *The **dimension** of a (complex) vector space is the number of elements in a basis of the vector space.*

This coincides with the usual use of the word "dimension." Let us run through some of our examples:

- $\mathbb{R}^3$, as a real vector space, is of dimension 3.
- In general, $\mathbb{R}^n$ has dimension n as a real vector space.
- $\mathbb{C}^n$ has dimension n as a complex vector space.
- $\mathbb{C}^n$ is of dimension $2n$ as a real vector space because every complex number is described by two real numbers.
- $Poly_n$ is isomorphic to $\mathbb{C}^{n+1}$; it is not hard to see that the dimension of $Poly_n$ is also $n+1$.
- $\mathbb{C}^{m \times n}$: the dimension is mn as a complex vector space.
- $Func(\mathbb{N}, \mathbb{C})$ has countably infinite dimension.
- $Func([a, b], \mathbb{C})$ has uncountably infinite dimension.
- The dimension of $\mathbb{V} \times \mathbb{V}'$ is the dimension of $\mathbb{V}$ plus the dimension of $\mathbb{V}'$.

The following proposition will make our lives easier:

Proposition 2.3.2 Any two complex vector spaces that have the same dimension are isomorphic. In particular, for each n, there is essentially only one complex vector space that is of dimension n: $\mathbb{C}^n$.

(It is easy to see why this is true. Let V and V' be any two vector spaces with the same dimension. Every $V \in \mathbb{V}$ can be written in a unique way as a linear combination of basis vectors in $\mathbb{V}$. Taking those unique coefficients and using them as coefficients for the linear combination of the basis elements of any basis of $\mathbb{V}'$ gives us a nice isomorphism from $\mathbb{V}$ to $\mathbb{V}'$.)

Because we will be concentrating on finite-dimensional vector spaces, we only concern ourselves with $\mathbb{C}^n$.

Sometimes we shall use more than one basis for a single vector space.

Example 2.3.5 Consider the basis

$$
\mathcal{B} = \left\{ \begin{bmatrix} 1 \\ -3 \end{bmatrix}, \begin{bmatrix} -2 \\ 4 \end{bmatrix} \right\} \tag{2.85}
$$

of $\mathbb{R}^2$. The vector $V = \begin{bmatrix} 7 \\ -17 \end{bmatrix}$ can be written as

$$
\begin{bmatrix} 7 \\ -17 \end{bmatrix} = 3 \begin{bmatrix} 1 \\ -3 \end{bmatrix} - 2 \begin{bmatrix} -2 \\ 4 \end{bmatrix}. \tag{2.86}
$$

The coefficients for V with respect to the basis $\mathcal{B}$ are 3 and -2. We write this as $V_{\mathcal{B}} = \begin{bmatrix} 3 \\ -2 \end{bmatrix}$. If $\mathcal{C}$ is the canonical basis of $\mathbb{R}^2$, then

$$
\begin{bmatrix} 7 \\ -17 \end{bmatrix} = 7 \begin{bmatrix} 1 \\ 0 \end{bmatrix} - 17 \begin{bmatrix} 0 \\ 1 \end{bmatrix}, \tag{2.87}
$$

i.e., $V_{\mathcal{C}} = V = \begin{bmatrix} 7 \\ -17 \end{bmatrix}$.

Let us consider another basis of $\mathbb{R}^2$:

$$
\mathcal{D} = \left\{ \begin{bmatrix} -7 \\ 9 \end{bmatrix}, \begin{bmatrix} -5 \\ 7 \end{bmatrix} \right\}. \tag{2.88}
$$

What are the coefficients of V with respect to $\mathcal{D}$? What is $V_{\mathcal{D}}$? A **change of basis matrix** or a **transition matrix** from basis $\mathcal{B}$ to basis $\mathcal{D}$ is a matrix $M_{\mathcal{D} \leftarrow \mathcal{B}}$ such that for any vector V, we have

$$
V_{\mathcal{D}} = M_{\mathcal{D} \leftarrow \mathcal{B}} \star V_{\mathcal{B}}. \tag{2.89}
$$

In other words, $M_{\mathcal{D} \leftarrow \mathcal{B}}$ is a way of getting the coefficients with respect to one basis from the coefficients with respect to another basis. For the above bases $\mathcal{B}$ and $\mathcal{D}$, the transition matrix is

$$
M_{\mathcal{D} \leftarrow \mathcal{B}} = \begin{bmatrix} 2 & -\frac{3}{2} \\ -3 & \frac{5}{2} \end{bmatrix}. \tag{2.90}
$$

So

$$
V_{\mathcal{D}} = M_{\mathcal{D} \leftarrow \mathcal{B}} V_{\mathcal{B}} = \begin{bmatrix} 2 & -\frac{3}{2} \\ -3 & \frac{5}{2} \end{bmatrix} \begin{bmatrix} 3 \\ -2 \end{bmatrix} = \begin{bmatrix} 9 \\ -14 \end{bmatrix}. \tag{2.91}
$$

Figure 2.6. The Hadamard matrix as a transition between two bases.

Checking, we see that

$$\begin{bmatrix} 7 \\ -17 \end{bmatrix} = 9 \begin{bmatrix} -7 \\ 9 \end{bmatrix} - 14 \begin{bmatrix} -5 \\ 7 \end{bmatrix}. \tag{2.92}$$

□

Given two bases of a finite-dimensional vector space, there are standard algorithms to find a transition matrix from one to the other. (We will not need to know how to find these matrices.)

In $\mathbb{R}^2$, the transition matrix from the canonical basis

$$\left\{ \begin{bmatrix} 1 \\ 0 \end{bmatrix}, \begin{bmatrix} 0 \\ 1 \end{bmatrix} \right\} \tag{2.93}$$

to this other basis

$$\left\{ \begin{bmatrix} \frac{1}{\sqrt{2}} \\ \frac{1}{\sqrt{2}} \end{bmatrix}, \begin{bmatrix} \frac{1}{\sqrt{2}} \\ -\frac{1}{\sqrt{2}} \end{bmatrix} \right\} \tag{2.94}$$

is the **Hadamard matrix**:

$$H = \frac{1}{\sqrt{2}} \begin{bmatrix} 1 & 1 \\ 1 & -1 \end{bmatrix} = \begin{bmatrix} \frac{1}{\sqrt{2}} & \frac{1}{\sqrt{2}} \\ \frac{1}{\sqrt{2}} & -\frac{1}{\sqrt{2}} \end{bmatrix}. \tag{2.95}$$

Exercise 2.3.3 Show that H times itself gives you the identity matrix. ∎

Because H multiplied by itself gives the identity matrix, we observe that the transition back to the canonical basis is also the Hadamard matrix. We might envision these transitions as in Figure 2.6.

It turns out that the Hadamard matrix plays a major role in quantum computing.

In physics, we are often faced with a problem in which it is easier to calculate something in a noncanonical basis. For example, consider a ball rolling down a ramp as depicted in Figure 2.7.

The ball will not be moving in the direction of the canonical basis. Rather it will be rolling downward in the direction of $+45°$, $-45°$ basis. Suppose we wish to calculate when this ball will reach the bottom of the ramp or what is the speed of the ball. To do this, we change the problem from one in the canonical basis to one in the other basis. In this other basis, the motion is easier to deal with. Once we have

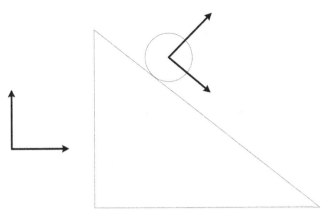

Figure 2.7. A ball rolling down a ramp and the two relevant bases.

completed the calculations, we change our results into the more understandable canonical basis and produce the desired answer. We might envision this as the flow-chart shown in Figure 2.8.

Throughout this text, we shall go from one basis to another basis, perform some calculations, and finally revert to the original basis. The Hadamard matrix will frequently be the means by which we change the basis.

2.4 INNER PRODUCTS AND HILBERT SPACES

We will be interested in complex vector spaces with additional structure. Recall that a state of a quantum system corresponds to a vector in a complex vector space. A need will arise to compare different states of the system; hence, there is a need to compare corresponding vectors or measure one vector against another in a vector space.

Consider the following operation that we can perform with two vectors in $\mathbb{R}^3$:

$$\left\langle \begin{bmatrix} 5 \\ 3 \\ -7 \end{bmatrix}, \begin{bmatrix} 6 \\ 2 \\ 0 \end{bmatrix} \right\rangle = [5, 3, -7] \star \begin{bmatrix} 6 \\ 2 \\ 0 \end{bmatrix} = (5 \times 6) + (3 \times 2) + (-7 \times 0) = 36.$$

$$(2.96)$$

Figure 2.8. Problem-solving flowchart.

In general, for any two vectors $V_1 = [r_0, r_1, r_2]^T$ and $V_2 = [r_0', r_1', r_2']^T$ in $\mathbb{R}^3$, we can form a real number by performing the following operation:

$$\langle V_1, V_2 \rangle = V_1^T \star V_2 = \sum_{j=0}^{2} r_j r_j'. \tag{2.97}$$

This is an example of an inner product of two vectors. An inner product in a complex (real) vector space is a binary operation that accepts two vectors as inputs and outputs a complex (real) number. This operation must satisfy certain properties spelled out in the following:

Definition 2.4.1 *An **inner product** (also called a **dot product** or **scalar product**) on a complex vector space $\mathbb{V}$ is a function*

$$\langle -, - \rangle : \mathbb{V} \times \mathbb{V} \longrightarrow \mathbb{C} \tag{2.98}$$

that satisfies the following conditions for all V, V_1, V_2, and V_3 in $\mathbb{V}$ and for a $c \in \mathbb{C}$:

(i) *Nondegenerate:*

$$\langle V, V \rangle \geq 0, \tag{2.99}$$

$$\langle V, V \rangle = 0 \text{ if and only if } V = \mathbf{0} \tag{2.100}$$

(i.e., the only time it "degenerates" is when it is 0).

(ii) *Respects addition:*

$$\langle V_1 + V_2, V_3 \rangle = \langle V_1, V_3 \rangle + \langle V_2, V_3 \rangle, \tag{2.101}$$

$$\langle V_1, V_2 + V_3 \rangle = \langle V_1, V_2 \rangle + \langle V_1, V_3 \rangle. \tag{2.102}$$

(iii) *Respects scalar multiplication:*

$$\langle c \cdot V_1, V_2 \rangle = \overline{c} \times \langle V_1, V_2 \rangle, \tag{2.103}$$

$$\langle V_1, c \cdot V_2 \rangle = c \times \langle V_1, V_2 \rangle. \tag{2.104}$$

(iv) *Skew symmetric:*

$$\langle V_1, V_2 \rangle = \overline{\langle V_2, V_1 \rangle}. \tag{2.105}$$

An inner product on real vector space $\langle \ , \ \rangle : \mathbb{V} \times \mathbb{V} \longrightarrow \mathbb{R}$ must satisfy the same properties. Because any $r \in \mathbb{R}$ satisfies $\overline{r} = r$, Properties (iii) and (iv) are simpler for a real vector space.

Definition 2.4.2 *A (complex) inner product space is a (complex) vector space along with an inner product.*

Let us list some examples of inner product spaces.

■ $\mathbb{R}^n$: The inner product is given as

$$\langle V_1, V_2 \rangle = V_1^T \star V_2. \tag{2.106}$$

■ $\mathbb{C}^n$: The inner product is given as

$$\langle V_1, V_2 \rangle = V_1^\dagger \star V_2. \tag{2.107}$$

■ $\mathbb{R}^{n \times n}$ has an inner product given for matrices $A, B \in \mathbb{R}^{n \times n}$ as

$$\langle A, B \rangle = Trace(A^T \star B), \tag{2.108}$$

where the **trace** of a square matrix C is given as the sum of the diagonal elements. That is,

$$Trace(C) = \sum_{i=0}^{n-1} C[i, i]. \tag{2.109}$$

■ $\mathbb{C}^{n \times n}$ has an inner product given for matrices $A, B \in \mathbb{C}^{n \times n}$ as

$$\langle A, B \rangle = Trace(A^\dagger \star B). \tag{2.110}$$

■ $Func(\mathbb{N}, \mathbb{C})$:

$$\langle f, g \rangle = \sum_{j=0}^{\infty} \overline{f(j)} g(j). \tag{2.111}$$

■ $Func([a, b], \mathbb{C})$:

$$\langle f, g \rangle = \int_a^b \overline{f(t)} g(t) \, dt. \tag{2.112}$$

Exercise 2.4.1 Let $V_1 = [2, 1, 3]^T$, $V_2 = [6, 2, 4]^T$, and $V_3 = [0, -1, 2]^T$. Show that the inner product in $\mathbb{R}^3$ respects the addition, i.e., Equations (2.101) and (2.102). ■

Exercise 2.4.2 Show that the function $\langle \ , \ \rangle : \mathbb{R}^n \times \mathbb{R}^n \longrightarrow \mathbb{R}$ given in Equation (2.106) satisfies all the properties of being an inner product on $\mathbb{R}^n$. ■

Exercise 2.4.3 Let $A = \begin{bmatrix} 1 & 2 \\ 0 & 1 \end{bmatrix}$, $B = \begin{bmatrix} 0 & -1 \\ -1 & 0 \end{bmatrix}$, and $C = \begin{bmatrix} 2 & 1 \\ 1 & 3 \end{bmatrix}$. Show that the inner product in $\mathbb{R}^{2 \times 2}$ respects addition (Equations (2.101) and (2.102)) with these matrices. ■

Exercise 2.4.4 Show that the function given for pairs of real matrices satisfies the inner product properties and converts the real vector space $\mathbb{R}^{n \times n}$ to a real inner product space. ■

Programming Drill 2.4.1 *Write a function that accepts two complex vectors of length n and calculates their inner product.*

The inner product of a complex vector with itself is a real number. We can observe this from the property that for all V_1, V_2, an inner product must satisfy

$$\langle V_1, V_2 \rangle = \overline{\langle V_2, V_1 \rangle}. \tag{2.113}$$

It follows that if $V_2 = V_1$, then we have

$$\langle V_1, V_1 \rangle = \overline{\langle V_1, V_1 \rangle}; \tag{2.114}$$

hence it is real.

Definition 2.4.3 *For every complex inner product space* $\mathbb{V}, \langle -, - \rangle$, *we can define a* **norm** *or* **length** *which is a function*

$$|\ | : \mathbb{V} \longrightarrow \mathbb{R} \tag{2.115}$$

defined as $|V| = \sqrt{\langle V, V \rangle}$.

Example 2.4.1 In $\mathbb{R}^3$, the norm of vector $[3, -6, 2]^T$ is

$$\left| \begin{bmatrix} 3 \\ -6 \\ 2 \end{bmatrix} \right| = \sqrt{\left\langle \begin{bmatrix} 3 \\ -6 \\ 2 \end{bmatrix}, \begin{bmatrix} 3 \\ -6 \\ 2 \end{bmatrix} \right\rangle} = \sqrt{3^2 + (-6)^2 + 2^2} = \sqrt{49} = 7. \tag{2.116}$$

$\square$

Exercise 2.4.5 Calculate the norm of $[4 + 3i, 6 - 4i, 12 - 7i, 13i]^T$. ∎

Exercise 2.4.6 Let $A = \begin{bmatrix} 3 & 5 \\ 2 & 3 \end{bmatrix} \in \mathbb{R}^{2\times2}$. Calculate the norm $|A| = \sqrt{\langle A, A \rangle}$. ∎

In general, the norm of the vector $[x, y, z]^T$ is

$$\left| \begin{bmatrix} x \\ y \\ z \end{bmatrix} \right| = \sqrt{\left\langle \begin{bmatrix} x \\ y \\ z \end{bmatrix}, \begin{bmatrix} x \\ y \\ z \end{bmatrix} \right\rangle} = \sqrt{x^2 + y^2 + z^2}. \tag{2.117}$$

This is the Pythagorean formula for the length of a vector. The intuition one should have is that the norm of a vector in any vector space is the length of the vector.

From the properties of an inner product space, it follows that a norm has the following properties for all $V, W \in \mathbb{V}$ and $c \in \mathbb{C}$:

   (i) Norm is nondegenerate: $|V| > 0$ if $V \neq \mathbf{0}$ and $|\mathbf{0}| = 0$.
   (ii) Norm satisfies the **triangle inequality**: $|V + W| \leq |V| + |W|$.
   (iii) Norm respects scalar multiplication: $|c \cdot V| = |c| \times |V|$.

Programming Drill 2.4.2 *Write a function that calculates the norm of a given complex vector.*

Given a norm, we can proceed and define a distance function.

Definition 2.4.4 *For every complex inner product space* $(\mathbb{V}, \langle\ ,\ \rangle)$, *we can define a* **distance function**

$$d(\ ,\ ): \mathbb{V} \times \mathbb{V} \longrightarrow \mathbb{R}, \tag{2.118}$$

where

$$d(V_1, V_2) = |V_1 - V_2| = \sqrt{\langle V_1 - V_2, V_1 - V_2 \rangle}. \tag{2.119}$$

Exercise 2.4.7 Let $V_1 = \begin{bmatrix} 3 \\ 1 \\ 2 \end{bmatrix}$ and $V_2 = \begin{bmatrix} 2 \\ 2 \\ -1 \end{bmatrix}$. Calculate the distance between these two vectors. ∎

The intuition is that $d(V_1, V_2)$ is the distance from the end of vector V_1 to the end of vector V_2. From the properties of an inner product space, it is not hard to show that a distance function has the following properties for all $U, V, W \in \mathbb{V}$:

(i) Distance is nondegenerate: $d(V, W) > 0$ if $V \neq W$ and $d(V, V) = 0$.
(ii) Distance satisfies the **triangle inequality**: $d(U, V) \leq d(U, W) + d(W, V)$.
(iii) Distance is symmetric: $d(V, W) = d(W, V)$.

Programming Drill 2.4.3 *Write a function that calculates the distance of two given complex vectors.*

Definition 2.4.5 *Two vectors V_1 and V_2 in an inner product space $\mathbb{V}$ are* **orthogonal** *if* $\langle V_1, V_2 \rangle = 0$.

The picture to keep in mind is that two vectors are orthogonal if they are perpendicular to each other.

Definition 2.4.6 *A basis* $\mathcal{B} = \{V_0, V_1, \ldots, V_{n-1}\}$ *for an inner product space $\mathbb{V}$ is called an* **orthogonal basis** *if the vectors are pairwise orthogonal to each other, i.e., $j \neq k$ implies $\langle V_j, V_k \rangle = 0$. An orthogonal basis is called an* **orthonormal basis** *if every vector in the basis is of norm 1, i.e.,*

$$\langle V_j, V_k \rangle = \delta_{j,k} = \begin{cases} 1, & \text{if } j = k, \\ 0, & \text{if } j \neq k. \end{cases} \tag{2.120}$$

$\delta_{j,k}$ *is called the* **Kronecker delta function**.

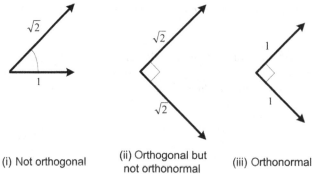

(i) Not orthogonal   (ii) Orthogonal but not orthonormal   (iii) Orthonormal

Figure 2.9. Three bases for $\mathbb{R}^2$.

Example 2.4.2 Consider the three bases for $\mathbb{R}^2$ shown in Figure 2.9. Formally, these bases are

(i) $\begin{bmatrix} 1 \\ 1 \end{bmatrix}, \begin{bmatrix} 1 \\ 0 \end{bmatrix},$

(ii) $\begin{bmatrix} 1 \\ 1 \end{bmatrix}, \begin{bmatrix} 1 \\ -1 \end{bmatrix},$

(iii) $\frac{1}{\sqrt{2}} \begin{bmatrix} 1 \\ 1 \end{bmatrix}, \frac{1}{\sqrt{2}} \begin{bmatrix} 1 \\ -1 \end{bmatrix}.$

$\square$

In $\mathbb{R}^3$, the standard inner product $\langle V, V' \rangle = V^T V'$ can be shown to be equivalent to

$$\langle V, V' \rangle = |V||V'| \cos \theta, \tag{2.121}$$

where θ is the angle between V and V'. When $|V'| = 1$, this equation reduces to

$$\langle V, V' \rangle = |V| \cos \theta. \tag{2.122}$$

Exercise 2.4.8 Let $V = [3, -1, 0]^T$ and $V' = [2, -2, 1]^T$. Calculate the angle θ between these two vectors. ■

Elementary trigonometry teaches us that when $|V'| = 1$, the number $\langle V, V' \rangle$ is the length of the projection of V onto the direction of V' (Figure 2.10).

Figure 2.10. The projection of V onto V'.

$\langle V, V' \rangle \cdot V'$ is the vector V' extended (or reduced) to meet the projection of V onto V'.

What does this mean in terms of $\mathbb{R}^3$? Let $V = [r_0, r_1, r_2]^T$ be any vector in $\mathbb{R}^3$. Let E_0, E_1, and E_2 be the canonical basis of $\mathbb{R}^3$. Then

$$V = \begin{bmatrix} r_0 \\ r_1 \\ r_2 \end{bmatrix} = \langle E_0, V \rangle \begin{bmatrix} 1 \\ 0 \\ 0 \end{bmatrix} + \langle E_1, V \rangle \begin{bmatrix} 0 \\ 1 \\ 0 \end{bmatrix} + \langle E_2, V \rangle \begin{bmatrix} 0 \\ 0 \\ 1 \end{bmatrix}. \tag{2.123}$$

In general, for any $V \in \mathbb{R}^n$,

$$V = \sum_{j=0}^{n-1} \langle E_j, V \rangle E_j. \tag{2.124}$$

We shall use the intuition afforded by $\mathbb{R}^3$ and $\mathbb{R}^n$ to understand this type of decomposition of vectors into sums of canonical vectors for other vector spaces.

Proposition 2.4.1 In $\mathbb{C}^n$, we also have that any V can be written as

$$V = \langle E_0, V \rangle E_0 + \langle E_1, V \rangle E_1 + \cdots + \langle E_{n-1}, V \rangle E_{n-1}. \tag{2.125}$$

It must be stressed that this is true for any orthonormal basis, not just the canonical one.

In $Func(\mathbb{N}, \mathbb{C})$ for an arbitrary function $g : \mathbb{N} \longrightarrow \mathbb{C}$ and for a canonical basis function $f_j : \mathbb{N} \longrightarrow \mathbb{C}$, we have

$$\langle f_j, g \rangle = \sum_{k=0}^{\infty} \overline{f_j(k)} g(k) = 1 \times g(j) = g(j). \tag{2.126}$$

And so any $g : \mathbb{N} \longrightarrow \mathbb{C}$ can be written as

$$g = \sum_{k=0}^{\infty} (\langle f_k, g \rangle f_k). \tag{2.127}$$

. . . .

Reader Tip. The following definitions will not be essential for us, but we include them so that the reader will be able to understand other texts. In our text, there is no reason to worry about them because we are restricting ourselves to finite-dimensional inner product spaces and they automatically satisfy these properties.   ♡

. . . .

Definition 2.4.7 *Within an inner product space* $\mathbb{V}, \langle \ , \ \rangle$ *(with the derived norm and a distance function), a sequence of vectors* $V_0, V_1, V_2, \ldots$ *is called a* **Cauchy sequence** *if for every* $\epsilon > 0$, *there exists an* $N_0 \in \mathbb{N}$ *such that*

$$\text{for all } m, n \geq N_0, \quad d(V_m, V_n) \leq \epsilon. \tag{2.128}$$

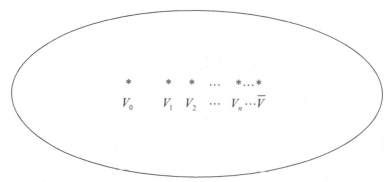

Figure 2.11. Completeness for a complex inner product space.

Definition 2.4.8 *A complex inner product space is called* **complete** *if for any Cauchy sequence of vectors* $V_0, V_1, V_2, \ldots$, *there exists a vector* $\bar{V} \in \mathbb{V}$ *such that*

$$\lim_{n \to \infty} |V_n - \bar{V}| = 0. \tag{2.129}$$

The intuition behind this is that a vector space with an inner product is complete if any sequence accumulating somewhere converges to a point (Figure 2.11).

Definition 2.4.9 *A* **Hilbert space** *is a complex inner product space that is complete.*

If completeness seems like an overly complicated notion, fear not. We do not have to worry about completeness because of the following proposition (which we shall not prove).

Proposition 2.4.2 Every inner product on a *finite*-dimensional complex vector space is automatically complete; hence, every finite-dimensional complex vector space with an inner product is automatically a Hilbert space.

Quantum computing in our text will only deal with finite-dimensional vector spaces and so we do not have to concern ourselves with the notion of completeness. However, in the culture of quantum mechanics and quantum computing, you will encounter the words "Hilbert space," which should no longer cause any anxiety.

2.5 EIGENVALUES AND EIGENVECTORS

Example 2.5.1   Consider the simple 2-by-2 real matrix

$$\begin{bmatrix} 4 & -1 \\ 2 & 1 \end{bmatrix}. \tag{2.130}$$

Notice that

$$\begin{bmatrix} 4 & -1 \\ 2 & 1 \end{bmatrix} \begin{bmatrix} 1 \\ 1 \end{bmatrix} = \begin{bmatrix} 3 \\ 3 \end{bmatrix} = 3 \begin{bmatrix} 1 \\ 1 \end{bmatrix}. \tag{2.131}$$

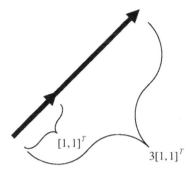

Figure 2.12. A vector before and after a matrix action.

Multiplying our matrix by this vector is nothing more than multiplying the vector by a scalar. We can see this in Figure 2.12.

In other words, when the matrix acts on this vector, it does not change the direction of the vector, but only its length.   □

Example 2.5.2   Consider the following matrix and vector:

$$\begin{bmatrix} 4 & -1 \\ 2 & 1 \end{bmatrix} \begin{bmatrix} 1 \\ 2 \end{bmatrix} = \begin{bmatrix} 2 \\ 4 \end{bmatrix} = 2 \begin{bmatrix} 1 \\ 2 \end{bmatrix}. \tag{2.132}$$

Again, the matrix acting on this vector does not change the vector's direction, rather its length as in Figure 2.13.   □

This is not always true for every vector, nor is it true for every matrix. However, when it is true, we assign such scalars and vectors special names.

Definition 2.5.1   *For a matrix A in $\mathbb{C}^{n \times n}$, if there is a number c in $\mathbb{C}$ and a vector $V \neq 0$ in $\mathbb{C}^n$ such that*

$$AV = c \cdot V, \tag{2.133}$$

*then c is called an **eigenvalue** of A and V is called an **eigenvector** of A associated with c. ("eigen-" is a German prefix that indicates possession.)*

Figure 2.13. Another vector before and after a matrix action.

Exercise 2.5.1 The following vectors

$$\left\{ \begin{bmatrix} 1 \\ 1 \\ 0 \end{bmatrix}, \begin{bmatrix} 1 \\ 0 \\ -1 \end{bmatrix}, \begin{bmatrix} 1 \\ 1 \\ 2 \end{bmatrix} \right\} \tag{2.134}$$

are eigenvectors of the matrix

$$\begin{bmatrix} 1 & -3 & 3 \\ 3 & -5 & 3 \\ 6 & -6 & 4 \end{bmatrix}. \tag{2.135}$$

Find the eigenvalues.   ∎

If a matrix A has eigenvalue c_0 with eigenvector V_0, then for any $c \in \mathbb{C}$ we have

$$A(cV_0) = cAV_0 = cc_0V_0 = c_0(cV_0), \tag{2.136}$$

which shows that cV_0 is also an eigenvector of A with eigenvalue c_0. If cV_0 and $c'V_0$ are two such eigenvectors, then because

$$A(cV_0 + c'V_0) = AcV_0 + Ac'V_0 = cAV_0 + c'AV_0$$
$$= c(c_0V_0) + c'(c_0V_0) = (c + c')(c_0V_0) = c_0(c + c')V_0, \tag{2.137}$$

we see that the addition of two such eigenvectors is also an eigenvector. We conclude the following:

Proposition 2.5.1 Every eigenvector determines a complex subvector space of the vector space. This space is known as the **eigenspace** associated with the given eigenvector.

Some matrices have many eigenvalues and eigenvectors and some matrices have none.

2.6 HERMITIAN AND UNITARY MATRICES

We shall need certain types of important square matrices and their properties.

A matrix $A \in \mathbb{R}^{n \times n}$ is called **symmetric** if $A^T = A$. In other words, $A[j, k] = A[k, j]$. Let us generalize this notion from the real numbers to the complex numbers.

Definition 2.6.1 *An n-by-n matrix A is called **hermitian** if $A^\dagger = A$. In other words, $A[j, k] = \overline{A[k, j]}$.*

Definition 2.6.2 *If A is a hermitian matrix then the operator that it represents is called* **self-adjoint**.

Example 2.6.1   The matrix

$$\begin{bmatrix} 5 & 4+5i & 6-16i \\ 4-5i & 13 & 7 \\ 6+16i & 7 & -2.1 \end{bmatrix} \tag{2.138}$$

is hermitian.   □

Exercise 2.6.1   Show that the matrix

$$\begin{bmatrix} 7 & 6+5i \\ 6-5i & -3 \end{bmatrix} \tag{2.139}$$

is hermitian.   ∎

Exercise 2.6.2   Show that A is hermitian if and only if $A^T = \overline{A}$.   ∎

Notice from the definition that the elements along the diagonal of a hermitian matrix must be real. The old notion of a symmetric matrix is a special case of hermitian that is limited to matrices with only real entries.

Proposition 2.6.1   If A is a hermitian n-by-n matrix, then for all V, $V' \in \mathbb{C}^n$ we have

$$\langle AV, V' \rangle = \langle V, AV' \rangle. \tag{2.140}$$

The proof is easy to see:

$$\langle AV, V' \rangle = (AV)^\dagger \star V' = V^\dagger A^\dagger V' = V^\dagger \star AV' = \langle V, AV' \rangle \tag{2.141}$$

where the first and the fourth equalities are from the definition of an inner product, the second equality is from the property of †, and the third equality is from the definition of a hermitian matrix.

Exercise 2.6.3   Prove the same proposition for symmetric real matrices.   ∎

Proposition 2.6.2   If A is a hermitian, then all eigenvalues are real.

To prove this, let A be a hermitian matrix with an eigenvalue $c \in \mathbb{C}$ and an eigenvector V. Consider the following sequence of equalities:

$$c\langle V, V \rangle = \langle V, cV \rangle = \langle V, AV \rangle = \langle AV, V \rangle = \langle cV, V \rangle = \overline{c}\langle V, V \rangle. \tag{2.142}$$

The first and fifth equalities are properties of the inner product. The second and fourth equalities are from the definition of eigenvalue. The third equality is from Proposition 2.6.1. Because V is nonzero, $c = \overline{c}$ and hence must be real.

Exercise 2.6.4   Prove that the eigenvalues of a symmetric matrix are real.   ∎

Proposition 2.6.3 For a given hermitian matrix, distinct eigenvectors that have distinct eigenvalues are orthogonal.

We prove this by looking at V_1 and V_2 that are distinct eigenvectors of a hermitian matrix A.

$$AV_1 = c_1 V_1 \quad \text{and} \quad AV_2 = c_2 V_2. \tag{2.143}$$

Then we have the following sequence of equalities:

$$c_2 \langle V_1, V_2 \rangle = \langle V_1, c_2 V_2 \rangle = \langle V_1, AV_2 \rangle = \langle AV_1, V_2 \rangle$$
$$= \langle c_1 V_1, V_2 \rangle = \overline{c}_1 \langle V_1, V_2 \rangle = c_1 \langle V_1, V_2 \rangle \tag{2.144}$$

where the first and fifth equalities are from properties of inner products, the second and fourth equalities are by definition of eigenvector, the third equality follows from the fact that A is hermitian, and the last equality is from the fact that eigenvalues of hermitian matrices are real. As the left side is equal to the right side, we may subtract one from the other to get 0:

$$c_1 \langle V_1, V_2 \rangle - c_2 \langle V_1, V_2 \rangle = (c_1 - c_2) \langle V_1, V_2 \rangle = 0. \tag{2.145}$$

Because c_1 and c_2 are distinct, $c_1 - c_2 \neq 0$. Hence, it follows that $\langle V_1, V_2 \rangle = 0$ and they are orthogonal.

We shall need one more important proposition about self-adjoint operators.

Definition 2.6.3 *A **diagonal matrix** is a square matrix whose only nonzero entries are on the diagonal. All entries off the diagonal are zero.*

Proposition 2.6.4 (The Spectral Theorem for Finite-Dimensional Self-Adjoint Operators.) Every self-adjoint operator A on a finite-dimensional complex vector space $\mathbb{V}$ can be represented by a diagonal matrix whose diagonal entries are the eigenvalues of A, and whose eigenvectors form an orthonormal basis for $\mathbb{V}$ (we shall call this basis an **eigenbasis**).

Hermitian matrices and their eigenbases will play a major role in our story. We shall see in Chapter 4 that associated with every physical observable of a quantum system there is a corresponding hermitian matrix. Measurements of that observable always lead to a state that is represented by one of the eigenvectors of the associated hermitian matrix.

Programming Drill 2.6.1 *Write a function that accepts a square matrix and tells if it is hermitian.*

Another fundamental type of matrix is unitary. A matrix A is **invertible** if there exists a matrix A^{-1} such that

$$A \star A^{-1} = A^{-1} \star A = I_n. \tag{2.146}$$

Unitary matrices are a type of invertible matrix. They are invertible and their inverse is their adjoint. This fact ensures that unitary matrices "preserve the geometry" of the space on which it is acting.

Definition 2.6.4 *An n-by-n matrix U is* **unitary** *if*

$$U \star U^\dagger = U^\dagger \star U = I_n. \tag{2.147}$$

It is important to realize that not all invertible matrices are unitary.

Example 2.6.2 For any θ, the matrix

$$\begin{bmatrix} \cos\theta & -\sin\theta & 0 \\ \sin\theta & \cos\theta & 0 \\ 0 & 0 & 1 \end{bmatrix} \tag{2.148}$$

is a unitary matrix. (You might have seen such a matrix when studying computer graphics. We shall see why in a few moments.) ☐

Exercise 2.6.5 Show that the matrix given in Equation (2.148) is unitary. ■

Example 2.6.3 The matrix

$$\begin{bmatrix} \frac{1+i}{2} & \frac{i}{\sqrt{3}} & \frac{3+i}{2\sqrt{15}} \\ \frac{-1}{2} & \frac{1}{\sqrt{3}} & \frac{4+3i}{2\sqrt{15}} \\ \frac{1}{2} & \frac{-i}{\sqrt{3}} & \frac{5i}{2\sqrt{15}} \end{bmatrix} \tag{2.149}$$

is a unitary matrix. ☐

Exercise 2.6.6 Show that the matrix given in Equation (2.149) is unitary. ■

Exercise 2.6.7 Show that if U and U' are unitary matrices, then so is $U \star U'$. (Hint: Use Equation (2.44)). ■

Proposition 2.6.5 Unitary matrices preserve inner products, i.e., if U is unitary, then for any $V, V' \in \mathbb{C}^n$, we have $\langle UV, UV' \rangle = \langle V, V' \rangle$.

This proposition is actually very easy to demonstrate:

$$\langle UV, UV' \rangle = (UV)^\dagger \star UV' = V^\dagger U^\dagger \star UV' = V^\dagger \star I \star V' = V^\dagger \star V' = \langle V, V' \rangle \tag{2.150}$$

where the first and fifth equalities are from the definition of the inner product, the second equality is from the properties of the adjoint, the third equality is from the definition of a unitary matrix, and the fourth equality is due to the face that I is the identity.

Because unitary matrices preserve inner products, they also preserve norms

$$|UV| = \sqrt{\langle UV, UV \rangle} = \sqrt{\langle V, V \rangle} = |V|. \tag{2.151}$$

In particular, if $|V| = 1$, then $|UV| = 1$. Consider the set of all vectors that have length 1. They form a ball around the origin (the zero of the vector space). We call this ball the **unit sphere** and imagine it as Figure 2.14.

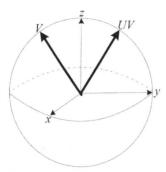

Figure 2.14. The unit sphere and the action of U on V.

If V is a vector on the unit sphere (in any dimension), then UV is also on the unit sphere. We shall see that a unitary matrix is a way of rotating the unit sphere.[7]

Exercise 2.6.8 Show that if U is a unitary matrix and V_1 and V_2 are in $\mathbb{C}^n$, then

$$d(UV_1, UV_2) = d(V_1, V_2), \tag{2.152}$$

i.e., U preserves distances. (An operator that preserves distances is called an **isometry**.) ∎

What does unitary really mean? As we saw, it means that it preserves the geometry. But it also means something else: If U is unitary and $UV = V'$, then we can easily form $U^\dagger$ and multiply both sides of the equation by $U^\dagger$ to get $U^\dagger U V = U^\dagger V'$ or $V = U^\dagger V'$. In other words, because U is unitary, there is a related matrix that can "undo" the action that U performs. $U^\dagger$ takes the result of U's action and gets back the original vector. In the quantum world, all actions (that are not measurements) are "undoable" or "reversible" in such a manner.

Hermitian matrices and unitary matrices will be very important in our text. The Venn diagram shown in Figure 2.15 is helpful.

Exercise 2.6.9 Show that I_n and $-1 \cdot I_n$ are both hermitian and unitary. ∎

Programming Drill 2.6.2 *Write a function that accepts a square matrix and tells if it is unitary.*

2.7 TENSOR PRODUCT OF VECTOR SPACES

At the conclusion of Section 2.2 we were introduced to the Cartesian product, which is one method of combining vector spaces. In this section, we study the tensor product, which is another, more important, method of combining vector spaces. If $\mathbb{V}$ describes one quantum system and $\mathbb{V}'$ describes another, then their tensor product describes both quantum systems as one. The tensor product is the fundamental building operation of quantum systems.

---

[7] These movements of the unit sphere are important in computer graphics.

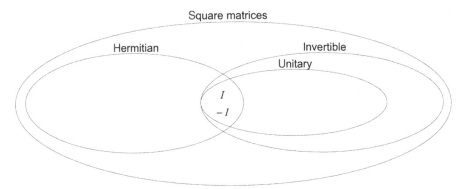

Figure 2.15. Types of matrices.

. . . .

Reader Tip. A brief warning is in order. The tensor product of two vector spaces is perhaps one of the most difficult subjects in this chapter, as well as one of the most essential. Do not be intimidated if you do not understand it the first time you read it. Everyone has a hard time with tensor products. We also suggest that you read this section in conjunction with Sections 3.4 and 4.5. All these three sections deal with the tensor product from slightly different viewpoints.   ♡

. . . .

Given two vector spaces $\mathbb{V}$ and $\mathbb{V}'$, we shall form the **tensor product** of two vector spaces, and denote it $\mathbb{V} \otimes \mathbb{V}'$. The tensor product is generated by the set of "tensors" of all vectors:

$$\{V \otimes V' | V \in \mathbb{V} \text{ and } V' \in \mathbb{V}'\}, \tag{2.153}$$

where $\otimes$ is just a symbol. A typical element of $\mathbb{V} \otimes \mathbb{V}'$ looks like this:

$$c_0(V_0 \otimes V_0') + c_1(V_1 \otimes V_1') + \cdots + c_{p-1}(V_{p-1} \otimes V_{p-1}'), \tag{2.154}$$

where $V_0, V_1, \ldots, V_{p-1}$ are elements of $\mathbb{V}$ and $V_0', V_1', \ldots, V_{p-1}'$ are elements of $\mathbb{V}'$. We might write this as

$$\sum_{i=0}^{p-1} c_i(V_i \otimes V_i'). \tag{2.155}$$

The operations on this vector space are straightforward. For a given $\sum_{i=0}^{p-1} c_i(V_i \otimes V_i')$ and $\sum_{i=0}^{q-1} c_i'(W_i \otimes W_i')$, addition is simply the addition of summations, i.e.,

$$\sum_{i=0}^{p-1} c_i(V_i \otimes V_i') + \sum_{i=0}^{q-1} c_i'(W_i \otimes W_i'). \tag{2.156}$$

The scalar multiplication for a given $c \in \mathbb{C}$ is

$$c \cdot \sum_{i=0}^{p-1} c_i(V_i \otimes V_i') = \sum_{i=0}^{p-1} (c \times c_i)(V_i \otimes V_i'). \tag{2.157}$$

We impose the following important rewriting rules for this vector space:

(i) The tensor must respect addition in both $\mathbb{V}$ and $\mathbb{V}'$:

$$(V_i + V_j) \otimes V_k' = V_i \otimes V_k' + V_j \otimes V_k', \tag{2.158}$$

$$V_i \otimes (V_j' + V_k') = V_i \otimes V_j' + V_i \otimes V_k'. \tag{2.159}$$

(ii) The tensor must respect the scalar multiplication in both $\mathbb{V}$ and $\mathbb{V}'$:

$$c \cdot (V_j \otimes V_k') = (c \cdot V_j) \otimes V_k' = V_j \otimes (c \cdot V_k'). \tag{2.160}$$

By following these rewriting rules and setting elements equal to each other, we form $\mathbb{V} \otimes \mathbb{V}'$.

Let us find a basis for $\mathbb{V} \otimes \mathbb{V}'$. Say, $\mathbb{V}$ has a basis $\mathcal{B} = \{B_0, B_1, \ldots, B_{m-1}\}$ and $\mathbb{V}'$ has a basis $\mathcal{B}' = \{B_0', B_1', \ldots, B_{n-1}'\}$. Given that every $V_i \in \mathbb{V}$ and $V_i' \in \mathbb{V}'$ can be written in a unique way for these bases, we can use the rewrite rules to "decompose" every element $\sum_{i=0}^{p-1} c_i (V_i \otimes V_i')$ in the tensor product. This will give us a basis for $\mathbb{V} \otimes \mathbb{V}'$. In detail, the basis for $\mathbb{V} \otimes \mathbb{V}'$ will be the set of vectors

$$\{B_j \otimes B_k' \mid j = 0, 1, \ldots, m-1 \text{ and } k = 0, 1, \ldots, n-1\}. \tag{2.161}$$

Every $\sum_{i=0}^{p-1} c_i (V_i \otimes V_i') \in \mathbb{V} \otimes \mathbb{V}'$ can be written as

$$c_{0,0}(B_0 \otimes B_0') + c_{1,0}(B_1 \otimes B_0') + \cdots + c_{m-1,n-1}(B_{m-1} \otimes B_{n-1}'). \tag{2.162}$$

The dimension of $\mathbb{V} \otimes \mathbb{V}'$ is the dimension of $\mathbb{V}$ times the dimension of $\mathbb{V}'$. (Remember that the dimension of $\mathbb{V} \times \mathbb{V}'$ is the dimension of $\mathbb{V}$ plus the dimension of $\mathbb{V}'$. So the tensor product of two vector spaces is usually a larger space than their Cartesian product.[8]) One should think of $\mathbb{V} \times \mathbb{V}'$ as the vector space whose states are the states of a system $\mathbb{V}$ *or* a system $\mathbb{V}'$ or both. $\mathbb{V} \otimes \mathbb{V}'$ is to be thought of as the vector space whose basic states are pairs of states, one from system $\mathbb{V}$ *and* one from the system $\mathbb{V}'$.

Given an element of $\mathbb{V}$

$$c_0 B_0 + c_1 B_1 + \cdots + c_{m-1} B_{m-1}, \tag{2.163}$$

and an element of $\mathbb{V}'$

$$c_0' B_0' + c_1' B_1' + \cdots + c_{n-1}' B_{n-1}', \tag{2.164}$$

we can associate[9] the following element of $\mathbb{V} \otimes \mathbb{V}'$:

$$(c_0 \times c_0')(B_0 \otimes B_0') + (c_0 \times c_1')(B_0 \otimes B_1') + \cdots + (c_{m-1} \times c_{n-1}')(B_{m-1} \otimes B_{n-1}'). \tag{2.165}$$

Let us step down from the abstract highland and see what $\mathbb{C}^m \otimes \mathbb{C}^n$ actually looks like. $\mathbb{C}^m \otimes \mathbb{C}^n$ is of dimension mn and hence is isomorphic to $\mathbb{C}^{m \times n}$. What is important is how $\mathbb{C}^m \otimes \mathbb{C}^n$ is isomorphic to $\mathbb{C}^{m \times n}$. If E_j is an element of the canonical basis of each vector space, then we might identify $E_j \otimes E_k$ with $E_{j \times k}$. It is not hard to see

---

[8] But not always! Remember that $1 \times 1 < 1 + 1$ and $1 \times 2 < 1 + 2$, etc.

[9] It is important to notice that this "association" is not a linear map; it is something called a **bilinear map**.

from the association given in Equation (2.165) that the **tensor product of vectors** is defined as follows:

$$
\begin{bmatrix} a_0 \\ a_1 \\ a_2 \\ a_3 \end{bmatrix} \otimes \begin{bmatrix} b_0 \\ b_1 \\ b_2 \end{bmatrix} = \begin{bmatrix} a_0 \cdot \begin{bmatrix} b_0 \\ b_1 \\ b_2 \end{bmatrix} \\ a_1 \cdot \begin{bmatrix} b_0 \\ b_1 \\ b_2 \end{bmatrix} \\ a_2 \cdot \begin{bmatrix} b_0 \\ b_1 \\ b_2 \end{bmatrix} \\ a_3 \cdot \begin{bmatrix} b_0 \\ b_1 \\ b_2 \end{bmatrix} \end{bmatrix} = \begin{bmatrix} a_0 b_0 \\ a_0 b_1 \\ a_0 b_2 \\ a_1 b_0 \\ a_1 b_1 \\ a_1 b_2 \\ a_2 b_0 \\ a_2 b_1 \\ a_2 b_2 \\ a_3 b_0 \\ a_3 b_1 \\ a_3 b_2 \end{bmatrix}.
\tag{2.166}
$$

In general, $\mathbb{C}^m \times \mathbb{C}^n$ is much smaller than $\mathbb{C}^m \otimes \mathbb{C}^n$.

Example 2.7.1 For example, consider $\mathbb{C}^2 \times \mathbb{C}^3$ and $\mathbb{C}^2 \otimes \mathbb{C}^3 = \mathbb{C}^6$. Consider the vector

$$
\begin{bmatrix} 8 \\ 12 \\ 6 \\ 12 \\ 18 \\ 9 \end{bmatrix} \in \mathbb{C}^6 = \mathbb{C}^2 \otimes \mathbb{C}^3.
\tag{2.167}
$$

It is not hard to see that this is simply

$$
\begin{bmatrix} 2 \\ 3 \end{bmatrix} \otimes \begin{bmatrix} 4 \\ 6 \\ 3 \end{bmatrix}.
\tag{2.168}
$$

$\square$

Example 2.7.2   In contrast to the above example,

$$
\begin{bmatrix} 8 \\ 0 \\ 0 \\ 0 \\ 0 \\ 18 \end{bmatrix} \in \mathbb{C}^6 = \mathbb{C}^2 \otimes \mathbb{C}^3 \tag{2.169}
$$

cannot be written as the tensor product of a vector from $\mathbb{C}^2$ and $\mathbb{C}^3$. In order to see this, consider the variables

$$
\begin{bmatrix} x \\ y \end{bmatrix} \otimes \begin{bmatrix} a \\ b \\ c \end{bmatrix} = \begin{bmatrix} xa \\ xb \\ xc \\ ya \\ yb \\ yc \end{bmatrix}. \tag{2.170}
$$

There are no solutions for the variable that will give you the required results. However, we can write the vector in Equation (2.169) as

$$
\begin{bmatrix} 8 \\ 0 \\ 0 \\ 0 \\ 0 \\ 18 \end{bmatrix} = \begin{bmatrix} 1 \\ 0 \end{bmatrix} \otimes \begin{bmatrix} 8 \\ 0 \\ 0 \end{bmatrix} + \begin{bmatrix} 0 \\ 6 \end{bmatrix} \otimes \begin{bmatrix} 0 \\ 0 \\ 3 \end{bmatrix}. \tag{2.171}
$$

This is a summation of two vectors.   □

For reasons that are made clear in Sections 3.4 and 4.5, we shall call a vector that can be written as the tensor of two vectors **separable**. In contrast, a vector that cannot be written as the tensor of two vectors (but can be written as the nontrivial sum of such tensors) shall be called **entangled**.

Exercise 2.7.1 Calculate the tensor product $\begin{bmatrix} 3 \\ 4 \\ 7 \end{bmatrix} \otimes \begin{bmatrix} -1 \\ 2 \end{bmatrix}$.   ∎

Exercise 2.7.2 State whether $[5, 6, 3, 2, 0, 1]^T$ is a tensor product of smaller vectors from $\mathbb{C}^3$ and $\mathbb{C}^2$.   ∎

We will need to know not only how to take the tensor product of two vectors, but also how to determine the **tensor product of two matrices**.[10] Consider two matrices

$$A = \begin{bmatrix} a_{0,0} & a_{0,1} \\ a_{1,0} & a_{1,1} \end{bmatrix} \quad \text{and} \quad B = \begin{bmatrix} b_{0,0} & b_{0,1} & b_{0,2} \\ b_{1,0} & b_{1,1} & b_{1,2} \\ b_{2,0} & b_{2,1} & b_{2,2} \end{bmatrix}. \tag{2.172}$$

From the association given in Equation (2.165), it can be seen that the tensor product $A \otimes B$ is the matrix that has every element of A, scalar multiplied with the entire matrix B. That is,

$$A \otimes B = \begin{bmatrix} a_{0,0} \cdot \begin{bmatrix} b_{0,0} & b_{0,1} & b_{0,2} \\ b_{1,0} & b_{1,1} & b_{1,2} \\ b_{2,0} & b_{2,1} & b_{2,2} \end{bmatrix} & a_{0,1} \cdot \begin{bmatrix} b_{0,0} & b_{0,1} & b_{0,2} \\ b_{1,0} & b_{1,1} & b_{1,2} \\ b_{2,0} & b_{2,1} & b_{2,2} \end{bmatrix} \\ a_{1,0} \cdot \begin{bmatrix} b_{0,0} & b_{0,1} & b_{0,2} \\ b_{1,0} & b_{1,1} & b_{1,2} \\ b_{2,0} & b_{2,1} & b_{2,2} \end{bmatrix} & a_{1,1} \cdot \begin{bmatrix} b_{0,0} & b_{0,1} & b_{0,2} \\ b_{1,0} & b_{1,1} & b_{1,2} \\ b_{2,0} & b_{2,1} & b_{2,2} \end{bmatrix} \end{bmatrix}$$

$$= \begin{bmatrix} a_{0,0} \times b_{0,0} & a_{0,0} \times b_{0,1} & a_{0,0} \times b_{0,2} & a_{0,1} \times b_{0,0} & a_{0,1} \times b_{0,1} & a_{0,1} \times b_{0,2} \\ a_{0,0} \times b_{1,0} & a_{0,0} \times b_{1,1} & a_{0,0} \times b_{1,2} & a_{0,1} \times b_{1,0} & a_{0,1} \times b_{1,1} & a_{0,1} \times b_{1,2} \\ a_{0,0} \times b_{2,0} & a_{0,0} \times b_{2,1} & a_{0,0} \times b_{2,2} & a_{0,1} \times b_{2,0} & a_{0,1} \times b_{2,1} & a_{0,1} \times b_{2,2} \\ a_{1,0} \times b_{0,0} & a_{1,0} \times b_{0,1} & a_{1,0} \times b_{0,2} & a_{1,1} \times b_{0,0} & a_{1,1} \times b_{0,1} & a_{1,1} \times b_{0,2} \\ a_{1,0} \times b_{1,0} & a_{1,0} \times b_{1,1} & a_{1,0} \times b_{1,2} & a_{1,1} \times b_{1,0} & a_{1,1} \times b_{1,1} & a_{1,1} \times b_{1,2} \\ a_{1,0} \times b_{2,0} & a_{1,0} \times b_{2,1} & a_{1,0} \times b_{2,2} & a_{1,1} \times b_{2,0} & a_{1,1} \times b_{2,1} & a_{1,1} \times b_{2,2} \end{bmatrix}. \tag{2.173}$$

[10] It should be clear that the tensor product of two vectors is simply a special case of the tensor product of two matrices.

Formally, the tensor product of matrices is a function

$$\otimes : \mathbb{C}^{m \times m'} \times \mathbb{C}^{n \times n'} \longrightarrow \mathbb{C}^{mn \times m'n'} \qquad (2.174)$$

and it is defined as

$$(A \otimes B)[j, k] = A[j/n, k/m] \times B[j \bmod n, k \bmod m]. \qquad (2.175)$$

Exercise 2.7.3   Calculate

$$\begin{bmatrix} 3+2i & 5-i & 2i \\ 0 & 12 & 6-3i \\ 2 & 4+4i & 9+3i \end{bmatrix} \otimes \begin{bmatrix} 1 & 3+4i & 5-7i \\ 10+2i & 6 & 2+5i \\ 0 & 1 & 2+9i \end{bmatrix}. \qquad (2.176)$$

∎

Exercise 2.7.4   Prove that the tensor product is "almost" commutative. Take two 2-by-2 matrices A and B. Calculate $A \otimes B$ and $B \otimes A$. In general, although they are not equal, they do have the same entries, and one can be transformed to the other with a "nice" change of rows and columns.   ∎

Exercise 2.7.5   Let $A = \begin{bmatrix} 1 & 2 \\ 0 & 1 \end{bmatrix}$, $B = \begin{bmatrix} 3 & 2 \\ -1 & 0 \end{bmatrix}$, and $C = \begin{bmatrix} 6 & 5 \\ 3 & 2 \end{bmatrix}$. Calculate $A \otimes (B \otimes C)$ and $(A \otimes B) \otimes C$ and show that they are equal.   ∎

Exercise 2.7.6   Prove that the tensor product is associative, i.e., for arbitrary matrices A, B, and C,

$$A \otimes (B \otimes C) = (A \otimes B) \otimes C. \qquad (2.177)$$

∎

Exercise 2.7.7   Let $A = \begin{bmatrix} 2 & 3 \end{bmatrix}$ and $B = \begin{bmatrix} 1 & 2 \\ 3 & 4 \end{bmatrix}$. Calculate $(A \otimes B)^{\dagger}$ and $A^{\dagger} \otimes B^{\dagger}$ and show that they are equal.   ∎

Exercise 2.7.8   Prove that $(A \otimes B)^{\dagger} = A^{\dagger} \otimes B^{\dagger}$.   ∎

Exercise 2.7.9   Let A, A', B, and B' be matrices of the appropriate sizes. Prove that

$$(A \star A') \otimes (B \star B') = (A \otimes B) \star (A' \otimes B'). \qquad (2.178)$$

∎

If A acts on V and B acts on V', then we define the action on their tensor product as

$$(A \otimes B) \star (V \otimes V') = A \star V \otimes B \star V'. \qquad (2.179)$$

Such "parallel" actions will arise over and over again.

Programming Drill 2.7.1   *Write a function that accepts two matrices and constructs their tensor product.*

. . . .

References: There are plenty of good references for basic linear algebra. Many of the more elementary ones, like Gilbert and Gilbert (2004), Lang (1986), and Penney (1998), contain many examples and intuitive drawings. Complex vector spaces are discussed in, e.g., Nicholson (1994) and O'Nan (1976). The tensor product is found only in more advanced texts, such as Lang (1993).

A history of the development of the subject can be found in Crowe (1994).

3

The Leap from Classical to Quantum

Everyone has lost their marbles!

Anonymous

Before we formally present quantum mechanics in all its wonders, we shall spend time providing some basic intuitions behind its core methods and ideas. Realizing that computer scientists feel comfortable with graphs and matrices, we shall cast quantum mechanical ideas in graph-theoretic and matrix-theoretic terms. Everyone who has taken a class in discrete structures knows how to represent a (weighted) graph as an adjacency matrix. We shall take this basic idea and generalize it in several straightforward ways. While doing this, we shall present a few concepts that are at the very core of quantum mechanics. In Section 3.1, the graphs are without weights. This will model classical deterministic systems. In Section 3.2, the graphs are weighted with real numbers. This will model classical probabilistic systems. In Section 3.3, the graphs are weighted with complex numbers and will model quantum systems. We conclude Section 3.3 with a computer science/graph-theoretic version of the double-slit experiment. This is perhaps the most important experiment in quantum mechanics. Section 3.4 discusses ways of combining systems to yield larger systems.

Throughout this chapter, we first present an idea in terms of a toy model, then generalize it to an abstract point, and finally discuss its connection with quantum mechanics, before moving on to the next idea.

3.1 CLASSICAL DETERMINISTIC SYSTEMS

We begin with a simple system described by a graph together with some toy marbles. Imagine the identical marbles as being placed on the vertices of a graph. The state of a system is described by how many marbles are on each vertex.

Example 3.1.1 Let there be 6 vertices in a graph and a total of 27 marbles. We might place 6 marbles on vertex 0, 2 marbles on vertex 1, and the rest as described by this picture.

$$0 \bullet \boxed{6} \qquad\qquad 1 \bullet \boxed{2} \qquad\qquad 2 \bullet \boxed{1}$$

$$(3.1)$$

$$3 \bullet \boxed{5} \qquad\qquad 4 \bullet \boxed{3} \qquad\qquad 5 \bullet \boxed{10}$$

We shall denote this state as $X = [6, 2, 1, 5, 3, 10]^T$. □

Example 3.1.2 The state $[5, 5, 0, 2, 0, 15]^T$ (in the same 6 vertex, 27 marble system) will correspond to

$$0 \bullet \boxed{5} \qquad\qquad 1 \bullet \boxed{5} \qquad\qquad 2 \bullet \boxed{0}$$

$$(3.2)$$

$$3 \bullet \boxed{2} \qquad\qquad 4 \bullet \boxed{0} \qquad\qquad 5 \bullet \boxed{15}$$

□

We are concerned not only with the states of the system, but also with the way the states change. How they change – or the **dynamics** of the system – can be represented by a graph with directed edges. We do not permit an arbitrary graph. Rather, we insist that every vertex in the graph has exactly one outgoing edge. This requirement will coincide with our demand that the system be deterministic. In other words, each marble must move to exactly one place.

Example 3.1.3 An example of the dynamics might be described by the following directed graph:

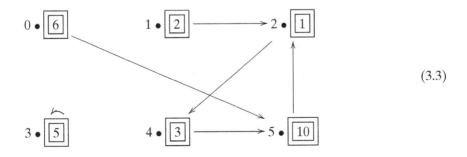

$$(3.3)$$

The idea is that if an arrow exists from vertex i to vertex j, then in one time click, all the marbles on vertex i will shift to vertex j.

This graph is easy to store in a computer as a Boolean adjacency matrix, M (for "marbles"):

$$
M = \begin{array}{c}
 \\
0 \\ 1 \\ 2 \\ 3 \\ 4 \\ 5
\end{array}
\begin{array}{cccccc}
0 & 1 & 2 & 3 & 4 & 5 \\
\left[\begin{array}{cccccc}
0 & 0 & 0 & 0 & 0 & 0 \\
0 & 0 & 0 & 0 & 0 & 0 \\
0 & 1 & 0 & 0 & 0 & 1 \\
0 & 0 & 0 & 1 & 0 & 0 \\
0 & 0 & 1 & 0 & 0 & 0 \\
1 & 0 & 0 & 0 & 1 & 0
\end{array}\right],
\end{array}
\tag{3.4}
$$

where $M[i, j] = 1$ if and only if there is an arrow from vertex j to vertex i.[1] The requirement that every vertex has exactly one outgoing edge corresponds to the fact that every column of the Boolean adjacency matrix contains exactly one 1. □

Let's say that we multiply M by a state of the system $X = [6, 2, 1, 5, 3, 10]^T$. Then we have

$$
MX = \begin{bmatrix}
0 & 0 & 0 & 0 & 0 & 0 \\
0 & 0 & 0 & 0 & 0 & 0 \\
0 & 1 & 0 & 0 & 0 & 1 \\
0 & 0 & 0 & 1 & 0 & 0 \\
0 & 0 & 1 & 0 & 0 & 0 \\
1 & 0 & 0 & 0 & 1 & 0
\end{bmatrix}
\begin{bmatrix}
6 \\ 2 \\ 1 \\ 5 \\ 3 \\ 10
\end{bmatrix}
=
\begin{bmatrix}
0 \\ 0 \\ 12 \\ 5 \\ 1 \\ 9
\end{bmatrix}
= Y.
\tag{3.5}
$$

To what does this correspond? If X describes the state of the system at time t, then Y is the state of the system at time $t + 1$, i.e., after one time click. We can see this clearly by looking at the formula for matrix multiplication:

$$
Y[i] = (MX)[i] = \sum_{k=0}^{5} M[i, k]X[k].
\tag{3.6}
$$

In plain English, this states that the number of marbles that will reach vertex i after one time step is the sum of all the marbles that are on vertices with edges connecting to vertex i.

Notice that the top two entries of Y are 0. This corresponds to the fact that there are no arrows going to vertex 0 or vertex 1.

Exercise 3.1.1 Using the dynamics given in Equation (3.4), determine what the state of the system would be if you start with the state $[5, 5, 0, 2, 0, 15]^T$.   ■

---

[1] Although most texts have $M[i, j] = 1$ if and only if there is an arrow from vertex i to vertex j, we shall need it to be the other way for reasons which will become apparent later.

In general, any simple directed graph with n vertices can be represented by an n-by-n matrix M having entries as

$$M[i, j] = 1 \text{ if and only if there is an edge from vertex } j \text{ to vertex } i.$$

$$= 1 \text{ if and only if there is a path of length 1 from vertex } j \text{ to vertex } i.$$

$$(3.7)$$

If $X = [x_0, x_1, \ldots, x_{n-1}]^T$ is a column vector that corresponds to placing x_i marbles on vertex i, and if $MX = Y$ where $Y = [y_0, y_1, \ldots, y_{n-1}]^T$, then there are y_j marbles on vertex j after one time click. M is thus a way of describing how the state of the marbles can change from time t to time $t + 1$.

As we shall soon see, (finite-dimensional) quantum mechanics works the same way. States of a system are represented by column vectors, and the way in which the system changes in one time click is represented by matrices. Multiplying a matrix with a column vector yields a subsequent state of the system.

Looking at the formula for Boolean matrix multiplication

$$M^2[i, j] = \bigvee_{k=0}^{n-1} M[i, k] \wedge M[k, j], \tag{3.8}$$

we observe that it really shows us how to go from vertex j to vertex i in *two* time clicks. The following picture is helpful:

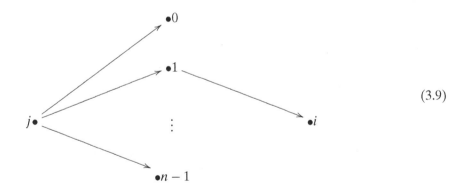

$$(3.9)$$

There will be a path of length 2 from vertex j to vertex i if there exists ($\bigvee$) some vertex k such that there is an arrow from vertex j to vertex k and ($\wedge$) an arrow from vertex k to vertex i.

Thus, we have that

$$M^2[i, j] = 1 \text{ if and only if there is a path of length 2 from vertex } j \text{ to vertex } i.$$

$$(3.10)$$

For an arbitrary k we have

$M^k[i, j] = 1$ if and only if there is a path of length k from vertex j to vertex i.

(3.11)

Exercise 3.1.2 For the matrix M given in Equation (3.4), calculate M^2, M^3, and M^6. If all the marbles start at vertex 2, where will all the marbles end up after 6 time steps? ∎

In general, multiplying an n-by-n matrix by itself several times will produce another matrix whose i, jth entry will indicate whether there is a path after several time clicks. Consider $X = [x_0, x_1, \ldots, x_{n-1}]^T$ to be the state where one places x_0 marbles on vertex 0, x_1 marbles on vertex 1, ..., x_{n-1} marbles on vertex $n - 1$. Then, after k steps, the state of the marbles is Y, where $Y = [y_0, y_1, \ldots, y_{n-1}]^T = M^k X$. In other words, y_j is the number of marbles on vertex j after k steps.

In quantum mechanics, if there are two or more matrices that manipulate states, the action of one followed by another is described by their product. We shall take different states of systems and multiply the states by various matrices (of the appropriate type) to obtain other ones. These new states will again be multiplied by other matrices until we attain the desired end state. In quantum computing, we shall start with an initial state, described by a vector of numbers. The initial state will essentially be the input to the system. Operations in a quantum computer will correspond to multiplying the vector with matrices. The output will be the state of the system when we are finished carrying out all the operations.

Summing up, we have learned the following:

- The states of a system correspond to column vectors (state vectors).
- The dynamics of a system correspond to matrices.
- To progress from one state to another in one time step, one must multiply the state vector by a matrix.
- Multiple step dynamics are obtained via matrix multiplication.

Exercise 3.1.3 What would happen if we relaxed the requirement that exactly one edge leaves each vertex, i.e., what would happen if we permitted any graph? ∎

Exercise 3.1.4 What would happen if we permitted not only 0's and 1's but also -1 in the adjacency matrix? Give an interpretation of this scenario in terms of marbles. ∎

Exercise 3.1.5 Consider the following graph representing city streets. Single-headed arrows ($\longrightarrow$) correspond to one-way streets and double-headed arrows ($\longleftrightarrow$) correspond to two-way streets.

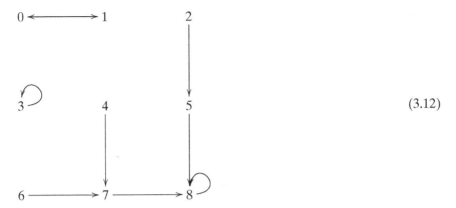

(3.12)

Imagine that it takes one time click to traverse an arrow. You may assume that ev-eryone must move at every time click. If every corner starts with exactly one person, where will everyone be after one time click? After two time clicks? After four time clicks?   ∎

Programming Drill 3.1.1   *Write a program that performs our little marble experi-ment. The program should allow the user to enter a Boolean matrix that describes the ways that marbles move. Make sure that the matrix follows our requirement. The user should also be permitted to enter a starting state of how many marbles are on each vertex. Then the user enters how many time clicks she wants to proceed. The com-puter should then calculate and output the state of the system after those time clicks. We will make changes to this program later in the chapter.*

3.2 PROBABILISTIC SYSTEMS

In quantum mechanics, there is an inherent indeterminacy in our knowledge of a physical state. Furthermore, states change with probabilistic laws. This simply means that the laws governing a system's evolution are given by describing how states tran-sition from one to another with a certain likelihood.

In order to capture these probabilistic scenarios, let us modify what we did in the last section. Instead of dealing with a bunch of marbles moving about, we shall work with a single marble. The state of the system will tell us the probabilities of the marble being on each vertex. For a three-vertex graph, a typical state might look like $X = \left[\frac{1}{5}, \frac{3}{10}, \frac{1}{2}\right]^T$. This will correspond to the fact that there is a one-fifth[2] chance that the marble is on vertex 0, a three-tenths chance that the marble is on vertex 1; and a half chance that the marble is on vertex 2. Because the marble must be somewhere on the graph, the sum of the probabilities is 1.

We must modify the dynamics as well. Rather than exactly one arrow leaving each vertex, we will have several arrows shooting out of each vertex with real num-bers between 0 and 1 as weights. These weights describe the probability of our marble moving from one vertex to another in one time click. We shall restrict our

---

[2] Although the theory works with any $r \in [0, 1]$, we shall deal only with fractions.

attention to weighted graphs that satisfy the following two conditions: a) the sum of all the weights leaving a vertex is 1 and b) the sum of all the weights entering a vertex is 1. This will correspond to the fact that the marble must both go and come from someplace (there might be loops).

Example 3.2.1　An example of such a graph is

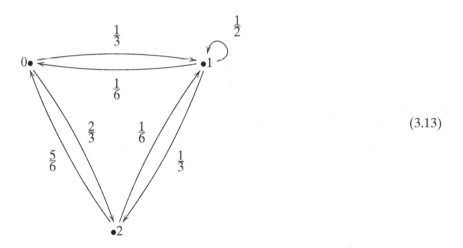

(3.13)

The adjacency matrix for this graph is

$$
M = \begin{bmatrix} 0 & \frac{1}{6} & \frac{5}{6} \\ \frac{1}{3} & \frac{1}{2} & \frac{1}{6} \\ \frac{2}{3} & \frac{1}{3} & 0 \end{bmatrix}.
$$

(3.14)

□

The adjacency matrices for our graphs will have real entries between 0 and 1 where the sums of the rows and the sums of the columns are all 1. Such matrices are called **doubly stochastic.**

Let us see how the states interact with the dynamics. Suppose we have a state $X = \left[\frac{1}{6}, \frac{1}{6}, \frac{2}{3}\right]^T$ that expresses an indeterminacy about the position of a marble: the probability is $\frac{1}{6}$ that the marble is on vertex 0, the probability is $\frac{1}{6}$ that the marble is on vertex 1, and the probability is $\frac{2}{3}$ that the marble is on vertex 2.

With this interpretation, we will calculate how a state changes:

$$
MX = \begin{bmatrix} 0 & \frac{1}{6} & \frac{5}{6} \\ \frac{1}{3} & \frac{1}{2} & \frac{1}{6} \\ \frac{2}{3} & \frac{1}{3} & 0 \end{bmatrix} \begin{bmatrix} \frac{1}{6} \\ \frac{1}{6} \\ \frac{2}{3} \end{bmatrix} = \begin{bmatrix} \frac{21}{36} \\ \frac{9}{36} \\ \frac{6}{36} \end{bmatrix} = Y.
$$

(3.15)

Notice that the sum of the entries of Y is 1. We might express this by saying

If the marble's position is
   $\frac{1}{6}$ chance on vertex 0,
   $\frac{1}{6}$ chance on vertex 1, and
   $\frac{2}{3}$ chance on vertex 2,
then, after following the arrows, the probability of the marble's position is
   $\frac{21}{36}$ chance on vertex 0,
   $\frac{9}{36}$ chance on vertex 1, and
   $\frac{6}{36}$ chance on vertex 2.

That is, if we have X expressing the probability of the position of a marble and M expressing the probability of the way the marble moves around, then $MX = Y = \left[\frac{21}{36}, \frac{9}{36}, \frac{6}{36}\right]^{T}$ is expressing the probability of the marble's location after moving. If X is the probability of the marble at time t, then MX is the probability of the marble at time $t + 1$.

Exercise 3.2.1   Let M be as in Equation (3.14) and let $X = \left[\frac{1}{2}, 0, \frac{1}{2}\right]^{T}$. Show that the entries of $Y = MX$ sum to 1.   ∎

Exercise 3.2.2   Let M be any n-by-n doubly stochastic matrix. Let X be an n-by-1 column vector. Let the result of $MX = Y$.

a) If the sum of the entries of X is 1, prove that the sum of the entries of Y is 1.

b) More generally, prove that if the sum of the entries of X is x, then the sum of the entries of Y is also x, i.e., M preserves the sum of the entries of a column vector multiplied at the right of M.   ∎

We shall multiply vectors not only on the right of a matrix, but on the left as well. We shall posit that a *row* vector will also correspond to a state of a system. Take a row vector where the sum of the entries is 1. Multiply it on the left of M. $W = \left[\frac{1}{3}, 0, \frac{2}{3}\right]$. Then we have

$$WM = \left[\frac{1}{3}, 0, \frac{2}{3}\right] \begin{bmatrix} 0 & \frac{1}{6} & \frac{5}{6} \\ \frac{1}{3} & \frac{1}{2} & \frac{1}{6} \\ \frac{2}{3} & \frac{1}{3} & 0 \end{bmatrix} = \left[\frac{4}{9}, \frac{5}{18}, \frac{5}{18}\right] = Z. \tag{3.16}$$

Notice that the sum of the entries of Z is 1.

Exercise 3.2.3   Let M be any n-by-n doubly stochastic matrix. Let W be a 1-by-n row vector. Then we have the resulting

$$WM = Z. \tag{3.17}$$

a) If the sum of the entries of W is 1, prove that the sum of the entries of Z is 1.

b) More generally, prove that if the sum of the entries of W is w, then the sum of the entries of Z is also w, i.e., M preserves the sum of the entries of a row vector multiplied on the left of M.   ∎

What can this possibly mean? The transpose of M

$$M^T = \begin{bmatrix} 0 & \frac{1}{3} & \frac{2}{3} \\ \frac{1}{6} & \frac{1}{2} & \frac{1}{3} \\ \frac{5}{6} & \frac{1}{6} & 0 \end{bmatrix} \tag{3.18}$$

corresponds to our directed graph with the arrows reversed:

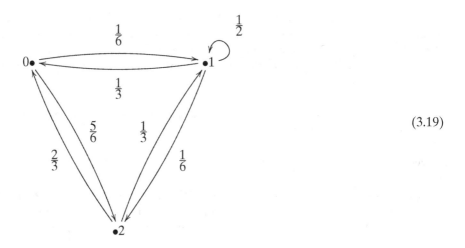

$$\tag{3.19}$$

Reversing the arrows is like traveling back in time or having the marble roll backward. A simple calculation shows that

$$M^T W^T = \begin{bmatrix} 0 & \frac{1}{3} & \frac{2}{3} \\ \frac{1}{6} & \frac{1}{2} & \frac{1}{3} \\ \frac{5}{6} & \frac{1}{6} & 0 \end{bmatrix} \begin{bmatrix} \frac{1}{3} \\ 0 \\ \frac{2}{3} \end{bmatrix} = \begin{bmatrix} \frac{4}{9} \\ \frac{5}{18} \\ \frac{5}{18} \end{bmatrix} = Z^T, \tag{3.20}$$

i.e.,

$$M^T W^T = (WM)^T = Z^T. \tag{3.21}$$

So if multiplying on the right of M takes states from time t to time $t + 1$, then multiplying on the left of M takes states from time t to time $t - 1$.

This *time symmetry* is one of the fundamental concepts of quantum mechanics and quantum computation. Our description of system dynamics is entirely symmetric: by replacing column vectors with row vectors, and forward evolution in time with backward evolution, the laws of dynamics still hold. We shall encounter row vectors in Chapter 4, and unravel their role. But let us now go back to M.

Let's multiply M by itself. $MM = M^2$:

$$
\begin{bmatrix} 0 & \frac{1}{6} & \frac{5}{6} \\ \frac{1}{3} & \frac{1}{2} & \frac{1}{6} \\ \frac{2}{3} & \frac{1}{3} & 0 \end{bmatrix}
\begin{bmatrix} 0 & \frac{1}{6} & \frac{5}{6} \\ \frac{1}{3} & \frac{1}{2} & \frac{1}{6} \\ \frac{2}{3} & \frac{1}{3} & 0 \end{bmatrix}
=
\begin{bmatrix} \frac{11}{18} & \frac{13}{36} & \frac{1}{36} \\ \frac{5}{18} & \frac{13}{36} & \frac{13}{36} \\ \frac{1}{9} & \frac{5}{18} & \frac{11}{18} \end{bmatrix}.
\tag{3.22}
$$

The following picture can help us understand matrix multiplication with probability entries:

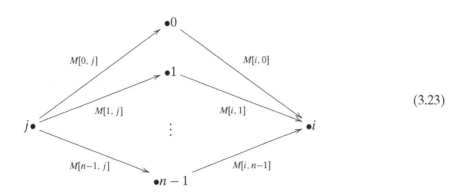

$$\tag{3.23}$$

In order to go from vertex j to vertex i in two steps,
one can go from vertex j to vertex 0 and (multiply) go to vertex i or (add)
one can go from vertex j to vertex 1 and (multiply) go to vertex i or (add)
$\vdots$
or (add)
one can go from vertex j to vertex $n - 1$ and (multiply) go to vertex i.

This is exactly the formula for multiplying matrices in Equation (2.37) on page 41. And so we can state

$$M^2[i, j] = \text{ the probability of going from vertex } j \text{ to vertex } i \text{ in 2 time clicks.}$$

$$\tag{3.24}$$

Exercise 3.2.4 Let

$$
M = \begin{bmatrix} \frac{1}{3} & \frac{2}{3} \\ \frac{2}{3} & \frac{1}{3} \end{bmatrix} \quad \text{and} \quad N = \begin{bmatrix} \frac{1}{2} & \frac{1}{2} \\ \frac{1}{2} & \frac{1}{2} \end{bmatrix}
$$

be two doubly stochastic matrices. Calculate $M \star N$ and show that this is again a doubly stochastic matrix. ∎

Exercise 3.2.5   Prove that the product of a doubly stochastic matrix with another doubly stochastic matrix is also a doubly stochastic matrix.   ■

In general, for an arbitrary positive integer k, we have

$$M^k[i, j] = \text{the probability of going from vertex } j \text{ to vertex } i \text{ in } k \text{ time clicks.}$$

(3.25)

If M is an n-by-n doubly stochastic matrix and X is an n-by-1 column vector whose entries sum to 1, then $M^k X = Y$ is expressing the probability of the position of a marble after k time clicks. That is, if $X = [x_0, x_1, \ldots, x_{n-1}]^T$ means that there is an x_i chance that a marble is on vertex i, then $M^k X = Y = [y_0, y_1, \ldots, y_{n-1}]^T$ means that after k time clicks, there is a y_j chance that the marble is on vertex j.

We are not constrained to multiply M by itself. We may also multiply M by another doubly stochastic matrix. Let M and N be two n-by-n doubly stochastic matrices corresponding to the weighted n vertex graphs G_M and G_N, respectively. Then $M \star N$ corresponds to an n-vertex graph whose weight is given as

$$(M \star N)[i, j] = \sum_{k=0}^{n-1} M[i, k]N[k, j].$$

(3.26)

In terms of a marble, this n-vertex graph corresponds to the sum of the probabilities of its shifting from vertex j to some vertex k in G_N and then shifting from vertex k to vertex i in G_M. So if M and N each describe some probability transition for going from one time click to the next, $M \star N$ will then describe a probability transition of going from time t to $t + 1$ to $t + 2$.

Example 3.2.2   Let us tackle a real example: **the stochastic billiard ball**. Consider the graph

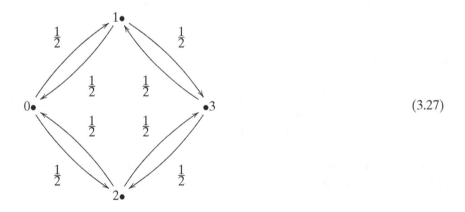

(3.27)

Corresponding to this graph is the matrix

$$A = \begin{bmatrix} 0 & \frac{1}{2} & \frac{1}{2} & 0 \\ \frac{1}{2} & 0 & 0 & \frac{1}{2} \\ \frac{1}{2} & 0 & 0 & \frac{1}{2} \\ 0 & \frac{1}{2} & \frac{1}{2} & 0 \end{bmatrix}. \tag{3.28}$$

Notice that A is a doubly stochastic matrix. Let us start with a single marble on vertex 0; that is, we shall start in state $[1, 0, 0, 0]^T$. After one time click, the system will be in state

$$\left[0, \frac{1}{2}, \frac{1}{2}, 0\right]^T. \tag{3.29}$$

A quick calculation shows that in another time click, the system will be in state

$$\left[\frac{1}{2}, 0, 0, \frac{1}{2}\right]^T. \tag{3.30}$$

Continuing in this fashion, we find that the marble acts like a billiard ball and continues to bounce back and forth between vertices 1,2 and 0,3. We shall meet a quantum version of this example in the next section. □

Exercise 3.2.6 Consider the following hypothetical situation at a hypothetical college. Thirty percent of all math majors become computer science majors after one year. Another 60% become physics majors after one year. After a year, 70% of the physics majors become math majors and 10% of the physics majors become computer science majors. In contrast to the other departments, computer science students are usually very happy: only 20% of them become math majors and 20% become physics majors after a year.

(a) Draw a graph that describes the situation.

(b) Give the corresponding adjacency matrix. Notice that it is a doubly stochastic matrix.

(c) If a student is majoring in one of these three areas, indicate her probable major after 2, 4, and 8 years. ∎

Before moving on to the next section, let us examine an interesting example. This shall be known as the **probabilistic double-slit experiment**. Consider Figure 3.1 where there is a diagram of a gun shooting bullets.

There are two slits in the wall. The shooter is a good enough shot to always get the bullets through one of the two slits. There is a 50% chance that the bullet will travel through the top slit. Similarly, there is a 50% chance the bullet will travel through the bottom slit. Once a bullet is through a slit, there are three targets to the right of each slit that the bullet can hit with equal probability. The middle target can get hit in one of two ways: from the top slit going down or from the bottom slit going up. It is assumed that it takes the bullet one time click to travel from the

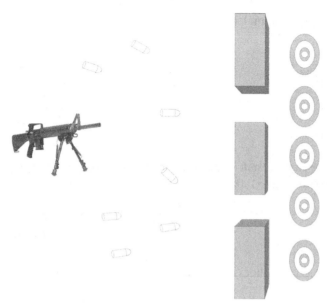

Figure 3.1. Double-slit experiment with bullets.

gun to the wall and one time click to travel from the wall to the targets. The picture corresponds to the following weighted graph:

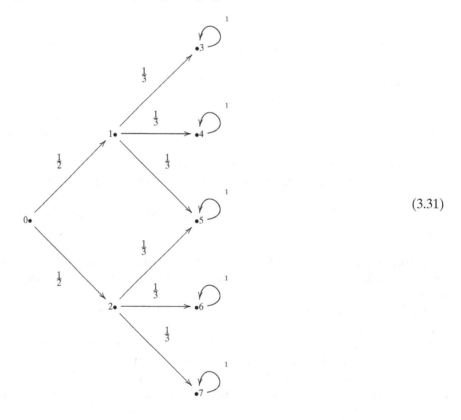

$$(3.31)$$

Notice that the vertex marked 5 can receive bullets from either of the two slits. Also notice that once a bullet is in position 3, 4, 5, 6, or 7, it will, with probability 1, stay there.

Corresponding to this graph is the matrix B (for "bullets"):

$$
B = \begin{bmatrix}
0 & 0 & 0 & 0 & 0 & 0 & 0 & 0 \\
\frac{1}{2} & 0 & 0 & 0 & 0 & 0 & 0 & 0 \\
\frac{1}{2} & 0 & 0 & 0 & 0 & 0 & 0 & 0 \\
0 & \frac{1}{3} & 0 & 1 & 0 & 0 & 0 & 0 \\
0 & \frac{1}{3} & 0 & 0 & 1 & 0 & 0 & 0 \\
0 & \frac{1}{3} & \frac{1}{3} & 0 & 0 & 1 & 0 & 0 \\
0 & 0 & \frac{1}{3} & 0 & 0 & 0 & 1 & 0 \\
0 & 0 & \frac{1}{3} & 0 & 0 & 0 & 0 & 1
\end{bmatrix}.
\tag{3.32}
$$

In words, B describes the way a bullet will move after one time click. The matrix B is not a doubly stochastic matrix. The sum of the weights entering vertex 0 is not 1. The sum of weights leaving vertices 3, 4, 5, 6, and 7 are more than 1. In order to convert this to a doubly stochastic matrix, our bullets would require the ability to go from right to left. In other words, the targets and the slits would have to be made of some type of elastic material that could cause the bullets to ricochet as in our stochastic billiard ball example. Rather than consider such a complicated scenario, we shall stick to this simplified version.

Let us calculate the probabilities for the bullet's position after two time clicks.

$$
B \star B = B^2 = \begin{bmatrix}
0 & 0 & 0 & 0 & 0 & 0 & 0 & 0 \\
0 & 0 & 0 & 0 & 0 & 0 & 0 & 0 \\
0 & 0 & 0 & 0 & 0 & 0 & 0 & 0 \\
\frac{1}{6} & \frac{1}{3} & 0 & 1 & 0 & 0 & 0 & 0 \\
\frac{1}{6} & \frac{1}{3} & 0 & 0 & 1 & 0 & 0 & 0 \\
\frac{1}{3} & \frac{1}{3} & \frac{1}{3} & 0 & 0 & 1 & 0 & 0 \\
\frac{1}{6} & 0 & \frac{1}{3} & 0 & 0 & 0 & 1 & 0 \\
\frac{1}{6} & 0 & \frac{1}{3} & 0 & 0 & 0 & 0 & 1
\end{bmatrix}.
\tag{3.33}
$$

So B^2 indicates the probabilities of the bullet's position after two time clicks.

If we are sure that we start with the bullet in position 0, i.e.,

$$
X = [1, 0, 0, 0, 0, 0, 0, 0]^T,
\tag{3.34}
$$

then after two time clicks, the state of the bullets will be

$$B^2 X = \left[0, 0, 0, \frac{1}{6}, \frac{1}{6}, \frac{1}{3}, \frac{1}{6}, \frac{1}{6}\right]^T. \tag{3.35}$$

The key idea is to notice that $B^2[5, 0] = \frac{1}{6} + \frac{1}{6} = \frac{1}{3}$ because the gun shoots the bullet from position 0; hence, there are two possible ways for the bullets to get to position 5. The possibilities sum to $\frac{1}{3}$. This is what we would expect. We revisit this example in the next section where strange things start happening!

Let us summarize what we should retain from this section:

- The vectors that represent states of a probabilistic physical system express a type of indeterminacy about the exact physical state of the system.
- The matrices that represent the dynamics express a type of indeterminacy about the way the physical system will change over time. Their entries enable us to compute the likelihood of transitioning from one state to the next.
- The way in which the indeterminacy progresses is simulated by matrix multiplication, just as in the deterministic scenario.

Programming Drill 3.2.1   *Modify your program from Programming Drill 3.1.1 so that the entries in the matrices can be fractions as opposed to Boolean values.*

Programming Drill 3.2.2   *What would happen if there were more than two slits? Write a program that asks a user to design a multislit experiment. The user notes the number of slits and the number of targets to measure the bullets. Then the user enters probabilities of the bullets' moving from each slit to each target. An appropriate matrix is set up and then the matrix is multiplied by itself. Have the program print the appropriate resulting matrix and vector.*

3.3 QUANTUM SYSTEMS

We are now ready to leave the world of classical probabilities and enter the world of the quantum. As mentioned earlier, quantum mechanics works with complex numbers. A weight is not given as a real number p between 0 and 1. Rather, it is given as a complex number c such that $|c|^2$ is a real number between 0 and 1.

What difference does it make how probabilities are given? What does it matter if a probability is given directly as a real number between 0 and 1, or indirectly as a complex number whose modulus squared is a real number between 0 and 1? The difference is – and this lies at the very core of quantum theory – that real number probabilities can only increase when added. In contrast, complex numbers can cancel each other and lower their probability. For example, if p_1 and p_2 are two real numbers between 0 and 1, then $(p_1 + p_2) \geq p_1$ and $(p_1 + p_2) \geq p_2$. Now let us look at the complex case. Let c_1 and c_2 be two complex numbers with associated squares of modulus $|c_1|^2$ and $|c_2|^2$. $|c_1 + c_2|^2$ need not be bigger than $|c_1|^2$ and it also does not need to be bigger than $|c_2|^2$.

Example 3.3.1   For example,[3] if $c_1 = 5 + 3i$ and $c_2 = -3 - 2i$, then $|c_1|^2 = 34$ and $|c_2|^2 = 13$ but $|c_1 + c_2|^2 = |2 + i|^2 = 5$. 5 is less than 34, and 5 is less than 13.   □

The fact that complex numbers may cancel each other out when added has a well-defined physical meaning in quantum mechanics (and in classical wave mechanics as well). It is referred to as **interference**[4] and it is one of the most important concepts in quantum theory.

Let us generalize our states and graphs from the previous section. For our states, rather than insisting that the sum of the entries in the column vector is 1, we shall require that the sum of the modulus squared of the entries be 1. (This makes sense because we are considering the probability as the modulus squared.) An example of such a state is

$$X = \left[\frac{1}{\sqrt{3}}, \frac{2i}{\sqrt{15}}, \sqrt{\frac{2}{5}} \right]^T. \tag{3.36}$$

Rather than talking about graphs with real number weights, we shall talk about graphs with complex number weights. Instead of insisting that the adjacency matrix of such a graph be a doubly stochastic matrix, we ask instead that the adjacency matrix be unitary.[5]

For example, consider the graph

$$\tag{3.37}$$

The corresponding unitary adjacency matrix is

$$U = \begin{bmatrix} \frac{1}{\sqrt{2}} & \frac{1}{\sqrt{2}} & 0 \\ \frac{-i}{\sqrt{2}} & \frac{i}{\sqrt{2}} & 0 \\ 0 & 0 & i \end{bmatrix}. \tag{3.38}$$

---

[3] The important point here is that the modulus squared is positive. For simplicity of calculation, we have chosen easy complex numbers.

[4] The clever reader might have considered something like "negative probability" to perform the same task as complex numbers. It turns out that much of quantum mechanics can, in fact, be done that way. However, it is not the standard way of introducing quantum theory, and we will not take that route.

[5] We defined a "unitary matrix" in Section 2.6. Remember: A matrix U is unitary if $U \star U^\dagger = I = U^\dagger \star U$.

Unitary matrices are related to doubly stochastic matrices as follows: the modulus squared of the all the complex entries in U forms a doubly stochastic matrix.[6] The i, jth element in U is denoted $U[i, j]$, and its modulus squared is denoted $|U[i, j]|^2$. By abuse of notation, we shall denote the entire matrix of modulus squares as $|U[i, j]|^2$:

$$|U[i, j]|^2 = \begin{bmatrix} \frac{1}{2} & \frac{1}{2} & 0 \\ \frac{1}{2} & \frac{1}{2} & 0 \\ 0 & 0 & 1 \end{bmatrix}. \tag{3.39}$$

It is easy to see that this is a doubly stochastic matrix.

Exercise 3.3.1   Find the $|U[i, j]|^2$ for the unitary matrix

$$U = \begin{bmatrix} \cos\theta & -\sin\theta & 0 \\ \sin\theta & \cos\theta & 0 \\ 0 & 0 & 1 \end{bmatrix}$$

for any θ. Check that it is doubly stochastic.   ■

Exercise 3.3.2   Given any unitary matrix, prove that the modulus squared of each of the entries forms a doubly stochastic matrix.   ■

Let us now see how unitary matrices act on states. Calculating $UX = Y$, we get

$$\begin{bmatrix} \frac{1}{\sqrt{2}} & \frac{1}{\sqrt{2}} & 0 \\ \frac{-i}{\sqrt{2}} & \frac{i}{\sqrt{2}} & 0 \\ 0 & 0 & i \end{bmatrix} \begin{bmatrix} \frac{1}{\sqrt{3}} \\ \frac{2i}{\sqrt{15}} \\ \sqrt{\frac{2}{5}} \end{bmatrix} = \begin{bmatrix} \frac{5+2i}{\sqrt{30}} \\ \frac{-2-\sqrt{5}i}{\sqrt{30}} \\ \sqrt{\frac{2}{5}}i \end{bmatrix}. \tag{3.40}$$

Notice that the sum of the modulus squares of Y is 1.

Exercise 3.3.3   Prove that a unitary matrix preserves the sum of the modulus squares of a column vector multiplied on its right.   ■

From the graph-theoretic point of view, it is easy to see what unitary means: the conjugate transpose of the U matrix is

$$U^\dagger = \begin{bmatrix} \frac{1}{\sqrt{2}} & \frac{i}{\sqrt{2}} & 0 \\ \frac{1}{\sqrt{2}} & \frac{-i}{\sqrt{2}} & 0 \\ 0 & 0 & -i \end{bmatrix}. \tag{3.41}$$

---

[6] In fact, it is a *symmetric* doubly stochastic matrix.

This matrix corresponds to the graph

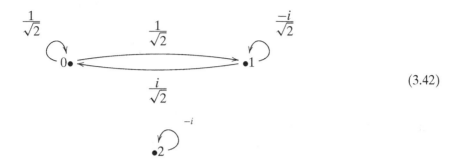

$$(3.42)$$

If U is the matrix that takes a state from time t to time $t + 1$, then $U^\dagger$ is the matrix that takes a state from time t to time $t - 1$. If we were to multiply $U^\dagger$ and U, we would obtain the identity matrix I_3. We can then have the following sequence of vectors in times steps:

$$V \longmapsto UV \longmapsto U^\dagger UV = I_3 V = V. \tag{3.43}$$

I_3 corresponds to the graph

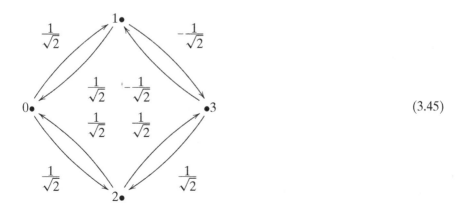

$$(3.44)$$

This means that if you perform some operation and then "undo" the operation, you will find yourself (with probability 1) in the same state with which you began.

Example 3.3.2 Let us revisit the stochastic billiard ball example. This time we shall make a quantum system out of it: **the quantum billiard ball**. Consider the graph

$$(3.45)$$

The matrix corresponding to this graph is

$$
A = \begin{bmatrix} 0 & \frac{1}{\sqrt{2}} & \frac{1}{\sqrt{2}} & 0 \\ \frac{1}{\sqrt{2}} & 0 & 0 & -\frac{1}{\sqrt{2}} \\ \frac{1}{\sqrt{2}} & 0 & 0 & \frac{1}{\sqrt{2}} \\ 0 & -\frac{1}{\sqrt{2}} & \frac{1}{\sqrt{2}} & 0 \end{bmatrix}.
\tag{3.46}
$$

Notice that this matrix is unitary. Let us start with a single marble on vertex 0, i.e., the state $[1, 0, 0, 0]^T$. After one time click, the system will be in the state

$$
\left[0, \sqrt{\frac{1}{2}}, \sqrt{\frac{1}{2}}, 0\right]^T
\tag{3.47}
$$

reflecting the 50-50 chance as in the stochastic billiard ball example. But what happens if we multiply this vector by A to determine the next state of the system? A quick calculation will show that after the next time click, the system will be *back in* state

$$
[1, 0, 0, 0]^T.
\tag{3.48}
$$

This is in stark contrast to what happened with the stochastic billiard ball. Here, the other paths cancel each other out (interference). We could have seen this by noticing that in order to find the state after two time clicks, we would have had to multiply our starting state with $A \star A$. However, $A \star A = A^2 = I_4$.   □

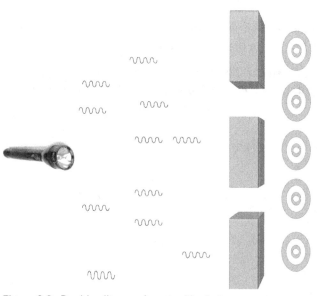

Figure 3.2. Double-slit experiment with photons.

In order to see the interference phenomenon more clearly, we shall revisit the **double-slit experiment** from Section 3.2. Rather than examine bullets, which are relatively large objects and hence adhere to the laws of classical physics, we shall study microscopic objects such as photons that follow the laws of quantum physics. Rather than a gun, we shall have a laser shoot photons. (Photons are elementary particles that are the basic ingredients of light.) We shall shoot photons through two slits as in Figure 3.2.

Again, we shall make the assumption that a photon will pass through one of the two slits. Each slit has a 50% chance of the photon's passing through it. To the right of each slit, there are three measuring devices. It is assumed that it takes one time click to go from the laser to the wall and one time click to go from the wall to the measuring devices. We are not interested in how large the slits are or how far the measuring devices are from the slits. Physicists are very adept at calculating many different aspects of this experiment. We are only interested in the setup.

The following weighted graph describes the setup of the experiment:

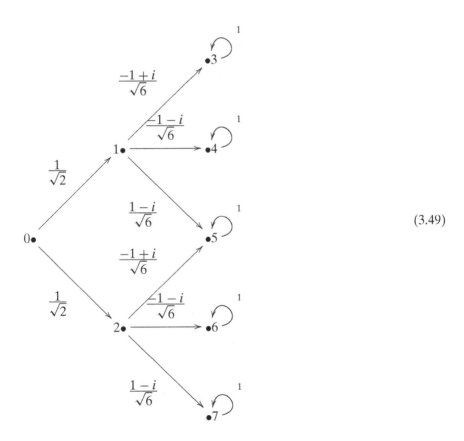

$$(3.49)$$

The modulus squared of $\frac{1}{\sqrt{2}}$ is $\frac{1}{2}$, which corresponds to the fact that there is a 50–50 chance of the photon's passing through either slit. $\left|\frac{\pm 1 \pm i}{\sqrt{6}}\right|^2 = \frac{1}{3}$, which corresponds to the fact that whichever slit the photon passes through, there is a $\frac{1}{3}$ chance of its hitting any of the three measuring devices to the right of that slit.[7]

The adjacency matrix, P (for "photons"), of this graph is

$$
P = \begin{bmatrix}
0 & 0 & 0 & 0 & 0 & 0 & 0 & 0 \\
\frac{1}{\sqrt{2}} & 0 & 0 & 0 & 0 & 0 & 0 & 0 \\
\frac{1}{\sqrt{2}} & 0 & 0 & 0 & 0 & 0 & 0 & 0 \\
0 & \frac{-1+i}{\sqrt{6}} & 0 & 1 & 0 & 0 & 0 & 0 \\
0 & \frac{-1-i}{\sqrt{6}} & 0 & 0 & 1 & 0 & 0 & 0 \\
0 & \frac{1-i}{\sqrt{6}} & \frac{-1+i}{\sqrt{6}} & 0 & 0 & 1 & 0 & 0 \\
0 & 0 & \frac{-1-i}{\sqrt{6}} & 0 & 0 & 0 & 1 & 0 \\
0 & 0 & \frac{1-i}{\sqrt{6}} & 0 & 0 & 0 & 0 & 1
\end{bmatrix}. \tag{3.50}
$$

This matrix is not unitary. The reason this matrix fails to be unitary is that we have not placed all the arrows in our graph. There are many more possible ways the photon can travel in a real-life physical situation. In particular, the photon might travel from right to left. The diagram and matrix would become too complicated if we put in all the transitions. We are simply trying to demonstrate the phenomenon of interference and we can accomplish that even with a matrix that is not quite unitary.

The modulus squared of the P matrix is exactly the same as that of the bullet's matrix, i.e.,

$$
|P[i, j]|^2 = \begin{bmatrix}
0 & 0 & 0 & 0 & 0 & 0 & 0 & 0 \\
\frac{1}{2} & 0 & 0 & 0 & 0 & 0 & 0 & 0 \\
\frac{1}{2} & 0 & 0 & 0 & 0 & 0 & 0 & 0 \\
0 & \frac{1}{3} & 0 & 1 & 0 & 0 & 0 & 0 \\
0 & \frac{1}{3} & 0 & 0 & 1 & 0 & 0 & 0 \\
0 & \frac{1}{3} & \frac{1}{3} & 0 & 0 & 1 & 0 & 0 \\
0 & 0 & \frac{1}{3} & 0 & 0 & 0 & 1 & 0 \\
0 & 0 & \frac{1}{3} & 0 & 0 & 0 & 0 & 1
\end{bmatrix}. \tag{3.51}
$$

In fact, we chose our complex numbers so that $|P[i, j]|^2$ would be equal to B of Section 3.2. This means that nothing strange happens after one time click.

---

[7] The actual complex number weights are not our concern here. If we wanted to calculate the actual numbers, we would have to measure the width of the slits, the distance between them, the distance from the slits to the measuring devices, etc. However, our goal here is to clearly demonstrate the interference phenomenon, and so we chose the above complex numbers simply because the modulus squared are exactly the same as in the bullet's case.

So far, everything looks normal. Let us see what happens if we calculate the transition matrix after *two* time clicks.

$$P^2 = \begin{bmatrix} 0 & 0 & 0 & 0 & 0 & 0 & 0 & 0 \\ 0 & 0 & 0 & 0 & 0 & 0 & 0 & 0 \\ 0 & 0 & 0 & 0 & 0 & 0 & 0 & 0 \\ \frac{-1+i}{\sqrt{12}} & \frac{-1+i}{\sqrt{6}} & 0 & 1 & 0 & 0 & 0 & 0 \\ \frac{-1-i}{\sqrt{12}} & \frac{-1-i}{\sqrt{6}} & 0 & 0 & 1 & 0 & 0 & 0 \\ 0 & \frac{1-i}{\sqrt{6}} & \frac{-1+i}{\sqrt{6}} & 0 & 0 & 1 & 0 & 0 \\ \frac{-1-i}{\sqrt{12}} & 0 & \frac{-1-i}{\sqrt{6}} & 0 & 0 & 0 & 1 & 0 \\ \frac{1-i}{\sqrt{12}} & 0 & \frac{1-i}{\sqrt{6}} & 0 & 0 & 0 & 0 & 1 \end{bmatrix}. \tag{3.52}$$

How do we interpret this in terms of probability? Let us look at the modulus squared of each of the entries.

$$|P^2[i, j]|^2 = \begin{bmatrix} 0 & 0 & 0 & 0 & 0 & 0 & 0 & 0 \\ 0 & 0 & 0 & 0 & 0 & 0 & 0 & 0 \\ 0 & 0 & 0 & 0 & 0 & 0 & 0 & 0 \\ \frac{1}{6} & \frac{1}{3} & 0 & 1 & 0 & 0 & 0 & 0 \\ \frac{1}{6} & \frac{1}{3} & 0 & 0 & 1 & 0 & 0 & 0 \\ 0 & \frac{1}{3} & \frac{1}{3} & 0 & 0 & 1 & 0 & 0 \\ \frac{1}{6} & 0 & \frac{1}{3} & 0 & 0 & 0 & 1 & 0 \\ \frac{1}{6} & 0 & \frac{1}{3} & 0 & 0 & 0 & 0 & 1 \end{bmatrix}. \tag{3.53}$$

This matrix is almost exactly the same as B^2 of Section 3.2, but with one glaring difference. $B^2[5, 0] = \frac{1}{3}$ because of the two ways of starting at position 0 and ending at position 5. We added the nonnegative probabilities $\frac{1}{6} + \frac{1}{6} = \frac{1}{3}$. However, with a photon that follows the laws of quantum mechanics, the complex numbers are added as opposed to their probabilities.

$$\frac{1}{\sqrt{2}}\left(\frac{-1+i}{\sqrt{6}}\right) + \frac{1}{\sqrt{2}}\left(\frac{1-i}{\sqrt{6}}\right) = \frac{-1+i}{\sqrt{12}} + \frac{1-i}{\sqrt{12}} = \frac{0}{\sqrt{12}} = 0, \tag{3.54}$$

thus giving us $|P^2[5, 0]|^2 = 0$. In other words, although there are two ways of a photon's going from vertex 0 to vertex 5, there will be no photon at vertex 5.

How is one to understand this phenomenon? For hundreds of years, physicists have had a simple explanation for interference: waves. A familiar observation such as two pebbles thrown into a pool of water will easily convince us that waves interfere, sometimes reinforcing each other, sometimes canceling each other. Thus, the double-slit experiment points to the wave-like nature of light. At the same time, another crucial experiment in quantum mechanics, namely the photoelectric effect, points toward a different direction: light is absorbed and emitted in discrete quantities – photons. It is as if light (and matter) has a double nature: on some occasions it acts as a beam of particles, and at other times it acts like a wave.

It is important to notice that the experiment can be done with a *single* photon shot from vertex 0. Even in this scenario, interference will still occur. What is going on here?

The naive probabilistic interpretation of the position of the photon following the bullet metaphor of the previous section is thus not entirely adequate. Let the state of the system be given by $X = [c_0, c_1, \ldots, c_{n-1}]^T \in \mathbb{C}^n$. It is incorrect to say that the probability of the photon's being in position k is $|c_k|^2$. Rather, to be in state X means that the particle is in some sense in *all* positions simultaneously. The photon passes through the top slit *and* the bottom slit simultaneously, and when it exits both slits, it can cancel *itself* out. A photon is not in *a* single position, rather it is in *many* positions, a **superposition**.

This might generate some justifiable disbelief. After all, we do not see things in many different positions. Our everyday experience tells us that things are in one position or (exclusive or!) another. How can this be? The reason we see particles in one particular position is because we have performed a **measurement**. When we measure something at the quantum level, the quantum object that we have measured is no longer in a superposition of states, rather it collapses to a single classical state. So we have to redefine what the state of a quantum system is: a system is in state X means that *after measuring* it, it will be found in position i with probability $|c_i|^2$.

What are we to make of these strange ideas? Are we really to believe them? Richard Feynman, in discussing the double-slit experiment (Feynman, 1963, Vol. III, page 1-1) waxes lyrical:

> We choose to examine a phenomenon which is impossible, *absolutely* impossible, to explain in any classical way, and which has in it the heart of quantum mechanics. In reality, it contains the *only* mystery. We cannot make the mystery go away by "explaining" how it works. We will just tell you how it works.

It is exactly this superposition of states that is the real power behind quantum computing. Classical computers are in one state at every moment. Imagine putting a computer in many different classical states simultaneously and then processing with *all* the states at once. This is the ultimate in parallel processing! Such a computer can only be conceived of in the quantum world.

Let us review what we have learned:

- States in a quantum system are represented by column vectors of complex numbers whose sum of moduli squared is 1.
- The dynamics of a quantum system is represented by unitary matrices and is therefore reversible. The "undoing" is obtained via the algebraic inverse, i.e., the adjoint of the unitary matrix representing forward evolution.

■ The probabilities of quantum mechanics are always given as the modulus square of complex numbers.

■ Quantum states can be superposed, i.e., a physical system can be in more than one basic state simultaneously.

Programming Drill 3.3.1 *Modify your program from Programming Drill 3.2.1 so that you allow the entries to be complex numbers as opposed to fractions.*

Programming Drill 3.3.2 *Modify your program from Programming Drill 3.2.2 so that you allow transitions from the many slits to the many measuring devices to be complex numbers. Your program should identify where there are interference phenomena.*

3.4 ASSEMBLING SYSTEMS

Quantum mechanics also deals with composite systems, i.e., systems that have more than one part. In this section, we learn how to combine several systems into one. We shall talk about assembling classical probabilistic systems. However, whatever is stated about probabilistic systems is also true for quantum systems.

Consider two different marbles. Imagine that a red marble follows the probabilities of the graph G_M:

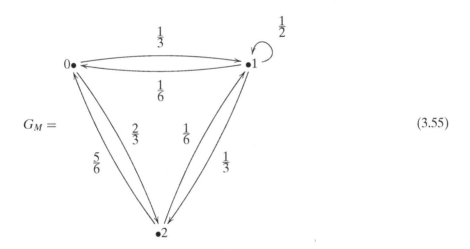

$$G_M = \qquad\qquad\qquad\qquad\qquad\qquad (3.55)$$

whose corresponding adjacency matrix is

$$M = \begin{bmatrix} 0 & \frac{1}{6} & \frac{5}{6} \\ \frac{1}{3} & \frac{1}{2} & \frac{1}{6} \\ \frac{2}{3} & \frac{1}{3} & 0 \end{bmatrix}. \qquad\qquad (3.56)$$

Furthermore, there is also a blue marble that follows the transitions given by the graph

$$
G_N = \quad \overset{\tfrac{1}{3}}{\underset{\tfrac{2}{3}}{\underset{a\bullet \;\underset{\longrightarrow}{\longleftarrow}\; \bullet b}{\overset{\tfrac{2}{3}}{}}}} \quad \overset{\tfrac{1}{3}}{}
\tag{3.57}
$$

i.e., the matrix

$$
N = \begin{bmatrix} \frac{1}{3} & \frac{2}{3} \\ \frac{2}{3} & \frac{1}{3} \end{bmatrix}.
\tag{3.58}
$$

How does a state for a *two*-marble system look? Because the red marble can be on one of three vertices and the blue marble can be on one of two vertices, there are $3 \times 2 = 6$ possible states of the combined system. This is the tensor product of a 3-by-1 vector with a 2-by-1 vector. A typical state might look like this:

$$
X = \begin{matrix} 0a \\ 0b \\ 1a \\ 1b \\ 2a \\ 2b \end{matrix} \begin{bmatrix} \frac{1}{18} \\ 0 \\ \frac{2}{18} \\ \frac{1}{3} \\ 0 \\ \frac{1}{2} \end{bmatrix},
\tag{3.59}
$$

which would correspond to the fact that there is a

$\frac{1}{18}$ chance of the red marble being on vertex 0 and the blue marble being on vertex a,

0 chance of the red marble being on vertex 0 and the blue marble being on vertex b,

$\frac{2}{18}$ chance of the red marble being on vertex 1 and the blue marble being on vertex a,

$\frac{1}{3}$ chance of the red marble being on vertex 1 and the blue marble being on vertex b,

0 chance of the red marble being on vertex 2 and the blue marble being on vertex a, and

$\frac{1}{2}$ chance of the red marble being on vertex 2 and the blue marble being on vertex b.

How does a system with these *two* marbles change? What is its dynamics? Imagine that the red marble is on vertex 1 and the blue marble is on vertex a. We may write this state as "1a." What is the probability of going from state 1a to state 2b? Obviously, the red marble must move from vertex 1 to vertex 2 and (multiply) the blue marble must move from vertex a to vertex b. The probability is $\frac{1}{3} \times \frac{2}{3} = \frac{2}{9}$. In general, for a system to go from state ij to a state $i'j'$ we must multiply the probability of going from state i to state i' with the probability of going from state j to state j'.

$$ij \xrightarrow{\ \ M[i',i] \times N[j',j]\ \ } i'j' \,. \tag{3.60}$$

For the changes of all states, we have to do this for all entries. We are really giving the tensor product of two matrices as defined in Equation (2.175) of Section 2.7.

$$M \otimes N = \begin{array}{c} \\ \mathbf{1} \\ \\ \\ \mathbf{2} \end{array}
\begin{bmatrix}
\mathbf{0} \begin{bmatrix} \frac{1}{3} & \frac{2}{3} \\ \frac{2}{3} & \frac{1}{3} \end{bmatrix} & \frac{1}{6} \begin{bmatrix} \frac{1}{3} & \frac{2}{3} \\ \frac{2}{3} & \frac{1}{3} \end{bmatrix} & \frac{5}{6} \begin{bmatrix} \frac{1}{3} & \frac{2}{3} \\ \frac{2}{3} & \frac{1}{3} \end{bmatrix} \\[12pt]
\frac{1}{3} \begin{bmatrix} \frac{1}{3} & \frac{2}{3} \\ \frac{2}{3} & \frac{1}{3} \end{bmatrix} & \frac{1}{2} \begin{bmatrix} \frac{1}{3} & \frac{2}{3} \\ \frac{2}{3} & \frac{1}{3} \end{bmatrix} & \frac{1}{6} \begin{bmatrix} \frac{1}{3} & \frac{2}{3} \\ \frac{2}{3} & \frac{1}{3} \end{bmatrix} \\[12pt]
\frac{2}{3} \begin{bmatrix} \frac{1}{3} & \frac{2}{3} \\ \frac{2}{3} & \frac{1}{3} \end{bmatrix} & \frac{1}{3} \begin{bmatrix} \frac{1}{3} & \frac{2}{3} \\ \frac{2}{3} & \frac{1}{3} \end{bmatrix} & 0 \begin{bmatrix} \frac{1}{3} & \frac{2}{3} \\ \frac{2}{3} & \frac{1}{3} \end{bmatrix}
\end{bmatrix}$$

$$=
\begin{array}{c} \mathbf{0a} \\ \mathbf{0b} \\ \mathbf{1a} \\ \mathbf{1b} \\ \mathbf{2a} \\ \mathbf{2b} \end{array}
\begin{bmatrix}
0 & 0 & \frac{1}{18} & \frac{2}{18} & \frac{5}{18} & \frac{10}{18} \\
0 & 0 & \frac{2}{18} & \frac{1}{18} & \frac{10}{18} & \frac{5}{18} \\
\frac{1}{9} & \frac{2}{9} & \frac{1}{6} & \frac{2}{6} & \frac{1}{18} & \frac{2}{18} \\
\frac{2}{9} & \frac{1}{9} & \frac{2}{6} & \frac{1}{6} & \frac{2}{18} & \frac{1}{18} \\
\frac{2}{9} & \frac{4}{9} & \frac{1}{9} & \frac{2}{9} & 0 & 0 \\
\frac{4}{9} & \frac{2}{9} & \frac{2}{9} & \frac{1}{9} & 0 & 0
\end{bmatrix}. \tag{3.61}$$

$$\begin{array}{cccccc} \mathbf{0a} & \mathbf{0b} & \mathbf{1a} & \mathbf{1b} & \mathbf{2a} & \mathbf{2b} \end{array}$$

The graph that corresponds to this matrix, $G_M \times G_N$ – called the **Cartesian product** of two weighted graphs – has 28 weighted arrows. We shall simply fill in those arrows that correspond to the third column of $M \otimes N$:

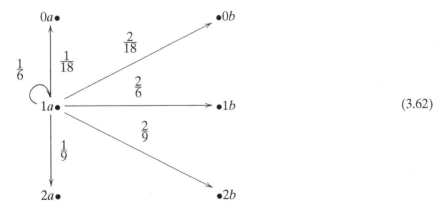

$$\tag{3.62}$$

Exercise 3.4.1 Complete the graph in Equation (3.62) on a large piece of paper.

◼

Exercise 3.4.2   Find the matrix and the graph that correspond to $N \otimes N$.   ■

In quantum theory, the states of two separate systems can be combined using the tensor product of two vectors and the changes of two systems are combined by using the tensor product of two matrices. The tensor product of the matrices will then act on the tensor product of the vectors. However, it must be stressed that in the quantum world there are many more possible states than just states that can be combined from smaller ones. In fact, the states that are not the tensor product of the smaller states are the more interesting ones. They are called **entangled states**. We shall see them again in Section 4.5. Similarly, there are many more actions on a combined quantum system than simply that of the tensor product of the individual system's actions.

In general, the Cartesian product of an n-vertex graph with an n'-vertex graph is an $(n \times n')$-vertex graph. If we have an n-vertex graph G and we are interested in m different marbles moving within this system, we would need to look at the graph

$$G^m = \underbrace{G \times G \times \cdots \times G}_{m \text{ times}}, \tag{3.63}$$

which will have n^m vertices. If M_G is the associated adjacency matrix, then we will be interested in

$$M_G^{\otimes m} = \underbrace{M_G \otimes M_G \otimes \cdots \otimes M_G}_{m \text{ times}}, \tag{3.64}$$

which will be a n^m-by-n^m matrix.

One might think of a bit as a two-vertex graph with a marble on the 0 vertex or a marble on the 1 vertex. If one wished to represent m bits with a single marble, one would need a 2^m vertex graph, or equivalently, a 2^m-by-2^m matrix. So there is exponential growth of the resources needed for the number of bits under discussion.

This exponential growth is actually one of the main reasons Richard Feynman started talking (Feynman, 1982) about quantum computing in the first place. He realized that because of this exponential growth, it would be hard for a classical computer to simulate such a system. He then asked whether a prospective quantum computer, with its inherent ability to perform massive parallel processing, might be able to accomplish the task. After all, Nature can keep up with herself! We discuss this exponential growth again in Section 5.1.

....
Reader Tip. It might be a good idea to flip through Section 2.7 again now that you have developed some intuition about the tensor product.   ♡
....

Let us summarize:

■ A composite system is represented by the Cartesian product of the transition graphs of its subsystems.

■ If two matrices act on the subsystems independently, then their tensor product acts on the states of their combined system.

■ There is an exponential growth in the amount of resources needed to describe larger and larger composite systems.

Exercise 3.4.3   Let

$$M = \begin{bmatrix} \frac{1}{3} & \frac{2}{3} \\ \frac{2}{3} & \frac{1}{3} \end{bmatrix} \quad \text{and} \quad N = \begin{bmatrix} \frac{1}{2} & \frac{1}{2} \\ \frac{1}{2} & \frac{1}{2} \end{bmatrix}.$$

Calculate $M \otimes N$ and find its associated graph. Compare this graph to $G_M \times G_N$. ■

Exercise 3.4.4   Prove a general theorem: given two square matrices M and N with associated weighted graphs G_M and G_N, show that the two graphs

$$G_{M \otimes N} \cong G_M \times G_N \tag{3.65}$$

are essentially the same (isomorphism of weighted graphs). ■

Exercise 3.4.5   Prove a general theorem: given two weighted graphs G and H with associated adjacency matrices M_G and M_H, show the equality of matrices

$$M_{G \times H} = M_G \otimes M_H. \tag{3.66}$$

■

Exercise 3.4.6   In Exercise 2.7.4, you proved the essential commutativity of the tensor product of matrices, that is, for matrices M and N, we have the following isomorphism:

$$M \otimes N \cong N \otimes M. \tag{3.67}$$

What does this correspond to in terms of marbles moving on graphs? ■

Exercise 3.4.7   In Exercise 2.7.9, you proved that for matrices of the appropriate sizes M, M', N, and N', we have the following equation:

$$(M \star M') \otimes (N \star N') = (M \otimes N) \star (M' \otimes N'). \tag{3.68}$$

What does this correspond to in terms of marbles moving on graphs? ■

....

References: The relationship between graphs and matrices can be found in any book of discrete mathematics, e.g., Grimaldi (2003), Ross and Wright (2003), and Rosen (2003). The connection between the number of paths in a graph and matrix multiplication can be found in many books, e.g., Section 11.3 of Ross and Wright (2003). The rest of this chapter consists of generalizations of this idea with a view toward basic quantum mechanics.

To learn elementary quantum mechanics, see the references at the end of Chapter 4.

The double-slit experiment is discussed in depth in Chapter 1 of Volume III of Feynman (1963). Feynman derives many of the properties of quantum mechanics from this simple experiment. Definitely worth the read!

To learn more about the tensor product of vector spaces, see the references at the end of Chapter 2.

4

Basic Quantum Theory

Reality is that which, when you stop believing in it, does not go away.

Philip K. Dick[1]

In Chapters 1 and 2 we developed the necessary mathematical apparatus and terminology that will be used throughout this book. Chapter 3 has provided some heuristics and gently led us to the threshold of quantum mechanics. It is now time to open the door, introduce the basic concepts and tools of the trade, and continue our journey to quantum computing.[2]

In Section 4.1 we spend a few words on the motivations behind quantum mechanics. We then introduce quantum states and how they are distinguishable from one another through observations. Section 4.2 describes observable physical quantities within the quantum framework. How observable quantities are measured is the topic of Section 4.3. The dynamics of quantum systems, i.e., their evolution in time, is the focus of Section 4.4. Finally, in Section 4.5, we revisit the tensor product and show how it describes the way in which larger quantum systems are assembled from smaller ones. In the process, we meet the crucial notion of entanglement, a feature of the quantum world that pops up again in the chapters ahead.

4.1 QUANTUM STATES

Why quantum mechanics? To answer this question, we have to hearken back in time to the dawn of the twentieth century. Classical mechanics still dominated the scene, with its double-pronged approach: **particles** and **waves**. Matter was considered to be

---

[1] The quotation is taken from Dick's 1978 lecture *How to build a Universe that does not fall apart two days later*, freely available on the Web at http://deoxy.org/pkd_how2build.htm.

[2] No attempt will be made to present the material in an exhaustive historical manner. The curious reader can refer to the references at the end of this chapter for a plethora of good, comprehensive introductions to quantum mechanics.

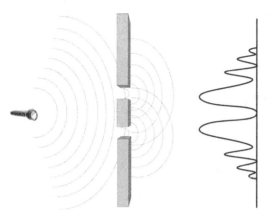

Figure 4.1. Young's double-slit experiment.

ultimately composed of microscopic particles, and light was thought of as continuous electromagnetic waves propagating in space.

The dichotomy – particles versus waves – was proven false by several ground-breaking experiments. For instance, the **diffraction experiment** shows that a beam of subatomic particles hitting a crystal diffract following a wave-like pattern, entirely similar to the diffraction pattern of light itself. By the mid-twenties, physicists started associating waves to all known particles, the so-called **matter waves** (the first proposal was made by French physicist Louis De Broglie in 1924 in his doctoral dissertation).

The **photoelectric effect** (observed by Hertz in 1887) showed that an atom hit by a beam of light may absorb it, causing some electrons to transition to a higher-energy orbital (i.e., farther from the nucleus). Later on, the absorbed energy may be released in the form of emitted light, causing the excited electrons to revert to a lower orbital. What the photoelectric effect unraveled was that light-matter trans-actions *always* occur through discrete packets of energy, known as **photons** (the concept was introduced by Einstein in his seminal 1905 paper, as a way to account for the photoelectric effect). Photons act as genuine particles that can get absorbed and emitted, one at a time.

Further experimental evidence from many quarters accumulated over time, strongly suggesting that the old duality particle–wave theory must be replaced by a new theory of the microscopic world in which *both matter and light manifest a particle-like and a wave-like behavior*. Time was ripe for the conceptual framework of quantum mechanics.

In Chapter 3 we met a toy version of the double-slit experiment; as it turns out, this was an actual experiment, indeed an entire series of related experiments, the first one being carried out with light by the English polymath Thomas Young around 1801. Before we move on, it is worth our while to revisit it briefly, as it contains most of the main ingredients that make up quantum's magic.

One shines light at a boundary with two slits that are very close to each other. The pattern of the light to the right of the boundary will have certain regions that are dark and certain others that are bright, as depicted in Figure 4.1.

The reason why there are regions on the screen with no light is that light waves are interfering with each other. Light is propagating as a single wave from its source;

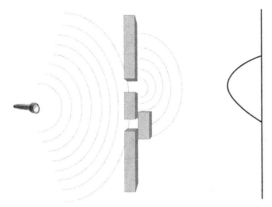

Figure 4.2. Young's double-slit experiment with one slit closed.

the two slits cause this wave to split into two independent ones, which can then interfere with each other when reaching the screen. Some regions are going to be darker, others are going to be brighter, depending on whether the two waves are in phase (positive interference) or out of phase (negative interference).

What would happen if we closed off one of the slits? In that case, there is no splitting and therefore no interference pattern whatsoever (Figure 4.2).

Two remarks on this seminal experiment are in order:

- As we have already pointed out in Chapter 3, the double-slit experiment can be done with just one photon at a time. Rather than spotting patterns of lighter or darker light on the screen, we are now looking for which region is more or less likely for the single photon to land. The same pattern can then be viewed as describing the probability for a certain region to get hit by the photon. The natural question then is, if there is a single photon why would there be any interference pattern? Yet, experiments have shown that such a pattern is there. Our photon is a true chameleon: sometimes it behaves as a particle and sometimes as a wave, depending on how it is observed.
- The double-slit experiment is not only about light: one can perform it equally well with electrons, protons, and even atomic nuclei, and they will all exhibit exactly the same interference behavior.[3] Once again, this clearly indicates that the rigid distinction between waves and particles as a paradigm of description of the physical world is untenable at the quantum level.

In the rest of this section, we are going to introduce the basic mathematical description of a quantum physical system. We shall restrict ourselves to two simple examples, to illustrate the basic machinery:

- a particle confined to a set of discrete positions on a line
- a single-particle spin system

---

[3] Such experiments have indeed been performed, only much later than Young's original version of the double-slit experiment. We invite you to read about this fascinating slice of experimental physics in Rodgers (2002).

Consider a subatomic particle on a line; moreover, let us suppose that it can only be detected at one of the equally spaced points $\{x_0, x_1, \ldots, x_{n-1}\}$, where $x_1 = x_0 + \delta x$, $x_2 = x_1 + \delta x$, $\ldots$, with δx some fixed increment.

$$x_0 \qquad x_1 \qquad \cdots \qquad x_i \qquad \cdots \qquad x_{n-1}$$

$$\text{(4.1)}$$

In real life, a particle can of course occupy any of the points of the line, not just a finite subset thereof. However, if we followed this route, the state space of our system would be infinite dimensional, requiring a considerably larger mathematical apparatus than the one covered in the last chapters. Whereas such an apparatus is vital for quantum mechanics, it is not needed for an exposition of quantum computing.[4] For our current exposition, we can thus assume that the set $\{x_0, x_1, \ldots, x_{n-1}\}$ is composed of a great many points (n large) and that δx is tiny, thereby providing a reasonably good approximation of a continuous system.

We are now going to associate to the current **state** of the particle an n-dimensional complex column vector $[c_0, c_1, \ldots, c_{n-1}]^T$.

The particle being at the point x_i shall be denoted as $|x_i\rangle$, using the Dirac **ket** notation. (Do not worry about the funny symbol: it will be explained momentarily.) To each of these n basic states, we shall associate a column vector:

$$|x_0\rangle \longmapsto [1, 0, \ldots 0]^T$$
$$|x_1\rangle \longmapsto [0, 1, \ldots 0]^T \qquad\qquad \text{(4.2)}$$
$$\vdots$$
$$|x_{n-1}\rangle \longmapsto [0, 0, \ldots 1]^T.$$

Observe that these vectors form the canonical basis of $\mathbb{C}^n$. From the standpoint of classical mechanics, the basic states in Equation (4.2) are all we shall ever need. Not so in quantum mechanics: experimental evidence testifies to the fact that the particle can be in a strange fuzzy blending of these states (think again of the double-slit!). To catch up with Nature, we shall make a bold leap by positing that *all* vectors in $\mathbb{C}^n$ represent a legitimate physical state of the particle.

What can all this possibly mean?

An arbitrary state, which we shall denote as $|\psi\rangle$, will be a linear combination of $|x_0\rangle, |x_1\rangle, \ldots, |x_{n-1}\rangle$, by suitable complex weights, $c_0, c_1, \ldots, c_{n-1}$, known as **complex amplitudes**,[5]

$$|\psi\rangle = c_0|x_0\rangle + c_1|x_1\rangle + \cdots + c_{n-1}|x_{n-1}\rangle. \qquad\qquad \text{(4.3)}$$

---

[4] We mention in passing that in computer simulation one must always turn a continuous physical system (classical or quantum) into a discrete one: computers cannot deal with infinities.

[5] This name comes from the fact that $|\psi\rangle$ is indeed a (complex) wave when we study its time evolution, as we shall see at the end of Section 4.3. Waves are characterized by their amplitude (think of the intensity of a sound wave) – hence the name above – as well as by their frequency (in case of sound waves, their pitch). As it turns out, the frequency of $|\psi\rangle$ plays a key role in the particle's momentum. You can think of Equation (4.3) as describing $|\psi\rangle$ as the overlap of n waves, the $|x_i\rangle$, each contributing with amplitude c_i.

Thus, every state of our system can be represented by an element of $\mathbb{C}^n$ as

$$|\psi\rangle \longmapsto [c_0, c_1, \ldots, c_{n-1}]^T. \tag{4.4}$$

We say that the state $|\psi\rangle$ is a **superposition** of the basic states. $|\psi\rangle$ represents the particle as being simultaneously in all $\{x_0, x_1, \ldots, x_{n-1}\}$ locations, or a blending of all the $|x_i\rangle$. There are, however, different possible blendings (much like in the recipe for baking an apple pie you can vary the proportions of the ingredients and obtain different flavors). The complex numbers $c_0, c_1, \ldots, c_{n-1}$ tell us precisely which superposition our particle is currently in. The norm square of the complex number c_i divided by the norm squared of $|\psi\rangle$ will tell us the probability that, *after* observing the particle, we will detect it at the point x_i:

$$p(x_i) = \frac{|c_i|^2}{||\psi\rangle|^2} = \frac{|c_i|^2}{\sum_j |c_j|^2}. \tag{4.5}$$

Observe that $p(x_i)$ is always a positive real number and $0 \leq p(x_i) \leq 1$, as any genuine probability should be.

When $|\psi\rangle$ is observed, we will find it in one of the basic states. We might write it as[6]

$$|\psi\rangle \rightsquigarrow |x_i\rangle. \tag{4.6}$$

Example 4.1.1 Let us assume that the particle can only be at the four points $\{x_0, x_1, x_2, x_3\}$. Thus, we are concerned with the state space $\mathbb{C}^4$. Let us also assume that now the state vector is

$$|\psi\rangle = \begin{bmatrix} -3 - i \\ -2i \\ i \\ 2 \end{bmatrix}. \tag{4.7}$$

We shall calculate the probability that our particle can be found at position x_2. The norm of $|\psi\rangle$ is given by

$$||\psi\rangle| = \sqrt{|-3-i|^2 + |-2i|^2 + |i|^2 + |2|^2} = 4.3589. \tag{4.8}$$

The probability is therefore

$$\frac{|i|^2}{(4.3589)^2} = 0.052632. \tag{4.9}$$

$\square$

---

[6] The wiggly line is used throughout this chapter to denote the state of a quantum system before and after measurement.

Exercise 4.1.1   Let us assume that the particle is confined to $\{x_0, x_1, \ldots, x_5\}$ and the current state vector is

$$|\psi\rangle = [2 - i, 2i, 1 - i, 1, -2i, 2]^T. \tag{4.10}$$

What is the likelihood of finding the particle at position x_3?   ∎

Kets can be added: if

$$|\psi\rangle = c_0|x_0\rangle + c_1|x_1\rangle + \cdots + c_{n-1}|x_{n-1}\rangle = [c_0, c_1, \ldots, c_{n-1}]^T \tag{4.11}$$

and

$$|\psi'\rangle = c_0'|x_0\rangle + c_1'|x_1\rangle + \cdots + c_{n-1}'|x_{n-1}\rangle = [c_0', c_1', \ldots, c_{n-1}']^T, \tag{4.12}$$

then

$$|\psi\rangle + |\psi'\rangle = (c_0 + c_0')|x_0\rangle + (c_1 + c_1')|x_1\rangle + \cdots + (c_{n-1} + c_{n-1}')|x_{n-1}\rangle$$
$$= [c_0 + c_0', c_1 + c_1', \ldots, c_{n-1} + c_{n-1}']^T. \tag{4.13}$$

Also, for a complex number $c \in \mathbb{C}$, we can scalar multiply a ket by c:

$$c|\psi\rangle = cc_0|x_0\rangle + cc_1|x_1\rangle + \cdots + cc_{n-1}|x_{n-1}\rangle = [cc_0, cc_1, \ldots, cc_{n-1}]^T. \tag{4.14}$$

What happens if we add a ket to itself?

$$|\psi\rangle + |\psi\rangle = 2|\psi\rangle = [c_0 + c_0, c_1 + c_1, \ldots, c_j + c_j, \ldots, c_{n-1} + c_{n-1}]^T$$
$$= [2c_0, 2c_1, \ldots, 2c_j, \ldots, 2c_{n-1}]^T. \tag{4.15}$$

The sum of the moduli squared is

$$S' = |2c_0|^2 + |2c_1|^2 + \cdots + |2c_{n-1}|^2 = 2^2|c_0|^2 + 2^2|c_1|^2 + \cdots + 2^2|c_{n-1}|^2$$
$$= 2^2(|c_0|^2 + |c_1|^2 + \cdots + |c_{n-1}|^2). \tag{4.16}$$

For the state $2|\psi\rangle$, the chance that the particle will be found in position j is

$$p(x_j) = \frac{|2c_j|^2}{S'} = \frac{2^2|c_j|^2}{2^2(|c_0|^2 + |c_1|^2 + \cdots + |c_{n-1}|^2)}$$
$$= \frac{|c_j|^2}{|c_0|^2 + |c_1|^2 + \cdots + |c_{n-1}|^2}. \tag{4.17}$$

In other words, the ket $2|\psi\rangle$ describes *the same physical system* as $|\psi\rangle$. Notice that we could replace 2 with an arbitrary $c \in \mathbb{C}$ and get the same results. Geometrically, the vector $|\psi\rangle$ and all its complex scalar multiples $c|\psi\rangle$, i.e., *the entire subspace generated by $|\psi\rangle$*, describe the same physical state. The length of $|\psi\rangle$ does not matter as far as physics goes.

Exercise 4.1.2   Let $|\psi\rangle$ be $[c_0, c_1, \ldots, c_{n-1}]^T$. Check that multiplying $|\psi\rangle$ by any complex number c will not alter the calculation of probabilities. (Hint: Factor out c in the ratio.)   ∎

Example 4.1.2   The vectors

$$|\psi_1\rangle = \begin{bmatrix} 1 + i \\ i \end{bmatrix} \quad \text{and} \quad |\psi_2\rangle = \begin{bmatrix} 2 + 4i \\ 3i - 1 \end{bmatrix} \tag{4.18}$$

differ by the factor $3 + i$ (verify it!), and are thus representatives of the same quantum state.   □

Exercise 4.1.3   Do the vectors $[1 + i, 2 - i]^T$ and $[2 + 2i, 1 - 2i]^T$ represent the same state?   ■

As we can multiply (or divide) a ket by any (complex) number and still have a representation of the same physical state, we may as well work with a **normalized** $|\psi\rangle$, i.e.,

$$\frac{|\psi\rangle}{\||\psi\rangle|} \tag{4.19}$$

which has length 1.[7]

Example 4.1.3   The vector $[2 - 3i, 1 + 2i]^T$ has length given by

$$\sqrt{|2 - 3i|^2 + |1 + 2i|^2} = 4.2426. \tag{4.20}$$

We can normalize it by simply dividing by its length:

$$\frac{1}{4.2426}[2 - 3i, 1 + 2i]^T = [0.47140 - 0.70711i, 0.23570 + 0.47140i]^T. \tag{4.21}$$

□

Exercise 4.1.4   Normalize the ket

$$|\psi\rangle = [3 - i, 2 + 6i, 7 - 8i, 6.3 + 4.9i, 13i, 0, 21.1]^T. \tag{4.22}$$

■

Exercise 4.1.5   (a) Verify that the two state vectors $[\frac{\sqrt{2}}{2}, \frac{\sqrt{2}}{2}]^T$ and $[\frac{\sqrt{2}}{2}, -\frac{\sqrt{2}}{2}]^T$ are each of length 1 in $\mathbb{C}^2$. (b) Find the vector on the unit ball of $\mathbb{C}^2$ representing the superposition (addition) of these two states.   ■

Given a normalized ket $|\psi\rangle$, the denominator of Equation (4.5) is 1, and hence, the equation reduces to

$$p(x_i) = |c_i|^2. \tag{4.23}$$

We are now done with our first motivating example. Let us move on to the second one. In order to talk about it, we need to introduce a property of subatomic particles called **spin**. As it turns out, spin will play a major role in our story, because it is the prototypical way to implement quantum bits of information, or qubits, which we shall encounter in Section 5.1.

---

[7] In Section 3.3, we limited ourselves to normalized complex vectors. Now you see why!

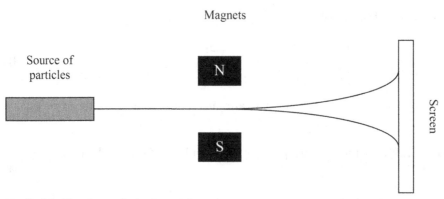

Figure 4.3. The Stern–Gerlach experiment.

What is spin? The **Stern–Gerlach experiment** (first performed in 1922) showed that an electron in the presence of a magnetic field will behave as if it were a charged spinning top: it will act as a small magnet and strive to align itself to the external field. The Stern–Gerlach experiment (as shown in Figure 4.3) consists of shooting a beam of electrons through a nonhomogeneous magnetic field oriented in a certain direction, say, vertically (z direction). As it happens, the field splits the beam into two streams, with opposite spin. Certain electrons will be found spinning one way, and certain others spinning the opposite way.

With respect to a classical spinning top, there are two striking differences:

- First, the electron does not appear to have an internal structure, by itself it is just a charged point. It acts as a spinning top but it is no top! Spin is therefore a new property of the quantum world, with no classical analog.
- Secondly, and quite surprisingly, all our electrons can be found either at the top of the screen or at the bottom, none in between. But, we had not prepared the "spinning" electrons in any way before letting them interact with the magnetic field. Classically, one would have expected them to have different magnetic components along the vertical axis, and therefore to be differently pulled by the field. There should be some in the middle of the screen. But there isn't. Conclusion: when the spinning particle is measured in a given direction, it can only be found in two states: it spins either clockwise or anticlockwise (as shown in Figure 4.4).

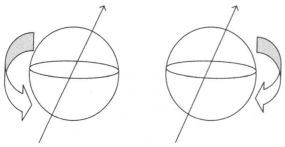

Figure 4.4. Particles with spin.

For each given direction in space, there are only two basic spin states. For the vertical axis, these states have a name: spin **up** $| \uparrow \rangle$ and spin **down** $| \downarrow \rangle$. The generic state will then be a superposition of up and down, or

$$|\psi\rangle = c_0 | \uparrow \rangle + c_1 | \downarrow \rangle. \tag{4.24}$$

Just like before, c_0 is the amplitude of finding the particle in the up state, and similarly for c_1.

Example 4.1.4 Consider a particle whose spin is described by the ket

$$|\psi\rangle = (3 - 4i) | \uparrow \rangle + (7 + 2i) | \downarrow \rangle. \tag{4.25}$$

The length of the ket is

$$\sqrt{|3 - 4i|^2 + |7 + 2i|^2} = 8.8318. \tag{4.26}$$

Therefore, the probability of detecting the spin of the particle in the up direction is

$$p(\uparrow) = \frac{|3 - 4i|^2}{8.8318^2} = \frac{25}{78}. \tag{4.27}$$

The probability of detecting the spin of the particle in state down is

$$p(\downarrow) = \frac{|7 + 2i|^2}{8.8318^2} = \frac{53}{78}. \tag{4.28}$$

□

Exercise 4.1.6 Let the spinning electron's current state be $|\psi\rangle = 3i| \uparrow \rangle - 2| \downarrow \rangle$. Find the probability that it will be detected in the up state. ∎

Exercise 4.1.7 Normalize the ket given in Equation (4.25). ∎

In Chapter 2, the inner product was introduced as an abstract mathematical idea. This product turned a vector space into a space with a *geometry*: angles, orthogonality, and distance were added to the canvas. Let us now investigate its physical meaning. The inner product of the state space gives us a tool to compute complex numbers known as **transition amplitudes**, which in turn will enable us to determine how likely the state of the system *before* a specific measurement (start state), will change to another (end state), *after* measurement has been carried out. Let

$$|\psi\rangle = \begin{bmatrix} c_0 \\ c_1 \\ \vdots \\ c_{n-1} \end{bmatrix} \quad \text{and} \quad |\psi'\rangle = \begin{bmatrix} c'_0 \\ c'_1 \\ \vdots \\ c'_{n-1} \end{bmatrix} \tag{4.29}$$

be two normalized states. We can extract the transition amplitude between state $|\psi\rangle$ and state $|\psi'\rangle$ by the following recipe: $|\psi\rangle$ will be our start state. The end state will be a row vector whose coordinates will be the complex conjugate of $|\psi'\rangle$ coordinates.

Such a state is called a **bra**, and will be denoted $\langle\psi'|$, or equivalently

$$\langle\psi'| = |\psi'\rangle^\dagger = \left[\overline{c_0'}, \overline{c_1'}, \dots, \overline{c_{n-1}'}\right]. \tag{4.30}$$

To find the transition amplitude we multiply them *as matrices* (notice that we put them side by side, forming a bra–ket, or bra(c)ket, i.e., their inner product):

$$\langle\psi'|\psi\rangle = \left[\overline{c_0'}, \overline{c_1'}, \dots, \overline{c_{n-1}'}\right] \begin{bmatrix} c_0 \\ c_1 \\ \vdots \\ c_{n-1} \end{bmatrix} = \overline{c_0'} \times c_0 + \overline{c_1'} \times c_1 + \cdots + \overline{c_{n-1}'} \times c_{n-1}. \tag{4.31}$$

We can represent the start state, the ending state, and the amplitude of going from the first to the second as the decorated arrow:

$$|\psi\rangle \xrightarrow{\quad\langle\psi'|\psi\rangle\quad} |\psi'\rangle . \tag{4.32}$$

This recipe is, of course, none other than the inner product of Section 2.4. What we have done is simply split the product into the bra–ket form. Although this is mathematically equivalent to our previous definition, it is quite handy for doing calculations, and moreover opens up an entirely new vista: it shifts the focus from *states* to *state transitions*.[8]

Note: The transition amplitude between two states may be zero. In fact, that happens precisely when the two states are orthogonal to one another. This simple fact hints at the physical content of orthogonality: orthogonal states are as far apart as they can possibly be. We can think of them as *mutually exclusive alternatives*: for instance, an electron can be in an arbitrary superposition of spin up and down, but after we measure it in the z direction, it will always be *either* up *or* down, never both up *and* down. If our electron was already in the up state before the z direction measurement, it will never transition to the down state as a result of the measurement.

Assume that we are given a normalized start state $|\psi\rangle$ and an orthonormal basis $\{|b_0\rangle, |b_1\rangle, \dots, |b_{n-1}\rangle\}$, representing a maximal list of mutually exclusive end states associated with some specific measurement of the system. In other words, we know beforehand that the result of our measurement will necessarily be one or the other of the states in the basis, but never a superposition of any of them. We show in Section 4.3 that for every complete measurement of a quantum system there is an associated orthonormal basis of all its possible outcomes.

---

[8] This line of thought has been pursued by some researchers, in the ambitious attempt to provide a satisfactory interpretation of quantum mechanics. For instance, Yakhir Aharonov and his colleagues have in recent years proposed a model called the two-vector formalism, in which the single vector description is replaced with the full bra-ket pair. The interested reader can consult Aharonov's recent book *Quantum Paradoxes* (Aharonov and Rohrlich, 2005).

We can express $|\psi\rangle$ in the basis $\{|b_0\rangle, |b_1\rangle, \ldots, |b_{n-1}\rangle\}$ as

$$|\psi\rangle = b_0|b_0\rangle + b_1|b_1\rangle + \cdots + b_{n-1}|b_{n-1}\rangle. \tag{4.33}$$

We invite you to check that $b_i = \langle b_i|\psi\rangle$ and that $|b_0|^2 + |b_1|^2 + \cdots + |b_{n-1}|^2 = 1$.

It is thus natural to read Equation (4.33) in the following way: each $|b_i|^2$ is the *probability* of ending up in state $|b_i\rangle$ after a measurement has been made.

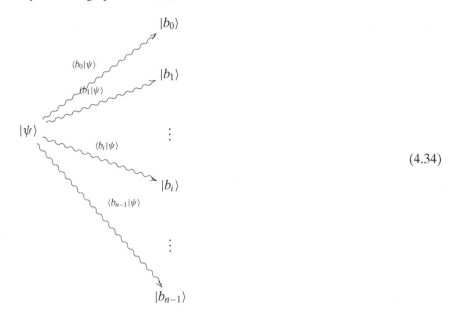

$$\tag{4.34}$$

Exercise 4.1.8 Check that the set $\{|x_0\rangle, |x_1\rangle \ldots, |x_{n-1}\rangle\}$ is an orthonormal basis for the state space of the particle on the line. Similarly, verify that $\{|\uparrow\rangle, |\downarrow\rangle\}$ is an orthonormal basis of the one-particle spin system. ∎

From now on, we shall use the row–column and the bra–ket notation introduced earlier interchangeably, as we deem fit.[9]

Let us work through a couple of examples together.

Example 4.1.5 Let us compute the bra corresponding to the ket $|\psi\rangle = [3, 1 - 2i]^T$. It is quite easy; we take the complex conjugate of all the entries, and list them: $\langle\psi| = [3, 1 + 2i]$. □

Example 4.1.6 Let us now compute the amplitude of the transition from $|\psi\rangle = \frac{\sqrt{2}}{2}[1, i]^T$ to $|\phi\rangle = \frac{\sqrt{2}}{2}[i, -1]^T$. We first need to write down the bra corresponding to the end state:

$$\langle\phi| = \frac{\sqrt{2}}{2}[-i, -1]. \tag{4.35}$$

---

[9] An historical note is in order: the bra–ket notation, which is now ubiquitous in quantum mechanics, was introduced by the great physicist Paul A.M. Dirac around 1930.

Now we can take their inner product:

$$\langle \phi, \psi \rangle = -i. \tag{4.36}$$

□

Exercise 4.1.9 Calculate the bra corresponding to the ket $|\psi\rangle = [3 + i, -2i]^T$. ∎

Exercise 4.1.10 Calculate the amplitude of the transition from $\frac{\sqrt{2}}{2}[i, -1]^T$ to $\frac{\sqrt{2}}{2}[1, -i]^T$. ∎

Observe that in the calculation of transition amplitudes via the inner product, the requirement that the representatives be normalized states can be easily removed by simply dividing the hermitian product by the product of the length of the two vectors (or equivalently, normalizing your states first, and then computing their inner product). Here is an example.

Example 4.1.7 Let us calculate the amplitude of the transition from $|\psi\rangle = [1, -i]^T$ to $|\phi\rangle = [i, 1]^T$. Both vectors have norm $\sqrt{2}$.

We can take their inner product first:

$$\langle \phi | \psi \rangle = [-i, 1][1, -i]^T = -2i. \tag{4.37}$$

and then divide it by the product of their norm:

$$\frac{-2i}{\sqrt{2} * \sqrt{2}} = -i. \tag{4.38}$$

Equivalently, we can first normalize them, and then take their product:

$$\left\langle \frac{1}{\sqrt{2}}\phi \Big| \frac{1}{\sqrt{2}}\psi \right\rangle = \left[\frac{-i}{\sqrt{2}}, \frac{1}{\sqrt{2}} \right]\left[\frac{1}{\sqrt{2}}, \frac{-i}{\sqrt{2}} \right]^T = -i. \tag{4.39}$$

The result is, of course, the same. We can concisely indicate it as

$$\frac{\langle \phi | \psi \rangle}{||\phi\rangle| \; ||\psi\rangle|}. \tag{4.40}$$

□

Let us pause one moment, and see where we are.

■ We have learned to associate a vector space to a quantum system. The dimension of this space reflects the amount of basic states of the system.
■ States can be superposed, by adding their representing vectors.
■ A state is left unchanged if its representing vector is multiplied by a complex scalar.
■ The state space has a geometry, given by its inner product. This geometry has a physical meaning: it tells us the likelihood for a given state to transition into another one after being measured. States that are orthogonal to one another are mutually exclusive.

Before moving on to the next sections, we invite you to write a simple computer simulation.

Programming Drill 4.1.1 *Write a program that simulates the first quantum system described in this section. The user should be able to specify how many points the particle can occupy (warning: keep the max number low, or you will fairly quickly run out of memory). The user will also specify a ket state vector by assigning its amplitudes. The program, when asked the likelihood of finding the particle at a given point, will perform the calculations described in Example 4.1.1. If the user enters two kets, the system will calculate the probability of transitioning from the first ket to the second, after an observation has been made.*

4.2 OBSERVABLES

Physics is, by and large, about observations: physical quantities like mass, momentum, velocity, etc., make sense only insofar as they can be observed in a quantifiable way. We can think of a physical system as specified by a double list: on the one hand, its state space, i.e., the collection of all the states it can possibly be found in (see the previous section), and on the other hand, the set of its **observables**, i.e., the physical quantities that can be observed in each state of the state space.

Each observable may be thought of as a specific question we pose to the system: if the system is currently in some given state $|\psi\rangle$, which values can we possibly observe?

In our quantum dictionary, we need to introduce the mathematical analog of an observable:

Postulate 4.2.1 *To each physical observable there corresponds a hermitian operator.*

Let us see what this postulate actually entails. First of all, an observable is a linear operator, which means that it maps states to states. If we apply the observable Ω to the state vector $|\psi\rangle$, the resulting state is now $\Omega|\psi\rangle$.

Example 4.2.1 Let $|\psi\rangle = [-1, -1 - i]^T$ be the start state in the two-dimensional spin state space. Now, let

$$\Omega = \begin{bmatrix} -1 & -i \\ i & 1 \end{bmatrix}. \tag{4.41}$$

This matrix acts as an operator on $\mathbb{C}^2$. Therefore, we can apply it to $|\psi\rangle$. The result is the vector $\Omega|\psi\rangle = [i, -1 - 2i]^T$. Observe that $|\psi\rangle$ and $\Omega|\psi\rangle$ are *not* scalar multiples of one another, and thus they do not represent the same state: Ω has modified the state of the system.   □

Secondly, as we already know from Chapter 2, the eigenvalues of a hermitian operator are all real. The physical meaning of this fact is established by the following:

Postulate 4.2.2 *The eigenvalues of a hermitian operator Ω associated with a physical observable are the only possible values observable can take as a result of measuring it on any given state. Furthermore, the eigenvectors of Ω form a basis for the state space.*

As we have said before, observables can be thought of as legitimate questions we can pose to quantum systems. *Each question admits a set of answers: the eigenvalues of the observable.* We learn in the next section how to compute the likelihood that one specific answer will come up out of the entire set.

Before delving into the subtler properties of observables, let us mention some real-life ones. In the case of the first quantum system of Section 4.1, namely, the particle on the line, the most obvious observable is **position**. As we have stated already, each observable represents a specific question we pose to the quantum system. Position asks: "Where can the particle be found?" Which hermitian operator corresponds to position? We are going to tell first how it acts on the basic states:

$$P(|x_i\rangle) = x_i|x_i\rangle. \tag{4.42}$$

In plain words, P acts as multiplication by position.

As the basic states form a basis, we can extend Equation 4.42 to arbitrary states:

$$P(|\psi\rangle) = P\left(\sum c_i|x_i\rangle\right) = \sum x_i c_i|x_i\rangle. \tag{4.43}$$

Here is the matrix representation of the operator in the standard basis:

$$P = \begin{bmatrix} x_0 & 0 & \cdots & 0 \\ 0 & x_1 & 0 & 0 \\ \vdots & \vdots & \ddots & \vdots \\ 0 & 0 & \cdots & x_{n-1} \end{bmatrix}. \tag{4.44}$$

P is simply the diagonal matrix whose entries are the x_i coordinates. Observe that P is trivially hermitian, its eigenvalues are the x_i values, and its normalized eigenvectors are precisely the basic state vectors that we met at the beginning of Section 4.1: $|x_0\rangle, |x_1\rangle, \ldots, |x_{n-1}\rangle$.

Exercise 4.2.1 Verify the last statement. [Hint: Do it by brute force (start with a generic vector, multiply it by the position operator, and assume that the result vector is a scalar multiple of the original one. Conclude that it must be one of the basis vectors).] ∎

There is a second natural question one may ask of our particle: What is your velocity? Actually, physicists ask a slightly different question: "What is your momentum?" where **momentum** is defined classically as *velocity times mass*. There is a quantum analog of this question, which is represented in our discrete model by the following operator (recall that δx is the increment of distance on the line):

$$M(|\psi\rangle) = -i * \hbar * \frac{|\psi(x + \delta x)\rangle - |\psi(x)\rangle}{\delta x}. \tag{4.45}$$

In words, momentum is, up to the constant $-i * \hbar$, the rate of change of the state vector from one point to the next.[10]

The constant $\hbar$ (pronounced **h bar**) that we have just met is a universal constant in quantum mechanics, known as the **reduced Planck constant**. Although it plays a fundamental role in modern physics (it is one of the universal constants of nature), for the purpose of the present discussion it can be safely ignored.

As it turns out, position and momentum are the most elementary questions we can ask of the particle: there are of course many more, such as energy, angular momentum, etc., but these two are in a sense the basic building blocks (most observables can be expressed in terms of position and momentum). We shall meet again position and momentum at the end of the next section.

Our second example of observables comes from the spin system. The typical question we might pose to such a system is: given a specific direction in space, in which way is the particle spinning? We can, for instance, ask: is the particle spinning up or down in the z direction? Left or right in the x direction? In or out in the y direction? The three spin operators corresponding to these questions are

$$S_z = \frac{\hbar}{2} \begin{bmatrix} 1 & 0 \\ 0 & -1 \end{bmatrix}, \qquad S_y = \frac{\hbar}{2} \begin{bmatrix} 0 & -i \\ i & 0 \end{bmatrix}, \qquad S_x = \frac{\hbar}{2} \begin{bmatrix} 0 & 1 \\ 1 & 0 \end{bmatrix}. \tag{4.46}$$

Each of the three spin operators comes equipped with its orthonormal basis. We have already met up and down, the eigenbasis of S_z. S_x has eigenbasis $\{| \leftarrow\rangle, | \rightarrow\rangle\}$, or left and right, and S_y has $\{| \swarrow\rangle, | \nearrow\rangle\}$, or in and out.

Exercise 4.2.2 Consider a particle in initial spin up. Apply S_x to it and determine the probability that the resulting state is still spin up.   ∎

. . . .

Reader Tip. The remainder of this section, although quite relevant for general quantum theory, is tangential to quantum computation, and can thus be safely skipped in a first reading (just take a look at the summary at the end of this section and proceed to Section 4.3).   ♡

. . . .

We are going to make some calculations with the operators described before in a little while; first, though, we need a few additional facts on observables and their associated hermitian matrices.

Up to this point, the collection of physical observables on a given quantum system is just a set. However, even an informal acquaintance with elementary physics

---

[10] The calculus-enabled reader would have easily recognized a one-step discrete version of the derivative in the momentum. Indeed, if δx goes to zero, momentum is precisely the derivative with respect to position of $|\psi\rangle$ times the scalar $-i * \hbar$.

teaches us that observable quantities can be added, multiplied, or multiplied by a scalar number to form other meaningful physical quantities, i.e., other examples of observables abound: think of momentum as mass times velocity, work as force times displacement, total energy of a particle in motion as the sum of its kinetic and potential energies, etc. We are thus naturally concerned with the following issue: to what extent can we manipulate quantum observables to obtain yet other observables?

Let us start our investigation from the first step, namely, multiplying an observable by a number (i.e., a scalar). There is no problem with carrying out this operation: indeed, if we scalar multiply a hermitian matrix by a real scalar (i.e., we multiply all its entries), the result is still hermitian.

Exercise 4.2.3   Verify the last statement.   ∎

Exercise 4.2.4   What about complex scalars? Try to find a hermitian matrix and a complex number such that their product fails to be hermitian.   ∎

Let us make the next move. What about the addition of two hermitian matrices? Suppose we are looking at two physical observables, represented respectively by the hermitians Ω_1 and Ω_2. Again, no problem: their sum $\Omega_1 + \Omega_2$ is the observable whose representative is the sum of the corresponding hermitian operators, $\Omega_1 + \Omega_2$, which happens to be hermitian.

Exercise 4.2.5   Check that the sum of two arbitrary hermitian matrices is hermitian.
                                                                                            ∎

From these two facts it ensues that the set of hermitian matrices of fixed dimension forms a real (but not a complex) vector space.

How about products? It is quite tempting to conclude that the product of two physical quantities, represented respectively by the hermitians Ω_1 and Ω_2, is an observable whose representative is the product (i.e., matrix composition) of Ω_1 and Ω_2. There are two substantial difficulties here. First, the order in which operators are applied to state vectors matters. Why? Well, simply because matrix multiplication, unlike multiplication of ordinary numbers or functions, is *not*, in general, a commutative operation.

Example 4.2.2   Let

$$\Omega_1 = \begin{bmatrix} 1 & -1-i \\ -1+i & 1 \end{bmatrix} \quad \text{and} \quad \Omega_2 = \begin{bmatrix} 0 & -1 \\ -1 & 2 \end{bmatrix}. \tag{4.47}$$

Their product $\Omega_2 \star \Omega_1$ is equal to

$$\Omega_2 \star \Omega_1 = \begin{bmatrix} 1-i & -1 \\ -3+2i & 3+i \end{bmatrix}, \tag{4.48}$$

whereas $\Omega_1 \star \Omega_2$ is equal to

$$\Omega_1 \star \Omega_2 = \begin{bmatrix} 1+i & -3-2i \\ -1 & 3-i \end{bmatrix}. \tag{4.49}$$

□

Exercise 4.2.6 Let $\Omega_1 = \begin{bmatrix} 1 & -i \\ i & 1 \end{bmatrix}$ and $\Omega_2 = \begin{bmatrix} 2 & 0 \\ 0 & 4 \end{bmatrix}$. Verify that both are hermitian. Do they commute with respect to multiplication? ■

The second difficulty is just as serious: in general, the product of hermitian operators is not guaranteed to be hermitian. Let us now investigate in a more rigorous way what it takes for the product of two hermitian operators to be hermitian. Notice that we have

$$\langle \Omega_1 \star \Omega_2 \phi, \psi \rangle = \langle \Omega_2 \phi, \Omega_1 \psi \rangle = \langle \phi, \Omega_2 \star \Omega_1 \psi \rangle, \tag{4.50}$$

where the first equality comes from the fact that Ω_1 is hermitian and the second equality comes from the fact that Ω_2 is hermitian. For $\Omega_1 \star \Omega_2$ to be hermitian, we would need that

$$\langle \Omega_1 \star \Omega_2 \phi, \psi \rangle = \langle \phi, \Omega_1 \star \Omega_2 \psi \rangle. \tag{4.51}$$

This in turn implies

$$\Omega_1 \star \Omega_2 = \Omega_2 \star \Omega_1, \tag{4.52}$$

or equivalently, the operator

$$[\Omega_1, \Omega_2] = \Omega_1 \star \Omega_2 - \Omega_2 \star \Omega_1 \tag{4.53}$$

must be the zero operator (i.e., the operator that sends every vector to the zero vector).

The operator $[\Omega_1, \Omega_2]$ is so important that it deserves its own name; it is called the **commutator** of Ω_1 and Ω_2. We have just learned that if the commutator is zero then the product (in whichever order) is hermitian. We are going to meet the commutator again in a little while. Meanwhile, let us familiarize ourselves with the commutator through a simple and very important example.

Example 4.2.3 Let us calculate the commutators of the three spin matrices (we shall deliberately ignore the constant factor $\frac{\hbar}{2}$):

$$[S_x, S_y] = \begin{bmatrix} 0 & 1 \\ 1 & 0 \end{bmatrix} \begin{bmatrix} 0 & -i \\ i & 0 \end{bmatrix} - \begin{bmatrix} 0 & -i \\ i & 0 \end{bmatrix} \begin{bmatrix} 0 & 1 \\ 1 & 0 \end{bmatrix} = 2i \begin{bmatrix} 1 & 0 \\ 0 & -1 \end{bmatrix}, \tag{4.54}$$

$$[S_y, S_z] = \begin{bmatrix} 0 & -i \\ i & 0 \end{bmatrix} \begin{bmatrix} 1 & 0 \\ 0 & -1 \end{bmatrix} - \begin{bmatrix} 1 & 0 \\ 0 & -1 \end{bmatrix} \begin{bmatrix} 0 & -i \\ i & 0 \end{bmatrix} = 2i \begin{bmatrix} 0 & 1 \\ 1 & 0 \end{bmatrix}, \tag{4.55}$$

$$[S_z, S_x] = \begin{bmatrix} 1 & 0 \\ 0 & -1 \end{bmatrix} \begin{bmatrix} 0 & 1 \\ 1 & 0 \end{bmatrix} - \begin{bmatrix} 0 & 1 \\ 1 & 0 \end{bmatrix} \begin{bmatrix} 1 & 0 \\ 0 & -1 \end{bmatrix} = 2i \begin{bmatrix} 0 & -i \\ i & 0 \end{bmatrix}. \qquad (4.56)$$

A bit more concisely,

$$[S_x, S_y] = 2i\,S_z, \quad [S_y, S_z] = 2i\,S_x, \quad [S_z, S_x] = 2i\,S_y. \qquad (4.57)$$

As we have just seen, none of the commutators are zero. The spin operators do not commute with each other. □

Now it is your turn.

Exercise 4.2.7 Explicitly calculate the commutator of the operators of Example 4.2.2. ■

Note: A moment's thought shows that the product of a hermitian operator with itself always commutes and so does the exponent operation. Therefore, given a single hermitian Ω, we automatically get the entire algebra of polynomials over Ω, i.e., all operators of the form

$$\Omega' = \alpha_0 + \alpha_1 \Omega + \alpha_2 \Omega^2 + \cdots + \alpha_{n-1} \Omega^{n-1}. \qquad (4.58)$$

All such operators commute with one another.

Exercise 4.2.8 Show that the commutator of two hermitian matrices is a hermitian matrix. ■

If the commutator of two hermitian operators is zero, or equivalently, the two operators commute, there is no difficulty in assigning their product (in whatever order) as the mathematical equivalent of the physical product of their associated observables. But what about the other cases, when the two operators do *not* commute? The Heisenberg's uncertainty principle, which we are going to meet at the end of this section, will provide an answer.

There is yet another aspect of the association between observables and hermitian operators that can provide substantial physical insight: we know from Chapter 2 that hermitian operators are precisely those operators that behave well with respect to the inner product, i.e.,

$$\langle \Omega\phi, \psi \rangle = \langle \phi, \Omega\psi \rangle \qquad (4.59)$$

for each pair $|\psi\rangle, |\phi\rangle$.

From this fact, it immediately derives that $\langle \Omega\psi, \psi \rangle$ is a real number for each $|\psi\rangle$, which we shall denote as $\langle \Omega \rangle_\psi$ (the subscript points to the fact that this quantity depends on the state vector). We can attach a physical meaning to the number $\langle \Omega \rangle_\psi$.

Postulate 4.2.3 $\langle \Omega \rangle_\psi$ is the **expected value** *of observing Ω repeatedly on the same state ψ.*

This postulate states the following: suppose that

$$\lambda_0, \lambda_1, \ldots, \lambda_{n-1} \tag{4.60}$$

is the list of eigenvalues of Ω. Let us prepare our quantum system so that it is in state $|\psi\rangle$ and let us observe the value of Ω. We are going to obtain one or another of the aforementioned eigenvalues. Now, let us start all over again many times, say, n times, and let us keep track of what was observed each time. At the end of our experiment, the eigenvalue λ_i has been seen p_i times, where $0 \le p_i \le n$ (in statistical jargon, its frequency is p_i/n). Now perform the calculation

$$\lambda_0 \times \frac{p_0}{n} + \lambda_1 \times \frac{p_1}{n} + \cdots + \lambda_{n-1} \times \frac{p_{n-1}}{n}. \tag{4.61}$$

If n is sufficiently large, this number (known in statistics as the estimated expected value of Ω) will be very close to $\langle \Omega\psi, \psi \rangle$.

Example 4.2.4 Let us calculate the expected value of the position operator on an arbitrary normalized state vector: let

$$|\psi\rangle = c_0|x_0\rangle + c_1|x_1\rangle + \cdots + c_{n-1}|x_{n-1}\rangle \tag{4.62}$$

be our state vector and

$$\langle P\psi, \psi \rangle = |c_0|^2 \times x_0 + |c_1|^2 \times x_1 + \cdots + |c_{n-1}|^2 \times x_{n-1}, \tag{4.63}$$

where

$$|c_0|^2 + |c_1|^2 + \cdots + |c_{n-1}|^2 = 1. \tag{4.64}$$

In particular, if $|\psi\rangle$ happens to be just $|x_i\rangle$, we simply get x_i (verify it!). In other words, the expected value of position on any of its eigenvectors $|x_i\rangle$ is the corresponding position x_i on the line.   □

Example 4.2.5 Let $|\psi\rangle = \left[\frac{\sqrt{2}}{2}, \frac{\sqrt{2}}{2}i\right]^T$ and $\Omega = \begin{bmatrix} 1 & -i \\ i & 2 \end{bmatrix}$.

Let us calculate $\Omega(|\psi\rangle)$:

$$\Omega(|\psi\rangle) = \begin{bmatrix} 1 & -i \\ i & 2 \end{bmatrix} \begin{bmatrix} \frac{\sqrt{2}}{2} \\ \frac{\sqrt{2}}{2}i \end{bmatrix} = \begin{bmatrix} \sqrt{2} \\ \frac{3}{2}\sqrt{2}i \end{bmatrix}. \tag{4.65}$$

The bra associated with $\Omega|\psi\rangle$ is $\left[\sqrt{2}, -\frac{3}{2}\sqrt{2}i\right]$. The scalar product $\langle \Omega\psi|\psi\rangle$, i.e., the average value of Ω on $|\psi\rangle$, is thus equal to

$$\left[\sqrt{2}, -\frac{3}{2}\sqrt{2}i\right]\left[\frac{\sqrt{2}}{2}, \frac{\sqrt{2}}{2}i\right]^T = 2.5. \tag{4.66}$$

□

Exercise 4.2.9 Repeat the steps of the previous example where

$$|\psi\rangle = \left[\frac{\sqrt{2}}{2}, -\frac{\sqrt{2}}{2}\right]^T \tag{4.67}$$

and

$$\Omega = \begin{bmatrix} 3 & 1+2i \\ 1-2i & -1 \end{bmatrix}.$$ (4.68)

■

We now know that the result of observing Ω repeatedly on a given state will be a certain frequency distribution on the set of its eigenvalues. In plain words, sooner or later we will encounter all its eigenvalues, some more frequently and some less. In the next section we compute the probability that a given eigenvalue of Ω will actually be observed on a given state. For now, we may be interested in knowing the spread of the distribution around its expected value, i.e., the **variance** of the distribution. A small variance will tell us that most of the eigenvalues are very close to the mean, whereas a large variance means just the opposite. We can define the variance in our framework in a few stages. First, we introduce the hermitian operator

$$\Delta_\psi(\Omega) = \Omega - \langle\Omega\rangle_\psi I$$ (4.69)

(I is the identity operator). The operator $\Delta_\psi(\Omega)$ acts on a generic vector $|\phi\rangle$ in the following fashion:

$$\Delta_\psi(\Omega)|\phi\rangle = \Omega(|\phi\rangle) - (\langle\Omega\rangle_\psi)|\phi\rangle.$$ (4.70)

So $\Delta_\psi(\Omega)$ just subtracts the mean from the result of Ω. What then is the mean of $\Delta_\psi(\Omega)$ itself on the normalized state $|\psi\rangle$? A simple calculation shows that it is precisely zero: $\Delta_\psi(\Omega)$ is the *demeaned* version of Ω.

Exercise 4.2.10   Verify the last statement.   ■

We can now define the variance of Ω at $|\psi\rangle$ as the expectation value of $\Delta_\psi(\Omega)$ squared (i.e., the operator $\Delta_\psi(\Omega)$ composed with itself):

$$Var_\psi(\Omega) = \langle(\Delta_\psi(\Omega)) \star (\Delta_\psi(\Omega))\rangle_\psi.$$ (4.71)

Admittedly, the definition looks at first sight rather obscure, although it is not so bad if we remember the usual definition of the variance of a random variable X as

$$Var(X) = E((X-\mu)^2) = E((X-\mu)(X-\mu)),$$ (4.72)

where E is the expected value function. The best course is to turn to a simple example to get a concrete feel for it.

Example 4.2.6 Let Ω be a 2-by-2 diagonal matrix with real entries:

$$\Omega = \begin{bmatrix} \lambda_1 & 0 \\ 0 & \lambda_2 \end{bmatrix},$$

and let

$$\langle \psi \rangle = \begin{bmatrix} c_1 \\ c_2 \end{bmatrix}. \tag{4.73}$$

Let us denote by μ (pronounced "mu") the mean of Ω on $|\psi\rangle$.

$$\Delta_\psi(\Omega) = \Omega - \langle \Omega \rangle_\psi I = \begin{bmatrix} \lambda_1 & 0 \\ 0 & \lambda_2 \end{bmatrix} - \begin{bmatrix} \mu & 0 \\ 0 & \mu \end{bmatrix} = \begin{bmatrix} \lambda_1 - \mu & 0 \\ 0 & \lambda_2 - \mu \end{bmatrix}.$$
$$\tag{4.74}$$

Now we calculate $\Delta_\psi(\Omega) \star \Delta_\psi(\Omega)$:

$$\Delta_\psi(\Omega) \star \Delta_\psi(\Omega) = \begin{bmatrix} \lambda_1 - \mu & 0 \\ 0 & \lambda_2 - \mu \end{bmatrix} \begin{bmatrix} \lambda_1 - \mu & 0 \\ 0 & \lambda_2 - \mu \end{bmatrix}$$

$$= \begin{bmatrix} (\lambda_1 - \mu)^2 & 0 \\ 0 & (\lambda_2 - \mu)^2 \end{bmatrix}. \tag{4.75}$$

Finally, we can compute the variance:

$$\langle (\Delta_\psi(\Omega))(\Delta_\psi(\Omega)) \rangle_\psi = \begin{bmatrix} \overline{c_1} & \overline{c_2} \end{bmatrix} \begin{bmatrix} (\lambda_1 - \mu)^2 & 0 \\ 0 & (\lambda_2 - \mu)^2 \end{bmatrix} \begin{bmatrix} c_1 \\ c_2 \end{bmatrix}$$

$$= |c_1|^2 \times (\lambda_1 - \mu)^2 + |c_2|^2 \times (\lambda_2 - \mu)^2. \tag{4.76}$$

We are now able to see that if both λ_1 and λ_2 are very close to μ, the term in the equation will be close to zero. Conversely, if either of the two eigenvalues is far from μ (it is immaterial whether above or below it, because we are taking squares), the variance will be a big real number. Conclusion: the variance does indeed inform us about the spread of the eigenvalues around their mean. □

Our reader may still be a bit unsatisfied after this example: after all, what it shows is that the definition of variance given above works as it should in the case of diagonal matrices. Actually, it is a known fact that all hermitian matrices can be diagonalized by switching to a basis of eigenvectors, so the example is comprehensive enough to legitimize our definition.

Example 4.2.7   Let us calculate the variance of the operator described in Example 4.2.5:

$$
\Delta_\psi(\Omega) = \Omega - \langle \Omega \rangle_\psi I = \begin{bmatrix} 1 & -i \\ i & 2 \end{bmatrix} - \begin{bmatrix} 2.5 & 0 \\ 0 & 2.5 \end{bmatrix} = \begin{bmatrix} -1.5 & -i \\ i & -0.5 \end{bmatrix}. \quad (4.77)
$$

We now compute $\Delta_\psi(\Omega) \star \Delta_\psi(\Omega)$:

$$
\Delta_\psi(\Omega) \star \Delta_\psi(\Omega) = \begin{bmatrix} -1.5 & -i \\ i & -0.5 \end{bmatrix} \begin{bmatrix} -1.5 & -i \\ i & -0.5 \end{bmatrix} = \begin{bmatrix} 3.25 & 2i \\ -2i & 1.25 \end{bmatrix}.
$$

$$(4.78)$$

Hence the variance is

$$
\langle (\Delta_\psi(\Omega))(\Delta_\psi(\Omega)) \rangle_\psi = \begin{bmatrix} \frac{\sqrt{2}}{2} & -\frac{\sqrt{2}}{2}i \end{bmatrix} \begin{bmatrix} 3.25 & 2i \\ -2i & 1.25 \end{bmatrix} \begin{bmatrix} \frac{\sqrt{2}}{2} \\ \frac{\sqrt{2}}{2}i \end{bmatrix} = 0.25.
$$

$$(4.79)$$

$\square$

Exercise 4.2.11   Calculate the variance of the position operator. Show that the variance of position on any of its eigenvectors is zero.   ■

Exercise 4.2.12   Calculate the variance of S_z on a generic spin state. Show that the variance of S_z reaches a maximum on the state $\frac{\sqrt{2}}{2}(|\downarrow\rangle + |\uparrow\rangle)$.   ■

Note: The variance of the same hermitian varies from state to state: In particular, on an eigenvector of the operator the variance is zero, and the expected value is just the corresponding eigenvalue: we can say that an observable is sharp on its eigenvectors (no ambiguity on the outcome).

Exercise 4.2.13   Prove the preceding statement. (Hint: Work out some examples first.)   ■

We have built all the machinery needed to introduce a fundamental theorem of quantum mechanics, known as Heisenberg's uncertainty principle. Let us begin with two observables, represented by the two hermitians Ω_1 and Ω_2, and a given state, say, $|\psi\rangle$. We can compute the variance of Ω_1 and Ω_2 on $|\psi\rangle$, obtaining $Var_\psi(\Omega_1)$ and $Var_\psi(\Omega_2)$. Do these two quantities relate in any way, and if so, how?

Let us see what the question actually means. We have two observables, and our hope would be to simultaneously minimize their variances, thereby getting a sharp outcome for both. If there were no correlation in the variances, we could expect a very sharp measure of both observables on some convenient state (such as a common eigenvector, if any such existed). Alas, this is not the case, as shown by the following.

Theorem 4.2.1 (Heisenberg's Uncertainty Principle). *The product of the variances of two arbitrary hermitian operators on a given state is always greater than or equal to one-fourth the square of the expected value of their commutator. In formulas:*

$$Var_\psi(\Omega_1) \times Var_\psi(\Omega_2) \geq \frac{1}{4}|\langle[\Omega_1, \Omega_2]\rangle_\psi|^2. \tag{4.80}$$

As promised, we have found our commutator once again. Heisenberg's principle tells us that the commutator *measures how good a simultaneous measure of two observables can possibly be.* In particular, if the commutator happens to be zero (or equivalently, if the observables commute), there is no limit (at least in principle) to our accuracy. In quantum mechanics, however, there are plenty of operators that do not commute: in fact, we have seen that the directional spin operators provide one such example.

Exercise 4.2.14 Use the calculation of the commutator in Example 4.2.3 and Heisenberg's principle to give an estimate of how accurate a simultaneous observation of spin in the z and x directions can be. ∎

Another typical example, related to our first quantum system, is given by the pair position–momentum, which we have also met in the last section. So far $|\psi\rangle$ for the particle on the line has been described in terms of its position eigenbasis, i.e., the collection $\{|x_i\rangle\}$. $|\psi\rangle$ can be written in many other orthonormal bases, corresponding to different observables. One of those is the momentum eigenbasis. This basis comes up when we think of $|\psi\rangle$ as a wave (a bit like a wave hovering over the line). We can thus decompose it into its basic frequencies, just as we can resolve a sound into its basic pure tones. These pure tones are precisely the elements of the momentum eigenbasis.

The image of $|\psi\rangle$ in the position basis is as different as it can possibly be from the one associated with the momentum eigenbasis. The position eigenbasis is made of "peaks," i.e., vectors that are zero everywhere except at a point (**Dirac's deltas**, in math jargon). Therefore, $|\psi\rangle$ is decomposed into a weighted sum of peaks. The momentum eigenbasis, on the other hand, is made of sinusoids, whose position is totally undetermined.

The commutator of the position–momentum pair captures well this inherent dissimilarity: it is not zero, and therefore our hope to keep the comforting traditional picture of a particle as a tiny billiard ball moving around in space is dashed. If we can pin down the particle position at a given point in time (i.e., if the variance of its position operator is very small), we are at a loss as to its momentum (i.e., the variance of its momentum operator is very big), and vice versa.

Let us sum up:

- Observables are represented by hermitian operators. The result of an observation is always an eigenvalue of the hermitian.
- The expression $\langle\psi|\Omega|\psi\rangle$ represents the expected value of observing Ω on $|\psi\rangle$.
- Observables in general do not commute. This means that the order of observation matters. Moreover, if the commutator of two observables is not zero, there is an intrinsic limit to our capability of measuring their values simultaneously.

Programming Drill 4.2.1 *Continue your simulation of a quantum system by adding observables to the picture: the user will input a square matrix of the appropriate size, and a ket vector. The program will verify that the matrix is hermitian, and if so, it will calculate the mean value and the variance of the observable on the given state.*

4.3 MEASURING

The act of carrying out an observation on a given physical system is called **measuring**. Just as a single observable represents a specific question posed to the system, measuring is the process consisting of *asking a specific question and receiving a definite answer.*

In classical physics, we implicitly assumed that

- the act of measuring would leave the system in whatever state it already was, at least in principle; and
- the result of a measurement on a well-defined state is predictable, i.e., if we know the state with absolute certainty, we can anticipate the value of the observable on that state.

Both these assumptions proved wrong, as research in the subatomic scale has repeatedly shown: systems *do* get perturbed and modified as a result of measuring them. Furthermore, only the probability of observing specific values can be calculated: measurement is inherently a nondeterministic process.

Let us briefly recapitulate what we know: an observable can only assume one of its eigenvalues as the result of an observation. So far though, nothing tells us how frequently we are going to see a specific eigenvalue, say, λ. Moreover, our framework does not tell us yet what happens to the state vector if λ is actually observed. We need an additional postulate to handle concrete measures:

Postulate 4.3.1 *Let Ω be an observable and $|\psi\rangle$ be a state. If the result of measuring Ω is the eigenvalue λ, the state after measurement will always be an eigenvector corresponding to λ.*

Example 4.3.1 Let us go back to Example 4.2.1: It is easy to check that the eigenvalues of Ω are $\lambda_1 = -\sqrt{2}$ and $\lambda_2 = \sqrt{2}$ and the corresponding normalized eigenvectors are $|e_1\rangle = [-0.924i, -0.383]^T$ and $|e_2\rangle = [-0.383i, 0.924]^T$.

Now, let us suppose that after an observation of Ω on $|\psi\rangle = \frac{\sqrt{2}}{2}[1, 1]^T$, the actual value observed is λ_1. The system has "collapsed" from $|\psi\rangle$ to $|e_1\rangle$.   □

Exercise 4.3.1 Find all the possible states the system described in Exercise 4.2.2 can transition into after a measurement has been carried out.   ∎

What is the probability that a normalized start state $|\psi\rangle$ will transition to a specific eigenvector, say, $|e\rangle$? We must go back to what we said in Section 4.1: the probability of the transition to the eigenvector is given by the square of the inner product of the two states: $|\langle e|\psi\rangle|^2$. This expression has a simple meaning: it is the *projection* of $|\psi\rangle$ along $|e\rangle$.

We are ready for a new insight into the real meaning of $\langle \Omega \rangle_\psi$ of the last section: first, let us recall that the normalized eigenvectors of Ω constitute an orthonormal basis of the state space. Therefore, we can express $|\psi\rangle$ as a linear combination in this basis:

$$|\psi\rangle = c_0|e_0\rangle + c_1|e_1\rangle + \cdots + c_{n-1}|e_{n-1}\rangle. \tag{4.81}$$

Now, let us compute the mean:

$$\langle \Omega \rangle_\psi = \langle \Omega\psi, \psi \rangle = |c_0|^2\lambda_0 + |c_1|^2\lambda_1 + \cdots + |c_{n-1}|^2\lambda_{n-1}. \tag{4.82}$$

(Verify this identity!)

As we can now see, $\langle \Omega \rangle_\psi$ is precisely the mean value of the probability distribution

$$(\lambda_0, p_0), (\lambda_1, p_1), \ldots, (\lambda_{n-1}, p_{n-1}), \tag{4.83}$$

where each p_i is the square of the amplitude of the collapse into the corresponding eigenvector.

Example 4.3.2   Let us go back to Example 4.3.1 and calculate the probabilities that our state vector will fall into one of the two eigenvectors:

$$p_1 = |\langle e_1|\psi\rangle|^2 = 0.5 \quad \text{and} \quad p_2 = |\langle e_2|\psi\rangle|^2 = 0.5. \tag{4.84}$$

Now, let us compute the mean value of the distribution:

$$p_1 \times \lambda_1 + p_2 \times \lambda_2 = 0, \tag{4.85}$$

which is precisely the value we could obtain by directly calculating $\langle \psi|\Omega|\psi\rangle$.

$\square$

Exercise 4.3.2   Perform the same calculations as in the last example, using Exercise 4.3.1. Then draw the probability distribution of the eigenvalues as in the previous example.   ∎

Note: As a result of the foregoing discussion, an important fact emerges. Suppose we ask a specific question (i.e., we choose an observable) and perform a measurement once. We get an answer, say, λ, and the system transitions to the corresponding eigenvector. Now, let us ask the same question immediately thereafter. What is going to happen? The system will give exactly the *same* answer, and stay where it is. All right, you may say. But, what about changing the question? The following example will clarify matters.

Example 4.3.3   Until now we have dealt with measurements relative to only one observable. What if there were more than one observable involved? With each observable there is a different set of eigenvectors the system can possibly collapse to after a measurement has taken place. As it turns out, the answers we get will *depend on which order we pose our questions*, i.e., which observable we measure first.

There is an intriguing experiment that one can easily perform in order to see some of these ideas in action (and have some fun in the process). Suppose you shoot a beam of light. Light is also a wave, and like all waves it vibrates during its journey (think of sea waves). There are two possibilities: either it vibrates along all possible

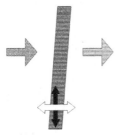

Figure 4.5. Light partially passing through one polarization sheet.

directions orthogonal to its line of propagation, or it does it only in a specific one. In the second case we say that light is **polarized**.[11] What kind of questions we can ask concerning polarization? We can set a specific direction, and ask: is light vibrating along this direction or its orthogonal?

For our experiment we need thin plastic semitransparent polarization sheets (they are fairly easy to obtain). Polarization sheets do two things: once you orient them in a specific direction, they measure the polarization of light in the orthogonal basis corresponding to that direction (let us call it the vertical–horizontal basis), and then filter out those photons that collapsed to one of the elements of the basis (Figure 4.5).

What if we had two sheets? If the two sheets were oriented in the same direction, there would be no difference whatsoever (why? because we are asking the same question; the photon will give once more the same exact answer). However, if we rotated the second sheet by 90°, then no light would pass through both sheets (Figure 4.6).

Placing the sheets orthogonal to each other ensures that the permitted half that passes through the left sheet is filtered out by the right sheet.

What happens if we add a *third* sheet? Placing a third sheet to the left or to the right of the other two sheets does not have any effect whatsoever. No light was permitted before and none will be allowed through the additional sheet. However, placing the third sheet in-between the other two *at an angle*, say, 45°, does have a remarkable effect (Figure 4.7).

Light will pass through all the three sheets! How can this be? Let us see what is going on here. The left sheet measures all the light relative to the up–down basis. The polarized light in the vertical polarization state that goes through is then considered to be a superposition with respect to the diagonal middle sheet measuring basis. The middle sheet recollapses the permitted half, filters some, and passes some through. But what is passed through is now in a diagonal polarization state. When this light passes through the right sheet, it is again in a superposition of the vertical–horizontal basis, and so it must collapse once more. Notice that only one-eighth of the original light passes through all three sheets.   □

---

[11] Polarization is a familiar phenomenon: fancy sun glasses are made on the basis of light polarization.

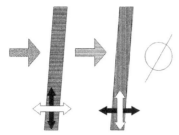

Figure 4.6. No light passing through two polarization sheets at orthogonal angels.

A brief summary is in order:

- The end state of the measurement of an observable is always one of its eigenvectors.
- The probability for an initial state to collapse into an eigenvector of the observable is given by the length squared of the projection.
- When we measure several observables, the order of measurements matters.

We have come a long way. We now have three main ingredients to cook up quantum dishes. We need one more, dynamics.

Programming Drill 4.3.1 *Next step in the simulation: when the user enters an observable and a state vector, the program will return the list of eigenvalues of the observable, the mean value of the observable on the state, and the probability that the state will transition to each one of the eigenstates. Optional: plot the corresponding probability distribution.*

4.4 DYNAMICS

Thus far, we have been concerned with static quantum systems, i.e., systems that do not evolve over time. To be sure, changes could still occur as a result of one or possibly many measurements, but the system itself was not time-dependent. In reality, of course, quantum systems do evolve over time, and we thus need to add a new hue to the canvas namely **quantum dynamics**. Just as hermitian operators represent physical observables, unitary operators introduce dynamics in the quantum arena.

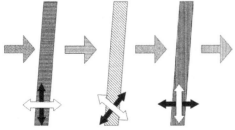

Figure 4.7. Light partially passing through three polarization sheets.

Postulate 4.4.1 *The evolution of a quantum system (that is not a measurement) is given by a unitary operator or transformation.*

That is, if U is a unitary matrix that represents a unitary operator and $|\psi(t)\rangle$ represents a state of the system at time t, then

$$|\psi(t+1)\rangle = U|\psi(t)\rangle \tag{4.86}$$

will represent the system at time $t+1$.

An important feature of unitary transformations is that they are closed under composition and inverse, i.e., the product of two arbitrary unitary matrices is unitary, and the inverse of a unitary transformation is also unitary. Finally, there is a multiplicative identity, namely, the identity operator itself (which is trivially unitary). In math jargon, one says that the set of unitary transformations constitutes a **group of transformations** with respect to composition.

Exercise 4.4.1 Verify that

$$U_1 = \begin{bmatrix} 0 & 1 \\ 1 & 0 \end{bmatrix} \quad \text{and} \quad U_2 = \begin{bmatrix} \frac{\sqrt{2}}{2} & \frac{\sqrt{2}}{2} \\ \frac{\sqrt{2}}{2} & -\frac{\sqrt{2}}{2} \end{bmatrix} \tag{4.87}$$

are unitary matrices. Multiply them and verify that their product is also unitary. ∎

We are now going to see how dynamics is determined by unitary transformations: assume we have a rule, $\mathfrak{U}$, that associates with each instant of time

$$t_0, t_1, t_2, \ldots, t_{n-1} \tag{4.88}$$

a unitary matrix

$$\mathfrak{U}[t_0], \mathfrak{U}[t_1], \ldots, \mathfrak{U}[t_{n-1}]. \tag{4.89}$$

Let us start with an initial state vector $|\psi\rangle$. We can apply $\mathfrak{U}[t_0]$ to $|\psi\rangle$, then apply $\mathfrak{U}[t_1]$ to the result, and so forth. We will obtain a sequence of state vectors

$$\mathfrak{U}[t_0]|\psi\rangle, \tag{4.90}$$

$$\mathfrak{U}[t_1]\mathfrak{U}[t_0]|\psi\rangle, \tag{4.91}$$

$$\vdots \tag{4.92}$$

$$\mathfrak{U}[t_{n-1}]\mathfrak{U}[t_{n-2}] \cdots \mathfrak{U}[t_0]|\psi\rangle. \tag{4.93}$$

Such a sequence is called the **orbit**[12] of $|\psi\rangle$ under the action of $\mathfrak{U}[t_i]$ at the time clicks $t_0, t_1, \ldots, t_{n-1}$.

$$
\begin{array}{ccccc}
\xrightarrow{\mathfrak{U}[t_0]} & & \xrightarrow{\mathfrak{U}[t_1]} & & \xrightarrow{\mathfrak{U}[t_2]} \\
|\psi\rangle & \mathfrak{U}[t_0]|\psi\rangle & \mathfrak{U}[t_1]\mathfrak{U}[t_0]|\psi\rangle & \mathfrak{U}[t_2]\mathfrak{U}[t_1]\mathfrak{U}[t_0]|\psi\rangle \\
\xleftarrow{\mathfrak{U}[t_0]^\dagger} & & \xleftarrow{\mathfrak{U}[t_1]^\dagger} & & \xleftarrow{\mathfrak{U}[t_2]^\dagger}
\end{array}
$$

$$
\begin{array}{c}
\xrightarrow{\quad\quad} \quad \xrightarrow{\quad\quad} \\
\cdots \quad \mathfrak{U}[t_{n-1}]\mathfrak{U}[t_{n-2}]\cdots\mathfrak{U}[t_0]|\psi\rangle. \\
\xleftarrow{\quad\quad} \quad \xleftarrow{\quad\quad}
\end{array} \tag{4.94}
$$

Observe that one can always go back, just like running a movie backward, simply by applying the inverses of $\mathfrak{U}[t_0], \mathfrak{U}[t_1], \ldots, \mathfrak{U}[t_{n-1}]$ in reverse order: evolution of a quantum system is *symmetric* with respect to time.

We can now preview how a quantum computation will look. A quantum computer shall be placed into an initial state $|\psi\rangle$, and we shall then apply a sequence of unitary operators to the state. When we are done, we will measure the output and get a final state. The next chapters are largely devoted to working out these ideas in detail.

Here is an exercise for you on dynamics:

Exercise 4.4.2 Go back to Example 3.3.2 (quantum billiard ball), keep the same initial state vector $[1, 0, 0, 0]^T$, but change the unitary map to

$$
\begin{bmatrix}
0 & \frac{1}{\sqrt{2}} & \frac{1}{\sqrt{2}} & 0 \\
\frac{i}{\sqrt{2}} & 0 & 0 & \frac{1}{\sqrt{2}} \\
\frac{1}{\sqrt{2}} & 0 & 0 & \frac{i}{\sqrt{2}} \\
0 & \frac{1}{\sqrt{2}} & -\frac{1}{\sqrt{2}} & 0
\end{bmatrix}. \tag{4.95}
$$

Determine the state of the system after three time steps. What is the chance of the quantum ball to be found at point 3? ∎

The reader may wonder how the sequence $\mathfrak{U}[t_i]$ of unitary transformations is actually selected in real-life quantum mechanics. In other words, given a concrete quantum system, how is its dynamics determined? How does the system change? The answer lies in an equation known as the **Schrödinger equation:**[13]

$$
\frac{|\psi(t + \delta t)\rangle - |\psi(t)\rangle}{\delta t} = -i\frac{2\pi}{h}\mathcal{H}|\psi(t)\rangle. \tag{4.96}
$$

---

[12] A small warning: one commonly thinks of an orbit as closed (a typical example is the orbit of the moon around the earth). In dynamics, this is not always the case: an orbit can be open or closed.

[13] The version shown here is actually the discretized version of the original equation, which is a differential equation obtained from the above by letting δt become infinitesimal. It is this discretized version (or variants thereof) that is usually employed in computer simulation of quantum systems.

A complete discussion of this fundamental equation goes beyond the scope of this introductory chapter. However, without going into technical details, we can at least convey its spirit. Classical mechanics taught physicists that the global energy of an isolated system is preserved throughout its evolution.[14] Energy is an observable, and therefore for a concrete quantum system it is possible to write down a hermitian matrix representing it (this expression will of course vary from system to system). This observable is called the **hamiltonian** of the system, indicated by $\mathcal{H}$ in Equation (4.96).

The Schrödinger equation states that the rate of variation of the state vector $|\psi(t)\rangle$ with respect to time at the instant t is equal (up to the scalar factor $\frac{2\pi}{h}$) to $|\psi(t)\rangle$ multiplied by the operator $-i * \mathcal{H}$. By solving the equation with some initial conditions one is able to determine the evolution of the system over time.

Time for a small recap:

- Quantum dynamics is given by unitary transformations.
- Unitary transformations are invertible; thus, all closed system dynamics are reversible in time (as long as no measurement is involved).
- The concrete dynamics is given by the Schrödinger equation, which determines the evolution of a quantum system whenever its hamiltonian is specified.

Programming Drill 4.4.1 *Add dynamics to your computer simulation of the particle on a grid: the user should input a number of time steps n, and a corresponding sequence of unitary matrices U_n of the appropriate size. The program will then compute the state vector after the entire sequence U_n has been applied.*

4.5 ASSEMBLING QUANTUM SYSTEMS

The opening section of this chapter described a simple quantum system: a particle moving in a confined one-dimensional grid (the set of points $\{x_0, x_1, \ldots, x_{n-1}\}$). Now, let us suppose that we are dealing with two particles confined to the grid. We shall make the following assumption: the points on the grid that can be occupied by the first particle will be $\{x_0, x_1, \ldots, x_{n-1}\}$. The second particle can be at the points $\{y_0, y_1, \ldots, y_{m-1}\}$.

$$x_0 \qquad x_1 \qquad \cdots \qquad x_{n-1} \qquad y_0 \qquad y_1 \qquad \cdots \qquad y_{m-1}$$

$$(4.97)$$

Can we lift the description we already have to this new setup? Yes. The details will keep us busy in this section.

Our answer will not be confined to the aforementioned system. Instead, it will provide us with a quantum version of a building block game, i.e., a way of assembling more complex quantum systems starting from simpler ones. This procedure

---

[14] For instance, a stone dropped from a height falls down in such a way that its kinetic energy plus its potential energy plus energy dissipated from attrition is constant.

lies at the very core of modern quantum physics: it enables physicists to model multiparticle quantum systems.[15]

We need one last expansion of our quantum dictionary: *assembling quantum systems means tensoring the state space of their constituents.*

Postulate 4.5.1 *Assume we have two independent quantum systems Q and Q', represented respectively by the vector spaces $\mathbb{V}$ and $\mathbb{V}'$. The quantum system obtained by merging Q and Q' will have the tensor product $\mathbb{V} \otimes \mathbb{V}'$ as a state space.*

Notice that the postulate above enables us to assemble as many systems as we like. The tensor product of vector spaces is associative, so we can progressively build larger and larger systems:

$$\mathbb{V}_0 \otimes \mathbb{V}_1 \otimes \cdots \otimes \mathbb{V}_k. \tag{4.98}$$

Let us go back to our example. To begin with, there are $n \times m$ possible basic states:

$|x_0\rangle \otimes |y_0\rangle$, meaning the first particle is at x_0 and the second particle at y_0.

$|x_0\rangle \otimes |y_1\rangle$, meaning the first particle is at x_0 and second particle at y_1.

$\vdots$

$|x_0\rangle \otimes |y_{m-1}\rangle$, meaning the first particle is at x_0 and the second particle at y_{m-1}.

$|x_1\rangle \otimes |y_0\rangle$, meaning the first particle is at x_1 and the second particle at y_0.

$\vdots$

$|x_i\rangle \otimes |y_j\rangle$, meaning the first particle is at x_i and the second particle at y_j.

$\vdots$

$|x_{n-1}\rangle \otimes |y_{m-1}\rangle$, meaning the first particle is at x_{n-1} and the second particle at y_{m-1}.

Now, let us write the generic state vector as a superposition of the basic states:

$$|\psi\rangle = c_{0,0}|x_0\rangle \otimes |y_0\rangle + \cdots + c_{i,j}|x_i\rangle \otimes |y_j\rangle + \cdots + c_{n-1,m-1}|x_{n-1}\rangle \otimes |y_{m-1}\rangle, \tag{4.99}$$

which is a vector in the $(n \times m)$-dimensional complex space $\mathbb{C}^{n \times m}$.

The quantum amplitude $|c_{i,j}|$ squared will give us the probability of finding the two particles at positions x_i and y_j, respectively, as shown by the following example.

Example 4.5.1 Assume $n = 2$ and $m = 2$ in the above. We are thus dealing with the state space $\mathbb{C}^4$ whose standard basis is

$$\{|x_0\rangle \otimes |y_0\rangle, \ |x_0\rangle \otimes |y_1\rangle, \ |x_1\rangle \otimes |y_0\rangle, \ |x_1\rangle \otimes |y_1\rangle\}. \tag{4.100}$$

---

[15] By thinking of fields such as the electromagnetic field as systems composed of infinitely many particles, this procedure makes field theory amenable to the quantum approach.

Now, let us consider the state vector for the two-particle system given by

$$|\psi\rangle = i|x_0\rangle \otimes |y_0\rangle + (1-i)|x_0\rangle \otimes |y_1\rangle + 2|y_1\rangle \otimes |x_0\rangle + (-1-i)|x_1\rangle \otimes |y_1\rangle.$$

$$(4.101)$$

What is the probability of finding the first particle at location x_1 and the second one at y_1? We look at the last amplitude in the list given before, and use the same recipe as in the one-particle system:

$$p(x_1, y_1) = \frac{|-1-i|^2}{|i|^2 + |1-i|^2 + |2|^2 + |-1-i|^2} = 0.2222. \tag{4.102}$$

$\square$

Exercise 4.5.1   Redo the steps of the last example when $n = m = 4$ and $c_{0,0} = c_{0,1} = \cdots = c_{3,3} = 1 + i$.   ∎

The same machinery can be applied to any other quantum system. For instance, it is instructive to generalize our spin example of Section 4.1 to a system where many particles are involved. You can try yourself.

Exercise 4.5.2   Write down the generic state vector for the system of two particles with spin. Generalize it to a system with n particles (this is important: it will be the physical realization for quantum registers!).   ∎

Now that we are a bit familiar with quantum assemblage, we are ready for the final puzzling surprise of quantum mechanics: **entanglement**. Entanglement will force us to abandon one last comforting faith, namely, that assembled complex systems can be understood completely in terms of their constituents.

The basic states of the assembled system are just the tensor product of basic states of its constituents. It would be nice if *each* generic state vector could be rewritten as the tensor product of two states, one coming from the first quantum subsystem and the other one from the second. It turns out that this is not true, as is easily shown by this example.

Example 4.5.2   Let us work on the simplest nontrivial two-particle system: each particle is allowed only two points. Consider the state

$$|\psi\rangle = |x_0\rangle \otimes |y_0\rangle + |x_1\rangle \otimes |y_1\rangle. \tag{4.103}$$

In order to clarify what is left out, we might write this as

$$|\psi\rangle = 1|x_0\rangle \otimes |y_0\rangle + 0|x_0\rangle \otimes |y_1\rangle + 0|x_1\rangle \otimes |y_0\rangle + 1|x_1\rangle \otimes |y_1\rangle. \tag{4.104}$$

Let us see if we can write $|\psi\rangle$ as the tensor product of two states coming from the two subsystems. Any vector representing the first particle on the line can be written as

$$c_0|x_0\rangle + c_1|x_1\rangle. \tag{4.105}$$

Similarly, any vector representing the second particle on the line can be written as

$$c_0'|y_0\rangle + c_1'|y_1\rangle. \tag{4.106}$$

Therefore, if $|\psi\rangle$ came from the tensor product of the two subsystems, we would have

$$(c_0|x_0\rangle + c_1|x_1\rangle) \otimes (c_0'|y_0\rangle + c_1'|y_1\rangle) = c_0c_0'|x_0\rangle \otimes |y_0\rangle + c_0c_1'|x_0\rangle \otimes |y_1\rangle$$
$$+ c_1c_0'|x_1\rangle \otimes |y_0\rangle + c_1c_1'|x_1\rangle \otimes |y_1\rangle. \tag{4.107}$$

For our $|\psi\rangle$ in Equation (4.104) this would imply that $c_0c_0' = c_1c_1' = 1$ and $c_0c_1' = c_1c_0' = 0$. However, these equations have no solution. We conclude that $|\psi\rangle$ cannot be rewritten as a tensor product.

Let us go back to $|\psi\rangle$ and see what it physically means. What would happen if we measured the first particle? A quick calculation will show that the first particle has a 50–50 chance of being found at the position x_0 or at x_1. So, what if it is, in fact, found in position x_0? Because the term $|x_0\rangle \otimes |y_1\rangle$ has a 0 coefficient, we know that there is no chance that the second particle will be found in position y_1. We must then conclude that the second particle can only be found in position y_0. Similarly, if the first particle is found in position x_1, then the second particle must be in position y_1. Notice that the situation is perfectly symmetrical with respect to the two particles, i.e., it would be the same if we measured the second one first. The individual states of the two particles are intimately related to one another, or **entangled**. The amazing side of this story is that the x_i's can be light years away from the y_j's. Regardless of their actual distance in space, a measurement's outcome for one particle will always determine the measurement's outcome for the other one.

The state $|\psi\rangle$ is in sharp contrast to other states like

$$|\psi'\rangle = 1|x_0\rangle \otimes |y_0\rangle + 1|x_0\rangle \otimes |y_1\rangle + 1|x_1\rangle \otimes |y_0\rangle + 1|x_1\rangle \otimes |y_1\rangle. \tag{4.108}$$

Here, finding the first particle at a particular position does not provide any clue as to where the second particle will be found (check it!). □

States that can be broken into the tensor product of states from the constituent subsystems (like $|\psi'\rangle$) are called **separable states**, whereas states that are unbreakable (like $|\psi\rangle$) are referred to as **entangled states**.

Exercise 4.5.3 Assume the same scenario as in Example 4.5.2 and let

$$|\phi\rangle = |x_0\rangle \otimes |y_1\rangle + |x_1\rangle \otimes |y_1\rangle. \tag{4.109}$$

Is this state separable? ■

A clear physical case of entanglement is in order. We must revert to spin. Just as there are laws of conservation of momentum, angular momentum, energy-mass, and other physical properties, so too there is a law of conservation of total spin of a quantum system. This means that in an isolated system the total amount of spin must stay the same. Let us fix a specific direction, say, the vertical one (z axis), and the corresponding spin basis, up and down. Consider the case of a quantum system,

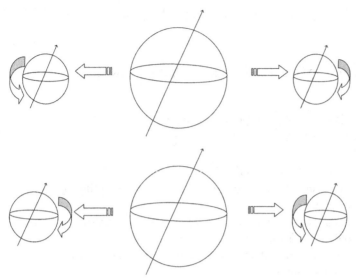

Figure 4.8. Two possible scenarios of a composite system where the total spin is zero.

such as a composite particle, whose total spin is zero. This particle might split up at some point in time into two other particles that do have spin (Figure 4.8).

The spin states of the two particles will now be entangled. The law of conservation of spin stipulates that because we began with a system of total spin zero, the sum of the spins of the two particles must cancel each other out. This amounts to the fact that if we measure the spin of the left particle along the z axis and we find it in state $|\uparrow_L\rangle$ (where the subscript is to describe which particle we are dealing with), then it must be that the spin of the particle on the right will be $|\downarrow_R\rangle$. Similarly, if the state of the left particle is $|\downarrow_L\rangle$, then the spin of the right particle must be $|\uparrow_R\rangle$.

We can describe this within our notation. In terms of vector spaces, the basis that describes the left particle is $\mathcal{B}_L = \{\uparrow_L, \downarrow_L\}$ and the basis that describes the right particle is $\mathcal{B}_R = \{\uparrow_R, \downarrow_R\}$. The basis elements of the entire system are

$$\{\uparrow_L \otimes \uparrow_R, \quad \uparrow_L \otimes \downarrow_R, \quad \downarrow_L \otimes \uparrow_R, \quad \downarrow_L \otimes \downarrow_R\}. \tag{4.110}$$

In such a vector space, our entangled particles can be described by

$$\frac{|\uparrow_L \otimes \downarrow_R\rangle + |\downarrow_L \otimes \uparrow_R\rangle}{\sqrt{2}}, \tag{4.111}$$

similar to Equation (4.104). As we said before, the combinations $|\uparrow_L \otimes \uparrow_R\rangle$ and $|\downarrow_L \otimes \downarrow_R\rangle$ cannot occur because of the law of conservation of spin. When one measures the left particle and it collapses to the state $|\uparrow_L\rangle$ then *instantaneously* the right particle will collapse to the state $|\downarrow_R\rangle$, *even if the right particle is millions of light-years away*.

How will entanglement arise in the tale that we are telling? We find in Chapter 6 that it plays a central role in algorithm design. It is also used extensively in Chapter 9 while discussing cryptography (Section 9.4) and teleportation (Section 9.5). Entanglement makes a final appearance in Chapter 11, in connection with decoherence.

What have we learned?

- We can use the tensor product to build complex quantum systems out of simpler ones.
- The new system cannot be analyzed simply in terms of states belonging to its subsystems. An entire set of new states has been created, which cannot be resolved into their constituents.

Programming Drill 4.5.1 *Expand the simulation of the last sections by letting the user choose the number of particles.*

....

References: There are many elementary introductions to quantum mechanics that are very readable. Here is a list of some of them: Chen (2003), Gillespie (1974), Martin (1982), Polkinghorne (2002), and White (1966).

Special mention must be made of the classic introduction by P.A.M. Dirac (1982). Seventy years after its first publication, it remains a classic that is worth reading.

For a more advanced and modern presentation see, e.g., Volume III of Feynman (1963), Hannabuss (1997), Sakurai (1994), or Sudbery (1986).

For a short history of the early development of quantum mechanics, see Gamow (1985).

5

Architecture

> *From the intrinsic evidence of his creation, the Great Architect of the Universe now begins to appear as a pure mathematician.*
>
> Sir James Jeans, *Mysterious Universe*

Now that we have the mathematical and physical preliminaries under our belt, we can move on to the nuts and bolts of quantum computing. At the heart of a classical computer is the notion of a bit and at the heart of quantum computer is a generalization of the concept of a bit called a qubit, which shall be discussed in Section 5.1. In Section 5.2, classical (logical) gates, which manipulate bits, are presented from a new and different perspective. From this angle, it is easy to formulate the notion of quantum gates, which manipulate qubits. As mentioned in Chapters 3 and 4, the evolution of a quantum system is reversible, i.e., manipulations that can be done must also be able to be undone. This "undoing" translates into reversible gates, which are discussed in Section 5.3. We move on to quantum gates in Section 5.4.

....

Reader Tip. Discussion of the actual physical implementation of qubits and quantum gates is dealt with in Chapter 11. ♡

....

5.1 BITS AND QUBITS

What is a **bit**?

Definition 5.1.1 *A **bit** is a unit of information describing a two-dimensional classical system.*

There are many examples of bits:

- A bit is electricity traveling through a circuit or not (or high and low).
- A bit is a way of denoting "true" or "false."
- A bit is a switch turned on or off.

All these examples are saying the same thing: a bit is a way of describing a system whose set of states is of size 2. We usually write these two possible states as 0 and 1, or F and T, etc.

As we have become adept at matrices, let us use them as a way of representing a bit. We shall represent 0 – or, better, the state $|0\rangle$ – as a 2-by-1 matrix with a 1 in the 0's row and a 0 in the 1's row:

$$|0\rangle = \begin{array}{c} \mathbf{0} \\ \mathbf{1} \end{array}\begin{bmatrix} 1 \\ 0 \end{bmatrix}. \tag{5.1}$$

We shall represent a 1, or state $|1\rangle$, as

$$|1\rangle = \begin{array}{c} \mathbf{0} \\ \mathbf{1} \end{array}\begin{bmatrix} 0 \\ 1 \end{bmatrix}. \tag{5.2}$$

Because these are two different representations (indeed orthogonal), we have an honest-to-goodness bit. We explore how to manipulate these bits in Section 5.2.

A bit can be either in state $|0\rangle$ or in state $|1\rangle$, which was sufficient for the classical world. Either electricity is running through a circuit or it is not. Either a proposition is true or it is false. Either a switch is on or it is off. But either/or is not sufficient in the quantum world. In that world, there are situations where we are in one state *and* in the other simultaneously. In the realm of the quantum, there are systems where a switch is both on *and* off at the same time. One quantum system can be in state $|0\rangle$ *and* in state $|1\rangle$ simultaneously. Hence we are led to the definition of a qubit:

Definition 5.1.2 *A* **quantum bit** *or a* **qubit** *is a unit of information describing a two-dimensional quantum system.*

We shall represent a qubit as a 2-by-1 matrix with complex numbers

$$\begin{array}{c} \mathbf{0} \\ \mathbf{1} \end{array}\begin{bmatrix} c_0 \\ c_1 \end{bmatrix}, \tag{5.3}$$

where $|c_0|^2 + |c_1|^2 = 1$. Notice that a classical bit is a special type of qubit. $|c_0|^2$ is to be interpreted as the probability that after measuring the qubit, it will be found in state $|0\rangle$. $|c_1|^2$ is to be interpreted as the probability that after measuring the qubit it will be found in state $|1\rangle$. Whenever we measure a qubit, it automatically becomes a bit. So we shall never "see" a general qubit. Nevertheless, they do exist and are the main characters in our tale. We might visualize this "collapsing" of a qubit to a bit as

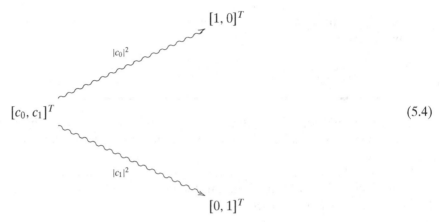

$$[1, 0]^T$$

$$|c_0|^2$$

$$[c_0, c_1]^T \tag{5.4}$$

$$|c_1|^2$$

$$[0, 1]^T$$

It is easy to see that the bits $|0\rangle$ and $|1\rangle$ are the canonical basis of $\mathbb{C}^2$. Thus, any qubit can be written as

$$\begin{bmatrix} c_0 \\ c_1 \end{bmatrix} = c_0 \cdot \begin{bmatrix} 1 \\ 0 \end{bmatrix} + c_1 \cdot \begin{bmatrix} 0 \\ 1 \end{bmatrix} = c_0|0\rangle + c_1|1\rangle. \tag{5.5}$$

Exercise 5.1.1 Write $V = \begin{bmatrix} 3+2i \\ 4-2i \end{bmatrix}$ as a sum of $|0\rangle$ and $|1\rangle$. ∎

Following the normalization procedures that we learned in Chapter 4 on page 109, any nonzero element of $\mathbb{C}^2$ can be converted into a qubit.

Example 5.1.1 The vector

$$V = \begin{bmatrix} 5+3i \\ 6i \end{bmatrix} \tag{5.6}$$

has norm

$$|V| = \sqrt{\langle V, V \rangle} = \sqrt{[5 - 3i, -6i] \begin{bmatrix} 5+3i \\ 6i \end{bmatrix}} = \sqrt{34 + 36} = \sqrt{70}. \tag{5.7}$$

So V describes the same physical state as the qubit

$$\frac{V}{\sqrt{70}} = \begin{bmatrix} \frac{5+3i}{\sqrt{70}} \\ \frac{6i}{\sqrt{70}} \end{bmatrix} = \frac{5+3i}{\sqrt{70}}|0\rangle + \frac{6i}{\sqrt{70}}|1\rangle. \tag{5.8}$$

After measuring the qubit $\frac{V}{\sqrt{70}}$, the probability of it being found in state $|0\rangle$ is $\frac{34}{70}$ and the probability of it being found in state $|1\rangle$ is $\frac{36}{70}$. □

Exercise 5.1.2 Normalize $V = \begin{bmatrix} 15 - 3.4i \\ 2.1 - 16i \end{bmatrix}$. ■

Let us look at several ways of denoting different qubits. $\frac{1}{\sqrt{2}}\begin{bmatrix} 1 \\ 1 \end{bmatrix}$ can be written as

$$\begin{bmatrix} \frac{1}{\sqrt{2}} \\ \frac{1}{\sqrt{2}} \end{bmatrix} = \frac{1}{\sqrt{2}}|0\rangle + \frac{1}{\sqrt{2}}|1\rangle = \frac{|0\rangle + |1\rangle}{\sqrt{2}}. \tag{5.9}$$

Similarly, $\frac{1}{\sqrt{2}}\begin{bmatrix} 1 \\ -1 \end{bmatrix}$ can be written as

$$\begin{bmatrix} \frac{1}{\sqrt{2}} \\ \frac{-1}{\sqrt{2}} \end{bmatrix} = \frac{1}{\sqrt{2}}|0\rangle - \frac{1}{\sqrt{2}}|1\rangle = \frac{|0\rangle - |1\rangle}{\sqrt{2}}. \tag{5.10}$$

It is important to realize that

$$\frac{|0\rangle + |1\rangle}{\sqrt{2}} = \frac{|1\rangle + |0\rangle}{\sqrt{2}}. \tag{5.11}$$

These are both ways of denoting $\begin{bmatrix} \frac{1}{\sqrt{2}} \\ \frac{1}{\sqrt{2}} \end{bmatrix}$. In contrast,

$$\frac{|0\rangle - |1\rangle}{\sqrt{2}} \neq \frac{|1\rangle - |0\rangle}{\sqrt{2}}. \tag{5.12}$$

The left state is the vector $\begin{bmatrix} \frac{1}{\sqrt{2}} \\ -\frac{1}{\sqrt{2}} \end{bmatrix}$ and the right state is the vector $\begin{bmatrix} -\frac{1}{\sqrt{2}} \\ \frac{1}{\sqrt{2}} \end{bmatrix}$. However, the two states are related:

$$\frac{|0\rangle - |1\rangle}{\sqrt{2}} = (-1)\frac{|1\rangle - |0\rangle}{\sqrt{2}}. \tag{5.13}$$

How are qubits to be implemented? In Chapter 11, several different methods are explored. We simply state some examples of implementations for the time being:

■ An electron in an atom might be in one of two different energy levels (ground state and excited state).
■ A photon might be in one of two polarized states.
■ A subatomic particle might have one of two spin directions.

There will be enough quantum indeterminacy and quantum superposition effects within all these systems to represent a qubit.

Computers with only one bit of storage are not very interesting. Similarly, we will need quantum devices with more than one qubit. Consider a byte, or eight bits. A typical byte might be

$$01101011. \tag{5.14}$$

If we were to follow the preceding method of describing bits, we would represent the bits as follows:

$$\begin{bmatrix} 1 \\ 0 \end{bmatrix}, \begin{bmatrix} 0 \\ 1 \end{bmatrix}, \begin{bmatrix} 0 \\ 1 \end{bmatrix}, \begin{bmatrix} 1 \\ 0 \end{bmatrix}, \begin{bmatrix} 0 \\ 1 \end{bmatrix}, \begin{bmatrix} 1 \\ 0 \end{bmatrix}, \begin{bmatrix} 0 \\ 1 \end{bmatrix}, \begin{bmatrix} 0 \\ 1 \end{bmatrix}. \tag{5.15}$$

We learned previously that in order to combine quantum systems, one should use the tensor product; hence, we can describe the byte in Equation (5.14) as

$$|0\rangle \otimes |1\rangle \otimes |1\rangle \otimes |0\rangle \otimes |1\rangle \otimes |0\rangle \otimes |1\rangle \otimes |1\rangle. \tag{5.16}$$

As a qubit, this is an element of

$$\mathbb{C}^2 \otimes \mathbb{C}^2 \otimes \mathbb{C}^2 \otimes \mathbb{C}^2 \otimes \mathbb{C}^2 \otimes \mathbb{C}^2 \otimes \mathbb{C}^2 \otimes \mathbb{C}^2. \tag{5.17}$$

This vector space may be denoted as $(\mathbb{C}^2)^{\otimes 8}$. This is a complex vector space of dimension $2^8 = 256$. Because there is essentially only one complex vector space of this dimension, this vector space is isomorphic to $\mathbb{C}^{256}$.

We can describe our byte in yet another way: as a $2^8 = 256$ row vector

$$\begin{array}{r} \mathbf{00000000} \\ \mathbf{00000001} \\ \vdots \\ \mathbf{01101010} \\ \mathbf{01101011} \\ \mathbf{01101100} \\ \vdots \\ \mathbf{11111110} \\ \mathbf{11111111} \end{array} \begin{bmatrix} 0 \\ 0 \\ \vdots \\ 0 \\ 1 \\ 0 \\ \vdots \\ 0 \\ 0 \end{bmatrix}. \tag{5.18}$$

Exercise 5.1.3 Express the three bits 101 or $|1\rangle \otimes |0\rangle \otimes |1\rangle \in \mathbb{C}^2 \otimes \mathbb{C}^2 \otimes \mathbb{C}^2$ as a vector in $(\mathbb{C}^2)^{\otimes 3} = \mathbb{C}^8$. Do the same for 011 and 111.   ■

This is fine for the classical world. However, for the quantum world, in order to permit superposition, a generalization is needed: every state of an eight-qubit system can be written as

$$
\begin{array}{cc}
00000000 \\
00000001 \\
\vdots \\
01101010 \\
01101011 \\
01101100 \\
\vdots \\
11111110 \\
11111111
\end{array}
\left[
\begin{array}{c}
c_0 \\
c_1 \\
\vdots \\
c_{106} \\
c_{107} \\
c_{108} \\
\vdots \\
c_{254} \\
c_{255}
\end{array}
\right],
\tag{5.19}
$$

where $\sum_{i=0}^{255} |c_i|^2 = 1$. Eight qubits together is called a **qubyte**.

In the classical world, it is necessary to indicate the state of each bit of a byte. This amounts to writing eight bits. In the quantum world, a state of eight qubits is given by writing 256 complex numbers. As we stated in Section 3.4, this exponential growth was one of the reasons researchers started giving thought to the notion of quantum computing. If one wanted to emulate a quantum computer with a 64-qubit register, one would need to store $2^{64} = 18,446,744,073,709,551,616$ complex numbers. This is way beyond our current storage capability.

Let us practice writing two qubits in ket notation. A qubit pair can be written as

$$
|0\rangle \otimes |1\rangle \quad \text{or} \quad |0 \otimes 1\rangle,
\tag{5.20}
$$

which means that the first qubit is in state $|0\rangle$ and the second qubit is in state $|1\rangle$. Because the tensor product is understood, we might also denote these qubits as $|0\rangle|1\rangle, |0, 1\rangle$, or $|01\rangle$. Yet another way to look at these two qubits as the 4-by-1 matrix is

$$
\begin{array}{c}
00 \\
01 \\
10 \\
11
\end{array}
\left[
\begin{array}{c}
0 \\
1 \\
0 \\
0
\end{array}
\right].
\tag{5.21}
$$

Exercise 5.1.4   What vector corresponds to the state $3|01\rangle + 2|11\rangle$?   ∎

Example 5.1.2   The qubit corresponding to

$$
\frac{1}{\sqrt{3}}
\left[
\begin{array}{c}
1 \\
0 \\
-1 \\
1
\end{array}
\right]
\tag{5.22}
$$

can be written as

$$\frac{1}{\sqrt{3}}|00\rangle - \frac{1}{\sqrt{3}}|10\rangle + \frac{1}{\sqrt{3}}|11\rangle = \frac{|00\rangle - |10\rangle + |11\rangle}{\sqrt{3}}. \tag{5.23}$$

□

A general state of a two-qubit system can be written as

$$|\psi\rangle = c_{0,0}|00\rangle + c_{0,1}|01\rangle + c_{1,0}|10\rangle + c_{1,1}|11\rangle. \tag{5.24}$$

The tensor product of two states is not commutative:

$$|0 \otimes 1\rangle = |0\rangle \otimes |1\rangle = |0, 1\rangle = |01\rangle \neq |10\rangle = |1, 0\rangle = |1\rangle \otimes |0\rangle = |1 \otimes 0\rangle. \tag{5.25}$$

The left ket describes the state in which the first qubit is in state 0 and the second qubit is in state 1. The right ket indicates that first qubit is in state 1 and the second qubit is in state 0.

Let us briefly revisit the notion of entanglement again. If the system is in the state

$$\frac{|11\rangle + |00\rangle}{\sqrt{2}} = \frac{1}{\sqrt{2}}|11\rangle + \frac{1}{\sqrt{2}}|00\rangle, \tag{5.26}$$

then that means that the the two qubits are entangled. That is, if we measure the first qubit and it is found in state $|1\rangle$ then we automatically know that the state of the second qubit is $|1\rangle$. Similarly, if we measure the first qubit and find it in state $|0\rangle$ then we know the second qubit is also in state $|0\rangle$.

5.2 CLASSICAL GATES

Classical logical gates are ways of manipulating bits. Bits enter and exit logical gates. We will need ways of manipulating qubits and will study classical gates from the point of view of matrices. As stated in Section 5.1, we represent n input bits as a 2^n-by-1 matrix and m output bits as a 2^m-by-1 matrix. How should we represent our logical gates? When one multiplies a 2^m-by-2^n matrix with a 2^n-by-1 matrix, the result is a 2^m-by-1 matrix. In symbols:

$$(2^m\text{-by-}2^n) \star (2^n\text{-by-}1) = (2^m\text{-by-}1). \tag{5.27}$$

So bits will be represented by column vectors and logic gates by matrices.

Let us try a simple example. Consider the NOT gate.

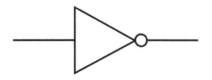

NOT takes as input one bit, or a 2-by-1 matrix, and outputs one bit, or a 2-by-1 matrix. NOT of $|0\rangle$ equals $|1\rangle$ and NOT of $|1\rangle$ equals $|0\rangle$. Consider the matrix

$$\text{NOT} = \begin{bmatrix} 0 & 1 \\ 1 & 0 \end{bmatrix}. \tag{5.28}$$

This matrix satisfies

$$\begin{bmatrix} 0 & 1 \\ 1 & 0 \end{bmatrix} \begin{bmatrix} 1 \\ 0 \end{bmatrix} = \begin{bmatrix} 0 \\ 1 \end{bmatrix} \quad \text{and} \quad \begin{bmatrix} 0 & 1 \\ 1 & 0 \end{bmatrix} \begin{bmatrix} 0 \\ 1 \end{bmatrix} = \begin{bmatrix} 1 \\ 0 \end{bmatrix}, \tag{5.29}$$

which is exactly what we want.

What about the other gates? Consider the AND gate. The AND gate is different from the NOT gate because AND accepts two bits and outputs one bit.

Because there are two inputs and one output, we will need a 2^1-by-2^2 matrix. Consider the matrix

$$\text{AND} = \begin{bmatrix} 1 & 1 & 1 & 0 \\ 0 & 0 & 0 & 1 \end{bmatrix}. \tag{5.30}$$

This matrix satisfies

$$\begin{bmatrix} 1 & 1 & 1 & 0 \\ 0 & 0 & 0 & 1 \end{bmatrix} \begin{bmatrix} 0 \\ 0 \\ 0 \\ 1 \end{bmatrix} = \begin{bmatrix} 0 \\ 1 \end{bmatrix}. \tag{5.31}$$

We can write this as

$$\text{AND}|11\rangle = |1\rangle. \tag{5.32}$$

In contrast, consider another 4-by-1 matrix:

$$\begin{bmatrix} 1 & 1 & 1 & 0 \\ 0 & 0 & 0 & 1 \end{bmatrix} \begin{bmatrix} 0 \\ 1 \\ 0 \\ 0 \end{bmatrix} = \begin{bmatrix} 1 \\ 0 \end{bmatrix}. \tag{5.33}$$

We can write this as

$$\text{AND}|01\rangle = |0\rangle. \tag{5.34}$$

Exercise 5.2.1   Calculate $AND|10\rangle$.   ■

What would happen if we put an arbitrary 4-by-1 matrix to the right of AND?

$$\begin{bmatrix} 1 & 1 & 1 & 0 \\ 0 & 0 & 0 & 1 \end{bmatrix} \begin{bmatrix} 3.5 \\ 2 \\ 0 \\ -4.1 \end{bmatrix} = \begin{bmatrix} 5.5 \\ -4.1 \end{bmatrix} \tag{5.35}$$

This is clearly nonsense. We are allowed only to multiply these classical gates with vectors that represent classical states, i.e., column matrices with a single 1 entry and all other entries 0. In the classical world, the bits are in only one state at a time and are described by such vectors. Only later, when we delve into quantum gates, will we have more room (and more fun).

The OR gate

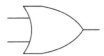

can be represented by the matrix

$$OR = \begin{bmatrix} 1 & 0 & 0 & 0 \\ 0 & 1 & 1 & 1 \end{bmatrix}. \tag{5.36}$$

Exercise 5.2.2   Show that this matrix performs the OR operation.   ■

The NAND gate

is of special importance because every logical gate can be composed of NAND gates. Let us try to determine which matrix would correspond to NAND. One way is to sit down and consider for which of the four possible input states of two bits (00, 01, 10, 11) does NAND output a 1 (answer: 00, 01, 10), and in which states does NAND output a 0 (answer: 11). From this, we realize that NAND can be written as

$$NAND = \begin{matrix} \mathbf{0} \\ \mathbf{1} \end{matrix} \begin{matrix} \mathbf{00} & \mathbf{01} & \mathbf{10} & \mathbf{11} \\ \begin{bmatrix} 0 & 0 & 0 & 1 \\ 1 & 1 & 1 & 0 \end{bmatrix} \end{matrix}. \tag{5.37}$$

Notice that the column names correspond to the inputs and the row names correspond to the outputs. 1 in the jth column and ith row means that on entry j the matrix/gate will output i.

There is, however, another way in which one can determine the NAND gate. The NAND gate is really the AND gate followed by the NOT gate.

In other words, we can perform the NAND operation by first performing the AND operation and then the NOT operation. In terms of matrices we can write this as

$$NOT \star AND = \begin{bmatrix} 0 & 1 \\ 1 & 0 \end{bmatrix} \star \begin{bmatrix} 1 & 1 & 1 & 0 \\ 0 & 0 & 0 & 1 \end{bmatrix} = \begin{bmatrix} 0 & 0 & 0 & 1 \\ 1 & 1 & 1 & 0 \end{bmatrix} = \text{NAND}.$$

(5.38)

Exercise 5.2.3 Find a matrix that corresponds to NOR. ∎

This way of thinking of NAND brings to light a general situation. When we perform a computation, we often have to carry out one operation followed by another.

(5.39)

We call this procedure performing **sequential** operations. If matrix A corresponds to performing an operation and matrix B corresponds to performing another operation, then the matrix $B \star A$ corresponds to performing the operation sequentially. Notice that $B \star A$ looks like the reverse of our picture which has, from left to right, A and then B. Do not be alarmed by this. The reason for this is because we read from left to right and hence we depict processes as flowing from left to right. We could have easily drawn the above figure as

(5.40)

with no confusion.[1] We shall follow the convention that computation flows from left to right and omit the heads of the arrows. And so a computation of A followed by B shall be denoted

(5.41)

---

[1] If the text were written in Arabic or Hebrew, this problem would not even arise.

Let us be formal with the number of inputs and the number of outputs. If A is an operation with m input bits and n output bits, then we shall draw this as

$$\overset{m}{\longrightarrow}\boxed{\quad A \quad}\overset{n}{\longrightarrow} \qquad (5.42)$$

The matrix A will be of size 2^n-by-2^m. Say, B takes the n outputs of A as input and outputs p bits, i.e.,

$$\overset{m}{\longrightarrow}\boxed{A}\overset{n}{\longrightarrow}\boxed{B}\overset{p}{\longrightarrow} \qquad (5.43)$$

then B is represented by a 2^p-by-2^n matrix B, and performing one operation sequentially followed by another operation corresponds to $B \star A$, which is a $(2^p$-by-$2^n) \star (2^n$-by-$2^m) = (2^p$-by-$2^m)$ matrix.

Besides sequential operations, there are **parallel** operations as well.

$$\boxed{\quad A \quad}$$
$$\qquad (5.44)$$
$$\boxed{\quad B \quad}$$

Here we have A acting on some bits and B on others. This will be represented by $A \otimes B$ (see Section 2.7). Let us be exact with the number of inputs and the number of outputs.

$$\overset{m}{\longrightarrow}\boxed{\quad A \quad}\overset{n}{\longrightarrow}$$
$$\qquad (5.45)$$
$$\overset{m'}{\longrightarrow}\boxed{\quad B \quad}\overset{n'}{\longrightarrow}$$

A will be of size 2^n-by-2^m. B will be of size $2^{n'}$-by-$2^{m'}$. Following Equation (2.174) in Section 2.7, $A \otimes B$ is of size $2^n 2^{n'} = 2^{n+n'}$-by-$2^m 2^{m'} = 2^{m+m'}$.

Exercise 5.2.4 In Exercise 2.7.4, we proved that $A \otimes B \cong B \otimes A$. What does this fact correspond to in terms of performing parallel operations on different bits? ∎

Combinations of sequential and parallel operations gates/matrices will be called **circuits**. We will, of course, construct some really complicated matrices, but they will all be decomposable into the sequential and parallel compositions of simple gates.

Exercise 5.2.5 In Exercise 2.7.9, we proved that for matrices of the appropriate sizes A, A', B, and B' we have the following equation:

$$(B \otimes B') \star (A \otimes A') = (B \star A) \otimes (B' \star A'). \qquad (5.46)$$

To what does this correspond in terms of performing different operations on different (qu)bits? (Hint: Consider the following figure.)

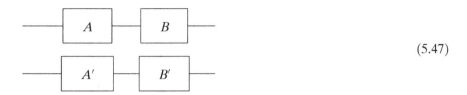

(5.47)

∎

Example 5.2.1 Let A be an operation that takes n inputs and gives m outputs. Let B take $p < m$ of these outputs and leave the other $m - p$ outputs alone. B outputs q bits.

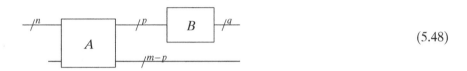

(5.48)

A is a 2^m-by-2^n matrix. B is a 2^q-by-2^p matrix. As nothing should be done to the $m - p$ bits, we might represent this as the 2^{m-p}-by-2^{m-p} identity matrix I_{m-p}. We do not draw any gate for the identity matrix. The entire circuit can be represented by the following matrix:

$$(B \otimes I_{m-p}) \star A.$$ (5.49)

□

Example 5.2.2 Consider the circuit.
   This is represented by

$$\text{OR} \star (\text{NOT} \otimes \text{AND}).$$ (5.50)

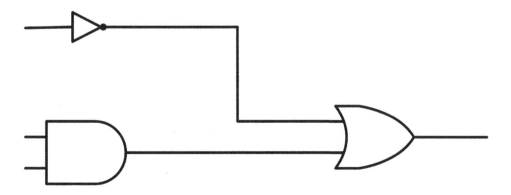

Let us see how the operations look like as matrices. Calculating, we get

$$
\mathrm{NOT} \otimes \mathrm{AND} = \begin{bmatrix} 0 & 1 \\ 1 & 0 \end{bmatrix} \otimes \begin{bmatrix} 1 & 1 & 1 & 0 \\ 0 & 0 & 0 & 1 \end{bmatrix} = \begin{bmatrix} 0 & 0 & 0 & 0 & 1 & 1 & 1 & 0 \\ 0 & 0 & 0 & 0 & 0 & 0 & 0 & 1 \\ 1 & 1 & 1 & 0 & 0 & 0 & 0 & 0 \\ 0 & 0 & 0 & 1 & 0 & 0 & 0 & 0 \end{bmatrix}.
$$
(5.51)

And so we get

$$
\mathrm{OR} \star (\mathrm{NOT} \otimes \mathrm{AND}) = \begin{bmatrix} 0 & 0 & 0 & 0 & 1 & 1 & 1 & 0 \\ 1 & 1 & 1 & 1 & 0 & 0 & 0 & 1 \end{bmatrix}.
$$
(5.52)

$\square$

Let us see if we can formulate DeMorgan's laws in terms of matrices. One of DeMorgan's laws states that $\neg(\neg P \wedge \neg Q) = P \vee Q$. Here is a pictorial representation.

In terms of matrices this corresponds to

$$
\mathrm{NOT} \star \mathrm{AND} \star (\mathrm{NOT} \otimes \mathrm{NOT}) = \mathrm{OR}.
$$
(5.53)

First, let us calculate the tensor product:

$$
\mathrm{NOT} \otimes \mathrm{NOT} = \begin{bmatrix} 0 & 1 \\ 1 & 0 \end{bmatrix} \otimes \begin{bmatrix} 0 & 1 \\ 1 & 0 \end{bmatrix} = \begin{bmatrix} 0 & 0 & 0 & 1 \\ 0 & 0 & 1 & 0 \\ 0 & 1 & 0 & 0 \\ 1 & 0 & 0 & 0 \end{bmatrix}.
$$
(5.54)

This DeMorgan's law corresponds to the following identity of matrices:

$$
\begin{bmatrix} 0 & 1 \\ 1 & 0 \end{bmatrix} \star \begin{bmatrix} 1 & 1 & 1 & 0 \\ 0 & 0 & 0 & 1 \end{bmatrix} \star \begin{bmatrix} 0 & 0 & 0 & 1 \\ 0 & 0 & 1 & 0 \\ 0 & 1 & 0 & 0 \\ 1 & 0 & 0 & 0 \end{bmatrix} = \begin{bmatrix} 1 & 0 & 0 & 0 \\ 0 & 1 & 1 & 1 \end{bmatrix}.
$$
(5.55)

Exercise 5.2.6   Multiply out these matrices and confirm the identity.   ■

Exercise 5.2.7   Formulate the other DeMorgan's law

$$\neg(\neg P \bigvee \neg Q) = P \bigwedge Q \tag{5.56}$$

in terms of matrices.   ■

Exercise 5.2.8   Write the matrix that would correspond to a one-bit adder. A one-bit adder adds the bits x, y, and c (a carry-bit from an earlier adder) and outputs the bits z and c' (a carry-bit for the next adder). There are three inputs and two outputs, so the matrix will be of dimension 2^2-by-2^3. (Hint: Mark the columns as $000, 001, 010, \ldots, 110, 111$, where column, say, 101 corresponds to $x = 1, y = 0, c = 1$. Mark the rows as $00, 01, 10, 11$, where row, say, 10, corresponds to $z = 1, c' = 0$. When $x = 1, y = 0, c = 1$, the output should be $z = 0$ and $c' = 1$. So place a 1 in the row marked 01 and a 0 in all other rows.)   ■

Exercise 5.2.9   In Exercise 5.2.8, you determined the matrix that corresponds to a one-bit adder. Check that your results are correct by writing the circuit in terms of classical gates and then converting the circuit to a big matrix.   ■

5.3 REVERSIBLE GATES

Not all the logical gates that we dealt with in Section 5.2 will work in quantum computers. In the quantum world, all operations that are not measurements are reversible and are represented by unitary matrices. The AND operation is not reversible. Given an output of $|0\rangle$ from AND, one cannot determine if the input was $|00\rangle$, $|01\rangle$, or $|10\rangle$. So from an output of the AND gate, one cannot determine the input and hence AND is not reversible. In contrast, the NOT gate and the identity gates are reversible. In fact, they are their own inverses:

$$\text{NOT} \star \text{NOT} = I_2 \qquad I_n \star I_n = I_n. \tag{5.57}$$

Reversible gates have a history that predates quantum computing. Our everyday computers lose energy and generate a tremendous amount of heat. In the 1960s, Rolf Landauer analyzed computational processes and showed that erasing information, as opposed to writing information, is what causes energy loss and heat. This notion has come to be known as the **Landauer's principle**.

In order to gain a real-life intuition as to why erasing information dissipates energy, consider a tub of water with a wall separating the two sides as in Figure 5.1.

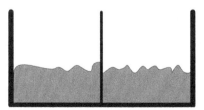

Figure 5.1. Tub with water in no state.

$|0\rangle$ $|1\rangle$

Figure 5.2. Tub with water in state $|0\rangle$ and state $|1\rangle$.

This tub is used as a way of storing a bit of information. If all the water is pushed to the left then the system is in state $|0\rangle$, and if all the water is pushed to the right then the system is in state $|1\rangle$, as in Figure 5.2.

What would correspond to erasing information in such a system? If there were a hole in the wall separating the 0 and 1 regions, then the water could seep out and we would not know what state the system would be in. One can easily place a turbine where the water is seeping out (see Figure 5.3) and generate energy. Hence, losing information means energy is being dissipated.

Notice, also, that writing information is a reversible procedure. If the tub is in no state and we push all the water to the left and set the water to state $|0\rangle$, all one needs to do is remove the wall and the water will go into both regions resulting in no state. This is shown in Figure 5.4. We have reversed the fact that information was written. In contrast, erasing information is not reversible. Start at state $|0\rangle$, and then remove the wall that separates the two parts of the tub. That is erasing the information. How could we return to the original state? There are two possible states to return to, as in Figure 5.5.

The obvious answer is that we should push all the water back to state $|0\rangle$. But the only way we know that $|0\rangle$ is the original state is if that information is copied to the brain. In that case, the system is both the tub and the brain, and we did not really erase the fact that state $|0\rangle$ was the original state. Our brain was still storing the information.

Let us reexamine this intuition by considering two people, Alice and Bob. If Alice writes a letter on an empty blackboard and then Bob walks into the room, he can then erase the letter that Alice wrote on the board and return the blackboard into its original pristine state. Thus, writing is reversible. In contrast, if there is a board with writing on it and Alice erases the board, then when Bob walks into the room he cannot write what was on the board. Bob does not know what was on the board before Alice erased it. So Alice's erasing was not reversible.

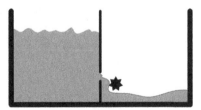

Figure 5.3. State $|0\rangle$ dissipating and creating energy.

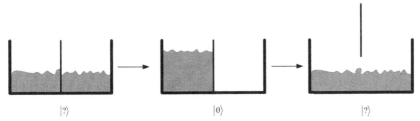

Figure 5.4. Reversibility of writing.

We have found that erasing information is an irreversible, energy-dissipating operation. In the 1970s, Charles H. Bennett continued along these lines of thought. If erasing information is the only operation that uses energy, then a computer that is reversible and does not erase would not use any energy. Bennett started working on reversible circuits and programs.

What examples of reversible gates are there? We have already seen that the identity gate and NOT gates are reversible. What else is there? Consider the following **controlled-NOT gate**:

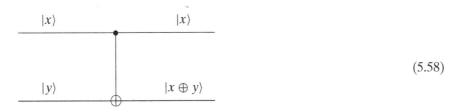

(5.58)

This gate has two inputs and two outputs. The top input is the control bit. It controls what the output will be. If $|x\rangle = |0\rangle$, then the bottom output of $|y\rangle$ will be the same as the input. If $|x\rangle = |1\rangle$, then the bottom output will be the opposite. If we write the top qubit first and then the bottom qubit, then the controlled-NOT gate takes $|x, y\rangle$ to $|x, x \oplus y\rangle$, where $\oplus$ is the binary exclusive or operation.

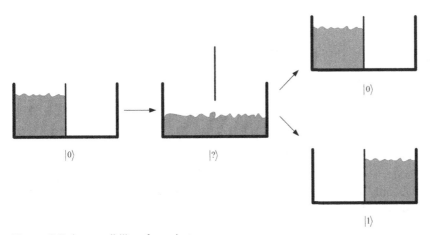

Figure 5.5. Irreversibility of erasing.

The matrix that corresponds to this reversible gate is

$$
\begin{array}{c}
\quad\quad \mathbf{00}\quad \mathbf{01}\quad \mathbf{10}\quad \mathbf{11} \\
\begin{array}{c}
\mathbf{00} \\ \mathbf{01} \\ \mathbf{10} \\ \mathbf{11}
\end{array}
\begin{bmatrix}
1 & 0 & 0 & 0 \\
0 & 1 & 0 & 0 \\
0 & 0 & 0 & 1 \\
0 & 0 & 1 & 0
\end{bmatrix}.
\end{array}
\tag{5.59}
$$

The controlled-NOT gate can be reversed by itself. Consider the following figure:

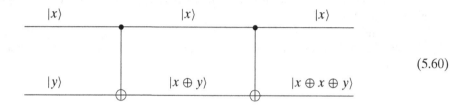

$$\tag{5.60}$$

State $|x, y\rangle$ goes to $|x, x \oplus y\rangle$, which further goes to $|x, x \oplus (x \oplus y)\rangle$. This last state is equal to $|x, (x \oplus x) \oplus y\rangle$ because $\oplus$ is associative. Because $x \oplus x$ is always equal to 0, this state reduces to the original $|x, y\rangle$.

Exercise 5.3.1 Show that the controlled-NOT gate is its own inverse by multiplying the corresponding matrix by itself and arriving at the identity matrix. ∎

An interesting reversible gate is the **Toffoli gate**:

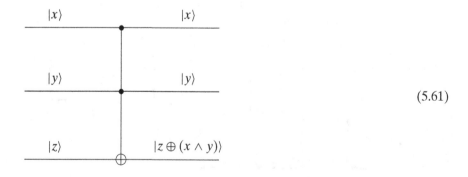

$$\tag{5.61}$$

This is similar to the controlled-NOT gate, but with two controlling bits. The bottom bit flips only when *both* of the top two bits are in state $|1\rangle$. We can write this operation as taking state $|x, y, z\rangle$ to $|x, y, z \oplus (x \wedge y)\rangle$.

Exercise 5.3.2 Show that the Toffoli gate is its own inverse. ∎

The matrix that corresponds to this gate is

$$
\begin{array}{c}
\begin{array}{cccccccc}
\mathbf{000} & \mathbf{001} & \mathbf{010} & \mathbf{011} & \mathbf{100} & \mathbf{101} & \mathbf{110} & \mathbf{111}
\end{array} \\
\begin{array}{c}
\mathbf{000} \\ \mathbf{001} \\ \mathbf{010} \\ \mathbf{011} \\ \mathbf{100} \\ \mathbf{101} \\ \mathbf{110} \\ \mathbf{111}
\end{array}
\left[
\begin{array}{cccccccc}
1 & 0 & 0 & 0 & 0 & 0 & 0 & 0 \\
0 & 1 & 0 & 0 & 0 & 0 & 0 & 0 \\
0 & 0 & 1 & 0 & 0 & 0 & 0 & 0 \\
0 & 0 & 0 & 1 & 0 & 0 & 0 & 0 \\
0 & 0 & 0 & 0 & 1 & 0 & 0 & 0 \\
0 & 0 & 0 & 0 & 0 & 1 & 0 & 0 \\
0 & 0 & 0 & 0 & 0 & 0 & 0 & 1 \\
0 & 0 & 0 & 0 & 0 & 0 & 1 & 0
\end{array}
\right].
\end{array}
\qquad (5.62)
$$

Example 5.3.1 The NOT gate has no controlling bit, the controlled-NOT gate has one controlling bit, and the Toffoli gate has two controlling bits. Can we go on with this? Yes. A gate with three controlling bits can be constructed from three Toffoli gates as follows:

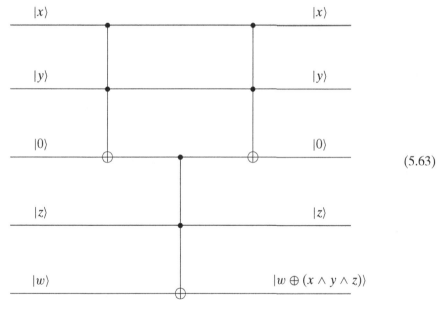

$$(5.63)$$

$\square$

One reason why the Toffoli gate is interesting is that it is universal. In other words, with copies of the Toffoli gate, you can make any logical gate. In particular, you can make a reversible computer using only Toffoli gates. Such a computer would, in theory, neither use any energy nor give off any heat.

In order to see that the Toffoli gate is universal, we will show that it can be used to make both the AND and NOT gates. The AND gate is obtained by setting the bottom $|z\rangle$ input to $|0\rangle$. The bottom output will then be $|x \wedge y\rangle$.

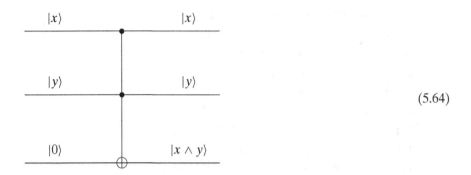

(5.64)

The NOT gate is obtained by setting the top two inputs to $|1\rangle$. The bottom output will be $|(1 \wedge 1) \oplus z\rangle = |1 \oplus z\rangle = |\neg z\rangle$.

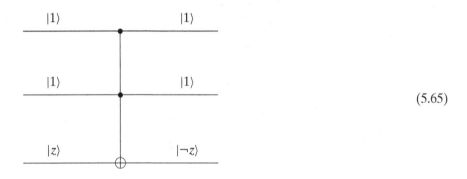

(5.65)

In order to construct all gates, we must also have a way of producing a fanout of values. In other words, a gate is needed that inputs a value and outputs two of the same values. This can be obtained by setting $|x\rangle$ to $|1\rangle$ and $|z\rangle$ to $|0\rangle$. This makes the output $|1, y, y\rangle$.

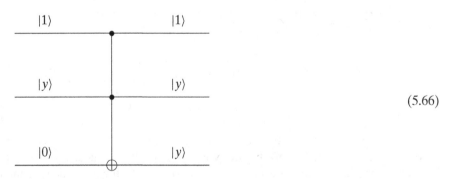

(5.66)

Exercise 5.3.3 Construct the NAND with one Toffoli gate. Construct the OR gate with two Toffoli gates. ∎

Another interesting reversible gate is the **Fredkin gate**. The Fredkin gate also has three inputs and three outputs.

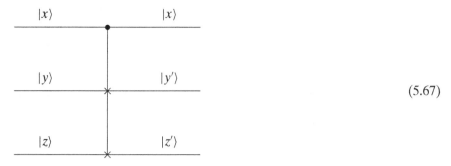

$$(5.67)$$

The top $|x\rangle$ input is the control input. The output is always the same $|x\rangle$. If $|x\rangle$ is set to $|0\rangle$, then $|y'\rangle = |y\rangle$ and $|z'\rangle = |z\rangle$, i.e., the values stay the same. If, on the other hand, the control $|x\rangle$ is set to $|1\rangle$, then the outputs are reversed: $|y'\rangle = |z\rangle$ and $|z'\rangle = |y\rangle$. In short, $|0, y, z\rangle \mapsto |0, y, z\rangle$ and $|1, y, z\rangle \mapsto |1, z, y\rangle$.

Exercise 5.3.4   Show that the Fredkin gate is its own inverse.   ■

The matrix that corresponds to the Fredkin gate is

	000	001	010	011	100	101	110	111
000	1	0	0	0	0	0	0	0
001	0	1	0	0	0	0	0	0
010	0	0	1	0	0	0	0	0
011	0	0	0	1	0	0	0	0
100	0	0	0	0	1	0	0	0
101	0	0	0	0	0	0	1	0
110	0	0	0	0	0	1	0	0
111	0	0	0	0	0	0	0	1

$$(5.68)$$

The Fredkin gate is also universal. By setting $|y\rangle$ to $|0\rangle$, we get the AND gate as follows:

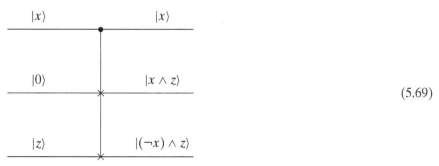

$$(5.69)$$

The NOT gate and the fanout gate can be obtained by setting $|y\rangle$ to $|1\rangle$ and $|z\rangle$ to $|0\rangle$. This gives us

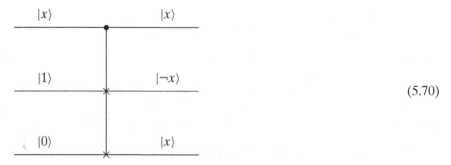

$$(5.70)$$

So both the Toffoli and the Fredkin gates are universal. Not only are both reversible gates; a glance at their matrices indicates that they are also unitary. In the next section, we look at other unitary gates.

5.4 QUANTUM GATES

Definition 5.4.1 *A **quantum gate** is simply an operator that acts on qubits. Such operators will be represented by unitary matrices.*

We have already worked with some quantum gates such as the identity operator I, the Hadamard gate H, the NOT gate, the controlled-NOT gate, the Toffoli gate, and the Fredkin gate. What else is there?

Let us look at some other quantum gates. The following three matrices are called **Pauli matrices** and are very important:

$$X = \begin{bmatrix} 0 & 1 \\ 1 & 0 \end{bmatrix}, \qquad Y = \begin{bmatrix} 0 & -i \\ i & 0 \end{bmatrix}, \qquad Z = \begin{bmatrix} 1 & 0 \\ 0 & -1 \end{bmatrix}. \qquad (5.71)$$

They occur everywhere in quantum mechanics and quantum computing.[2] Note that the X matrix is nothing more than our NOT matrix. Other important matrices that will be used are

$$S = \begin{bmatrix} 1 & 0 \\ 0 & i \end{bmatrix} \quad \text{and} \quad T = \begin{bmatrix} 1 & 0 \\ 0 & e^{i\pi/4} \end{bmatrix}. \qquad (5.72)$$

Exercise 5.4.1   Show that each of these matrices are unitary.   ∎

Exercise 5.4.2   Show the action of each of these matrices on an arbitrary qubit $[c_0, c_1]^T$.   ∎

---

[2] Sometimes the notation σ_x, σ_y, and σ_z is used for these matrices.

Exercise 5.4.3 These operations are intimately related to each other. Prove the following relationships between the operations:

(i) $X^2 = Y^2 = Z^2 = I$,
(ii) $H = \frac{1}{\sqrt{2}}(X + Z)$,
(iii) $X = HZH$,
(iv) $Z = HXH$,
(v) $-1Y = HYH$,
(vi) $S = T^2$,
(vii) $-1Y = XYX$. ∎

There are still other quantum gates. Let us consider a one-qubit quantum gate with an interesting name. The gate is called the **square root of NOT** and is denoted $\sqrt{NOT}$. The matrix representation of this gate is

$$\sqrt{NOT} = \frac{1}{\sqrt{2}} \begin{bmatrix} 1 & -1 \\ 1 & 1 \end{bmatrix}. \tag{5.73}$$

The first thing to notice is that this gate is not its own inverse, that is,

$$\sqrt{NOT} \neq \sqrt{NOT}^\dagger. \tag{5.74}$$

In order to understand why this gate has such a strange name, let us multiply $\sqrt{NOT}$ by itself:

$$\sqrt{NOT} \star \sqrt{NOT} = (\sqrt{NOT})^2 = \begin{bmatrix} 0 & -1 \\ 1 & 0 \end{bmatrix}, \tag{5.75}$$

which is very similar to the NOT gate. Let us put the qubits $|0\rangle$ and $|1\rangle$ through $\sqrt{NOT}$ gate twice. We get

$$|0\rangle = [1, 0]^T \mapsto \left[\frac{1}{\sqrt{2}}, \frac{1}{\sqrt{2}}\right]^T \mapsto [0, 1]^T = |1\rangle \tag{5.76}$$

and

$$|1\rangle = [0, 1]^T \mapsto \left[-\frac{1}{\sqrt{2}}, \frac{1}{\sqrt{2}}\right]^T \mapsto [-1, 0]^T = -1|0\rangle. \tag{5.77}$$

Remembering that $|0\rangle$ and $-1|0\rangle$ both represent the same state, we are confident in saying that the square of $\sqrt{NOT}$ performs the same operation as the NOT gate, and hence the name.

There is one other gate we have not discussed: the measurement operation. This is not unitary or, in general, even reversible. This operation is usually performed at the end of a computation when we want to measure qubits (and find bits). We shall denote it as

$$\tag{5.78}$$

There is a beautiful geometric way of representing one-qubit states and operations. Remember from Chapter 1, page 18, that for a given complex number $c = x + yi$ whose modulus is 1, there is a nice way of visualizing c as an arrow of length 1 from the origin to the circle of radius 1.

$$|c|^2 = c \times \bar{c} = (x + yi) \times (x - yi) = x^2 + y^2 = 1. \tag{5.79}$$

In other words, every complex number of radius 1 can be identified by the angle ϕ that the vector makes with the positive x axis.

There is an analogous representation of a qubit as an arrow from the origin to a three-dimensional sphere. Let us see how it works. A generic qubit is of the form

$$|\psi\rangle = c_0|0\rangle + c_1|1\rangle, \tag{5.80}$$

where $|c_0|^2 + |c_1|^2 = 1$. Although at first sight there are four real numbers involved in the qubit given in Equation (5.80), it turns out that there are only two actual degrees of freedom to the three-dimensional ball (as latitude and longitude on the Earth). Let us rewrite the qubit in Equation (5.80) in polar form:

$$c_0 = r_0 \, e^{i\phi_0} \tag{5.81}$$

and

$$c_1 = r_1 \, e^{i\phi_1}, \tag{5.82}$$

and so Equation (5.80) can be rewritten as

$$|\psi\rangle = r_0 \, e^{i\phi_0}|0\rangle + r_1 \, e^{i\phi_1}|1\rangle. \tag{5.83}$$

There are still four real parameters: r_0, r_1, ϕ_0, ϕ_1. However, a quantum physical state does not change if we multiply its corresponding vector by an arbitrary complex number (of norm 1, see Chapter 4, page 109). We can therefore obtain an equivalent expression for the qubit in Equation (5.80), where the amplitude for $|0\rangle$ is real, by "killing" its phase:

$$e^{-i\phi_0}|\psi\rangle = e^{-i\phi_0}(r_0 \, e^{i\phi_0}|0\rangle + r_1 \, e^{i\phi_1}|1\rangle) = r_0|0\rangle + r_1 \, e^{i(\phi_1 - \phi_0)}|1\rangle. \tag{5.84}$$

We now have only three real parameters, namely, r_0, r_1, and $\phi = \phi_1 - \phi_0$. But we can do better: using the fact that

$$1 = |c_0|^2 + |c_1|^2 = |r_0 \, e^{i\phi_0}|^2 + |r_1 \, e^{i\phi_1}|^2 = |r_0|^2|e^{i\phi_0}|^2 + |r_1|^2|e^{i\phi_1}|^2, \tag{5.85}$$

we get that

$$r_0^2 + r_1^2 = 1. \tag{5.86}$$

We can rename them as

$$r_0 = \cos(\theta) \quad \text{and} \quad r_1 = \sin(\theta). \tag{5.87}$$

Summing up, the qubit in Equation (5.80) is now in the canonical representation

$$|\psi\rangle = \cos(\theta)|0\rangle + e^{i\phi} \sin(\theta)|1\rangle, \tag{5.88}$$

with only two real parameters remaining.

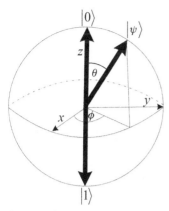

Figure 5.6. Bloch sphere.

What is the range of the two angles θ and ϕ? We invite you to show that $0 \leq \phi < 2\pi$ and $0 \leq \theta \leq \frac{\pi}{2}$ are enough to cover all possible qubits.

Exercise 5.4.4 Prove that every qubit in the canonical representation given in Equation (5.88) with $\theta > \frac{\pi}{2}$ is equivalent to another one where θ lies in the first quadrant of the plane. (Hint: Use a bit of trigonometry and change ϕ according to your needs.) ∎

As only two real numbers are necessary to identify a qubit, we can map it to an arrow from the origin to the three-dimensional sphere of $\mathbb{R}^3$ of radius 1 known as the **Bloch sphere**, as shown in Figure 5.6.

Every qubit can be represented by two angles that describe such an arrow. The two angles will correspond to the latitude (θ) and the longitude (ϕ) needed to specify any position on Earth. The standard parametrization of the unit sphere is

$$x = \cos\phi \sin\theta, \tag{5.89}$$

$$y = \sin\phi \sin\theta, \tag{5.90}$$

$$z = \cos\theta. \tag{5.91}$$

where $0 \leq \phi < 2\pi$ and $0 \leq \theta \leq \pi$.

However, there is a caveat: suppose we use this representation to map our qubit on the sphere. Then, the points (θ, ϕ) and $(\pi - \theta, \phi + \pi)$ represent the same qubit, up to the factor -1. Conclusion: the parametrization would map the same qubit twice, on the upper hemisphere and on the lower one. To mitigate this problem, we simply double the "latitude" to cover the entire sphere at "half speed":

$$x = \cos\phi \sin 2\theta, \tag{5.92}$$

$$y = \sin 2\theta \sin\phi, \tag{5.93}$$

$$z = \cos 2\theta. \tag{5.94}$$

Let us spend a few moments familiarizing ourselves with the Bloch sphere and its geometry. The north pole corresponds to the state $|0\rangle$ and the south pole corresponds to the state $1\rangle$. These two points can be taken as the geometrical image of the good old-fashioned bit. But there are many more qubits out there, and the Bloch sphere clearly shows it.

The precise meaning of the two angles in Equation (5.88) is the following: ϕ is the angle that $|\psi\rangle$ makes from x along the equator and θ is half the angle that $|\psi\rangle$ makes with the z axis.

When a qubit is measured in the standard basis, it collapses to a bit, or equivalently, to the north or south pole of the Bloch sphere. The probability of which pole the qubit will collapse to depends exclusively on how high or low the qubit is pointing, i.e., to its *latitude*. In particular, if the qubit happens to be on the equator, there is a 50–50 chance of it collapsing to either $|0\rangle$ or $|1\rangle$. As the angle θ expresses the qubit's latitude, it controls its chance of collapsing north or south.

Exercise 5.4.5   Consider a qubit whose θ is equal to $\frac{\pi}{4}$. Change it to $\frac{\pi}{3}$ and picture the result. Then compute its likelihood of collapsing to the south pole after being observed.   ■

Take an arbitrary arrow and rotate it around the z axis; in the geographical metaphor, you are changing its *longitude:*

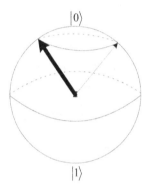

Notice that the probability of which classical state it will collapse to is not affected. Such a state change is called a **phase change**. In the representation given in Equation (5.88), this corresponds to altering the phase parameter $e^{i\phi}$.

Before we move on, one last important item: just as $|0\rangle$ and $|1\rangle$ sit on opposite sides of the sphere, so an arbitrary pair of orthogonal qubits is mapped to antipodal points of the Bloch sphere.

Exercise 5.4.6   Show that if a qubit has latitude 2θ and longitude ϕ on the sphere, its orthogonal lives in the antipode $\pi - 2\theta$ and $\pi + \phi$.   ■

That takes care of states of a qubit. What about the dynamics? The Bloch sphere is interesting in that every unitary 2-by-2 matrix (i.e., a one-qubit operation) can be visualized as a way of manipulating the sphere. We have seen in Chapter 2, page 66, that every unitary matrix is an isometry. This means that such a matrix maps qubits to qubits and the inner product is preserved. Geometrically, this corresponds to a rotation or an inversion of the Bloch sphere.

The X, Y, and Z Pauli matrices are ways of "flipping" the Bloch sphere $180°$ about the x, y, and z axes respectively. Remember that X is nothing more than the

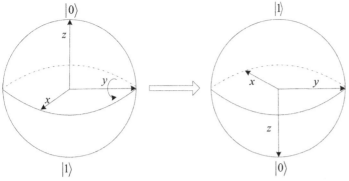

Figure 5.7. A rotation of the Bloch sphere at y.

NOT gate, and takes $|0\rangle$ to $|1\rangle$ and vice versa. But it does more; it takes everything above the equator to below the equator. The other Pauli matrices work similarly. Figure 5.7 shows the action of the Y operation.

There are times when we are not interested in performing a total 180° flip but just want to turn the Bloch sphere θ degrees along a particular direction.

The first such gates are the **phase shift** gates. It is defined as

$$R(\theta) = \begin{bmatrix} 1 & 0 \\ 0 & e^{\theta} \end{bmatrix}. \tag{5.95}$$

This gate performs the following operation on an arbitrary qubit:

$$\cos(\theta')|0\rangle + e^{i\phi}\sin(\theta')|1\rangle = \begin{bmatrix} \cos(\theta') \\ e^{i\phi}\sin(\theta') \end{bmatrix} \mapsto \begin{bmatrix} \cos(\theta') \\ e^{\theta}e^{i\phi}\sin(\theta') \end{bmatrix}. \tag{5.96}$$

This corresponds to a rotation that leaves the latitude alone and just changes the longitude. The new state of the qubit will remain unchanged. Only the phase will change.

There are also times when we want to rotate a particular number of degrees around the x, y, or z axis. These three matrices will perform the task:

$$R_x(\theta) = \cos\frac{\theta}{2}I - i\sin\frac{\theta}{2}X = \begin{bmatrix} \cos\frac{\theta}{2} & -i\sin\frac{\theta}{2} \\ -i\sin\frac{\theta}{2} & \cos\frac{\theta}{2} \end{bmatrix}, \tag{5.97}$$

$$R_y(\theta) = \cos\frac{\theta}{2}I - i\sin\frac{\theta}{2}Y = \begin{bmatrix} \cos\frac{\theta}{2} & -\sin\frac{\theta}{2} \\ \sin\frac{\theta}{2} & \cos\frac{\theta}{2} \end{bmatrix}, \tag{5.98}$$

$$R_z(\theta) = \cos\frac{\theta}{2}I - i\sin\frac{\theta}{2}Z = \begin{bmatrix} e^{-i\theta/2} & 0 \\ 0 & e^{i\theta/2} \end{bmatrix}. \tag{5.99}$$

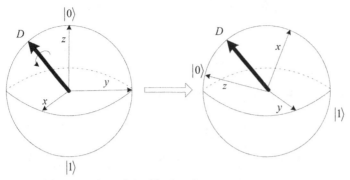

Figure 5.8. A rotation of the Bloch sphere at D.

There are rotations around axes besides the x, y, and z axes. Let $D = (D_x, D_y, D_z)$ be a three-dimensional vector of size 1 from the origin. This determines an axis of the Bloch sphere around which we can spin (see Figure 5.8). The rotation matrix is given as

$$R_D(\theta) = \cos\frac{\theta}{2} I - i \sin\frac{\theta}{2}(D_x X + D_y Y + D_z Z). \tag{5.100}$$

As we have just seen, the Bloch sphere is a very valuable tool when it comes to understanding qubits and one-qubit operations. What about n-qubits? It turns out there is a higher-dimensional analog of the sphere, but coming to grips with it is not easy. Indeed, it is a current research challenge to develop new ways of visualizing what happens when we manipulate several qubits at once. Entanglement, for instance, lies beyond the scope of the Bloch sphere (as it involves at least two qubits).

There are still other quantum gates. One of the central features of computer science is an operation that is done only under certain conditions and not under others. This is equivalent to an IF–THEN statement. If a certain (qu)bit is true, then a particular operation should be performed, otherwise the operation is not performed. For every n-qubit unitary operation U, we can create a unitary $(n + 1)$-qubit operation **controlled-**U or $^C U$.

$$
\begin{array}{c}
|x\rangle \qquad\qquad\qquad |x\rangle \\
\rule{3cm}{0.4pt}\bullet\rule{3cm}{0.4pt} \\
\rlap{} \\
\underset{n}{\rule{1.5cm}{0.4pt}}\boxed{U}\underset{n}{\rule{1.5cm}{0.4pt}}
\end{array}
\tag{5.101}
$$

This operation will perform the U operation if the top $|x\rangle$ input is a $|1\rangle$ and will simply perform the identity operation if $|x\rangle$ is $|0\rangle$.

For the simple case of

$$U = \begin{bmatrix} a & b \\ c & d \end{bmatrix}, \tag{5.102}$$

the controlled-U operation can be seen to be

$$
{}^C U = \begin{bmatrix} 1 & 0 & 0 & 0 \\ 0 & 1 & 0 & 0 \\ 0 & 0 & a & b \\ 0 & 0 & c & d \end{bmatrix}.
\tag{5.103}
$$

This same construction works for matrices larger than 2-by-2.

Exercise 5.4.7   Show that the constructed ${}^C U$ works as it should when the top qubit is set to $|0\rangle$ or set to $|1\rangle$.   ■

Exercise 5.4.8   Show that if U is unitary, then so is ${}^C U$.   ■

Exercise 5.4.9   Show that the Toffoli gate is nothing more than ${}^C({}^C\text{NOT})$.   ■

It is well known that every logical circuit can be simulated using only the AND gate and the NOT gate. We say that {AND, NOT} forms a set of **universal logical gates**. The NAND gate by itself is also a universal logical gate. We have also seen in Section 5.3 that both the Toffoli gate and the Fredkin gate are each universal logic gates. This leads to the obvious question: are there sets of quantum gates that can simulate all quantum gates? In other words, are there **universal quantum gates**? The answer is yes.[3] One set of universal quantum gates is

$$
\left\{ H, {}^C\text{NOT}, R\left(\cos^{-1}\left(\frac{3}{5} \right) \right) \right\},
\tag{5.104}
$$

that is, the Hadamard gate, the controlled-NOT gate, and this phase shift gate.

There is also a quantum gate called the **Deutsch gate**, $D(\theta)$, depicted as

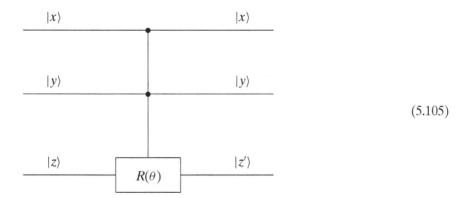

$$\tag{5.105}$$

[3] We must clarify what we mean by "simulate." In the classical world, we say that one circuit *Circ* simulates another circuit *Circ'* if for any possible inputs, the output for *Circ* will be the same for *Circ'*. Things in the quantum world are a tad more complicated. Because of the probabilistic nature of quantum computation, the outputs of a circuit are always probabilistic. So we have to reformulate what we mean when we talk about simulate. We shall not worry about this here.

which is very similar to the Toffoli gate. If the inputs $|x\rangle$ and $|y\rangle$ are both $|1\rangle$, then the phase shift operation $R(\theta)$ will act on the $|z\rangle$ input. Otherwise, the $|z'\rangle$ will simply be the same as the $|z\rangle$. When θ is not a rational multiple of π, $D(\theta)$ by itself is a universal three-qubit quantum gate. In other words, $D(\theta)$ will be able to mimic every other quantum gate.

Exercise 5.4.10   Show that the Toffoli gate is nothing more than $D(\frac{\pi}{2})$.   ■

Throughout the rest of this text, we shall demonstrate many of the operations that can be performed with quantum gates. However, there are limitations to what can be done with them. For one thing, every operation must be reversible. Another limitation is a consequence of the the the **No-Cloning Theorem.** This theorem says that it is impossible to clone an exact quantum state. In other words, it is impossible to make a copy of an arbitrary quantum state without first destroying the original. In "computerese," this says that we can "cut" and "paste" a quantum state, but we cannot "copy" and "paste" it. "Move is possible. Copy is impossible."

What is the difficulty? How would such a cloning operation look? Let $\mathbb{V}$ represent a quantum system. As we intend to clone states in this system, we shall "double" this vector space and deal with $\mathbb{V} \otimes \mathbb{V}$. A potential cloning operation would be a linear map (indeed unitary!)

$$C : \mathbb{V} \otimes \mathbb{V} \longrightarrow \mathbb{V} \otimes \mathbb{V}, \tag{5.106}$$

that should take an arbitrary state $|x\rangle$ in the first system and, perhaps, nothing in the second system and clone $|x\rangle$, i.e.,

$$C(|x\rangle \otimes 0) = (|x\rangle \otimes |x\rangle). \tag{5.107}$$

This seems like a harmless enough operation, but is it? If C is a candidate for cloning, then certainly on the basic states

$$C(|0\rangle \otimes |0\rangle) = |0\rangle \otimes |0\rangle \quad \text{and} \quad C(|1\rangle \otimes |0\rangle) = |1\rangle \otimes |1\rangle. \tag{5.108}$$

Because C must be linear, we should have that

$$C((c_1|0\rangle + c_2|1\rangle) \otimes |0\rangle) = c_1|0\rangle \otimes |0\rangle + c_2|1\rangle \otimes |1\rangle, \tag{5.109}$$

for an arbitrary quantum state, i.e., an arbitrary *superposition* of $|0\rangle$ and $|1\rangle$. Suppose we start with $\frac{|x\rangle+|y\rangle}{\sqrt{2}}$. Cloning such a state would mean that

$$C\left(\frac{|x\rangle + |y\rangle}{\sqrt{2}} \otimes 0\right) = \left(\frac{|x\rangle + |y\rangle}{\sqrt{2}} \otimes \frac{|x\rangle + |y\rangle}{\sqrt{2}}\right). \tag{5.110}$$

However, if we insist that C is a quantum operation, then C must be linear,[4] and hence, must respect the addition and the scalar multiplication in $\mathbb{V} \otimes \mathbb{V}$. If C was

---

[4] Just a reminder: C being linear means that

$$C(|\phi\rangle + |\psi\rangle) = C(|\phi\rangle) + C(|\psi\rangle) \tag{5.111}$$

and

$$C(c|\phi\rangle) = cC(|\phi\rangle). \tag{5.112}$$

linear, then

$$C\left(\frac{|x\rangle + |y\rangle}{\sqrt{2}} \otimes 0\right) = C\left(\frac{1}{\sqrt{2}}(|x\rangle + |y\rangle) \otimes 0\right) = \frac{1}{\sqrt{2}}C((|x\rangle + |y\rangle) \otimes 0)$$

$$= \frac{1}{\sqrt{2}}(C(|x\rangle \otimes 0 + |y\rangle \otimes 0)) = \frac{1}{\sqrt{2}}(C(|x\rangle \otimes 0) + C(|y\rangle \otimes 0))$$

$$= \frac{1}{\sqrt{2}}((|x\rangle \otimes |x\rangle) + (|y\rangle \otimes |y\rangle)) = \frac{(|x\rangle \otimes |x\rangle) + (|y\rangle \otimes |y\rangle)}{\sqrt{2}}.$$

$$(5.113)$$

But

$$\left(\frac{|x\rangle + |y\rangle}{\sqrt{2}} \otimes \frac{|x\rangle + |y\rangle}{\sqrt{2}}\right) \neq \frac{(|x\rangle \otimes |x\rangle) + (|y\rangle \otimes |y\rangle)}{\sqrt{2}}. \qquad (5.114)$$

So C is not a linear map,[5] and hence is not permitted.

In contrast to cloning, there is no problem **transporting** arbitrary quantum states from one system to another. Such a transporting operation would be a linear map

$$T : \mathbb{V} \otimes \mathbb{V} \longrightarrow \mathbb{V} \otimes \mathbb{V}, \qquad (5.115)$$

that should take an arbitrary state $|x\rangle$ in the first system and, say, nothing in the second system, and transport $|x\rangle$ to the second system, leaving nothing in the first system, i.e.,

$$T(|x\rangle \otimes 0) = (0 \otimes |x\rangle). \qquad (5.116)$$

We do not run into the same problem as earlier if we transport a superposition of states. In detail,

$$T\left(\frac{|x\rangle + |y\rangle}{\sqrt{2}} \otimes 0\right) = T\left(\frac{1}{\sqrt{2}}(|x\rangle + |y\rangle) \otimes 0\right)$$

$$= \frac{1}{\sqrt{2}}T((|x\rangle + |y\rangle) \otimes 0) = \frac{1}{\sqrt{2}}T((|x\rangle \otimes 0) + (|y\rangle \otimes 0))$$

$$= \frac{1}{\sqrt{2}}(T(|x\rangle \otimes 0) + T(|y\rangle \otimes 0)) = \frac{1}{\sqrt{2}}((0 \otimes |x\rangle) + (0 \otimes |y\rangle))$$

$$= \frac{(|0 \otimes (|x\rangle + |y\rangle))}{\sqrt{2}} = 0 \otimes \frac{(|x\rangle + |y\rangle)}{\sqrt{2}}. \qquad (5.117)$$

This is exactly what we would expect from a transporting operation.[6]

Fans of Star Trek have long known that when Scotty "beams" Captain Kirk down from the Starship Enterprise to the planet Zygon, he is transporting Captain Kirk to Zygon. The Kirk of the Enterprise gets destroyed and only the Zygon Kirk survives. Captain Kirk is not being cloned. He is being transported. (Would we really want many copies of Captain Kirk all over the Universe?)

---

[5] C is, however, a legitimate set map.
[6] In fact, we will show how to transport arbitrary quantum states at the end of Chapter 9.

The reader might see an apparent contradiction in what we have stated. On the one hand, we have stated that the Toffoli and Fredkin gates can mimic the fanout gate. The matrices for the Toffoli and Fredkin gates are unitary, and hence they are quantum gates. On the other hand, the no-cloning theorem says that no quantum gates can mimic the fanout operation. What is wrong here? Let us carefully examine the Fredkin gate. We have seen how this gate performs the cloning operation

$$(x, 1, 0) \qquad \mapsto \qquad (x, \neg x, x). \tag{5.118}$$

However, what would happen if the x input was in a superposition of states say, $\frac{|0\rangle + |1\rangle}{\sqrt{2}}$, while leaving $y = 1$ and $z = 0$. This would correspond to the state

$$
\begin{array}{cccccccc}
\mathbf{000} & \mathbf{001} & \mathbf{010} & \mathbf{011} & \mathbf{100} & \mathbf{101} & \mathbf{110} & \mathbf{111}
\end{array}^{T}
$$
$$
\begin{bmatrix} 0 & 0 & \frac{1}{\sqrt{2}} & 0 & 0 & 0 & \frac{1}{\sqrt{2}} & 0 \end{bmatrix}. \tag{5.119}
$$

Multiplying this state with the Fredkin gate gives us

$$
\begin{array}{c}
 \\
\mathbf{000} \\
\mathbf{001} \\
\mathbf{010} \\
\mathbf{011} \\
\mathbf{100} \\
\mathbf{101} \\
\mathbf{110} \\
\mathbf{111}
\end{array}
\begin{array}{c}
\begin{array}{cccccccc}
\mathbf{000} & \mathbf{001} & \mathbf{010} & \mathbf{011} & \mathbf{100} & \mathbf{101} & \mathbf{110} & \mathbf{111}
\end{array} \\
\begin{bmatrix}
1 & 0 & 0 & 0 & 0 & 0 & 0 & 0 \\
0 & 1 & 0 & 0 & 0 & 0 & 0 & 0 \\
0 & 0 & 1 & 0 & 0 & 0 & 0 & 0 \\
0 & 0 & 0 & 1 & 0 & 0 & 0 & 0 \\
0 & 0 & 0 & 0 & 1 & 0 & 0 & 0 \\
0 & 0 & 0 & 0 & 0 & 0 & 1 & 0 \\
0 & 0 & 0 & 0 & 0 & 1 & 0 & 0 \\
0 & 0 & 0 & 0 & 0 & 0 & 0 & 1
\end{bmatrix}
\end{array}
\begin{bmatrix}
0 \\ 0 \\ \frac{1}{\sqrt{2}} \\ 0 \\ 0 \\ 0 \\ 0 \\ \frac{1}{\sqrt{2}} \\ 0
\end{bmatrix}
=
\begin{bmatrix}
0 \\ 0 \\ \frac{1}{\sqrt{2}} \\ 0 \\ 0 \\ 0 \\ \frac{1}{\sqrt{2}} \\ 0
\end{bmatrix}. \tag{5.120}
$$

The resulting state is

$$\frac{|0, 1, 0\rangle + |1, 0, 1\rangle}{\sqrt{2}}. \tag{5.121}$$

So, whereas on a classical bit x, the Fredkin gate performs the fanout operation, on a superposition of states the Fredkin gate performs the following very strange operation:

$$\left(\frac{|0\rangle + |1\rangle}{\sqrt{2}}, 1, 0 \right) \qquad \mapsto \qquad \frac{|0, 1, 0\rangle + |1, 0, 1\rangle}{\sqrt{2}}. \tag{5.122}$$

This strange operation is not a fanout operation. Thus, the no-cloning theorem safely stands.

Exercise 5.4.11 Do a similar analysis for the Toffoli gate. Show that the way we set the Toffoli gate to perform the fanout operation does not clone a superposition of states. ∎

. . . .

Reader Tip. The no-cloning theorem is of major importance in Chapter 9.   ♡
. . . .

. . . .

References: The basics of qubits and quantum gates can be found in any text-book on quantum computing. They were first formulated by David Deutsch in 1989 (Deutsch, 1989).

Section 5.2 is simply a reformulation of basic computer architecture in terms of matrices.

The history of reversible computation can be found in Bennett (1988). The readable article (Landauer, 1991) by one of the forefathers of reversible computation is strongly recommended.

The no-cloning theorem was first proved in Dieks (1982) and Wootters and Zurek (1982).

6

Algorithms

Computer Science is no more about computers than astronomy is about telescopes.

E.W. Dijkstra

Algorithms are often developed long before the machines they are supposed to run on. Classical algorithms predate classical computers by millennia, and similarly, there exist several quantum algorithms before any large-scale quantum computers have seen the light of day. These algorithms manipulate qubits to solve problems and, in general, they solve these tasks more efficiently than classical computers.

Rather than describing the quantum algorithms in the chronological order in which they were discovered, we choose to present them in order of increasing difficulty. The core ideas of each algorithm are based on previous ones. We start at tutorial pace, introducing new concepts in a thorough way. Section 6.1 describes Deutsch's algorithm that determines a property of functions from $\{0, 1\}$ to $\{0, 1\}$. In Section 6.2 we generalize this algorithm to the Deutsch–Jozsa algorithm, which deals with a similar property for functions from $\{0, 1\}^n$ to $\{0, 1\}$. Simon's periodicity algorithm is described in Section 6.3. Here we determine patterns of a function from $\{0, 1\}^n$ to $\{0, 1\}^n$. Section 6.4 goes through Grover's search algorithm that can search an unordered array of size n in $\sqrt{n}$ time as opposed to the usual n time. The chapter builds up to the ground-breaking Shor's factoring algorithm done in Section 6.5. This quantum algorithm can factor numbers in polynomial time. There are no known classical algorithms that can perform this feat in such time.

....

Reader Tip. This chapter may be a bit overwhelming on the first reading. After reading Section 6.1, the reader can move on to Section 6.2 or Section 6.4. Shor's algorithm can safely be read after Section 6.2. ♡

....

170

6.1 DEUTSCH'S ALGORITHM

All quantum algorithms work with the following basic framework:

- The system will start with the qubits in a particular classical state.
- From there the system is put into a superposition of many states.
- This is followed by acting on this superposition with several unitary operations.
- And finally, a measurement of the qubits.

Of course, there will be several variations of this theme. Nevertheless, it will be helpful to keep this general scheme in mind as we proceed.

The simplest quantum algorithm is Deutsch's algorithm, which is a nice algorithm that solves a slightly contrived problem. This algorithm is concerned with functions from the set $\{0, 1\}$ to the set $\{0, 1\}$. There are four such functions that might be visualized as

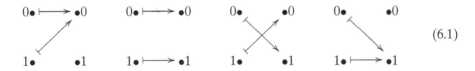

(6.1)

Call a function $f : \{0, 1\} \longrightarrow \{0, 1\}$ **balanced** if $f(0) \neq f(1)$, i.e., it is one to one. In contrast, call a function **constant** if $f(0) = f(1)$. Of the four functions, two are balanced and two are constant.

Deutsch's algorithm solves the following problem: Given a function $f : \{0, 1\} \longrightarrow \{0, 1\}$ as a black box, where one can evaluate an input, but cannot "look inside" and "see" how the function is defined, determine if the function is balanced or constant.

With a classical computer, one would have to first evaluate f on one input, then evaluate f on the second input, and finally, compare the outputs. The following decision tree shows what a classical computer must do:

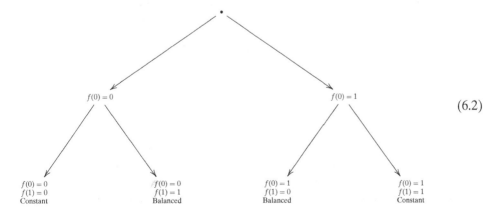

(6.2)

The point is that with a classical computer, f must be evaluated twice. Can we do better with a quantum computer?

A quantum computer can be in a superposition of two basic states at the same time. We shall use this superposition of states to evaluate both inputs at one time.

In classical computing, evaluating a given function f corresponds to performing the following operation:

$$x \quad \boxed{f} \quad f(x) \qquad (6.3)$$

As we discussed in Chapter 5, such a function can be thought of as a matrix acting on the input. For instance, the function

$$
\begin{array}{cc}
0\bullet & \bullet 0 \\
& \diagdown\diagup \\
& \diagup\diagdown \\
1\bullet & \bullet 1
\end{array}
\qquad (6.4)
$$

is equivalent to the matrix

$$
\begin{array}{c}
\;\mathbf{0}\;\;\mathbf{1} \\
\begin{array}{c}\mathbf{0}\\\mathbf{1}\end{array}
\begin{bmatrix} 0 & 1 \\ 1 & 0 \end{bmatrix}.
\end{array}
\qquad (6.5)
$$

Multiplying state $|0\rangle$ on the right of this matrix would result in state $|1\rangle$, and multiplying state $|1\rangle$ on the right of this matrix would result in state $|0\rangle$. The column name is to be thought of as the input and the row name as the output.

Exercise 6.1.1 Describe the matrices for the other three functions from $\{0, 1\}$ to $\{0, 1\}$. ∎

However, this will not be enough for a quantum system. Such a system demands a little something extra: every gate must be unitary (and thus reversible). Given the output, we must be able to find the input. If f is the name of the function, then the following black-box U_f will be the quantum gate that we shall employ to evaluate input:

$$
\begin{array}{ccc}
|x\rangle & \boxed{} & |x\rangle \\
& U_f & \\
|y\rangle & & |y \oplus f(x)\rangle
\end{array}
\qquad (6.6)
$$

The top input, $|x\rangle$, will be the qubit value that one wishes to evaluate and the bottom input, $|y\rangle$, controls the output. The top output will be the same as the input qubit $|x\rangle$ and the bottom output will be the qubit $|y \oplus f(x)\rangle$, where $\oplus$ is XOR, the exclusive-or operation (binary addition modulo 2.) We are going to write from left to right the top qubit first and then the bottom. So we say that this function takes the state $|x, y\rangle$ to the state $|x, y \oplus f(x)\rangle$. If $y = 0$, this simplifies $|x, 0\rangle$ to $|x, 0 \oplus f(x)\rangle = |x, f(x)\rangle$. This gate can be seen to be reversible as we may demonstrate by simply looking at the following circuit:

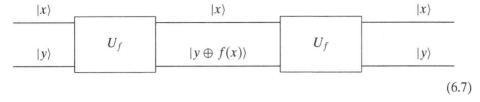

$$(6.7)$$

State $|x, y\rangle$ goes to $|x, y \oplus f(x)\rangle$, which further goes to

$$|x, (y \oplus f(x)) \oplus f(x)\rangle = |x, y \oplus (f(x) \oplus f(x))\rangle = |x, y \oplus 0\rangle = |x, y\rangle, \quad (6.8)$$

where the first equality is due to the associativity of $\oplus$ and the second equality holds because $\oplus$ is idempotent. From this we see that U_f is its own inverse.

In quantum systems, evaluating f is equivalent to multiplying a state by the unitary matrix U_f. For function (6.4), the corresponding unitary matrix, U_f, is

$$
\begin{array}{c}
\begin{array}{cccc} \mathbf{00} & \mathbf{01} & \mathbf{10} & \mathbf{11} \end{array} \\
\begin{array}{c} \mathbf{00} \\ \mathbf{01} \\ \mathbf{10} \\ \mathbf{11} \end{array}
\begin{bmatrix}
0 & 1 & 0 & 0 \\
1 & 0 & 0 & 0 \\
0 & 0 & 1 & 0 \\
0 & 0 & 0 & 1
\end{bmatrix}.
\end{array}
\qquad (6.9)
$$

Remember that the top column name corresponds to the input $|x, y\rangle$ and the left-hand row name corresponds to the outputs $|x', y'\rangle$. A 1 in the xy column and the $x'y'$ row means that for input $|x, y\rangle$, the output will be $|x', y'\rangle$.

Exercise 6.1.2 What is the adjoint of the matrix given in Equation (6.9)? Show that this matrix is its own inverse. ∎

Exercise 6.1.3 Give the unitary matrices that correspond to the other three functions from $\{0, 1\}$ to $\{0, 1\}$. Show that each of the matrices is its own adjoint and hence all are reversible and unitary. ∎

Let us remind ourselves of the task at hand. We are given such a matrix that expresses a function but we cannot "look inside" the matrix to "see" how it is defined. We are asked to determine if the function is balanced or constant.

Let us take a first stab at a quantum algorithm to solve this problem. Rather than evaluating f twice, we shall try our trick of superposition of states. Instead of having the top input to be either in state $|0\rangle$ or in state $|1\rangle$, we shall put the top input in state

$$\frac{|0\rangle + |1\rangle}{\sqrt{2}}, \qquad (6.10)$$

which is "half-way" $|0\rangle$ and "half-way" $|1\rangle$. The Hadamard matrix can place a qubit in such a state.

$$H|0\rangle = \begin{bmatrix} \frac{1}{\sqrt{2}} & \frac{1}{\sqrt{2}} \\ \frac{1}{\sqrt{2}} & -\frac{1}{\sqrt{2}} \end{bmatrix} \begin{bmatrix} 1 \\ 0 \end{bmatrix} = \begin{bmatrix} \frac{1}{\sqrt{2}} \\ \frac{1}{\sqrt{2}} \end{bmatrix} = \frac{|0\rangle + |1\rangle}{\sqrt{2}}. \qquad (6.11)$$

The obvious (but not necessarily correct) state to put the bottom input into is state $|0\rangle$. Thus we have the following quantum circuit:

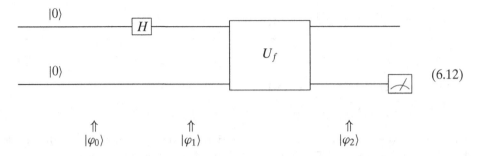

(6.12)

The $|\varphi_j\rangle$ at the bottom of the quantum circuit will be used to describe the state of the qubits at each time click.

In terms of matrices this circuit corresponds to

$$U_f(H \otimes I)(|0\rangle \otimes |0\rangle) = U_f(H \otimes I)(|0, 0\rangle).$$

(6.13)

The tensor product $|0, 0\rangle$ can be written as

$$\begin{matrix} \mathbf{00} \\ \mathbf{01} \\ \mathbf{10} \\ \mathbf{11} \end{matrix} \begin{bmatrix} 1 \\ 0 \\ 0 \\ 0 \end{bmatrix}$$

(6.14)

and the entire circuit is then

$$U_f(H \otimes I) \begin{matrix} \mathbf{00} \\ \mathbf{01} \\ \mathbf{10} \\ \mathbf{11} \end{matrix} \begin{bmatrix} 1 \\ 0 \\ 0 \\ 0 \end{bmatrix}.$$

(6.15)

We shall carefully examine the states of the system at every time click. The system starts in

$$|\varphi_0\rangle = |0\rangle \otimes |0\rangle = |0, 0\rangle.$$

(6.16)

We then apply the Hadamard matrix only to the top input – leaving the bottom input alone – to get

$$|\varphi_1\rangle = \left[\frac{|0\rangle + |1\rangle}{\sqrt{2}} \right] |0\rangle = \frac{|0, 0\rangle + |1, 0\rangle}{\sqrt{2}}.$$

(6.17)

After multiplying with U_f, we have

$$|\varphi_2\rangle = \frac{|0, f(0)\rangle + |1, f(1)\rangle}{\sqrt{2}}.$$ (6.18)

For function (6.4), the state $|\varphi_2\rangle$ would be

$$|\varphi_2\rangle = \begin{array}{c} \\ 00 \\ 01 \\ 10 \\ 11 \end{array} \begin{array}{cccc} \mathbf{00} & \mathbf{01} & \mathbf{10} & \mathbf{11} \\ \left[\begin{array}{cccc} 0 & 1 & 0 & 0 \\ 1 & 0 & 0 & 0 \\ 0 & 0 & 1 & 0 \\ 0 & 0 & 0 & 1 \end{array}\right] \end{array} \begin{array}{c} 00 \\ 01 \\ 10 \\ 11 \end{array} \left[\begin{array}{c} \frac{1}{\sqrt{2}} \\ 0 \\ \frac{1}{\sqrt{2}} \\ 0 \end{array}\right] = \begin{array}{c} 00 \\ 01 \\ 10 \\ 11 \end{array} \left[\begin{array}{c} 0 \\ \frac{1}{\sqrt{2}} \\ \frac{1}{\sqrt{2}} \\ 0 \end{array}\right] = \frac{|0, 1\rangle + |1, 0\rangle}{\sqrt{2}}.$$ (6.19)

Exercise 6.1.4 Using the matrices calculated in Exercise 6.1.3, determine the state $|\varphi_2\rangle$ for the other three functions. ■

If we measure the top qubit, there will be a 50–50 chance of finding it in state $|0\rangle$ and a 50–50 chance of finding it in state $|1\rangle$. Similarly, there is no real information to be gotten by measuring the bottom qubit. So the obvious algorithm does not work. We need a better trick.

Let us take another stab at solving our problem. Rather than leaving the bottom qubit in state $|0\rangle$, let us put it in the superposition state:

$$\frac{|0\rangle - |1\rangle}{\sqrt{2}} = \left[\begin{array}{c} \frac{1}{\sqrt{2}} \\ -\frac{1}{\sqrt{2}} \end{array}\right].$$ (6.20)

Notice the minus sign. Even though there is a negation, this state is also "half-way" in state $|0\rangle$ and "half-way" in state $|1\rangle$. This change of phase will help us get our desired results. We can get to this superposition of states by multiplying state $|1\rangle$ with the Hadamard matrix. We shall leave the top qubit as an ambiguous $|x\rangle$.

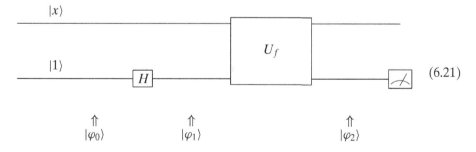

(6.21)

In terms of matrices, this becomes

$$U_f(I \otimes H)|x, 1\rangle.$$ (6.22)

Let us look carefully at how the states of the qubits change.

$$|\varphi_0\rangle = |x, 1\rangle. \tag{6.23}$$

After the Hadamard matrix, we have

$$|\varphi_1\rangle = |x\rangle \left[\frac{|0\rangle - |1\rangle}{\sqrt{2}} \right] = \frac{|x, 0\rangle - |x, 1\rangle}{\sqrt{2}}. \tag{6.24}$$

Applying U_f, we get

$$|\varphi_2\rangle = |x\rangle \left[\frac{|0 \oplus f(x)\rangle - |1 \oplus f(x)\rangle}{\sqrt{2}} \right] = |x\rangle \left[\frac{|f(x)\rangle - |\overline{f(x)}\rangle}{\sqrt{2}} \right], \tag{6.25}$$

where $\overline{f(x)}$ means the opposite of $f(x)$. Therefore, we have

$$|\varphi_2\rangle = \begin{cases} |x\rangle \left[\frac{|0\rangle - |1\rangle}{\sqrt{2}} \right], & \text{if } f(x) = 0, \\ |x\rangle \left[\frac{|1\rangle - |0\rangle}{\sqrt{2}} \right], & \text{if } f(x) = 1. \end{cases} \tag{6.26}$$

Remembering that $a - b = (-1)(b - a)$, we might write this as

$$|\varphi_2\rangle = (-1)^{f(x)}|x\rangle \left[\frac{|0\rangle - |1\rangle}{\sqrt{2}} \right]. \tag{6.27}$$

What would happen if we evaluate either the top or the bottom state? Again, this does not really help us. We do not gain any information if we measure the top qubit or the bottom qubit. The top qubit will be in state $|x\rangle$ and the bottom qubit will be either in state $|0\rangle$ or in state $|1\rangle$. We need something more.

Now let us combine both these attempts to actually give Deutsch's algorithm.

Deutsch's algorithm works by putting *both* the top and the bottom qubits into a superposition. We will also put the results of the top qubit through a Hadamard matrix.

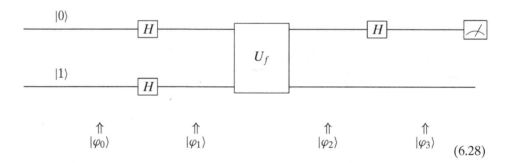

$$(H \otimes I)U_f(H \otimes H)|0, 1\rangle \tag{6.28}$$

In terms of matrices this becomes

$$(H \otimes I)U_f(H \otimes H)|0, 1\rangle \tag{6.29}$$

or

$$(H \otimes I)U_f(H \otimes H) \begin{matrix} \mathbf{00} \\ \mathbf{01} \\ \mathbf{10} \\ \mathbf{11} \end{matrix} \begin{bmatrix} 0 \\ 1 \\ 0 \\ 0 \end{bmatrix}. \tag{6.30}$$

At each point of the algorithm the states are as follows:

$$|\varphi_0\rangle = |0, 1\rangle, \tag{6.31}$$

$$|\varphi_1\rangle = \left[\frac{|0\rangle + |1\rangle}{\sqrt{2}}\right]\left[\frac{|0\rangle - |1\rangle}{\sqrt{2}}\right] = \frac{+|0, 0\rangle - |0, 1\rangle + |1, 0\rangle - |1, 1\rangle}{2} = \begin{matrix} \mathbf{00} \\ \mathbf{01} \\ \mathbf{10} \\ \mathbf{11} \end{matrix} \begin{bmatrix} +\frac{1}{2} \\ -\frac{1}{2} \\ +\frac{1}{2} \\ -\frac{1}{2} \end{bmatrix}. \tag{6.32}$$

We saw from our last attempt at solving this problem that when we put the bottom qubit into a superposition and then multiply by U_f, we will be in the superposition

$$(-1)^{f(x)}|x\rangle\left[\frac{|0\rangle - |1\rangle}{\sqrt{2}}\right]. \tag{6.33}$$

Now, with $|x\rangle$ in a superposition, we have

$$|\varphi_2\rangle = \left[\frac{(-1)^{f(0)}|0\rangle + (-1)^{f(1)}|1\rangle}{\sqrt{2}}\right]\left[\frac{|0\rangle - |1\rangle}{\sqrt{2}}\right]. \tag{6.34}$$

For example, if $f(0) = 1$ and $f(1) = 0$, the top qubit becomes

$$\frac{(-1)|1\rangle + (+1)|1\rangle}{\sqrt{2}} = (-1)\left[\frac{|0\rangle - |1\rangle}{\sqrt{2}}\right]. \tag{6.35}$$

Exercise 6.1.5 For each of the other three functions from the set $\{0, 1\}$ to the set $\{0, 1\}$, describe what $|\varphi_2\rangle$ would be. ∎

For a general function f, let us look carefully at

$$(-1)^{f(0)}|0\rangle + (-1)^{f(1)}|1\rangle. \tag{6.36}$$

If f is constant, this becomes either

$$+1(|0\rangle + |1\rangle) \text{ or } -1(|0\rangle + |1\rangle) \tag{6.37}$$

(depending on being constantly 0 or constantly 1).

If f is balanced, it becomes either

$$+1(|0\rangle - |1\rangle) \text{ or } -1(|0\rangle - |1\rangle) \tag{6.38}$$

(depending on which way it is balanced).

Summing up, we have that

$$|\varphi_2\rangle = \begin{cases} (\pm 1)\left[\frac{|0\rangle + |1\rangle}{\sqrt{2}}\right]\left[\frac{|0\rangle - |1\rangle}{\sqrt{2}}\right], & \text{if } f \text{ is constant}, \\ (\pm 1)\left[\frac{|0\rangle - |1\rangle}{\sqrt{2}}\right]\left[\frac{|0\rangle - |1\rangle}{\sqrt{2}}\right], & \text{if } f \text{ is balanced}. \end{cases} \tag{6.39}$$

Remembering that the Hadamard matrix is its own inverse that takes $\frac{|0\rangle + |1\rangle}{\sqrt{2}}$ to $|0\rangle$ and takes $\frac{|0\rangle - |1\rangle}{\sqrt{2}}$ to $|1\rangle$, we apply the Hadamard matrix to the top qubit to get

$$|\varphi_3\rangle = \begin{cases} (\pm 1)|0\rangle\left[\frac{|0\rangle - |1\rangle}{\sqrt{2}}\right], & \text{if } f \text{ is constant}, \\ (\pm 1)|1\rangle\left[\frac{|0\rangle - |1\rangle}{\sqrt{2}}\right], & \text{if } f \text{ is balanced}. \end{cases} \tag{6.40}$$

For example, if $f(0) = 1$ and $f(1) = 0$, then we get

$$|\varphi_3\rangle = -1|1\rangle\left[\frac{|0\rangle - |1\rangle}{\sqrt{2}}\right]. \tag{6.41}$$

Exercise 6.1.6 For each of the other three functions from the set $\{0, 1\}$ to the set $\{0, 1\}$, calculate the value of $|\varphi_3\rangle$. ∎

Now, we simply measure the top qubit. If it is in state $|0\rangle$, then we know that f is a constant function, otherwise it is a balanced function. This was all accomplished with only one function evaluation as opposed to the two evaluations that the classical algorithm demands.

Notice that although the ± 1 tells us even more information, namely, which of the two balanced functions or two constant functions we have, measurement will not grant us this information. Upon measuring, if the function is balanced, we will measure $|1\rangle$ regardless if the state was $(-1)|1\rangle$ or $(+1)|1\rangle$.

The reader might be bothered by the fact that the output of the top qubit of U_f should not change from being the same as the input. However, the inclusion of the Hadamard matrices changes things around, as we saw in Section 5.3. This is the essence of the fact that the top and the bottom qubits are entangled.

Did we perform a magic trick here? Did we gain information that was not there? Not really. There are four possible functions, and we saw in decision tree (6.2) that with a classical computer we needed two bits of information to determine which of the four functions we were given. What we are really doing here is *changing around the information*. We might determine which of the four functions is the case by asking the following two questions: "Is the function balanced or constant?" and "What is the value of the function on 0?" The answers to these two questions uniquely describe each of the four functions, as described by the following decision tree:

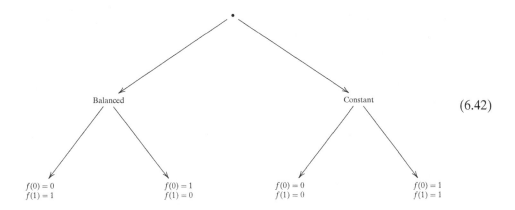

(6.42)

The Hadamard matrices are changing the question that we are asking (change of basis). The intuition behind the Deutsch algorithm is that we are really just performing a change of basis problem as discussed at the end of Section 2.3. We might rewrite quantum circuit (6.28) as

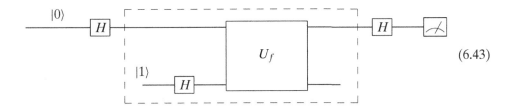

(6.43)

We start in the canonical basis. The first Hadamard matrix is used as a change of basis matrix to go into a balanced superposition of basic states. While in this noncanonical basis, we evaluate f with the bottom qubit in a superposition. The last Hadamard matrix is used as a change of basis matrix to revert back to the canonical basis.

6.2 THE DEUTSCH–JOZSA ALGORITHM

Let us generalize the Deutsch algorithm to other functions. Rather than talking about functions $f : \{0, 1\} \longrightarrow \{0, 1\}$, let us talk about functions with a larger domain. Consider functions $f : \{0, 1\}^n \longrightarrow \{0, 1\}$, which accept a string of n 0's and 1's and outputs a zero or one. The domain might be thought of as any natural number from 0 to $2^n - 1$.

We shall call a function $f : \{0, 1\}^n \longrightarrow \{0, 1\}$ **balanced** if exactly half of the inputs go to 0 (and the other half go to 1). Call a function **constant** if *all* the inputs go to 0 or *all* the inputs go to 1.

Exercise 6.2.1 How many functions are there from $\{0, 1\}^n$ to $\{0, 1\}$? How many of them are balanced? How many of them are constant? ∎

The Deutsch–Jozsa algorithm solves the following problem: Suppose you are given a function from $\{0, 1\}^n$ to $\{0, 1\}$ which you can evaluate but cannot "see" the way it is defined. Suppose further that you are assured that the function is either balanced or constant. Determine if the function is balanced or constant. Notice that when $n = 1$, this is exactly the problem that the Deutsch algorithm solved.

Classically, this problem can be solved by evaluating the function on different inputs. The best case scenario is when the first two different inputs have different outputs, which assures us that the function is balanced. In contrast, to be sure that the function is constant, one must evaluate the function on more than half the possible inputs. So the worst case scenario requires $\frac{2^n}{2} + 1 = 2^{n-1} + 1$ function evaluations. Can we do better?

In the last section, we solved the problem by entering into a superposition of two possible input states. In this section, we solve the problem by entering a superposition of all 2^n possible input states.

The function f will be given as a unitary matrix that we shall depict as

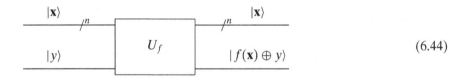

$$(6.44)$$

with n qubits (denoted as ———/^{n}———) as the top input and output. For the rest of this chapter, a binary string is denoted by a boldface letter. So we write the top input as $|\mathbf{x}\rangle = |x_0 x_1 \ldots x_{n-1}\rangle$. The bottom entering control qubit is $|y\rangle$. The top output is $|\mathbf{x}\rangle$ which will not be changed by U_f. The bottom output of U_f is the single qubit $|y \oplus f(\mathbf{x})\rangle$. Remember that although $\mathbf{x}$ is n bits, $f(\mathbf{x})$ is one bit and hence we can use the binary operation $\oplus$. It is not hard to see that U_f is its own inverse.

Example 6.2.1 Consider the following balanced function from $\{0, 1\}^2$ to $\{0, 1\}$:

$$(6.45)$$

This function shall be represented by the following 8-by-8 unitary matrix:

$$
\begin{array}{c}
\begin{array}{cccccccc}
\mathbf{00,0} & \mathbf{00,1} & \mathbf{01,0} & \mathbf{01,1} & \mathbf{10,0} & \mathbf{10,1} & \mathbf{11,0} & \mathbf{11,1}
\end{array} \\
\begin{array}{c}
\mathbf{00,0} \\ \mathbf{00,1} \\ \mathbf{01,0} \\ \mathbf{01,1} \\ \mathbf{10,0} \\ \mathbf{10,1} \\ \mathbf{11,0} \\ \mathbf{11,1}
\end{array}
\left[
\begin{array}{cccccccc}
 & 1 & & & & & & \\
1 & & & & & & & \\
 & & & & 1 & & & \\
 & & & 1 & & & & \\
 & & & & & 1 & & \\
 & & & & & & 1 & \\
 & & & & & & & 1 \\
 & & & & & & & 1
\end{array}
\right]
\end{array}
\tag{6.46}
$$

(the zeros are omitted for readability). □

Exercise 6.2.2 Consider the balanced function from $\{0,1\}^2$ to $\{0,1\}$:

$$\tag{6.47}$$

Give the corresponding 8-by-8 unitary matrix. ■

Exercise 6.2.3 Consider the function from $\{0,1\}^2$ to $\{0,1\}$ that always outputs a 1. Give the corresponding 8-by-8 unitary matrix. ■

In order to place a single qubit in a superposition of $|0\rangle$ and $|1\rangle$, we used a single Hadamard matrix. To place n qubits in a superposition, we are going to use the tensor product of n Hadamard matrices. What does such a tensor product look like? It will be helpful to do some warm-up exercises. Let us calculate H, $H \otimes H$ which we may write as $H^{\otimes 2}$, and $H \otimes H \otimes H = H^{\otimes 3}$; and look for a pattern. Our goal will be to find a pattern for $H^{\otimes n}$.

Remember that the Hadamard matrix is defined as

$$
H = \frac{1}{\sqrt{2}}
\begin{array}{c}
\begin{array}{cc} \mathbf{0} & \mathbf{1} \end{array} \\
\begin{array}{c} \mathbf{0} \\ \mathbf{1} \end{array}
\left[
\begin{array}{cc}
1 & 1 \\
1 & -1
\end{array}
\right]
\end{array}.
\tag{6.48}
$$

Notice that $H[i, j] = \frac{1}{\sqrt{2}}(-1)^{i \wedge j}$, where i and j are the row and column numbers in binary and $\wedge$ is the AND operation. We might then write the Hadamard matrix as

$$H = \frac{1}{\sqrt{2}} \begin{array}{c} \\ 0 \\ 1 \end{array} \begin{bmatrix} (-1)^{0 \wedge 0} & (-1)^{0 \wedge 1} \\ (-1)^{1 \wedge 0} & (-1)^{1 \wedge 1} \end{bmatrix}. \tag{6.49}$$

Notice that we are thinking of 0 and 1 as both Boolean values and numbers that are exponents. (Remember: $(-1)^0 = 1$ and $(-1)^1 = -1$.) With this trick in mind we can then calculate

$$H^{\otimes 2} = H \otimes H = \frac{1}{\sqrt{2}} \begin{array}{c} \\ 0 \\ 1 \end{array} \begin{bmatrix} (-1)^{0 \wedge 0} & (-1)^{0 \wedge 1} \\ (-1)^{1 \wedge 0} & (-1)^{1 \wedge 1} \end{bmatrix} \otimes \frac{1}{\sqrt{2}} \begin{array}{c} \\ 0 \\ 1 \end{array} \begin{bmatrix} (-1)^{0 \wedge 0} & (-1)^{0 \wedge 1} \\ (-1)^{1 \wedge 0} & (-1)^{1 \wedge 1} \end{bmatrix}$$

$$= \frac{1}{\sqrt{2}} * \frac{1}{\sqrt{2}} \begin{array}{c} \\ 00 \\ 01 \\ 10 \\ 11 \end{array} \begin{bmatrix} (-1)^{0 \wedge 0} * (-1)^{0 \wedge 0} & (-1)^{0 \wedge 0} * (-1)^{0 \wedge 1} & (-1)^{0 \wedge 1} * (-1)^{0 \wedge 0} & (-1)^{0 \wedge 1} * (-1)^{0 \wedge 1} \\ (-1)^{0 \wedge 0} * (-1)^{1 \wedge 0} & (-1)^{0 \wedge 0} * (-1)^{1 \wedge 1} & (-1)^{0 \wedge 1} * (-1)^{1 \wedge 0} & (-1)^{0 \wedge 1} * (-1)^{1 \wedge 1} \\ (-1)^{1 \wedge 0} * (-1)^{0 \wedge 0} & (-1)^{1 \wedge 0} * (-1)^{0 \wedge 1} & (-1)^{1 \wedge 1} * (-1)^{0 \wedge 0} & (-1)^{1 \wedge 1} * (-1)^{0 \wedge 1} \\ (-1)^{1 \wedge 0} * (-1)^{1 \wedge 0} & (-1)^{1 \wedge 0} * (-1)^{1 \wedge 1} & (-1)^{1 \wedge 1} * (-1)^{1 \wedge 0} & (-1)^{1 \wedge 1} * (-1)^{1 \wedge 1} \end{bmatrix} \tag{6.50}$$

When we multiply $(-1)^x$ by $(-1)^y$, we are not interested in $(-1)^{x+y}$. Rather, we are interested in the parity of x and y. So we shall not add x and y but take their exclusive-or ($\oplus$). This leaves us with

$$H^{\otimes 2} = \frac{1}{2} \begin{array}{c} \\ 00 \\ 01 \\ 10 \\ 11 \end{array} \begin{bmatrix} (-1)^{0 \wedge 0 \oplus 0 \wedge 0} & (-1)^{0 \wedge 0 \oplus 0 \wedge 1} & (-1)^{0 \wedge 1 \oplus 0 \wedge 0} & (-1)^{0 \wedge 1 \oplus 0 \wedge 1} \\ (-1)^{0 \wedge 0 \oplus 1 \wedge 0} & (-1)^{0 \wedge 0 \oplus 1 \wedge 1} & (-1)^{0 \wedge 1 \oplus 1 \wedge 0} & (-1)^{0 \wedge 1 \oplus 1 \wedge 1} \\ (-1)^{1 \wedge 0 \oplus 0 \wedge 0} & (-1)^{1 \wedge 0 \oplus 0 \wedge 1} & (-1)^{1 \wedge 1 \oplus 0 \wedge 0} & (-1)^{1 \wedge 1 \oplus 0 \wedge 1} \\ (-1)^{1 \wedge 0 \oplus 1 \wedge 0} & (-1)^{1 \wedge 0 \oplus 1 \wedge 1} & (-1)^{1 \wedge 1 \oplus 1 \wedge 0} & (-1)^{1 \wedge 1 \oplus 1 \wedge 1} \end{bmatrix}$$

$$= \frac{1}{2} \begin{array}{c} \\ 00 \\ 01 \\ 10 \\ 11 \end{array} \begin{bmatrix} 1 & 1 & 1 & 1 \\ 1 & -1 & 1 & -1 \\ 1 & 1 & -1 & -1 \\ 1 & -1 & -1 & 1 \end{bmatrix}. \tag{6.51}$$

Exercise 6.2.4 Prove by induction that the scalar coefficient of $H^{\otimes n}$ is

$$\frac{1}{\sqrt{2^n}} = 2^{-\frac{n}{2}}. \tag{6.52}$$

∎

Thus, we have reduced the problem to determining if the exponent of (-1) is odd or even. The only time that this exponent should change is when the (-1) is in the lower-right-hand corner of a matrix. When we calculate $H^{\otimes 3}$ we will again multiply each entry of $H^{\otimes 2}$ by the appropriate element of H. If we are in the lower-right-hand corner, i.e., the $(1, 1)$ position, then we should toggle the exponent of (-1).

The following operation will be helpful. We define

$$\langle\ ,\ \rangle : \{0,1\}^n \times \{0,1\}^n \longrightarrow \{0,1\} \tag{6.53}$$

as follows: Given two binary strings of length n, $\mathbf{x} = x_0 x_1 x_2 \ldots x_{n-1}$ and $\mathbf{y} = y_0 y_1 y_2 \ldots y_{n-1}$, we say

$$\langle \mathbf{x}, \mathbf{y} \rangle = \langle x_0 x_1 x_2 \ldots x_{n-1}, y_0 y_1 y_2 \ldots y_{n-1} \rangle$$
$$= (x_0 \wedge y_0) \oplus (x_1 \wedge y_1) \oplus \cdots \oplus (x_{n-1} \wedge y_{n-1}). \tag{6.54}$$

Basically, this gives the parity of the number of times that both bits are at 1.[1]

If $\mathbf{x}$ and $\mathbf{y}$ are binary strings of length n, then $\mathbf{x} \oplus \mathbf{y}$ is the pointwise (bitwise) exclusive-or operation, i.e.,

$$\mathbf{x} \oplus \mathbf{y} = x_0 \oplus y_0, x_1 \oplus y_1, \ldots, x_{n-1} \oplus y_{n-1}. \tag{6.55}$$

The function $\langle\ ,\ \rangle : \{0,1\}^n \times \{0,1\}^n \longrightarrow \{0,1\}$ satisfies the following properties:

(i)

$$\langle \mathbf{x} \oplus \mathbf{x}', \mathbf{y} \rangle = \langle \mathbf{x}, \mathbf{y} \rangle \oplus \langle \mathbf{x}', \mathbf{y} \rangle, \tag{6.56}$$

$$\langle \mathbf{x}, \mathbf{y} \oplus \mathbf{y}' \rangle = \langle \mathbf{x}, \mathbf{y} \rangle \oplus \langle \mathbf{x}, \mathbf{y}' \rangle. \tag{6.57}$$

(ii)

$$\langle 0 \cdot \mathbf{x}, \mathbf{y} \rangle = \langle 0^n, \mathbf{y} \rangle = 0, \tag{6.58}$$

$$\langle \mathbf{x}, 0 \cdot \mathbf{y} \rangle = \langle \mathbf{x}, 0^n \rangle = 0. \tag{6.59}$$

With this notation, it is easy to write $H^{\otimes 3}$ as

$$\frac{1}{2\sqrt{2}} \begin{array}{c} \\ \begin{array}{c} 000 \\ 001 \\ 010 \\ 011 \\ 100 \\ 101 \\ 110 \\ 111 \end{array} \end{array}
\begin{bmatrix}
(-1)^{\langle 000,000\rangle} & (-1)^{\langle 000,001\rangle} & (-1)^{\langle 000,010\rangle} & (-1)^{\langle 000,011\rangle} & (-1)^{\langle 000,100\rangle} & (-1)^{\langle 000,101\rangle} & (-1)^{\langle 000,110\rangle} & (-1)^{\langle 000,111\rangle} \\
(-1)^{\langle 001,000\rangle} & (-1)^{\langle 001,001\rangle} & (-1)^{\langle 001,010\rangle} & (-1)^{\langle 001,011\rangle} & (-1)^{\langle 001,100\rangle} & (-1)^{\langle 001,101\rangle} & (-1)^{\langle 001,110\rangle} & (-1)^{\langle 001,111\rangle} \\
(-1)^{\langle 010,000\rangle} & (-1)^{\langle 010,001\rangle} & (-1)^{\langle 010,010\rangle} & (-1)^{\langle 010,011\rangle} & (-1)^{\langle 010,100\rangle} & (-1)^{\langle 010,101\rangle} & (-1)^{\langle 010,110\rangle} & (-1)^{\langle 010,111\rangle} \\
(-1)^{\langle 011,000\rangle} & (-1)^{\langle 011,001\rangle} & (-1)^{\langle 011,010\rangle} & (-1)^{\langle 011,011\rangle} & (-1)^{\langle 011,100\rangle} & (-1)^{\langle 011,101\rangle} & (-1)^{\langle 011,110\rangle} & (-1)^{\langle 011,111\rangle} \\
(-1)^{\langle 100,000\rangle} & (-1)^{\langle 100,001\rangle} & (-1)^{\langle 100,010\rangle} & (-1)^{\langle 100,011\rangle} & (-1)^{\langle 100,100\rangle} & (-1)^{\langle 100,101\rangle} & (-1)^{\langle 100,110\rangle} & (-1)^{\langle 100,111\rangle} \\
(-1)^{\langle 101,000\rangle} & (-1)^{\langle 101,001\rangle} & (-1)^{\langle 101,010\rangle} & (-1)^{\langle 101,011\rangle} & (-1)^{\langle 101,100\rangle} & (-1)^{\langle 101,101\rangle} & (-1)^{\langle 101,110\rangle} & (-1)^{\langle 101,111\rangle} \\
(-1)^{\langle 110,000\rangle} & (-1)^{\langle 110,001\rangle} & (-1)^{\langle 110,010\rangle} & (-1)^{\langle 110,011\rangle} & (-1)^{\langle 110,100\rangle} & (-1)^{\langle 110,101\rangle} & (-1)^{\langle 110,110\rangle} & (-1)^{\langle 110,111\rangle} \\
(-1)^{\langle 111,000\rangle} & (-1)^{\langle 111,001\rangle} & (-1)^{\langle 111,010\rangle} & (-1)^{\langle 111,011\rangle} & (-1)^{\langle 111,100\rangle} & (-1)^{\langle 111,101\rangle} & (-1)^{\langle 111,110\rangle} & (-1)^{\langle 111,111\rangle}
\end{bmatrix}$$

with column headers $000\ \ 001\ \ 010\ \ 011\ \ 100\ \ 101\ \ 110\ \ 111$.

---

[1] This is reminiscent of the definition of an inner product. In fact, it *is* an inner product, but on an interesting vector space. The vector space is not a complex vector space, nor a real vector space. It is a vector space over the field with exactly two elements $\{0, 1\}$. This field is denoted $\mathbb{Z}_2$ or $\mathbb{F}_2$. The set of elements of the vector space is $\{0, 1\}^n$, the set of bit strings of length n, and the addition is pointwise $\oplus$. The zero element is the string of n zeros. Scalar multiplication is obvious. We shall not list all the properties of this inner product space but we strongly recommend that you do so. Meditate on a basis and on the notions of orthogonality, dimension, etc.

$$= \frac{1}{2\sqrt{2}} \begin{array}{c} \\ \begin{matrix} 000 \\ 001 \\ 010 \\ 011 \\ 100 \\ 101 \\ 110 \\ 111 \end{matrix} \end{array} \begin{bmatrix} 1 & 1 & 1 & 1 & 1 & 1 & 1 & 1 \\ 1 & -1 & 1 & -1 & 1 & -1 & 1 & -1 \\ 1 & 1 & -1 & -1 & 1 & 1 & -1 & -1 \\ 1 & -1 & -1 & 1 & 1 & -1 & -1 & 1 \\ 1 & 1 & 1 & 1 & -1 & -1 & -1 & -1 \\ 1 & -1 & 1 & -1 & -1 & 1 & -1 & 1 \\ 1 & 1 & -1 & -1 & -1 & -1 & 1 & 1 \\ 1 & -1 & -1 & 1 & -1 & 1 & 1 & -1 \end{bmatrix}. \tag{6.60}$$

where the column headers are $000\ 001\ 010\ 011\ 100\ 101\ 110\ 111$.

From this, we can write a general formula for $H^{\otimes n}$ as

$$H^{\otimes n}[\mathbf{i}, \mathbf{j}] = \frac{1}{\sqrt{2^n}} (-1)^{\langle \mathbf{i}, \mathbf{j} \rangle}, \tag{6.61}$$

where $\mathbf{i}$ and $\mathbf{j}$ are the row and column numbers in binary.

What happens if we multiply a state with this matrix? Notice that all the elements of the leftmost column of $H^{\otimes n}$ are $+1$. So if we multiply $H^{\otimes n}$ with the state

$$|\mathbf{0}\rangle = |00\ldots0\rangle = \begin{array}{c} 00000000 \\ 00000001 \\ 00000010 \\ \vdots \\ 11111110 \\ 11111111 \end{array} \begin{bmatrix} 1 \\ 0 \\ 0 \\ \vdots \\ 0 \\ 0 \end{bmatrix}, \tag{6.62}$$

we see that this will equal the leftmost column of $H^{\otimes n}$:

$$H^{\otimes n}|\mathbf{0}\rangle = H^{\otimes n}[-, \mathbf{0}] = \frac{1}{\sqrt{2^n}} \begin{array}{c} 00000000 \\ 00000001 \\ 00000010 \\ \vdots \\ 11111110 \\ 11111111 \end{array} \begin{bmatrix} 1 \\ 1 \\ 1 \\ \vdots \\ 1 \\ 1 \end{bmatrix} = \frac{1}{\sqrt{2^n}} \sum_{\mathbf{x} \in \{0,1\}^n} |\mathbf{x}\rangle. \tag{6.63}$$

For an arbitrary basic state $|\mathbf{y}\rangle$, which can be represented by a column vector with a single 1 in position $\mathbf{y}$ and 0's everywhere else, we will be extracting the $\mathbf{y}$th column of $H^{\otimes n}$:

$$H^{\otimes n}|\mathbf{y}\rangle = H^{\otimes n}[-, \mathbf{y}] = \frac{1}{\sqrt{2^n}} \sum_{\mathbf{x} \in \{0,1\}^n} (-1)^{\langle \mathbf{x}, \mathbf{y} \rangle} |\mathbf{x}\rangle. \tag{6.64}$$

Let us return to the problem at hand. We are trying to tell whether the given function is balanced or constant. In the last section, we were successful by placing the bottom control qubit in a superposition. Let us see what would happen if we did the same thing here.

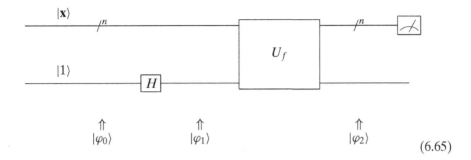

(6.65)

In terms of matrices this amounts to

$$U_f(I \otimes H)|\mathbf{x}, 1\rangle. \tag{6.66}$$

For an arbitrary $\mathbf{x} = x_0 x_1 x_2 \ldots x_{n-1}$ as an input in the top n qubits, we will have the following states:

$$|\varphi_0\rangle = |\mathbf{x}, 1\rangle. \tag{6.67}$$

After the bottom Hadamard matrix, we have

$$|\varphi_1\rangle = |\mathbf{x}\rangle \left[\frac{|0\rangle - |1\rangle}{\sqrt{2}} \right] = \left[\frac{|\mathbf{x}, 0\rangle - |\mathbf{x}, 1\rangle}{\sqrt{2}} \right]. \tag{6.68}$$

Applying U_f we get

$$|\varphi_2\rangle = |\mathbf{x}\rangle \left[\frac{|f(\mathbf{x}) \oplus 0\rangle - |f(\mathbf{x}) \oplus 1\rangle}{\sqrt{2}} \right] = |\mathbf{x}\rangle \left[\frac{|f(\mathbf{x})\rangle - |\overline{f(\mathbf{x})}\rangle}{\sqrt{2}} \right], \tag{6.69}$$

where $\overline{f(\mathbf{x})}$ means the opposite of $f(\mathbf{x})$.

$$|\varphi_2\rangle = \begin{cases} |\mathbf{x}\rangle \left[\frac{|0\rangle - |1\rangle}{\sqrt{2}} \right], & \text{if } f(\mathbf{x}) = 0 \\ \\ |\mathbf{x}\rangle \left[\frac{|1\rangle - |0\rangle}{\sqrt{2}} \right], & \text{if } f(\mathbf{x}) = 1 \end{cases} = (-1)^{f(\mathbf{x})} |\mathbf{x}\rangle \left[\frac{|0\rangle - |1\rangle}{\sqrt{2}} \right]. \tag{6.70}$$

This is almost exactly like Equation (6.27) in the last section. Unfortunately, it is just as unhelpful.

Let us take another stab at the problem and present the Deutsch–Jozsa algorithm. This time, we shall put $|\mathbf{x}\rangle = |x_0 x_1 \cdots x_{n-1}\rangle$ into a superposition in which all

2^n possible strings have equal probability. We saw that we can get such a superposition by multiplying $H^{\otimes n}$ by $|\mathbf{0}\rangle = |000\cdots 0\rangle$. Thus, we have

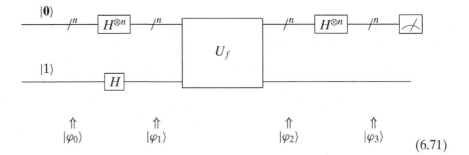

$$(6.71)$$

In terms of matrices this amounts to

$$(H^{\otimes n} \otimes I)U_f(H^{\otimes n} \otimes H)|\mathbf{0}, 1\rangle. \qquad (6.72)$$

Each state can be written as

$$|\varphi_0\rangle = |\mathbf{0}, 1\rangle, \qquad (6.73)$$

$$|\varphi_1\rangle = \left[\frac{\sum_{\mathbf{x}\in\{0,1\}^n}|\mathbf{x}\rangle}{\sqrt{2^n}}\right]\left[\frac{|0\rangle - |1\rangle}{\sqrt{2}}\right] \qquad (6.74)$$

(as in Equation (6.63)). After applying the U_f unitary matrix, we have

$$|\varphi_2\rangle = \left[\frac{\sum_{\mathbf{x}\in\{0,1\}^n}(-1)^{f(\mathbf{x})}|\mathbf{x}\rangle}{\sqrt{2^n}}\right]\left[\frac{|0\rangle - |1\rangle}{\sqrt{2}}\right]. \qquad (6.75)$$

Finally, we apply $H^{\otimes n}$ to the top qubits that are already in a superposition of different $\mathbf{x}$ states to get a superposition of a superposition

$$|\varphi_3\rangle = \left[\frac{\sum_{\mathbf{x}\in\{0,1\}^n}(-1)^{f(\mathbf{x})}\sum_{\mathbf{z}\in\{0,1\}^n}(-1)^{\langle\mathbf{z},\mathbf{x}\rangle}|\mathbf{z}\rangle}{2^n}\right]\left[\frac{|0\rangle - |1\rangle}{\sqrt{2}}\right] \qquad (6.76)$$

from Equation (6.64). We can combine parts and "add" exponents to get

$$|\varphi_3\rangle = \left[\frac{\sum_{\mathbf{x}\in\{0,1\}^n}\sum_{\mathbf{z}\in\{0,1\}^n}(-1)^{f(\mathbf{x})}(-1)^{\langle\mathbf{z},\mathbf{x}\rangle}|\mathbf{z}\rangle}{2^n}\right]\left[\frac{|0\rangle - |1\rangle}{\sqrt{2}}\right] \qquad (6.77)$$

$$= \left[\frac{\sum_{\mathbf{x}\in\{0,1\}^n}\sum_{\mathbf{z}\in\{0,1\}^n}(-1)^{f(\mathbf{x})\oplus\langle\mathbf{z},\mathbf{x}\rangle}|\mathbf{z}\rangle}{2^n}\right]\left[\frac{|0\rangle - |1\rangle}{\sqrt{2}}\right].$$

Now the top qubits of state $|\varphi_3\rangle$ are measured. Rather than figuring out what we will get after measuring the top qubit, let us ask the following question: What is the probability that the top qubits of $|\varphi_3\rangle$ will collapse to the state $|\mathbf{0}\rangle$? We can answer this by setting $\mathbf{z} = \mathbf{0}$ and realizing that $\langle \mathbf{z}, \mathbf{x}\rangle = \langle \mathbf{0}, \mathbf{x}\rangle = 0$ for all $\mathbf{x}$. In this case, we have reduced $|\varphi_3\rangle$ to

$$\left[\frac{\sum_{\mathbf{x}\in\{0,1\}^n}(-1)^{f(\mathbf{x})}|\mathbf{0}\rangle}{2^n} \right] \left[\frac{|0\rangle - |1\rangle}{\sqrt{2}} \right]. \tag{6.78}$$

So, the probability of collapsing to $|\mathbf{0}\rangle$ is totally dependent on $f(\mathbf{x})$. If $f(\mathbf{x})$ is constant at 1, the top qubits become

$$\frac{\sum_{\mathbf{x}\in\{0,1\}^n}(-1)|\mathbf{0}\rangle}{2^n} = \frac{-(2^n)|\mathbf{0}\rangle}{2^n} = -1|\mathbf{0}\rangle. \tag{6.79}$$

If $f(\mathbf{x})$ is constant at 0, the top qubits become

$$\frac{\sum_{\mathbf{x}\in\{0,1\}^n}1|\mathbf{0}\rangle}{2^n} = \frac{2^n|\mathbf{0}\rangle}{2^n} = +1|\mathbf{0}\rangle. \tag{6.80}$$

And finally, if f is balanced, then half of the $\mathbf{x}$'s will cancel the other half and the top qubits will become

$$\frac{\sum_{\mathbf{x}\in\{0,1\}^n}(-1)^{f(\mathbf{x})}|\mathbf{0}\rangle}{2^n} = \frac{0|\mathbf{0}\rangle}{2^n} = 0|\mathbf{0}\rangle. \tag{6.81}$$

When measuring the top qubits of $|\varphi_3\rangle$, we will only get $|\mathbf{0}\rangle$ if the function is constant. If anything else is found after being measured, then the function is balanced.

In conclusion, we have solved the – admittedly contrived – problem in one function evaluation as opposed to the $2^{n-1} + 1$ function evaluations needed in classical computations. That is an exponential speedup!

Exercise 6.2.5 What would happen if we were tricked and the given function was neither balanced nor constant? What would our algorithm produce? ∎

6.3 SIMON'S PERIODICITY ALGORITHM

Simon's algorithm is about finding patterns in functions. We will use methods that we already learned in previous sections, but we will also employ other ideas. This algorithm is a combination of quantum procedures as well as classical procedures.

Suppose that we are given a function $f : \{0, 1\}^n \longrightarrow \{0, 1\}^n$ that we can evaluate but it is given to us as a black box. We are further assured that there exists a secret (hidden) binary string $\mathbf{c} = c_0 c_1 c_2 \cdots c_{n-1}$, such that for all strings $\mathbf{x}, \mathbf{y} \in \{0, 1\}^n$, we have

$$f(\mathbf{x}) = f(\mathbf{y}) \quad \text{if and only if} \quad \mathbf{x} = \mathbf{y} \oplus \mathbf{c}, \tag{6.82}$$

where $\oplus$ is the bitwise exclusive-or operation. In other words, the values of f repeat themselves in some pattern and the pattern is determined by **c**. We call **c** the **period** of f. The goal of Simon's algorithm is to determine **c**.

Example 6.3.1   Let us work out an example. Let $n = 3$. Consider $\mathbf{c} = 101$. Then we are going to have the following requirements on f:

- $000 \oplus 101 = 101$; hence, $f(000) = f(101)$.
- $001 \oplus 101 = 100$; hence, $f(001) = f(100)$.
- $010 \oplus 101 = 111$; hence, $f(010) = f(111)$.
- $011 \oplus 101 = 110$; hence, $f(011) = f(110)$.
- $100 \oplus 101 = 001$; hence, $f(100) = f(001)$.
- $101 \oplus 101 = 000$; hence, $f(101) = f(000)$.
- $110 \oplus 101 = 011$; hence, $f(110) = f(011)$.
- $111 \oplus 101 = 010$; hence, $f(111) = f(010)$.

$\square$

Exercise 6.3.1   Work out the requirements on f if $\mathbf{c} = 011$.   ∎

Notice that if $\mathbf{c} = 0^n$, then the function is one to one. Otherwise the function is two to one.

The function f will be given as a unitary operation that can be visualized as

$$(6.83)$$

where $|\mathbf{x}, \mathbf{y}\rangle$ goes to $|\mathbf{x}, \mathbf{y} \oplus f(\mathbf{x})\rangle$. U_f is again its own inverse. Setting $\mathbf{y} = 0^n$ would give us an easy way to evaluate $f(\mathbf{x})$.

How would one solve this problem classically? We would have to evaluate f on different binary strings. After each evaluation, check to see if that output has already been found. If one finds two inputs $\mathbf{x_1}$ and $\mathbf{x_2}$ such that $f(\mathbf{x_1}) = f(\mathbf{x_2})$, then we are assured that

$$\mathbf{x_1} = \mathbf{x_2} \oplus \mathbf{c} \qquad (6.84)$$

and can obtain **c** by $\oplus$-ing both sides with $\mathbf{x_2}$:

$$\mathbf{x_1} \oplus \mathbf{x_2} = \mathbf{x_2} \oplus \mathbf{c} \oplus \mathbf{x_2} = \mathbf{c}. \qquad (6.85)$$

If the function is a two-to-one function, then we will not have to evaluate more than half the inputs before we get a repeat. If we evaluate more than half the strings and still cannot find a match, then we know that f is one to one and that $\mathbf{c} = 0^n$. So, in the worst case, $\frac{2^n}{2} + 1 = 2^{n-1} + 1$ function evaluations will be needed. Can we do better?

The quantum part of Simon's algorithm basically consists of performing the following operations several times:

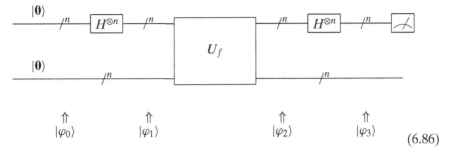

$$(6.86)$$

In terms of matrices this is

$$(H^{\otimes n} \otimes I)U_f(H^{\otimes n} \otimes I)|0, 0\rangle. \tag{6.87}$$

Let us look at the states of the system. We start at

$$|\varphi_0\rangle = |0, 0\rangle. \tag{6.88}$$

We then place the input in a superposition of all possible inputs. From Equation (6.63) we know that it looks like

$$|\varphi_1\rangle = \frac{\sum_{\mathbf{x} \in \{0,1\}^n} |\mathbf{x}, \mathbf{0}\rangle}{\sqrt{2^n}}. \tag{6.89}$$

Evaluation of f on all these possibilities gives us

$$|\varphi_2\rangle = \frac{\sum_{\mathbf{x} \in \{0,1\}^n} |\mathbf{x}, f(\mathbf{x})\rangle}{\sqrt{2^n}}. \tag{6.90}$$

And finally, let us apply $H^{\otimes n}$ to the top output, as in Equation (6.64):

$$|\varphi_3\rangle = \frac{\sum_{\mathbf{x} \in \{0,1\}^n} \sum_{\mathbf{z} \in \{0,1\}^n} (-1)^{\langle \mathbf{z}, \mathbf{x} \rangle} |\mathbf{z}, f(\mathbf{x})\rangle}{2^n}. \tag{6.91}$$

Notice that for each input $\mathbf{x}$ and for each $\mathbf{z}$, we are assured by the one who gave us the function that the ket $|\mathbf{z}, f(\mathbf{x})\rangle$ is the same ket as $|\mathbf{z}, f(\mathbf{x} \oplus \mathbf{c})\rangle$. The coefficient for this ket is then

$$\frac{(-1)^{\langle \mathbf{z}, \mathbf{x} \rangle} + (-1)^{\langle \mathbf{z}, \mathbf{x} \oplus \mathbf{c} \rangle}}{2^n}. \tag{6.92}$$

Let us examine this coefficient in depth. We saw that $\langle -, - \rangle$ is an inner product and from Equation (6.57)

$$\frac{(-1)^{\langle \mathbf{z}, \mathbf{x} \rangle} + (-1)^{\langle \mathbf{z}, \mathbf{x} \oplus \mathbf{c} \rangle}}{2^n} = \frac{(-1)^{\langle \mathbf{z}, \mathbf{x} \rangle} + (-1)^{\langle \mathbf{z}, \mathbf{x} \rangle \oplus \langle \mathbf{z}, \mathbf{c} \rangle}}{2^n}$$

$$= \frac{(-1)^{\langle \mathbf{z}, \mathbf{x} \rangle} + (-1)^{\langle \mathbf{z}, \mathbf{x} \rangle}(-1)^{\langle \mathbf{z}, \mathbf{c} \rangle}}{2^n}. \tag{6.93}$$

So, if $\langle \mathbf{z}, \mathbf{c} \rangle = 1$, the terms of the numerator of this coefficient will cancel each other out and we would get $\frac{0}{2^n}$. In contrast, if $\langle \mathbf{z}, \mathbf{c} \rangle = 0$, the sum will be $\frac{\pm 2}{2^n} = \pm 1$. Hence, upon measuring the top qubits, we will only find those binary strings such that $\langle \mathbf{z}, \mathbf{c} \rangle = 0$.

This algorithm becomes completely clear only after we look at a concrete example.

....

Reader Tip. Warning: admittedly, working out all the gory details of an example can be a bit scary. We recommend that the less meticulous reader move on to the next section for now. Return to this example on a calm sunny day, prepare a good cup of your favorite tea or coffee, and go through the details: the effort will pay off.   ♡

....

Consider the function $f : \{0, 1\}^3 \longrightarrow \{0, 1\}^3$ defined as

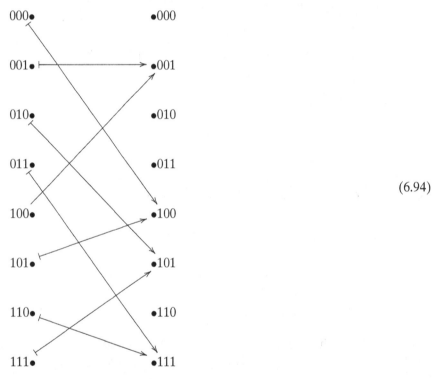

(6.94)

Let us go through the states of the algorithm with this function:

$$|\varphi_0\rangle = |\mathbf{0}, \mathbf{0}\rangle = |\mathbf{0}\rangle \otimes |\mathbf{0}\rangle, \tag{6.95}$$

$$|\varphi_1\rangle = \frac{\sum_{\mathbf{x} \in \{0,1\}^3} |\mathbf{x}\rangle}{\sqrt{8}} \otimes |\mathbf{0}\rangle. \tag{6.96}$$

We might also write this as

$$|\varphi_1\rangle = \frac{1}{\sqrt{8}}(|000\rangle \otimes |000\rangle + |001\rangle \otimes |000\rangle + |010\rangle \otimes |000\rangle + |011\rangle \otimes |000\rangle$$

$$+ |100\rangle \otimes |000\rangle + |101\rangle \otimes |000\rangle + |110\rangle \otimes |000\rangle + |111\rangle \otimes |000\rangle).$$

After applying U_f, we have

$$|\varphi_2\rangle = \frac{\sum_{\mathbf{x}\in\{0,1\}^3}|\mathbf{x}\rangle \otimes |f(\mathbf{x})\rangle}{\sqrt{8}} \tag{6.97}$$

or

$$|\varphi_2\rangle = \frac{1}{\sqrt{8}}(|000\rangle \otimes |100\rangle + |001\rangle \otimes |001\rangle + |010\rangle \otimes |101\rangle + |011\rangle \otimes |111\rangle$$
$$+ |100\rangle \otimes |001\rangle + |101\rangle \otimes |100\rangle + |110\rangle \otimes |111\rangle + |111\rangle \otimes |101\rangle).$$

Then applying $H^{\otimes n} \otimes I$ we get

$$|\varphi_3\rangle = \frac{\sum_{\mathbf{x}\in\{0,1\}^3}\sum_{\mathbf{z}\in\{0,1\}^3}(-1)^{\langle\mathbf{z},\mathbf{x}\rangle}|\mathbf{z}\rangle \otimes |f(\mathbf{x})\rangle}{8}. \tag{6.98}$$

This amounts to

$$|\varphi_3\rangle = \frac{1}{8}((+1)|000\rangle \otimes |f(000)\rangle + (+1)|000\rangle \otimes |f(001)\rangle + (+1)|000\rangle \otimes |f(010)\rangle + (+1)|000\rangle \otimes |f(011)\rangle$$
$$+ (+1)|000\rangle \otimes |f(100)\rangle + (+1)|000\rangle \otimes |f(101)\rangle + (+1)|000\rangle \otimes |f(110)\rangle + (+1)|000\rangle \otimes |f(111)\rangle$$

$$+ (+1)|001\rangle \otimes |f(000)\rangle + (-1)|001\rangle \otimes |f(001)\rangle + (+1)|001\rangle \otimes |f(010)\rangle + (-1)|001\rangle \otimes |f(011)\rangle$$
$$+ (+1)|001\rangle \otimes |f(100)\rangle + (-1)|001\rangle \otimes |f(101)\rangle + (+1)|001\rangle \otimes |f(110)\rangle + (-1)|001\rangle \otimes |f(111)\rangle$$

$$+ (+1)|010\rangle \otimes |f(000)\rangle + (+1)|010\rangle \otimes |f(001)\rangle + (-1)|010\rangle \otimes |f(010)\rangle + (-1)|010\rangle \otimes |f(011)\rangle$$
$$+ (+1)|010\rangle \otimes |f(100)\rangle + (+1)|010\rangle \otimes |f(101)\rangle + (-1)|010\rangle \otimes |f(110)\rangle + (-1)|010\rangle \otimes |f(111)\rangle$$

$$+ (+1)|011\rangle \otimes |f(000)\rangle + (-1)|011\rangle \otimes |f(001)\rangle + (-1)|011\rangle \otimes |f(010)\rangle + (+1)|011\rangle \otimes |f(011)\rangle$$
$$+ (+1)|011\rangle \otimes |f(100)\rangle + (-1)|011\rangle \otimes |f(101)\rangle + (-1)|011\rangle \otimes |f(110)\rangle + (+1)|011\rangle \otimes |f(111)\rangle$$

$$+ (+1)|100\rangle \otimes |f(000)\rangle + (+1)|100\rangle \otimes |f(001)\rangle + (+1)|100\rangle \otimes |f(010)\rangle + (+1)|100\rangle \otimes |f(011)\rangle$$
$$+ (-1)|100\rangle \otimes |f(100)\rangle + (-1)|100\rangle \otimes |f(101)\rangle + (-1)|100\rangle \otimes |f(110)\rangle + (-1)|100\rangle \otimes |f(111)\rangle$$

$$+ (+1)|101\rangle \otimes |f(000)\rangle + (-1)|101\rangle \otimes |f(001)\rangle + (+1)|101\rangle \otimes |f(010)\rangle + (-1)|101\rangle \otimes |f(011)\rangle$$
$$+ (-1)|101\rangle \otimes |f(100)\rangle + (+1)|101\rangle \otimes |f(101)\rangle + (-1)|101\rangle \otimes |f(110)\rangle + (+1)|101\rangle \otimes |f(111)\rangle$$

$$+ (+1)|110\rangle \otimes |f(000)\rangle + (+1)|110\rangle \otimes |f(001)\rangle + (-1)|110\rangle \otimes |f(010)\rangle + (-1)|110\rangle \otimes |f(011)\rangle$$
$$+ (-1)|110\rangle \otimes |f(100)\rangle + (-1)|110\rangle \otimes |f(101)\rangle + (+1)|110\rangle \otimes |f(110)\rangle + (+1)|110\rangle \otimes |f(111)\rangle$$

$$+ (+1)|111\rangle \otimes |f(000)\rangle + (-1)|111\rangle \otimes |f(001)\rangle + (-1)|111\rangle \otimes |f(010)\rangle + (+1)|111\rangle \otimes |f(011)\rangle$$
$$+ (-1)|111\rangle \otimes |f(100)\rangle + (+1)|111\rangle \otimes |f(101)\rangle + (+1)|111\rangle \otimes |f(110)\rangle + (-1)|111\rangle \otimes |f(111)\rangle).$$

Notice that the coefficients follow the exact pattern as $H^{\otimes 3}$ on page 184.

Evaluating the function f gives us

$$|\varphi_3\rangle = \frac{1}{8}((+1)|000\rangle \otimes |100\rangle + (+1)|000\rangle \otimes |001\rangle + (+1)|000\rangle \otimes |101\rangle + (+1)|000\rangle \otimes |111\rangle$$
$$+ (+1)|000\rangle \otimes |001\rangle + (+1)|000\rangle \otimes |100\rangle + (+1)|000\rangle \otimes |111\rangle + (+1)|000\rangle \otimes |101\rangle$$

$$+ (+1)|001\rangle \otimes |100\rangle + (-1)|001\rangle \otimes |001\rangle + (+1)|001\rangle \otimes |101\rangle + (-1)|001\rangle \otimes |111\rangle$$
$$+ (+1)|001\rangle \otimes |001\rangle + (-1)|001\rangle \otimes |100\rangle + (+1)|001\rangle \otimes |111\rangle + (-1)|001\rangle \otimes |101\rangle$$

$$+ (+1)|010\rangle \otimes |100\rangle + (+1)|010\rangle \otimes |001\rangle + (-1)|010\rangle \otimes |101\rangle + (-1)|010\rangle \otimes |111\rangle$$
$$+ (+1)|010\rangle \otimes |001\rangle + (+1)|010\rangle \otimes |100\rangle + (-1)|010\rangle \otimes |111\rangle + (-1)|010\rangle \otimes |101\rangle$$

$$+ (+1)|011\rangle \otimes |100\rangle + (-1)|011\rangle \otimes |001\rangle + (-1)|011\rangle \otimes |101\rangle + (+1)|011\rangle \otimes |111\rangle$$
$$+ (+1)|011\rangle \otimes |001\rangle + (-1)|011\rangle \otimes |100\rangle + (-1)|011\rangle \otimes |111\rangle + (+1)|011\rangle \otimes |101\rangle$$

$$+ (+1)|100\rangle \otimes |100\rangle + (+1)|100\rangle \otimes |001\rangle + (+1)|100\rangle \otimes |101\rangle + (+1)|100\rangle \otimes |111\rangle$$
$$+ (-1)|100\rangle \otimes |001\rangle + (-1)|100\rangle \otimes |100\rangle + (-1)|100\rangle \otimes |111\rangle + (-1)|100\rangle \otimes |101\rangle$$

$$+ (+1)|101\rangle \otimes |100\rangle + (-1)|101\rangle \otimes |001\rangle + (+1)|101\rangle \otimes |101\rangle + (-1)|101\rangle \otimes |111\rangle$$
$$+ (-1)|101\rangle \otimes |001\rangle + (+1)|101\rangle \otimes |100\rangle + (-1)|101\rangle \otimes |111\rangle + (+1)|101\rangle \otimes |101\rangle$$

$$+ (+1)|110\rangle \otimes |100\rangle + (+1)|110\rangle \otimes |001\rangle + (-1)|110\rangle \otimes |101\rangle + (-1)|110\rangle \otimes |111\rangle$$
$$+ (-1)|110\rangle \otimes |001\rangle + (-1)|110\rangle \otimes |100\rangle + (+1)|110\rangle \otimes |111\rangle + (+1)|110\rangle \otimes |101\rangle$$

$$+ (+1)|111\rangle \otimes |100\rangle + (-1)|111\rangle \otimes |001\rangle + (-1)|111\rangle \otimes |101\rangle + (+1)|111\rangle \otimes |111\rangle$$
$$+ (-1)|111\rangle \otimes |001\rangle + (+1)|111\rangle \otimes |100\rangle + (+1)|111\rangle \otimes |111\rangle + (-1)|111\rangle \otimes |101\rangle).$$

Combining like terms and canceling out gives us

$$|\varphi_3\rangle = \frac{1}{8}((+2)|000\rangle \otimes |100\rangle + (+2)|000\rangle \otimes |001\rangle + (+2)|000\rangle \otimes |101\rangle + (+2)|000\rangle \otimes |111\rangle$$
$$+ (+2)|010\rangle \otimes |100\rangle + (+2)|010\rangle \otimes |001\rangle + (-2)|010\rangle \otimes |101\rangle + (-2)|010\rangle \otimes |111\rangle$$
$$+ (+2)|101\rangle \otimes |100\rangle + (-2)|101\rangle \otimes |001\rangle + (+2)|101\rangle \otimes |101\rangle + (-2)|101\rangle \otimes |111\rangle$$
$$+ (+2)|111\rangle \otimes |100\rangle + (-2)|111\rangle \otimes |001\rangle + (-2)|111\rangle \otimes |101\rangle + (+2)|111\rangle \otimes |111\rangle)$$

or

$$|\varphi_3\rangle = \frac{1}{8}((+2)|000\rangle \otimes (|100\rangle + |001\rangle + |101\rangle + |111\rangle)$$
$$+ (+2)|010\rangle \otimes (|100\rangle + |001\rangle - |101\rangle - |111\rangle)$$
$$+ (+2)|101\rangle \otimes (|100\rangle - |001\rangle + |101\rangle - |111\rangle)$$
$$+ (+2)|111\rangle \otimes (|100\rangle - |001\rangle - |101\rangle + |111\rangle)).$$

When we measure the top output, we will get, with equal probability, 000, 010, 101, or 111. We know that for all these, the inner product with the missing **c** is 0. This gives us the set of equations:

(i) $\langle 000, \mathbf{c} \rangle = 0$
(ii) $\langle 010, \mathbf{c} \rangle = 0$
(iii) $\langle 101, \mathbf{c} \rangle = 0$
(iv) $\langle 111, \mathbf{c} \rangle = 0$.

If we write $\mathbf{c}$ as $\mathbf{c} = c_1 c_2 c_3$, then Equation (ii) tells us that $c_2 = 0$. Equation (iii) tells us that $c_1 \oplus c_3 = 0$ or that either $c_1 = c_3 = 0$ or $c_1 = c_3 = 1$. Because we know that $\mathbf{c} \neq 000$, we come to the conclusion that $\mathbf{c} = 101$.

Exercise 6.3.2 Do a similar analysis for the function f defined as

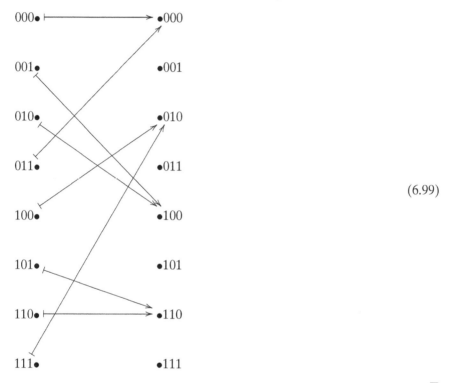

(6.99)

After running Simon's algorithm several times, we will get n different $\mathbf{z}_i$ such that $\langle \mathbf{z}_i, \mathbf{c} \rangle = 0$. We then put these results into a classical algorithm that solves "linear equations." They are linear equations; rather than using the usual + operation, we use $\oplus$ on binary strings. Here is a nice worked-out example.

Example 6.3.2 Imagine that we are dealing with a case where $n = 7$. That means we are given a function $f : \{0, 1\}^7 \longrightarrow \{0, 1\}^7$. Let us assume that we ran the algorithm 7 times and we get the following results:

(i) $\langle 1010110, \mathbf{c} \rangle = 0$
(ii) $\langle 0010001, \mathbf{c} \rangle = 0$
(iii) $\langle 1100101, \mathbf{c} \rangle = 0$

(iv) $\langle 0011011, \mathbf{c} \rangle = 0$
(v) $\langle 0101001, \mathbf{c} \rangle = 0$
(vi) $\langle 0011010, \mathbf{c} \rangle = 0$
(vii) $\langle 0110111, \mathbf{c} \rangle = 0$.

To clear the first column of 1's, we are going to "add" (really pointwise exclusive or) the first equation to the third equation. This gives us

(i) $\langle 1010110, \mathbf{c} \rangle = 0$
(ii) $\langle 0010001, \mathbf{c} \rangle = 0$
(iii) $\langle 0110011, \mathbf{c} \rangle = 0$
(iv) $\langle 0011011, \mathbf{c} \rangle = 0$
(v) $\langle 0101001, \mathbf{c} \rangle = 0$
(vi) $\langle 0011010, \mathbf{c} \rangle = 0$
(vii) $\langle 0110111, \mathbf{c} \rangle = 0$.

To clear the second column of 1's, we are going to "add" the third equation to the fifth and seventh equations. This gives us

(i) $\langle 1010110, \mathbf{c} \rangle = 0$
(ii) $\langle 0010001, \mathbf{c} \rangle = 0$
(iii) $\langle 0110011, \mathbf{c} \rangle = 0$
(iv) $\langle 0011011, \mathbf{c} \rangle = 0$
(v) $\langle 0011010, \mathbf{c} \rangle = 0$
(vi) $\langle 0011010, \mathbf{c} \rangle = 0$
(vii) $\langle 0000100, \mathbf{c} \rangle = 0$.

To clear the third column of 1's, we are going to "add" the second equation to Equations (i), (iii), (iv), (v), and (vi). This gives us

(i) $\langle 1000111, \mathbf{c} \rangle = 0$
(ii) $\langle 0010001, \mathbf{c} \rangle = 0$
(iii) $\langle 0100010, \mathbf{c} \rangle = 0$
(iv) $\langle 0001010, \mathbf{c} \rangle = 0$
(v) $\langle 0001011, \mathbf{c} \rangle = 0$
(vi) $\langle 0001011, \mathbf{c} \rangle = 0$
(vii) $\langle 0000100, \mathbf{c} \rangle = 0$.

To clear the fourth column of 1's, we are going to "add" Equation (iv) to Equations (v) and (vi). We are going to clear the fifth column by adding Equation (vii) to Equation (i). This gives us

(i) $\langle 1000011, \mathbf{c} \rangle = 0$
(ii) $\langle 0010001, \mathbf{c} \rangle = 0$
(iii) $\langle 0100010, \mathbf{c} \rangle = 0$
(iv) $\langle 0001010, \mathbf{c} \rangle = 0$
(v) $\langle 0000001, \mathbf{c} \rangle = 0$
(vi) $\langle 0000001, \mathbf{c} \rangle = 0$
(vii) $\langle 0000100, \mathbf{c} \rangle = 0$.

And finally, to clear the seventh column of 1's, we are going to "add" Equation
(v) to Equations (i), (ii), and (vi). We get

(i) $\langle 1000010, \mathbf{c} \rangle = 0$
(ii) $\langle 0010000, \mathbf{c} \rangle = 0$
(iii) $\langle 0100010, \mathbf{c} \rangle = 0$
(iv) $\langle 0001010, \mathbf{c} \rangle = 0$
(v) $\langle 0000001, \mathbf{c} \rangle = 0$
(vi) $\langle 0000000, \mathbf{c} \rangle = 0$
(vii) $\langle 0000100, \mathbf{c} \rangle = 0$.

We can interpret these equations as

(i) $c_1 \oplus c_6 = 0$
(ii) $c_3 = 0$
(iii) $c_2 \oplus c_6 = 0$
(iv) $c_4 \oplus c_6 = 0$
(v) $c_7 = 0$
(vi)
(vii) $c_5 = 0$.

Notice that if $c_6 = 0$, then $c_1 = c_2 = c_4 = 0$ and that if $c_6 = 1$, then $c_1 = c_2 = c_4 = 1$.
Because we are certain that f is not one to one and $\mathbf{c} \neq 0000000$, we can conclude
that $\mathbf{c} = 1101010$.   □

Exercise 6.3.3 Solve the following linear equations in a similar manner:

(i) $\langle 11110000, \mathbf{c} \rangle = 0$
(ii) $\langle 01101001, \mathbf{c} \rangle = 0$
(iii) $\langle 10010110, \mathbf{c} \rangle = 0$
(iv) $\langle 00111100, \mathbf{c} \rangle = 0$
(v) $\langle 11111111, \mathbf{c} \rangle = 0$
(vi) $\langle 11000011, \mathbf{c} \rangle = 0$
(vii) $\langle 10001110, \mathbf{c} \rangle = 0$
(viii) $\langle 01110001, \mathbf{c} \rangle = 0$.

(Hint: The answer is $\mathbf{c} = 10011001$.)   ■

In conclusion, for a given periodic f, we can find the period $\mathbf{c}$ in n function evaluations. This is in contrast to the $2^{n-1} + 1$ needed with the classical algorithm.

· ·

Reader Tip. We shall see this concept of finding the period of a function in Section
6.5 when we present Shor's algorithm.   ♡

· ·

6.4 GROVER'S SEARCH ALGORITHM

How do you find a needle in a haystack? You look at each piece of hay separately
and check each one to see if it is the desired needle. That is not very efficient.

The computer science version of this problem is about unordered arrays instead of haystacks. Given an unordered array of m elements, find a particular element. Classically, in the worst case, this takes m queries. On average, we will find the desired element in $m/2$ queries. Can we do better?

Lov Grover's search algorithm does the job in $\sqrt{m}$ queries. Although this is not the exponential speedup of the Deutsch–Jozsa algorithm and Simon's algorithm, it is still very good. Grover's algorithm has many applications to database theory and other areas.

Because, over the past few sections, we have become quite adept at functions, let us look at the search problem from the point of view of functions. Imagine that you are given a function $f : \{0, 1\}^n \longrightarrow \{0, 1\}$ and you are assured that there exists exactly one binary string $\mathbf{x_0}$ such that

$$
f(\mathbf{x}) = \begin{cases} 1, & \text{if } \mathbf{x} = \mathbf{x_0}, \\ 0, & \text{if } \mathbf{x} \neq \mathbf{x_0}. \end{cases} \tag{6.100}
$$

We are asked to find $\mathbf{x_0}$. Classically, in the worst case, we would have to evaluate all 2^n binary strings to find the desired $\mathbf{x_0}$. Grover's algorithm will demand only $\sqrt{2^n} = 2^{\frac{n}{2}}$ evaluations.

f will be given to us as the unitary matrix U_f that takes $|\mathbf{x}, y\rangle$ to $|\mathbf{x}, f(\mathbf{x}) \oplus y\rangle$. For example, for $n = 2$, if f is the unique function that "picks out" the binary string 10, then U_f looks like

$$
\begin{array}{c c}
 & \begin{matrix} \mathbf{00,0} & \mathbf{00,1} & \mathbf{01,0} & \mathbf{01,1} & \mathbf{10,0} & \mathbf{10,1} & \mathbf{11,0} & \mathbf{11,1} \end{matrix} \\
\begin{matrix} \mathbf{00,0} \\ \mathbf{00,1} \\ \mathbf{01,0} \\ \mathbf{01,1} \\ \mathbf{10,0} \\ \mathbf{10,1} \\ \mathbf{11,0} \\ \mathbf{11,1} \end{matrix} &
\begin{bmatrix}
1 & & & & & & & \\
 & 1 & & & & & & \\
 & & 1 & & & & & \\
 & & & 1 & & & & \\
 & & & & & 1 & & \\
 & & & & 1 & & & \\
 & & & & & & 1 & \\
 & & & & & & & 1
\end{bmatrix}
\end{array}. \tag{6.101}
$$

Exercise 6.4.1 Find the matrices that correspond to the other three functions from $\{0, 1\}^2$ to $\{0, 1\}$ that have exactly one element $\mathbf{x}$ with $f(\mathbf{x}) = 1$. ∎

As a first try at solving this problem, we might try placing $|\mathbf{x}\rangle$ into a superposition of all possible strings and then evaluating U_f.

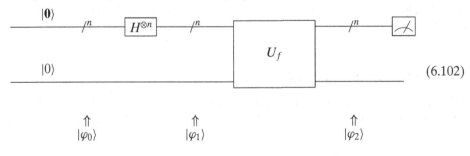

$$ \tag{6.102} $$

In terms of matrices this becomes

$$U_f(H^{\otimes n} \otimes I)|0, 0\rangle. \tag{6.103}$$

The states are

$$|\varphi_0\rangle = |0, 0\rangle, \tag{6.104}$$

$$|\varphi_1\rangle = \left[\frac{\sum_{\mathbf{x} \in \{0,1\}^n} |\mathbf{x}\rangle}{\sqrt{2^n}} \right] |0\rangle, \tag{6.105}$$

and

$$|\varphi_2\rangle = \frac{\sum_{\mathbf{x} \in \{0,1\}^n} |\mathbf{x}, f(\mathbf{x})\rangle}{\sqrt{2^n}}. \tag{6.106}$$

Measuring the top qubits will, with equal probability, give one of the 2^n binary strings. Measuring the bottom qubit will give $|0\rangle$ with probability $\frac{2^n - 1}{2^n}$, and $|1\rangle$ with probability $\frac{1}{2^n}$. If you are lucky enough to measure $|1\rangle$ on the bottom qubit, then, because the top and the bottom are entangled, the top qubit will have the correct answer. However, it is improbable that you will be so lucky. We need something new.

Grover's search algorithm uses two tricks. The first, called **phase inversion**, changes the phase of the desired state. It works as follows. Take U_f and place the bottom qubit in the superposition

$$\frac{|0\rangle - |1\rangle}{\sqrt{2}} \tag{6.107}$$

state. This is similar to quantum circuit (6.21). For an arbitrary $\mathbf{x}$, this looks like

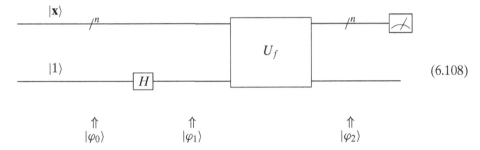

$$\tag{6.108}$$

In terms of matrices this becomes

$$U_f(I_n \otimes H)|\mathbf{x}, 1\rangle. \tag{6.109}$$

Because both U_f and H are unitary operations, it is obvious that phase inversion is a unitary operation.

The states are

$$|\varphi_0\rangle = |\mathbf{x}, 1\rangle, \tag{6.110}$$

$$|\varphi_1\rangle = |\mathbf{x}| \left[\frac{|0\rangle - |1\rangle}{\sqrt{2}} \right] = \left[\frac{|\mathbf{x}, 0\rangle - |\mathbf{x}, 1\rangle}{\sqrt{2}} \right], \tag{6.111}$$

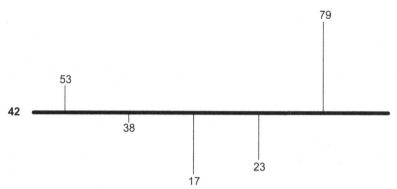

Figure 6.1. Five numbers and their average

and

$$|\varphi_2\rangle = |\mathbf{x}\rangle \left[\frac{|f(\mathbf{x}) \oplus 0\rangle - |f(\mathbf{x}) \oplus 1\rangle}{\sqrt{2}} \right] = |\mathbf{x}\rangle \left[\frac{|f(\mathbf{x})\rangle - |\overline{f(\mathbf{x})}\rangle}{\sqrt{2}} \right]. \qquad (6.112)$$

Remembering that $a - b = (-1)(b - a)$, we may write

$$|\varphi_2\rangle = (-1)^{f(\mathbf{x})} |\mathbf{x}\rangle \left[\frac{|0\rangle - |1\rangle}{\sqrt{2}} \right] = \begin{cases} -1|\mathbf{x}\rangle \left[\frac{|0\rangle - |1\rangle}{\sqrt{2}} \right], & \text{if } \mathbf{x} = \mathbf{x_0}, \\ +1|\mathbf{x}\rangle \left[\frac{|0\rangle - |1\rangle}{\sqrt{2}} \right], & \text{if } \mathbf{x} \neq \mathbf{x_0}. \end{cases} \qquad (6.113)$$

How does this unitary operation act on states? If $|\mathbf{x}\rangle$ starts off in a equal superposition of four different states, i.e., $\left[\frac{1}{2}, \frac{1}{2}, \frac{1}{2}, \frac{1}{2} \right]^T$, and f chooses the string "10," then after performing a phase inversion, the state looks like $\left[\frac{1}{2}, \frac{1}{2}, -\frac{1}{2}, \frac{1}{2} \right]^T$. Measuring $|\mathbf{x}\rangle$ does not give any information: both $|\frac{1}{2}|^2$ and $|-\frac{1}{2}|^2$ are equal to $+\frac{1}{4}$. Changing the phase from positive to negative separates the phases, but does not separate them enough. We need something else.

What is needed is a way of boosting the phase separation of the desired binary string from the other binary strings. The second trick is called **inversion about the mean** or **inversion about the average**. This is a way of boosting the separation of the phases. A small example will be helpful. Consider a sequence of integers: $53, 38, 17, 23$, and 79. The average of these numbers is $a = 42$. We might picture these numbers as in Figure 6.1.

The average is the number such that the sum of the lengths of the lines above the average is the same as the sum of the lengths of the lines below. Suppose we wanted to change the sequence so that each element of the original sequence above the average would be the same distance from the average but below. Furthermore, each element of the original sequence below the average would be the same distance from the average but above. In other words, we are inverting each element around the average. For example, the first number, 53 is $a - 53 = -11$ units away from the average. We must add $a = 42$ to -11 and get $a + (a - 53) = 31$. The second element of the original sequence, 38, is $a - 38 = 4$ units below the average and will go to

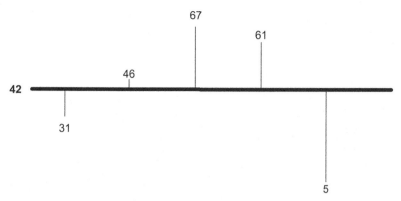

Figure 6.2. After an inversion about the mean.

$a + (a - 38) = 46$. In general, we shall change each element v to

$$v' = a + (a - v) \tag{6.114}$$

or

$$v' = -v + 2a. \tag{6.115}$$

The above sequence becomes $31, 46, 67, 61$, and 5. Notice that the average of this sequence remains 42 as in Figure 6.2.

Exercise 6.4.2 Consider the following number: $5, 38, 62, 58, 21$, and 35. Invert these numbers around their mean. ■

Let us write this in terms of matrices. Rather than writing the numbers as a sequence, consider a vector $V = [53, 38, 17, 23, 79]^T$. Now consider the matrix

$$A = \begin{bmatrix} \frac{1}{5} & \frac{1}{5} & \frac{1}{5} & \frac{1}{5} & \frac{1}{5} \\ \frac{1}{5} & \frac{1}{5} & \frac{1}{5} & \frac{1}{5} & \frac{1}{5} \\ \frac{1}{5} & \frac{1}{5} & \frac{1}{5} & \frac{1}{5} & \frac{1}{5} \\ \frac{1}{5} & \frac{1}{5} & \frac{1}{5} & \frac{1}{5} & \frac{1}{5} \\ \frac{1}{5} & \frac{1}{5} & \frac{1}{5} & \frac{1}{5} & \frac{1}{5} \end{bmatrix}. \tag{6.116}$$

It is easy to see that A is a matrix that finds the average of a sequence:

$$AV = [42, 42, 42, 42, 42]^T. \tag{6.117}$$

In terms of matrices, the formula $v' = -v + 2a$ becomes

$$V' = -V + 2AV = (-I + 2A)V. \tag{6.118}$$

Let us calculate

$$(-I + 2A) = \begin{bmatrix} (-1 + \frac{2}{5}) & \frac{2}{5} & \frac{2}{5} & \frac{2}{5} & \frac{2}{5} \\ \frac{2}{5} & (-1 + \frac{2}{5}) & \frac{2}{5} & \frac{2}{5} & \frac{2}{5} \\ \frac{2}{5} & \frac{2}{5} & (-1 + \frac{2}{5}) & \frac{2}{5} & \frac{2}{5} \\ \frac{2}{5} & \frac{2}{5} & \frac{2}{5} & (-1 + \frac{2}{5}) & \frac{2}{5} \\ \frac{2}{5} & \frac{2}{5} & \frac{2}{5} & \frac{2}{5} & (-1 + \frac{2}{5}) \end{bmatrix}. \tag{6.119}$$

And, as expected,

$$(-I + 2A)V = V', \tag{6.120}$$

or in our case,

$$(-I + 2A)[53, 38, 17, 23, 79]^T = [31, 46, 67, 61, 5]^T. \tag{6.121}$$

Let us generalize: rather than dealing with five numbers, let us deal with 2^n numbers. Given n qubits, there are 2^n possible states. A state is a 2^n vector. Consider the following 2^n-by-2^n matrix:

$$A = \begin{bmatrix} \frac{1}{2^n} & \frac{1}{2^n} & \cdots & \frac{1}{2^n} \\ \frac{1}{2^n} & \frac{1}{2^n} & \cdots & \frac{1}{2^n} \\ \vdots & \vdots & \ddots & \vdots \\ \frac{1}{2^n} & \frac{1}{2^n} & \cdots & \frac{1}{2^n} \end{bmatrix}. \tag{6.122}$$

Exercise 6.4.3   Prove that $A^2 = A$.   ∎

Multiplying any state by A will give a state where each amplitude will be the average of all the amplitudes. Building on this, we form the following 2^n-by-2^n matrix

$$-I + 2A = \begin{bmatrix} -1 + \frac{2}{2^n} & \frac{2}{2^n} & \cdots & \frac{2}{2^n} \\ \frac{2}{2^n} & -1 + \frac{2}{2^n} & \cdots & \frac{2}{2^n} \\ \vdots & \vdots & \ddots & \vdots \\ \frac{2}{2^n} & \frac{2}{2^n} & \cdots & -1 + \frac{2}{2^n} \end{bmatrix}. \tag{6.123}$$

Multiplying a state by $-I + 2A$ will invert amplitudes about the mean.

We must show that $-I + 2A$ is a unitary matrix. First, observe that the adjoint of $-I + 2A$ is itself. Then, using the properties of matrix multiplication and realizing that matrices act very much like polynomials, we have

$$(-I + 2A) \star (-I + 2A) = +I - 2A - 2A + 4A^2$$

$$= I - 4A + 4A^2 = I - 4A + 4A = I, \tag{6.124}$$

where the first equality is from distributivity of matrix multiplication, the second equality comes from combining like terms, and the third equality is from the fact that $A^2 = A$. We conclude that $(-I + 2A)$ is a unitary operation and acts on states by inverting the numbers about the mean.

When considered separately, phase inversion and inversion about the mean are each innocuous operations. However, when combined, they are a very powerful operation that separates the amplitude of the desired state from those of all the other states.

Example 6.4.1 Let us do an example that shows how both these techniques work together. Consider the vector

$$[10, 10, 10, 10, 10]^T. \tag{6.125}$$

We are always going to perform a phase inversion to the fourth of the five numbers. There is no difference between the fourth number and all the other numbers. We start by doing a phase inversion to the fourth number and get

$$[10, 10, 10, -10, 10]^T. \tag{6.126}$$

The average of these five numbers is $a = 6$. Calculating the inversion about the mean we get

$$-v + 2a = -10 + (2 \times 6) = 2 \tag{6.127}$$

and

$$-v + 2a = 10 + (2 \times 6) = 22. \tag{6.128}$$

Thus, our five numbers become

$$[2, 2, 2, 22, 2]^T. \tag{6.129}$$

The difference between the fourth element and all the others is $22 - 2 = 20$.

Let us do these two operations again to our five numbers. Another phase inversion on the fourth element gives us

$$[2, 2, 2, -22, 2]^T. \tag{6.130}$$

The average of these numbers is $a = -2.8$. Calculating the inversion about the mean we get

$$-v + 2a = -2 + (2 \times -2.8) = -7.6 \tag{6.131}$$

and

$$-v + 2a = 22 + (2 \times -2.8) = 16.4. \tag{6.132}$$

Hence, our five numbers become

$$[-7.6, -7.6, -7.6, 16.4, -7.6]^T. \tag{6.133}$$

The difference between the fourth element and all the others is $16.4 + 7.6 = 24$. We have further separated the numbers. This was all done with unitary operations. □

Exercise 6.4.4   Do the two operations again on this sequence of five numbers. Did our results improve?   ■

How many times should these operations be done? $\sqrt{2^n}$ times. If you do it more than that, the process will "overcook" the numbers. The proof that $\sqrt{2^n}$ times is needed is beyond this text. Suffice it to say that the proof actually uses some very pretty geometry (well worth looking into!).

We are ready to state Grover's algorithm:

Step 1. Start with a state $|0\rangle$

Step 2. Apply $H^{\otimes n}$

Step 3. Repeat $\sqrt{2^n}$ times:

   Step 3a. Apply the phase inversion operation: $U_f(I \otimes H)$

   Step 3b. Apply the inversion about the mean operation: $-I + 2A$

Step 4. Measure the qubits.

We might view this algorithm as

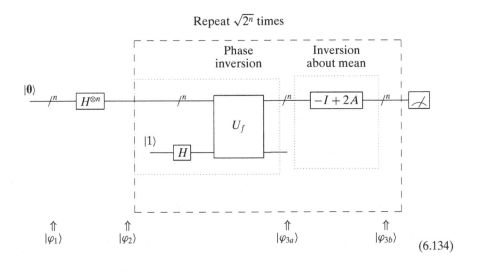

$$(6.134)$$

Example 6.4.2   Let us look at an example of an execution of this algorithm. Let f be a function that picks out the string "101." The states after each step will be

$$|\varphi_1\rangle = \begin{array}{cccccccc} \mathbf{000} & \mathbf{001} & \mathbf{010} & \mathbf{011} & \mathbf{100} & \mathbf{101} & \mathbf{110} & \mathbf{111} \\ [\ 0 & 0 & 0 & 0 & 0 & 0 & 0 & 0\ ] \end{array}^T,$$

$$(6.135)$$

$$|\varphi_2\rangle = \begin{array}{cccccccc} \mathbf{000} & \mathbf{001} & \mathbf{010} & \mathbf{011} & \mathbf{100} & \mathbf{101} & \mathbf{110} & \mathbf{111} \\ \left[\dfrac{1}{\sqrt{8}},\right. & \dfrac{1}{\sqrt{8}}, & \dfrac{1}{\sqrt{8}}, & \dfrac{1}{\sqrt{8}}, & \dfrac{1}{\sqrt{8}}, & \dfrac{1}{\sqrt{8}}, & \dfrac{1}{\sqrt{8}}, & \left.\dfrac{1}{\sqrt{8}}\right] \end{array}^T, \tag{6.136}$$

$$|\varphi_{3a}\rangle = \begin{array}{cccccccc} \mathbf{000} & \mathbf{001} & \mathbf{010} & \mathbf{011} & \mathbf{100} & \mathbf{101} & \mathbf{110} & \mathbf{111} \\ \left[\dfrac{1}{\sqrt{8}},\right. & \dfrac{1}{\sqrt{8}}, & \dfrac{1}{\sqrt{8}}, & \dfrac{1}{\sqrt{8}}, & \dfrac{1}{\sqrt{8}}, & -\dfrac{1}{\sqrt{8}}, & \dfrac{1}{\sqrt{8}}, & \left.\dfrac{1}{\sqrt{8}}\right] \end{array}^T. \tag{6.137}$$

The average of these numbers is

$$a = \frac{7 * \frac{1}{\sqrt{8}} - \frac{1}{\sqrt{8}}}{8} = \frac{\frac{6}{\sqrt{8}}}{8} = \frac{3}{4\sqrt{8}}. \tag{6.138}$$

Calculating the inversion about the mean we have

$$-v + 2a = -\frac{1}{\sqrt{8}} + \left(2 \times \frac{3}{4\sqrt{8}}\right) = \frac{1}{2\sqrt{8}} \tag{6.139}$$

and

$$-v + 2a = \frac{1}{\sqrt{8}} + \left(2 \times \frac{3}{4\sqrt{8}}\right) = \frac{5}{2\sqrt{8}}. \tag{6.140}$$

Thus, we have

$$|\varphi_{3b}\rangle = \begin{array}{cccccccc} \mathbf{000} & \mathbf{001} & \mathbf{010} & \mathbf{011} & \mathbf{100} & \mathbf{101} & \mathbf{110} & \mathbf{111} \\ \left[\dfrac{1}{2\sqrt{8}},\right. & \dfrac{1}{2\sqrt{8}}, & \dfrac{1}{2\sqrt{8}}, & \dfrac{1}{2\sqrt{8}}, & \dfrac{1}{2\sqrt{8}}, & \dfrac{5}{2\sqrt{8}}, & \dfrac{1}{2\sqrt{8}}, & \left.\dfrac{1}{2\sqrt{8}}\right] \end{array}^T. \tag{6.141}$$

A phase inversion will give us

$$|\varphi_{3a}\rangle = \begin{array}{cccccccc} \mathbf{000} & \mathbf{001} & \mathbf{010} & \mathbf{011} & \mathbf{100} & \mathbf{101} & \mathbf{110} & \mathbf{111} \\ \left[\dfrac{1}{2\sqrt{8}},\right. & \dfrac{1}{2\sqrt{8}}, & \dfrac{1}{2\sqrt{8}}, & \dfrac{1}{2\sqrt{8}}, & \dfrac{1}{2\sqrt{8}}, & -\dfrac{5}{2\sqrt{8}}, & \dfrac{1}{2\sqrt{8}}, & \left.\dfrac{1}{2\sqrt{8}}\right] \end{array}^T. \tag{6.142}$$

The average of these numbers is

$$a = \frac{7 * \frac{1}{2\sqrt{8}} - \frac{5}{2\sqrt{8}}}{8} = \frac{1}{8\sqrt{8}}. \tag{6.143}$$

Calculating for the inversion about the mean we have

$$-v + 2a = -\frac{1}{2\sqrt{8}} + \left(2 \times \frac{1}{8\sqrt{8}}\right) = -\frac{1}{4\sqrt{8}} \tag{6.144}$$

and

$$-v + 2a = \frac{5}{2\sqrt{8}} + \left(2 \times \frac{1}{8\sqrt{8}}\right) = \frac{11}{4\sqrt{8}}. \tag{6.145}$$

Hence, we have

$$|\varphi_{3b}\rangle = \begin{bmatrix} \overset{\mathbf{000}}{\frac{-1}{4\sqrt{8}}}, & \overset{\mathbf{001}}{\frac{-1}{4\sqrt{8}}}, & \overset{\mathbf{010}}{\frac{-1}{4\sqrt{8}}}, & \overset{\mathbf{011}}{\frac{-1}{4\sqrt{8}}}, & \overset{\mathbf{100}}{\frac{-1}{4\sqrt{8}}}, & \overset{\mathbf{101}}{\frac{11}{4\sqrt{8}}}, & \overset{\mathbf{110}}{\frac{-1}{4\sqrt{8}}}, & \overset{\mathbf{111}}{\frac{-1}{4\sqrt{8}}} \end{bmatrix}^T.$$

(6.146)

For the record, $\frac{11}{4\sqrt{8}} = 0.97227$ and $\frac{-1}{4\sqrt{8}} = -0.08839$. Squaring the numbers gives us the probability of measuring the corresponding states. When we measure the state in Step 4, we will most likely get the state

$$|\varphi_4\rangle = \begin{bmatrix} \overset{\mathbf{000}}{0} & \overset{\mathbf{001}}{0} & \overset{\mathbf{010}}{0} & \overset{\mathbf{011}}{0} & \overset{\mathbf{100}}{0} & \overset{\mathbf{101}}{1} & \overset{\mathbf{110}}{0} & \overset{\mathbf{111}}{0} \end{bmatrix}^T,$$

(6.147)

which is exactly what we wanted.   □

Exercise 6.4.5 Do a similar analysis for the case where $n = 4$ and f chooses the "1101" string.   ■

A classical algorithm will search an unordered array of size m in m steps. Grover's algorithm will take time $\sqrt{m}$. This is what is referred to as a quadratic speedup. Although this is very good, it is not the holy grail of computer science: an exponential speedup. In the next section we shall meet an algorithm that does have such a speedup.

What if we relax the requirements that there be only one needle in the haystack? Let us assume that there are t objects that we are looking for (with $t \leq \frac{2^n}{2}$). Grover's algorithm still works, but now one must go through the loop $\frac{\pi}{4}\sqrt{\frac{2^n}{t}}$ times. There are many other types of generalizations and assorted changes that one can do with Grover's algorithm. Several references are given at the end of the chapter. We discuss some complexity issues with Grover's algorithm at the end of Section 8.3.

6.5 SHOR'S FACTORING ALGORITHM

The problem of factoring integers is very important. Much of the World Wide Web's security is based on the fact that it is "hard" to factor integers on classical computers. Peter Shor's amazing algorithm factors integers in polynomial time and really brought quantum computing into the limelight.

Shor's algorithm is based on the following fact: the factoring problem can be reduced to finding the period of a certain function. In Section 6.3 we learned how to find the period of a function. In this section, we employ some of those periodicity techniques to factor integers.

We shall call the number we wish to factor N. In practice, N will be a large number, perhaps hundreds of digits long. We shall work out all the calculations for the numbers 15 and 371. For exercises, we ask the reader to work with the number 247. We might as well give away the answer and tell you that the only nontrivial factors of 247 are 19 and 13.

We assume that the given N is not a prime number but is a composite number. There now exists a deterministic, polynomial algorithm that determines if N is prime

(Agrawal, Kayal, and Saxena, 2004). So we can easily check to see if N is prime before we try to factor it.

....

Reader Tip. There are several different parts of this algorithm and it might be too much to swallow in one bite. If you are stuck at a particular point, may we suggest skipping to the next part of the algorithm. At the end of this section, we summarize the algorithm.   ♡

....

Modular Exponentiation.   Before we go on to Shor's algorithm, we have to remind ourselves of some basic number theory. We begin by looking at some **modular arithmetic.** For a positive integer N and any integer a, we write a Mod N for the remainder (or residue) of the quotient a/N. (For C/C++ and Java programmers, Mod is recognizable as the % operation.)

Example 6.5.1   Some examples:

■ 7 Mod 15 = 7 because 7/15 = 0 remainder 7.
■ 99 Mod 15 = 9 because 99/15 = 6 remainder 9.
■ 199 Mod 15 = 4 because 199/15 = 13 remainder 4.
■ 5,317 Mod 371 = 123 because 5,317/371 = 14 remainder 123.
■ 2,3374 Mod 371 = 1 because 2,3374/371 = 63 remainder 1.
■ 1,446 Mod 371 = 333 because 1,446/371 = 3 remainder 333.   □

Exercise 6.5.1   Calculate

  (i)   244,443 Mod 247
  (ii) 18,154 Mod 247
  (iii) 226,006 Mod 247.   ■

We write

$$a \equiv a' \text{ Mod } N \quad \text{if and only if } (a \text{ Mod } N) = (a' \text{ Mod } N), \tag{6.148}$$

or equivalently, if N is a divisor of $a - a'$, i.e., $N|(a - a')$.

Example 6.5.2   Some examples:

■ $17 \equiv 2$ Mod 15
■ $126 \equiv 1,479,816$ Mod 15
■ $534 \equiv 1,479$ Mod 15
■ $2,091 \equiv 236$ Mod 371
■ $3,350 \equiv 2237$ Mod 371
■ $3,325,575 \equiv 2,765,365$ Mod 371.   □

Exercise 6.5.2   Show that

  (i) $1,977 \equiv 1$ Mod 247
  (ii) $16,183 \equiv 15,442$ Mod 247
  (iii) $2,439,593 \equiv 238,082$ Mod 247.

■

With Mod understood we can start discussing the algorithm. Let us randomly choose an integer a that is less than N but does not have a nontrivial factor in common with N. One can test for such a factor by performing Euclid's algorithm to calculate $GCD(a, N)$. If the GCD is not 1, then we have found a factor of N and we are done. If the GCD is 1, then a is called **co-prime** to N and we can use it. We shall need to find the powers of a modulo N, that is,

$$a^0 \text{ Mod } N, \quad a^1 \text{ Mod } N, \quad a^2 \text{ Mod } N, \quad a^3 \text{ Mod } N, \quad \ldots \tag{6.149}$$

In other words, we shall need to find the values of the function

$$f_{a,N}(x) = a^x \text{ Mod } N. \tag{6.150}$$

Some examples are in order.

Example 6.5.3 Let $N = 15$ and $a = 2$. A few simple calculations show that we get the following:

x	0	1	2	3	4	5	6	7	8	9	10	11	12	$\cdots$
$f_{2,15}(x)$	1	2	4	8	1	2	4	8	1	2	4	8	1	$\cdots$

$$\tag{6.151}$$

For $a = 4$, we have

x	0	1	2	3	4	5	6	7	8	9	10	11	12	$\cdots$
$f_{4,15}(x)$	1	4	1	4	1	4	1	4	1	4	1	4	1	$\cdots$

$$\tag{6.152}$$

For $a = 13$, we have

x	0	1	2	3	4	5	6	7	8	9	10	11	12	$\cdots$
$f_{13,15}(x)$	1	13	4	7	1	13	4	7	1	13	4	7	1	$\cdots$

$$\tag{6.153}$$

$\square$

The first few outputs of $f_{13,15}$ function can be viewed as the bar graph in Figure 6.3.

Example 6.5.4 Let us work out some examples with $N = 371$. This is a little harder and probably cannot be done with a handheld calculator. The numbers simply get too large. However, it is not difficult to write a small program, use MATLAB or Microsoft Excel. Trying to calculate $a^x \text{ Mod } N$ by first calculating a^x will not go very far, because the numbers will usually be beyond range. Rather, the trick is to calculate $a^x \text{ Mod } N$ from $a^{x-1} \text{ Mod } N$ by using the standard number theoretic fact

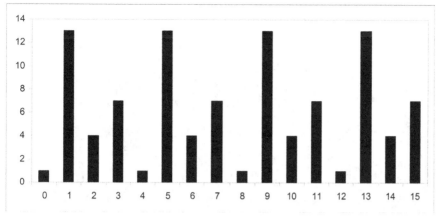

Figure 6.3. The first few outputs of $f_{13,15}$.

that

$$\text{if } a \equiv a' \text{ Mod } N \text{ and } b \equiv b' \text{ Mod } N, \text{ then } a \times b \equiv a' \times b' \text{ Mod } N. \quad (6.154)$$

Or, equivalently

$$a \times b \text{ Mod } N = (a \text{ Mod } N) \times (b \text{ Mod } N) \text{ Mod } N. \quad (6.155)$$

From this fact we get the formula

$$a^x \text{ Mod } N = a^{x-1} \times a \text{ Mod } N = ((a^{x-1} \text{ Mod } N) \times (a \text{ Mod } N)) \text{ Mod } N. \quad (6.156)$$

Because $a < N$ and $a \text{ Mod } N = a$, this reduces to

$$a^x \text{ Mod } N = ((a^{x-1} \text{ Mod } N) \times a) \text{ Mod } N. \quad (6.157)$$

Using this, it is easy to iterate to get the desired results. For $N = 371$ and $a = 2$, we have

x	0	1	2	3	4	5	6	7	$\cdots$	78	$\cdots$	155	156	157	158	$\cdots$
$f_{2,371}(x)$	1	2	4	8	16	32	64	128	$\cdots$	211	$\cdots$	186	1	2	4	$\cdots$

$$(6.158)$$

For $N = 371$ and $a = 6$, we have

x	0	1	2	3	4	5	6	7	$\cdots$	13	$\cdots$	25	26	27	28	$\cdots$
$f_{6,371}(x)$	1	6	36	216	183	356	281	202	$\cdots$	370	$\cdots$	62	1	6	36	$\cdots$

$$(6.159)$$

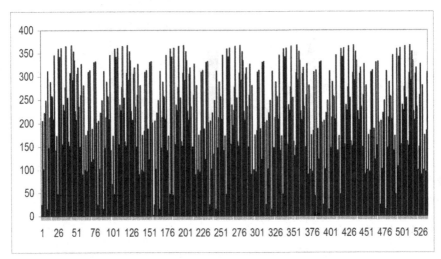

Figure 6.4. The output of $f_{24,371}$.

For $N = 371$ and $a = 24$, we have

x	0	1	2	3	4	5	6	7	$\cdots$	39	$\cdots$	77	78	79	80	$\cdots$
$f_{24,371}(x)$	1	24	205	97	102	222	134	248	$\cdots$	160	$\cdots$	201	1	24	205	$\cdots$

$$(6.160)$$

$\square$

We can see the results of $f_{24,371}$ as a bargraph in Figure 6.4.

Exercise 6.5.3   Calculate the first few values of $f_{a,N}$ for $N = 247$ and

(i) $a = 2$
(ii) $a = 17$
(iii) $a = 23$.

$\blacksquare$

In truth, we do not really need the values of this function, but rather we need to find the **period** of this function, i.e., we need to find the smallest r such that

$$f_{a,N}(r) = a^r \text{ Mod } N = 1. \qquad (6.161)$$

It is a theorem of number theory that for any co-prime $a \leq N$, the function $f_{a,N}$ will output a 1 for some $r < N$. After it hits 1, the sequence of numbers will simply repeat. If $f_{a,N}(r) = 1$, then

$$f_{a,N}(r + 1) = f_{a,N}(1) \qquad (6.162)$$

and in general

$$f_{a,N}(r + s) = f_{a,N}(s). \qquad (6.163)$$

Example 6.5.5 Charts (6.151), (6.152), and (6.153) show us that the periods for $f_{2,15}$, $f_{4,15}$, and $f_{13,15}$ are 4, 2, and 4, respectively. Charts (6.158), (6.159), and (6.160) show us that the periods for $f_{2,371}$, $f_{6,371}$, and $f_{24,371}$ are 156, 26, and 78, respectively. In fact, it is easy to see the periodicity of $f_{24,371}$ in Figure 6.4.   □

Exercise 6.5.4 Find the period of the functions $f_{2,247}$, $f_{17,247}$, and $f_{23,247}$.   ■

The Quantum Part of the Algorithm. For small numbers like 15, 371, and 247, it is fairly easy to calculate the periods of these functions. But what about a large N that is perhaps hundreds of digits long? This will be beyond the ability of any conventional computers. We will need a quantum computer with its ability to be in a superposition to calculate $f_{a,N}(x)$ for *all* needed x.

How do we get a quantum circuit to find the period? First we have to show that there is a quantum circuit that can implement the function $f_{a,N}$. The output of this function will always be less than N, and so we will need $n = \log_2 N$ output bits. We will need to evaluate $f_{a,N}$ for at least the first N^2 values of x and so will need at least

$$m = \log_2 N^2 = 2 \log_2 N = 2n \tag{6.164}$$

input qubits. The quantum circuit that we would get will be the operator $U_{f_{a,N}}$, which we may visualize as

$$
\begin{array}{c}
|\mathbf{x}\rangle \quad /^m \quad \boxed{U_{f_{a,N}}} \quad /^m \quad |\mathbf{x}\rangle \\
|\mathbf{y}\rangle \quad /^n \qquad\qquad /^n \quad |\mathbf{y} \oplus f_{a,N}(\mathbf{x})\rangle
\end{array}
\tag{6.165}
$$

where $|\mathbf{x}, \mathbf{y}\rangle$ goes to $|\mathbf{x}, \mathbf{y} \oplus f_{a,N}(\mathbf{x})\rangle = |\mathbf{x}, \mathbf{y} \oplus a^{\mathbf{x}} \text{ Mod } N\rangle$.[2] How is this circuit formed? Rather than destroying the flow of the discussion, we leave that technical discussion for a mini appendix at the end of this section.

With $U_{f_{a,N}}$, we can go on to use it in the following quantum algorithm. The first thing is to evaluate *all* the input at one time. From earlier sections, we know how to put $\mathbf{x}$ into an equally weighted superposition. (In fact, the beginning of this algorithm is very similar to Simon's algorithm.) We shall explain all the various parts of this quantum circuit:

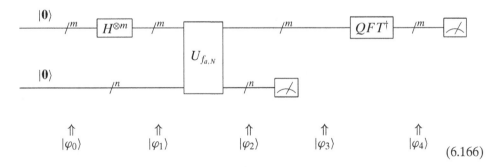

$$\tag{6.166}$$

---

[2] Until now, we have thought of x as any number and now we are dealing with x as its binary expansion $\mathbf{x}$. This is because we are thinking of x as described in a (quantum) computer. We shall use both notations interchangeably.

In terms of matrices this is

$$(Measure \otimes I)(QFT^\dagger \otimes I)(I \otimes Measure)U_{f_{a,N}}(H^{\otimes m} \otimes I)|\mathbf{0}_m, \mathbf{0}_n\rangle, \quad (6.167)$$

where $\mathbf{0}_m$ and $\mathbf{0}_n$ are qubit strings of length m and n, respectively.

Let us look at the states of the system. We start at

$$|\varphi_0\rangle = |\mathbf{0}_m, \mathbf{0}_n\rangle. \tag{6.168}$$

We then place the input in an equally weighted superposition of all possible inputs:

$$|\varphi_1\rangle = \frac{\sum_{\mathbf{x}\in\{0,1\}^m} |\mathbf{x}, \mathbf{0}_n\rangle}{\sqrt{2^m}}. \tag{6.169}$$

Evaluation of f on all these possibilities gives us

$$|\varphi_2\rangle = \frac{\sum_{\mathbf{x}\in\{0,1\}^m} |\mathbf{x}, f_{a,N}(\mathbf{x})\rangle}{\sqrt{2^m}} = \frac{\sum_{\mathbf{x}\in\{0,1\}^m} |\mathbf{x}, a^{\mathbf{x}} \text{ Mod } N\rangle}{\sqrt{2^m}}. \tag{6.170}$$

As the examples showed, these outputs repeat and repeat. They are periodic. We have to figure out what is the period. Let us meditate on what was just done. It is right here where the fantastic power of quantum computing is used. We have evaluated *all* the needed values at one time! Only quantum parallelism can perform such a task.

Let us pause and look at some examples.

Example 6.5.6   For $N = 15$, we will have $n = 4$ and $m = 8$. For $a = 13$, the state $|\varphi_2\rangle$ will be

$$\frac{|0, 1\rangle + |1, 13\rangle + |2, 4\rangle + |3, 7\rangle + |4, 1\rangle + \cdots + |254, 4\rangle + |255, 7\rangle}{\sqrt{256}}. \tag{6.171}$$

$\square$

Example 6.5.7   For $N = 371$, we will have $n = 9$ and $m = 18$. For $a = 24$, the state $|\varphi_2\rangle$ will be

$$\frac{|0, 1\rangle + |1, 24\rangle + |2, 205\rangle + |3, 97\rangle + |4, 102\rangle + \cdots + |2^{18} - 1, 24^{2^{18}-1} \text{ Mod } 371\rangle}{\sqrt{2^{18}}}. \tag{6.172}$$

$\square$

Exercise 6.5.5   Write the state $|\varphi_2\rangle$ for $N = 247$ and $a = 9$.   ∎

Going on with the algorithm, we measure the bottom qubits of $|\varphi_2\rangle$, which is in a superposition of many states. Let us say that after measuring the bottom qubits we find

$$a^{\overline{\mathbf{x}}} \text{ Mod } N \tag{6.173}$$

for some $\bar{\mathbf{x}}$. However, by the periodicity of $f_{a,N}$ we also have that

$$a^{\bar{\mathbf{x}}} \equiv a^{\bar{\mathbf{x}}+r} \text{ Mod } N \tag{6.174}$$

and

$$a^{\bar{\mathbf{x}}} \equiv a^{\bar{\mathbf{x}}+2r} \text{ Mod } N. \tag{6.175}$$

In fact, for any $s \in \mathbb{Z}$ we have

$$a^{\bar{\mathbf{x}}} \equiv a^{\bar{\mathbf{x}}+sr} \text{ Mod } N. \tag{6.176}$$

How many of the 2^m superpositions $\mathbf{x}$ in $|\varphi_2\rangle$ have $a^{\bar{\mathbf{x}}}$ Mod N as the output? Answer: $\lfloor \frac{2^m}{r} \rfloor$. So

$$|\varphi_3\rangle = \frac{\sum_{a^{\mathbf{x}} \equiv a^{\bar{\mathbf{x}}} \text{ Mod } N} |\mathbf{x}, a^{\bar{\mathbf{x}}} \text{ Mod } N\rangle}{\lfloor \frac{2^m}{r} \rfloor}. \tag{6.177}$$

We might also write this as

$$|\varphi_3\rangle = \frac{\sum_{j=0}^{2^m/r-1} |t_0 + jr, a^{\bar{\mathbf{x}}} \text{ Mod } N\rangle}{\left[\frac{2^m}{r}\right]}, \tag{6.178}$$

where t_0 is the first time that $a^{t_0} \equiv a^{\bar{\mathbf{x}}}$ Mod N, i.e., the first time that the measured value occurs. We shall call t_0 the **offset** of the period for reasons that will soon become apparent.

It is important to realize that this stage employs entanglement in a serious fashion. The top qubits and the bottom qubits are entangled in a way that when the top is measured, the bottom stays the same.

Example 6.5.8 Continuing Example 6.5.6, let us say that after measurement of the bottom qubits, 7 is found. In that case $|\varphi_3\rangle$ would be

$$\frac{|3, 7\rangle + |7, 7\rangle + |11, 7\rangle + |15, 7\rangle + \cdots + |251, 7\rangle + |255, 7\rangle}{\left[\frac{256}{4}\right]}. \tag{6.179}$$

For example, if we looked at the $f_{13,15}$ rather than the bargraph in Figure 6.3, we would get the bargraph shown in Figure 6.5. □

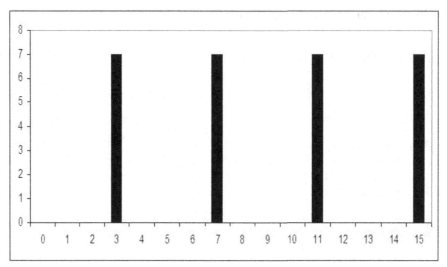

Figure 6.5. $f_{13,15}$ after a measurement of 7.

Example 6.5.9   Continuing Example 6.5.7, let us say that after measurement of the bottom qubits we find 222 (which is 24^5 Mod 371.) In that case $|\varphi_3\rangle$ would be

$$\frac{|5, 222\rangle + |83, 222\rangle + |161, 222\rangle + |239, 222\rangle + \cdots}{\left[\frac{2^{18}}{78}\right]}. \qquad (6.180)$$

We can see the result of this measurement in Figure 6.6   □

Exercise 6.5.6   Continuing Exercise 6.5.5, let us say that after measuring the bottom qubits, 55 is found. What would $|\varphi_3\rangle$ be?   ∎

The final step of the quantum part of the algorithm is to take such a superposition and return its period. This will be done with a type of **Fourier transform**. We do not

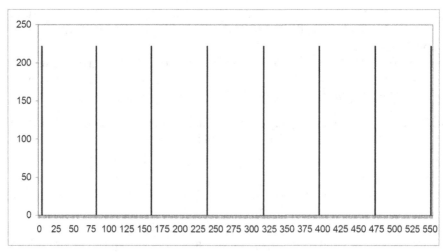

Figure 6.6. $f_{24,371}$ after a measurement of 222.

assume the reader has seen this before and some motivation is in order. Let us step away from our task at hand and talk about evaluating polynomials. Consider the polynomial

$$P(x) = a_0 + a_1 x^1 + a_2 x^2 + a_3 x^3 + \cdots + a_{n-1} x^{n-1}. \tag{6.181}$$

We can represent this polynomial with a column vector $[a_0, a_1, a_2, \ldots, a_{n-1}]^T$. Suppose we wanted to evaluate this polynomial at the numbers $x_0, x_1, x_2, \ldots, x_{n-1}$, i.e., we wanted to find $P(x_0)$, $P(x_1)$, $P(x_2)$, $\ldots$, $P(x_{n-1})$. A simple way of performing the task is with the following matrix multiplication:

$$
\begin{bmatrix}
1 & x_0 & x_0^2 & \cdots & x_0^j & \cdots & x_0^{n-1} \\
1 & x_1 & x_1^2 & \cdots & x_1^j & \cdots & x_1^{n-1} \\
1 & x_2 & x_2^2 & \cdots & x_2^j & \cdots & x_2^{n-1} \\
\vdots & & \vdots & & \vdots & & \vdots \\
1 & x_k & x_k^2 & \cdots & x_k^j & \cdots & x_k^{n-1} \\
\vdots & & \vdots & & \vdots & & \vdots \\
1 & x_{n-1} & x_{n-1}^2 & \cdots & x_{n-1}^j & \cdots & x_{n-1}^{n-1}
\end{bmatrix}
\begin{bmatrix}
a_0 \\ a_1 \\ a_2 \\ \vdots \\ a_j \\ \vdots \\ a_{n-1}
\end{bmatrix}
=
\begin{bmatrix}
P(x_0) \\ P(x_1) \\ P(x_2) \\ \vdots \\ P(x_k) \\ \vdots \\ P(x_{n-1})
\end{bmatrix}. \tag{6.182}
$$

The matrix on the left, where every row is a geometric series, is called the **Vandermonde matrix** and is denoted $\mathcal{V}(x_0, x_1, x_2, \ldots, x_{n-1})$. There is no restriction on the type of numbers we are permitted to use in the Vandermonde matrix, and hence, we are permitted to use complex numbers. In fact, we shall need them to be powers of one of the Mth roots of unity, ω_M^1 (see page 26 of Chapter 1 for a quick reminder). Because M is fixed throughout this discussion, we shall simply denote this as ω. There is also no restriction on the size of the Vandermonde matrix. Letting $M = 2^m$, which is the amount of numbers that can be described with the top qubits, there is a need for the Vandermonde matrix to be an M-by-M matrix. We would like to evaluate the polynomials at $\omega^0 = 1, \omega, \omega^2, \ldots, \omega^{M-1}$. To do this, we need to look at $\mathcal{V}(\omega^0, \omega^1, \omega^2, \ldots, \omega^{M-1})$. In order to evaluate $P(x)$ at the Mth roots of unity, we must multiply

$$
\begin{bmatrix}
1 & 1 & 1 & \cdots & 1 & \cdots & 1 \\
1 & \omega^1 & \omega^2 & \cdots & \omega^j & \cdots & \omega^{M-1} \\
1 & \omega^2 & \omega^{2\times2} & \cdots & \omega^{2j} & \cdots & \omega^{2(M-1)} \\
\vdots & & \vdots & & \vdots & & \vdots \\
1 & \omega^k & \omega^{k2} & \cdots & \omega^{kj} & \cdots & \omega^{k(M-1)} \\
\vdots & & \vdots & & \vdots & & \vdots \\
1 & \omega^{M-1} & \omega^{(M-1)2} & \cdots & \omega^{(M-1)j} & \cdots & \omega^{(M-1)(M-1)}
\end{bmatrix}
\begin{bmatrix}
a_0 \\ a_1 \\ a_2 \\ \vdots \\ a_j \\ \vdots \\ a_{M-1}
\end{bmatrix}
=
\begin{bmatrix}
P(\omega^0) \\ P(\omega^1) \\ P(\omega^2) \\ \vdots \\ P(\omega^k) \\ \vdots \\ P(\omega^{M-1})
\end{bmatrix}.
$$

$$\tag{6.183}$$

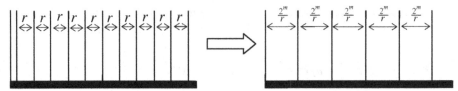

Figure 6.7. The action of $DFT^\dagger$.

$[P(\omega^0), P(\omega^1), P(\omega^2), \ldots, P(\omega^k), \ldots, P(\omega^{M-1})]^T$ is the vector of the values of the polynomial at the Mth roots of unity.

Let us define the **discrete Fourier transform**, denoted DFT, as

$$DFT = \frac{1}{\sqrt{M}} \mathcal{V}(\omega^0, \omega^1, \omega^2, \ldots, \omega^{M-1}). \tag{6.184}$$

Formally, DFT is defined as

$$DFT[j, k] = \frac{1}{\sqrt{M}} \omega^{jk}. \tag{6.185}$$

It is easy to see that DFT is a unitary matrix: the adjoint of this matrix, $DFT^\dagger$, is formally defined as

$$DFT^\dagger[j, k] = \frac{1}{\sqrt{M}} \overline{\omega^{kj}} = \frac{1}{\sqrt{M}} \omega^{-jk}. \tag{6.186}$$

To show that DFT is unitary, let us multiply

$$(DFT \star DFT^\dagger)[j, k] = \frac{1}{M} \sum_{i=0}^{M-1} (\omega^{ji} \omega^{-ik}) = \frac{1}{M} \sum_{i=0}^{M-1} \omega^{-i(k-j)}. \tag{6.187}$$

If $k = j$, i.e., if we are along the diagonal, this becomes

$$\frac{1}{M} \sum_{i=0}^{M-1} \omega^0 = \frac{1}{M} \sum_{i=0}^{M-1} 1 = 1. \tag{6.188}$$

If $k \neq j$, i.e., if we are off the diagonal, then we get a geometric progression which sums to 0. And so $DFT \star DFT^\dagger = I$.

What task does $DFT^\dagger$ perform? Our text will not get into the nitty-gritty of this important operation, but we shall try to give an intuition of what is going on. Let us forget about the normalization $\frac{1}{\sqrt{M}}$ for a moment and think about this intuitively. The matrix DFT acts on polynomials by evaluating them on different equally spaced points of the circle. The outcomes of those evaluations will necessarily have periodicity because the points go around and around the circle. So multiplying a column vector with DFT takes a sequence and outputs a periodic sequence. If we start with a periodic column vector, then the DFT will transform the periodicity. Similarly, the inverse of the Fourier transform, $DFT^\dagger$, will also change the periodicity. Suffice it to say that the $DFT^\dagger$ does two tasks as shown in Figure 6.7:

- It modifies the period from r to $\frac{2^m}{r}$.
- It eliminates the offset.

Circuit (6.166) requires a variant of a DFT called a **quantum Fourier transform** and denoted as QFT. Its inverse is denoted $QFT^\dagger$. The $QFT^\dagger$ performs the same operation but is constructed in a way that is more suitable for quantum computers. (We shall not delve into the details of its construction.) The quantum version is very fast and made of "small" unitary operators that are easy for a quantum computer to implement.[3]

The final step of the circuit is to measure the top qubits. For our presentation, we shall make the simplifying assumption that r evenly divides into 2^m. Shor's actual algorithm does not make this assumption and goes into details about finding the period for any r. When we measure the top qubit we will find it to be some multiple of $\frac{2^m}{r}$. That is, we will measure

$$x = \frac{\lambda 2^m}{r} \tag{6.191}$$

for some whole number λ. We know 2^m, and after measuring we will also know x. We can divide the whole number x by 2^m and get

$$\frac{x}{2^m} = \frac{\lambda 2^m}{r 2^m} = \frac{\lambda}{r}. \tag{6.192}$$

One can then reduce this number to an irreducible fraction and take the denominator to be the long sought-after r. If we do not make the simplifying assumption that r evenly divides into 2^m, then we might have to perform this process several times and analyze the results.

From the Period to the Factors.   Let us see how knowledge of the period r will help us find a factor of N. We shall need a period that is an even number. There is a theorem of number theory that tells us that for the majority of a, the period of $f_{a,N}$ will be an even number. If, however, we do choose an a such that the period is an odd number, simply throw that a away and choose another one. Once an even r is found so that

$$a^r \equiv 1 \bmod N, \tag{6.193}$$

---

[3] There are slight variations of Shor's algorithm: For one, rather than using the $H^{\otimes m}$ to put the m qubits in a superposition in the beginning of circuit (6.166), we could have used QFT and get the same results. However, we leave it as is because at this point the reader has familiarity with the Hadamard matrix.

Another variation is not measuring the bottom qubits before performing the $QFT^\dagger$ operation. This makes the mathematics slightly more complicated. We leave it as is for simplicity sakes.

However, if we take both of these variants, our quantum circuit would look like

$$\tag{6.189}$$

This would have been more in line with our discussion at the end of Section 2.3, where we wrote about solving problems using

$$Translation \mapsto Calculation \mapsto Reverse\ Translation \tag{6.190}$$

where QFT and $QFT^\dagger$ would be our two translations.

we may subtract 1 from both sides of the equivalence to get

$$a^r - 1 \equiv 0 \text{ Mod } N, \tag{6.194}$$

or equivalently

$$N | (a^r - 1). \tag{6.195}$$

Remembering that $1 = 1^2$ and $x^2 - y^2 = (x + y)(x - y)$ we get that

$$N | (\sqrt{a^r} + 1)(\sqrt{a^r} - 1) \tag{6.196}$$

or

$$N | (a^{\frac{r}{2}} + 1)(a^{\frac{r}{2}} - 1). \tag{6.197}$$

(If r was odd, we would not be able to evenly divide by 2.) This means that any factor of N is also a factor of either $(a^{\frac{r}{2}} + 1)$ or $(a^{\frac{r}{2}} - 1)$ or both. Either way, a factor for N can be found by looking at

$$\text{GCD}((a^{\frac{r}{2}} + 1), N) \tag{6.198}$$

and

$$\text{GCD}((a^{\frac{r}{2}} - 1), N). \tag{6.199}$$

Finding the GCD can be done with the classical Euclidean algorithm. There is, however, one caveat. We must make sure that

$$a^{\frac{r}{2}} \neq -1 \text{ Mod } N \tag{6.200}$$

because if $a^{\frac{r}{2}} \equiv -1 \text{ Mod } N$, then the right side of Equation (6.197) would be 0. In that case we do not get any information about N and must throw away that particular a and start over again.

Let us work out some examples.

Example 6.5.10   In chart (6.151), we saw that the period of $f_{2,15}$ is 4, i.e., $2^4 \equiv 1 \text{ Mod } 15$. From Equation (6.197), we get that

$$15 | (2^2 + 1)(2^2 - 1). \tag{6.201}$$

And, hence, we have that GCD$(5, 15) = 5$ and GCD$(3, 15) = 3$.   □

Example 6.5.11   In chart (6.159), we saw that the period of $f_{6,371}$ is 26, i.e., $6^{26} \equiv 1 \text{ Mod } 371$. However, we can also see that $6^{\frac{26}{2}} = 6^{13} \equiv 370 \equiv -1 \text{ Mod } 371$. So we cannot use $a = 6$.   □

Example 6.5.12   In chart (6.160), we saw that the period of $f_{24,371}$ is 78, i.e., $24^{78} \equiv 1 \text{ Mod } 371$. We can also see that $24^{\frac{78}{2}} = 24^{39} \equiv 160 \neq -1 \text{ Mod } 371$. From Equation (6.197), we get that

$$371 | (24^{39} + 1)(24^{39} - 1). \tag{6.202}$$

And, thus, GCD$(161, 371) = 7$ and GCD$(159, 371) = 53$ and $371 = 7 * 53$.   □

Exercise 6.5.7 Use the fact that the period of $f_{7,247}$ is 12 to determine the factors of 247. ∎

Shor's Algorithm. We are, at last, ready to put all the pieces together and formally state **Shor's algorithm**:

Input: A positive integer N with $n = \lceil \log_2 N \rceil$.

Output: A factor p of N if it exists.

Step 1. Use a polynomial algorithm to determine if N is prime or a power of prime. If it is a prime, declare that it is and exit. If it is a power of a prime number, declare that it is and exit.

Step 2. Randomly choose an integer a such that $1 < a < N$. Perform Euclid's algorithm to determine $\text{GCD}(a, N)$. If the GCD is not 1, then return it and exit.

Step 3. Use quantum circuit (6.166) to find a period r.

Step 4. If r is odd or if $a^{\frac{r}{2}} \equiv -1 \text{ Mod } N$, then return to Step 2 and choose another a.

Step 5. Use Euclid's algorithm to calculate $\text{GCD}((a^{\frac{r}{2}} + 1), N)$ and $\text{GCD}((a^{\frac{r}{2}} - 1), N)$. Return at least one of the nontrivial solutions.

What is the worst case complexity of this algorithm? To determine this, one needs to have an in-depth analysis of the details of how $U_{f_{a,N}}$ and $QFT^{\dagger}$ are implemented. One would also need to know what percentage of times things can go wrong. For example, what percentage of a would $f_{a,N}$ have an odd period? Rather than going into the gory details, let us just state that Shor's algorithm works in

$$O(n^2 \log n \, \log \log n) \tag{6.203}$$

number of steps, where n is the number of bits needed to represent the number N. That is polynomial in terms of n. This is in contrast to the best-known classical algorithms that demand

$$O(e^{cn^{1/3} \, \log^{2/3} n}) \tag{6.204}$$

steps, where c is some constant. This is exponential in terms of n. Shor's quantum algorithm is indeed faster.

Appendix: Implementing $U_{f_{a,N}}$ with quantum gates. In order for $U_{f_{a,N}}$ to be implemented with unitary matrices, we need to "break up" the operations into small little jobs. This is done by splitting up x. Let us write x in binary. That is,

$$\mathbf{x} = x_{n-1}x_{n-2} \cdots x_2 x_1 x_0. \tag{6.205}$$

Formally, x as a number is

$$x = x_{n-1}2^{n-1} + x_{n-2}2^{n-2} + \cdots + x_2 2^2 + x_1 2 + x_0. \tag{6.206}$$

Using this description of x, we can rewrite our function as

$$f_{a,N}(x) = a^x \bmod N = a^{x_{n-1}2^{n-1} + x_{n-2}2^{n-2} + \cdots + x_2 2^2 + x_1 2 + x_0} \bmod N \qquad (6.207)$$

or

$$a^{x_{n-1}2^{n-1}} \times a^{x_{n-2}2^{n-2}} \times \cdots \times a^{x_2 2^2} \times a^{x_1 2} \times a^{x_0} \bmod N. \qquad (6.208)$$

We can convert this formula to an inductive definition[4] of $f_{a,N}(x)$. We shall define $y_0, y_1, y_2, \ldots, y_{n-2}, y_{n-1}$, where $y_{n-1} = f_{a,N}(x)$: the base case is

$$y_0 = a^{x_0}. \qquad (6.209)$$

If we have y_{j-1}, then to get y_j we use the trick from Equation (6.157):

$$y_j = y_{j-1} \times a^{x_j 2^j} \bmod N. \qquad (6.210)$$

Notice that if $x_j = 0$ then $y_j = y_{j-1}$. In other words, whether or not we should multiply y_{j-1} by $a^{2^j} \bmod N$ is dependent on whether or not $x_j = 1$. It turns out that as long as a and N are co-prime, the operation of multiplying a number times $a^{2^j} \bmod N$ is reversible and, in fact, unitary. So for each j, there is a unitary operator

$$U_{a^{2^j} \bmod N} \qquad (6.211)$$

that we shall write as $U_{a^{2^j}}$. As we want to perform this operation conditionally, we will need controlled-$U_{a^{2^j}}$, or $^C U_{a^{2^j}}$, gates. Putting this all together, we have the following quantum circuit that implements $f_{a,N}$ in a polynomial number of gates:

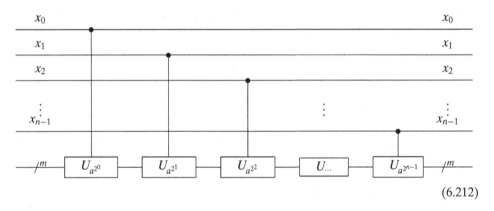

$$(6.212)$$

Even if a real implementation of large-scale quantum computers is years away, the design and study of quantum algorithms is something that is ongoing and is an exciting field of interest.

. . . .

References:

(i) A version of Deutsch's algorithm was first stated in Deutsch (1985).
(ii) Deutsch–Jozsa was given in Deutsch and Jozsa (1992).
(iii) Simon's algorithm was first presented in Simon (1994).

---

[4] This inductive definition is nothing more than the modular-exponentiation algorithm given in, say, Section 31.6 of Corman et al. (2001) or Section 1.2 of Dasgupta, Papadimitriou, and Vazirani (2006).

(iv) Grover's search algorithm was originally presented in Grover (1997). Further developments of the algorithm can be found in Chapter 6 of Nielsen and Chuang (2000). For nice applications of Grover's algorithm to graph theory, see Cirasella (2006).

(v) Shor's algorithm was first announced in Shor (1994). There is also a very readable presentation of it in Shor (1997). There are several slight variations to the algorithm and there are many presentations at different levels of complexity. Chapter 5 of Nielsen and Chuang (2000) goes through it thoroughly. Chapter 10 of Dasgupta, Papadimitriou, and Vazirani (2006) goes from an introduction to quantum computing through Shor's algorithm in 20 pages.

Every quantum computer textbook works through several algorithms. See, e.g., Hirvensalo (2001) and Kitaev, Shen, and Vyalyi (2002) and, of course, Nielsen and Chuang (2000). There is also a very nice short article by Shor that discusses several algorithms (Shor, 2002). Dorit Aharonov has written a nice survey article that goes through many of the algorithms (Aharonov, 1998)

Peter Shor has written a very interesting article on the seeming paucity of quantum algorithms in Shor (2003).

7

Programming Languages

The computer programmer is a creator of universes for which he alone is the lawgiver... universes of virtually unlimited complexity can be created in the form of computer programs.... They compliantly obey their laws and vividly exhibit their obedient behavior. No playwright, no stage director, no emperor, however powerful, has ever exercised such absolute authority to arrange a stage or a field of battle and to command such unswervingly dutiful actors or troops.

J. Weizmann, *Computer Power and Human Reason: From Judgement to Calculation*

In this chapter we are going to describe **quantum programming**, i.e., the art and science of programming a quantum computer. In Section 7.1, we briefly sketch what it means to program a quantum computing device. Section 7.2 covers a simple version of quantum assembler, based on the so-called QRAM architecture. Section 7.3 describes possible steps leading to higher-level programming languages and constructs. We conclude this chapter with Section 7.4, a short discussion on quantum emulators.

7.1 PROGRAMMING IN A QUANTUM WORLD

As you are about to read this chapter, you have undoubtedly been exposed to computer programming in a variety of flavors, and are perhaps already an accomplished programmer of real-life applications. Programming a classical machine carries an immediate, unambiguous sense. However, we are going to leave the familiar world of binary chips, and learn how to program some as yet unspecified quantum hardware. Thus, it is appropriate to spend a minute pondering what it can possibly mean to write code for a quantum computing device.

As we all know, programming a computer means to tell it to carry out certain actions in a specific language that the machine understands, either directly or through the intermediary of an interpreter. A program is a set of instructions, planning out the behavior of the computing machine. Stripped of all its complexity, this set of instructions prescribes how to manipulate data in a controlled fashion, as summarized by the following slogan:

$$\boxed{DATA + CONTROL = PROGRAMMING}$$

Control here means that the program is built from a small set of basic instructions and a set of control structures (conditionals, jumps, loops, etc.).

This scheme carries over to the world of quantum computers. We can assume in the following that a machine sits in front of us; also, the machine is a computer that operates at least partially at the quantum level. For the time being, you can imagine that our computer comprises a quantum device, with an input area of *quantum data*, represented by an addressable set of qubits, together with a set of prebuilt *operations* that can manipulate quantum data. These operations are of two types: unitary operations, which will evolve quantum data, and measuring, which will inspect the value of data. We shall also assume that we can assemble more and more complicated operations out of the basic ones. Loosely speaking, the set of instructions that specify such assemblages will be our quantum programs. Here is the updated "quantum" slogan:

$$\boxed{QUANTUM\ DATA + CONTROL = QUANTUM\ PROGRAMMING}$$

Let us now imagine that we have a concrete problem to solve, where additional quantum speedup might be highly beneficial, and that after some pondering we have come up with some effective quantum algorithm, perhaps similar to those we have already encountered in Chapter 6.

A basic ingredient is still missing, namely, a *programming language for writing down our instructions*. Such a language will enable us to control the quantum computing device and implement our quantum algorithm.[1]

7.2 QUANTUM ASSEMBLY PROGRAMMING

Nowadays, there is a plethora of programming languages for classical machines. Most programmers write their source code in one or more of the high-level programming languages, such as C++, Perl, or Java. Quite often a developer ignores the architecture of the machines he/she is working with, or how the underlying operating system will handle the requests of the program. There is an obvious advantage in this state of affairs: we can concentrate on the task at hand, and simply let

---

[1] We have deliberately separated algorithms from the language in which they are implemented to emphasize the fact that the focus of quantum programming is not quantum algorithms per se, but the way they are expressed in a quantum language (thus, we can think of the description of the algorithms in Chapter 6 as given in some sort of quantum pseudo-code). In real life, though, there is a tight synergy between algorithm design and the choice of a specific programming language, as every experienced software engineer knows well: a good language's choice fosters good algorithm's design.

the interpreter/compiler take care of what goes on under the hood. It should be remembered though that somebody has to have the know-how necessary to build such interpreters–compilers; simply, this expertise has been confined to a relatively small subgroup within the vast community of software developers. We should bear in mind, though, that things were not always this way: only a few decades ago assembler was pretty much the only game in town. Before those times, the only option was crude machine language.[2]

In our exploration of quantum programming languages we shall not begin with raw **quantum machine language**, a territory at the frontier between quantum hardware and quantum software; we touch this area a bit in Chapter 11. It goes without saying that to be able to program at the true quantum machine level, a vast amount of know-how in the fields of quantum physics and quantum engineering is required. The future quantum developer will not be expected to have such an in-depth expertise, just as modern-day programmers have for the most part a scanty knowledge of hardware issues. Furthermore, the need for a quantum programming language that is to some extent machine independent is rather obvious: the algorithms presented in Chapter 6 have clearly nothing to do with specific physical implementations. We should thus be able to specify them much in the same way as we are used to with classical algorithms. To do all these we need, at a minimum, a **quantum assembler**.

Although we can describe a quantum assembler without entering into the specifics of quantum hardware, we still need to select an architecture for the underlying quantum machine.[3]

There are at least three quite different, although provably equivalent, candidate architectures for quantum computation.[4] In Chapter 5, as you may recall, quantum gates were introduced. By combining quantum gates, one ends up with a computation model known as **quantum circuits**. Here is how:

- The first ingredient is an input device, through which we can feed quantum data.
- The second ingredient is a set of basic gates. Gates can be applied sequentially and in parallel, forming an acyclic-directed graph known as quantum circuit.
- The third ingredient is a device that enables us to carry out measurements. The result of this operation will be a sequence of standard bits that can be read off and further displayed, stored, and manipulated.

For a description of quantum circuits, their graphical notation, and some examples, you can refer back to Chapters 5 and 6.

We could describe a quantum assembler using quantum circuits as our background architecture. Notice that in the model we have just presented, measuring occurs only at the very end of the computing process. This is not a theoretical limitation

---

[2] Assembler and machine language are often confused. Indeed, for most practical purposes, they can be safely identified. Nevertheless, assembler represents a minimum of abstraction: register have names, and so do basic machine operations, such as ADD, PUSH, and REMOVE.

[3] It is exactly the same in the classical case. In any compiler design class, finite state machines, registers, heaps, stacks are introduced in order to illustrate what happens in response to specific commands.

[4] As a matter of fact, there are at least four: the last one is described in Raussendorf and Briegel (2001). In this model, there is no network involved. Instead, a cluster of entangled qubit is the starting point. Information is extracted via a sequence of one-qubit measurements. We are indebted to Stefano Bettelli for pointing this out.

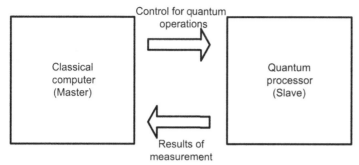

Figure 7.1. A simplified QRAM machine.

of the quantum circuits architecture, as it can be formally shown that measurements can always be pushed to the end. However, it is perhaps a bit awkward from the programming standpoint, as developers generally wish to inspect their variables anywhere during the computation.

As a second option, we could choose the **quantum Turing machine** model, which is presented in Chapter 8. These are precisely the quantum analog of Turing machines. Much like classical Turing machines, this model is very convenient for discussing quantum complexity classes and other theoretical computer science issues, but is not conducive to the design of algorithms or programming languages.

A third more convenient alternative, which we shall therefore adopt throughout this chapter, is known as **Quantum Random Access Memory Model (QRAM)**. The QRAM is made of the following parts:

- A classical computer, playing the role of the master.
- A quantum computing device (either internal or external), that can be accessed by the master computer on request.

Figure 7.1 is a simplified sketch of a QRAM machine.

The idea behind the QRAM is that the programmer writes classical code in a standard classical language, say, C. When she needs the extra quantum power, she will add a few lines of quantum assembler to her code.[5] This q-assembler is the way to access and use the quantum device. Notice that the programmer is not required to know anything about the internals of the quantum device. There is no need to know how qubits are physically stored, initialized, manipulated, or measured. The only information she may need concerns the capacity of the device, i.e., the maximum size of available quantum memory. Everything else will happen by means of a **Quantum Hardware Interface**, or **QHI**, which will translate assembler commands issued by the master into explicit actions performed by the quantum device.

As you have certainly not failed to notice, the description of the QRAM model has been very vague (there are just two empty boxes in the picture). Let us flesh

---

[5] This concept is not far-fetched: think of a graphic developer programming a sophisticated 3D game. When she needs to carry out computationally intensive operations, such as fast matrix multiplications for repositioning her objects in the scene, she can take advantage of a graphic accelerator via a few snippets of code embedded in the main program.

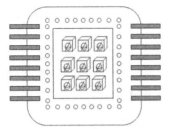

Figure 7.2. A 9-qubit register.

it out a bit . . . The first box is a classical computer. Inside the master computer, the control register will be used to store q-assembler instruction (after all, the instructions themselves are encodable as sequences of bits!). When the control pointer is on one or the other of the quantum instructions, the master will use the quantum hardware interface to push it over to the servant device. What is inside the second box? Essentially two things: a set of quantum data storage registers (we are going to introduce them in a minute) and utilities that apply operations on the storage.

Note: Let us recall in passing that the no-cloning theorem will prevent quantum assembler from having *copying instructions*. There is no way to copy the content of a register to another one, a familiar and pervasive operation in ordinary assemblers.

The first thing our programmer will do is to ask the quantum device through the quantum hardware interface to initialize an addressable sequence of qubits. These transactions happen through an interface known as the **quantum register**, or **q-register**.

Definition 7.2.1 *A **quantum register** is an interface to an addressable sequence of qubits (see Figure 7.2). Each q-register has a unique identifier by which it is referred.*

For the purpose of this discussion, we can safely think of the quantum register as an array of adjacent qubits. Where and how they are actually stored in the quantum chip is irrelevant in this context.

What is the actual size of the register, and how many registers are available? Both questions will be left unanswered, as they depend on the progress made in quantum hardware. For the time being, we can think of each register as having a fixed size, and a numerical code, by which it can be addressed.

After the quantum register has been initialized and manipulated, the programmer can issue a command that will measure selected portions thereof. The quantum device will perform the requested measurement, and it will return a classical value that can be displayed and/or stored somewhere in the main program (e.g., as an array of classical bits). This is depicted in Figure 7.3.

The loop-back arrow in Figure 7.3 means that the same pipeline can be repeated as many times as needed.

As we have already mentioned, in this model measuring is interleaved with other commands: our quantum programmer can ask *at any time* after initialization for the value of an arbitrary section of the register.[6]

---

[6] With one important caveat: whenever she observes parts of the register, she destroys its state.

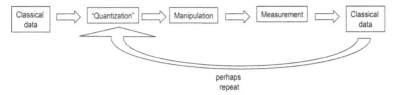

Figure 7.3. Flowchart of quantum control.

We are now armed with the necessary understanding to begin the design of a quantum assembler for the QRAM model. The toy assembler we are going to describe is not standard in any way.[7] It is here just for illustration purposes: real-life q-assemblers may differ from the one in this section.[8] For a thorough presentation of a quantum assembler in a real-life QRAM setting, you can read the article by R. Nagarajan, N. Papanikolaou, and D. Williams (2005).

Let us begin. In the following we shall denote by the letters $R1$, $R2$, ..., the identifiers (numerical codes) of the available q-registers. We shall also assume, for the sake of our discussion, that all registers are of size 8, i.e., they can store the quantum analog of a byte, a **qubyte**. The prefix R will stand for the code of an unspecified q-register.

We are now going to list the set of basic instructions comprising our language. The QRAM architecture enables the calling program to push each individual instruction over to the quantum chip one at a time.

We need a way to initialize q-registers. More specifically, we need to pass a bit array from the main program to a given q-register, and ask the quantum device to initialize it accordingly.

■ Initialize the register R:
INITIALIZE R [INPUT]

The optional INPUT is a *classical* array of bits, whose size matches the size of the register (i.e., a byte). If it is not specified, it is assumed to be filled with zeros.

Example 7.2.1 The example below initializes a register R of eight qubits; it then reinitializes it using as input the bit array $B = [00001111]$.

⋮

var B=[00001111] // before invoking quantum assembler

⋮

INITIALIZE R1
INITIALIZE R1 B

⋮   □

We shall assume that the default initialization procedure "cools off" all the qubits to the ground state $|0\rangle$. In other words, if we initialize a q-register of size

---

[7] As a matter of fact, we extracted it from a few extant proposals of imperative quantum languages, by discarding their high-level constructs.

[8] They almost certainly will, by taking advantage of a specific target hardware. The same happens in the classical case. There is no universal assembly language, but a family or closely related languages, each geared toward a specific platform.

5, the joint state is $|00000\rangle$. If, on the other hand, we do provide an INPUT such as [00101], the system will take care of initializing our register to $|00101\rangle$.

Let us proceed. Once we have a register, we can address its individual qubits for manipulation. For instance, $R[0]$ will denote its first qubit, and so on. As a convenience, though, we shall enrich our assembler with the capability of selecting a subregister variable, which we can use later on for our needs. Subregister variables will be denoted by the prefix letter S.

■ Select from R the subregister made up of NUMQUBITS qubits starting at R[OFFSET]. Store the address in the variable S.
   SELECT S R OFFSET NUMQUBITS

Example 7.2.2 We can iterate the instruction, extracting a subregister from an existing one:

$\vdots$

INITIALIZE R1
SELECT S R1 2 3

$\vdots$

In this fragment of quantum assembler we have initialized a quantum register, and we have then extracted a subregister formed by the qubits of index 2, 3, 4 and represented by the variable S (notice that we assume indices starting from 0, just like C arrays). □

Exercise 7.2.1 Consider the snippet of program:
INITIALIZE R1 [01110001]
SELECT S1 R1 2 4
SELECT S2 S1 0 2

$\vdots$

Which qubits of $R1$ have we selected in $S2$?   ■

As we have already mentioned, the second essential ingredient is the basic unitary transformations, known as gates (we have dedicated Section 5.4 to quantum gates; our reader is referred there for details):

$$\mathbf{GATES} = \{G_0, G_1, \dots, G_{n-1}\}. \tag{7.1}$$

Note: Different choices[9] of basic quantum gates can be made, as long as the set **GATES** is a **universal set of gates**, i.e., it generates *all* unitary transformations on a finite-dimensional Hilbert space via successive applications of composition and tensoring. In practice, gates like Hadamard that are constantly used should be part of the primitives, so **GATES** does not necessarily have to be a minimal generating set (redundancy is allowed).

---

[9] In the design of real-life quantum assembler, the choice would be dictated, at least in part, by which gates are easily implementable on the target hardware.

In the following exercises and examples we shall adopt the following set of gates:

$$\mathbf{GATES} = \{H, R_\theta, I_n, CNOT\}, \tag{7.2}$$

where H, R_θ, I_n, and $CNOT$ denote the Hadamard, the phase shift by an angle θ, the $n \times n$ identity matrix, and the controlled-NOT gate, respectively.

- The basic instruction will look like
  APPLY U R

where U will be a suitable unitary gate matching the size of the register R.

Most classical assemblers have some support for **macros**, and here we shall take the same course. We need ways to build new unitary transformations by concatenating more basic building blocks and by taking inverses (Remember: Unitary transformations are closed by composition and inverse!). The resulting transformation is given a name, and each time we intend to use it, it will be expanded inline by the assembler into its constituents. Let us now see how:

- The composition operation, that executes sequentially from right to left two unitary transformations U_1 and U_2, and saves the result in a variable U:
  U CONCAT U$_1$ U$_2$
- The tensor product (alias the parallelization) of operations: U is the result of tensoring U_1 and U_2:
  U TENSOR U$_1$ U$_2$
- The inverse: U is the result of taking the inverse of U_1 (i.e., the transformation that "undoes" U_1):
  U INVERSE U$_1$

Note: Why the identity matrix? The simple reason is that it is needed to pad unitary transformations to the appropriate size. Suppose, for instance, that you have a q-register of four qubits, but you want to manipulate only the first two, via, say, Hadamard. What you are going to do is to tensor H with I_2, which leaves the third and fourth qubit unchanged.

Example 7.2.3 Let us express some simple unitary transformations in our assembler:

U$_1$ CONCAT R$_{\frac{\pi}{4}}$ R$_{\frac{\pi}{2}}$
U$_2$ CONCAT U$_1$ U$_1$
U$_3$ CONCAT U$_2$ H

Which unitary transformation corresponds to U_3? We just follow the sequence of matrix operations:

$$U_3 = U_2 \star H = (U_1 \star U_1) \star H$$

$$= (R_{\frac{\pi}{4}} \star R_{\frac{\pi}{2}}) \star (R_{\frac{\pi}{4}} \star R_{\frac{\pi}{2}}) \star H$$

$$= R_{\frac{\pi}{4}} \star R_{\frac{\pi}{2}} \star R_{\frac{\pi}{4}} \star R_{\frac{\pi}{2}} \star H. \tag{7.3}$$

We are now to going to replace each gate with the corresponding matrix:

$$U_3 = \frac{1}{\sqrt{2}} \begin{bmatrix} 1 & 0 \\ 0 & e^{i\frac{\pi}{4}} \end{bmatrix} \begin{bmatrix} 1 & 0 \\ 0 & e^{i\frac{\pi}{2}} \end{bmatrix} \begin{bmatrix} 1 & 0 \\ 0 & e^{i\frac{\pi}{4}} \end{bmatrix} \begin{bmatrix} 1 & 0 \\ 0 & e^{i\frac{\pi}{2}} \end{bmatrix} \begin{bmatrix} 1 & 1 \\ 1 & -1 \end{bmatrix}$$

$$= \begin{bmatrix} 0.70711 & 0.70711 \\ -0.70711i & 0.70711i \end{bmatrix}. \tag{7.4}$$

□

It is your turn: in the following exercise we are going to use tensoring.

Exercise 7.2.2   Here is a snippet of quantum code:

$\vdots$

U$_1$ TENSOR CNOT CNOT
U$_2$ CONCAT U$_1$ U$_1$

$\vdots$

Which unitary transformation corresponds to the variable U_2? On how many qubits does it act?   ■

Exercise 7.2.3   Write down the assembler code that generates the following unitary transformation in terms of the basic gates set **GATES**:

$$U = \begin{bmatrix} 1 & 0 & 0 & 0 \\ 0 & -1 & 0 & 0 \\ 0 & 0 & 1 & 0 \\ 0 & 0 & 0 & -1 \end{bmatrix}. \tag{7.5}$$

What is the action of U on a 2-qubit subregister?   ■

Let us move forward. We need to measure a register:

■ Measure the register R and put the results in the classical variable RES, pointing to a bit array:
   MEASURE R RES

Example 7.2.4   Here is a fragment of a program in quantum assembler:
INITIALIZE R 2
U TENSOR H H
APPLY U R
MEASURE R RES

We can now read the bit array *RES*. What is the chance that we find the sequence 11? Let us read the code one line at time.

(i) The first instruction allocates a 2-qubit register named R and initializes it to $|00\rangle$.

(ii) The second line creates a unitary matrix U of size 4×4:

$$U = H \otimes H = \frac{1}{2} * \begin{bmatrix} 1 & 1 & 1 & 1 \\ 1 & -1 & 1 & -1 \\ 1 & 1 & -1 & -1 \\ 1 & -1 & -1 & 1 \end{bmatrix}. \tag{7.6}$$

(iii) The third line applies U to R:

$$\frac{1}{2} \begin{bmatrix} 1 & 1 & 1 & 1 \\ 1 & -1 & 1 & -1 \\ 1 & 1 & -1 & -1 \\ 1 & -1 & -1 & 1 \end{bmatrix} \begin{bmatrix} 1 \\ 0 \\ 0 \\ 0 \end{bmatrix} = \begin{bmatrix} \frac{1}{2} \\ \frac{1}{2} \\ \frac{1}{2} \\ \frac{1}{2} \end{bmatrix} = \frac{1}{2}|00\rangle + \frac{1}{2}|01\rangle + \frac{1}{2}|10\rangle + \frac{1}{2}|11\rangle.$$

$$\tag{7.7}$$

(iv) Finally, the last line measures the q-register R and stores the result in the bit array *RES*. What is the probability that $RES = |11\rangle$? We simply calculate it from the coefficient of $|11\rangle$:

$$|\frac{1}{2}|^2 = \frac{1}{4} = 0.25. \tag{7.8}$$

This is no surprise: the parallel application of H to the two qubits puts the register in a balanced superposition of the four basic states. □

In the last example, measurement was the last step. The following exercise shows a bit of code where gates and measurement are interleaved, and measurement is restricted to a subregister.

Exercise 7.2.4 Consider the quantum assembler code:

INITIALIZE R 2
U TENSOR H I$_2$
APPLY U R
SELECT S1 R 0 1
MEASURE S1 RES
APPLY CNOT R
MEASURE R RES

We can now read the bit array *RES*. What is the chance that we find the bit sequence 10? ■

So far, there is a glaring omission: no control structures, such as the familiar conditional jumps. The reason is that they are dispensable. If our programmer wants to implement a if–then–else, she can issue a measurement statement, get back a bit array, and use a *classical conditional structure* (if, while, case, etc.) to branch out. For instance, going back to the last exercise, she could add a statement such as

IF(RES==[10]) THEN APPLY CNOT R ELSE APPLY H R

The exact syntax of the conditional would depend on the classical "host" language, i.e., the language she adopts to run the master machine.

Exercise 7.2.5   Go back to the last exercise. After initialization (first instruction), add a while loop that includes all other instructions in the while block and stops only when $RES = [10]$. Is it guaranteed that the program will always terminate? ■

What we have presented so far is a rather minimalist q-assembler: it contains only one data type, namely **quantum binary strings**. However, we have accomplished what we set forth to do: we now have a quantum language that can express quantum algorithms (try your hand with the following exercise).

Exercise 7.2.6   Write a program that implements Deutsch's algorithm described in Chapter 6. ■

In the next section, we investigate how we could expand it with more sophisticated constructs.

Programming Drill 7.2.1   *Write a lexical analyzer for the quantum assembler described in this section. You can use a large variety of tools, including Lex on UNIX, Bison on Linux, JavaCC for Java, or Parsec for Haskell.*

7.3 TOWARD HIGHER-LEVEL QUANTUM PROGRAMMING

The quantum assembler described in the last section is sufficient, at least in principle, to implement quantum algorithms such as the ones seen in Chapter 6. Just like everything in classical computing is ultimately represented as a sequence of bits, in quantum computing the basic constituents are sequences of qubits. However, in classical computation we have a vast array of languages that provide several built-in data types, such as integers, floating numbers, character strings, and the capability of creating new user-defined types (such as structures in C, or objects in C++, Java, or Perl). It would be great if the same happened here.

Indeed, even from the standpoint of the algorithms we presented, this need emerges quite naturally: Shor's algorithm, for instance, is about *integers*, not bit sequences. An implementation in quantum assembler would entail representing integers as sequences of bits, and thus as sequences of qubits (via the usual identification of 0 with $|0\rangle$ and of 1 with $|1\rangle$), all done explicitly by us. Similarly, if one wants to add two integers, one must find a unitary transformation that corresponds to addition, and moreover write it as a sequence of basic gates.

To gauge what is involved here, it is worth exploring how classical operations can be implemented as unitary transformations. Let us start with a boolean map

$$f : \{0,1\}^n \longrightarrow \{0,1\}^n, \tag{7.9}$$

in other words, a map from a sequence of n bits to itself. We intend to produce a map

$$U_f : \mathbb{C}^{2^n} \longrightarrow \mathbb{C}^{2^n}, \tag{7.10}$$

such that its "restriction" to regular bit sequences, when we identify the bit sequence $b_1 \ldots b_N$ with the corresponding qubit sequence $|b_1\rangle \ldots |b_N\rangle = |b_1 \ldots b_N\rangle$, is precisely f: $f(|b_1 \ldots b_N\rangle) = |f(b_1 \ldots b_N)\rangle$.

If f were an invertible map, it would have been easy: in this case, it suffices to extend f linearly by defining U_f as

$$U_f(c_0|0 \ldots 00\rangle + c_1|0 \ldots 01\rangle + \cdots + c_{2^n-1}|1 \ldots 11\rangle)$$
$$= c_0|f(0 \ldots 00)\rangle + c_1|f(0 \ldots 01)\rangle + \cdots + c_{2^n-1}|f(1 \ldots 11)\rangle. \tag{7.11}$$

As you can easily check, U_f is not only linear, but unitary, and thus within reach of our quantum device.

Exercise 7.3.1 Verify that f invertible implies that U_f is a unitary map. ∎

Unfortunately, if f is not invertible, U_f fails to be unitary.

Exercise 7.3.2 Provide a simple example of the fact that a noninvertible f generates, following the recipe given in Equation (7.11), a nonunitary map. ∎

Luckily, things are not so bad. There is a way around, that comes at some price, as it requires extra quantum memory. Let us see how it works. The basic idea is that we can *turn an irreversible function from bit sequences to bit sequences into a reversible one*, by carrying the input along with the result:

$$U_f : |\mathbf{x}\rangle|\mathbf{y}\rangle \longmapsto |\mathbf{x}\rangle|f(\mathbf{x}) \oplus \mathbf{y}\rangle. \tag{7.12}$$

In particular, for $\mathbf{y} = \mathbf{0}$, we get

$$U_f : |\mathbf{x}\rangle|\mathbf{0}\rangle \longmapsto |\mathbf{x}\rangle|f(\mathbf{x}) \oplus \mathbf{0}\rangle = |\mathbf{x}\rangle|f(\mathbf{x})\rangle. \tag{7.13}$$

If $\mathbf{x_1} \neq \mathbf{x_2}$, where $\mathbf{x_1}, \mathbf{x_2}$ are two bit sequences of the same length n,

$$U_f(|\mathbf{x_1}\rangle|\mathbf{0}\rangle) = |\mathbf{x_1}\rangle|f(\mathbf{x_1})\rangle \neq |\mathbf{x_2}\rangle|f(\mathbf{x_2})\rangle = U_f(|\mathbf{x_2}\rangle|\mathbf{0}\rangle). \tag{7.14}$$

U_f is injective on the standard basis padded with zeros. As a matter of fact, U_f is reversible on all inputs.

Exercise 7.3.3   Prove that U_f is a reversible map from $c^{2^{2n}}$ to itself.   ∎

We can thus extend it by linearity on a generic input, using the recipe given in Equation (7.11).

The map U_f associated with the function f should sound familiar to you if you have gone through Chapter 6: it is indeed the same map that was used to represent classical functions in many of the algorithms.

Observe that our input register has doubled its length: each time we wish to apply f to an input $|x\rangle$, we must pad it with a sequence of 0s as long as the input itself.

A simple example will illustrate the foregoing.

Example 7.3.1   Consider the boolean function f given by the following table:

x	$f(x)$
00	00
01	00
10	01
11	11

(7.15)

The function f is clearly not invertible. Let us turn it into a reversible one.

x, y	$x, f(x) \oplus y$	x, y	$x, f(x) \oplus y$
0000	0000	1000	1001
0001	0001	1001	1000
0010	0010	1010	1011
0011	0011	1011	1010
0100	0100	1100	1111
0101	0101	1101	1110
0110	0110	1110	1101
0111	0111	1111	1100

(7.16)

Now, we can simply extend the foregoing chart by linearity to obtain the desired U_f:

$$U_f(c_0|0000\rangle + c_1|0001\rangle + \cdots + c_{15}|1111\rangle) = c_0|0000\rangle + c_1|0001\rangle + \cdots + c_{15}|1100\rangle.$$

(7.17)

To compute f on the input 11, we simply "pad" it with the appropriate number of zeros (in this case two) and set our register to $|1100\rangle$. Now, we apply U_f to it and get 1111. Finally, we measure the subregister given by its last two indexes, obtaining 11, as desired.   □

It may seem as an idle and a bit silly exercise to go through this roundabout way, simply to carry out classical computation which could be safely performed on a classical machine in a snapshot. But it is not so: think again the role that U_f played in Deutsch's algorithm. We can use it to compute f on a *superposition of classical inputs*. For instance, if f stands for some arithmetical operation, we can now perform it on *all* classical inputs, in one single step: applying U_f.

Exercise 7.3.4   Consider the set of positive integers $\{0, 1, \ldots, 15\}$. In other words, the numbers that one can express with four bits. Write the unitary map that corresponds to the map $f(n) = n + 2$, if $n \leq 13$, and $f(n) = n$, otherwise.   ■

The trick described earlier has two main costs:

■ The reversibilization operation we performed by hand requires explicit calculations of f on all the input values, and the table grows exponentially in the size of the input. That is, of course, unacceptable because such a preprocessing would erode all the benefits of quantum speedup (not to mention the unpleasant fact that to carry out simple arithmetical operations via U_f, we must already compute all f's values!).
■ The extra qubits one needs to allocate. As it stands, it could create a big quantum memory issue, in case we needed to carry out several operations in a row.

As for the first issue, there are effective ways to turn an irreversible function into a reversible one in polynomial time, at least for certain function classes, without explicit calculations. The key idea is that one analyses the function in terms of its recursive definition, and uses that representation to rebuild it as a reversible one. We shall not pursue this fascinating topic here, but you can find some useful references in Bennett (1988).

Concerning the second item, there is an elegant solution, due to Bennett, known as the **quantum scratch pad**. Here is how it works: suppose you apply the function g to the output of function f:

$$|x, 0, 0\rangle \longmapsto |x, f(x), 0\rangle \longmapsto |x, f(x), g(f(x))\rangle \longmapsto |x, 0, g(f(x))\rangle. \quad (7.18)$$

Notice that in the last step we have just "undone" $|x, f(x)\rangle$ by applying the inverse of U_f. Now, the unused zero qubit can be recycled for future computations.

Exercise 7.3.5   Try to use the scratch-pad trick to compute $f \circ f$ where f is as in Exercise 7.3.4.   ∎

What have we learned? Suppose that we want to represent a classical data type such as Int, and its basic operations, on our quantum device. The steps involved are as follows:

- Represent the data type in the usual way, as bit sequences.
- Represent each of its operations as a unitary map, by turning it first into a reversible map.
- Analyze the unitary operations obtained in the previous item as quantum circuits, i.e., decompose them in terms of quantum gates.[10]

The use of our quantum assembler makes these steps entirely our responsibility. A bit cumbersome, isn't it? We can then envision future quantum languages where all this happens under the hood, at the compiler level. For instance, our programmer declares a classical variable of type integer and initializes it to some value:

$$Int \ \ n = 3. \tag{7.19}$$

She then decides to "quantize" it, so she creates a "quantum integer value" qn, of type QInt, and sets it equal to n. She then applies some gate G to qn, measure it, and stores the value back into n.

QInt qn= n

⋮

APPLY G qn
MEASURE qn n

We are going to conclude this section with a very sketchy survey on where we actually are, as far as designing higher-level quantum languages. The interested reader can consult the three excellent surveys by P. Selinger (2004b), by J. Gay (2005), and one by R. Rüdiger (2007) for fairly comprehensive views.

Classical higher-level languages are classified into broad groups, the broadest and most famous one being **imperative programming**. This class contains most of the languages that are commonly used in the workplace. A typical program is mainly a sequence of commands, interspersed with flow control statements. C, C++, Java, PERL, Python, and many, many others, all fit within this programming paradigm.

Some of the first proposals of quantum languages have been inspired by the imperative model. A typical example is **QCL**, written by Bernhard Ömer. QCL has a C-like syntax, augmented by a new QReg type, which lets the programmer access quantum registers. There is an important difference with respect to the registers we have encountered in the previous section: here, *registers are variables*. Just like

---

[10]   We have already mentioned that only certain classes of functions can been effectively turned into reversible maps and realized as quantum circuits. This point is critical, else the potentially huge benefits of quantum speedup could be easily eroded by these preprocessing steps.

in classical high-level languages, you do not need to specify any concrete memory location. You just say: "give me a register of size N," and the compiler takes care of allocating quantum memory. In the same spirit, in QCL unitary gates are operators (they look and feel like C functions). A QCL developer can write familiar classical C-like code, interspersed with instantiation and manipulation of q-registers.

⋮

qureg R[4]; // 4-qubit quantum register

⋮

H(R[2]); // Hadamard operation on the third qubit of the register

⋮

QCL is more than quantum assembler with memory management, as it supports user-defined operators and functions, much in a same way as in modern classical languages. Here is a simple example:

⋮

operator myop (qureg q)
H(q); // Hadamard transform on q
Not(q); // the NOT gate on q
CPhase(pi, q); // Controlled phase shift on q; it rotates it if q = 1111 …

QCL is not just a specification of a quantum language. An implementation in C++ exists and is downloadable at Ömer's Web site.

Programming Drill 7.3.1 *Download and install QCL, and then write an implementation of Grover's algorithm.*

An imperative quantum language akin to QCL is **Q**, by S. Bettelli and others. Q takes the stance of *promoting operators to full-fledged objects*, like in C++. Unlike QCL, which is in a sense self-contained, Q looks like an extension of C++, enriched by QRegisters and QOperators.

For a comparison of QCL and Q, you can read the joint interview of Ömer and Bettelli (the reference is in Rüdiger (2007), where they expound their guiding design philosophies.

In spite of their popularity, imperative languages are by no means the only option available; for instance, Prolog is a language that belongs to the so-called **logic programming** class, where a program is a specification of properties and relations in a fragment of first-order logic, and then queries such as: Is it true that the variable a enjoys the property P? As of the time of this writing, no quantum logic programming language has been proposed yet, but things may change in the future.

A third subclass is known as **functional programming**. Here a program can be seen as the specification of a function. The program will be provided with an acceptable value for the function and it will compute the return value. The prototypical example is LISP, a language you may have met already if you have taken a class on expert systems. There are many other functional programming languages, such as

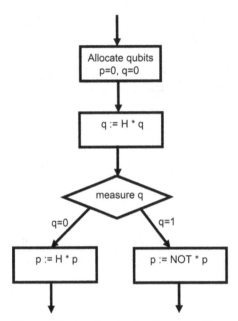

Figure 7.4. A snippet of a Quantum Flow-chart (QFC) program.

ML, Miranda, or Haskell. These languages are very powerful and extremely flexible, but not very popular in the industrial world.[11] Their chief users are academicians and industrial researchers working in the areas of theoretical computer science and artificial intelligence. It thus comes as no surprise that some of the first proposals for a high-level quantum programming language are functional languages. There are, however, other deeper motivations: functional languages, classical or quantum, lend themselves nicely to compile-time-type checking and correctness proofs. For languages in this category, there is an extensive body of work on denotational and operational semantics, that can be used as a baseline for the designer of new quantum languages.

The "quantum slogan" at page 221 says that quantum programming is quantum data plus control. But, *what kind of control?* Peter Selinger (2004b) has proposed a functional quantum programming language, known as **QFC**, which combines quantum data and classical control. Selinger's variant of the quantum slogan is

$$\boxed{\textit{QUANTUM DATA AND CLASSICAL CONTROL}}$$

Control is specified using a flowchart type of syntax. Figure 7.4 is a flowchart of a program.

---

[11] Though things are rapidly changing: the newly popular Ruby is an OOP imperative language which incorporates some features of the functional paradigm (most notably the capability of writing meta-programs. The web framework Rails, entirely written in Ruby, is based on Ruby's meta-programming features). We expect that mixed languages similar to Ruby will play an important role in the future of IT, as programs will process not only data, but other programs as well.

The same program in text syntax is

new qbit p, q : = 0 // initializes two qubits to |0⟩
q * = H   //multiply the second qubit by Hadamard
measure q then   //start conditional: measures second qubit
{p * = H}   //if the result is 0, apply Hadamard to the first qubit
else   //if the result is 1
{p * = NOT}   // flips the first qubit

Exercise 7.3.6   Download Selinger's paper on QFC, and write down a simple program that (1) initializes three qubits to zero, (2) applies Hadamard to the first one, and (3) measures the first qubit. If it is zero, it flips the second qubit; else, it maximally entangles the second and the third.   ∎

In classical functional programming, the distinction between data and control is blurred: programs themselves can be handled as data, naturally generating metaprogramming patterns (i.e., programs that manipulate other programs, or even themselves). Indeed, this feature is one of the strongest edges of the functional paradigm. Recently, Grattage and Alterlich have proposed a new functional quantum programming language, known as **QML** (see Grattage and Altenkirch, 2005), for which the claim is made that *both* data and control are quantum.[12]

7.4 QUANTUM COMPUTATION BEFORE QUANTUM COMPUTERS

For the time being, there are no quantum computers available aside a few experimental devices that operate on very small qubit registers (more on this in Chapter 11).

Nevertheless, things are not too gloomy: we can still emulate quantum computers on classical ones, as long as their quantum data storage is small. As we will learn in Chapter 8, in principle quantum machines can be successfully simulated by Turing machines, and thus by ordinary computers. Unfortunately, this emulation grows exponentially in the size of the qubit register, making it soon unfeasible. However, if we work with programs involving only a small amount of qubits, a successful emulation can be run on your desktop.

What is actually required to build a quantum emulator from scratch? As we have seen in Section 7.2, a quantum computing device consists of quantum registers and operations acting on them. To simulate a quantum register, we first need to simulate individual qubits. Now, via the standard representation, a qubit is just a (normalized) pair of complex numbers. Some languages, such as MATLAB or Maple, already come equipped with complex numbers (see the MATLAB Appendix for a tutorial on using MATLAB for quantum computing emulations). With others, you

---

[12] To which extent the claim is correct is, at the time of writing, debatable. On the one hand, QML does provide new conditional constructs, such as the new "quantum if" statements. On the other hand, such conditional constructs cannot be nested, restricting considerably the notion of control as it commonly intended.

can either use suitable external libraries or define them yourself. A quantum register of size N can be represented as an array of 2^N complex numbers, whereas a unitary transformation of the register will be represented by a $2^N \times 2^N$ matrix (as you can imagine, things get out of hand pretty fast!).

You can find a list of numerous quantum emulators at the Quantiki Web site http://www.quantiki.org/wiki/index.php/Main_Page. You just have to choose the language. Even better, you can build your own!

Programming Drill 7.4.1 *Design and implement a quantum computer emulator in the language of your choice. (Hint: If you have done consistently all other programming drills, you are almost done.)*

....

References: QRAM was first introduced in Knill (1996). According to the survey on quantum programming languages by Peter Selinger (2004a), Knill's paper is also the first known paper on quantum programming.

These are nice survey articles on quantum programming: Bettelli, Calarco, and Serafini (2001), Gay (2005), and Selinger (2004a).

8

Theoretical Computer Science

The meaning of the world is the separation of wish and fact.
Kurt Gödel, quoted in Hao Wang's *A Logical*
Journey: From Gödel to Philosophy, page 309[1]

In a sense, theoretical computer science is uniquely qualified to study quantum computing. After all, Alan Turing and the other founders of theoretical computer science studied formal computation long before engineers actually produced a real-life computer. At present, large-scale quantum computers are not a reality yet. Nevertheless, the theoretical analysis of quantum computability and complexity is well on its way.

In Section 8.1, we start with a quick review of some of the basics of deterministic and nondeterministic Turing machines and the complexity classes that they engender. However, we shall discuss them in a way that is easily generalizable for our purposes. Section 8.2 moves on to probabilistic Turing machines and their zoo of complexity classes. Our main objective is found in Section 8.3, where we meet quantum Turing machines and their complexity classes. We shall also state some basic theorems and ideas about quantum computation.

8.1 DETERMINISTIC AND NONDETERMINISTIC COMPUTATIONS

Theoretical computer science deals with the question, "What is computable?" We must immediately qualify the question: "computable according to *which* model of computation?" It turns out that if we omit the question of efficiency, all sufficiently complicated formal models of computation can simulate each other. However, in order to fix our ideas and notation, we have to stick with one and work with it. For historical reasons, we choose the Turing machine model.

We are going to assume that our reader already knows the basic "yoga" of Turing machines (see Figure 8.1). The simple facts are that a Turing machine is a device

---

[1] We are indebted to John D. Barrow for the source of this quote.

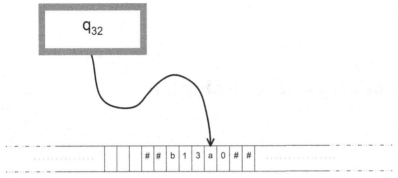

Figure 8.1. Turing machine.

with a two-way infinite tape that serves as a place to read input, write output, do scrap work, and to store a potentially infinite amount of information. The tape is split into a one-dimensional infinite array of boxes, each of which can hold exactly one symbol at a time. The machine can be in one of a finite set of states at any given moment and "see" one box at a time. It can move along the tape in any of two directions: left (L) or right (R). At each time step, the machine can read one box on the tape, write on that box, move, and change states.

Formally, a **deterministic Turing machine** M is a 6-tuple

$$M = (Q, \Sigma, q_{start}, q_{accept}, q_{reject}, \delta), \tag{8.1}$$

where Q is a finite set of states, Σ is a nonempty finite alphabet that includes a symbol # which we call "blank"; $q_{start}, q_{accept}, q_{reject}$ are all elements of Q; and a **transition function** δ,

$$\delta : Q \times \Sigma \longrightarrow Q \times \Sigma \times \{L, R\}. \tag{8.2}$$

For a given $q \in Q$ and $\sigma \in \Sigma$ if $\delta(q, \sigma) = (q', \sigma', D)$, we mean that

If Turing machine M is in state q and the eye encounters symbol σ, then the machine should exchange symbol σ for σ', move one box in the direction $D \in \{L, R\}$, and enter state $q' \in Q$.

Equivalently, we can write the function δ as

$$\delta' : Q \times \Sigma \times Q \times \Sigma \times \{L, R\} \longrightarrow \{0, 1\}, \tag{8.3}$$

where

$$\delta'(q, \sigma, q', \sigma', D) = 1 \quad \text{if and only if} \quad \delta(q, \sigma) = (q', \sigma', D). \tag{8.4}$$

Because for every $q \in Q$ and $\sigma \in \Sigma$, δ has exactly one output $(q', \sigma', D) \in Q \times \Sigma \times \{L, R\}$, our (deterministic) transition functions must satisfy the following requirement:

$$(\forall q \in Q)(\forall \sigma \in \Sigma) \sum_{q' \in Q, \sigma' \in \Sigma, D \in \{L, R\}} \delta'(q, \sigma, q', \sigma', D) = 1. \tag{8.5}$$

It is not hard to see that any δ is equivalent to a δ' that satisfies Equation (8.5).

The set of all words in Σ without blanks is denoted $(\Sigma - \{\#\})^*$. An input string from this set is placed on the tape at a specific starting place. The rest of boxes on the tape are assumed to have blanks. The Turing machine is then "let loose" from state q_{start} and follows the rules that are described by δ'. There are three possibilities that can occur to such a machine: (1) the Turing machine can reach state q_{accept}, (2) the Turing machine can reach state q_{reject}, or (3) the Turing machine can enter an infinite loop and never reach q_{accept} or q_{reject}. Think of a Turing machine as solving a decision problem by being presented with an input and then examining which state the machine will enter. Each such machine determines a language $L \subseteq (\Sigma - \{\#\})^*$ of those words that the machine accepts.

Although there are many other models of computation, we are comfortable with the deterministic Turing machine because of the following thesis:

Thesis. The **Classical Church–Turing Thesis** states that any problem that is intuitively computable can be computed by a deterministic Turing machine.

This thesis cannot be proved because it is impossible to give an exact definition of what is meant by "intuitively computable." However, most researchers agree that the thesis is a true statement.

In this chapter, we work through several examples and present some exercises involving Turing machines that follow the same theme. These machines are build up to a crescendo until we reach a Turing machine version of the double-slit experiment.

Example 8.1.1   Consider the following problem: a word of odd length in the alphabet $\Sigma = \{0, 1, \#\}$ is given as input and we are asked if this string contains a "1." Words that have at least one "1" are accepted and words that are all "0's" are rejected. We are deciding the language

$$L = \{w \in \Sigma^* : |w| = 2m + 1, (\exists i)w_i = \text{"1"}\}. \tag{8.6}$$

The usual convention is that the head of the Turing machine is at the leftmost letter of the input, but we shall be slightly unconventional and assume that the head is reading the center symbol of the odd-length string.

Let us describe a deterministic Turing machine to solve this problem. The machine should start with its head in the center.[2] The head should move to the left looking for a "1." If the left end of the word is reached, then the head should move to the right searching for a "1." If a "1" is found, then the computer should enter q_{accept}. If the head reaches the right end of the word without finding a "1," then the machine goes into state q_{reject}. By convention, if the machine enters a halting state, then the head just stays there. This Turing machine will not change anything on the tape.[3]

---

[2]   We have the adopted the convention that if the word is empty it is rejected.

[3]   In fact, what we have described is a two-way finite automaton. This example does not require the full definition of a Turing machine.

Formally, the set of states will be $Q = \{q_{start}, q_{accept}, q_{reject}, q_L, q_R\}$ and δ is defined by the following table:

δ	0	1	#	
q_{start}	q_L, L	q_{accept}	q_{reject}	(8.7)
q_L	q_L, L	q_{accept}	q_R, R	
q_R	q_R, R	q_{accept}	q_{reject}	

Each row tells what should be done in that state. The columns describe which symbol is seen. The entry tells us which state to enter and in which direction to move. In words, the search begins by going to q_L that continually moves to the left. When the machine hits #, the state enters q_R that always moves to the right. At any time, if a "1" is found, the machine enters q_{accept}. A **configuration** (also called a **snapshot**, or **instantaneous description**) of a Turing machine contains the complete information of the machine at a particular time step. There are three pieces of information that have to be described:

- the tape's contents,
- the state of the machine, and
- the position of the head of the Turing machine.

We shall summarize all three pieces of information by writing the contents of the tape and the state exactly to the left of the position that the machine is reading. An example of a configuration is

$$\#00001001q_{45}0010101\#, \tag{8.8}$$

which means that #000010010010101# is on the tape, the state is q_{45}, and the head is reading the ninth symbol which is a "0." (We will later need the obvious fact that all the configurations can be put in lexicographical order.)

A typical computation, i.e., a sequence of configurations, might look like this:

$$\#000q_{start}0010\# \longmapsto \#00q_L00010\# \longmapsto \#0q_L000010\# \longmapsto \#q_L0000010\# \longmapsto$$

$$q_L\#0000010\# \longmapsto \#q_R0000010\# \longmapsto \#0q_R000010\# \longmapsto \#00q_R00010\# \longmapsto$$

$$\#000q_R0010\# \longmapsto \#0000q_R010\# \longmapsto \#00000q_R10\# \longmapsto \#00000q_{accept}10\#. \tag{8.9}$$

In the worst-case scenario, for an input of size n, the machine will have to perform $n + \frac{n}{2}$ operations before a "1" is found or before it realizes that no "1" is in the word. We shall revisit this example in the next section. □

Exercise 8.1.1 Write a deterministic Turing machine that determines if the input string has a substring "101." You might have to begin by moving off the center a little. For an input of size n, how many moves does the Turing machine have to make in the worst case?   ■

What can and cannot be computed is not our exclusive interest. Another important issue is what can be computed *efficiently*. We shall be looking at different sets of problems of various degrees of difficulty. A **complexity class** is a set of problems that can all be solved by a certain model of computation within certain efficiency bounds. By examining and comparing different complexity classes, we shall derive principles about different models of computation.

The number of computational time steps that a machine must undergo before it enters an accepting or rejecting state is the number of steps for the computation. The number will usually depend on the size of the input. Hence we describe a function from the size of an input to the number of steps in the computation. Such a function might be a polynomial. If every input to a problem can be solved within a polynomial number of steps, then the problem is said to be solvable in a polynomial number of steps.

> **Complexity Class.** **P** is the set of problems that can be solved by a deterministic Turing machine in a **P**olynomial number of steps.

This complexity class is important because of the following thesis:

Thesis. The **Cook–Karp Thesis** states that problems that are "tractably computable" can be computed by a deterministic Turing machine in polynomial time, i.e., are in **P**.

This thesis also cannot be proved because it is impossible to give an exact definition of what we informally mean by "tractably computable." In fact, one would be hard-pressed to argue that a problem that demands n^{100} steps for an input of size n is tractable. Nevertheless, n^{100} is a function that grows slower than any nontrivial exponential function (including 1.001^n).

Exercise 8.1.2   Find the least n such that $1.001^n \geq n^{100}$.   ■

There are other interesting models of computation. A **nondeterministic Turing machine** is similar to a deterministic Turing machine, but we eliminate the requirement that at every step of the computation, the machine proceeds to exactly one subsequent step. In other words, for a given $q \in Q$ and a $\sigma \in \Sigma$, the machine can enter into a subset (possibly empty) of $Q \times \Sigma \times \{L, R\}$. Formally, a nondeterministic Turing machine M is a 6-tuple

$$M = (Q, \Sigma, q_{start}, q_{accept}, q_{reject}, \delta), \tag{8.10}$$

where $Q, \Sigma, q_{start}, q_{accept}, q_{reject}$ are as before and δ is a function

$$\delta : Q \times \Sigma \longrightarrow \wp(Q \times \Sigma \times \{L, R\}), \tag{8.11}$$

where $\wp$ is the powerset function. For a given $q \in Q$ and $\sigma \in \Sigma$ if $(q', \sigma', D) \in \delta(q, \sigma)$, we mean that

> If Turing machine M is in state q and the eye encounters symbol σ, then *one of the actions that the machine could perform* is to exchange symbol σ for σ', move one box in the direction $D \in \{L, R\}$, and enter state $q' \in Q$.

Just as we rewrote function (8.2), we might also rewrite function (8.11) as

$$\bar{\delta} : Q \times \Sigma \longrightarrow \{0, 1\}^{Q \times \Sigma \times \{L, R\}}, \tag{8.12}$$

where $\{0, 1\}^{Q \times \Sigma \times \{L, R\}}$ is the set of functions from $Q \times \Sigma \times \{L, R\}$ to $\{0, 1\}$. Whereas δ in function (8.11) chooses a subset of $Q \times \Sigma \times \{L, R\}$, $\bar{\delta}$ in function (8.12) chooses the characteristic function of the same subset. We may write this $\bar{\delta}$ similar to function (8.3):

$$\delta' : Q \times \Sigma \times Q \times \Sigma \times \{L, R\} \longrightarrow \{0, 1\}, \tag{8.13}$$

but this time we do not insist on the requirement that δ' must satisfy Equation (8.5). In other words,

$$(\forall q \in Q)(\forall \sigma \in \Sigma) \sum_{q' \in Q, \sigma' \in \Sigma, D \in \{L, R\}} \delta'(q, \sigma, q', \sigma', D) = 0, \text{ or } 1, \text{ or } 2, \text{ or } \ldots, \text{ or } n.$$
$$\tag{8.14}$$

The largest n is $|Q \times \Sigma \times \{L, R\}|$.

Exercise 8.1.3 Show that every nondeterministic Turing machine is equivalent to a nondeterministic Turing machine that bifurcates into exactly two states at every time step. Another way of stating this is that the summation in Equation (8.14) is exactly 2. ∎

In nondeterministic Turing machines, a computation can perform one of several different tasks at each time step. We say that a word is accepted by such a machine M if there exists a computational path that ends in q_{accept}.

Complexity Class. NP is the set of problems that can be solved by **N**ondeterministic Turing machines in a **P**olynomial number of steps.

Because every deterministic Turing machine is also a nondeterministic Turing machine (i.e., any δ' that satisfies Equation (8.5) also satisfies Equation (8.14)), every problem that can be solved in polynomial time by a deterministic Turing machine can also be solved by a nondeterministic Turing machine in polynomial time. Hence, **P** $\subseteq$ **NP**. The million-dollar question is whether **P** = **NP**. Alas, this question shall not be answered in this text.

If a problem has a "yes" answer, then the **complement of the problem** has a "no" answer, and vice versa. Hence, we define the following:

> **Complexity Class.** **coP** is the set of problems whose **co**mplements can be solved by a deterministic Turing machine in a **P**olynomial number of steps.

> **Complexity Class.** **coNP** is the set of problems whose **co**mplements can be solved by a **N**ondeterministic Turing machine in a **P**olynomial number of steps.

If we can solve a problem with a deterministic Turing machine, then by swapping the q_{accept} and the q_{reject} states, we can solve the complement of the problem. From this we know that **P = coP**. Notice that this trick does not work for nondeterministic Turing machines: a nondeterministic Turing machine accepts a word if there exists *at least one* computational path that ends with an accepting state. If a computation has *all but one* path ending with an accepting state, then the word would be accepted. If we swapped the accepting and rejecting states, then *all but one* path would end in a rejecting state and exactly one path would end in an accepting state. Because of the single accepting state, the computation would also be accepted. So a word would be accepted by both a problem in **NP** and its corresponding problem in **coNP**. This cannot be. In conclusion, although it is known that **P = coP**, we do not know if **NP = coNP**. In fact, most researchers believe that **NP ≠ coNP**. For the same reason that **P ⊆ NP**, we have that

$$\mathbf{P = coP \subseteq coNP}. \tag{8.15}$$

We are interested in not only how much time a computation uses but also how much of the Turing machine's infinite tape is used.

> **Complexity Class.** **PSPACE** is the set of problems that can be solved by deterministic Turing machines using a **P**olynomial number of **SPACE**s on the tape.

We could have written the same definition using a nondeterministic Turing machine. It is a consequence of Savitch's theorem[4] that when looking at space (as opposed to time), the distinction between deterministic polynomial space and nondeterministic polynomial space is not essential.

Because a (nondeterministic) Turing machine can change only one box per time step, machines that use $p(n)$ time steps to solve a problem cannot use more than $p(n)$ spaces of its infinite tape. Hence, we have **NP ⊆ PSPACE**. For similar reasons, **coNP ⊆ PSPACE**.

---

[4] Savitch's theorem states that any nondeterministic computation that uses $f(n)$ space can be simulated by a deterministic computation that uses at most $(f(n))^2$ space. If $f(n)$ is a polynomial, then $(f(n))^2$ is also a polynomial. See, e.g., page 306 of Sipser (2005) or page 149 of Papadimitriou (1994).

We may summarize the inclusions of the complexity classes that we have defined so far as follows:

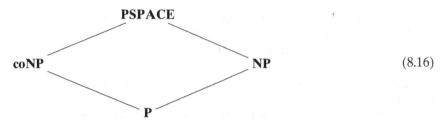

$$(8.16)$$

A line between one complexity class and another means that the lower one is included in the higher one. It must be stressed that it is unknown if any of these inclusions are proper inclusions.

8.2 PROBABILISTIC COMPUTATIONS

Probabilistic computations occur when there is a random choice among several possible transitions during a computation. Probabilities can be described with real numbers in the interval $[0, 1] \subseteq \mathbb{R}$. No computer's memory can hold an arbitrary real number,[5] and so this set is beyond our bounds. Some tractable computable subset of $[0, 1]$ is needed. Consider the set $\widetilde{\mathbb{R}} \subseteq \mathbb{R}$ of **tractably computable real numbers**. These are real numbers such that a deterministic Turing machine can calculate their nth digit in polynomial time. We shall be concerned with

$$\widetilde{[0, 1]} = [0, 1] \bigcap \widetilde{\mathbb{R}}. \tag{8.17}$$

A probabilistic Turing machine is a Turing machine that randomly performs one of several tasks at each time step. Formally, a **probabilistic Turing machine** is a 6-tuple

$$M = (Q, \Sigma, q_{start}, q_{accept}, q_{reject}, \delta), \tag{8.18}$$

where everything is as before except the transition function δ. δ is now a function

$$\delta : Q \times \Sigma \longrightarrow \widetilde{[0, 1]}^{\widetilde{Q \times \Sigma \times \{L, R\}}}, \tag{8.19}$$

where $\widetilde{[0, 1]}^{\widetilde{Q \times \Sigma \times \{L, R\}}}$ is the set of functions from the set of all possible actions, $Q \times \Sigma \times \{L, R\}$, to $\widetilde{[0, 1]}$. For a given state and symbol, δ will describe the probabilities of the moves that the machine can make. An arbitrary function from $Q \times \Sigma \times \{L, R\}$ to $\widetilde{[0, 1]}$ is not good enough. We must also restrict δ so that the sum of all the probabilities is equal to 1. δ is restricted as follows: as an analogy to functions (8.3) and (8.13), we define

$$\delta' : Q \times \Sigma \times Q \times \Sigma \times \{L, R\} \longrightarrow \widetilde{[0, 1]}, \tag{8.20}$$

---

[5] An arbitrary real number might have an infinite expansion. One could encode any language in that expansion.

where

$$\delta'(q, \sigma, q', \sigma', D) = r \in \widetilde{[0, 1]} \tag{8.21}$$

if and only if

$$\delta(q, \sigma) \text{ is the function that takes } (q', \sigma', D) \text{ to } r \in \widetilde{[0, 1]}. \tag{8.22}$$

It is not hard to see that for every δ there is a unique δ' that performs the same job. However, we insist that δ' satisfy the following requirement (analogous to Equations (8.5) and (8.14)):

$$(\forall q \in Q)(\forall \sigma \in \Sigma) \sum_{q' \in Q, \sigma' \in \Sigma, D \in \{L, R\}} \delta'(q, \sigma, q', \sigma', D) = 1. \tag{8.23}$$

This means that at every state and when viewing every symbol, the sum of all the probabilities of possible moves is equal to 1.

How does this machine work? At every time step, the machine will be in a certain state, say q_6, and will be looking at a certain symbol, say σ_{16}, on the tape. The function δ gives the nonzero probabilities where we list all possibilities in lexicographical order using the ordering of Q, Σ, and $\{L, R\}$.

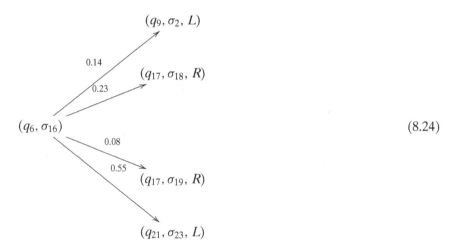

$$(8.24)$$

A real number between 0 and 1 is randomly chosen. This real number will determine which operation the Turing machine should perform. For example, if the real number is 0.12, which is between 0.0 and 0.14, then the machine will perform the (q_9, σ_2, L) operation. If the real number is 0.39, which is between $0.14 + 0.23$ and $0.14 + 0.23 + 0.08$, then the machine will perform the (q_{17}, σ_{19}, R) operation.

Exercise 8.2.1 Following the spirit of Exercise 8.1.3, show that every probabilistic Turing machine is equivalent to a Turing machine that can enter one of exactly two configurations. The machine can choose one of these two configurations by flipping a fair coin or by looking at a tape with a random sequence of "0's" and "1's." The machine will choose one operation if there is a "0" and the other one if there is a "1." (Hint: Write the probability r as a finite binary sequence.) ■

As with a regular Turing machine, the input will be placed on the tape, the computer will be put in the q_{start} state, and then the machine will "run." At each time step, an arbitrary real number is randomly chosen and the Turing machine performs the appropriate next action. At some point, the computer might enter a halting state and stop.

Exercise 8.2.1 Following Example 8.1.1, let us describe a probabilistic Turing machine that solves the same problem. Because we are dealing with probabilistic algorithms, we shall permit false negatives, i.e., the machine might report that there is no "1" when, in fact, there is one.

We place the probability of performing a given action to the left of the action.

δ	0	1	#
q_{start}	$\frac{1}{2} : q_L, L; \quad \frac{1}{2} : q_R, R$	$1 : q_{accept}$	$1 : q_{reject}$
q_L	$1 : q_L, L$	$1 : q_{accept}$	$1 : q_{reject}$
q_R	$1 : q_R, R$	$1 : q_{accept}$	$1 : q_{reject}$

$$(8.25)$$

How does this work? When the computer starts, 50% of the time the head moves to the left and 50% of the time it moves to the right. The machine will examine $\frac{n}{2} + 1$ boxes and hence will give a correct answer more than half the time. The machine will have to go through $\frac{n}{2}$ time steps in the worst case. ■

Exercise 8.2.2 Describe a probabilistic Turing machine that does not generate any false negatives. The machine should start by randomly moving to the left or to the right. However, regardless of direction, if it hits the left end or the right end of the word without finding a "1," it should reverse itself. Make sure that the machine does not end up in an infinite loop! Show that in the worst case, there will have to be $\frac{3n}{2}$ time steps. ■

Exercise 8.2.3 Describe a probabilistic Turing machine that determines if there is a substring "101" in the input string. Do the same for a solution that permits false negatives and one that does not permit false negatives. ■

Let us look at the different complexity classes that are defined for probabilistic Turing machines. Because of the probabilistic nature of the execution of such a Turing machine, there is a chance that when you execute the same program on the same input, there will be a different final state, i.e., there is a chance that the Turing machine will produce an error. An input should be accepted by a Turing machine, but the machine rejects it (false negative), or an input should be rejected and the machine accepts it (false positive).

We shall also restrict our attention to those probabilistic Turing machines that stop within a polynomial number of time steps in the length of the input.

In terms of permitting errors, the largest class of problems that we will be interested in are those that can be solved by probabilistic Turing machines that allow some false negatives and some false positives.

Complexity Class. **BPP** is the set of problems that can be solved by a **P**robabilistic Turing machine in **P**olynomial time with the possibility of some errors. To be precise, if M is a probabilistic Turing machine that decides $L \in$ **BPP** and if x is a word, then

$$x \in L \Rightarrow Prob(M \text{ accepts } x) > \frac{2}{3} \qquad (8.26)$$

and

$$x \notin L \Rightarrow Prob(M \text{ rejects } x) > \frac{2}{3}. \qquad (8.27)$$

We shall discuss the use of the fraction $\frac{2}{3}$ presently.

A smaller set of problems are those that can be solved with a probabilistic Turing machine that permits false positives but does not permit false negatives.

Complexity Class. **RP** is the set of problems that can be solved by a probabilistic (i.e. **R**andom) Turing machine in **P**olynomial time with only the possibility of false negatives. In other words, if M is a probabilistic Turing machine that decides $L \in$ **RP** and if x is a word, then

$$x \in L \Rightarrow Prob(M \text{ accepts } x) > \frac{2}{3} \qquad (8.28)$$

and

$$x \notin L \Rightarrow Prob(M \text{ rejects } x) = 1. \qquad (8.29)$$

We can also consider problems that can be solved by probabilistic Turing machines that permit only false positives.

Complexity Class. **coRP** is the set of problems that can be solved by a **P**robabilistic Turing machine in **P**olynomial time with only the possibility of false positives. In other words, if M is a probabilistic Turing machine that decides $L \in$ **coRP** and if x is a word, then

$$x \in L \Rightarrow Prob(M \text{ accepts } x) = 1 \qquad (8.30)$$

and

$$x \notin L \Rightarrow Prob(M \text{ rejects } x) > \frac{2}{3}. \qquad (8.31)$$

The easiest problems are those that can be solved by probabilistic Turing machines in which no errors are permitted.

Complexity Class. **ZPP** is the set of problems that can be solved by a **P**robabilistic Turing machine in **P**olynomial time with **Z**ero error. In other words, if M is a probabilistic Turing machine that decides $L \in$ **ZPP** and if x is a word, then there is a less than 50% chance that the machine will finish in a "do not know" state, otherwise if the machine does know

$$x \in L \Rightarrow Prob(M \text{ accepts } x) = 1 \tag{8.32}$$

and

$$x \notin L \Rightarrow Prob(M \text{ rejects } x) = 1. \tag{8.33}$$

It is a fact that **RP** $\bigcap$ **coRP** = **ZPP**.[6]

If we can solve a problem with no errors (**ZPP**), then we can definitely solve the problem permitting false negatives (**RP**) and we can definitely solve the problem permitting false positives (**coRP**). Furthermore, if we can solve a problem permitting only false negatives (**RP**), then we can definitely solve the problem permitting both false negatives and false positives (**BPP**). A similar argument can be made for **coRP**. Thus we have the following inclusion diagram:

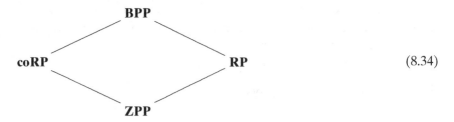

$$\tag{8.34}$$

It must be stressed that it is unknown if any of these inclusions are proper inclusions.

One might wonder why the fraction $\frac{2}{3}$ plays such an important role here. In fact, we could have used any fraction greater than $\frac{1}{2}$ and the classes of problems would have been the same. The reason for this is the **amplification lemma**.[7] The idea is that one can execute the Turing machine a polynomial amount of times and accept or reject the input depending on the results of the majority of executions. This method provides exponential growth in the likelihood of excluding false positives and false negatives.

Let us relate the complexity classes of this section with those of Section 8.1. One can consider a deterministic Turing machine a probabilistic Turing machine that does not make any guesses and always comes up with the right answer. From this, we have that **P** $\subseteq$ **ZPP**. Another way of thinking about $L \in$ **RP** is that if $x \in L$, then at least two-thirds of the computational paths end in q_{accept}, and if $x \notin L$, then

---

[6] See, e.g., page 256 of Papadimitriou (1994).

[7] E.g., see Zachos (1982), page 369 of Sipser (2005), or page 259 of Papadimitriou (1994).

all the computational paths end in q_{reject}. Similarly, one can think of $L \in \mathbf{NP}$ as stating that if $x \in L$, then at least one of the computational paths ends in q_{accept}, and if $x \notin L$, then all the computational paths end in q_{reject}. Because two-thirds of the computational paths (of an **RP** computation) are greater than one computational path (of an **NP** computation), it is not hard to see that $\mathbf{RP} \subseteq \mathbf{NP}$. Similarly, $\mathbf{coRP} \subseteq \mathbf{coNP}$.

For every $L \in \mathbf{BPP}$, we can create a machine that traverses all the computational paths and keeps track of the paths ending in q_{accept} and q_{reject}. There is no reason to save the path once it is calculated, so we might as well reuse the space. Such a machine will take a very long time to calculate an answer, but it will use only a polynomial amount of space. From this, it can be seen that $\mathbf{BPP} \subseteq \mathbf{PSPACE}$. By a similar analysis, it can be seen that $\mathbf{NP} \subseteq \mathbf{PSPACE}$ and $\mathbf{coNP} \subseteq \mathbf{PSPACE}$.

We can sum up our results with the following diagram.

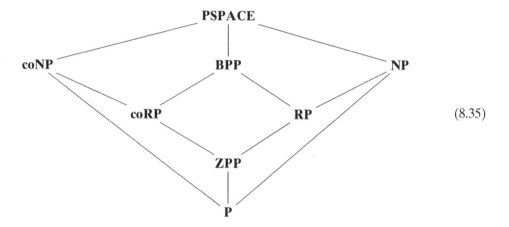

(8.35)

Again, it must be stressed that it is unknown if any of these inclusions are proper inclusions. The relationship between **BPP** and **NP** is also unknown.

Because probabilistic Turing machines are so general and because they permit some error ("noise"), we have the following thesis:

Thesis. The **Strong Church–Turing Thesis** states that any efficient computation that can be performed by *any* physical machine can be simulated by a probabilistic Turing machine in polynomial time, i.e., in **BPP**.

We reexamine this thesis at the end of the next section.

8.3 QUANTUM COMPUTATIONS

As you have probably guessed, quantum Turing machines will have something to do with complex numbers. As in the last section, general complex numbers $\mathbb{C}$ are beyond the reach of a finite machine. Thus, we are in need of the subset of all **tractably computable complex numbers** $\widetilde{\mathbb{C}} \subseteq \mathbb{C}$. $\widetilde{\mathbb{C}}$ consists of those complex numbers such that the nth digit of their real and imaginary parts can be deterministically computed in polynomial time.[8]

At last, we come to the definition of a **quantum Turing machine**. A quantum Turing machine is a 6-tuple

$$M = (Q, \Sigma, q_{start}, q_{accept}, q_{reject}, \delta') \tag{8.38}$$

where everything is as before except the transition function δ' (analogous to functions (8.3),(8.13), and (8.20))

$$\delta' : Q \times \Sigma \times Q \times \Sigma \times \{L, R\} \longrightarrow \widetilde{\mathbb{C}}. \tag{8.39}$$

We require[9] that δ' satisfy (analogous to Equations (8.5), (8.14), and (8.23))

$$(\forall q \in Q)(\forall \sigma \in \Sigma) \sum_{q' \in Q, \sigma' \in \Sigma, D \in \{L, R\}} |\delta'(q, \sigma, q', \sigma', D)|^2 = 1. \tag{8.40}$$

In plain English, a quantum Turing machine is like a probabilistic Turing machine but the probabilities are given as complex number amplitudes.[10] And we require that for any particular $q \in Q$ and $\sigma \in \Sigma$, the sum of those squared norms of the amplitudes equals 1. This can be visualized by a diagram similar to diagram (8.24) but with complex numbers. Another way of thinking about it is to consider what configuration the machine is in and what configurations it will enter with the actions. The complex numbers determine the probabilities of which configuration it

---

[8] We do this for the reasons given in the last section. It was proven in Adleman, DeMarrais, and Huang (1997) that any quantum Turing machine can be simulated by a machine that uses only the numbers

$$\left\{-1, -\frac{4}{5}, -\frac{3}{5}, 0, \frac{3}{5}, \frac{4}{5}, 1\right\} \tag{8.36}$$

or, if irrationals are permitted,

$$\left\{-1, -\frac{1}{\sqrt{2}}, 0, \frac{1}{\sqrt{2}}, 1\right\}. \tag{8.37}$$

[9] This requirement is not strictly needed because we are going to impose a much stronger requirement presently. (It is left in the text to make the connection between classic probabilistic Turing machines and quantum Turing machines.) Furthermore, we can permit arbitrary tractably computable complex numbers and then calculate probabilities with a normalization trick as we did in Section 4.1 on page 103.

[10] The clever reader will notice the progression of δ's in this chapter. They were all the same functions, except they take values in different sets. We went from $\{0, 1\}$ to real numbers (of the appropriate type) to complex numbers (of the appropriate type.) This progression is exactly the same as the progression of entries in the adjacency matrices of the weighted graphs discussed in Chapter 3. That makes sense; after all, the different systems discussed in Chapter 3 were introduced to bring to light the different types of computational power. However, the analogy highlights a problem with Chapter 3. Just as we restricted the values of the real and complex numbers in this chapter to *tractably computable* real and complex numbers, so too we should have restricted the values of the entries in the matrices of classical probabilistic systems and quantum systems. However, we wrote it as is for simplicity's sake.

will change as follows:

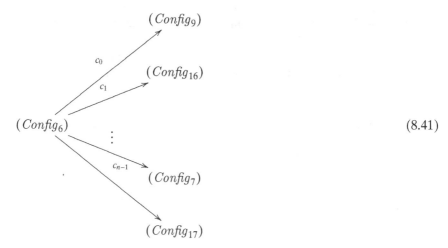

$$(8.41)$$

A quantum Turing machine works differently than a probabilistic Turing machine. Rather than carrying out one of the possibilities, it performs *all* the operations and enters a superposition of *all* the resulting states. The quantum Turing machine will collapse to a single configuration only when it is measured. In fact, if we observe the state and the contents of the tape of the quantum Turing machine after each step, then a quantum Turing machine will be the same as a probabilistic Turing machine. The difference is that when we *do not* observe the state and the contents of the tape, the probabilities of performing one operation followed by another sum up *as complex numbers* (a short review of Section 3.3 would be in order). Hence when we do not observe, there will be interference and superposition of contents of the tape.

Bernstein and Vazirani (1997) have many conventions that they insist their quantum Turing machine follow. There are many different reasons for this. Although these conventions are important for their work, we shall ignore most of them because we want to show only the basic workings of a quantum Turing machine.

There are, of course, many variants of quantum Turing machines, such as machines with many tapes and many tracks. It was shown in Yao (1993) that many of these are polynomially equivalent to the quantum Turing machine described earlier.

Many of the properties that one would want in a Turing machine, such as iteration, subroutines, and looping, are shown to exist with a quantum Turing machine in Bernstein and Vazirani (1997). Some of them are done with great effort. All these different properties are combined to show that one can actually construct a universal quantum Turing machine, i.e., a quantum Turing machine that can simulate[11] every other quantum Turing machine. With such a universal quantum Turing machine, we acquire many results similar to those of classical recursion theory.

---

[11] The notion of simulation has to be suitably adjusted because of the probabilistic nature of the computation. We cannot simply state that one machine outputs as the other. There must be a statement about "how far away" the simulated output is from the real one.

There is another way of thinking about quantum Turing machines. For a given machine, there is the set of all possible configurations of that machine. We can form a countably infinite dimensional complex vector space $\mathfrak{C}$ from these configurations. The vectors in this vector space will be finite complex linear combinations of configurations.[12] One can think of a vector as a countably infinite sequence of complex numbers indexed by the configurations of the Turing machine, where all but a finite number of the complex numbers are 0.

$$
\begin{matrix}
\textit{Config}_0 \\
\textit{Config}_1 \\
\textit{Config}_2 \\
\vdots \\
\textit{Config}_j \\
\vdots
\end{matrix}
\begin{bmatrix}
c_0 \\
c_1 \\
c_2 \\
\vdots \\
c_j \\
\vdots
\end{bmatrix}
\tag{8.42}
$$

A classical state of a quantum Turing machine will be a vector for which all but one complex number is 0 and the unique nonzero c_i is 1. This states that the configuration of the Turing machine is $\textit{Config}_i$. An arbitrary vector in $\mathfrak{C}$ will correspond to a superposition of classical configurations that can be written as

$$
|\psi\rangle = \sum_j c_j |\textit{Config}_j\rangle,
\tag{8.43}
$$

where the sum is over a finite set.

This is fine for states of the system. How does the system itself change? We shall make a countably infinite "matrix" U_M

$$
U_M : \mathfrak{C} \longrightarrow \mathfrak{C}.
\tag{8.44}
$$

Every row and column of this matrix will correspond to a possible configuration of the machine.

$$
U_M =
\begin{matrix}
 \\
\textit{Config}_0 \\
\textit{Config}_1 \\
\textit{Config}_2 \\
\vdots \\
\textit{Config}_i \\
\vdots
\end{matrix}
\begin{matrix}
\textit{Config}_0 & \textit{Config}_1 & \textit{Config}_2 & \cdots & \textit{Config}_j \\
\begin{bmatrix}
c_{0,0} & c_{0,1} & c_{0,2} & \cdots & c_{0,j} & \cdots \\
c_{1,0} & c_{1,1} & c_{1,2} & \cdots & c_{1,j} & \cdots \\
c_{2,0} & c_{2,1} & c_{2,2} & \cdots & c_{2,j} & \cdots \\
\vdots & \vdots & \vdots & \ddots & \vdots & \\
c_{i,0} & c_{i,1} & c_{i,2} & \cdots & c_{i,i} & \cdots \\
\vdots & \vdots & \vdots & & \vdots & \ddots
\end{bmatrix}
\end{matrix}
\tag{8.45}
$$

---

[12] This complex vector space is an inner product space but not a Hilbert space because of the finiteness in the definition. If we relax the finiteness requirement, then the inner product space is, in fact, complete and thus a Hilbert space.

The entries of the matrix will be the complex numbers that describe the amplitude of going from one configuration to another. That is, $c_{i,j}$ will be the amplitude described by δ' that would change configuration j into configuration i as depicted in diagram (8.41). Obviously, most of the entries of this matrix will be 0.

Definition 8.3.1 *A quantum Turing machine is* **well formed** *if the constructed U_M preserves the inner product (is an isometry) in $\mathfrak{C}$.*

With a well-formed quantum Turing machine, one is back into the familiar world of unitary matrices. If we let $|Config_I\rangle$ be the initial configuration, then $U_M|Config_I\rangle$ will be a configuration or a superposition of configurations after one time step. $U_M^2|Config_I\rangle$ will be the (superposition of) configuration(s) after two steps. If the Turing machine runs in time $t(n)$, then we would have to observe the state

$$\underbrace{U_M \circ U_M \circ \cdots \circ U_M}_{t(n) \text{ times}} |Config_I\rangle = U_M^{t(n)}|Config_I\rangle. \tag{8.46}$$

Example 8.3.1 There is nothing particularly quantum about the set $\mathfrak{C}$ of configurations and the matrix acting upon it. In fact, the same can be done for a deterministic Turing machine. In the deterministic case, we will only be concerned with vectors that have exactly one entry as 1 and all others as 0 (note that this is not a subvector space of $\mathfrak{C}$ because it is not closed under addition). The U_M will be such that every column has exactly one 1 and the remaining entries 0. $\square$

Exercise 8.3.1 Do a similar analysis to the one in Example 8.3.1 for a reversible deterministic Turing machine and for a probabilistic Turing machine. ∎

Example 8.3.2 In the spirit of Examples 8.1.1 and 8.2.1, let us describe a quantum Turing machine that solves the same problem.

δ	0	1	#
q_{start}	$\frac{1}{\sqrt{2}} : q_L, L \quad \frac{1}{\sqrt{2}} : q_R, R$	$1 : q_{accept}$	$1 : q_{reject}$
q_L	$1 : q_L, L$	$1 : q_{accept}$	$1 : q_{reject}$
q_R	$1 : q_R, R$	$1 : q_{accept}$	$1 : q_{reject}$

$$\tag{8.47}$$

This quantum Turing machine does not start by moving either to the right or to the left. Rather it moves *both* to the right *and* to the left simultaneously.

A typical computation might look like this:

$$|\#000q_{start}0010\#\rangle \longmapsto \frac{|\#00q_L00010\#\rangle + |\#0000q_R010\#\rangle}{\sqrt{2}} \longmapsto$$

$$\frac{|\#0q_L000010\#\rangle + |\#00000q_R10\#\rangle}{\sqrt{2}} \longmapsto \frac{|\#q_L0000010\#\rangle + |\#00000q_{accept}10\#\rangle}{\sqrt{2}}. \tag{8.48}$$

It is obvious that the machine will solve this problem without false positives or false negatives in $\frac{n}{2}$ steps. Again, we want to stress that this is not really a quantum Turing machine because it does not satisfy all the conventions laid down in Bernstein and Vazirani (1997).

We feel confident in identifying this as "a Turing machine version of the double-slit experiment." The double-slit experiment is performed by physicists who are interested in where a photon lands. A photon exhibits the superposition phenomenon, and hence the photon passes through both slits simultaneously. We are computer scientists and solve searching problems. This problem is solved in $\frac{n}{2}$ time by splitting into a simultaneous superposition of two computational paths. (Of course, it is not really the double-split experiment because there is no interference, only superposition.)   □

Let us summarize what we have done in Examples 8.1.1, 8.2.1, and 8.3.2 and in Exercise 8.2.2. For the same problem, i.e., given a string to determine if it contains a "1," we formulated deterministic, probabilistic, and quantum Turing machines. Some of these machines solved the problem without error and some of them gave us probabilistic solutions. The problems were solved in the following time.[13]

Turing Machine Running Time		
	Exact	Probable
Deterministic	$n + \frac{n}{2}$	NA
Probabilistic	$n + \frac{n}{2}$	$\frac{n}{2}$
Quantum	$\frac{n}{2}$	NA

(8.49)

Exercise 8.3.2   Write a quantum Turing machine that determines if there is a substring "101" on the tape.   ■

A quantum Turing machine is just one model of quantum computation. In Chapters 5 and 6 we dealt with another one, namely, quantum circuits. (The QRAM model, dealt with in Chapter 7, is yet another way of describing quantum computations.) In the classical case, logical circuits and deterministic Turing machines are polynomially equivalent. That means that each model can implement the other with only polynomial amount of "overhead." Yao (1993) proved a similar result for the quantum case. That is, quantum circuits and quantum Turing machines are polynomially equivalent.

The following simple example shows how a quantum Turing machine would implement a common quantum circuit:

---

[13] We have deliberately omitted the nondeterministic case from our chart. The reason is that a nondeterministic Turing machine can also solve the problem in $\frac{n}{2}$ steps. This is just as fast as the quantum Turing machine and would have "stolen its thunder." We should remind the reader that nondeterminism is a mathematical fiction whereas the laws of quantum mechanics are a physical fact.

Example 8.3.3 Many of the algorithms in Chapter 6 required that we apply $H^{\otimes n}$ to a string of qubits. Let us show how one would do this with a quantum Turing machine. Suppose that a string of n "0's" and "1's" are on a tape and that the head is pointing to the rightmost symbol of the string.

δ	0	1	$\#$	
q_{start}	$(\frac{1}{\sqrt{2}} : 0, q_{start}, L)$	$(\frac{1}{\sqrt{2}} : 0, q_{start}, L)$	$1 : q_{stop}$	(8.50)
	$(\frac{1}{\sqrt{2}} : 1, q_{start}, L)$	$(-\frac{1}{\sqrt{2}} : 1, q_{start}, L)$		

Basically, the quantum Turing machine will go through the string and change the "0's" or "1's" the way a Hadamard matrix would. (This is a simplification of Theorem 8.4.1 of Bernstein and Vazirani (1997). Ours is simpler because we have not followed all their conventions.) □

Let us have a look at complexity classes for quantum Turing machines. As in Section 8.2, because of the probabilistic nature of the computations, there is the possibility of false positives and false negatives. We are led to the following three definitions:

Complexity Class. BQP is the set of problems that can be solved by a **Q**uantum Turing machine in **P**olynomial time with **Z**ero error. In other words, if M is a quantum Turing machine that decides $L \in$ **BQP** and if x is a word, then

$$x \in L \Rightarrow Prob(M \text{ accepts } x) > \frac{2}{3} \qquad (8.51)$$

and

$$x \notin L \Rightarrow Prob(M \text{ rejects } x) > \frac{2}{3}. \qquad (8.52)$$

It was proven in Bennett et al. (1997) that the same amplification lemma that worked for probabilistic complexity classes also works for **BQP**. Hence, the fraction $\frac{2}{3}$ is not of major significance.

Complexity Class. ZQP is the set of problems that can be solved by a **Q**uantum Turing machine in **P**olynomial time with **Z**ero error. In other words, if M is a quantum Turing machine that decides $L \in$ **ZQP** and if x is a word, then there is a less than 50% chance that the machine will finish in a "do not know" state, otherwise if the machine does know then

$$x \in L \Rightarrow Prob(M \text{ accepts } x) = 1 \qquad (8.53)$$

and

$$x \notin L \Rightarrow Prob(M \text{ rejects } x) = 1. \qquad (8.54)$$

Complexity Class. **EQP** is the set of problems that can be solved with a **Q**uantum Turing machine in **P**olynomial time **E**xactly (without error). In other words, if M is a quantum Turing machine that decides $L \in$ **EQP** and if x is a word, then

$$x \in L \Rightarrow Prob(M \text{ accepts } x) = 1 \qquad (8.55)$$

and

$$x \notin L \Rightarrow Prob(M \text{ rejects } x) = 1. \qquad (8.56)$$

It should be obvious that

$$\textbf{EQP} \subseteq \textbf{ZQP} \subseteq \textbf{BQP}. \qquad (8.57)$$

Now relate these complexity classes with those of Sections 8.1 and 8.2. Because a deterministic Turing machine can be seen as a type of quantum Turing machine, we have that **P** $\subseteq$ **EQP**. Given that we can have a quantum Turing machine simulate a probabilistic Turing machine by using the Hadamard matrix as a fair coin toss, we have that **BPP** $\subseteq$ **BQP**. Also, for the same reason that **BPP** can be mimicked by a machine that uses only polynomial amount of space, so too **BQP** can be mimicked by such a machine. Such a machine is the theoretical version of a quantum emulator. The fact that every problem in **BQP** can be simulated by something in **PSPACE** shows that every quantum computation can be simulated by a classical computer. Of course, the simulation will probably use exponential time if it was to be exact.[14] Summing up, we have the following:

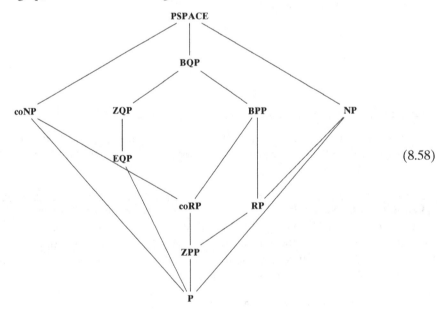

$$(8.58)$$

---

[14] We can also make the obvious definition of **QSPACE**. It was shown in Watrous (1999) that **QSPACE**$(f(n)) \subseteq$ **SPACE**$((f(n))^2)$. This is analogous to Savitch's theorem about nondeterministic computation.

It is unknown if any of these inclusions are proper inclusions. There is much still open about the relationships among these complexity classes.

Because of Shor's algorithm and the belief that there is no polynomial probabilistic algorithm to factor numbers, it is strongly believed that $\mathbf{BPP} \subsetneq \mathbf{BQP}$. It should be noticed that if it were to be proved that $\mathbf{BPP} \neq \mathbf{BQP}$, then we would know that $\mathbf{P} \neq \mathbf{PSPACE}$, which has been an open problem for a very long time.

It should be noted that Shor's algorithm is not the only algorithm that we saw that has an exponential speedup. As we saw in Chapter 6, the Deutsch–Jozsa algorithm and Simon's algorithm also had exponential speedups over any known classical algorithm.

If a large-scale quantum computer is ever built, then there would be evidence that the strong Church–Turing Thesis would be invalidated. Such a quantum computer will be a physical machine that can perform a computation (e.g., factoring large numbers) for which there are no known polynomial time probabilistic machines. (Of course, someone might create such a probabilistic machine in the future.)

It is to be stressed that although Shor's algorithm solves the factoring problem, factoring is not believed to be an NP-complete problem. The factoring problem, as a decision problem, is an $\mathbf{NP}$ problem (and a $\mathbf{coNP}$ problem) but has never been shown to be harder than any known $\mathbf{NP}$-complete problem. In terms of quantum computers, this means that even if there were a large-scale quantum computer, we would not be able to use Shor's algorithm to solve all known $\mathbf{NP}$-complete problems.

Some researchers believe that the fact that there is a quantum algorithm for the factoring problem is a "fluke" and not something that should be expected for many problems. They believe that methods similar to Shor's algorithm will not be very helpful for other hard problems.

In contrast to Shor's algorithm, Grover's algorithm can be very interesting in terms of $\mathbf{NP}$ problems. Although the speedup using Grover's algorithm is from n to $\sqrt{n}$, which is quadratic and not exponential, it is still significant. Consider your favorite $\mathbf{NP}$ problem. The search space for such a problem is, in general, either $n!$ or 2^n. One can set up Grover's algorithm to search through the problem's search space. So if the problem is SAT, we can use Grover's algorithm to search through all 2^n possible valuations of the n variables in the formula. If the problem is HAMILTONIAN GRAPH, then search through all $n!$ paths on the graph to find one that is hamiltonian. In fact, we are solving a search problem rather than a decision problem.[15]

Let us perform some calculations to show how significant Grover's speedup can be. Say, we would like to solve some $\mathbf{NP}$ problem whose search space is 2^n. Imagine a quantum computer running Grover's algorithm that can perform 1,000 function evaluations per second. This quantum computer will have to perform $\sqrt{2^n}$ function evaluations. Contrast this with a classical computer running a brute-force search through all 2^n possible members of the search space. We shall assume that

---

[15] We showed that we can solve an $\mathbf{NP}$ problem in $O(2^{\frac{n}{2}})$ time using Grover's algorithm. We are led to the obvious question of whether we can do better. It has been shown in Bennett (1997) that relative to an oracle chosen uniformly at random with probability 1, the class of $\mathbf{NP}$ cannot be solved by quantum Turing machines in $o(2^{\frac{n}{2}})$ time.

this classical computer is 100 times faster than the quantum computer, i.e., it can perform 100,000 function evaluations per second. The following table shows how these two algorithms compare on different values of n:

	Classical Brute-Force Search		Quantum Grover's Algorithm Search	
n	2^n ops	Time	$\sqrt{2^n}$ ops	Time
5	32	0.00032 second	5.656854249	0.00566 second
10	1,024	0.01024 second	32	0.032 second
15	32,768	0.32768 second	181.019336	0.18102 second
20	1,048,576	10.48576 seconds	1,024	1,024 seconds
25	33,554,432	335.54432 seconds	5792.618751	5.79261 seconds
30	1,073,741,824	10737.41824 seconds	32,768	32.768 seconds
40	1.09951E+12	127.25829 days	1,048,576	1048.576 seconds
50	1.1259E+15	356.77615 years	33,554,432	33554.432 seconds
60	1.15292E+18	365338.7788 years	1,073,741,824	12.42756 days
70	1.18059E+21	374106909.5 years	34,359,738,368	397.68215 days
100	1.26765E+30	4.01694E+17 years	1.1259E+15	35677.61512 years
125	4.25353E+37	1.34786E+25 years	6.52191E+18	206666822.3 years

(8.59)

We can see that for $n = 15$, the quantum computer will run faster than the classical computer. We conclude that Grover's algorithm might have major significance when dealing with "hard" computer problems.

Exercise 8.3.3   Write a short program or use either MATLAB or Microsoft Excel to determine the exact n when the slower quantum computer running Grover's algorithm runs faster than the classical computer running a brute-force algorithm. ■

Exercise 8.3.4   Perform a similar analysis to that shown in table (8.59) for an **NP** problem whose search space is $n!$. ■

. . . .

References: For general Turing machines, see Davis, Weyuker, and Sigal (1994) or Garey and Johnson (1979). Another excellent text is Sipser (2005).

For probabilistic Turing machines, see Section 10.2 of Sipser (2005) or Chapter 11 of Papadimitriou (1994). For general complexity theory, see Papadimitriou (1994).

For Section 8.3, we mostly followed Bernstein and Vazirani (1997). Their definition of a quantum Turing machine is a variant of the one formulated in Deutsch (1985). Much was gained from the following survey papers: Cleve (1999), Fortnow (2003), and Vazirani (2002).

Scott Aaronson has a very interesting blog "Shtetl-Optimized" that looks at current issues in quantum computability and complexity theory: http://www.scottaaronson.com/blog/. Well worth the read. He is also the "Zookeeper" at a Web page (http://qwiki.caltech.edu/wiki/Complexity_Zoo) that has more than 400 different complexity classes. These are great places to start learning more about this topic.

9

Cryptography

> *We dance round in a ring and suppose,*
> *But the Secret sits in the middle and knows.*
> Robert Frost, *The Secret Sits* (1942)

In this chapter we explore the merging of quantum computation and classical cryptography. This is a new and exciting field of pure and applied research known as **quantum cryptography**.

We begin with the basics of classical cryptography in Section 9.1. Section 9.2 demonstrates a quantum cryptographic protocol that uses two different bases. We improve on this in Section 9.3, where a protocol with one basis is employed. Section 9.4 shows how to use entanglement to secretly send a message. We conclude with Section 9.5, in which teleportation is demonstrated.

9.1 CLASSICAL CRYPTOGRAPHY

Before delving into quantum cryptography, we need to familiarize ourselves with the core ideas of classical cryptography. A good place to start is the following definition.

Definition 9.1.1 **Cryptography** *is the art of concealing messages.*

Indeed, this is precisely what the etymology reveals: "Cryptography" is a compound of two Greek words, *crypton*[1] and *graphein*, which mean, respectively, hidden and writing.

Turning an ordinary message into an indecipherable one is called **encryption**. The opposite action, i.e., restoring the original message, is **decryption**. The original message is generally referred to as the **plaintext**, and the encrypted message is the **ciphertext**. A method for encryption is often referred to as an **encryption protocol**.

---

[1] Now you know where the Kryptonite got its name. It is rare to find and hence is "hidden." It usually stays concealed unless Lex Luthor gets hold of it!

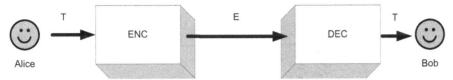

Figure 9.1. A basic communication scheme.

The history of cryptography is a very long one. As soon as people started sending messages to each other that were not intended for the public, the need for privacy arose. At the very moment encryption ideas and techniques were devised by some smart individual, another one, just as smart set out to break them. Thus, **cryptology** was born.

To present encryption and decryption methods, we need to set the scene. First, we need two characters – the **sender** of messages and the **receiver**. In the standard cryptology literature, these two are named Alice and Bob. Alice wants to send a message to Bob, say, a string of plaintext T. We assume that Alice and Bob are physically separated and that they can communicate with each other over some kind of **insecure channel**.[2]

Alice uses an encryption algorithm – let's call it ENC – that turns T into some encrypted text E. We can think of ENC as some computable function, taking T and an additional parameter K_E, known as the **encryption key**, as inputs. ENC computes the encrypted message E, which is transmitted to Bob.

$$ENC(T, K_E) = E. \tag{9.1}$$

Bob receives E (assuming there is no noise involved) and applies a decryption algorithm, DEC, to the encrypted message to reconstruct T. DEC requires a **decryption key** K_D as input.

$$DEC(E, K_D) = T. \tag{9.2}$$

The entire scheme is shown in Figure 9.1.

Summing up, $ENC(-, K_E)$ and $DEC(-, K_D)$ are a pair of computable functions such that for every message T, the following equation holds:

$$DEC(ENC(T, K_E), K_D) = T. \tag{9.3}$$

What does this equation tell us? It states that as long as we use the right keys, we can always retrieve the original message intact without any loss of information.

Exercise 9.1.1 Does Equation (9.3) imply that $ENC(-, K_E)$ and $DEC(-, K_D)$ are a pair of bijective functions that are inverse to each other? ■

Let us now examine a concrete example of an encryption protocol, a method known as the **Caesar's protocol**.[3] Arrange the letters of the English alphabet on a

---

[2] Why insecure? First of all, if the channel were foolproof beyond any reasonable doubt, we would have no story. Why bother with cryptography if no one else can spy on the message? Second, in the context of secure message transmission, *every* channel must be assumed insecure unless proven safe.

[3] Julius Caesar apparently used an encryption technique like this one to communicate with his generals during his military campaigns. See Suetonius' *Life of Julius Caesar*, Paragraph 56.

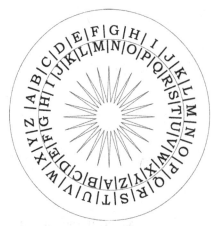

Figure 9.2. A children's encryption toy.

circle, so that the order is

$$\ldots, A, B, C, \ldots, X, Y, Z, A, B, \ldots \qquad (9.4)$$

Let $ENC = DEC = \text{shift}(-, -)$, where $\text{shift}(T, n) = T'$, the string obtained from T by shifting each character n steps clockwise if n is positive, or counterclockwise if it is negative (for instance, shift("MOM," 3) ="PRP"). Children actually make a helpful toy for this encryption protocol as depicted in Figure 9.2. This toy consists of two concentric circles with the alphabet written clockwise on each circle. The circles can be turned until the desired letters are matched up. With this encryption protocol, the decryption key is just the encryption key with the sign changed: $K_D = -K_E$.

Exercise 9.1.2 Decipher the following message "JNTGMNF VKRIMHZKTIAR BL YNG." (Hint: Use Figure 9.2.) ∎

Programming Drill 9.1.1 *Implement the encryption and decryption of text with the Caesar's protocol. Using ASCII makes this particularly easy.*

To make our story a bit more exciting, we need a third character, Eve, the **eavesdropper**, who can intercept the encrypted message and try to decode it. As previously noted, Alice is using an insecure channel (such as a public telephone wire) to transmit messages to Bob. Eve can thus tap into the channel and eavesdrop on its content. The protocol we have just presented is quite primitive and would not stand Eve's scrutiny for too long.

Imagine that you are Eve and that by tapping into the insecure channel you can save fairly long encrypted messages from Alice. How would you discover the encryption mechanism? If you were Eve, you might have a hunch about the weak side of the simple-minded protocol we have just introduced. The weakness lies in the fact that the original message and the encrypted one are *highly correlated*. By calculating simple statistics on the encrypted text, Eve may easily find her way back to the original text. Aside from her malicious purposes, Eve works exactly like an archeologist decoding an ancient unknown language.

To counter Eve's insight, Alice and Bob change their protocol. Their ideal strategy is to create an encrypted message E that bears no statistical correlation with the original message T. How can this be accomplished? Here is a surprisingly simple answer: a straightforward protocol known as the **One-Time-Pad protocol** or **Vernam cipher**.

As we are computer scientists, for the rest of this chapter, we shall refer to T as a binary string of length n. Alice tosses a coin n times and generates a sequence of random bits that she uses as her random key K. Assuming Alice and Bob both share K, they can exchange messages by means of the following protocol:

Step 1. Alice calculates $E = T \oplus K$, where $\oplus$ stands for the bitwise XOR operation.[4]

Step 2. Alice sends E along a public insecure channel.

Step 3. Bob retrieves E and calculates T from $T = E \oplus K$.

In this notation that we have introduced,

$$K_E = K_D = K, \tag{9.5}$$

$$ENC(T, K) = DEC(T, K) = T \oplus K, \tag{9.6}$$

and

$$DEC(ENC(T, K), K) = DEC(T \oplus K, K)$$
$$= (T \oplus K) \oplus K = T \oplus (K \oplus K) = T. \tag{9.7}$$

Example 9.1.1 The following table shows an example of an implementation of the One-Time-Pad protocol:

One-Time-Pad Protocol							
Original message T		0	1	1	0	1	1
Encryption key K	$\oplus$	1	1	1	0	1	0
Encrypted message E		1	0	0	0	0	1
Public channel		$\Downarrow$	$\Downarrow$	$\Downarrow$	$\Downarrow$	$\Downarrow$	$\Downarrow$
Received message E		1	0	0	0	0	1
Decryption key K	$\oplus$	1	1	1	0	1	0
Decrypted message T		0	1	1	0	1	1

$$\tag{9.8}$$

□

---

[4] A quick reminder on XOR: it is simply bitwise addition modulo two. $01001101 \oplus 11110001 = 10111100$.

Exercise 9.1.3 Find a friend and flip a coin to get an encryption key K. Then use K to send a message. See if it works.   ∎

Programming Drill 9.1.2 *Implement the One-Time-Pad protocol.*

Exercise 9.1.4 Suppose Alice generates only one pad key K, and uses it to encrypt two messages T_1 and T_2 (we are assuming they have exactly the same length). Show that by intercepting E_1 and E_2, Eve can get $T_1 \oplus T_2$ and hence is closer to the original text.   ∎

There are a couple of issues with the One-Time-Pad protocol:

1. As Exercise 9.1.4 shows, the generation of a new key K is required each time a new message is sent. If the same key is used twice, the text can be discovered through statistical analysis, and hence the name "One-Time-Pad."

2. The protocol is secure only insofar as the key K is not intercepted by Eve (remember, Alice and Bob must share the same pad in order to communicate). We see in the next section that quantum computing comes to the rescue for this crucial issue.

So far, we have assumed that the pair of keys K_E and K_D are kept secret. In fact, only one key was needed because knowledge of the first key implies knowledge of the second and vice versa.[5] A cryptographic protocol where the two keys are computable from one another, thus requiring that *both* keys be kept secret, is said to be **private key**.

There is yet another game in town: in the 1970s, Ronald Rivest, Adi Shamir, and Leonard Adleman introduced one of the first examples of **public-key cryptography**, now simply known as **RSA** (Rivest, Shamir, and Adleman, 1978). In public-key protocols, the knowledge of one key does not enable us to calculate the second one. To be precise, the requirement is that the computation of the second key from the first should be hard.[6]

Now, suppose that Bob has computed such a pair of keys K_E and K_D. Furthermore, suppose that brute force trial and error to find K_D given K_E is totally infeasible by Eve or anyone else (for instance, there could be an endless list of candidate keys). Bob's course of action is as follows: he places the encryption key K_E, in some public domain, where *anyone* can get it. He can safely advertise his protocol, i.e., the knowledge of $ENC(-, -)$ and $DEC(-, -)$. At the same time, he guards the decryption key for himself. When Alice wants to send a message to Bob, she simply uses K_E on her message. Even if Eve intercepts the encrypted text, she cannot retrieve Bob's decryption key, and so the message is safe. This scheme is shown in Figure 9.3.

Let us rephrase the foregoing: once Bob has his magic pair of keys, he finds himself with two computable functions

$$F_E(-) = ENC(-, K_E) \tag{9.9}$$
$$F_D(-) = DEC(-, K_D) \tag{9.10}$$

---

[5] In Caesar's protocol, the decryption key is just the encryption key with changed sign, whereas in the One-Time-Pad protocol, the two keys are exactly the same.

[6] By "hard," we mean that the number of computational steps to get from the first key to the second key is more than polynomial in the length of the first key.

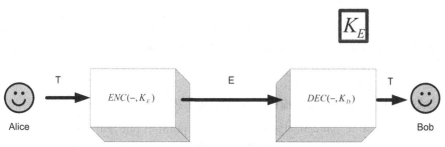

Figure 9.3. A cryptographic communication scheme with a public K_E.

such that F_D is the inverse of F_E but cannot easily be calculated from knowledge of F_E. A function like F_E, which is easy to compute yet hard to invert without extra information, is known as a **trapdoor function**. The name is quite suggestive: like a trapdoor in an old-fashioned Gothic castle, it opens under your feet but does not let you come back easily. So a trapdoor function is what Bob needs.[7]

Public-key cryptography has pros and cons. On the plus side, it solves the key distribution problem that hinders private-key protocols. If Alice wants to send a message to Bob, she does not need to know Bob's private key. On the minus side, all public-key protocols to date rely on the fact that the computation of the private key from the public key *appears* to be hard. This just means that as of yet, there are no known algorithms that do the job. The possibility is still open for some breakthrough result in computational complexity that would put all existing public-key cryptographic schemes out of business.[8] Finally, public-key protocols tend to be considerably slower than their private-key peers.

In light of the aforementioned, cryptographers devised a marriage of the two approaches to achieve the best of both worlds: public-key cryptography is used only to distribute a key K_E of some private-key protocol, rather than an entire text message. Once Alice and Bob safely share K_E, they can continue their conversation using the faster private-key scheme. Therefore, for the rest of this chapter, our only concern is to communicate a binary K_E of the appropriate length.

Before ending this section, we must expand on the picture of cryptography we have sketched so far. Secure communication of messages is only one of the issues at stake. Here are two others:

Intrusion Detection. Alice and Bob would like to determine whether Eve is, in fact, eavesdropping.

Authentication. We would like to ensure that nobody is impersonating Alice and sending false messages.

We shall show how to implement protocols that include the first of these features. The second feature is also discussed within the context of quantum cryptography but is outside the purview of this text.

---

[7] Where can Bob find trapdoor functions? There are, at present, quite a few public-key protocols about, drawing their techniques from advanced mathematics such as number theory (prime factorization) or algebraic curves theory (elliptic curves). We invite you to read about them in Koblitz (1994). (Caution: be prepared to perform some calculations!)

[8] Quantum computing itself offers unprecedented opportunities for breaking codes, as the celebrated result by Shor amply shows (see Section 6.5). For a discussion of the relationship between quantum computing and computational complexity, see Section 8.3.

Exercise 9.1.5   Suppose Alice and Bob communicate using some kind of public-key protocol. Alice has a pair of keys (one public, one private), and so does Bob. Devise a way in which Alice and Bob can communicate simultaneously while authenticating their messages. (Hint: Think of encoding one message "inside" another.)   ■

9.2 QUANTUM KEY EXCHANGE I: THE BB84 PROTOCOL

While discussing the One-Time-Pad protocol, we pointed out that the problem of securely transmitting the key is a serious one. During the 1980s, two authors came up with a clever idea that exploits quantum mechanics. This idea formed the basis of the first **quantum key exchange (QKE)** protocol.

Before presenting QKE in some detail, let us first see if we can guess which features of the quantum world are appealing to cryptographers. In the classical case, Eve is somewhere along the insecure channel listening for some bits of information. What can she do?

1. She can make copies of arbitrary portions of the encrypted bit stream and store them somewhere to be used for later analysis and investigations.

2. Eve can listen without affecting the bitstream, i.e., her eavesdropping does not leave traces.

Now, assume that Alice sends qubits, rather than bits, over some channel.[9]

$1'$. Eve cannot make perfect copies of the qubit stream: the no-cloning theorem discussed in Section 5.4 prevents this from happening.

$2'$. The very act of measuring the qubit stream alters it.

At first sight, the points raised above seem like limitations, but from the point of view of Alice and Bob, they actually turn out to be great opportunities. How? For one thing, the no-cloning theorem hampers Eve's ability to use past messages to conduct her analysis. Even more important, each time she measures the qubit stream, she disturbs it, allowing Alice and Bob to detect her presence along the channel.

The first quantum key exchange protocol was introduced by Charles Bennett and Gilles Brassard in 1984, and hence the name **BB84**. This section describes this important protocol.

Alice's goal is to send Bob a key via a quantum channel. Just as in the One-Time-Pad protocol, her key is a sequence of random (classical) bits obtained, perhaps, by tossing a coin. Alice will send a qubit each time she generates a new bit of her key. But which qubit should she send?

In this protocol, Alice will employ two different orthogonal bases shown in Figure 9.4:

$$+ = \{| \rightarrow \rangle, | \uparrow \rangle\} = \left\{ [1, 0]^T, [0, 1]^T \right\} \tag{9.11}$$

---

[9] This chapter is not concerned with hardware implementation of quantum cryptography. That topic is tackled in Chapter 11. For the time being, suffice it to note that any two-dimensional quantum system (like spin or photon polarization) could be employed for transmission.

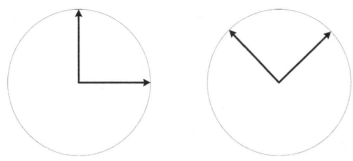

Figure 9.4. Two bases used for BB84.

and

$$X = \{|\searrow\rangle, |\nearrow\rangle\} = \left\{ \frac{1}{\sqrt{2}}[-1, 1]^T, \frac{1}{\sqrt{2}}[1, 1]^T \right\}. \tag{9.12}$$

We shall refer to the first basis as the "plus" basis and the second as the "times" basis. Essentially, they are two alternative vocabularies that Alice and Bob will use to communicate.

In these vocabularies, the states $|0\rangle$ and $|1\rangle$ shall be described by the following table:

State / Basis	+	X
$|0\rangle$	$|\rightarrow\rangle$	$|\nearrow\rangle$
$|1\rangle$	$|\uparrow\rangle$	$|\searrow\rangle$

(9.13)

For example, in the $+$ basis, a $|\rightarrow\rangle$ will correspond to a $|0\rangle$. If Alice wants to work in the X basis and wants to convey a $|1\rangle$, she will send a $|\searrow\rangle$. Similarly, if Alice sends a $|\uparrow\rangle$ and Bob measures a $|\uparrow\rangle$ in the $+$ basis, he should record a $|1\rangle$.

This is fine for basic states, but what about superpositions? If Bob measures photons using the $+$ basis, he will only see photons as $|\rightarrow\rangle$ or $|\uparrow\rangle$. What if Alice sends a $|\nearrow\rangle$ and Bob measures it in the $+$ basis? Then it will be in a superposition of states

$$|\nearrow\rangle = \frac{1}{\sqrt{2}}|\uparrow\rangle + \frac{1}{\sqrt{2}}|\rightarrow\rangle. \tag{9.14}$$

In other words, after measurement, there is a 50–50 chance of Bob's recording a $|0\rangle$ or a $|1\rangle$. Again, Alice could use the X basis, intending to send a $|0\rangle$, and Bob has a 50–50 chance of recording a $|1\rangle$ and a 50–50 chance of recording a $|0\rangle$. In all, there are four possible superpositions:

- $|\searrow\rangle$ with respect to $+$ will be $\frac{1}{\sqrt{2}}|\uparrow\rangle - \frac{1}{\sqrt{2}}|\rightarrow\rangle$.
- $|\nearrow\rangle$ with respect to $+$, will be $\frac{1}{\sqrt{2}}|\uparrow\rangle + \frac{1}{\sqrt{2}}|\rightarrow\rangle$.
- $|\uparrow\rangle$ with respect to X, will be $\frac{1}{\sqrt{2}}|\nearrow\rangle + \frac{1}{\sqrt{2}}|\searrow\rangle$.
- $|\rightarrow\rangle$ with respect to X, will be $\frac{1}{\sqrt{2}}|\nearrow\rangle - \frac{1}{\sqrt{2}}|\searrow\rangle$.

Exercise 9.2.1 Work out what $|\leftarrow\rangle$, $|\downarrow\rangle$, $|\swarrow\rangle$, and $|\searrow\rangle$ would be in terms of the two bases. ∎

Armed with this vocabulary and the inherent indeterminacy of the two bases, Alice and Bob are ready to start communicating. Here are the steps of the protocol:

Step 1. Alice flips a coin n times to determine which classical bits to send. She then flips the coin another n times to determine in which of the two bases to send those bits. She then sends the bits in their appropriate basis.

For example, if n is 12, we might have something like this:

Step 1: Alice sends n random bits in random bases

Bit number	1	2	3	4	5	6	7	8	9	10	11	12
Alice's random bits	0	1	1	0	1	1	1	0	1	0	1	0
Alice's random bases	+	+	X	+	+	+	X	+	X	X	X	+
Alice sends	→	↑	↖	→	↑	↑	↖	→	↖	↗	↖	→
Quantum channel	⇓	⇓	⇓	⇓	⇓	⇓	⇓	⇓	⇓	⇓	⇓	⇓

$$(9.15)$$

Step 2. As the sequence of qubits reaches Bob, he does not know which basis Alice used to send them, so to determine the basis by which to measure them he also tosses a coin n times. He then goes on to measure the qubit in those random bases.

In our example, we might have something like this:

Step 2: Bob receives n random bits in random measurements

Bit number	1	2	3	4	5	6	7	8	9	10	11	12
Bob's random bases	X	+	X	X	+	X	+	+	X	X	X	+
Bob observes	↗	↑	↖	↖	↑	↗	↑	→	↖	↗	↖	→
Bob's bits	0	1	1	1	1	0	1	0	1	0	1	0

$$(9.16)$$

Here is the catch: for about half of the time, Bob's basis will be the same as Alice's, in which case his result after measuring the qubit will be identical to Alice's original bit. The other half of the time, though, Bob's basis will differ from Alice's. In that case, the result of Bob's measurement will agree with Alice's original bit about 50% of the time.

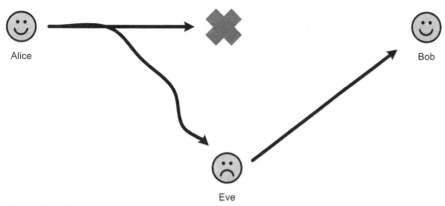

Figure 9.5. Eve "cutting" the quantum wire and transmitting her own message.

Programming Drill 9.2.1   *Write functions that mimic Alice, Bob, and their inter-actions.* **Alice** *should generate two random bit strings of the same length. Call one* **BitSent** *and the other* **SendingBasis**.

Bob *will be a function that generates a random bit string of the same length called* **ReceivingBasis**.

All three of these bit strings should be sent to an "all-knowing" function named **Knuth**. *This function must look at all three and create a fourth bit string named* **BitReceived**. *This is defined by the following instruction:*

$$
BitReceived[i] = \begin{cases} BitSent[i], & if \, SendingBasis[i] = ReceivingBasis[i], \\ random\{0, 1\}, & otherwise. \end{cases} \tag{9.17}
$$

This $random\{0, 1\}$ *is the classical analog of a qubit collapsing to a bit.*

Knuth *must furthermore evaluate the percentage of bits that* **Bob** *receives accu-rately.*

Let us continue with the protocol: If evil Eve is eavesdropping, she must be read-ing the information that Alice transmits and sending that information onward to Bob, as shown in Figure 9.5.

Eve also does not know in which basis Alice sent each qubit, so she must act like Bob. She will also toss a coin each time. If Eve's basis is identical to Alice's, her measure will be accurate and she will, in turn, send accurate information on to Bob. If, on the other hand, her basis is different from Alice's, her bit will be in agreement with Alice's only 50% of the time. However, here's the rub: the qubit has now col-lapsed to one of the two elements of *Eve's basis*. Because of the no-cloning theorem, Eve does not have the luxury of making a copy of the original qubit and then send-ing it on (after her probe), so she just sends the qubit after her observation. Now

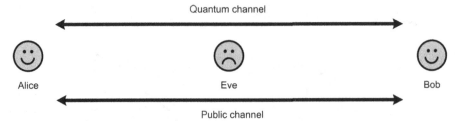

Figure 9.6. Alice and Bob communicating on quantum and public channels, with Eve eavesdropping.

Bob will receive it in the wrong basis. What are his chances of getting the same bit Alice has? Answer: His chances are 50–50.[10]

Therefore if Eve intercepts and measures each qubit sent, she will negatively affect Bob's chances of agreement with Alice.

Exercise 9.2.2   Give an estimate of how frequently Bob's bit will agree with Alice's if Eve is constantly eavesdropping.   ∎

By computing some simple statistics, a potential intrusion by Eve would be detected. This suggests how to complete BB84. Let us examine the details.

After Bob has finished decoding the qubit stream, he has in his hands a bit stream of length n. Bob and Alice will discuss which of the n bits were sent and received in the same basis. They can do this on a public channel, such as a telephone line. Figure 9.6 is helpful.

Step 3. Bob and Alice publicly compare which basis they used chose at each step. For instance, he can tell her $X, +, X, X, \ldots$. Alice replies by telling him when he was right, and when he was not. Each time they disagreed, Alice and Bob scratch out the corresponding bit. Proceeding this way until the end, they are each left with a subsequence of bits that were sent and received in the same basis. If Eve was not listening to the quantum channel, this subsequence should be exactly identical. On average, this subsequence is of length $\frac{n}{2}$.

Step 3: Alice and Bob publicly compare bases used											
Bit number	1	2	3	4	5	6	7	8	9	10	11	12
Alice's random bases	+	+	X	+	+	+	X	+	X	X	X	+
Public channel	↕	↕	↕	↕	↕	↕	↕	↕	↕	↕	↕	↕
Bob's random bases	X	+	X	X	+	X	+	+	X	X	X	+
Which agree?		✓	✓		✓			✓	✓	✓	✓	✓
Shared secret keys		1	1		1			0	1	0	1	0

(9.18)

---

[10] Eve does, in fact, have other options. For example, she can "listen in" with a third basis. However, such considerations would take us too far afield.

Programming Drill 9.2.2 *Continuing with the last programming drill, write a function named* **Knuth2** *that accepts all three-bit strings and creates a bit string (of possibly shorter length) called* **AgreedBits***, which is a substring of both* **BitSent** *and* **BitReceived***.*

But what if Eve was eavesdropping? Alice and Bob would also like to engage in some intrusion detection. They want to know if Eve (or anyone else) was listening in. They do this by comparing some of the bits of the subsequence.

Step 4. Bob randomly chooses half of the $\frac{n}{2}$ bits and publicly compares them with Alice. If they disagree by more than a tiny percentage (that could be attributed to noise), they know that Eve was listening in and then sending what she received. In that case, they scratch the whole sequence and try something else. If the exposed sequence is mostly similar, it means that either Eve has great guessing ability (improbable) or Eve was not listening in. In that case, they simply scratch out the revealed test subsequence and what remains is the unrevealed secret private key.

Step 4: Alice and Bob publicly compare half of the remaining bits												
Bit number	1	2	3	4	5	6	7	8	9	10	11	12
Shared secret keys		1	1		1			0	1	0	1	0
Randomly chosen to compare			✓						✓	✓		✓
Public channel			↕						↕	↕		↕
Shared secret keys		1	1		1			0	1	0	1	0
Which agree?			✓						✓	✓		✓
Unrevealed secret keys:		1			1			0			1	

In this protocol, Step 3 has eliminated half of the original qubits sent. So if we begin with n qubits, only $\frac{n}{2}$ qubits will be available after Step 3. Furthermore, Alice and Bob publicly display half of the resulting qubits in Step 4. This leaves us with $\frac{n}{4}$ of the original qubits. Do not be disturbed about this, as Alice can make her qubit stream as large as she needs. Hence, if Alice is interested in sending an m bit key, she simply starts with a $4m$ qubit stream.

9.3 QUANTUM KEY EXCHANGE II: THE B92 PROTOCOL

In the previous section, we introduced the first quantum key exchange protocol. Alice had two distinct orthogonal bases at her disposal. It turns out that the use of two different bases is redundant, provided one employs a slightly slicker means of measuring. This simplification results in another quantum key distribution protocol, known as **B92**. **B** stands for its inventor, Charles Bennett, and 1992 is the year it was published.

The main idea in B92 is that Alice uses only one *nonorthogonal* basis. Let us work out the protocol with the following example:

$$\{|\rightarrow\rangle\,|\,\nearrow\rangle\} = \left\{[1, 0]^T, \frac{1}{\sqrt{2}}[1, 1]^T\right\}. \tag{9.19}$$

Exercise 9.3.1 Verify that these two vectors are, in fact, not orthogonal. ∎

Before going into detail, we need to pause and reflect a little. We know that all observables have an orthogonal basis of eigenvectors. This means that if we consider a nonorthogonal basis, there is no observable whose basis of eigenvectors is the one we have chosen. In turn, this means that there is no single experiment whose resulting states are precisely the members of our basis. Stated differently, no single experiment can be set up for the specific purpose of discriminating unambiguously between the nonorthogonal states of the basis.

Alice takes $|\rightarrow\rangle$ to be 0 and $|\nearrow\rangle$ to be 1. Using this language, we can begin the protocol.

Step 1. Alice flips a coin n times and transmits to Bob the n random bits in the appropriate polarization with a quantum channel.

Here is an example.

Step 1: Alice sends n random bits in the $\angle$ basis												
Bit number	1	2	3	4	5	6	7	8	9	10	11	12
Alice's random bits	0	0	1	0	1	0	1	0	1	1	1	0
Alice's qubits	→	→	↗	→	↗	→	↗	→	↗	↗	↗	→
Quantum channel	⇓	⇓	⇓	⇓	⇓	⇓	⇓	⇓	⇓	⇓	⇓	⇓

$$\tag{9.20}$$

Step 2. For each of the n qubits, Bob measures the received qubits in either the $+$ basis or the X basis. He flips a coin to determine which basis to use.

There are several possible scenarios that can occur:

- If Bob uses the $+$ basis and observes a $|\uparrow\rangle$, then he knows that Alice must have sent a $|\nearrow\rangle = |1\rangle$ because if Alice had sent a $|\rightarrow\rangle$, Bob would have received a $|\rightarrow\rangle$.
- If Bob uses the $+$ basis and observes a $|\rightarrow\rangle$, then it is not clear to him which qubit Alice sent. She could have sent a $|\rightarrow\rangle$ but she could also have sent a $|\nearrow\rangle$ that collapsed to a $|\rightarrow\rangle$. Because Bob is in doubt, he will omit this bit.
- If Bob uses the X basis and observes a $|\nwarrow\rangle$, then he knows that Alice must have sent a $|\rightarrow\rangle = |0\rangle$ because if Alice had sent a $|\nearrow\rangle$, Bob would have received a $|\nearrow\rangle$.
- If Bob uses the X basis and observes a $|\nearrow\rangle$, then it is not clear to him which qubit Alice sent. She could have sent a $|\nearrow\rangle$ but she could also have sent a $|\rightarrow\rangle$ that collapsed to a $|\nearrow\rangle$. Because Bob is in doubt, he will omit this bit.

Continuing the example, we have the following:

Step 2: Bob receives n random bits in a random basis												
Bit number	1	2	3	4	5	6	7	8	9	10	11	12
Alice's random bits	→	→	↗	→	↗	→	↗	→	↗	↗	↗	→
Quantum channel	⇓	⇓	⇓	⇓	⇓	⇓	⇓	⇓	⇓	⇓	⇓	⇓
Bob's random bases	X	+	X	X	+	X	+	+	X	+	X	+
Bob's observations	↖	→	↗	↖	↑	↖	→	→	↗	↑	↗	→
Bob's bits	0	?	?	0	1	0	?	?	?	1	?	?

$$(9.21)$$

There are two possible bases that Bob could have used to measure. For each basis, there are two types of results. For half of those four results, the bit sent is certain. For the other half, there is uncertainty. Bob must omit the uncertain ones and keep the others hidden. He must inform Alice of this.

Step 3. Bob publicly tells Alice which bits were uncertain and they both omit them.

At this point, Alice and Bob know which bits are secret, so they may use those. But there is one more step if they want to detect whether or not Eve was listening in. They can, as in Step 4 of BB84, sacrifice half their hidden bits and publicly compare them. If they do not agree for a significant number, then they know that evil Eve has been doing her wicked deeds and the entire bit string should be ignored.

Programming Drill 9.3.1 *Write three functions that mimic Alice, Bob, and their interactions. Use functions named **Alice92**, **Bob92**, and **Knuth92**. They should create bit strings that perform the B92 protocol.*

9.4 QUANTUM KEY EXCHANGE III: THE EPR PROTOCOL

In 1991, Artur K. Ekert proposed a completely different type of quantum key distribution protocol based on entanglement (Ekert, 1991). We shall present a simplified version of the protocol and then point to the original version.

We remind the reader that it is possible to place two qubits in the following entangled state[11]:

$$\frac{|00\rangle + |11\rangle}{\sqrt{2}}.$$

$$(9.22)$$

---

[11] In the real world, the entangled pairs will probably be in a state

$$\frac{|01\rangle + |10\rangle}{\sqrt{2}}.$$

$$(9.23)$$

as explained on page 136 of Chapter 4. When one is measured, they will both collapse to opposite values. We shall deal with the slightly easier version given in Equation (9.22). It will become apparent that if we use Equation (9.23), then Alice and Bob will have inverted bit strings. But if we use the simplified one given in Equation (9.22), they will share the exact same bit string.

We saw in Section 4.5 that when one of the qubits is measured, they both will collapse to the same value.

Suppose Alice wants to send Bob a secret key. A sequence of entangled pairs of qubits can be generated and each of our communicators can be sent one of the pairs. When Alice and Bob are ready to communicate, they can measure their respective qubits. It does not matter who measures first, because whoever does it first will collapse the other qubit to the same random value. We are done! Alice and Bob now have a sequence of random bits that no one else has.

There are more sophisticated protocols that will be useful to detect eavesdroppers or if the qubits fell out of entanglement. As in BB84, rather than measure a qubit in one basis, we can measure it in two different bases, say X and +.

Following the vocabulary of X and + of Section 9.2, we present the protocol.

Step 1. Alice and Bob are each assigned one of each of the pairs of a sequence of entangled qubits.

When they are ready to communicate, they move on to Step 2.

Step 2. Alice and Bob separately choose a random sequence of bases to measure their particles. They then measure their qubits in their chosen basis.

An example might look like this:

Step 2: Alice and Bob measure in each of their random bases												
Bit number	1	2	3	4	5	6	7	8	9	10	11	12
Alice's random bases	X	X	+	+	X	+	X	+	+	X	+	X
Alice's observations	↗	↖	→	↑	↗	→	↖	→	→	↗	→	↗
Bob's random bases	X	+	+	X	X	+	+	+	+	X	X	+
Bob's observations	↗	→	→	↗	↗	→	↑	→	→	↗	↖	→

$$(9.24)$$

Step 3. Alice and Bob publicly compare what bases were used and keep only those bits that were measured in the same basis.

Step 3: Alice and Bob publicly compare their bases												
Bit number	1	2	3	4	5	6	7	8	9	10	11	12
Alice's random bases	X	X	+	+	X	+	X	+	+	X	+	X
Public channel	↕	↕	↕	↕	↕	↕	↕	↕	↕	↕	↕	↕
Bob's random bases	X	+	+	X	X	+	+	+	+	X	X	+
Which agree?	✓		✓		✓	✓		✓	✓	✓		

$$(9.25)$$

If everything worked fine, Alice and Bob share a totally random secret key. But problems could have occurred. The entangled pairs could have been exposed to the environment and become disentangled,[12] or wicked Eve could have taken hold of one of the pairs, measured them, and sent along disentangled qubits.

We solve this problem by doing what we did in Step 4 of BB84. Alice or Bob randomly choose half of the remaining qubits and publicly compare the bits (not the bases). If they agree, then the last quarter of hidden qubits are probably good. If more than a small part disagree (from noise), then we must suspect Eve is up to her evil ways and our friendly communicators must throw away the entire sequence.

Ekert's original protocol is even more sophisticated. For Step 2, rather than measuring the qubits in two different bases, they will be measured in three different bases. As in BB84, Alice and Bob will publicly compare the results of half of their measured sequences to detect if the qubits are still entangled. They will then perform certain tests on the results to determine if they were still entangled. If not, then they throw away the entire sequence.

The test that they will perform is based on John Bell's famous **Bell's inequality**,[13] which is central to the foundations of quantum mechanics.

Bell's inequality is a way of describing the results of measurements on three different bases of two particles. If the particles are independent of each other, like classical objects, then the measurements will satisfy the inequality. If the particles are not independent of each other, i.e., they are entangled particles, then Bell's inequality *fails*.

Ekert proposed to use Bell's inequality to test Alice and Bob's bit sequences to make sure that when they were measured they were, in fact, entangled. This is done by publicly comparing a randomly chosen part of the sequences. We are going to look at one of three possible directions x, y, and z of spin of particles. If the revealed part of the sequence respects Bell's inequality, then we know that the qubits are not entangled (i.e., are independent) and they are acting like classical objects. In such a case, we throw away the entire sequence and start over. If the revealed portion fails Bell's inequality, then we can assume that the whole sequence was measured when it was in a quantum entangled state, and hence the sequence is still private.

9.5 QUANTUM TELEPORTATION

In the last section, we became experts at dealing with entangled qubits. We would like to use this expertise to perform quantum teleportation.

Definition 9.5.1 **Quantum teleportation** *is the process by which the state of an arbitrary qubit is transferred from one location to another.*

---

[12] Entanglement is indeed a volatile property. See Chapter 11 for a further discussion of entanglement and what happens when it is exposed to the environment.

[13] In fact, a similar inequality that describes classical independent objects was noticed in the nineteenth century by one of the forefathers of computer science, George Boole. Boole called them "conditions of possible experience." See Pitowsky (1994).

It is important to realize that what we describe in this section is not science fiction. Quantum teleportation has already been performed in the laboratory. The future of teleportation is, indeed, something to look forward to.

Recall that in Section 5.4 we met the no-cloning theorem, which states that we are not able to make a copy of the state of an arbitrary qubit. That means that when the state of the original qubit is teleported to another location, the state of the original will necessarily be destroyed. As stated on page 166, "Move is possible. Copy is impossible."

Before moving on to the protocol, some preliminaries must be dealt with. In our journey, we have found that working with a cleverly chosen noncanonical basis and switching between the canonical basis and the noncanonical basis is helpful. When working with a single qubit, we worked with the canonical basis

$$\{|0\rangle, |1\rangle\} \tag{9.26}$$

and the noncanonical basis

$$\left\{ \frac{|0\rangle + |1\rangle}{\sqrt{2}}, \frac{|0\rangle - |1\rangle}{\sqrt{2}} \right\}. \tag{9.27}$$

The teleportation algorithm will work with two entangled qubits, one held by Alice and one held by Bob. The obvious canonical basis for this four-dimensional space is

$$\{|0_A 0_B\rangle, |0_A 1_B\rangle, |1_A 0_B\rangle, |1_A 1_B\rangle\}. \tag{9.28}$$

A noncanonical basis, called the **Bell basis** in honor of John Bell, consists of the following four vectors:

$$|\Psi^+\rangle = \frac{|0_A 1_B\rangle + |1_A 0_B\rangle}{\sqrt{2}}, \tag{9.29}$$

$$|\Psi^-\rangle = \frac{|0_A 1_B\rangle - |1_A 0_B\rangle}{\sqrt{2}}, \tag{9.30}$$

$$|\Phi^+\rangle = \frac{|0_A 0_B\rangle + |1_A 1_B\rangle}{\sqrt{2}}, \tag{9.31}$$

$$|\Phi^-\rangle = \frac{|0_A 0_B\rangle - |1_A 1_B\rangle}{\sqrt{2}}. \tag{9.32}$$

Every vector in this basis is entangled.

In order to show that these vectors form a basis, we must show that they are linearly independent (we leave this to the reader) and that every vector in $\mathbb{C}^2 \otimes \mathbb{C}^2$ can be written as a linear combination of vectors from the Bell basis. Rather than showing it for every vector in $\mathbb{C}^2 \otimes \mathbb{C}^2$, we show it is true for every vector in the canonical basis of $\mathbb{C}^2 \otimes \mathbb{C}^2$:

$$|0_A 0_B\rangle = \frac{1}{\sqrt{2}}(|\Phi^+\rangle + |\Phi^-\rangle), \tag{9.33}$$

$$|1_A 1_B\rangle = \frac{1}{\sqrt{2}}(|\Phi^+\rangle - |\Phi^-\rangle), \tag{9.34}$$

$$|0_A 1_B\rangle = \frac{1}{\sqrt{2}}(|\Psi^+\rangle + |\Psi^-\rangle), \tag{9.35}$$

$$|1_A 0_B\rangle = \frac{1}{\sqrt{2}}(|\Psi^+\rangle - |\Psi^-\rangle). \tag{9.36}$$

Because every vector in $\mathbb{C}^2 \otimes \mathbb{C}^2$ is a linear combination of canonical basis vectors and every canonical basis vector is a linear combination of Bell basis vectors, we have that the Bell basis is, in fact, a basis.

How are the Bell basis vectors formed? In the two-dimensional case, we saw that the elements of the noncanonical basis can be formed using the Hadamard matrix. Remember that H does the following:

$$|0\rangle \longmapsto \frac{|0\rangle + |1\rangle}{\sqrt{2}} \quad \text{and} \quad |1\rangle \longmapsto \frac{|0\rangle - |1\rangle}{\sqrt{2}}. \tag{9.37}$$

In the four-dimensional case, we need something a little more complicated:

$$
\begin{array}{c}
|x\rangle \quad \boxed{H} \quad \bullet \\
|y\rangle \quad\quad\quad \oplus
\end{array}
\tag{9.38}
$$

It can easily be seen that this quantum circuit with the appropriate inputs creates the elements of the Bell basis:

$$|00\rangle \longmapsto |\Phi^+\rangle, \qquad |01\rangle \longmapsto |\Psi^+\rangle, \qquad |10\rangle \longmapsto |\Phi^-\rangle, \qquad |11\rangle \longmapsto |\Psi^-\rangle. \tag{9.39}$$

We now have enough tool in our toolbox to move ahead with the quantum teleportation protocol. Alice has a qubit $|\psi\rangle = \alpha|0\rangle + \beta|1\rangle$ in an arbitrary state that she would like to teleport to Bob.

Step 1. Two entangled qubits are formed as $|\Phi^+\rangle$. One is given to Alice and one is given to Bob.

We may envision these three qubits as three lines.

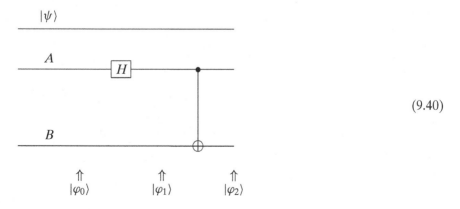

(9.40)

The top two lines are in Alice's possession and the bottom line is in Bob's possession. The states are as follows:

$$|\varphi_0\rangle = |\psi\rangle \otimes |0_A\rangle \otimes |0_B\rangle = |\psi\rangle \otimes |0_A 0_B\rangle, \tag{9.41}$$

$$|\varphi_1\rangle = |\psi\rangle \otimes \frac{|0_A\rangle + |1_A\rangle}{\sqrt{2}} \otimes |0_B\rangle, \tag{9.42}$$

$$|\varphi_2\rangle = |\psi\rangle \otimes |\Phi^+\rangle = |\psi\rangle \otimes \frac{|0_A 0_B\rangle + |1_A 1_B\rangle}{\sqrt{2}} \tag{9.43}$$

$$= (\alpha|0\rangle + \beta|1\rangle) \otimes \frac{|0_A 0_B\rangle + |1_A 1_B\rangle}{\sqrt{2}}$$

$$= \frac{\alpha|0\rangle(|0_A 0_B\rangle + |1_A 1_B\rangle) + \beta|1\rangle(|0_A 0_B\rangle + |1_A 1_B\rangle)}{\sqrt{2}}.$$

Step 2. Alice lets her $|\psi\rangle$ interact with her entangled qubit. Steps 1, 2, and 3 can be seen in the following diagram:

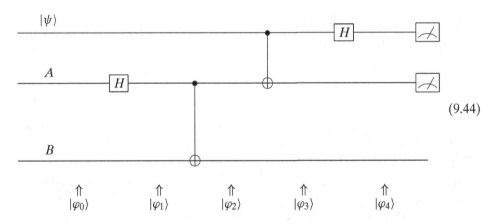

$$(9.44)$$

We have

$$|\varphi_3\rangle = \frac{\alpha|0\rangle(|0_A 0_B\rangle + |1_A 1_B\rangle) + \beta|1\rangle(|1_A 0_B\rangle + |0_A 1_B\rangle)}{\sqrt{2}},$$

$$|\varphi_4\rangle = \frac{1}{2}(\alpha(|0\rangle + |1\rangle)(|0_A 0_B\rangle + |1_A 1_B\rangle) + \beta(|0\rangle - |1\rangle)(|1_A 0_B\rangle + |0_A 1_B\rangle)$$

$$= \frac{1}{2}(\alpha(|000\rangle + |011\rangle + |100\rangle + |111\rangle) + \beta(|010\rangle + |001\rangle - |110\rangle - |101\rangle)).$$

$$(9.45)$$

Regrouping these triplets $|xyz\rangle$ in terms of $|xy\rangle$, which is in Alice's possession, we have

$$|\alpha_4\rangle = \frac{1}{2}(|00\rangle(\alpha|0\rangle + \beta|1\rangle) + |01\rangle(\beta|0\rangle + \alpha|1\rangle)$$
$$+ |10\rangle(\alpha|0\rangle - \beta|1\rangle) + |11\rangle(-\beta|0\rangle + \alpha|1\rangle)). \tag{9.46}$$

So the system of three qubits is now in a superposition of four possible states.

Step 3. Alice measures her two qubits and determines to which of the four possible states the system collapses.

At the moment Alice measures her two qubits; all three qubits collapse to one of four possibilities. So if she measures $|10\rangle$ then the third qubit is in state $\alpha|0\rangle - \beta|1\rangle$.

There are two problems to deal with:

(a) Alice knows this state but Bob does not; and
(b) Bob has $\alpha|0\rangle - \beta|1\rangle$, not the desired $\alpha|0\rangle + \beta|1\rangle$. Both problems are solved by Step 4.

Step 4. Alice sends copies of her two bits (not qubits) to Bob who uses that information to achieve the desired state $|\psi\rangle$.

In other words, if Bob receives $|10\rangle$ from Alice, he then knows that his qubit is in state

$$\alpha|0\rangle - \beta|1\rangle = \begin{bmatrix} \alpha \\ -\beta \end{bmatrix}; \tag{9.47}$$

hence he should act on his qubit with the following matrix:

$$\begin{bmatrix} 1 & 0 \\ 0 & -1 \end{bmatrix}\begin{bmatrix} \alpha \\ -\beta \end{bmatrix} = \begin{bmatrix} \alpha \\ \beta \end{bmatrix} = \alpha|0\rangle + \beta|1\rangle = |\psi\rangle. \tag{9.48}$$

In detail, Bob must apply the following matrices upon receiving information from Alice:

Bob's reconstruction matrices				
Bits received	$|00\rangle$	$|01\rangle$	$|10\rangle$	$|11\rangle$
Matrix to apply	$\begin{bmatrix} 1 & 0 \\ 0 & 1 \end{bmatrix}$	$\begin{bmatrix} 0 & 1 \\ 1 & 0 \end{bmatrix}$	$\begin{bmatrix} 1 & 0 \\ 0 & -1 \end{bmatrix}$	$\begin{bmatrix} 0 & 1 \\ -1 & 0 \end{bmatrix}$

$$\tag{9.49}$$

After applying the matrix, Bob will have the same qubit that Alice had.

The following space–time diagram might be helpful. We use the convention that straight arrows correspond to the movement of bits and curvy arrows correspond to qubits on the move.

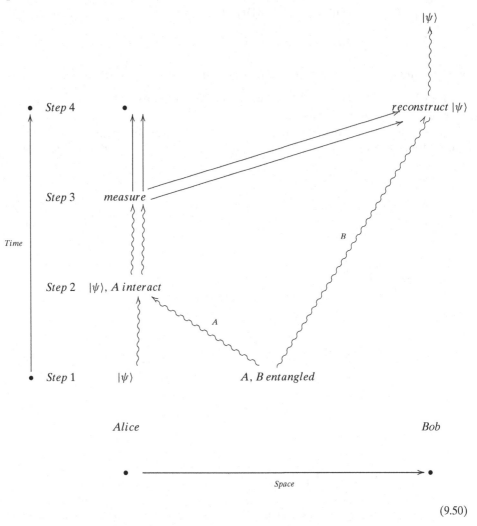

$$(9.50)$$

Notice that $|\psi\rangle$ moves from the lower-left corner in Alice's possession to the upper-right corner in Bob's possession. Mission accomplished!

Several points should be made about this protocol:

- Alice is no longer in possession of $|\psi\rangle$. She has only two classical bits.
- As we have seen, to "teleport" a single quantum particle, Alice has to send two classical bits. Without receiving them, there is no way that Bob can know what he has. These classical bits travel along a classical channel and thus they propagate at finite speed (less than the speed of light). Entanglement, in spite of its undisputable magic, does *not* allow you to communicate faster than the speed of light. Einstein's theory of relativity would not permit such communication.

■ α and β were arbitrary complex numbers satisfying $|\alpha|^2 + |\beta|^2 = 1$. They could have had an infinite decimal expansion. And yet, this potentially infinite amount of information has gone from Alice to Bob across the universe by passing only two bits. However, it is important to realize that this potentially infinite amount of information is passed as a *qubit* and useless to Bob. As soon as he measures the qubit, it will collapse to a bit.

■ Someone might argue that calling all the foregoing teleportation is a bit of a stretch. Indeed, no particle has been moved at all. However, from the point of view of quantum mechanics, two particles having exactly the same quantum state are, from the standpoint of physics, indistinguishable and can therefore be treated as the same particle. If you are configured like Captain Kirk down to the minutest details, you *are* Captain Kirk!

Exercise 9.5.1 What about Eve? She can certainly tap into the classical channel and snatch the two bits. But will it be useful to her? ■

Exercise 9.5.2 There was nothing special about Alice using $|\Phi^+\rangle$ to entangle her $|\psi\rangle$. She could have just as easily used any of the other three Bell vectors. Work out the result if she had used $|\Phi^-\rangle$. ■

. . . .

References: A comprehensive text on classical cryptography is Schneier (1995). For a more mathematical treatment, see Koblitz (1994). A general introduction to quantum cryptography is Lomonaco (2001).

BB84 was first described in Bennett and Brassard (1984). **B92** was the first presentation of Bennett (1992). The EPR protocol was first described in Ekert (1991).

A short history of quantum cryptography can be found in Brassard and Crépeau (1993), and a bibliography in Brassard (1993).

Quantum teleportation was first presented in Bennett et al. (1993).

10

Information Theory

I find that a great part of the information I have
was acquired by looking up something
and finding something else on the way.

Franklin P. Adams

The topic of this chapter is **quantum information**, i.e., information in the quantum world. The material that is presented here lies at the core of a variety of areas within the compass of quantum computation, such as quantum cryptography, described in Chapter 9, and quantum data compression. As quantum information extends and modifies concepts developed in classical information theory, a brief review of the mathematical notion of information is in order.

In Section 10.1, we recall the basics of classical information theory. Section 10.2 generalizes this work to get quantum information theory. Section 10.3 discusses classical and quantum data compression. We conclude with a small section on error-correcting codes.

10.1 CLASSICAL INFORMATION AND SHANNON ENTROPY

What *is* information really? In the mid-forties, an American mathematician named Claude Shannon set out to establish a mathematical theory of information on a firm basis. To see this, we use Alice and Bob. Alice and Bob are exchanging messages. Let us say that Alice can only send one of four different messages coded by the letters A, B, C, and D.

In our story, the meaning of the four letters is as following:

Symbol	Meaning
A	"I feel sad now"
B	"I feel angry now"
C	"I feel happy now"
D	"I feel bored now"

(10.1)

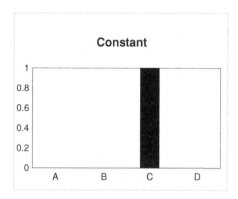
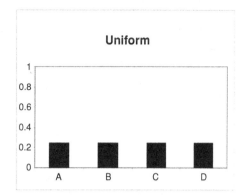
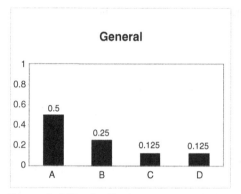

Figure 10.1. Three possible probability distributions.

Bob is a careful listener, so he keeps track of the frequency of each letter. By observing N consecutive messages from Alice, he reports the following:

A appeared N_A times

B appeared N_B times

C appeared N_C times

D appeared N_D times

where $N_A + N_B + N_C + N_D = N$. Bob concludes that the **probability** of each letter showing up is given by

$$p(A) = \frac{N_A}{N}, \quad p(B) = \frac{N_B}{N}, \quad p(C) = \frac{N_C}{N}, \quad \text{and} \quad p(D) = \frac{N_D}{N}. \quad (10.2)$$

The table that associates with each basic symbol its probability is known as the **probability distribution Function** (pdf for short) of the source. Of course, the probability distribution may have different shapes (Figure 10.1). For instance, Alice may be always happy (or at least say so to Bob), so that the pdf looks like

$$p(A) = \frac{0}{N} = 0, \quad p(B) = \frac{0}{N} = 0, \quad p(C) = \frac{N}{N} = 1, \quad \text{and} \quad p(D) = \frac{0}{N} = 0. \quad (10.3)$$

Such a pdf is called the **constant** distribution. In this case, Bob knows with certainty that the next symbol he will receive from Alice is C. It stands to reason that in this scenario C does not bring any new *information*: its information content is zero.

On the opposite side of the spectrum, let us assume that Alice is very moody, in fact totally unpredictable, as far as her emotional state goes. The pdf will then look like

$$p(A) = \frac{1}{4}, \quad p(B) = \frac{1}{4}, \quad p(C) = \frac{1}{4}, \quad \text{and} \quad p(D) = \frac{1}{4}. \tag{10.4}$$

Such a pdf is called the **uniform** distribution. In this case, when Bob will observe the new symbol from Alice, he will gain information, indeed the maximum amount of information this limited alphabet could convey.

These two scenarios are just two extremes among infinitely many others. For instance, the pdf might look like

$$p(A) = \frac{1}{2}, \quad p(B) = \frac{1}{4}, \quad p(C) = \frac{1}{8}, \quad \text{and} \quad p(D) = \frac{1}{8}. \tag{10.5}$$

It is quite obvious that this general scenario stands in between the other two, in the sense that its outcome is less certain than the one afforded by the constant pdf, but more so than the uniform pdf.

We have just found a deep connection between *uncertainty* and *information*. The more uncertain the outcome, the more Bob will gain information by knowing the outcome. What Bob can predict beforehand does not count: only novelty brings forth information![1] The uniform probability distribution represents the greatest uncertainty about the outcome: everything can happen with equal likelihood; likewise, its information content is the greatest.

It now becomes clear what we need: a way to quantify the amount of uncertainty in a given probability distribution. Shannon, building on classical statistical thermodynamics, introduced precisely such a measure.

Definition 10.1.1 *The **Shannon entropy** of a source with probability distribution* $\{p_i\}$ *is the quantity*

$$H_S = -\sum_{i=1}^{n} p_i \times \log_2(p_i) = \sum_{i=1}^{n} p_i \times \log_2\left(\frac{1}{p_i}\right), \tag{10.6}$$

where the following convention has been adopted: $0 \times \log_2(0) = 0$.[2]

Note: The minus sign is there to make sure that entropy is always positive or zero, as shown by the following exercise.

Exercise 10.1.1 Prove that Shannon entropy is always positive or zero.   ■

---

[1] After all, this is just common sense. Would you bother reading a daily newspaper if you knew its content beforehand?

[2] The calculus savvy reader will promptly recognize the soundness of this convention: the limit of the function $y = x \log_2(x)$ is zero as x approaches zero. There is another more philosophical motivation: if a symbol is never sent, its contribution to the calculation of entropy should be zero.

Why should we believe that the formula presented in Equation (10.6) does indeed capture the uncertainty of the source? The better course is to calculate H for each of the aforementioned scenarios above.

Let us compute the entropy for the constant pdf:

$$H_S = -0 \times \log_2(0) - 0 \times \log_2(0) - 1 \times \log_2(1) - 0 \times \log_2(0)$$
$$= -\log_2(1) = 0. \tag{10.7}$$

As we see, the entropy is as low as it can be, just as we would expect. When the entropy equals zero, that means there is absolutely no uncertainty in the source.

Let us move to the uniform pdf:

$$H_S = -\frac{1}{4} \times \log_2\left(\frac{1}{4}\right) - \frac{1}{4} \times \log_2\left(\frac{1}{4}\right) - \frac{1}{4} \times \log_2\left(\frac{1}{4}\right) - \frac{1}{4} \times \log_2\left(\frac{1}{4}\right)$$
$$= -\log_2\left(\frac{1}{4}\right) = 2. \tag{10.8}$$

This makes sense. After all, because Bob has no real previous information, he needs no less than two bits of information to describe which letter is being sent to him.

And now the general scenario:

$$H_S = -\frac{1}{2} \times \log_2\left(\frac{1}{2}\right) - \frac{1}{4} \times \log_2\left(\frac{1}{4}\right) - \frac{1}{8} \times \log_2\left(\frac{1}{8}\right)$$
$$- \frac{1}{8} \times \log_2\left(\frac{1}{8}\right) = 1.75. \tag{10.9}$$

We have thus verified, at least for the preceding examples, that the entropy formula does indeed classify the amount of uncertainty of the system.

Exercise 10.1.2 Create a fourth scenario that is strictly in between the general pdf in Equation (10.9) and the uniform distribution. In other words, determine a pdf for the four-symbol source whose entropy verifies $1.75 < H < 2$. ∎

Exercise 10.1.3 Find a pdf for the four-symbol source so that the entropy will be less than 1 but strictly positive. ∎

Summing up, we can recapitulate the above into two complementary slogans:

Greater entropy means greater uncertainty

Greater entropy means more information (10.10)

Programming Drill 10.1.1 *Write a simple program that lets the user choose how many letters the source alphabet has, and then enter the probability distribution. The program should visualize it, and compute its Shannon entropy.*

10.2 QUANTUM INFORMATION AND VON NEUMANN ENTROPY

The previous section dealt with the transmission of classical information, i.e., information that can be encoded as a *stream of bits*. We are now going to investigate to what extent things change when we are concerned with sources emitting *streams of qubits*.

As it turns out, there is a quantum analog of entropy, known as **von Neumann entropy**. Just as Shannon entropy measures the amount of order in a classical system, von Neumann entropy will gauge order in a given quantum system. Let us set the quantum scenario first. Alice has chosen as her quantum alphabet a set of normalized states in $\mathbb{C}^m$:

$$\{|w_1\rangle, |w_2\rangle, \ldots, |w_n\rangle\}. \tag{10.11}$$

If she wishes to notify Bob of her moods, as in the previous section, she can choose four normalized states in some state space. Even the single qubit space is quite roomy (there are infinitely many distinct qubits), so she could select the following set:

$$\left\{|A\rangle = |0\rangle, \ |B\rangle = |1\rangle, \ |C\rangle = \frac{1}{\sqrt{2}}|0\rangle + \frac{1}{\sqrt{2}}|1\rangle, \ |D\rangle = \frac{1}{\sqrt{2}}|0\rangle - \frac{1}{\sqrt{2}}|1\rangle\right\}. \tag{10.12}$$

Notice that Alice does not have to choose an orthogonal set of states, they simply need to be distinct.

Now, let us assume that she sends to Bob her states with probabilities:

$$p(|w_1\rangle) = p_1, \quad p(|w_2\rangle) = p_2, \ldots, p(|w_n\rangle) = p_n. \tag{10.13}$$

We can associate with the table above a linear operator, known as the **density operator**,[3] defined by the following expression:

$$D = p_1|w_1\rangle\langle w_1| + p_2|w_2\rangle\langle w_2| + \cdots + p_n|w_n\rangle\langle w_n|. \tag{10.14}$$

D does not look like anything we have met so far. It is the weighted sum of a basic expression of the form $|w\rangle\langle w|$, i.e., *products of a bra with their associated ket*. To get some sense for what D actually does, let us study first how its building blocks operate. $|w_i\rangle\langle w_i|$ acts on a ket vector $|v\rangle$ in the following way:

$$|w_i\rangle\langle w_i|(|v\rangle) = (\langle w_i|v\rangle)|w_i\rangle. \tag{10.15}$$

In plain words, the result of applying $|w_i\rangle\langle w_i|$ to a generic ket $|v\rangle$ is simply the projection of $|v\rangle$ onto $|w_i\rangle$, as shown in Figure 10.2. The length of the projection is the scalar product $\langle w_i|v\rangle$ (we are here using the fact that all w_i's are normalized).

---

[3] The origin of the density operator lies in statistical quantum mechanics. The formalism that we have presented thus far works well if we assume that the quantum system is in a well-defined state. Now, when studying large ensembles of quantum particles, the most we can assume is that we know the probability distribution of the quantum states of the individual particles, i.e., we know that a randomly selected particle will be in state $|w_1\rangle$ with probability p_1, etc.

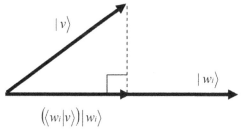

$$\bigl(\langle w_i | v \rangle\bigr) | w_i \rangle$$

Figure 10.2. The projection of $|v\rangle$ onto $|w_i\rangle$.

Exercise 10.2.1   Assume Alice always sends only one vector, say, w_1. Show that D in this case just looks like $|w_1\rangle\langle w_1|$. ∎

Now that we know how each component acts on a ket, it is not difficult to understand the entire action of D. It acts on ket vectors on the left:

$$D|v\rangle = p_1\langle w_1|v\rangle|w_1\rangle + p_2\langle w_2|v\rangle|w_2\rangle + \cdots + p_n\langle w_n|v\rangle|w_n\rangle. \tag{10.16}$$

In words, D is the sum of projections onto all the $|w_i\rangle$'s, weighted by their respective probabilities.

Exercise 10.2.2   Show that the action we have just described makes D a linear operator on kets (check that it preserves sums and scalar multiplication). ∎

As D is now a legitimate linear operator on the ket space, it can be represented by a matrix, once a basis is specified. Here is an example:

Example 10.2.1   Let $|w_1\rangle = \frac{1}{\sqrt{2}}|0\rangle + \frac{1}{\sqrt{2}}|1\rangle$ and $|w_2\rangle = \frac{1}{\sqrt{2}}|0\rangle - \frac{1}{\sqrt{2}}|1\rangle$. Assume that $|w_1\rangle$ is sent with probability $p_1 = \frac{1}{4}$ and $|w_2\rangle$ is sent with probability $p_2 = \frac{3}{4}$. Let us now describe the corresponding density matrix in the standard basis. In order to do so, we just compute the effect of D on the two basis vectors:

$$
\begin{aligned}
D(|0\rangle) &= \frac{1}{4}\langle w_1|0\rangle|w_1\rangle + \frac{3}{4}\langle w_2|0\rangle|w_2\rangle = \left(\frac{1}{4}\frac{1}{\sqrt{2}}\right)|w_1\rangle + \left(\frac{3}{4}\frac{1}{\sqrt{2}}\right)|w_2\rangle \\
&= \frac{1}{4\sqrt{2}}\left(\frac{1}{\sqrt{2}}|0\rangle + \frac{1}{\sqrt{2}}|1\rangle\right) + \frac{3}{4\sqrt{2}}\left(\frac{1}{\sqrt{2}}|0\rangle - \frac{1}{\sqrt{2}}|1\rangle\right) \\
&= \left(\frac{1}{8}|0\rangle + \frac{3}{8}|0\rangle\right) + \left(\frac{1}{8}|1\rangle - \frac{3}{8}|1\rangle\right) = \frac{1}{2}|0\rangle - \frac{1}{4}|1\rangle \tag{10.17}
\end{aligned}
$$

$$
\begin{aligned}
D(|1\rangle) &= \frac{1}{4}\langle w_1|1\rangle|w_1\rangle + \frac{3}{4}\langle w_2|1\rangle|w_2\rangle = \left(\frac{1}{4}\frac{1}{\sqrt{2}}\right)|w_1\rangle - \left(\frac{3}{4}\frac{1}{\sqrt{2}}\right)|w_2\rangle \\
&= \frac{1}{4\sqrt{2}}\left(\frac{1}{\sqrt{2}}|0\rangle + \frac{1}{\sqrt{2}}|1\rangle\right) - \frac{3}{4\sqrt{2}}\left(\frac{1}{\sqrt{2}}|0\rangle - \frac{1}{\sqrt{2}}|1\rangle\right) \\
&= \left(\frac{1}{8}|0\rangle - \frac{3}{8}|0\rangle\right) + \left(\frac{1}{8}|1\rangle + \frac{3}{8}|1\rangle\right) = -\frac{1}{4}|0\rangle + \frac{1}{2}|1\rangle. \tag{10.18}
\end{aligned}
$$

The density matrix is thus

$$D = \begin{bmatrix} \frac{1}{2} & -\frac{1}{4} \\ -\frac{1}{4} & \frac{1}{2} \end{bmatrix}. \tag{10.19}$$

$\square$

Exercise 10.2.3 Write the density matrix of the alphabet in Equation (10.12), where

$$p(|A\rangle) = \frac{1}{2}, \, p(|B\rangle) = \frac{1}{6}, \, p(|C\rangle) = \frac{1}{6}, \text{ and } p(|D\rangle) = \frac{1}{6}. \tag{10.20}$$

$\blacksquare$

D also acts on bra vectors on the right, using a mirror recipe:

$$\langle v|D = p_1 \langle v|w_1\rangle\langle w_1| + p_2 \langle v|w_2\rangle\langle w_2 + \cdots + p_n \langle v|w_n\rangle\langle w_n|. \tag{10.21}$$

What we have just found, namely, that D can operate on *both* bras and kets at the same time, suggests that we combine the action on the left and the right in one shot. Given any state $|v\rangle$, we can form

$$\langle v|D|v\rangle = p_1 |\langle v|w_1\rangle|^2 + p_2 |\langle v|w_2\rangle|^2 + \cdots + p_n |\langle v|w_n\rangle|^2. \tag{10.22}$$

The meaning of the number $\langle v|D|v\rangle$ will become apparent in a moment. Suppose Alice sends a state and Bob performs a measurement whose possible outcomes is the set of orthonormal states

$$\{|v_1\rangle, |v_2\rangle, \ldots, |v_n\rangle\}. \tag{10.23}$$

Let us compute the probability that Bob observes the state $|v_i\rangle$.

Alice sends $|w_1\rangle$ with probability p_1. Each time Bob receives $|w_1\rangle$, the probability that the outcome is $|v_i\rangle$ is precisely $|\langle v_i|w_1\rangle|^2$. Thus $p_1 |\langle v_i|w_1\rangle|^2$ is the probability that Alice has sent $|w_1\rangle$ *and* Bob has observed $|v_i\rangle$. Similarly for $|w_2\rangle, \ldots, |w_n\rangle$. Conclusion: $\langle v_i|D|v_i\rangle$ is the probability that Bob will see $|v_i\rangle$ *regardless* of which state Alice has sent him.

Example 10.2.2 Assume Alice has a quantum alphabet consisting of only two symbols, the vectors

$$|w_1\rangle = \frac{1}{\sqrt{2}}|0\rangle + \frac{1}{\sqrt{2}}|1\rangle \tag{10.24}$$

and

$$|w_2\rangle = |0\rangle. \tag{10.25}$$

Notice that, unlike Example 10.2.1, here the two states are not orthogonal. Alice sends $|w_1\rangle$ with frequency $p_1 = \frac{1}{3}$ and $|w_2\rangle$ with frequency $p_2 = \frac{2}{3}$. Bob uses the standard basis $\{|0\rangle, |1\rangle\}$ for his measurements.

The density operator is

$$D = \frac{1}{3}|\omega_1\rangle\langle\omega_1| + \frac{2}{3}|\omega_2\rangle\langle\omega_2|. \tag{10.26}$$

Let us write down the density matrix in the standard basis:

$$D(|0\rangle) = \frac{1}{3\sqrt{2}}\left(\frac{1}{\sqrt{2}}|0\rangle + \frac{1}{\sqrt{2}}|1\rangle\right) + \frac{2}{3}|0\rangle = \frac{5}{6}|0\rangle + \frac{1}{6}|1\rangle, \tag{10.27}$$

$$D(|1\rangle) = \frac{1}{3\sqrt{2}}\left(\frac{1}{\sqrt{2}}|0\rangle + \frac{1}{\sqrt{2}}|1\rangle\right) + 0|0\rangle = \frac{1}{6}|0\rangle + \frac{1}{6}|1\rangle. \tag{10.28}$$

The density matrix is thus

$$D = \begin{bmatrix} \frac{5}{6} & \frac{1}{6} \\ \frac{1}{6} & \frac{1}{6} \end{bmatrix}. \tag{10.29}$$

Now we can calculate $\langle 0|D|0\rangle$ and $\langle 1|D|1\rangle$:

$$\langle 0|D|0\rangle = [1, 0]\begin{bmatrix} \frac{5}{6} & \frac{1}{6} \\ \frac{1}{6} & \frac{1}{6} \end{bmatrix}\begin{bmatrix} 1 \\ 0 \end{bmatrix} = \frac{5}{6}, \tag{10.30}$$

$$\langle 1|D|1\rangle = [0, 1]\begin{bmatrix} \frac{5}{6} & \frac{1}{6} \\ \frac{1}{6} & \frac{1}{6} \end{bmatrix}\begin{bmatrix} 0 \\ 1 \end{bmatrix} = \frac{1}{6}. \tag{10.31}$$

If we calculate Shannon entropy with respect to this basis, we get

$$-\frac{1}{6}\log_2\left(\frac{1}{6}\right) - \frac{5}{6}\log_2\left(\frac{5}{6}\right) = 0.65. \tag{10.32}$$

$\square$

Even though Alice is sending $|w_i\rangle$'s, from Bob's standpoint, the source behaves as an emitter of states

$$|v_1\rangle, |v_2\rangle, \ldots, |v_n\rangle \tag{10.33}$$

with probability distribution given by

$$\langle v_1|D|v_1\rangle, \langle v_2|D|v_2\rangle, \ldots, \langle v_n|D|v_n\rangle. \tag{10.34}$$

It would be tempting to conclude that the source has entropy given by the same recipe as in the classical case:

$$-\sum_i \langle v_i|D|v_i\rangle \times \log_2\left(\langle v_i|D|v_i\rangle\right). \tag{10.35}$$

However, things are a bit more complicated and more interesting also. Bob can choose different measurements, each associated with its own orthonormal basis. The probability distribution will change as he changes basis, as shown by the following example.

Example 10.2.3   Suppose Bob settles for the basis

$$|v_1\rangle = \frac{1}{\sqrt{2}}|0\rangle + \frac{1}{\sqrt{2}}|1\rangle, \tag{10.36}$$

$$|v_2\rangle = \frac{1}{\sqrt{2}}|0\rangle - \frac{1}{\sqrt{2}}|1\rangle. \tag{10.37}$$

Let us calculate $\langle v_1|D|v_1\rangle$ and $\langle v_2|D|v_2\rangle$ (the density matrix is the same as in Example 10.2.2):

$$\langle v_1|D|v_1\rangle = \begin{bmatrix} \frac{1}{\sqrt{2}}, & \frac{1}{\sqrt{2}} \end{bmatrix} \begin{bmatrix} \frac{5}{6} & \frac{1}{6} \\ \frac{1}{6} & \frac{1}{6} \end{bmatrix} \begin{bmatrix} \frac{1}{\sqrt{2}} \\ \frac{1}{\sqrt{2}} \end{bmatrix} = \frac{2}{3}, \tag{10.38}$$

$$\langle v_2|D|v_2\rangle = \begin{bmatrix} \frac{1}{\sqrt{2}}, & -\frac{1}{\sqrt{2}} \end{bmatrix} \begin{bmatrix} \frac{5}{6} & \frac{1}{6} \\ \frac{1}{6} & \frac{1}{6} \end{bmatrix} \begin{bmatrix} \frac{1}{\sqrt{2}} \\ -\frac{1}{\sqrt{2}} \end{bmatrix} = \frac{1}{3}. \tag{10.39}$$

Let us calculate the Shannon entropy for this pdf:

$$-\frac{1}{3}\log_2\left(\frac{1}{3}\right) - \frac{2}{3}\log_2\left(\frac{2}{3}\right) = 0.9183. \tag{10.40}$$

Compared to Equation (10.32), the Shannon entropy, as perceived by Bob, has increased, because the pdf is less sharp than before. The source, however, *hasn't changed at all*: quite simply, Bob has replaced his "pair of glasses" (i.e., his measurement basis) with a new one!   □

Exercise 10.2.4   Write the matrix of the general density operator D described by Equation 10.14 in the standard basis of $\mathbb{C}^m$, and verify that it is always hermitian. Verify that the **trace** of this matrix, i.e., the sum of its diagonal entries, is 1.   ■

We can ask ourselves if there is a privileged basis, among the ones Bob can choose. Put differently, is there a basis that minimizes the calculation of Shannon entropy in Equation (10.35)? It turns out that such a basis does exist. Because the density operator is hermitian, we saw using the spectral theorem for self-adjoint operators on page 64, that it can be put in diagonal form. Assuming that its eigenvalues are

$$\lambda_1, \lambda_2, \ldots, \lambda_m, \tag{10.41}$$

we can then define the von Neumann entropy as follows:

Definition 10.2.1 *The **von Neumann entropy**[4] for a quantum source represented by a density operator D is given by*

$$H_V = - \sum_1^m \lambda_i log_2(\lambda_i),$$ (10.42)

where $\lambda_1, \lambda_2, \ldots, \lambda_m$ are the eigenvalues of D.

If Bob selects the basis

$$\{|e_1\rangle, |e_2\rangle, \ldots, |e_m\rangle\}$$ (10.43)

of orthonormal eigenvectors of D corresponding to the eigenvalues listed in Equation (10.41), the von Neumann entropy is precisely identical to the calculation of Shannon entropy in Equation (10.40) with respect to the basis of eigenvectors. Why? If you compute

$$\langle e_1 | D | e_1 \rangle,$$ (10.44)

you get

$$\langle e_1 | \lambda_1 e_1 \rangle = \lambda_1$$ (10.45)

(we have used the orthonormality of $|e_1\rangle$).

The same holds true for all eigenvectors: the eigenvalue λ_i is the *probability* that Bob will observe $|e_i\rangle$ when he measures incoming states in the eigenvector basis!

Example 10.2.4 Let us continue the investigation we began in Example 10.2.2. The density matrix D has eigenvalues

$$\lambda_1 = 0.1273 \quad \text{and} \quad \lambda_2 = 0.8727$$ (10.46)

corresponding to the normalized eigenvectors

$$|e_1\rangle = +0.2298|0\rangle - 0.9732|1\rangle \quad \text{and} \quad |e_2\rangle = -0.9732|0\rangle - 0.2298|1\rangle.$$ (10.47)

The von Neumann entropy of D is given by

$$H_V(D) = -0.1273 * \log_2(0.1273) - 0.8727 * \log_2(0.8727) = 0.5500.$$ (10.48)

Let us verify that von Neumann's entropy is identical to Shannon's entropy when calculated with respect to the orthonormal basis of eigenvectors of D:

$$\langle e_1 | D | e_1 \rangle = [0.2298, -0.9732] \begin{bmatrix} \frac{5}{6} & \frac{1}{6} \\ \frac{1}{6} & \frac{1}{6} \end{bmatrix} \begin{bmatrix} 0.2298 \\ -0.9732 \end{bmatrix} = 0.1273,$$ (10.49)

---

[4] Most texts introduce von Neumann entropy using the so-called Trace operator, and then recover our expression by means of diagonalization. We have sacrificed mathematical elegance for the sake of simplicity, and also because for the present purposes the explicit formula in terms of the eigenvalues is quite handy.

$$\langle e_2 | D | e_2 \rangle = [-0.9732, -0.2298] \begin{bmatrix} \frac{5}{6} & \frac{1}{6} \\ \frac{1}{6} & \frac{1}{6} \end{bmatrix} \begin{bmatrix} -0.9732 \\ -0.2298 \end{bmatrix} = 0.8727. \qquad (10.50)$$

Observe that the sum of eigenvalues $0.8727 + 0.1273$ is 1, and both eigenvalues are positive, as befits true probabilities. Also notice that the entropy is lower than the one calculated using the other two bases; it can indeed be proven that it is as low as it can possibly be.   □

Exercise 10.2.5   Go through all the steps of Examples 10.2.1, 10.2.2, and 10.2.3, assuming that Alice sends the same states, but with equal probability.

Note that for this exercise, you will need to calculate eigenvectors and eigenvalues. In Chapter 2 we stated what eigenvalues and eigenvectors are, but not how to compute them for a given symmetric or hermitian matrix. To complete this exercise, you have two equally acceptable options:

1. Look up any standard reference on linear algebra for the eigenvalues formula (search for "characteristic polynomial").

2. Use a math library to do the work for you. In MATLAB, for instance, the function *eig* is the appropriate one (Mathematica and Maple come equipped with similar functions).   ■

As we have said, Alice is at liberty in choosing her alphabet. What would happen if she selected a set of orthogonal vectors? The answer is in the following pair of exercises.

Exercise 10.2.6   Go back to Example 10.2.1. The two states $|w_1\rangle$ and $|w_2\rangle$ are a pair of orthonormal vectors, and thus an orthonormal basis for the one qubit space. Show that they are eigenvectors for the density matrix given in Equation (10.19), and thus Bob's best choice for measuring incoming messages.   ■

Exercise 10.2.7   This exercise is just the generalization of the previous one, in a more formal setting. Suppose Alice chooses from a set of orthonormal state vectors

$$\{|w_1\rangle, |w_2\rangle, \ldots, |w_n\rangle\} \qquad (10.51)$$

with frequencies

$$p_1, p_2, \ldots, p_n \qquad (10.52)$$

to code her messages. Prove that in this scenario each of the $|w_i\rangle$'s is a normalized eigenvector of the density matrix with eigenvalue p_i. Conclude that in this case the source behaves like a classical source (provided of course that Bob knows the orthonormal set and uses it to measure incoming states).   ■

In the wake of the two foregoing exercises, we now know that orthogonal quantum alphabets are the less surprising ones. Let us go back briefly to Example 10.2.2: there Alice's choice is a nonorthogonal set. If you calculate explicitly its von Neumann entropy, you will find that it is equal to 0.55005, whereas the classical entropy for a source of bits such that $p(0) = \frac{1}{3}$ and $p(1) = \frac{2}{3}$ is 0.91830.

We have just unraveled yet another distinct feature of the quantum world: if we stick to the core idea that entropy measures order, then we come to the inescapable conclusion that the quantum source above exhibits more order than its classical counterpart. Where does this order come from? If the alphabet is orthogonal, the two numbers are the same. Therefore, this apparent magic is due to the fact that there is additional room in the quantum via superposition of alternatives.[5] Our discovery is a valuable one, also in light of the important connection between entropy and data compression, the topic of the next section.

Programming Drill 10.2.1 *Write a program that lets the user choose how many qubits the alphabet of the quantum source consists of, enter the probability associated with each qubit, and compute von Neumann entropy as well as the orthonormal basis for the associated density matrix.*

10.3 CLASSICAL AND QUANTUM DATA COMPRESSION

In this section, we introduce the basic ideas of data compression for bit and qubit streams. Let us begin with bits first.

What is data compression? Alice has a message represented by a stream of bits. She wants to encode it either for storage or for transmission in such a way that the encoded stream is shorter than the original message. She has two main options:

- **Lossless data compression**, meaning that her compression algorithm must have an inverse that perfectly reconstruct her message.
- **Lossy data compression**, if she allows a loss of information while compressing her data.

In data compression, a notion of similarity between strings is always assumed, i.e., a function that enables us to compare different strings (in our scenario, the message before compression and the one after it has been decompressed):

$$\mu : \{0, 1\}^* \times \{0, 1\}^* \longrightarrow \mathbb{R}^+ \tag{10.53}$$

such that

- $\mu(s, s) = 0$ (a string is identical to itself), and
- $\mu(s_1, s_2) = \mu(s_2, s_1)$ (symmetry of similarity).[6]

Armed with such a notion of similarity, we can now define compression.

---

[5] The difference between entropy in classical and quantum domains becomes even sharper when we consider *composite sources*. There entanglement creates a new type of order that is reflected by the global entropy of the system. If you want to know more about this phenomenon, go to Appendix E at the end of the book.

[6] There are several notions of similarity used by the data compression community, depending on the particular needs one may have. Most are actually distances, meaning that they satisfy the triangular inequality, besides the two conditions mentioned here.

Definition 10.3.1 *Let μ be a measure of similarity for binary strings, ϵ a fixed threshold, and len( ) the length of a binary string. A* **compression scheme** *for a given source S is a pair of functions (ENC, DEC) from the set of finite binary strings to itself, such that*

- $len(ENC(s)) < len(s)$ *on average, and*
- $\mu(s, DEC(ENC(s))) \leq \epsilon$ *for all sequences.*

If $\mu(s, DEC(ENC(s))) = 0$ for all strings, then the compression scheme is lossless.

In the first item, we said "on average," in other words, for most messages sent by the source. It is important to realize that compression schemes are always coupled with a source: if the source's pdf changes, a scheme may become useless.

Which of the two options listed in Definition 10.3.1 is actually chosen depends on the problem at hand. For instance, if the sender wants to transmit an image, she may decide to go for lossy compression, as small detail losses hardly affect the reconstructed image.[7] On the other hand, if she is transmitting or storing, say, the source code of a program, every single bit may count. Alice here does not have the luxury to waste bits; she must resort to lossless compression.[8] As a rule of thumb, lossy compression allows you to achieve much greater compression (its requirements are less stringent!), so if you are not concerned with exact reconstruction, that is the obvious way to go.

There is a fundamental connection between Shannon entropy and data compression. Once again, let us build our intuition by working with the general pdf given in Section 10.1.

Note: We make an assumption throughout this section: the source is independently distributed. This simply means that each time Alice sends a fresh new symbol, the probability stays the same and there is no correlation with previous sent symbols.

Alice must transmit one of four symbols. Using the binary alphabet 0, 1, she can encode her A, B, C, D using $\log_2(4) = 2$ bits. Suppose she follows this coding

A	00
B	01
C	10
D	11

(10.54)

How many bits will she send on average per symbol?

$$2 \times \frac{1}{2} + 2 \times \frac{1}{4} + 2 \times \frac{1}{8} + 2 \times \frac{1}{8} = 2 \tag{10.55}$$

Doesn't sound too good, does it? Alice can definitely do better than that. How? The core idea is quite simple: she will use an encoding that uses *fewer* bits for

---

[7] The extremely popular JPEG and MPEG formats, for images and videos, respectively, are two popular examples of lossy compression algorithms.

[8] ZIP is a widely popular application based on the so-called Lempel–Ziv lossless compression algorithm, generally used to compress text files.

symbols that have a *higher* probability. After a little thinking, Alice comes up with this encoding:

A	0
B	11
C	100
D	101

$$(10.56)$$

Let us now compute the average number of bits per symbol Alice is going to transmit using this encoding:

$$1 \times \frac{1}{2} + 2 \times \frac{1}{4} + 3 \times \frac{1}{8} + 3 \times \frac{1}{8} = 1.75. \tag{10.57}$$

As you have already noticed, this is precisely the value we have found for the entropy of the source.

Exercise 10.3.1 Try to determine the most efficient coding for a four-symbol source whose pdf looks like

$$P(A) = \frac{1}{2}, \ P(B) = \frac{1}{6}, \ P(C) = \frac{1}{6}, \text{ and } P(D) = \frac{1}{6}. \tag{10.58}$$

∎

What we have just seen is far from accidental: indeed, it represents a concrete example of a general fact discovered by Shannon, namely, an entropy-related bound on how good compression can be for a given source.

Theorem 10.3.1 (Shannon's Noiseless Channel Coding Theorem). *Let a source S emit symbols from an alphabet with a given probability distribution. A message of length n, with n sufficiently large, sent over a noiseless channel can be compressed on average without loss of information to a minimum of $H(S) \times n$ bits.*

We shall not provide a formal proof of Shannon's theorem, only the underlying heuristics behind it. Imagine for simplicity's sake that the source transmits only binary sequences. If the length n of the message is large enough, most sequences will have a distribution of 0's and 1's, which will approximately correspond to their respective probability. These well-behaved sequences are called **typical**, and all together they form a subset of all messages, known as the **typical set**. For instance, suppose that 1 appears with probability $p = \frac{1}{3}$ and 0 with probability $p = \frac{2}{3}$. A typical sequence of length, say, 90, would have exactly 30 bits set to 1.

How many typical sequences are there? It turns out that their number is roughly given by $2^{H(S)n}$. As you can see from Figure 10.3, this is a proper subset of the set of all sequences of length n (the entire set has 2^n elements), as long as $H < 1$.

An ideal compression strategy is then the following:

■ Create a lookup table for all the typical sequences of length n. The key for the table needs exactly $H(S)n$ bits. This lookup table is shared by Alice and Bob.

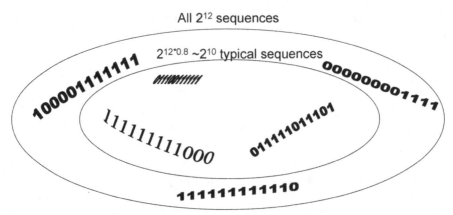

Figure 10.3. $p(0) = \frac{1}{4}$, $p(1) = \frac{3}{4}$, $n = 12$, $H(S) = 0.81128$.

■ When a message of length n is sent, Alice sends one bit to inform Bob that the sequence is typical, and the bits to look up the result. If the sequence is not typical, Alice sends the bit that says "not typical," and the original sequence.

For n large enough, almost all sequences will be typical or near typical, so the average number of bits transmitted will get very close to Shannon's bound.

Exercise 10.3.2 Assume that the source emits 0 with probability $\frac{n_0}{n}$ and 1 with probability $1 - \frac{n_0}{n}$. Count how many typical sequences of length n are there. (Hint: Start with some concrete example, setting $n = 2, 3, \ldots$. Then generalize.) ■

Programming Drill 10.3.1 *Write a program that accepts a pdf for 0 and 1, a given length n, and produces as output the list of all typical sequences of length n.*

Note: Shannon's theorem does *not* say that all sequences will be compressed, only that what the average compression rate for an optimal compression scheme will be. Indeed, a universal recipe for lossless compression of all binary sequences does not exist, as you can easily show doing the following exercise.

Exercise 10.3.3 Prove that there is no bijective map f from the set of finite binary strings to itself such that for each sequence s, $length(f(s)) < length(s)$. (Hint: Start from a generic sequence s_0. Apply f to it. Now iterate. What happens to the series of sequences $\{s_0, f(s_0), f(f(s_0)), \ldots\}$?) ■

Shannon's theorem establishes a bound for lossless compression algorithms, but it does not provide us with one. In some cases, as we have seen in the previous examples, we can easily find the optimal protocol by hand. In most situations though, we must resort to suboptimal protocols. The most famous and basic one is known as **Huffman's algorithm**.[9] You may have met it already in an Algorithms and Data Structures class.

---

[9] Huffman's algorithm is actually optimal, i.e., it reaches Shannon's bound, but only for special pdfs.

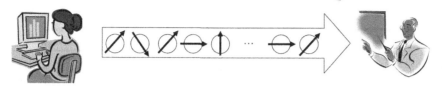

Figure 10.4. Alice sending messages to Bob in a four-qubit alphabet.

Programming Drill 10.3.2 *Implement Huffman's algorithm, and then experiment with it by changing the pdf of the source. For which source types does it perform poorly?*

It is now time to discuss qubit compression. As we already mentioned in the beginning of Section 10.3, Alice is now emitting sequences of qubits with certain frequencies to send her messages. More specifically, assume that Alice draws from a qubit alphabet $\{|q_1\rangle, \ldots, |q_k\rangle\}$ of k distinct but not necessarily orthogonal qubits, with frequency $p_1, \ldots, p_k$. A typical message of length n could look like

$$|q_1 q_1 q_3 \cdots q_2\rangle; \tag{10.59}$$

in other words, any such message will be a point of the tensor product $\mathbb{C}^2 \otimes \mathbb{C}^2 \otimes \cdots \otimes \mathbb{C}^2 = \mathbb{C}^{2^n}$. If you recall Alice's story, she was sending bits to inform Bob about her moods, as depicted in Figure 10.4. Alice is sending out streams of particles with spin.

We would like to know if there are ways for Alice to compress her quantum messages to shorter qubit strings.

We need to define first what a quantum compressor is, and see if and how the connection between entropy and compression carries over to the quantum world. To do so, we must upgrade our vocabulary: whereas in classical data compression we talk about compression/decompression *functions* and *typical subsets*, here we shall replace them with compression/decompression *unitary maps* and *typical subspaces*, respectively.

Definition 10.3.2 *A $k - n$ **quantum data compression scheme** for an assigned quantum source is specified by a change-of-basis unitary transformation*

$$QC : \mathbb{C}^{2^n} \longrightarrow \mathbb{C}^{2^n} \tag{10.60}$$

and its inverse

$$QC^{-1} : \mathbb{C}^{2^n} \longrightarrow \mathbb{C}^{2^n}. \tag{10.61}$$

The **fidelity** *of the quantum compressor is defined as follows: consider a message from the source of length n, say, $|m\rangle$. Let $P_k(QC(|m\rangle))$ be the truncation of the transformed message to a compressed version consisting of the first k qubits (the length of $P_k(QC(|m\rangle))$ is therefore k). Now, pad it with $n - k$ zeros, getting $Pi(QC(|m\rangle))00\ldots0\rangle$. The fidelity is the probability*

$$\langle QC^{-1}(|P_k(QC(|m\rangle))00\ldots0\rangle)|m\rangle|^2, \tag{10.62}$$

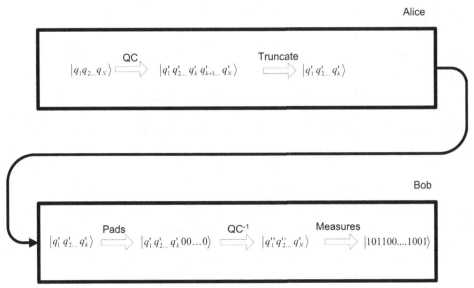

Figure 10.5. A quantum compression scheme.

i.e., the likelihood that the original message will be perfectly retrieved after the receiver pads the compressed message, applies the inverse maps and finally measures it.

In plain words, a quantum compressor is a unitary (and therefore invertible) map such that most transformed messages have only k significant qubits, i.e., they lie almost completely within a k-dimensional subspace known as the **typical subspace**.

If Alice owns such a quantum compressor, she and Bob have a well-defined strategy to compress qubit streams (shown in Figure 10.5):

Step 1. She applies the compressor to her message. The result's amplitudes can be safely set to zero except for the ones corresponding to the typical subspace. After a rearrangement, the amplitudes have been listed so that the first k belong to the subspace and the other $n - k$ are the ones that are negligible and can be thus set to zero.

Step 2. Alice truncates her message to the significant k qubits, and sends it to Bob.

Step 3. Bob appends to the received message the missing zeros (padding step), and

Step 4. Bob changes back the padded message to the original basis.

Step 5. He then measures the message and reads it.

How and where is Alice to find her quantum processor? As before, to build up our intuition, we are going to analyze a concrete example. Let us go back to Example 10.2.2 and use the same setup. Alice's quantum alphabet consists of the two vectors $|w_1\rangle$ and $|w_2\rangle$, which she sends with frequency $\frac{1}{3}$ and $\frac{2}{3}$, respectively. A message of length n will look like

$$|\psi_1 \psi_2 \dots \psi_n\rangle, \tag{10.63}$$

where

$$|\psi_i\rangle = |w_1\rangle \quad \text{or} \quad |\psi_i\rangle = |w_2\rangle. \tag{10.64}$$

Suppose that Alice, before sending the message, changes basis. Instead of the canonical basis, she chooses the eigenvector basis of the density matrix, i.e., the vectors $|e_1\rangle$ and $|e_2\rangle$ that we explicitly computed in Example 10.2.4.

Alice's message can be described in this basis as

$$c_1|e_1 e_1 \dots e_1\rangle + c_2|e_1 e_1 \dots e_2\rangle + \dots + c_{2^n}|e_2 e_2 \dots e_2\rangle. \tag{10.65}$$

What is the benefit of this change of basis? As a vector, the message is still a point in $\mathbb{C}^{2^n}$, and so its length has not changed. However, something quite interesting is happening here. We are going to find out that quite a few of the c_i's are indeed so small that they can be discarded. Let us calculate first the projections of $|w_1\rangle$ and $|w_2\rangle$ along the eigenvectors e_1 and e_2:

$$|\langle e_1|w_1\rangle| = 0.526, \quad |\langle e_1|w_2\rangle| = 0.230, \quad |\langle e_2|w_1\rangle| = 0.851, \quad \text{and} \quad |\langle e_2|w_2\rangle| = 0.973. \tag{10.66}$$

We have just discovered that the projection of either $|w_1\rangle$ or $|w_2\rangle$ along $|e_1\rangle$ is smaller than their components along $|e_2\rangle$.

Using the projections of Equation (10.66), we can now calculate the components c_i in the eigenbasis decomposition of a generic message. For instance, the message $|w_1 w_1 w_1 w_1 w_1 w_1 w_1 w_1 w_2 w_2\rangle$ has the component along $|e_1 e_1 e_1 e_1 e_1 e_1 e_1 e_1 e_1 e_1\rangle$ equal to

$$|c_1| = (|\langle e_1|w_1\rangle|)^8 (|\langle e_1|w_2\rangle|)^2 = 3.08 * 10^{-4}. \tag{10.67}$$

Exercise 10.3.4 Assume the same setup as the previous one, and consider the message $|v_1\rangle|v_1\rangle|v_1\rangle|v_1\rangle|v_2\rangle|v_1\rangle|v_1\rangle|v_1\rangle|v_1\rangle|v_2\rangle$. What is the value of the component along $|e_2\rangle|e_2\rangle|e_2\rangle|e_1\rangle|e_1\rangle|e_2\rangle|e_2\rangle|e_2\rangle|e_1\rangle|e_1\rangle$? ∎

Many of the coefficients c_i are dispensable, as we anticipated (see Figure 10.6.)

The significant coefficients turn out to be the ones that are associated with typical sequences of eigenvectors, i.e., sequences whose relative proportions of $|e_1\rangle$ and $|e_2\rangle$ are consistent with their probabilities, calculated in Equations (10.49) and (10.50). The set of all these typical sequences spans a subspace of $\mathcal{C}^{2^n}$, the typical subspace we were looking for. Its dimension is given by $2^{N \times H(S)}$, where $H(S)$ is the von Neumann entropy of the source. Alice and Bob now have a strategy for compressing and decompressing qubit sequences, following the recipe sketched earlier in Steps 1–5.

We have just shown a specific example. However, what Alice found out can be generalized and formally proved, leading to the quantum analog of Shannon's coding theorem, due to Benjamin Schumacher (1995b).

Theorem 10.3.2 (**Schumacher's Quantum Coding Theorem.**) *A qubit stream of length n emitted from a given quantum source QS of known density can be compressed on average to a qubit stream of length $n \times H(QS)$, where $H(QS)$ is the von Neumann entropy of the source. The fidelity approaches one as n goes to infinity.*

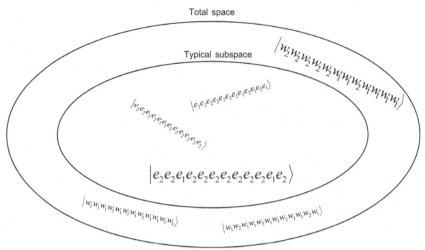

Figure 10.6. Source as in Example 10.2.2: $p(|w_1\rangle) = \frac{1}{3}$, $p(|w_2\rangle) = \frac{2}{3}$, $n = 12$, $H(S) = 0.54999$.

Note: In a sense, the bound $n \times H(QS)$ represents the best we can do with quantum sources. This theorem is particularly exciting in light of what we have seen at the end of the last section, namely, that von Neumann entropy can be lower than classical entropy. This means that, at least in principle, quantum compression schemes can be designed that compress quantum information in a tighter way than classical information can be in the classical world.

However, this magic comes at a price: whereas in the classical arena one can create purely lossless data compression schemes, this is not necessarily so in the quantum domain. Indeed, if Alice chooses her quantum alphabet as a set of nonorthogonal states, there is no measurement on Bob's side whose eigenvectors are precisely Alice's "quantum letters." This means that perfect reconstruction of the message cannot be ensured. There is a trade-off here: the quantum world is definitely more spacious than our own macroscopic world, thereby allowing for new compression schemes, but at the same time it is also fuzzy, carrying an unavoidable element of intrinsic indeterminacy that cannot be ignored.

Programming Drill 10.3.3 *Write a program that lets the user enter two qubits and their corresponding probabilities. Then calculate the density matrix, diagonalize it, and store the corresponding eigenbasis. The user will then enter a quantum message. The program will write the message in the eigenbasis and return the truncated part belonging to the typical subspace.*

10.4 ERROR-CORRECTING CODES

There is yet another aspect of information theory that cannot be ignored. Information is always sent or stored through some physical medium. In either case, random errors may happen: our valuable data can degrade over time.

Errors occur with classical data, but the problem is even more serious in the quantum domain: as we shall see in Chapter 11, a new phenomenon known as decoherence makes this issue absolutely critical for the very existence of a reliable quantum computer.

As a way to mitigate this unpleasant state of affairs, information theory researchers have developed a large variety of techniques to *detect* errors, as well as to *correct* them. In this last section we briefly showcase one of these techniques, both in its classical version and in its quantum version.

As we have just said, our enemy here is random errors. By their very definition, they are unpredictable. However, frequently we can anticipate which *types* of errors our physical devices are subjected to. This is important: by means of this knowledge we can often elaborate adequate defense strategies.

Suppose you send a single bit, and you expect a bit flip error 25% of the time. What would you do? A valid trick is simply repetition. Let us thus introduce an elementary **repetition code**:

$$\frac{\begin{array}{ll} 0 & 000 \end{array}}{\begin{array}{ll} 1 & 111 \end{array}} \tag{10.68}$$

We have simply repeated a bit three times. One can decode the triplet by **majority law**: if at least two of the qubits are zeros, it is zero; else, it is one.

Exercise 10.4.1   What is the probability of incorrectly decoding one bit?   ■

Now, let us move on to qubit messages. Qubits are less "rigid" than bits, so new types of errors can occur: for instance, aside qubit-flips

$$\alpha|0\rangle + \beta|1\rangle \longmapsto \beta|0\rangle + \alpha|1\rangle \tag{10.69}$$

signs can be flipped too:

$$\alpha|0\rangle + \beta|1\rangle \longmapsto \alpha|0\rangle - \beta|1\rangle. \tag{10.70}$$

Exercise 10.4.2   Go back to Chapter 5 and review the Block sphere representation of qubits. What is the geometric interpretation of sign flip?   ■

To be sure, when dealing with qubits other types of errors can occur, not just "jumpy" errors (i.e., discrete ones). For instance, either α or β could change by a small amount. For example, α might have a change of phase by $15°$. For the sake of simplicity though, we shall only envision bit and sign flips.

If we are looking for the quantum analog of the repetition code given in Equation (10.68), we must make sure that we can detect both types of errors. There is a code that does the job, due to Peter W. Shor (1995), known as the **9-qubit code**[10]:

$$\frac{|0\rangle \quad (|000\rangle + |111\rangle) \otimes (|000\rangle + |111\rangle) \otimes (|000\rangle + |111\rangle)}{|1\rangle \quad (|000\rangle - |111\rangle) \otimes (|000\rangle - |111\rangle) \otimes (|000\rangle - |111\rangle)} \tag{10.71}$$

[10] 9-qubit code is the first known quantum code.

Why nine qubits? $3 \times 3 = 9$: by employing the majority rule twice, once for qubit flip and once for sign, we can correct both.

Exercise 10.4.3   Suppose that a sign flip occurs 25% of the times, and a single qubit flip 10% of the times. Also suppose that these two errors are independent of each other. What is the likelihood that we incorrectly decode the original qubit?   ■

We have barely scraped the tip of an iceberg. Quantum error-correction is a flourishing area of quantum computing, and a number of interesting results have already emerged. If, as we hope, this small section has whetted your appetite, you can look into the references and continue your journey beyond the basics.

....

References: The first formulation of the basic laws of information theory is contained in the seminal (and readable!) paper "The mathematical theory of communication" written by Claude Shannon (Shannon, 1948). This paper is freely available online. A good reference for information theory and Shannon's theorem is Ash (1990).

Huffman's algorithm can be found, e.g., on pages 385–393 of Corman et al. (2001).

An excellent all-round reference on data compression is the text by Sayood (2005). For Schumacher's theorem, take a look at the PowerPoint presentation by Nielsen.

Finally, Knill et al. (2002) is a panoramic survey of quantum error-correction.

11

Hardware

> *The machine does not isolate man from the great problems*
> *of nature, but plunges him more deeply into them.*
>
> Antoine de Saint Exupery, *Wind, Sand, and Stars*

In this chapter, we discuss a few hardware issues and proposals. Most certainly you have wondered (perhaps more than once!) whether all we have presented up to now is nothing more than elegant speculation, with no practical impact for the real world.

To bring things down to earth, we must address a very basic question: *do we actually know how to build a quantum computer?*

It turns out that the implementation of quantum computing machines represents a formidable challenge to the communities of engineers and applied physicists. However, there is some hope in sight: quite recently, some simple quantum devices consisting of a few qubits have been successfully built and tested. Considering the amount of resources that have been poured into this endeavor from different quarters (academia, private sector, and the military), it would not be entirely surprising if noticeable progress were made in the near future.

In Section 11.1 we spell out the hurdles that stand in the way, chiefly related to the quantum phenomenon known as decoherence. We also enumerate the wish list of desirable features for a quantum device. Sections 11.2 and 11.3 are devoted to describing two of the major proposals around: the ion trap and optical quantum computers. The last section mentions two other proposals, and lists some milestones that have been achieved so far. We conclude with some musings on the future of quantum ware.

A small disclaimer is in order. Quantum hardware is an area of research that requires, by its very nature, a deep background in quantum physics and quantum engineering, way beyond the level we have asked of our reader. The presentation will have perforce a rather elementary character. Refer to the bibliography for more advanced references.

Note to the Reader: We would have loved to assign exercises such as "build a quantum microcontroller for your robot," or "assemble a network of quantum

Figure 11.1. A PC that is uncoupled from the environment.

chips," or something along these lines. Alas, we cannot. Nor, without violating the aforementioned disclaimer, could we ask you to carry out sophisticated calculations concerning modulations of electromagnetic fields, or similar matters. Thus, there are only few exercises scattered in this chapter (do not skip them though: your effort will be rewarded).

11.1 QUANTUM HARDWARE: GOALS AND CHALLENGES

In Chapter 6 we described the generic architecture of a quantum computing device: we need a number of addressable qubits, the capability of initializing them properly, applying a sequence of unitary transformation to them, and finally measuring them.

Initialization of a quantum computer is similar to initialization of a classical one: at the beginning of our computation, we set the machine in a **well-defined state**. It is absolutely crucial that the machine stay in the state we have put it in, till we modify it in a controlled way by means of known computational steps. For a classical computer, this is in principle quite easy to do[1]: a classical computer can be thought of as an *isolated system*. Influences from the environment can theoretically be reduced to zero. You might keep Figure 11.1 in mind.

The case of a quantum computer is rather different. As we have already seen, one of the core features of quantum mechanics is entanglement: if a system S is composed of two subsystems S_1 and S_2, their states may become entangled. In practice, this means that we cannot ignore what happens to S_2 if we are interested in the way S_1 evolves (and vice versa). Moreover, this odd phenomenon happens regardless of how physically separated the two subsystems actually are. How is this relevant to the task of building a quantum computer? The machine and its environment become entangled, preventing the evolution of the state of the quantum register from depending exclusively on which gates are applied to it. To fix our ideas, let us suppose that the quantum register in our device is a sequence of 1,000 electrons, qubits being encoded as their spin state. In this scenario, initialization means setting all the electrons to some defined spin state, as in Figure 11.2. For instance, they could be all in spin up, or all in spin down. The key point is that we need to control the global state of the register. In physics jargon, a well-defined state is known as **pure state**, as in Figure 11.2.

---

[1] In reality, of course, classical machines are also prone to errors.

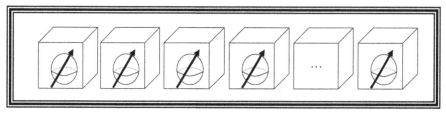

Figure 11.2. An uncoupled register initialized to spin up.

When we take our register out of isolation, these electrons tend to couple with the billions of other electrons in the environment, shifting to some superposition of spin up and spin down, as in Figure 11.3.

The problem here lies in that we have absolutely no idea about the precise initial state of the environment's electrons, nor do we know the details of their interaction with the electrons in the quantum register. After a while, the global state of the register is no longer pure; rather, it has become a probabilistic mix of pure states, or what is known in quantum jargon as a **mixed state**.[2] Pure states and mixed states have a different status in quantum mechanics. *There is always a specific measurement that invariably returns true on a pure state*. Instead, there is no such thing for mixed states, as shown by the following exercise.

Exercise 11.1.1 Consider the pure state $|\psi\rangle = \frac{|0\rangle+|1\rangle}{\sqrt{2}}$, and the mixed state obtained by tossing a coin and setting it equal to $|0\rangle$ if the result is heads, or $|1\rangle$ if the result is tails.[3] Devise an experiment that discriminates between these two states. Hint: What would happen if we measured the qubit in the following basis?

$$\left\{ \frac{|0\rangle + |1\rangle}{\sqrt{2}}, \frac{|0\rangle - |1\rangle}{\sqrt{2}} \right\} \tag{11.1}$$

∎

Where precisely lies the difference between pure and mixed states?
Consider the following family of spin states:

$$|\psi_\theta\rangle = \frac{|0\rangle + \exp(i\theta)|1\rangle}{\sqrt{2}}. \tag{11.2}$$

For every choice of the angle θ, there is a distinct pure state. Each of these states is characterized by a specific **relative phase**, i.e., by the difference between the angles of the components of $|0\rangle$ and $|1\rangle$ in the polar representation.[4] How can we physically detect their difference? A measurement in the standard basis would not do (the probabilities with respect to this basis haven't been affected). However, a change

---

[2] The density matrix, which we introduced in Section 10.2 in order to talk about entropy, is also the fundamental tool for studying mixed states. Indeed, a single pure quantum state $|\psi\rangle$ is associated with the special form of the density operator $|\psi\rangle\langle\psi|$, whereas an arbitrary mixed state can be represented by a generic density operator.

[3] For the readers of Section 10.2: the mixed state is represented by the density matrix $\frac{|0\rangle\langle0|+|1\rangle\langle1|}{2}$.

[4] It is only this relative phase that has some physical impact, as we are going to see in a minute. Indeed, multiplying both components by $\exp(i\theta)$ would simply rotate them by the same angle and generate an entirely equivalent physical state, as we pointed out in Section 4.1.

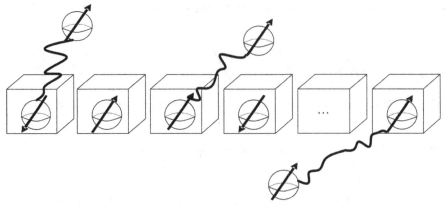

Figure 11.3. The qubits decohered as a result of coupling with the environment.

of basis will do. Observe $|\psi_\theta\rangle$ along the x axis, and compute the average spin value along this direction[5]: $\langle\psi_\theta|S_x|\psi_\theta\rangle$. As you can verify for yourself in the next exercise, *the average depends on θ*!

Exercise 11.1.2   Calculate $\langle\psi_\theta|S_x|\psi_\theta\rangle$. For which value of θ is the average maximum? ∎

If you now consider the mixed state of the last exercise, namely the one you get by tossing a coin and deciding for either $|0\rangle$ or $|1\rangle$, the relative phase and its concomitant information is *lost*. It is precisely the lack of relative phase that separates pure states and mixed ones. One way states change from pure to mixed is through uncontrollable interaction with the environment.

Definition 11.1.1   *The loss of purity of the state of a quantum system as the result of interaction with the environment is known as* **decoherence**.

We are not going to provide a full account of decoherence[6]. However, it is well worth sketching how it works, as it is our formidable challenger in the path to real-life quantum computation (the *Art of War* states: "know thy enemy!").

In all our descriptions of quantum systems, we have implicitly assumed that they are isolated from their environment. To be sure, they can interact with the external world. For instance, an electron can be affected by an electromagnetic field, but the interaction is, as it were, under control. The evolution of the system is described by its hamiltonian (see Section 4.4), which may include components accounting for external influences. Therefore, as long as we know the hamiltonian and the

---

[5] The formula for the average as well as the hermitian S_x were described in Section 4.2.

[6] Decoherence has been known since the early days of quantum mechanics. However, in recent times it has received a great deal of attention, not only in relation to quantum computing, but as a formidable tool for understanding how our familiar classical world emerges out of the uncanny quantum world. How come we do not normally see interference when dealing with macroscopic objects? An answer is provided by decoherence: large objects tend to decohere very fast, thereby losing their quantum features. An intriguing survey of decoherence as a way of accounting for classical behavior of macroscopic objects is Zurek (2003).

initial state, it is totally predictable. Under such circumstances, the system will always evolve from pure states to other pure states. The only unpredictable factor is measurement. Summing up: *we always implictly assumed that we knew exactly how the environment affects the quantum system.*

Let us now turn to a more realistic scenario: our system, say, a single electron spin, is immersed in a vast environment. Can we model this extended system? Yes, we can, by thinking of the environment as a huge quantum system, assembled out of its components.

To understand what happens, let us start small. Instead of looking at the entire environment, we shall restrict ourselves to interactions with a *single external* electron. Let us go back to our electron of a moment ago, and let us assume that it has become entangled with another electron to form the global state

$$|\psi_{global}\rangle = \frac{|00\rangle + \exp(i\theta)|11\rangle}{\sqrt{2}}. \tag{11.3}$$

Now, let us *only* measure the spin of our electron in the x direction, just as we have done before. This step corresponds to the observable $S_x \otimes I$, i.e., the tensor of S_x with the identity on the second electron: we must therefore compute

$$\langle \psi_{global}|(S_x \otimes I)|\psi_{global}\rangle. \tag{11.4}$$

Let us do it. In matrix notation (written in the standard basis),

$$|\psi_{global}\rangle = \frac{1}{\sqrt{2}}[1, 0, 0, \exp(i\theta)]^T \tag{11.5}$$

and (we are ignoring here the constant factor $\frac{\hbar}{2}$)

$$S_x \otimes I = \begin{bmatrix} 0 & 1 \\ 1 & 0 \end{bmatrix} \otimes \begin{bmatrix} 1 & 0 \\ 0 & 1 \end{bmatrix}; \tag{11.6}$$

thus we are simply evaluating

$$\left[\frac{1}{\sqrt{2}}, 0, 0, \exp(-i\theta)\frac{1}{\sqrt{2}}\right] \begin{bmatrix} 0 & 0 & 1 & 0 \\ 0 & 0 & 0 & 1 \\ 1 & 0 & 0 & 0 \\ 0 & 1 & 0 & 0 \end{bmatrix} \left[\frac{1}{\sqrt{2}}, 0, 0, \exp(i\theta)\frac{1}{\sqrt{2}}\right]^T = 0. \tag{11.7}$$

The net result of our calculation is that the phase is apparently gone: there is no a trace of θ in the average value! We say this – apparently – for a reason: the phase is simply hiding behind the curtain afforded by entanglement. To "smoke the phase out," we have to perform a measurement on *both* electrons. How? We simply compute the average of $S_x \otimes S_x$ on $|\psi_{global}\rangle$. The value now does indeed depend on θ, as you can check in the following exercise:

Exercise 11.1.3 Compute $\langle \psi_{global}|S_x \otimes S_x|\psi_{global}\rangle$. ∎

It is time to wrap up what we have learned. We were able to recover the precious phase information only after measuring the second electron. Now, imagine our electron interacting with a great many peers from the environment, in an unknown manner. If we could track them all down, and measure their respective states, just like we have done above, there would be no issue. Alas, we cannot: our phase is irretrievably lost, turning our pure state into a mixed one. Note that decoherence does not cause any real collapse of the state vector. The information is still out there, marooned, as it were, in the vast quantum ocean.

Decoherence presents us with a two-pronged challenge:

- On the one hand, adopting basic quantum systems that are very prone to "hook up" with the environment (electrons are a very good example, as they tend to interact with other peers in their vicinity) makes it quite difficult to manage the state of our machine.
- On the other hand, we *do* need to interact with the quantum device after all, to initialize it, apply gates, and so on. We are part of the environment. A quantum system that tends to stay aloof (photons are the primary example) makes it difficult to access its state.

How serious is the challenge afforded by decoherence? How quick are its effects? The answer varies, depending on the implementation one chooses (for instance, for single-ion qubits, as described in the next section, it is a matter of seconds). But it is serious enough to raise major concerns. You can read a leisurely account in the sprightly *Scientific American* article "Quantum Bug" by Graham P. Collins.

How can we even hope to build a reliable quantum computing device if decoherence is such a big part of quantum life? It sounds like a Catch-22, doesn't it? There are, however, two main answers:

- A possible way out is *fast gates execution*: one tries to make decoherence sufficiently slow in comparison to our control, so that one has time to safely apply quantum gates first. By striving to beat Nature in the speed race, at least on very short runs, we can still hope to get meaningful results.
- The other strategy is *fault-tolerance*. How can one practically achieve fault-tolerance? In Section 10.4, we have briefly sketched the topic of quantum error-correcting codes. The rationale is that using a certain redundancy, we can thwart at least some types of errors. Also, another possible strategy under the redundancy umbrella is repeating a calculation enough times, so that random errors cancel each other out.[7]

We conclude this section with an important wish list for candidate quantum computers that has been formulated by David P. DiVincenzo of IBM.

DiVincenzo's Wish List

- The quantum machine must have a sufficiently large number of individually addressable qubits.

---

[7] Caveat: one cannot repeat *too many* times, else the benefits of quantum parallelism will get totally eroded!

- It must be possible to initialize all the qubits to the zero state, i.e., $|00 \cdots 000\rangle$.
- The error rate in doing computations should be reasonably low, i.e., decoherence time must be substantially longer than gate operation time.
- We should be able to perform elementary logical operations between pairs of qubits.
- Finally, we should be able to reliably read out the results of measurements.

These five points spell out the challenge that every prospective implementation of a quantum computing device must meet. We are now going to see a few of the proposals that have emerged in the last ten odd years.

11.2 IMPLEMENTING A QUANTUM COMPUTER I: ION TRAPS

Before we start discussing concrete implementations, let us remind ourselves that a qubit is a state vector in a two-dimensional Hilbert space. Therefore, any physical quantum system whose state space has dimension 2^N can, at least in principle, be used to store an addressable sequence of N qubits (a q-register, in the notation of Chapter 7).

What are the options?

Generally, the standard strategy is to look for quantum systems with a two-dimensional state space. One can then implement q-registers by assembling a number of copies of such systems. The canonical two-dimensional quantum systems are particles with spin. Electrons, as well as single atoms, have spin. There is thus plenty of room in nature for encoding qubits. Spin is not the only one: another natural choice is excited states of atoms, as we are going to see in a moment.

Let us first summmarize all the steps we need:

- Initialize all particles to some well-defined state.
- Perform controlled qubit rotations on a single particle (this step will implement a single-qubit gate).
- Be able to mix the states of two particles (this step aims at implementing a universal two-qubit gate).
- Measure the state of each individual particle.
- Keep the system of particles making up our q-register as insulated as possible from the environment, at least for the short period of time when quantum gates are applied.

The first proposal for quantum hardware is known as the **ion trap**. It is the oldest one, going back to the mid-nineties, and it is still the most popular candidate for quantum hardware.[8]

The core idea is simple: as you may recall from your chemistry classes, an **ion** is an electrically charged atom. Ions can be of two types: they are either positive ion, or **cations**, having lost one or more electrons. Or they are negative ions, or **anions**, having acquired some electrons. Ionized atoms can be acted upon by means

---

[8] The first quantum gate, the controlled-NOT, was experimentally realized with trapped ions by C. Monroe and D. Wineland in 1995. They followed a proposal by Cirac and Zoller put forward a year earlier.

Figure 11.4. An ion in a trap.

of an electromagnetic field, as they are electrically charged; more precisely, we can confine our ionized atom in a specific volume, known as ion trap (Figure 11.4).

In practice, experiments have been conducted with positive ions of calcium: Ca^+. First, the metal is brought to its gaseous state. Next, the single atoms are stripped of some of their electrons, and third, by means of a suitable electromagnetic field, the resulting ions are confined to the trap.

How are qubits encoded? An atom can be in a **excited state** or in a **ground state** (Figure 11.5).

These two states represent two energy levels of the atom and they form an orthogonal basis for a two-dimensional Hilbert space. As we have seen in Chapter 4 (photoelectric effect), if we pump energy into an atom that is in ground state by making it absorb a photon, it will raise to its excited state. Conversely, the atom can lose its energy by emitting a photon. This process is known as **optical pumping** and it is performed using a laser, i.e., a coherent beam of light. The reason for using a laser is that it has an extremely high resolution, allowing the operator to "hit" single ions and thereby achieving a good control of the quantum register. Through optical pumping we can initialize our register to some initial state with a high degree of fidelity (almost 100%).

Next, we need to manipulate the register. As we mentioned in Section 7.2, there is a considerable degree of freedom in quantum computing when it comes to which particular set of gates is implemented, as long as the set is complete. The particular choice depends on the hardware architecture: one chooses gates that are easy to implement and provide a good degree of fidelity. In the ion trap model, the usual choice is as follows:

- Single-qubit rotation: By "hitting" the single ion with a laser pulse of a given amplitude, frequency, and duration, one can rotate its state appropriately.
- Two-qubit gates: The ions in the trap are, in a sense, strung together by what is known as their common vibrational modes. Again, using a laser one can affect their common mode, achieving the desired entanglement (see the paper

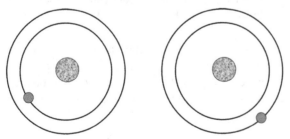

Figure 11.5. Ground and excited states.

by Holzscheiter for details). The original choice for a two-qubit gate was the controlled-NOT gate, which was proposed in 1995 by Cirac and Zoller (1995). Recently, several other more reliable schemes have been implemented.

The last step is measurement. Essentially, the same mechanism we use for setting the qubits can be employed for readouts. How? Aside from the two main long-lived states $|0\rangle$ and $|1\rangle$ (ground and excited), the ion can enter a short-lived state, let us call it $|s\rangle$ ("s" is for short), when gently hit by a pulse. Think of $|s\rangle$ as sitting in the middle between the other two. If the ion is in the ground state and gets pushed to $|s\rangle$ it will revert to ground and emit a photon. On the other hand, if it is in an the excited state, it will not. By repeating the transition many times, we can detect the photons emitted (if any) and thus establish where the qubit is.

To conclude this section, let us list the main strengths and weaknesses of the ion trap model:

- On the plus side, this mode has long coherence time, in the order of 1–10 seconds. Secondly, the measurements are quite reliable, very close to 100%. Finally, one can transport qubits around in the computer, which is a nice feature to have (remember, no copying allowed, so moving things around is good).

- On the minus side, the ion trap is slow, in terms of gate time (slow here means that it takes tens of milliseconds). Secondly, it is not apparent how to scale the optical part to thousands of qubits.

11.3 IMPLEMENTING A QUANTUM COMPUTER II: LINEAR OPTICS

The second implementation of a quantum machine we are going to consider is **linear optics**. Here, one builds a quantum machine out of sheer light!

To build a quantum computer, the very first step is to clearly state how we are going to implement qubits. Now, as we said in Section 5.1, every quantum system that has dimension 2 is, in principle, a valid candidate. Quanta of light, alias photons, are good enough, thanks to the physical phenomenon known as **polarization** (see Section 4.3). We have all seen polarization at work: a beam of light passes through a polarization filter, and the result is a coherent beam of light, i.e., an electromagnetic wave that vibrates along a specific plane.

As photon can be polarized, one can stipulate how qubits are implemented: a certain polarization axis, say vertical polarization, will model $|0\rangle$, whereas $|1\rangle$ will be represented by horizontal polarization.

So much for qubits. Initialization here is straightforward: a suitable polarization filter will do. Gates are less trivial, particularly entanglement gates, as photons have a tendency to stay aloof. It therefore pays to be on the economical side, i.e., to implement some small universal set of quantum gates. We have met the controlled-NOT gate in Chapter 5. If one were to follow the simple-minded route, controlled-NOT would require a two-photon interaction. This happens very seldom, and makes this venue quite impractical. But, as it often happens, there is a way around.

To create controlled-NOT, we need control and target inputs and we need more optical tools. Specifically, we need mirrors, polarizing beam splitters, additional ancillary photons, and single-photon detectors. This approach is known as **linear optics quantum computing**, or **LOQC**, as it uses only linear optics principles and

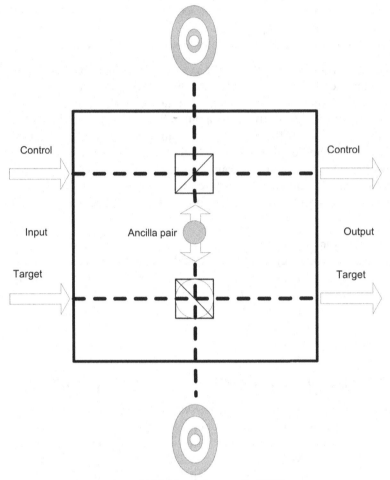

Figure 11.6. Basic idea of LOQC-based controlled-NOT gate.

methodologies. In LOQC, the nonlinearity of measurements arises from the detection of additional, ancillary photons. Figure 11.6 is a schematic picture of a LOQC controlled-NOT gate (details can be found in Pittman, Jacobs, and Franson (2004).

Measurement of the final output presents no difficulties. A combination of polarization filters and single-photon detectors will do.

Before we quit this section let us point out strengths and weaknesses of the optical scheme:

- On the plus side, light *travels*. This means that quantum gates and quantum memory devices can be easily connected via optical fibers. In other approaches, like the ion trap, this step can be a quite complex process. This plus is indeed a big one, as it creates a great milieu for distributed quantum computing.
- On the minus side, unlike electrons and other matter particles, it is not easy for photons to become entangled. This is actually a plus, as it prevents entanglement with its environment (decoherence), but it also makes gate creation a bit more challenging.

11.4 IMPLEMENTING A QUANTUM COMPUTER III: NMR AND SUPERCONDUCTORS

Aside the two models described in the last sections, there are currently several other proposals under investigation, and more may emerge soon. We mention in passing two others that have received a lot of attention in the last years.

Nuclear Magnetic Resonance (**NMR**). The idea here is to encode qubits not as single particles or atoms, but as global spin states of many molecules in some fluid. These molecules float in a cup, which is placed in an NMR machine, quite akin to the devices used in hospitals for magnetic resonance imaging. This large ensemble of molecules has plenty of built-in redundancy, which allows it to maintain coherence for a relatively long time span (several seconds).

The first two-qubit NMR computers were demonstrated in 1998 by J.A. Jones and M. Mosca at Oxford University and at the same time by Isaac L. Chuang at IBM's Almaden Research Center, together with coworkers at Stanford University and MIT. Berggren quoted in the references.

Superconductor Quantum Computers (**SQP**). Whereas NMR uses fluids, SQP employs superconductors.[9] How? By means of **Josephson junctions** – thin layers of nonconducting material sandwiched between two pieces of superconducting metal. At very low temperatures, electrons within a superconductor become, as they were, friends, and pair up to form a "superfluid" flowing with no resistance and traveling through the medium as a single, uniform wave pattern. This wave leaks into the insulating middle. The current flows back and forth through the junction much like a ping-pong ball, in a rhythmic fashion.

How are qubits implemented? Through what is now known as the **Josephson junction qubit**. In this implementation, the $|0\rangle$ and $|1\rangle$ states are represented by the two lowest-frequency oscillations of the currents flowing back and forth through the junction. The frequency of these oscillations is very high, being of the order of billions of times per second.

Where are we now?

In 2001 the first execution of Shor's algorithm was carried out at IBM's Almaden Research Center and Stanford University. They factored the number 15: not an impressive number by any means, but a definite start! (By the way, the answer was $15 = 5 * 3$.)

In 2005, using NMR, a 12-qubit quantum register was benchmarked. So far at least, scalability seems to be a major hurdle. Progress has been made almost a qubit at a time, in the last few years. On the positive side, new proposals and methodologies crop up in a continuous stream.

If you wish to know more about recent news in quantum hardware research, probably the best course is to take a look at the **NIST Road Map**. NIST, the **US National Institute of Science and Technology**, a major force in the ongoing effort to implement quantum computing machines, has recently released a comprehensive road map listing all major directions toward quantum hardware, as well as comparison tables pointing at weaknesses and strengths of each individual approach. You can download it at NIST Web site: http: //qist.lanl.gov/qcomp_map.shtml.

---

[9] A superconductor is matter at very low temperature, exhibiting so-called superconductivity properties.

As you can imagine from this brief survey, people are pretty busy at the moment, trying to make the magic quantum work.

It is worth mentioning that as of the time of this writing (late 2007), there are already three companies whose main business is developing quantum computing technologies: D-Wave Systems, MagicQ, and Id Quantique. Recently (February 13, 2007), D-Wave has publicly demonstrated a prototypical quantum computer, known as Orion, at the Historical Museum in Mountain View, CA. Orion was apparently able to play the popular Sudoku game. D-Wave's announcement has generated some expected and healthy skepticism among academic researchers.

11.5 FUTURE OF QUANTUM WARE

At last, the future. The great physicist Niels Bohr, a major protagonist in the development of quantum mechanics, had a great punch line: "Prediction is always hard, especially of the future."[10]

We could not agree more. What we think is safe to say is that there is a reasonable likelihood that quantum computing may become a reality in the future, perhaps even in the relatively near future. If that happens, it is also quite likely that many areas of information technology will be affected. Certainly, the first thought goes to communication and cryptography. These areas are noticeably ahead, in that some concrete quantum encryption systems have been implemented and tested.

Assuming that sizeable quantum devices will be available at some point in time, there is yet another important area of computer science where one can reasonably expect some impact of quantum computation, namely, artificial intelligence. It has been suggested in some quarters that the phenomenon of consciousness has some links with the quantum (see, for instance, the tantalizing paper by Paola Zizzi or either of these two books by Sir Roger Penrose, 1994, 1999). Some people even go as far as saying that our brain may be better modeled as an immense quantum computing network than are traditional neural networks (although this opinion is not shared by most contemporary neuroscientists and cognitive scientists). Be that as it may, a new area of research has already been spawned that merges traditional artificial intelligence with quantum computing. The interaction happens both ways: for instance, artificial intelligence methodologies such as genetic algorithms have been proposed as a way to design quantum algorithms. Essentially, genes encode candidate circuits and selection and mutation do the rest. This is an important direction, as for now our understanding of quantum algorithm design is still rather limited. On the other hand, quantum computing suggests new tools for artificial intelligence. A typical example is quantum neural networks. Here, the idea is to replace activation maps with complex valued ones, akin to what we have seen in Section 3.3.

Beyond these relatively tame predictions, there is the vast expanse of science fiction out there. Interestingly, quantum computing has already percolated into science fiction (the nextQuant blog maintains a current list of science fiction works with quantum computing themes). For instance, the well-known science fiction writer Greg Egan has written a new book called *Schild's Ladder* (Egan, 2002), in which he

---

[10] The same line is sometimes attributed to Yogi Berra.

speculates about the role of quantum computing devices in the far future to enhance mind capabilities. True? False?

All too often, the dreams of today are the reality of tomorrow.

. . . .

References: Literature in the topics covered by this chapter abounds, although it is a bit difficult for nonexperts to keep track of it. Here are just a few useful pointers:

For decoherence, Wojciech H. Zurek has an excellent readable paper: Zurek (2003).

David P. DiVincenzo's rules can be found in DiVincenzo.

The ion trap model is discussed in a number of places. A good general reference is the paper by M. Holzscheiter.

Optical computers are clearly and elegantly presented in a paper by Pittman, Jacobs, and Franson (2004).

For NMR computing, see Vandersypen et al. (2001).

An article by Karl Berggren (2004) provides a good introduction to superconductor quantum computing.

Appendix A
Historical Bibliography of Quantum Computing

Jill Cirasella

This bibliographic essay reviews seminal papers in quantum computing. Although quantum computing is a young science, its researchers have already published thousands of noteworthy articles, far too many to list here. Therefore, this appendix is not a comprehensive chronicle of the emergence and evolution of the field but rather a guided tour of some of the papers that spurred, formalized, and furthered its study.

Quantum computing draws on advanced ideas from computer science, physics, and mathematics, and most major papers were written by researchers conversant in all three fields. Nevertheless, all the articles described in this appendix can be appreciated by computer scientists.

A.1 READING SCIENTIFIC ARTICLES

Do not be deterred if an article seems impenetrable. Keep in mind that professors and professionals also struggle to understand these articles, and take comfort in this epigram usually attributed to the great physicist Richard Feynman: "If you think you understand quantum mechanics, you don't understand quantum mechanics."

Some articles are difficult to understand not only because quantum theory is devilishly elusive but also because scientific writing can be opaque. Fortunately, there are techniques for tackling scientific articles, beginning with these preliminary steps:

- **Read the title.** It may contain clues about the article's purpose or findings.
- **Read the abstract.** It summarizes the article and will help you recognize important points when you read them.
- **Read the introduction and conclusion.** Usually in plain language, the introduction and conclusion will help you decode the rest of the article.
- **Skim the article.** Skim to get a sense of the article's structure, which will help you stay oriented while you read.

Once you understand an article's purpose and structure, you are ready to read the full article. To maximize comprehension and minimize frustration, follow these tips:

- **Read actively.** Take notes while you read. Underline key phrases; mark important passages; record important points; sketch arguments and proofs; and reproduce calculations. (Of course, don't write on anything owned by a library; make copies instead.)
- **Don't dwell.** Skim or skip difficult parts and return to them later. They might make more sense after you have read subsequent sections.
- **Consult the bibliography.** If something confuses you, one of the cited articles might explain it better or provide helpful background information.
- **Read the article multiple times.** You'll understand more with each pass.
- **Know when to stop.** Don't obsess over an article. At some point, you will have gotten as much as you are going to get (for the time being). Some or even most of the article might still elude you; nevertheless, you will know more after reading the article than you did before you started, and you will then be better equipped to read other articles.
- **Talk about the article.** Mull over the article with other students, and ask your professor if you need help. After you have finished the article, keep talking about it. Explain it to your class, to your study group, or even to someone unfamiliar with the field. After all, the best way to learn something is to teach it to someone else!

A.2 MODELS OF COMPUTATION

Richard Feynman was the first to suggest, in a talk in 1981, that quantum-mechanical systems might be more powerful than classical computers. In this lecture, reproduced in the *International Journal of Theoretical Physics* in 1982 (Feynman, 1982), Feynman asked what kind of computer could simulate physics and then argued that only a quantum computer could simulate quantum physics efficiently. He focused on quantum physics rather than classical physics because, as he colorfully put it, "nature isn't classical, dammit, and if you want to make a simulation of nature, you'd better make it quantum mechanical, and by golly it's a wonderful problem, because it doesn't look so easy" (p. 486).

Around the same time, in "Quantum mechanical models of Turing machines that dissipate no energy" (Benioff, 1982) and related articles, Paul Benioff demonstrated that quantum-mechanical systems could model Turing machines. In other words, he proved that quantum computation is at least as powerful as classical computation. But is quantum computation *more* powerful than classical computation?

David Deutsch explored this question and more in his 1985 paper "Quantum theory, the Church–Turing principle and the universal quantum computer" (Deutsch, 1985). First, he introduced quantum counterparts to both the Turing machine and the universal Turing machine. He then demonstrated that the universal quantum computer can do things that the universal Turing machine cannot, including generate genuinely random numbers, perform some parallel calculations in a single register, and perfectly simulate physical systems with finite-dimensional state spaces.

In 1989, in "Quantum computational networks" (Deutsch, 1989), Deutsch described a second model for quantum computation: quantum circuits. He demonstrated that quantum gates can be combined to achieve quantum computation in the same way that Boolean gates can be combined to achieve classical computation. He then showed that quantum circuits can compute anything that the universal quantum computer can compute, and vice versa.

Andrew Chi-Chih Yao picked up where Deutsch left off and addressed the complexity of quantum computation in his 1993 paper "Quantum circuit complexity" (Yao, 1993). Specifically, he showed that any function that can be computed in polynomial time by a quantum Turing machine can also be computed by a quantum circuit of polynomial size. This finding allowed researchers to focus on quantum circuits, which are easier than quantum Turing machines to design and analyze.

Also in 1993, Ethan Bernstein and Umesh Vazirani presented "Quantum complexity theory" (Bernstein and Vazirani, 1993), in which they described a universal quantum Turing machine that can efficiently simulate any quantum Turing machine. (As with so many quantum articles, the final version of the paper did not appear until several years later, in the *SIAM Journal of Computing*; Bernstein and Vazirani, 1997). As its title suggests, Bernstein and Vazirani's paper kick-started the study of quantum complexity theory.

A.3 QUANTUM GATES

In 1995, a cluster of articles examined which sets of quantum gates are adequate for quantum computation – that is, which sets of gates are sufficient for creating any given quantum circuit. Of these papers, the one that was cited the most in later works was "Elementary gates for quantum computation" (Barenco et al., 1995), in which Adriano Barenco et al. showed that any quantum circuit can be constructed using nothing more than quantum gates on one qubit and controlled exclusive-OR gates on two qubits. Though that paper was arguably the most influential, other articles were important as well, including "Two-bit gates are universal for quantum computation" (DiVincenzo, 1995), in which David DiVincenzo proved that two-qubit quantum gates are adequate; "Conditional quantum dynamics and logic gates" (Barenco, Deutsch, Ekert, and Jozsa, 1995), in which Adriano Barenco, David Deutsch, Artur Ekert, and Richard Jozsa showed that quantum controlled-NOT gates and one-qubit gates are together adequate; and "Almost any quantum logic gate is universal" (Lloyd, 1995), in which Seth Lloyd showed that almost any quantum gate with two or more inputs is universal (i.e., by itself adequate).

A.4 QUANTUM ALGORITHMS AND IMPLEMENTATIONS

In 1992, David Deutsch and Richard Jozsa coauthored "Rapid solution of problems by quantum computation" (Deutsch and Jozsa, 1992), in which they presented an algorithm that determines whether a function f is constant over all inputs (i.e., either equal to 1 for all x or equal to 0 for all x) or balanced (i.e., equal to 1 for half of the values of x and equal to 0 for the other half). The Deutsch–Jozsa algorithm was the first quantum algorithm to run faster, in all cases, than its classical counterparts. So, even though the problem is somewhat contrived, the algorithm is notable and the article is worth reading. Also worth reading is "Experimental realization of a quantum algorithm" (Chuang et al., 1998), in which Isaac L. Chuang et al. detailed how they used bulk nuclear magnetic resonance techniques to implement a simplified version of the Deutsch–Jozsa algorithm.

In "Quantum complexity theory" (Bernstein and Vazirani, 1993) (also mentioned before), Bernstein and Vazirani were the first to identify a problem that can be solved in polynomial time by a quantum algorithm but requires superpolynomial time classically. The following year, Daniel R. Simon introduced a problem that a quantum algorithm can solve *exponentially* faster than any known classical algorithm. His research inspired Peter W. Shor, who then invented two quantum algorithms that outshone all others: polynomial-time algorithms for finding prime factors and discrete logarithms, problems widely believed to require exponential time on classical computers. Simon and Shor both presented their discoveries at the 1994 IEEE Symposium on the Foundations of Computer Science (in "On the power of quantum computation" (Simon, 1994) and "Algorithms for quantum computation: Discrete logarithms and factoring" (Shor, 1994), respectively) and published the final versions of their papers in a special quantum-themed issue of *SIAM Journal of Computing* (Simon, 1997, and Shor, 1997, respectively).

Shor's factorization algorithm in particular heightened excitement and even generated anxiety about the power and promise of quantum computing. Specifically, the algorithm caused a furor because it threatened the security of information encrypted according to the widely used cryptosystem developed by Ronald L. Rivest, Adi Shamir, and Leonard M. Adleman. RSA cryptography, as it is known, relies on the presumed difficulty of factoring large numbers, a problem that is not known to require exponential time but for which no classical polynomial-time algorithm exists. Rivest, Shamir, and Adleman described the cryptosystem in 1978 in "A method for obtaining digital signatures and public-key cryptosystems" (Rivest, Shamir, and Adleman, 1978), an article that is brief, elegant, and still very relevant to anyone interested in Shor's algorithm, cryptography, or complexity theory.

Of course, to pose a practical threat to RSA cryptography, Shor's algorithm must be implemented on quantum computers that can hold and manipulate large numbers, and these do not exist yet. That said, Isaac L. Chuang and his research team made headlines when they factored the number 15 on a quantum computer with seven qubits. Their 2001 précis of their accomplishment, "Experimental realization of Shor's quantum factoring algorithm using nuclear magnetic resonance" (Vandersypen et al., 2001), is a well-illustrated reminder of just how astonishing Shor's algorithm is.

Another highly influential quantum algorithm is Lov K. Grover's algorithm for searching an unordered list, described in both "A fast quantum mechanical algorithm for database search" (Grover, 1996) and "Quantum mechanics helps in searching for a needle in a haystack" (Grover, 1997). Unlike Shor's algorithm, Grover's algorithm solves a problem for which there are polynomial-time classical algorithms; however, Grover's algorithm does it quadratically faster than classical algorithms can. With Grover's algorithm, as with the algorithms mentioned earlier, Isaac L. Chuang was at the experimental fore; in 1998, he, Neil Gershenfeld, and Mark Kubinec reported on the first implementation of Grover's algorithm in "Experimental implementation of fast quantum searching" (Chuang, Gershenfeld, and Kubinec, 1998).

There are of course more quantum algorithms than those discussed earlier. However, there are far fewer than researchers had hoped there would be by now, and research in quantum algorithms has not kept pace with research in other aspects of quantum computing and quantum information. In 2003, Peter W. Shor addressed this stagnation in a short article called "Why haven't more quantum algorithms been found?" (Shor, 2003). Although unsure of the answer to that question, Shor offered several possible explanations, including the possibility that computer scientists have not yet developed intuitions for quantum behavior. The article should be required reading for all computer science students, whose intuitions are still being formed.

A.5 QUANTUM CRYPTOGRAPHY

As mentioned before, Shor's factorization algorithm has yet to be implemented on more than a few qubits. But if the efficient factorization of large numbers becomes possible, RSA cryptography will need to be replaced by a new form of cryptography, one that will not be foiled by classical or quantum computers. Conveniently, such a method already exists; in fact, it was developed before Shor invented his factorization algorithm. Coincidentally, it too relies on quantum mechanics.

The cryptographic method in question is quantum key distribution, which was introduced in 1984 by Charles H. Bennett and Gilles Brassard in "Quantum cryptography: Public key distribution and coin tossing" (Bennett and Brassard, 1984) and is thus commonly referred to as BB84. In short, quantum key distribution is secure not because messages are encrypted in some difficult-to-decrypt way but rather because eavesdroppers cannot intercept messages undetected, regardless of computational resources.

Although quantum key distribution is the most famous cryptographic application of quantum mechanics, it is not the only one, and it was not the first. In the 1960s, Stephen Wiesner conceived of two applications: a way to send two messages, only one of which can be read, and a way to design money that cannot be counterfeited. His ideas were largely unknown until 1983, when he described them in an article called "Conjugate coding" (Wiesner, 1983).

Needless to say, the papers mentioned earlier were not the only milestones in the development of quantum cryptography. Curious readers should consult these two installments of *SIGACT News'* "Cryptology column": "Quantum cryptography: A bibliography" by Gilles Brassard (1993) and "25 years of quantum cryptography" by Gilles Brassard and Claude Crépeau Brassard and Crépeau (1993). Since the publication of those articles, quantum cryptography has matured from theory and experiments to commercially available products; developments are frequently announced by manufacturers such as MagiQ Technologies (http://www.magiqtech.com/), id Quantique (http://www.idquantique.com/), and Smart Quantum (http://www.smartquantum.com/).

A.6 QUANTUM INFORMATION

Secure channels of communication are of course crucial, but security is not the only consideration in the transfer of information. Accordingly, quantum cryptography is just one of several topics in the burgeoning field of quantum information. Other topics include quantum error correction, fault-tolerant quantum computation, quantum data compression, and quantum teleportation.

Information needs to be protected not just from eavesdroppers but also from errors caused by channel noise, implementation flaws, and, in the quantum case, decoherence. Peter W. Shor, a trailblazer not just of quantum algorithms but also of quantum error correction and fault-tolerant quantum computation, was the first to describe a quantum error-correcting method. In his 1995 article "Scheme for reducing decoherence in quantum computer memory" (Shor, 1995), he demonstrated that encoding each qubit of information into nine qubits could provide some protection against decoherence. At almost the same time but without knowledge of Shor's article, Andrew M. Steane wrote "Error correcting codes in quantum theory" (Steane, 1997), which achieved similar results. Very shortly thereafter, Shor and A.R. Calderbank presented improved results in "Good quantum error-correcting codes exist" (Calderbank and Shor, 1996). In the late 1990s, when research on quantum error correction and fault-tolerant quantum computation ballooned, Shor, Steane, and Calderbank remained among the major contributors.

Error is not the only thing information theorists strive to reduce; they also seek to reduce the space required to represent information. The landmark paper on the classical representation and compression of data was "A mathematical theory of communication" by Claude E. Shannon (1948), the "father" of information theory. In this 1948 paper, Shannon showed that it is possible, up to a certain limit, to compress data without loss of information; beyond that limit, some information is necessarily lost. (Seminal in so many ways, this paper also laid the groundwork for classical error-correcting codes.)

Almost 50 years later, Benjamin Schumacher developed a quantum version of Shannon's theorem. Schumacher first described his finding in an article called "Quantum coding," which he submitted to *Physical Review A* in 1993 but which was not published until 1995 (Schumacher, 1995). In the (unfortunate but not uncommon) lag between submission and publication, he and Richard Jozsa published "A new proof of the quantum noiseless coding theorem" (Jozsa and Schumacher, 1994), which offered a simpler proof than the original article.

Not everything in quantum information theory has a precedent in classical information theory. In 1993, Charles H. Bennett et al., dazzled the scientific community and delighted science fiction fans by showing that quantum teleportation is theoretically possible. In "Teleporting an unknown quantum state via dual classical and Einstein–Podolsky–Rosen channels" (Bennett et al., 1993), they described how an unknown quantum state could be disassembled and then reconstructed perfectly in another location. The first researchers to verify this method of teleportation experimentally were Dik Bouwmeester et al., who reported their achievement in 1997 in "Experimental quantum teleportation" (Bouwmeester, 1997).

A.7 MORE MILESTONES?

Quantum computing continues to entice and engross researchers, who will no doubt continue to ask challenging questions, discover inventive and elegant solutions, identify stumbling blocks, and achieve experimental triumphs. To learn how to apprise yourself of developments, consult Appendix D, "Keeping abreast of quantum news: Quantum computing on the Web and in the literature."

Appendix B
Answers to Selected Exercises

CHAPTER 1

Ex. 1.1.1:

$$x^4 + 2x^2 + 1 = (x^2 + 1)(x^2 + 1) = 0. \tag{B.1}$$

As neither of the factors have real solutions, there are no real solutions to the entire equation.

Ex. 1.1.2: $-i$.

Ex. 1.1.3: $-1 - 3i$; $-2 + 14i$.

Ex. 1.1.4: Simply multiply out $(-1 + i)^2 + 2(-1 + i) + 2$ and show that it equals 0.

Ex. 1.2.1: $(-5, 5)$.

Ex. 1.2.2: Setting $c_1 = (a_1, b_1)$, $c_2 = (a_2, b_2)$, and $c_3 = (a_3, b_3)$. Then we have

$$
\begin{aligned}
c_1 \times (c_2 \times c_3) &= (a_1, b_1) \times (a_2 a_3 - b_2 b_3, a_2 b_3 + a_3 b_2) \\
&= (a_1(a_2 a_3 - b_2 b_3) - b_1(a_2 b_3 + a_3 b_2), a_1(a_2 b_3 + a_3 b_2) + (a_2 a_3 - b_2 b_3)b_1) \\
&= (a_1 a_2 a_3 - a_1 b_2 b_3 - b_1 a_2 b_3 - b_1 b_2 a_3, a_1 a_2 b_3 + a_1 b_2 a_3 + b_1 a_2 a_3 - b_1 b_2 b_3) \\
&= (a_1 a_2 - b_1 b_2, a_1 b_2 + b_1 a_2) \times (a_3, b_3) \\
&= ((a_1, b_1) \times (a_2, b_2)) \times (a_3, b_3) = (c_1 \times c_2) \times c_3. \tag{B.2}
\end{aligned}
$$

Ex. 1.2.3: $\frac{-3 - 3i}{2}$.

Ex. 1.2.4: 5.

Ex. 1.2.5: Setting $c_1 = (a_1, b_1)$ and $c_2 = (a_2, b_2)$. Then

$$
\begin{aligned}
|c_1||c_2| &= \sqrt{a_1^2 + b_1^2}\sqrt{a_2^2 + b_2^2} = \sqrt{(a_1^2 + b_1^2)(a_2^2 + b_2^2)} \\
&= \sqrt{a_1^2 a_2^2 + b_1^2 a_2^2 + b_1^2 b_2^2 + a_1^2 b_2^2} = \sqrt{(a_1 a_2 - b_1 b_2)^2 + (a_1 b_2 + a_2 b_1)^2} \\
&= |(a_1 a_2 - b_1 b_2, a_1 b_2 + a_2 b_1)| = |c_1 c_2|. \tag{B.3}
\end{aligned}
$$

Ex. 1.2.6: This can be carried out algebraically like Exercise 1.2.5. One should also think of this geometrically after reading Section 1.3. Basically this says that any side of a triangle is not greater than the sum of the other two sides.

Ex. 1.2.7: Examine it!

Ex. 1.2.8: Too easy.

Ex. 1.2.9: $(a_1, b_1)(-1, 0) = (-1a_1 - 0b_1, 0a_1 - 1b_1) = (-a_1, -b_1)$.

Ex. 1.2.10: Setting $c_1 = (a_1, b_1)$ and $c_2 = (a_2, b_2)$. Then

$$\overline{c_1} + \overline{c_2} = (a_1, -b_1) + (a_2, -b_2) = (a_1 + a_2, -(b_1 + b_2)) = \overline{c_1 + c_2}. \tag{B.4}$$

Ex. 1.2.11: Setting $c_1 = (a_1, b_1)$ and $c_2 = (a_2, b_2)$. Then

$$\overline{c_1} \times \overline{c_2} = (a_1, -b_1) \times (a_2, -b_2) = (a_1 a_2 - b_1 b_2, -a_1 b_2 - a_2 b_1), \tag{B.5}$$

$$(a_1 a_2 - b_1 b_2, -(a_1 b_2 + a_2 b_1)) = \overline{c_1 \times c_2}. \tag{B.6}$$

Ex. 1.2.12: Although the map is bijective, it is not a field isomorphism because it does not respect the multiplication, i.e., in general,

$$-\overline{(c_1 \times c_2)} \neq -\overline{c_1} \times -\overline{c_2} = \overline{c_1 \times c_2}. \tag{B.7}$$

Ex. 1.3.1: $3 + 0i$.

Ex. 1.3.2: $1 - 2i$.

Ex. 1.3.3: $1.5 + 2.6i$.

Ex. 1.3.4: $5i$.

Ex. 1.3.5: If $c = a + bi$, the effect of multiplying by r_0 is just $r_0 a + r_0 bi$. The vector in the plane has been stretched by the constant factor r_0. You can see it better in polar coordinates: only the magnitude of the vector has changed, the angle stays the same. The effect on the plane is an overall dilation by r_0, and no rotation.

Ex. 1.3.6: The best way to grasp this exercise it to pass to the polar representation: let $c = (\rho, \theta)$ and $c_0 = (\rho_0, \theta_0)$. Their product is $(\rho \rho_0, \theta + \theta_0)$. This is true for all c. The plane has been dilated by the factor ρ_0 and rotated by the angle θ_0.

Ex. 1.3.7: $2i$.

Ex. 1.3.8: $(1 - i)^5 = -4 + 4i$.

Ex. 1.3.9: $1.0842 + 0.2905i, -0.7937 + 0.7937i, -0.2905 - 1.0842i$.

Ex. 1.3.12:

$$\frac{c_1}{c_2} = \frac{\rho_1}{\rho_2} e^{i(\theta_1 - \theta_2)}. \tag{B.8}$$

Ex. 1.3.15: Let $c_0 = d_0 + d_1 i$ be our constant complex number and $x = a + bi$ be an arbitrary complex input. Then $(a + d_0) + (b + d_1)i$, i.e. the translation of x by c_0.

Ex. 1.3.17: Set $a'' = (aa' + b'c)$, $b'' = (a'b + b'd)$, $c'' = (ac' + cd')$, and $d'' = (bc' + dd')$ to get the composition of the two transformations.

Ex. 1.3.18: $a = 1, b = 0, c = 0, d = 1$. Notice that $ad - bc = 1$, so the condition is satisfied.

Ex. 1.3.19: The transformation $\frac{dx - b}{-cx + a}$ will do. Notice that it is still Möbius because

$$da - (-b)(-c) = da - bc = ad - bc. \tag{B.9}$$

CHAPTER 2

Ex. 2.1.1:

$$\begin{bmatrix} 12 + 5i \\ 6 + 6i \\ 2.53 - 6i \\ 21.4 + 3i \end{bmatrix}. \tag{B.10}$$

Ex. 2.1.2:

$$(V + (W + X))[j] = V[j] + (W + X)[j] = V[j] + (W[j] + X[j])$$
$$= (V[j] + W[j]) + X[j] = (V + W)[j] + X[j]$$
$$= ((V + W) + X)[j]. \tag{B.11}$$

Ex. 2.1.3:

$$\begin{bmatrix} 132.6 - 13.6i \\ -14 - 56i \\ 48 - 12i \\ 32 - 42i \end{bmatrix}. \tag{B.12}$$

Ex. 2.1.4:

$$((c_1 + c_2) \cdot V)[j] = ((c_1 + c_2) \times (V[j]) = ((c_1 \times (V[j])) + (c_2 \times (V[j]))$$
$$= (c_1 \cdot V)[j] + (c_2 \cdot V)[j] = ((c_1 \cdot V) + (c_2 \cdot V))[j]. \tag{B.13}$$

Ex. 2.2.1: They are both equal to $\begin{bmatrix} 12 \\ -24 \\ 6 \end{bmatrix}$.

Ex. 2.2.3: For property (vi):

$$\begin{bmatrix} -2 + 6i & -12 + 6i \\ -12 - 4i & -18 + 4i \end{bmatrix}. \tag{B.14}$$

For property (viii):

$$\begin{bmatrix} 5 + 3i & 3 + 12i \\ -6 + 10i & 17i \end{bmatrix}. \tag{B.15}$$

Ex. 2.2.4: Property (v) has the unit 1. Property (vi) is done as follows:

$$(c_1 \cdot (c_2 \cdot A))[j, k] = c_1 \times ((c_2 \cdot A)[j, k]) = c_1 \times (c_2 \times A[j, k])$$
$$= (c_1 \times c_2) \times A[j, k] = ((c_1 \times c_2) \cdot A)[j, k]. \quad \text{(B.16)}$$

Property (viii) is similar to this and similar to Exercise 2.1.4.

Ex. 2.2.5:

$$\begin{bmatrix} 6 - 3i & 0 & 1 \\ 2 + 12i & 5 + 2.1i & 2 + 5i \\ -19i & 17 & 3 - 4.5i \end{bmatrix} ; \quad \begin{bmatrix} 6 + 3i & 2 - 12i & 19i \\ 0 & 5 - 2.1i & 17 \\ 1 & 2 - 5i & 3 + 4.5i \end{bmatrix} ;$$

$$\begin{bmatrix} 6 + 3i & 0 & 1 \\ 2 - 12i & 5 - 2.1i & 2 - 5i \\ 19i & 17 & 3 + 4.5i \end{bmatrix} . \quad \text{(B.17)}$$

Ex. 2.2.6:

$$\overline{(c \cdot A)}[j, k] = \overline{(c \times (A[j, k])} = \overline{c} \times \overline{(A[j, k])} = (\overline{c} \cdot \overline{A})[j, k]. \quad \text{(B.18)}$$

Ex. 2.2.7: We shall only do Property (ix). The others are similar.

$$(c \cdot A)^{\dagger} = \overline{(c \cdot A)}^T = (\overline{c} \cdot \overline{A})^T = \overline{c} \cdot \overline{A}^T = \overline{c} \cdot A^{\dagger}. \quad \text{(B.19)}$$

Ex. 2.2.8:

$$\begin{bmatrix} 37 - 13i & 10 & 50 - 44i \\ 12 + 3i & 6 + 28i & 3 + 4i \\ 31 + 9i & -6 + 32i & 4 - 60i \end{bmatrix} . \quad \text{(B.20)}$$

Ex. 2.2.9:

$$((A \star B)^T)[j, k] = (A \star B)[k, j] = \sum_{i=0}^{n} A[k, i] \times B[i, j] = \sum_{i=0}^{n} B[i, j] \times A[k, i]$$

$$= \sum_{i=0}^{n} B^T[j, i] \times A^T[i, k] = (B^T \star A^T)[j, k]. \quad \text{(B.21)}$$

Ex. 2.2.10:

$$\begin{bmatrix} 26 + 52i & 9 - 7i & 48 + 21i \\ 60 - 24i & 1 - 29i & 15 - 22i \\ 26 & 14 & 20 + 22i \end{bmatrix} . \quad \text{(B.22)}$$

Ex. 2.2.11:

$$(A \star B)^\dagger = \overline{(A \star B)}^T = (\overline{A} \star \overline{B})^T = \overline{B}^T \star \overline{A}^T = B^\dagger \star A^\dagger. \tag{B.23}$$

Ex. 2.2.13: Every member of $Poly_5$ can be written as

$$c_0 + c_1 x + c_2 x^2 + c_3 x^3 + c_4 x^4 + c_5 x^5 + 0x^6 + 0x^7. \tag{B.24}$$

It is obvious that this subset is closed under addition and scalar multiplication.

Ex. 2.2.14: Given two matrices

$$\begin{bmatrix} x & y \\ -y & x \end{bmatrix} \quad \text{and} \quad \begin{bmatrix} x' & y' \\ -y' & x' \end{bmatrix}, \tag{B.25}$$

their sum is

$$\begin{bmatrix} x + x' & y + y' \\ -(y + y') & x + x' \end{bmatrix}, \tag{B.26}$$

and so the set is closed under addition. Similar for scalar multiplication. This sum is also equal to

$$f(x + yi) + f(x' + y'i) = f((x + x') + (y + y')i). \tag{B.27}$$

Ex. 2.2.17: A given pair $\left\langle \begin{bmatrix} c_0 \\ c_1 \\ \vdots \\ c_{m-1} \end{bmatrix}, \begin{bmatrix} c'_0 \\ c'_1 \\ \vdots \\ c'_{n-1} \end{bmatrix} \right\rangle$ goes to

$$[c_0, c_1, \cdots, c_{m-1}, c'_0, c'_1, \cdots, c'_{n-1}]^T. \tag{B.28}$$

Ex. 2.2.18: An element $[c_0, c_1, \cdots, c_{m-1}]^T$ of $\mathbb{C}^m$ can be seen as the element

$$\left\langle \begin{bmatrix} c_0 \\ c_1 \\ \vdots \\ c_{m-1} \end{bmatrix}, \begin{bmatrix} 0 \\ 0 \\ \vdots \\ 0 \end{bmatrix} \right\rangle \text{ of } \mathbb{C}^m \times \mathbb{C}^n.$$

Ex. 2.3.1:

$$2 \cdot [1, 2, 3]^T + [1, -4, -4]^T = [3, 0, 2]^T. \tag{B.29}$$

Ex. 2.3.2: The canonical basis can easily be written as a linear combination of these vectors.

Ex. 2.4.1: Both sides of Equation (2.101) are 11 and both sides of Equation (2.102) are 31.

Ex. 2.4.3: We shall show it for Equation (2.101).

$$(A + B)^T = \begin{bmatrix} 1 & -1 \\ 1 & 1 \end{bmatrix}; \quad (A + B)^T \star C = \begin{bmatrix} 1 & -2 \\ 3 & 4 \end{bmatrix}; \tag{B.30}$$

and the Trace of this matrix is 5. The right-hand side is $Trace(A^T \star C) = 7$ added to $Trace(B^T \star C) = -2$ for a sum of 5.

Ex. 2.4.5: $\sqrt{439}$.

Ex. 2.4.6: $\sqrt{47}$.

Ex. 2.4.7: $\sqrt{11}$.

Ex. 2.4.8:

$$\langle V, V' \rangle = |V||V'| \cos \theta, \tag{B.31}$$

$$8 = 3\sqrt{10} \cos \theta, \tag{B.32}$$

$$\cos \theta = 0.843, \tag{B.33}$$

$$\theta = 32.51°. \tag{B.34}$$

Ex. 2.5.1: Their eigenvalues are –2, –2, and 4, respectively.

Ex. 2.6.1: Look at it.

Ex. 2.6.2: The key idea is that you take the transpose of both sides of

$$\overline{A}^T = A \tag{B.35}$$

and remember that the T operation is idempotent.

Ex. 2.6.3: The proof is the same as the hermitian case but with the dagger replaced with the transpose operation.

Ex. 2.6.4: The proof is analogous to the hermitian case.

Ex. 2.6.5: Multiply it out by its adjoint and remember the basic trigonometric identity:

$$\sin^2 \theta + \cos^2 \theta = 1. \tag{B.36}$$

Ex. 2.6.6: Multiply it by its adjoint to get the identity.

Ex. 2.6.7: If U is unitary, then $U \star U^\dagger = I$. Similarly, if U' is unitary, then $U' \star U'^\dagger = I$. Combining these we get that

$$(U \star U') \star (U \star U')^\dagger = (U \star U') \star (U'^\dagger \star U^\dagger) = U \star U' \star U'^\dagger \star U^\dagger$$
$$= U \star I \star U^\dagger = U \star U^\dagger = I. \tag{B.37}$$

Ex. 2.6.8:

$$d(UV_1, UV_2) = |UV_1 - UV_2| = |U(V_1 - V_2)| = |V_1 - V_2| = d(V_1, V_2). \tag{B.38}$$

Ex. 2.6.9: It is a simple observation and they are their own adjoint.

Ex. 2.7.1:

$$[-3, 6, -4, 8, -7, 14]^T. \tag{B.39}$$

Ex. 2.7.2: No. We are looking for values such that

$$[z, y, z]^T \times [a, b]^T = [5, 6, 3, 2, 0, 1]^T. \tag{B.40}$$

That would imply that $za = 0$ and which means either $z = 0$ or $a = 0$. If $z = 0$, then we would not have $zb = 1$ and if $a = 0$ we would not have $xa = 5$. So no such values exist.

Ex. 2.7.3:

$$
\begin{bmatrix}
3+2i & 1+18i & 29-11i & 5-i & 19+17i & 18-40i & 2i & -8+6i & 14+10i \\
26+26i & 18+12i & -4+19i & 52 & 30-6i & 15+23i & -4+20i & 12i & -10+4i \\
0 & 3+2i & -12+31i & 0 & 5-i & 19+43i & 0 & 2i & -18+4i \\
0 & 0 & 0 & 12 & 36+48i & 60-84i & 6-3i & 30+15i & 9-57i \\
0 & 0 & 0 & 120+24i & 72 & 24+60i & 66-18i & 36-18i & 27+24i \\
0 & 0 & 0 & 0 & 12 & 24+108i & 0 & 6-3i & 39+48i \\
2 & 6+8i & 10-14i & 4+4i & -4+28i & 48-8i & 9+3i & 15+45i & 66-48i \\
20+4i & 12 & 4+10i & 32+48i & 24+24i & -12+28i & 84+48i & 54+18i & 3+51i \\
0 & 2 & 4+18i & 0 & 4+4i & -28+44i & 0 & 9+3i & -9+87i
\end{bmatrix}.
$$

$$(B.41)$$

Ex. 2.7.5: Both associations equal

$$
\begin{bmatrix}
18 & 15 & 12 & 10 & 36 & 30 & 24 & 20 \\
9 & 6 & 6 & 4 & 18 & 12 & 12 & 8 \\
-6 & -5 & 0 & 0 & -12 & -10 & 0 & 0 \\
-3 & -2 & 0 & 0 & -6 & -4 & 0 & 0 \\
0 & 0 & 0 & 0 & 18 & 15 & 12 & 10 \\
0 & 0 & 0 & 0 & 9 & 6 & 6 & 4 \\
0 & 0 & 0 & 0 & -6 & -5 & 0 & 0 \\
0 & 0 & 0 & 0 & -3 & -2 & 0 & 0
\end{bmatrix}.
$$

$$(B.42)$$

Ex. 2.7.6: For $A \in \mathbb{C}^{m \times m'}$, $B \in \mathbb{C}^{n \times n'}$, and $C \in \mathbb{C}^{p \times p'}$ we have

$$
\begin{aligned}
(A \otimes (B \otimes C))[j,k] &= A[j/(np), k/(n'p')] \times (B \otimes C)[j \bmod (np), k \bmod (n'p')] \\
&= A[j/(np), k/(n'p')] \times B[(j \bmod (np))/p, (k \bmod (n'p'))/p'] \\
&\quad \times C[(j \bmod (np)) \bmod p, (k \bmod (n'p')) \bmod p'] \\
&= A[(j/p)/n, (k/p')/n'] \times B[(j/p) \bmod n, (k/p') \bmod n'] \\
&\quad \times C[j \bmod p, k \bmod p'] = (A \otimes B)[j/p, k/p',] \\
&\quad \times C[j \bmod p, k \bmod p'] = ((A \otimes B) \otimes C)[j,k].
\end{aligned}
$$

$$(B.43)$$

The center equality follows from these three identities that can easily be checked:

$$j/(np) = (j/n)/p, \tag{B.44}$$

$$(j \bmod (np))/p = (j/p) \bmod n, \tag{B.45}$$

$$(j \bmod (np)) \bmod p = j \bmod p. \tag{B.46}$$

Ex. 2.7.7: They are both equal to

$$\begin{bmatrix} 2 & 6 \\ 4 & 8 \\ 3 & 9 \\ 6 & 12 \end{bmatrix}. \tag{B.47}$$

Ex. 2.7.8: For $A \in \mathbb{C}^{m \times m'}$ and $B \in \mathbb{C}^{n \times n'}$, we have

$$(A \otimes B)^\dagger[j, k] = \overline{(A \otimes B)[k, j]} = \overline{(A[k/n, j/n'] \times B[k \bmod n, j \bmod n'])}$$

$$= \overline{A[k/n, j/n']} \times \overline{B[k \bmod n, j \bmod n']}$$

$$= A^\dagger[j/n', k/n] \times B^\dagger[j \bmod n', k \bmod n]$$

$$= (A^\dagger \otimes B^\dagger)[j, k]. \tag{B.48}$$

Ex. 2.7.9: For $A \in \mathbb{C}^{m \times m'}$, $A' \in \mathbb{C}^{m' \times m''}$, $B \in \mathbb{C}^{n \times n'}$, and $B' \in \mathbb{C}^{n' \times n''}$ we will have $(A \star A') \in \mathbb{C}^{m \times m''}$, $(B \star B') \in \mathbb{C}^{n \times n''}$, $(A \otimes B) \in \mathbb{C}^{mn \times m'n'}$, and $(A' \otimes B') \in \mathbb{C}^{m'n' \times m''n''}$.

$$((A \otimes B) \star (A' \otimes B'))[j, k] = \sum_{t=0}^{m'n'-1} ((A \otimes B)[j, t] \times (A' \otimes B')[t, k])$$

$$= \sum_{t=0}^{m'n'-1} (A[j/n, t/n'] \times B[j \bmod n, t \bmod n']$$

$$\times A'[t/n', k/n''] \times B'[t \bmod n', k \bmod n'']). \tag{B.49}$$

These $m'n'$ terms can be rearranged as follows:

$$\left(\sum_{i=0}^{m'-1} A[j/n, i] \times A'[i, k/n'] \right) \times \left(\sum_{i=0}^{n'-1} B[j \bmod n, i] \times B'[i, k \bmod n'] \right)$$

$$= (A \star A')[j/n, k/n'] \times (B \star B')[j \bmod n, k \bmod n']$$

$$= ((A \star A') \otimes (B \star B'))[j, k]. \tag{B.50}$$

CHAPTER 3

Ex. 3.1.1:

$$[0, 0, 20, 2, 0, 5]^T. \tag{B.51}$$

Ex. 3.1.2:

$$MM = M^2 = \begin{bmatrix} 0 & 0 & 0 & 0 & 0 & 0 \\ 0 & 0 & 0 & 0 & 0 & 0 \\ 1 & 0 & 0 & 0 & 1 & 0 \\ 0 & 0 & 0 & 1 & 0 & 0 \\ 0 & 1 & 0 & 0 & 0 & 1 \\ 0 & 0 & 1 & 0 & 0 & 0 \end{bmatrix}, \tag{B.52}$$

$$MMM = M^2 M = MM^2 = M^3 = \begin{bmatrix} 0 & 0 & 0 & 0 & 0 & 0 \\ 0 & 0 & 0 & 0 & 0 & 0 \\ 0 & 0 & 1 & 0 & 0 & 0 \\ 0 & 0 & 0 & 1 & 0 & 0 \\ 1 & 0 & 0 & 0 & 1 & 0 \\ 0 & 1 & 0 & 0 & 0 & 1 \end{bmatrix}, \tag{B.53}$$

$$M^6 = M^3 M^3 = \begin{bmatrix} 0 & 0 & 0 & 0 & 0 & 0 \\ 0 & 0 & 0 & 0 & 0 & 0 \\ 0 & 0 & 1 & 0 & 0 & 0 \\ 0 & 0 & 0 & 1 & 0 & 0 \\ 1 & 0 & 0 & 0 & 1 & 0 \\ 0 & 1 & 0 & 0 & 0 & 1 \end{bmatrix}. \tag{B.54}$$

They all end up in vertex 2.

Ex. 3.1.3: The marbles in each vertex would "magically" multiply themselves and the many copies of the marbles would go to each vertex that has an edge connecting them. Think nondeterminism!

Ex. 3.1.4: The marbles would "magically" disappear.

Ex. 3.1.5: The adjacency matrix is

$$A = \begin{bmatrix} 0 & 1 & 0 & 0 & 0 & 0 & 0 & 0 & 0 \\ 1 & 0 & 0 & 0 & 0 & 0 & 0 & 0 & 0 \\ 0 & 0 & 0 & 0 & 0 & 0 & 0 & 0 & 0 \\ 0 & 0 & 0 & 1 & 0 & 0 & 0 & 0 & 0 \\ 0 & 0 & 0 & 0 & 0 & 0 & 0 & 0 & 0 \\ 0 & 0 & 1 & 0 & 0 & 0 & 0 & 0 & 0 \\ 0 & 0 & 0 & 0 & 0 & 0 & 0 & 0 & 0 \\ 0 & 0 & 0 & 0 & 1 & 0 & 1 & 0 & 0 \\ 0 & 0 & 0 & 0 & 0 & 1 & 0 & 1 & 1 \end{bmatrix}, \tag{B.55}$$

$$A^2 = \begin{bmatrix} 1 & 0 & 0 & 0 & 0 & 0 & 0 & 0 & 0 \\ 0 & 1 & 0 & 0 & 0 & 0 & 0 & 0 & 0 \\ 0 & 0 & 0 & 0 & 0 & 0 & 0 & 0 & 0 \\ 0 & 0 & 0 & 1 & 0 & 0 & 0 & 0 & 0 \\ 0 & 0 & 0 & 0 & 0 & 0 & 0 & 0 & 0 \\ 0 & 0 & 0 & 0 & 0 & 0 & 0 & 0 & 0 \\ 0 & 0 & 0 & 0 & 0 & 0 & 0 & 0 & 0 \\ 0 & 0 & 0 & 0 & 0 & 0 & 0 & 0 & 0 \\ 0 & 0 & 1 & 0 & 1 & 1 & 1 & 1 & 1 \end{bmatrix}; \quad A^4 = \begin{bmatrix} 1 & 0 & 0 & 0 & 0 & 0 & 0 & 0 & 0 \\ 0 & 1 & 0 & 0 & 0 & 0 & 0 & 0 & 0 \\ 0 & 0 & 0 & 0 & 0 & 0 & 0 & 0 & 0 \\ 0 & 0 & 0 & 1 & 0 & 0 & 0 & 0 & 0 \\ 0 & 0 & 0 & 0 & 0 & 0 & 0 & 0 & 0 \\ 0 & 0 & 0 & 0 & 0 & 0 & 0 & 0 & 0 \\ 0 & 0 & 0 & 0 & 0 & 0 & 0 & 0 & 0 \\ 0 & 0 & 0 & 0 & 0 & 0 & 0 & 0 & 0 \\ 0 & 0 & 1 & 0 & 1 & 1 & 1 & 1 & 1 \end{bmatrix}. \tag{B.56}$$

If we start in state $X = [1, 1, 1, 1, 1, 1, 1, 1, 1]^T$, then $AX = [1\ 1\ 0\ 1\ 0\ 1\ 0\ 2\ 3]^T$, and $A^2 X = A^4 X = [1\ 1\ 0\ 1\ 0\ 0\ 0\ 0\ 6]^T$.

Ex. 3.2.1:

$$Y = \left[\frac{5}{12}, \frac{3}{12}, \frac{4}{12}\right]^T. \tag{B.57}$$

Ex. 3.2.2: We are given that $\sum_i M[i, k] = 1$ and $\sum_i X[i] = 1$. Then we have

$$\sum_i Y[i] = \sum_i (MX)[i] = \sum_i \sum_k (M[i, k]X[k])$$

$$= \sum_k \sum_i (M[i, k]X[k]) = \sum_k (\sum_i M[i, k])X[k] = \sum_k (1 \times X[k]) = 1.$$

$$(\text{B.58})$$

Ex. 3.2.3: This is done almost exactly like Exercise 3.2.2.

Ex. 3.2.4:

$$M \star N = \begin{bmatrix} \frac{1}{2} & \frac{1}{2} \\ \frac{1}{2} & \frac{1}{2} \end{bmatrix}. \tag{B.59}$$

Ex. 3.2.5: Let M and N be two doubly stochastic matrices. We shall show that the jth row of $M \star N$ sums to 1 for any j. (The computation for the kth column is similar.)

$$\sum_i (M \star N)[j, i] = \sum_i \sum_k (M[j, k] \times N[k, i]) = \sum_k \sum_i (M[j, k] \times N[k, i])$$

$$= \sum_k \left[M[j, k] \times (\sum_i N[k, i]) \right] = \sum_k [M[j, k] \times (1)] = 1. \quad (\text{B.60})$$

Ex. 3.2.6: Let m stand for math, p stand for physics, and c stand for computer science. Then the corresponding adjacency matrix is

$$A = \begin{array}{c} m \\ p \\ c \end{array} \begin{array}{c} m \quad p \quad c \\ \begin{bmatrix} 0.1 & 0.7 & 0.2 \\ 0.6 & 0.2 & 0.2 \\ 0.3 & 0.1 & 0.6 \end{bmatrix} \end{array}; \quad A^2 = \begin{bmatrix} 0.49 & 0.23 & 0.28 \\ 0.24 & 0.48 & 0.28 \\ 0.27 & 0.29 & 0.44 \end{bmatrix}; \tag{B.61}$$

$$A^4 = \begin{bmatrix} 0.3709 & 0.3043 & 0.3248 \\ 0.3084 & 0.3668 & 0.3248 \\ 0.3207 & 0.3289 & 0.3504 \end{bmatrix}; \quad A^8 = \begin{bmatrix} 0.335576 & 0.331309 & 0.333115 \\ 0.33167 & 0.335215 & 0.333115 \\ 0.332754 & 0.333476 & 0.33377 \end{bmatrix}. $$

$$(\text{B.62})$$

To calculate the probable majors, multiply these matrices by $[1, 0, 0]^T$, $[0, 1, 0]^T$, and $[0, 0, 1]^T$.

Ex. 3.3.1:

$$\begin{bmatrix} \cos^2 \theta & \sin^2 \theta & 0 \\ \sin^2 \theta & \cos^2 \theta & 0 \\ 0 & 0 & 1 \end{bmatrix}. \tag{B.63}$$

The fact that it is doubly stochastic follows from the trigonometric identity

$$\sin^2 \theta + \cos^2 \theta = 1. \tag{B.64}$$

Ex. 3.3.2: Let U be a unitary matrix. U being unitary means that

$$(U \star U^\dagger)[j, k] = \sum_i (U[j, i] \times U^\dagger[i, k]) = \sum_i \left(U[j, i] \times \overline{U[k, i]} \right) = \delta_{j,k}, \tag{B.65}$$

where $\delta_{j,k}$ is the Kronecker delta function. We shall show that the sum of the jth row of the modulus squared elements is 1. A similar proof shows the same for the kth column.

$$\sum_k |U[j, k]|^2 = \sum_k \left(U[j, k] \times \overline{U[j, k]} \right) = \delta_{j,j} = 1. \tag{B.66}$$

The first equality follows from Equation (1.49).

Ex. 3.3.3: Let U be unitary and X be a column vector such that $\sum_j |X[j]|^2 = x$.

$$\sum_j |(U \star X)[j]|^2 = \sum_j \left| \sum_k (U[j, k] \times X[j]) \right|^2 = \sum_j \sum_k |(U[j, k] \times X[j])|^2$$

$$= \sum_j \sum_k \left[(U[j, k] \times X[j]) \times \overline{(U[j, k] \times X[j])} \right]$$

$$= \sum_j \sum_k (|U[j, k]|^2 \times |X[j]|^2) = 1 \times x = x, \tag{B.67}$$

which follows from the solution to Exercise 3.3.2.

Ex. 3.4.2:

$$N \otimes N = \begin{bmatrix} \frac{1}{9} & \frac{2}{9} & \frac{2}{9} & \frac{4}{9} \\ \frac{2}{9} & \frac{1}{9} & \frac{4}{9} & \frac{2}{9} \\ \frac{2}{9} & \frac{4}{9} & \frac{1}{9} & \frac{2}{9} \\ \frac{4}{9} & \frac{2}{9} & \frac{2}{9} & \frac{1}{9} \end{bmatrix}. \tag{B.68}$$

Ex. 3.4.3:

$$M \otimes N = \begin{bmatrix} \frac{1}{6} & \frac{1}{6} & \frac{2}{6} & \frac{2}{6} \\ \frac{1}{6} & \frac{1}{6} & \frac{2}{6} & \frac{2}{6} \\ \frac{2}{6} & \frac{2}{6} & \frac{1}{6} & \frac{1}{6} \\ \frac{2}{6} & \frac{2}{6} & \frac{1}{6} & \frac{1}{6} \end{bmatrix}. \tag{B.69}$$

Ex. 3.4.4: For $M \in \mathbb{C}^{m \times m'}$ and $N \in \mathbb{C}^{n \times n'}$, we will have $M \otimes N \in \mathbb{C}^{mn \times m'n'}$. The edge from j to k in $G_{M \otimes N}$ will have weight

$$M[j/n, k/n'] \times N[j \bmod n, k \bmod n'] \tag{B.70}$$

and will correspond to the pairs of edges

$$\langle j/n \longrightarrow k/n', j \bmod n \longrightarrow k \bmod n' \rangle. \tag{B.71}$$

Ex. 3.4.5: This is very similar to Exercise 3.4.4.

Ex. 3.4.6: "One marble traveling on the M graph and one marble traveling on the N graph" is the same as "One marble on the N graph and one marble on the M graph."

Ex. 3.4.7: It basically means that "A marble moves from the M graph to the M' graph and a marble moves from the N graph to the N' graph." It is the same as saying "Two marbles move from the M and N graph to the M' and N' graph, respectively. See the graph given in Equation (5.47).

CHAPTER 4

Ex. 4.1.1: The length of $|\psi\rangle$ is $|\psi\rangle| = 4.4721$. We get $p(x_3) = \frac{1}{4.4721^2} \cdot p(x_4) = \frac{4}{4.4721^2}$.

Ex. 4.1.2: This was done in the text where $c = 2$. The general problem is exactly the same.

Ex. 4.1.3: If they represented the same state, there would be a complex scalar c such that the second vector is the first one times c. The first component of the second vector is $2 \star (1 + i)$, and $1 + i$ is the first component of the first vector. However, if we multiply the second component, we get $2(2 - i) = 4 - 2i$, not $1 - 2i$. Hence, they do not represent the same state.

Ex. 4.1.9: $\langle \psi | = [3 - i, 2i]$.

Ex. 4.2.2: $S_x |\uparrow\rangle = |\downarrow\rangle$. (It flips them!) If we measure spin in state down, it will stay there; therefore, the probability to find it still in state up is zero.

Ex. 4.2.3: Taking $A[j, k] = \overline{A[k, j]}$ as the definition of hermitian, we consider $r \cdot A$, where r is a scalar.

$$(r \cdot A)[j, k] = r \times A[j, k] = r \times \overline{A[k, j]} = \overline{(r \cdot A)[k, j]}. \tag{B.72}$$

We used the fact that for any real $r, r = \bar{r}$.

Ex. 4.2.4: Let $M = \begin{bmatrix} 0 & 1 \\ 1 & 0 \end{bmatrix}$. M is certainly hermitian (in fact, real symmetric). Multiply it by i:

$$N = i M = \begin{bmatrix} 0 & i \\ i & 0 \end{bmatrix}. \tag{B.73}$$

Now, N is not hermitian: the adjoint of N is $\begin{bmatrix} 0 & -i \\ -i & 0 \end{bmatrix}$, whereas every hermitian is its own adjoint.

Ex. 4.2.5 Let A and A' be two hermitian matrices.

$$(A + A')[j, k] = A[j, k] + A'[j, k] = \overline{A[k, j]} + \overline{A'[k, j]}$$
$$= \overline{A[k, j] + A'[k, j]} = \overline{(A + A')[k, j]}. \tag{B.74}$$

Ex. 4.2.6 Both matrices are trivially hermitian by direct inspection (the first one has i and $-i$ on the nondiagonal elements, and the second is diagonal with real entries). Let us calculate their products:

$$\Omega_1 \star \Omega_2 = \begin{bmatrix} 2 & -4i \\ 2i & 4 \end{bmatrix}, \tag{B.75}$$

$$\Omega_2 \star \Omega_1 = \begin{bmatrix} 2 & -2i \\ 4i & 4 \end{bmatrix}. \tag{B.76}$$

They do not commute.

Ex. 4.2.7

$$[\Omega_1, \Omega_2] = \Omega_1 \star \Omega_2 - \Omega_2 \star \Omega_1$$

$$= \begin{bmatrix} 1+i & -3-2i \\ -1 & 3-i \end{bmatrix} - \begin{bmatrix} 1-i & -1 \\ -3+2i & 3+i \end{bmatrix} = \begin{bmatrix} 2i & -2-2i \\ 2-2i & -2i \end{bmatrix}. \tag{B.77}$$

CHAPTER 5

Ex. 5.1.1:

$$(3 + 2i)|0\rangle + (4 - 2i)|1\rangle. \tag{B.78}$$

Ex. 5.1.2:

$$(0.67286 - 0.15252i)|0\rangle + (0.09420 - 0.71772i)|1\rangle. \tag{B.79}$$

Ex. 5.1.3:

$$|1\rangle \otimes |0\rangle \otimes |1\rangle = \begin{matrix} 000 \\ 001 \\ 010 \\ 011 \\ 100 \\ 101 \\ 110 \\ 111 \end{matrix} \begin{bmatrix} 0 \\ 0 \\ 0 \\ 0 \\ 0 \\ 1 \\ 0 \\ 0 \end{bmatrix}; \quad |011\rangle = \begin{matrix} 000 \\ 001 \\ 010 \\ 011 \\ 100 \\ 101 \\ 110 \\ 111 \end{matrix} \begin{bmatrix} 0 \\ 0 \\ 0 \\ 1 \\ 0 \\ 0 \\ 0 \\ 0 \end{bmatrix}; \quad |1,1,1\rangle = \begin{matrix} 000 \\ 001 \\ 010 \\ 011 \\ 100 \\ 101 \\ 110 \\ 111 \end{matrix} \begin{bmatrix} 0 \\ 0 \\ 0 \\ 0 \\ 0 \\ 0 \\ 0 \\ 1 \end{bmatrix}.$$

(B.80)

Ex. 5.1.4:

$$\begin{matrix} 00 \\ 01 \\ 10 \\ 11 \end{matrix} \begin{bmatrix} 0 \\ 3 \\ 0 \\ 2 \end{bmatrix}.$$

(B.81)

Ex. 5.2.1:

$$\begin{bmatrix} 1 & 1 & 1 & 0 \\ 0 & 0 & 0 & 1 \end{bmatrix} \begin{bmatrix} 0 \\ 0 \\ 1 \\ 0 \end{bmatrix} = \begin{bmatrix} 1 \\ 0 \end{bmatrix} = |0\rangle.$$

(B.82)

Ex. 5.2.2:

$$\begin{bmatrix} 1 & 0 & 0 & 0 \\ 0 & 1 & 1 & 1 \end{bmatrix} \begin{bmatrix} w \\ x \\ y \\ z \end{bmatrix} = \begin{bmatrix} 0 \\ 1 \end{bmatrix} = |1\rangle.$$

(B.83)

if and only if either x or y or z is 1.

Ex. 5.2.3:

$$NOR = NOT \star OR = \begin{bmatrix} 0 & 1 \\ 1 & 0 \end{bmatrix} \begin{bmatrix} 1 & 0 & 0 & 0 \\ 0 & 1 & 1 & 1 \end{bmatrix} = \begin{bmatrix} 0 & 1 & 1 & 1 \\ 1 & 0 & 0 & 0 \end{bmatrix}.$$

(B.84)

Ex. 5.2.4: It means that it does not matter which operation is the "top" and which is the "bottom," i.e., the wires can be crossed as follows:

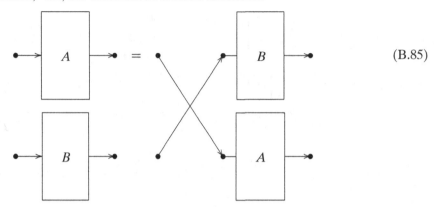

$$\text{(B.85)}$$

Ex. 5.2.5: It means that we can think of the diagram as doing parallel operations, each of which contain two sequential operations, or equivalently, we can think of the diagram as representing two sequential operations, each consisting of two parallel operations. Either way, the action of the operations are the same.

Ex. 5.2.7:

$$NOT \star OR \star (NOT \otimes NOT)$$

$$= \begin{bmatrix} 0 & 1 \\ 1 & 0 \end{bmatrix} \star \begin{bmatrix} 1 & 0 & 0 & 0 \\ 0 & 1 & 1 & 1 \end{bmatrix} \star \begin{bmatrix} 0 & 1 \\ 1 & 0 \end{bmatrix} \otimes \begin{bmatrix} 0 & 1 \\ 1 & 0 \end{bmatrix} = \begin{bmatrix} 1 & 1 & 1 & 0 \\ 0 & 0 & 0 & 1 \end{bmatrix}$$

$$= AND. \tag{B.86}$$

Ex. 5.2.8:

	000	001	010	011	100	101	110	111
00	1	0	0	0	0	0	0	0
01	0	0	0	1	0	1	1	0
10	0	1	1	0	1	0	0	0
11	0	0	0	0	0	0	0	1

$$\text{(B.87)}$$

Ex. 5.3.2:

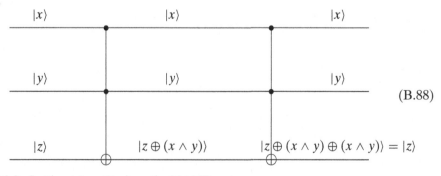

$$\text{(B.88)}$$

Ex. 5.3.3: Setting $|z\rangle = |1\rangle$ gives the NAND gate.

Ex. 5.3.4: Combining a Fredkin gate followed by a Fredkin gate gives the following:

$$|0, y, z\rangle \longmapsto |0, y, z\rangle \longmapsto |0, y, z\rangle \tag{B.89}$$

and

$$|1, y, z\rangle \longmapsto |1, z, y\rangle \longmapsto |1, y, z\rangle. \tag{B.90}$$

Ex. 5.4.1: Except for Y all of them are their own conjugate. Simple multiplication shows that one gets the identity.

Ex. 5.4.2:

$$\begin{bmatrix} 0 & 1 \\ 1 & 0 \end{bmatrix} \begin{bmatrix} c_0 \\ c_1 \end{bmatrix} = \begin{bmatrix} c_1 \\ c_0 \end{bmatrix}, \tag{B.91}$$

$$\begin{bmatrix} 0 & -i \\ i & 0 \end{bmatrix} \begin{bmatrix} a_0 + b_0 i \\ a_1 + b_1 i \end{bmatrix} = \begin{bmatrix} b_1 - a_1 i \\ -b_0 + a_0 i \end{bmatrix}. \tag{B.92}$$

Ex. 5.4.9: One way of doing this is to show that both gates have the same matrix that performs the action.

CHAPTER 6

Exercise	$0\bullet \longmapsto \bullet 0$ $1\bullet \longmapsto \bullet 1$	$0\bullet \longmapsto \bullet 0$ $1\bullet \quad\quad \bullet 1$	$0\bullet \quad\quad \bullet 0$ $1\bullet \longmapsto \bullet 1$
6.1.1 :	$\begin{matrix} & 0 & 1 \\ 0 & 1 & 0 \\ 1 & 0 & 1 \end{matrix}$	$\begin{matrix} & 0 & 1 \\ 0 & 1 & 1 \\ 1 & 0 & 0 \end{matrix}$	$\begin{matrix} & 0 & 1 \\ 0 & 0 & 0 \\ 1 & 1 & 1 \end{matrix}$
6.1.3	$\begin{bmatrix} 1 & 0 & 0 & 0 \\ 0 & 1 & 0 & 0 \\ 0 & 0 & 0 & 1 \\ 0 & 0 & 1 & 0 \end{bmatrix}$	$\begin{matrix} & 00 & 01 & 10 & 11 \\ 00 & 1 & 0 & 0 & 0 \\ 01 & 0 & 1 & 0 & 0 \\ 10 & 0 & 0 & 1 & 0 \\ 11 & 0 & 0 & 0 & 1 \end{matrix}$	$\begin{matrix} & 00 & 01 & 10 & 11 \\ 00 & 0 & 1 & 0 & 0 \\ 01 & 1 & 0 & 0 & 0 \\ 10 & 0 & 0 & 0 & 1 \\ 11 & 0 & 0 & 1 & 0 \end{matrix}$
6.1.4 :	$\frac{|0,0\rangle + |1,1\rangle}{\sqrt{2}}$	$\frac{|0,0\rangle + |1,0\rangle}{\sqrt{2}}$	$\frac{|0,1\rangle + |1,1\rangle}{\sqrt{2}}$
6.1.5 :	$\left[\frac{|0\rangle - |1\rangle}{\sqrt{2}} \right] \left[\frac{|0\rangle - |1\rangle}{\sqrt{2}} \right]$	$\left[\frac{|0\rangle + |1\rangle}{\sqrt{2}} \right] \left[\frac{|0\rangle - |1\rangle}{\sqrt{2}} \right]$	$\left[\frac{-|0\rangle - |1\rangle}{\sqrt{2}} \right] \left[\frac{|0\rangle - |1\rangle}{\sqrt{2}} \right]$
6.1.6 :	$+1|1\rangle \left[\frac{|0\rangle - |1\rangle}{\sqrt{2}} \right]$	$+1|0\rangle \left[\frac{|0\rangle - |1\rangle}{\sqrt{2}} \right]$	$-1|0\rangle \left[\frac{|0\rangle - |1\rangle}{\sqrt{2}} \right]$

$$\tag{B.93}$$

Ex 6.1.2: The conjugation of this matrix is the same as the original. If you multiply it by itself, you get I_4.

Ex. 6.2.1: $2^{(2^n)}$, $_{2^n}C_{2^{n-1}} = \frac{(2^n)!}{((2^{n-1})!)^2}$ and 2.

Ex. 6.2.2:

$$
\begin{array}{c}
\begin{array}{cccccccc}
00,0 & 00,1 & 01,0 & 01,1 & 10,0 & 10,1 & 11,0 & 11,1
\end{array} \\
\begin{array}{c}
00,0 \\ 00,1 \\ 01,0 \\ 01,1 \\ 10,0 \\ 10,1 \\ 11,0 \\ 11,1
\end{array}
\left[
\begin{array}{cccccccc}
1 & & & & & & & \\
 & 1 & & & & & & \\
 & & 1 & & & & & \\
 & & & 1 & & & & \\
 & & & & & 1 & & \\
 & & & & 1 & & & \\
 & & & & & & & 1 \\
 & & & & & & 1 &
\end{array}
\right].
\end{array}
\tag{B.94}
$$

Ex. 6.2.3:

$$
\begin{array}{c}
\begin{array}{cccccccc}
00,0 & 00,1 & 01,0 & 01,1 & 10,0 & 10,1 & 11,0 & 11,1
\end{array} \\
\begin{array}{c}
00,0 \\ 00,1 \\ 01,0 \\ 01,1 \\ 10,0 \\ 10,1 \\ 11,0 \\ 11,1
\end{array}
\left[
\begin{array}{cccccccc}
 & 1 & & & & & & \\
1 & & & & & & & \\
 & & & 1 & & & & \\
 & & 1 & & & & & \\
 & & & & & 1 & & \\
 & & & & 1 & & & \\
 & & & & & & & 1 \\
 & & & & & & 1 &
\end{array}
\right].
\end{array}
\tag{B.95}
$$

Ex. 6.2.4: We saw for $n = 1$, the scalar coefficient is $2^{-\frac{1}{2}}$. Assume it is true for $n = k$. That is the scalar coefficient of $H^{\otimes k}$ is $2^{-\frac{k}{2}}$. For $n = k + 1$, that coefficient will be multiplied by $2^{-\frac{1}{2}}$ to get

$$
2^{-\frac{k}{2}} 2^{-\frac{1}{2}} = 2^{-(\frac{k}{2} + \frac{1}{2})} = 2^{-\frac{k+1}{2}}.
\tag{B.96}
$$

Ex. 6.2.5: It depends how far away the function is from being balanced or constant. If it is close to constant than we will *probably* get $|0\rangle$ when we measure the top qubit. If it is close to constant, then we will *probably* get $|1\rangle$. Otherwise it will be random.

Ex. 6.3.1:

- $000 \oplus 011 = 011$; hence, $f(000) = f(011)$.
- $001 \oplus 011 = 010$; hence, $f(001) = f(010)$.
- $010 \oplus 011 = 001$; hence, $f(010) = f(001)$.
- $011 \oplus 011 = 000$; hence, $f(011) = f(000)$.
- $100 \oplus 011 = 111$; hence, $f(100) = f(111)$.
- $101 \oplus 011 = 110$; hence, $f(101) = f(110)$.
- $110 \oplus 011 = 101$; hence, $f(110) = f(101)$.
- $111 \oplus 011 = 101$; hence, $f(111) = f(101)$.

Ex. 6.4.1: For the function that "picks out" 00, we have

	00,0	00,1	01,0	01,1	10,0	10,1	11,0	11,1
00,0		1						
00,1	1							
01,0			1					
01,1				1				
10,0					1			
10,1						1		
11,0							1	
11,1								1

$$\text{(B.97)}$$

For the function that "picks out" 01, we have

	00,0	00,1	01,0	01,1	10,0	10,1	11,0	11,1
00,0	1							
00,1		1						
01,0				1				
01,1			1					
10,0					1			
10,1						1		
11,0							1	
11,1								1

$$\text{(B.98)}$$

For the function that "picks out" 11, we have

	00,0	00,1	01,0	01,1	10,0	10,1	11,0	11,1
00,0	1							
00,1		1						
01,0			1					
01,1				1				
10,0					1			
10,1						1		
11,0								1
11,1							1	

$$\text{(B.99)}$$

Ex. 6.4.2: The average is 36.5. The inverted numbers are 68, 35, 11, 15, 52, and 38.

Ex. 6.4.3:

$$(A \star A)[i, j] = \sum_k A[i, k] \times A[k, j] = \sum_k \left(\frac{1}{2^n} \times \frac{1}{2^n} \right)$$

$$= 2^n \times \left(\frac{1}{2^n} \times \frac{1}{2^n} \right) = \frac{1}{2^n} = A[i, j]. \qquad \text{(B.100)}$$

Ex. 6.5.1: 160, 123, and 1.

Ex. 6.5.2: The remainders of the pairs are 1, 128, and 221.

Ex. 6.5.4: The periods are 36, 18, and 18.

Ex. 6.5.7: $GCD(7^6 + 1, 247) = GCD(117650, 247) = 13$ and $GCD(7^6 - 1, 247) = GCD(117648, 247) = 19$. $13 \times 19 = 247$.

CHAPTER 7

Ex. 7.2.2:

$$U1 = CNOT \otimes CNOT; \quad U2 = U1 \star U1$$

$$= (CNOT \otimes CNOT) \star (CNOT \otimes CNOT). \tag{B.101}$$

$$CNOT = \begin{bmatrix} 1 & 0 & 0 & 0 \\ 0 & 1 & 0 & 0 \\ 0 & 0 & 0 & 1 \\ 0 & 0 & 1 & 0 \end{bmatrix}. \tag{B.102}$$

$$CNOT \otimes CNOT = \begin{bmatrix} 1 & 0 & 0 & 0 & 0 & 0 & 0 & 0 & 0 & 0 & 0 & 0 & 0 & 0 & 0 & 0 \\ 0 & 1 & 0 & 0 & 0 & 0 & 0 & 0 & 0 & 0 & 0 & 0 & 0 & 0 & 0 & 0 \\ 0 & 0 & 0 & 1 & 0 & 0 & 0 & 0 & 0 & 0 & 0 & 0 & 0 & 0 & 0 & 0 \\ 0 & 0 & 1 & 0 & 0 & 0 & 0 & 0 & 0 & 0 & 0 & 0 & 0 & 0 & 0 & 0 \\ 0 & 0 & 0 & 0 & 1 & 0 & 0 & 0 & 0 & 0 & 0 & 0 & 0 & 0 & 0 & 0 \\ 0 & 0 & 0 & 0 & 0 & 1 & 0 & 0 & 0 & 0 & 0 & 0 & 0 & 0 & 0 & 0 \\ 0 & 0 & 0 & 0 & 0 & 0 & 0 & 1 & 0 & 0 & 0 & 0 & 0 & 0 & 0 & 0 \\ 0 & 0 & 0 & 0 & 0 & 0 & 1 & 0 & 0 & 0 & 0 & 0 & 0 & 0 & 0 & 0 \\ 0 & 0 & 0 & 0 & 0 & 0 & 0 & 0 & 0 & 0 & 0 & 0 & 1 & 0 & 0 & 0 \\ 0 & 0 & 0 & 0 & 0 & 0 & 0 & 0 & 0 & 0 & 0 & 0 & 0 & 1 & 0 & 0 \\ 0 & 0 & 0 & 0 & 0 & 0 & 0 & 0 & 0 & 0 & 0 & 0 & 0 & 0 & 0 & 1 \\ 0 & 0 & 0 & 0 & 0 & 0 & 0 & 0 & 0 & 0 & 0 & 0 & 0 & 0 & 1 & 0 \\ 0 & 0 & 0 & 0 & 0 & 0 & 0 & 0 & 1 & 0 & 0 & 0 & 0 & 0 & 0 & 0 \\ 0 & 0 & 0 & 0 & 0 & 0 & 0 & 0 & 0 & 1 & 0 & 0 & 0 & 0 & 0 & 0 \\ 0 & 0 & 0 & 0 & 0 & 0 & 0 & 0 & 0 & 0 & 0 & 1 & 0 & 0 & 0 & 0 \\ 0 & 0 & 0 & 0 & 0 & 0 & 0 & 0 & 0 & 0 & 1 & 0 & 0 & 0 & 0 & 0 \end{bmatrix}. \tag{B.103}$$

$(CNOT \otimes CNOT) \star (CNOT \otimes CNOT) =$

$$\begin{bmatrix} 1 & 0 & 0 & 0 & 0 & 0 & 0 & 0 & 0 & 0 & 0 & 0 & 0 & 0 & 0 & 0 \\ 0 & 1 & 0 & 0 & 0 & 0 & 0 & 0 & 0 & 0 & 0 & 0 & 0 & 0 & 0 & 0 \\ 0 & 0 & 1 & 0 & 0 & 0 & 0 & 0 & 0 & 0 & 0 & 0 & 0 & 0 & 0 & 0 \\ 0 & 0 & 0 & 1 & 0 & 0 & 0 & 0 & 0 & 0 & 0 & 0 & 0 & 0 & 0 & 0 \\ 0 & 0 & 0 & 0 & 1 & 0 & 0 & 0 & 0 & 0 & 0 & 0 & 0 & 0 & 0 & 0 \\ 0 & 0 & 0 & 0 & 0 & 1 & 0 & 0 & 0 & 0 & 0 & 0 & 0 & 0 & 0 & 0 \\ 0 & 0 & 0 & 0 & 0 & 0 & 1 & 0 & 0 & 0 & 0 & 0 & 0 & 0 & 0 & 0 \\ 0 & 0 & 0 & 0 & 0 & 0 & 0 & 1 & 0 & 0 & 0 & 0 & 0 & 0 & 0 & 0 \\ 0 & 0 & 0 & 0 & 0 & 0 & 0 & 0 & 1 & 0 & 0 & 0 & 0 & 0 & 0 & 0 \\ 0 & 0 & 0 & 0 & 0 & 0 & 0 & 0 & 0 & 1 & 0 & 0 & 0 & 0 & 0 & 0 \\ 0 & 0 & 0 & 0 & 0 & 0 & 0 & 0 & 0 & 0 & 1 & 0 & 0 & 0 & 0 & 0 \\ 0 & 0 & 0 & 0 & 0 & 0 & 0 & 0 & 0 & 0 & 0 & 1 & 0 & 0 & 0 & 0 \\ 0 & 0 & 0 & 0 & 0 & 0 & 0 & 0 & 0 & 0 & 0 & 0 & 1 & 0 & 0 & 0 \\ 0 & 0 & 0 & 0 & 0 & 0 & 0 & 0 & 0 & 0 & 0 & 0 & 0 & 1 & 0 & 0 \\ 0 & 0 & 0 & 0 & 0 & 0 & 0 & 0 & 0 & 0 & 0 & 0 & 0 & 0 & 1 & 0 \\ 0 & 0 & 0 & 0 & 0 & 0 & 0 & 0 & 0 & 0 & 0 & 0 & 0 & 0 & 0 & 1 \end{bmatrix}. \qquad (B.104)$$

Ex. 7.2.3: Observe that U can be divided into four squares: the left on top is just the 2-by-2 identity, the right on top and the left at the bottom are both the 2-by-2 zero matrix, and finally the right at the bottom is the phase shift matrix R_{180}. Thus, $U = I_2 \otimes R_{180}$, and it acts on 2 qubits, leaving the first untouched and shift the phase of the second by 180.

CHAPTER 8

Ex. 8.1.2: $n = 1{,}417{,}122$.

Ex. 8.1.3: The best way to show this is with a series of trees that show how to split up at each step. If at a point, the Turing machine splits into $n > 2$ states, then perform something like the following substitution. If $n = 5$, split it into four steps as follows:

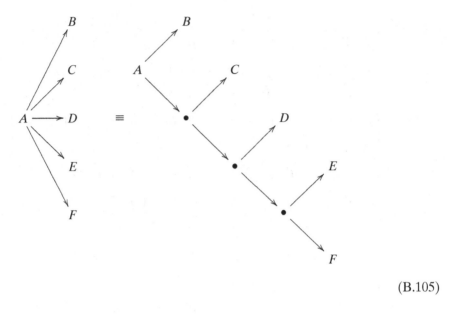

$$(\text{B}.105)$$

If $n = 2$, then no change has to be made. If $n = 1$, then do the following substitution:

$$A \longrightarrow B \quad \equiv \quad \begin{array}{c} B \\ \nearrow \\ A \\ \searrow \\ B \end{array} \qquad (\text{B}.106)$$

And finally, if $n = 0$, make the following substitution:

$$A \quad \equiv \quad \begin{array}{c} A \\ \nearrow \\ A \\ \searrow \\ A \end{array} \qquad (\text{B}.107)$$

Ex. 8.2.1: Following Exercise 8.1.3, every Turing machine can be made into one that at every step splits into exactly two configurations. When a real number is generated to determine which action the probabilistic Turing machine should perform, convert that real number to binary. Let that binary expansion determine which action to perform. If "0," then go up. If "1," then go down.

Ex 8.3.1: For a reversible Turing machine, every row of the matrix U will need to have exactly one 1 with the remaining entries 0. For a probabilistic Turing machine, every column of the matrix U will need to sum to 1.

Ex. 8.3.3: We see from the table in the text that Grover's algorithm starts getting quicker somewhere between 10 and 15. A little analysis gives us the following table:

	Classical Brute-Force Search		**Quantum Grover's Algorithm**	
n	2^n ops	Time	$\sqrt{2^n}$ ops	Time
10	1,024	0.01024 second	32	0.032 second
11	2,048	0.02048 second	45.254834	0.045254834 second
12	4,096	0.04096 second	64	0.064 second
13	8,192	0.08192 second	90.50966799	0.090509668 second
14	1,6384	0.16384 second	128	0.128 second
15	3,2768	0.32768 second	181.019336	0.181019336 second

(B.108)

Already at $n = 14$, Grover's algorithm is quicker.

Ex. 8.3.4:

	Classical Brute-Force Search		**Quantum Grover's Algorithm Search**	
n	$n!$ ops	Time	$\sqrt{n!}$ ops	Time
5	120	0.0012 second	10.95445115	0.010954451 second
10	3628800	36.288 seconds	1904.940944	1.904940944 seconds
15	1.30767E+12	151.3512 days	1143535.906	0.013235369 days
20	2.4329E+18	770940.1248 years	1559776269	18.05296607 days
25	1.55112E+25	4.91521E+12 years	3.93843E+12	124.8012319 years
30	2.65253E+32	8.40536E+19 years	1.62866E+16	516090.7443 years
40	8.15915E+47	2.58548E+35 years	9.0328E+23	2.86232E+13 years
50	3.04141E+64	9.63764E+51 years	1.74396E+32	5.52629E+21 years
60	8.32099E+81	2.63676E+69 years	9.12194E+40	2.89057E+30 years
70	1.1979E+100	3.79578E+87 years	1.09447E+50	3.46816E+39 years
100	9.3326E+157	2.9573E+145 years	9.66055E+78	3.06124E+68 years
125	1.8827E+209	5.9658E+196 years	4.339E+104	1.37494E+94 years

(B.109)

CHAPTER 9

Ex 9.1.1: No. It implies that $ENC(-, K_E)$ is injective (one-to-one) and that $DEC(-, K_D)$ is surjective (onto).

Ex 9.1.2: "QUANTUM CRYPTOGRAPHY IS FUN."

Ex 9.2.1:

- $|\leftarrow\rangle$ with respect to $+$ will be $-1|\rightarrow\rangle$.
- $|\downarrow\rangle$ with respect to $+$ will be $-1|\uparrow\rangle$.
- $|\nearrow\rangle$ with respect to $+$ will be $-\frac{1}{\sqrt{2}}|\uparrow\rangle - \frac{1}{\sqrt{2}}|\rightarrow\rangle$.
- $|\searrow\rangle$ with respect to $+$ will be $-\frac{1}{\sqrt{2}}|\uparrow\rangle + \frac{1}{\sqrt{2}}|\rightarrow\rangle$.
- $|\leftarrow\rangle$ with respect to X will be $-\frac{1}{\sqrt{2}}|\nearrow\rangle + \frac{1}{\sqrt{2}}|\searrow\rangle$.
- $|\downarrow\rangle$ with respect to X will be $-\frac{1}{\sqrt{2}}|\nearrow\rangle - \frac{1}{\sqrt{2}}|\searrow\rangle$.
- $|\nearrow\rangle$ with respect to X will be $-1|\nearrow\rangle$.
- $|\searrow\rangle$ with respect to X will be $-1|\searrow\rangle$.

CHAPTER 10

Ex 10.1.1: All probabilities p_i are positive numbers between 0 and 1. Therefore, all the logarithms $\log_2(p_i)$ are negative or zero, and so are all terms $p_i \log_2(p_i)$. Their sum is negative or zero and therefore entropy is always positive (it reaches zero only if one of the probabilities is 1).

Ex 10.1.3: Choose $p(A) = \frac{3}{4}$, $p(B) = \frac{1}{4}$, and $P(C) = p(D) = 0$. We get $H(S) = 0.81128$.

Ex 10.2.1: In Equation (10.14), D is defined as the sum of the projectors $|w_i\rangle\langle w_i|$ weighted by their probabilities. If Alice always send one state, say $|w_1\rangle$, that means that all the $p_i = 0$, except $p_1 = 1$. Replace them in D and you will find $D = 1|w_1\rangle\langle w_1|$.

Ex 10.2.3: Let us first write down the density operator:

$$D = \frac{1}{2}|0\rangle\langle 0| + \frac{1}{6}|1\rangle\langle 1| + \frac{1}{6}\left(\frac{1}{\sqrt{2}}|0\rangle + \frac{1}{\sqrt{2}}|1\rangle\right)\left(\frac{1}{\sqrt{2}}\langle 0| + \frac{1}{\sqrt{2}}\langle 1|\right)$$

$$+ \frac{1}{6}\left(\frac{1}{\sqrt{2}}|0\rangle - \frac{1}{\sqrt{2}}|1\rangle\right)\left(\frac{1}{\sqrt{2}}\langle 0| - \frac{1}{\sqrt{2}}\langle 1|\right) \tag{B.110}$$

Now, let us calculate $D(|0\rangle)$ and $D(|1\rangle)$:

$$D(|0\rangle) = \frac{2}{3}|0\rangle, \quad \text{and} \quad D(|1\rangle) = \frac{1}{3}|1\rangle. \tag{B.111}$$

Thus the matrix (we shall use the same letter D) in the standard basis is

$$D = \begin{bmatrix} \frac{2}{3} & 0 \\ 0 & \frac{1}{3} \end{bmatrix}. \tag{B.112}$$

Ex 10.4.1: Suppose you send "000" (i.e., the code for "0"). What are the chances that the message gets decoded wrongly? For that to happen, at least two flips must have occurred: "110," "011," "101," and "111." Now, the first three cases occur with probability $(0.25)^2 (0.75)$, and the last one with probability $(0.25)^3$ (under the assumption that flips occur independently).

The total probability is therefore $3 * (0.25)^2 (0.75) + (0.25)^3 = 0.15625$.

Similarly when you send "111."

CHAPTER 11

Ex 11.1.1: At first sight, the pure state

$$|\psi\rangle = \frac{1}{\sqrt{2}}|0\rangle + \frac{1}{\sqrt{2}}|1\rangle \tag{B.113}$$

and the mixed state obtained by having $|0\rangle$ or $|1\rangle$ with equal probability seem to be undistinguishable. If you measure $|\psi\rangle$ in the standard basis, you will get 50% of the time $|0\rangle$ and 50% of the time $|1\rangle$. However, if you measure $|\psi\rangle$ in the basis consisting of $|\psi\rangle$ itself, and its orthogonal

$$|\phi\rangle = \frac{1}{\sqrt{2}}|0\rangle - \frac{1}{\sqrt{2}}|1\rangle, \tag{B.114}$$

you will always detect $|\psi\rangle$. But, measuring the mixed state in that basis, you will get $|\psi\rangle$ 50% of the times and $|\phi\rangle$ 50% of the times. The change of basis discriminates between the two states.

Ex 11.1.2: Let us carry out the calculation of the average A. $|\psi\rangle$ is, in the standard basis, the column vector $[1, e^{i\theta}]^T$. Thus the average is

$$A = \frac{1}{\sqrt{2}} \begin{bmatrix} 1, & e^{-i\theta} \end{bmatrix} \frac{\hbar}{2} \begin{bmatrix} 0 & 1 \\ 1 & 0 \end{bmatrix} \frac{1}{\sqrt{2}} \begin{bmatrix} 1, e^{i\theta} \end{bmatrix}^T. \tag{B.115}$$

Multiplying, we get

$$A = \frac{\hbar}{4}(e^{-i\theta} + e^{i\theta}), \tag{B.116}$$

which simplifies to

$$A = \frac{\hbar}{2} \cos(\theta). \tag{B.117}$$

A does indeed depend on θ, and reaches a maximum at $\theta = 0$.

Ex 11.1.3: Let us compute the tensor product of S_x with itself first (we shall ignore the factor $\frac{\hbar}{2}$):

$$S_x \otimes S_x = \begin{bmatrix} 0 & 0 & 0 & 1 \\ 0 & 0 & 1 & 0 \\ 0 & 1 & 0 & 0 \\ 1 & 0 & 0 & 0 \end{bmatrix}. \tag{B.118}$$

We can now calculate the average:

$$\frac{1}{2}e^{-i\theta} + \frac{1}{2}e^{i\theta} = \cos(\theta) \tag{B.119}$$

(using the Euler formula). We have indeed recovered the hidden phase θ!

Appendix C
Quantum Computing Experiments
with MATLAB

C.1 PLAYING WITH MATLAB

There is no better way to learn than playing. After all, that is how children learn. In this appendix, we are going to provide the basic guidelines for "playing the quantum computing game" with the help of the MATLAB environment.

....

Reader Tip. This is not a full MATLAB tutorial. We assume that a fully functional version of MATLAB is already installed on your machine and that you know how to start a session, perform some basic calculations, save them, and quit. You should also know what M-files are and how to load them. For a crash brush up, you can read the online tutorial by MathWorks: http://www.mathworks.com/academia/student_center/tutorials/launchpad.html.   ♡

....

C.2 COMPLEX NUMBERS AND MATRICES

We began this book by saying that complex numbers are fundamental for both quantum mechanics and quantum computing, so we are going to familiarize ourselves with the way they are dealt with in MATLAB.

To begin with, we need to declare complex number variables. This is easy: a complex has a real part and an imaginary part, both double. The imaginary part is declared by using the "i" or "j" character.[1] For example, to declare the complex variable $c = 5 + 5i$, just type

⟩ c = 5 + 5i

and the computer will respond with

$c = 5.000 + 5.000i$

---

[1] Signal processing engineers tend to use "j" to denote the imaginary unit, hence the notation.

Or, equivalently,

⟩ c = 5 + 5j
$c = 5.000 + 5.000i$

Adding and multiplying complex numbers are entirely straightforward:

⟩ d = 3 − 2i
$d = 3 − 2i$

⟩ s = c + d
$s = 8 + 3i$

⟩ p = c * d
$p = 25 + 5i$

There is also a handy complex conjugate:

⟩ c1 = conj(c)
$c1 = 5.000 − 5.000i$

You may get the real and imaginary parts of a complex number by typing

⟩ re = real(c)
$re = 5$

⟩ im = imag(c)
$im = 5$

One can switch from Cartesian representation to polar representation:

⟩ r = abs(c)
$r = 7.0711$

⟩ a = angle(c)
$a = 0.78540.$

And back from polar to Cartesian:

⟩ c = r * exp(i * a)
$c1 = 5.0000 + 5.0000i$

It is extremely useful to plot a complex number. MATLAB has a lot of tools for mathematical visualization. We are going to present just one option here: the function **compass**:

⟩ compass(re, im)

The computer will output a picture of a complex number as an arrow as in Figure 1.1 on page 16. The compass function plots the complex number as a vector springing from the origin. The function can take several complex vectors at once (refer to the online MathWorks documentation).

Our second ingredient is complex matrices. MATLAB is extremely powerful in dealing with matrices; indeed, the name MATLAB means **MATrix LABoratory**. What about vectors? Well, vectors are matrices.[2] Nevertheless, first things first, so let us start with row and column vectors:

⟩ bra = [1, 2 − i, 3i]

$bra = 1 + 0i \ 2 − 1i \ 0 + 3i$

⟩ ket = bra′

$1 + 0i$
$2 + 1i$
$0 − 3i$

As you can see, the operator ′ on a complex matrix M is its adjoint (if the matrix is real, it is simply the transpose).

For the dot product (bra-ket), you just multiply them (there is, however, a dot( ) function):

⟩ bra ∗ ket

$ans = 15$

The norm function is built-in:

⟩ norm(ket)

$ans = 3.8730$

So much for vectors. Let us declare a matrix, say, Hadamard:

⟩ H = 1/sqrt(2) ∗ [1 1; 1 − 1]

$H =$
0.70711   0.70711
0.70711   − 0.70711

Now, we can calculate its inverse (as we found out already, H happens to be its own inverse):

⟩ inv(H)

$ans =$
0.70711 0.70711
0.70711   − 0.70711

MATLAB provides a trace function:

⟩ trace(H)

$ans = 0$

The product is straightforward. (Caveat: If you make a dimensional mismatch, MATLAB will return an error!)

---

[2] A big caveat: In MATLAB matrices and vectors start at 1, not 0!

⟩ H * I
ans =
0.70711 0.70711
0.70711 − 0.70711

We have met the tensor product several times throughout our text. Luckily, there is a primitive for it: it is called **kron**, as the tensor product of matrices is often referred to as the **Kronecker product**:

⟩ kron(H, I)
ans =
0.70711 0.00000 0.70711 0.00000
0.00000 0.70711 0.00000 0.70711
0.70711 0.00000 − 0.70711 − 0.00000
0.00000 0.70711 − 0.00000 − 0.70711

We have used eigenvalues and eigenvectors throughout our text. How to compute them? Worry not! MATLAB comes to rescue. The command [E, V] =eig(M) returns two matrices: E, whose columns are the eigenvectors of M, and V, a diagonal matrix whose diagonal elements are the eigenvalues of M.

⟩ [V, D] = eig(H)
V =
0.38268 − 0.92388
− 0.92388 − 0.38268
D =
− 1 0
0 1

There is so much more to aid you in complex algebra. A quick Google search will showcase numerous tutorials on complex matrices manipulation. You can also find more by typing HELP at the prompt.

C.3 QUANTUM COMPUTATIONS

We are now ready for quantum computation. Here, we have two options: the first one is to implement step by step a quantum computer emulator, following the indications of Section 7.4.

The second option is to learn how to use an existing emulator, and read the source code (MATLAB applications are collections of M-files, it is quite easy to inspect them and modify the code as we deem fit). There are a few quantum emulators in MATLAB. A very good and quite documented library is **Quack**, developed by Peter Rohde at the Department of Physics of University of Queensland, Australia. We are going to show a few things that Quack can do, and then it is your game: you can download it, learn the few examples, and start playing right away.[3]

---

[3] Although Quack is not at present a huge library, it is not a toy either. It contains functionality for quantum computation that goes beyond the scope of this book. But do not get deterred: you can use what you need, and perhaps, learn more as you go along.

The first thing one needs to do is to initialize Quack:

⟩ quack

Welcome to Quack! version pi/4 for MATLAB
by Peter Rohde
Centre for Quantum Computer Technology, Brisbane, Australia
http : //www.physics.uq.edu.au/people/rohde/

Now, we initialize a two-qubit register to the ground state($|00\rangle$):

⟩ init_state(2)

Just for fun, let us change the first qubit

⟩ prepare_one(1)

To see what happens, print the circuit history:

⟩ print_hist
{
$[1, 1] = |1 > -$
$[2, 1] = |0 > -$
}

Note: Ignore the left side of the circuit (it is there just to keep track of which cells contain the information). The right side of the equation contains the entry points of the circuit (in this case two qubits, initialized to $|1\rangle$, and $|0\rangle$ respectively). As we shall see momentarily, the circuit grows by concatenating gates and measurements.

Let us measure now the first qubit:

⟩ Z_measure(1)

$ans = -1$

and the second:

⟩ Z_measure(2)

$ans = 1$

Notice that the answer is -1 for $|1\rangle$ and 1 for $|0\rangle$. This may be a bit confusing at first, but is consistent with the spin notation: $|1\rangle$ simply means spin down along the z axis.

⟩ print_hist
{
$[1, 1] = |1 > - < Z| - - - - -$
$[2, 1] = |0 > - - - - - - < Z| -$
}

How about applying a controlled-NOT using the first qubit as control?

⟩ cnot(1, 2)

Better check what is happening . . .

⟩ print_hist

```
{
[1, 1] = |1 > − − < Z| − − − − − o −
[2, 1] = |0 > − − − − − − < Z| − X −
}
```

And now let us apply Hadamard on the second qubit:

⟩ H(2)

⟩ print_hist

```
{
[1, 1] = |1 > − − < Z| − − − − − o − − −
[2, 1] = |0 > − − − − − − < Z| − X − H −
}
```

What if we liked to shift the phase of the first qubit? T (see Section 5.4, it is there for you):

⟩ T(1)

⟩ print_hist

```
{
[1, 1] = |1 > − − < Z| − − − − − o − − − T −
[2, 1] = |0 > − − − − − − < Z| − X − H − − −
}
```

Let us perform some measurement. This time we are going to measure the second qubit, again along the z axis (i.e., in the standard basis):

⟩ Z_measure(2)

ans = 1

Hint: Pause a moment, jot down the steps, and try to follow what happened.

We have written a simple circuit, provided an input, and measured the results. Now it is all up to you: there are plenty of other gates, initialization routines, and measurement options in Quack, which you can dig up by reading the documentation. Investigate what is already there and play. (By the way, Quack can be easily extended in a number of ways. For instance, you can provide a simple GUI for designing circuits. You may want to start a mini project and create your personalized quantum computing lab).

Have fun!

Appendix D
Keeping Abreast of Quantum News:
Quantum Computing on the Web
and in the Literature

Jill Cirasella

This book covers many major developments in quantum computing, but the field is still young, and there will no doubt be many more developments in the future. These future developments will include research discoveries, of course, but they will also include trends in industry, surges in media coverage, and tides of public interest. This appendix describes tools that can help you track quantum developments of all kinds.

D.1 KEEPING ABREAST OF POPULAR NEWS

There are scores of newspapers, magazines, and other popular news sources, any one of which might run a story about the newest quantum development. How will you know if one does? You can keep an eye on your favorite news sources, but you will miss many stories that way. A better tactic is to use a news aggregator, such as Google News (http://news.google.com/), which allows you to search current and past stories from a multitude of news sources. You can add Google News to your stable of frequently visited sites, but the most efficient way to use it is to set up an alert or RSS feed and let the news come to you. After you perform a Google News search that yields good results, simply click "Alerts" to set up an alert that will notify you by e-mail of new stories that satisfy your search. Alternatively, click "RSS" to set up an RSS feed that will deliver those stories directly to your RSS reader.

In addition to the mainstream news, blogs devoted to quantum topics can be excellent sources of information. In fact, a blog whose focus overlaps with your interests can serve as a compass for navigating quantum news. Because new blogs are started all the time and existing blogs are often left to languish, there is little point in recommending individual blogs. Use tools such as Technorati (http://www.technorati.com/) and Google Blog Search (http://blogsearch.google.com/) to search for blog posts of interest and to identify blogs worth reading regularly. Look for blogs that offer insightful analyses of news stories and easy-to-understand distillations of scientific discoveries.

Occasionally, you will need to step back from the news and brush up on background information. The best site for refreshers is Quantiki (http://www.quantiki.

org/), a wiki with tutorials and encyclopedia-style articles about quantum information. As with all wikis, anyone can edit Quantiki entries, which means that anyone can (knowingly or unknowingly) insert errors, inconsistencies, and nonsense. So, although Quantiki is full of valid and valuable information, you cannot assume that everything written there is correct. In other words, Quantiki is a wonderful and informative site, but if you need to be absolutely certain of something, look it up somewhere else too. The same is true of the popular, omnidisciplinary Wikipedia (http://en.wikipedia.org/), which is pocked by errors and vandalism but nevertheless has some excellent entries on quantum computing.

D.2 KEEPING ABREAST OF SCIENTIFIC LITERATURE

Are news articles, wiki entries, and blog posts sufficient to satisfy your curiosity? Or do you want to track a topic more closely and read about developments in researchers' own words? If the latter, familiarize yourself with one or more of the following tools for tracking the scholarly literature of quantum computing. (For tips on how to read scientific articles, see Appendix A.) The single best source for up-to-the-minute articles about quantum computing is arXiv (http://arxiv.org/), an online archive of hundreds of thousands of scientific articles. Among quantum computing researchers, there is a strong culture of sharing articles on arXiv as soon as they are completed, often months (sometimes years) before they are published in journals or conference proceedings.

There are several ways to use arXiv to stay current with quantum computing. You can periodically visit arXiv and search for articles relevant to your interests. Alternatively, you can browse recent additions to arXiv's quantum physics archive, quant-ph, which includes quantum computing articles. If you prefer automatic notifications, you can sign up for arXiv's e-mail listing service or subscribe to the RSS feed of new quant-ph submissions.

Because articles on arXiv are posted by their authors, the articles have not been vetted by peer reviewers or cleaned up by editors. That said, arXiv has an endorsement system for authors, so there is some assurance that articles on arXiv are written by reliable researchers.

Posting to arXiv is voluntary, and some researchers do not, or do not always, post their articles. Thus, arXiv is not a comprehensive record of quantum computing research; indeed, no single resource is a comprehensive record of the field. That said, there exist databases that index all articles published in high-quality science journals. These databases are excellent aids to anyone who wants to systematically track research on a certain topic or focus on findings that have passed a stringent peer review process. The two biggest and best databases of this kind are Scopus and Web of Science, both extraordinarily expensive and therefore usually available only through academic libraries. If you have access to Scopus or Web of Science, you can periodically visit and perform searches, or you can perform a search once and then turn that search into an e-mail alert or RSS feed. If you are interested in multiple topics, you can set up multiple e-mail alerts or RSS feeds.

If you do not have access to either of these databases, your best option is Google Scholar (http://scholar.google.com/), a free Google tool for searching for journal articles and other kinds of scholarly literature. Google Scholar's coverage has gaps and its search features are not very sophisticated, but it is nevertheless remarkably powerful and delightfully easy to use.

Once you find out about an article, how do you find the article itself? Sometimes, the tool that makes you aware of the article's existence also leads you to the text of the article. For example, arXiv contains not just information about articles but also the articles themselves. But this is not always the case. For example, although Scopus and Web of Science contain a wealth of information about articles, they do not contain actual articles. In other words, they are indexing databases, not full-text databases. Meanwhile, Google Scholar is a hybrid: some results link to the full text of articles, some link to abstracts, and some are just citations with no links.

Luckily, many libraries subscribe to numerous full-text databases and employ tools that link from article citations to articles themselves. As a result, the full text of an article is often only a few clicks away from the article information in Scopus, Web of Science, or Google Scholar. Of course, different libraries subscribe to different databases and choose different technologies for linking between databases; ask your librarian about the tools available to you. Also, keep in mind that most journals are available both electronically and in print. If your library does not have electronic access to the article you want, it might have a print copy; again, talk to your librarian about how to determine definitively whether or not your library has a certain article.

Inevitably, your library will not have every article you want – what then? Perhaps the article (or a version of it) is freely available on arXiv, the author's homepage, an institutional repository, or elsewhere. In general, a search of both Google and Google Scholar is sufficient to determine whether an article is freely available on-line. If you do not find the article but do find a publisher's page offering to sell you the article, do not pay! Rather, request the article through interlibrary loan, a free service at many libraries.

D.3 THE BEST WAY TO STAY ABREAST?

No single tool is sufficient to keep you fully informed about quantum computing. Different tools have different strengths, and you should familiarize yourself with those that best satisfy your needs and curiosities. For example, if you are tracking a specific problem or technology, scientific articles are best. Furthermore, if you value seeing new research as soon as it is released, keep an eye on arXiv. If you are curious about which developments cause a stir and how they fit into scientific and social contexts, pay attention to popular news stories and quantum blogs.

If your interest in quantum computing is casual, stay abreast however and whenever suits you. But if quantum computing is your passion or specialty, read broadly. You never know what will excite your curiosity, provide an insight, or inspire a big idea.

Appendix E
Selected Topics for Student Presentations

Although its history is relatively recent, quantum computing is already, by all standards, a very broad area of research. There is simply no way we can cover anything more than a relatively small fraction of its interesting topics. There are also many fascinating themes that are not exactly part of quantum computing per se, but are nevertheless closely related to it.

In this appendix, we list a number of suggestions for further exploration, covering some items we omitted from our text. It is our sincere hope that students will find them useful for their presentations or perhaps inspire them to select others that they can discover on their own.

Note to the student: Now it is your turn! The best way to really learn something is to teach it. There is no substitute for spending hours preparing a lecture and getting ideas straight so that you can present them. Knowing that other people will be asking you questions and learning from you will force you to understand the material at a deeper level.

You are urged to choose a subject from an area that you find interesting. Much time and energy is going to be spent learning, understanding, and preparing, so you might as well enjoy your choice from the start.

For each of these topics, there are many different levels on which you can go about making a presentation. You can present a superficial lecture in which the bare outline of the idea is discussed, or you can get into the "nitty-gritty" of the technical details. Obviously, the superficial route is the easier one, but not much will be gained from such an exercise. We urge you to understand and present a topic with the utmost detail and depth. A presentation with a lot of hand waving is noticeably deficient. In contrast, one with equations and nice diagrams demonstrates understanding and knowledge. Do not just throw a few equations on the blackboard: show how they are derived. Develop charts and diagrams. Obviously, if the presentation is done in a classroom setting, there are time considerations as well.

How do you go about preparing for such a task? The first thing to do is to look for a popular account of the topic. This can be in a nontechnical magazine or on Web page. Some of the subjects are historical; hence, a look into a few encyclopedias might be helpful. Many nontechnical articles have suggestions for further reading. Once an introductory article is understood, you should move on to deeper, more detailed material. This is the safest and most effective way for you to go forward in your research.

Note to the teacher: If you are going to insist that students make presentations, we recommend that they choose their topics as early as possible in the semester. The more time they are given to prepare, the better the presentation will be. One possible way of arranging this is to have your students give their presentations at the end of the semester. There is, however, another way. You can have students' presentations scattered throughout the semester at the appropriate times. For example, when Chapter 4 is done, you might have a student lecture on the different ways of interpreting quantum theory (Presentation E.4.1). Before starting Shor's algorithm, a student might make a presentation on RSA (Presentation E.6.4) or classical factoring algorithms (Presentation E.6.3). This will explain the importance of Shor's algorithm and place it in its historical context. Having the presentations throughout the semester demands a lot of flexibility and juggling from the teacher and the students (they have to present them at the time you prefer) but it can be done.

We have found that some students get lost in the morass of literature on a subject (regrettably, in this Web-centered world, to many students "doing research" means going to Google's home page). We suggest that a few weeks after the students choose their topics, a private meeting be held with each one during which they present the articles they plan to use. At that meeting, they can also be told how much depth is expected from their presentation.

Note on the presentations: For each topic discussed, we

- give a short explanation of what the topic is and how it is related to quantum computing (when it is not obvious);
- give a short list of possible subtopics to include in your presentation; and
- recommend some starting places to look for information about the topic.

Our list is arranged to follow the chapters of the text. However, there are many items that could have easily fit in other places as well. It is important to realize that our list is in no way comprehensive. There are many other areas that we could have mentioned but did not. Feel free to find your own topic of choice.

E.1 COMPLEX NUMBERS

E.1.1 The History of Complex Numbers

We use complex numbers to help us describe parts of quantum theory. However, complex numbers have a long and distinguished history (they go back to the sixteenth century). At first they began as a mathematical curiosity, but as time went on, researchers progressively realized that complex numbers are ubiquitous and important.

Make sure your presentation contains the basic facts about some of the main players in this field and what their contribution was.

A good place to start is any of the many history of mathematics textbooks available, such as Eves (1976). Might we also suggest Mazur (2002) and Nahin (1998).

E.1.2 Geometry of the Complex Plane

In Section 1.3, we briefly introduced some basic complex functions, such as the exponential and polynomials. Maps from the complex plane to itself have a geometry: for instance, the map $x \longmapsto x + c_0$, where c_0 is a constant complex number, represents a translation of the plane.

In this presentation you should describe in detail (with examples!) the geometry of simple complex maps, such as the square function, exponential, and inverse. Some of this can be presented nicely with a computer graphics presentation.

Any basic textbook in complex analysis will do, but perhaps the classic *Geometry of Complex Numbers* (Schwerdtfeger, 1980) is the best entry point.

E.1.3 The Riemannian Sphere and Möbius Transformations

The complex plane can be turned into a sphere! Indeed, by adding a point at infinity, we can identify the plane with the so-called Riemann sphere. This is a representation that is both pervasive and extremely fruitful in thinking of the complex domain. The Riemann sphere model is not static: some special complex maps turn into rotations of the sphere. We have briefly met such maps at the end of Chapter 1: the Möbius transformations.

In your presentation you should explicitly describe the charting map from the extended complex plane to the sphere in details, and then proceed to illustrate the basic rotations of the sphere (use examples!).

The same references of the previous item apply here (in fact, Presentations E.1.2 and E.1.3 could be done in sequence).

E.2 COMPLEX VECTOR SPACES

E.2.1 Matrices in Computer Graphics

Many of the ideas from linear algebra that we needed for quantum computing are also used for computer graphics. States of a graphical system are represented by vectors and two- and three-dimensional transformations are represented by matrices.

Assuming the linear algebra presented in Chapter 2, one can proceed with a nice presentation describing the way researchers who deal with computer graphics work with these ideas. A nice computer presentation is always pleasant.

A good place to start is any comprehensive computer graphics textbook.

E.2.2 History of Vector Spaces

Although the ideas of vector spaces in particular and linear algebra in general seem simple now, their development was a long and torturous path. The ideas of higher-dimensional vectors were greeted with skepticism and ridicule. Eventually the mathematics and physics communities saw the importance of these ideas and embraced them completely.

A nice presentation should include a mini biography of some of the main players and what they accomplished. A talk should include the work of Sir William Rowan Hamilton, Hermann Grassmann, Josia Gibbs, and several others.

A good place to start is one of the many history of mathematics textbooks available, such as Eves (1976). There is a also a fascinating history of this subject by Michael J. Crowe (1994), which is definitely worth the read.

E.3 THE LEAP FROM CLASSICAL TO QUANTUM

E.3.1 Huygens' Principle and Wave Mechanics

The concept of interference has a long history. In 1678 the Dutch physicist Christiaan Huygens presented the wave theory of light, a model that dominated optics up to the discovery of quanta. In his revolutionary treatise, Huygens described the way a wave front propagates – the so-called **Huygens' principle**. In the early 1900s the English physicist Thomas Young introduced the double-slit experiment, which we have encountered in Chapter 3. This seminal experiment validated the wave model of light.

In this presentation you should clearly articulate the evolution of wave mechanics from Huygens to Schrödinger, and illustrate with diagrams how it explains known optical phenomena such as refraction and interference.

References? Plenty. Any good physics text will do. But, if we have to recommend a single book, perhaps *Wave Phenomena* by D.H. Towne is the one (Towne, 1989).

E.3.2 Quantum Erasers

With the understanding of the double-slit experiment, one can move on to one of the most fascinating experiments at the cutting edge of research. In the double-slit experiment, the photon passes through both slits simultaneously. Now consider a way of "tagging" the photon so that we would know which slit the photon went through. Such a "tagging" would eliminate the interference phenomenon. Now consider what would happen if we had some type of way to "erase" or remove the "tag" once the photon passed the slits. In that case, the photon would have the interference phenomenon. The amazing part is that whether or not a photon will go into both slits will depend on whether the "eraser" is present *after* it passes through the slit(s).

A presentation should explain the types of tags and erasers used. Some nice diagrams are a good idea. There are also many variations and improvements to this experiment that should be discussed. This is also related to the Elitzur–Vaidman bomb-tester experiment.

There are many articles in popular science magazines. They can point to more technical articles.

E.4 BASIC QUANTUM THEORY

E.4.1 Interpreting Quantum Theory

There are many different schools of thought of how one should interpret some of the less classical aspects of quantum theory. Some examples of the more popular schools are Bohr's Copenhagen interpretation, Everett's many worlds interpretation, and Bohm's wave function interpretation (to name a few). Many questions in the foundations of quantum theory come down to asking what really exists and what doesn't, the so-called ontological issues. Other issues are the measurement problem and how should one interpret nonlocality.

A presentation should include several of these different schools and how they deal with a few of the foundational issues of quantum mechanics.

There are many popular books on the topic, e.g., Herbert (1987) or Pagels (1982). There are also a few great articles on the Web at the *Stanford Encyclopedia of Philosophy*. These articles should lead you to more detailed articles. Any of the books by Roger Penrose (1994, 1999, 2005) would be worth looking into.

E.4.2 The EPR Paradox

In 1935, Albert Einstein and two younger colleagues wrote a paper entitled "Can quantum-mechanical description of physical reality be considered complete?" Einstein, Podolsky, and Rosen (1935). In this short paper, the authors give a simple thought experiment in which they attempt to prove that quantum mechanics as we have it is incomplete. They do this by considering two particles "entangled" and going off in two directions. By measuring one particle, one can determine facts about the other particle without disturbing it.

A presentation should include the historical context of the thought experiment (Schrödinger's observation about entanglement); conservation of momentum; Bohm's version of the thought experiment (conservation of spin); how EPR relates to the tensor product of two Hilbert spaces; a discussion of hidden variables; and possible solutions to the paradox.

A nice place to start looking into this is a paper on *Stanford Encyclopedia of Philosophy* by Arthur Fine that is very readable. See also Pagels (1982). The original EPR paper is not too difficult.

E.4.3 Bell's Theorem

In 1964, John Bell wrote a paper (Bell, 1964, reprinted in Bell, 1987) that took the EPR paradox one step further. Bell shows that by doing some statistical analysis on measurement of two entangled particles, one can show that quantum mechanics is fundamentally nonlocal.

A presentation should include the explanation of the terms local, nonlocal; what is the inequality; some variations of the inequality; Clause and Aspects experiments; and variations of the experiments.

There is a short discussion of Bell's theorem in Section 9.4. There is much popular literature on this topic. Alas, much of it is silly and resorts to cheap "mysticism."

For two nice presentations, see Pagels (1982) and Gribbin (1984). That should get you started.

E.4.4 Kochen–Specker Theorem

This is one of the most powerful and shocking theorems in the foundations of quantum theory. Quantum mechanics says that before a measurement, a property is in a superposition of basic states. Only after a measurement is there a collapse to a basic state. One might be tempted to say that a property is really in an unknown basic state before a measurement and the observer finds what basic state it *was* in after measurement. The Kochen–Specker theorem shows that it is impossible for this to be true. Before a measurement, the spin of a particle is in a superposition until it is measured.

Begin by explaining why the theorem is important. The theorem is proven by looking at a graph-coloring problem. A formal proof of this statement would be too complicated. However, giving nice geometrical intuitive pictures would be helpful. Show that it is possible to color the graph in two dimensions and then show how "there is not enough room" in three dimensions. Kernaghan's proof (Kernaghan, 1994) with 20 vectors is fairly easy to present.

Unfortunately, there is a dearth of easy literature on this important theorem. A good place to start looking is a nice article by Carsten Held in *the Stanford Encyclopedia of Philosophy*.

E.4.5 Schrödinger's Cat

This is a thought experiment that shows that the quantum weirdness of the microworld can cross over into the macroworld. By looking at a fairly mischievous contraption where a cat is placed in a box with a radioactive particle that is in a superposition of being "half-way" alive and "half-way" dead, the cat is placed in a superposition of being "half-way" alive and dead.

A presentation should include the basic construction; some history of the thought experiment; some variations of the ideas; a discussion of "Wigner's Friend"; and some possible answers to this puzzle. Do not harm any animals while making your presentation!

There are many popular articles and books that one can start looking into, e.g., Herbert (1987) and Gribbin (1984).

E.5 ARCHITECTURE

E.5.1 Maxwell's Demon, Landauer's Principle, and the Physics of Information

These are several ideas at the crossroads of information theory and statistical mechanics. Maxwell's demon is a seeming paradox that shows that one can create energy with information. Landauer's principle concerns itself with the relationship of energy and erasing information. Both of these ideas are the starting point to a field that is called the physics of information. The basic theme of this field is studying information from the physical point of view and studying physics from the informational point of view. One of their oft-quoted mottos is "It from bit," i.e., the physical world is created from information. David Deutsch has taken this idea a little further and written a paper (available on the Web) titled "It from qubit."

A presentation can be historical. Go through the major players in this story and the advances they made.

There are several papers by Charles H. Bennett and Rolf Landauer freely available on the Web, e.g., Bennett (1988) and Landauer (1991). David Deutsch's "It from qubit" is available. There is also an excellent book titled *Grammatical Man: Information, Entropy, Language and Life* by Jeremy Campbell (1982). It is a popular history of information theory. Definitely worth reading!

E.5.2 Classical Reversible Computation

With the ideas about energy use and losing information, several researchers went on to develop machines that are reversible and theoretically do not use energy.

A presentation can show some basic circuits; some reversible algorithms; and a discussion of the actual physical implementations of reversible computations and some of the problems they had.

There are many popular articles that are good places to start. See also Bennett's history of reversible computation (Bennett, 1988).

E.5.3 More Quantum Gates and Universal Quantum Gates

In the text we talked about several different quantum gates (Toffoli, controlled-NOT, Pauli, etc.). There are, however, many others.

A well-rounded presentation should include a list of new quantum gates, as well as their actions. For one-qubit gates, the geometry of their action on the Bloch sphere should be articulated (a large children's ball and a magic marker is a must for this presentation!).

There are also many other results concerning which sets of gates form universal sets. Here, you should identify one or two universal sets and explicitly show how familiar gates can be obtained from them. For instance, how can you get a pair of qubits maximally entangled from your chosen universal set?

The best place to begin is Nielsen and Chuang (2000).

E.6 ALGORITHMS

E.6.1 Probabilistic Algorithms

Some of the algorithms given in our text have a probabilistic flavor to them. Many students might be unfamiliar with this programming paradigm. It turns out that for certain problems if one does some clever guessing, there are ways of solving algorithmic problems.

A presentation should contain a few different algorithms; what they solve; what is a classic deterministic algorithm to solve the same problem; a comparison of complexity issues. A few computer simulations are easy.

A nice place to start looking for such algorithms are in Chapter 5 of Corman et al. (2001). There is also a more theoretical discussion in Chapter 10 of Sipser (2005).

E.6.2 Hidden Subgroup Problem

All the algorithms presented in this text, besides Grover's algorithm, can be stated as examples of a single computational problem. Some familiarity with basic group theory is necessary for the statement of this problem.

Definition E.6.1 (The Hidden Subgroup Problem). *Given a group G and a set function $f : G \longrightarrow S$ such that we are assured that there exists a subgroup $H \subseteq G$ such that f factors through the quotient G/H, i.e.,*

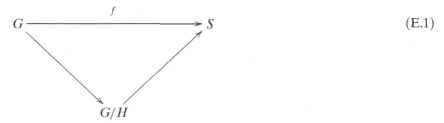

$$(E.1)$$

or in other words, that f is constant on different cosets of G, the goal is to find H.

Notice that this is a computational problem and not really a mathematical problem. Mathematically, H is simply $f^{-1}(f(e))$.

A presentation should include a statement and an explanation of the problem; how each of the algorithms in Chapter 6 (besides Grover's) can be seen as an instance of the problem; methods used to solve the general problem.

A good place to begin is Nielsen and Chuang (2000) and Hirvensalo (2001).

E.6.3 Classical Factoring Algorithms

Shor's algorithm is the first algorithm that can factor numbers in polynomial time. However, there are classical algorithms that factor large numbers. One of the algorithms is Pollard's rho heuristic. There are several others.

The presentation should have a nice statement of the problem; some discussion of the mathematical preliminaries necessary to understand the algorithm; the algorithms themselves; and the expected running time of the algorithm. One should also discuss how large are the numbers that can successfully be factored by such an algorithm. A computer implementation would be nice.

A nice place to start looking for material is Section 31.9 of Corman et al. (2001).

E.6.4 Fourier Transforms

In the text, we mentioned the Fourier transform with its use in Shor's algorithm. There are, however, many other uses for the Fourier transform in computer science.

They are used for multiplying numbers more efficiently; they are used to find patterns; and many other tasks.

A presentation should go through different versions of the Fourier transform such as the discrete Fourier transform, the fast Fourier transform, the quantum Fourier transform. A discussion of complexity issues is also important. Mention algorithms that use Fourier transforms. A computer simulation of one or more algorithms is not hard.

A few good places to start looking are Chapter 7 of Baase (1988), Chapter 30 of Corman et al. (2001), or Chapter 2 of Dasgupta, Papadimitriou, and Vazirani (2006).

E.7 PROGRAMMING LANGUAGES

E.7.1 SQRAM: A Full-Fledged Quantum Assembler

As we wrote in Chapter 7, our q-assembler is just a toy language to introduce the basic concepts of q-programming. There is, however, at least one attempt to describe a concrete full-fledged quantum assembler that would run on a special type of QRAM, the so-called sequential QRAM, or SQRAM.

After carefully reading Nagarajan, Papanikolaou, and Williams (2005), you should present the SQRAM model in detail, as well as the language it supports. Perhaps you could write a few simple programs for illustration purposes, and describe how the SQRAM machine executes them.

Can you think of additional desirable features?

E.7.2 QCL and Q: A Comparison

The languages by Ömer and Bettelli are two successful attempts to design an imperative quantum language. They share a number of similarities, but also some difference in the basic design philosophy.

Your presentations should clearly describe the basic features of the two proposals, and make explicit their intent.

The main references are Ömer (2000) and Bettelli, Calarco, and Serafini (2001). In an interview in Rüdiger (2007), Ömer and Bettelli have presented their views on designing a quantum programming language.

E.7.3 Functional Quantum Programming: QML

As we mentioned in passing in Section 7.3, quite recently there was a new proposal of a quantum functional language, known as QML, which attempts to provide quantum control constructs. Try to present its syntax and discuss its quantum control features, particularly the "quantum if." Do these constructs qualify for quantum control?

This presentation should be undertaken by students who have had some previous exposure to functional programming, and possibly to Haskell.

There is an entire Web site dedicated to this language, where you can find all necessary references (and more): http://sneezy.cs.nott.ac.uk/QML.

E.8 THEORETICAL COMPUTER SCIENCE

E.8.1 Primality Testing

Primality testing is concerned with telling if a given positive integer is a prime number or a composite number. With the knowledge of all the complexity classes mentioned in Sections 8.1 and 8.2, it is interesting to look at one problem and see how, over the past several decades, progress has been made in solving this problem. Although this problem is related to the factoring problem, it should not be confused with it. Obviously if a number is prime, there will not be any nontrivial factors. However, primality testing is a decision problem and factoring is a search problem.

A presentation should include some early results of primality testing, i.e., that it is in **coNP** (obvious) and **NP** (Pratt certificates) and then at least state some of the algorithms that show the problem is in the probabilistic polynomial time complexity classes. A presentation should conclude with the recent result that PRIMES is, in fact, in **P**.

Some early results are shown in Corman et al. (2001). There is a nice discussion of probabilistic complexity classes and primality testing in Papadimitriou (1994) and Sipser (2005). The result that PRIMES is in **P** is in Agrawal, Kayal, and Saxena (2004).

E.8.2 Quantum Finite Automata

One of the simplest types of computing machines is finite automaton. These are simple (virtual) devices that can recognize regular languages. Just as there is a generalization of a classical Turing machine to a quantum Turing machine, so too, there is a generalization of the notion of a classical finite automaton to a quantum finite automaton (QFA).

A presentation should include a clear definition of a QFA; a discussion of the different types of QFAs; what type of languages they recognize; their relationships with quantum Turing machines, quantum pushdown automata, and classical two-way finite automata.

Information for such a presentation will be mostly found in research articles easily found on xxx.lanl.gov.

E.8.3 QUANTUM ORACLE COMPUTATIONS

One of the more advanced topics in theoretical computer science is oracle computation; that is, the study of one type of computation "relative to" another. The extra knowledge given by an oracle changes the basic facts about complexity classes. For a given complexity class **C** and an oracle A, one constructs the complexity class $\mathbf{C}^A$. If A is a general member of a complexity class **A**, then we can discuss the complexity class $\mathbf{C}^A$. These new complexity classes are helpful in discussing the relative strength of complexity classes.

A presentation should start with some classical results of oracle computation. For example, there exists sets A and B such that

$$P^A = NP^A \quad \text{and} \quad P^B \neq NP^B, \tag{E.2}$$

and move on to define what does it mean for a quantum Turing machine to have an oracle. Move on to list and perhaps prove some of the results. Explain what a random oracle is and why they are important.

A good place to start is the survey papers Cleve (1999); Fortnow (2003); Vazirani (2002).

E.9 CRYPTOGRAPHY

E.9.1 RSA

One of the earliest public key cryptographic protocols is RSA. This protocol is used throughout the World Wide Web and is the current standard on public key cryptographic systems. RSA uses the fact that multiplication is computationally "easy" and factoring is computationally "hard."

The presentation should include a statement what the RSA protocol does; the mathematical preliminaries necessary to understand the protocol; how the protocol works; how the protocol would be destroyed if an efficient polynomial algorithm for factoring was found; and the present way it is implemented. A computer simulation is both easy and nice.

Many algorithms textbooks and discrete mathematics textbooks have chapters on the RSA protocol.

E.9.2 Quantum Authentication

How can one be sure that the message just received was indeed sent by the one who claims it? As it turns out, quantum cryptography can help. Again, just like in other areas, the magic of entanglement plays a major role.

An interesting paper by D. Richard Kuhn of NIST (Kuhn, 2003) can be used, both as a baseline and for the good references to related work.

E.10 INFORMATION THEORY

E.10.1 Quantum Games

Quantum games is a new area of research that straddles between game theory and quantum computing. It was started by David Meyer in 1999 as a coin flip game between Captain Picard of Enterprise Starship and Q, his "quantum opponent." The catch is that a qubit is used as the quantum coin. Whereas Captain Picard is allowed only to apply classical flips, Q has a full range of quantum strategies at his disposal. Q always wins.

For the hands-on reader, this presentation could also be an opportunity to write a piece of quantum code. How about implementing a simulator of Meyer's game?

You can begin by reading the enjoyable *Physics World* online article: Lee and Johnson (2002). At the end, you will find a number of references to get further along.

E.10.2 Quantum Entropy of Composite Systems

In Chapter 10, we have seen how quantum entropy measures the amount of order of a given quantum system. Suppose now you are looking at a composite quantum system S. There is a way to define the entropies of the subsystems if the entropy of S is known. They are called residual entropies. The interesting thing is that, unlike the classical case, the entropy of S can be smaller than the sum of the entropies of its parts. This is because of entanglement, a new form of order of the quantum world.

Your presentation should clearly articulate the notion of residual entropy and show an example of the above.

A good reference is the "Notes on quantum information theory" by Sam Lomonaco (1996). (Caveat: The level of math sophistication is a bit higher than the one of Chapter 10. This is a good presentation for a math-oriented class).

E.10.3 Quantum Error-Correcting Codes

The last section of Chapter 10 was just meant to whet your appetite. There is much more on the topic of quantum error-correction and error-detection, and thus a nice opportunity for a great presentation.

Start with the survey paper by Knill et al. (2002). Although the tone of the paper is rather informal, it is packed with good stuff. A suggestion would be to review the first three sections, and go on to Section 6, where techniques for constructing codes are presented, in particular stabilizer codes.

E.11 HARDWARE

E.11.1 Decoherence and the Emergence of the Classical World

In the first section we have introduced decoherence as a formidable opponent in our quest for quantum hardware. Decoherence is part of life, and it also has a bright side: it is perhaps the key to the emergence of the macroscopic physical world.

For this presentation, you can present the excellent survey paper (Zurek, 2003). A Google search with key words decoherence + classical world will provide other useful references (in particular, an excellent site is www.decoherence.info).

E.11.2 A Comparison of Extant Approaches to Quantum Hardware

In Chapter 11, we have briefly showcased a few approaches for quantum hardware. If this topic captivates you, it is worth preparing a presentation comparing all the known proposals to date. As we mentioned at the end of Section 11.3, NIST has a major ongoing effort toward implementing quantum devices, and it has made available a Quantum Roadmap (http://qist.lanl.gov/qcomp_map.shtml), divided into several sections, each dedicated to a specific proposal. As our introduction of nuclear magnetic resonance was sketchy at best, perhaps it could be your starting point (you should highlight its strengths and weaknesses).

E.11.3 Current Implementations of Quantum Cryptography

In Chapter 9 we familiarized ourselves with a few quantum cryptography protocols. But, where are we in real life? As it turns out, a number of experiments have been carried out. In fact, currently there are a few commercially available quantum cryptographic communicating devices.

In this presentation, you should showcase a few milestones and the roadmap for the future of quantum cryptography.

Where to start? A good entry point is the Quantum Cryptography Roadmap, available at the Los Alamos Laboratories', Web site: http://qist.lanl.gov/qcrypt_map.shtml. It is subdivided in several sections, each addressing a core method of QKD.

Bibliography

L.M. Adleman, J. DeMarrais, and M.-D. A. Huang. Quantum computability. *SIAM Journal on Computing*, 26(5):1524–1540, 1997.

M. Agrawal, N. Kayal, and N. Saxena. PRIMES in P. *Annals of Mathematics 2*, 160(2):781–793, 2004. Available at http://www.cse.iitk.ac.in/users/manindra/.

D. Aharonov. Quantum computation. December 1998. Available at www.arxiv.org/quant-ph/9812037.

Y. Aharonov and D. Rohrlich. *Quantum Paradoxes: Quantum Theory for the Perplexed*. Wiley-VCH, Weinheim, 2005.

R.B. Ash. *Information Theory*. Dover Publications, New York, 1990.

S. Baase. *Computer Algorithms: Introduction to Design and Analysis, Second Edition*. Addison-Wesley, Reading, Mass, 1988.

J. Bak and D.J. Newman. *Complex Analysis, Second Edition*. Springer, New York, 1996.

A. Barenco, C.H. Bennett, R. Cleve, D.P. DiVincenzo, N. Margolus, P.W. Shor, T. Sleator, J.A. Smolin, and H. Weinfurter. Elementary gates for quantum computation. *Physical Review A*, 52(5):3457–3467, 1995.

A. Barenco, D. Deutsch, A. Ekert, and R. Jozsa. Conditional quantum dynamics and logic gates. *Physical Review Letters*, 74(20):4083–4086, 1995.

H. Bass, H. Cartan, P. Freyd, A. Heller, and S. MacLane. Samuel Eilenberg (1913–1998). *Notices of American Mathematical Society*, 45(10):1344–1352, 1998.

J.S. Bell. On the Einstein–Podolsky–Rosen paradox. *Physics*, 1:195–200, 1964.

J.S. Bell. *Speakable and Unspeakable in Quantum Mechanics*. Cambridge University Press, Cambridge, UK, 1987.

P. Benioff. Quantum mechanical models of Turing machines that dissipate no energy. *Physical Review Letters*, 48(23):1581–1585, 1982.

C.H. Bennett. Notes on the history of reversible computation. *IBM Journal of Research and Development*, 32(1):16–23, 1988.

C.H. Bennett. Quantum cryptography using any two nonorthogonal states. *Physical Review Letters*, 68:3121, 1992.

C.H. Bennett, E. Bernstein, G. Brassard, and U. Vazirani. Strengths and weaknesses of quantum computing. *SIAM Journal on Computing*, 26(5):1510–1523, 1997.

C.H. Bennett and G. Brassard. Quantum cryptography: Public key distribution and coin tossing. In *Proceedings of IEEE International Conference on Computers Systems and Signal Processing*, pages 175–179, Bangalore, India, December 1984.

C.H. Bennett, G. Brassard, C. Crépeau, R. Jozsa, A. Peres, and W.K. Wootters. Teleporting an unknown quantum state via dual classical and Einstein–Podolsky–Rosen channels. *Physical Review Letters*, 70(13):1895–1899, March 1993.

K.K. Berggren. Quantum computing with superconductors. *Proceedings of the IEEE*, 92(10), October 2004.

E. Bernstein and U. Vazirani. Quantum complexity theory. In *STOC '93: Proceedings of the Twenty-Fifth Annual ACM Symposium on Theory of Computing*, pages 11–20, ACM, New York, 1993.

E. Bernstein and U. Vazirani. Quantum complexity theory. *SIAM Journal on Computing*, 26(5):1411–1473, 1997.

S. Bettelli, T. Calarco, and L. Serafini. Toward an architecture for quantum programming. *CoRR*, 2001. Available at http://arxiv.org/abs/cs.PL/0103009.

D. Bouwmeester, J.-W. Pan, K. Mattle, M. Eibl, H. Weinfurter, and A. Zeilinger. Experimental quantum teleportation. *Nature*, 390:575–579, 1997.

G. Brassard. Cryptology column–quantum cryptography. A bibliography. *SIGACT News*, 24(3):16–20, 1993.

G. Brassard and C. Crépeau. Cryptology column – 25 years of quantum cryptography. *SIGACT News*, 27(3):13–24, 1993.

A.R. Calderbank and P.W. Shor. Good quantum error-correcting codes exist. *Physical Review A*, 54(2):1098–1105, August 1996.

J. Campbell. *Grammatical Man: Information, Entropy, Language and Life*. Simon & Schuster, New York, July 1982.

M. Chester. *Primer of Quantum Mechanics*. Dover Publications, Mineola, N.Y., 2003.

I.L. Chuang, N. Gershenfeld, and M. Kubinec. Experimental implementation of fast quantum searching. *Physical Review Letters*, 80 (15):3408–3411, 1998.

I.L. Chuang, L.M.K. Vandersypen, X. Zhou, D.W. Leung, and S. Lloyd. Experimental realization of a quantum algorithm. *Nature*, 393:143–146, 1998.

J.I. Cirac and P. Zoller. Quantum computations with cold trapped ions. *Physical Review Letters*, 74:4091–4094, 1995.

J. Cirasella. Classical and quantum algorithms for finding cycles. 2006. Available at http://www.illc.uva.nl/Publications/ResearchReports/MoL-2006-06.text.pdf.

R. Cleve. An introduction to quantum complexity theory. Available at http://arxiv.org/abs/quant-ph/9906111, 1999.

G.P. Collins. Quantum bug: Qubits might spontaneously decay in seconds. An article from *Scientific American* available at http://www.sciam.com.

T.H. Corman, C.E. Leiserson, R.E. Rivest, and C. Stein. *Introduction to Algorithms, Second Edition*. The MIT Press, Cambridge, Mass., 2001.

M.J. Crowe. *A History of Vector Analysis: The Evolution of the Idea of a Vectorial System*. Dover Publications, Mineola, N.Y., 1994.

S. Dasgupta, C.H. Papadimitriou, and U. Vazirani. *Algorithms*. McGraw-Hill Science/Engineering/Math, New York, 2006.

M.D. Davis, E.J. Weyuker, and R. Sigal. *Computability, Complexity, and Languages: Fundamentals of Theoretical Computer Science*. Morgan Kaufmann, Boston, 1994.

D. Deutsch. Quantum theory, the Church–Turing principle and the universal quantum computer. *Proceedings of the Royal Society of London, Series A*, 400(1818):97–117, 1985. Available at http://www.qubit.org/oldsite/resource/deutsch85.pdf.

D. Deutsch. Quantum computational networks. *Proceedings of the Royal Society of London, Series A*, 425(1868):73–90, 1989.

D. Deutsch and R. Jozsa. Rapid solution of problems by quantum computation. *Proceedings of the Royal Society of London, Series A*, 439:553–558, October 1992.

D. Dieks. Comunicating by EPR devices. *Physical Letters A*, 92(6):271–272, 1982.

P.A.M. Dirac. *The Principles of Quantum Mechanics* (The International Series of Monographs on Physics). Oxford University Press, Oxford, UK, 1982.

D.P. DiVincenzo. The physical implementation of quantum computation. http://arxiv.org/abs/quant-ph/0002077.

D.P. DiVincenzo. Two-bit gates are universal for quantum computation. *Physical Review A*, 51(2):1015–1022, 1995.

G. Egan. *Schild's Ladder*. Harper Collins Publishers, New York, 2002.

A. Einstein, B. Podolsky, and N. Rosen. Can quantum-mechanical description of physical reality be considered complete? *Physical Review*, 47:777–780, May 1935.

A.K. Ekert. Quantum cryptography based on Bell's theorem. *Physical Review Letters*, 67:661–663, 1991.

H. Eves. *An Introduction to the History of Numbers, Fourth Edition*. Holt, Rinehart and Winston, New York, 1976.

R.P. Feynman. *Feynman Lectures on Physics (3 Volume Set)*. Addison-Wesley, Boston, 1963.

R.P. Feynman. Simulating physics with computers. *International Journal of Theoretical Physics*, 21(6/7):467–488, 1982.

L. Fortnow. One complexity theorist's view of quantum computing. *Theoretical Computer Science*, 292(3):597–610, 2003.

G. Gamow. *Thirty Years That Shook Physics: The Story of Quantum Theory*. Dover Publications, Mineda, N.Y., 1985.

M.R. Garey and D.S. Johnson. *Computers and Intractability: A Guide to the Theory of NP-Completeness*. WH Freeman & Co., New York, 1979.

S.J. Gay. Quantum programming languages: Survey and bibliography. *Bulletin of the EATCS*, 86:176–196, 2005. Available at http://dblp.uni-trier.de/db/journals/eatcs/eatcs86.html#Gay05.

J. Gilbert and L. Gilbert. *Linear Algebra and Matrix Theory, Second Edition*. Thomson, Brooks/Cole, San Diego, 2004.

D.T. Gillespie. *A Quantum Mechanics Primer: An Introduction to the Formal Theory of Non-relativistic Quantum Mechanics*. John Wiley & Sons, New York, 1974.

J. Grattage and T. Altenkirch. QML: Quantum data and control. February 2005. Available at http://www.cs.nott.ac.uk/ txa/publ/jqpl.pdf.

J. Gribbin. *In Search of Schrodinger's Cat: Quantum Physics and Reality*. Bantam, New York, 1984.

R.P. Grimaldi. *Discrete and Combinatorial Mathematics: An Applied Introduction, Fifth Edition*. Addison-Wesley, Boston, 2003.

L.K. Grover. A fast quantum mechanical algorithm for database search. In *STOC '96: Proceedings of the Twenty-Eighth Annual ACM Symposium on Theory of Computing*, pages 212–219, ACM, New York, 1996.

L.K. Grover. Quantum mechanics helps in searching for a needle in a haystack. *Physical Review Letters*, 79(2):325–328, 1997.

K. Hannabuss. *An Introduction to Quantum Theory*. Oxford University Press, New York, 1997.

N. Herbert. *Quantum Reality: Beyond the New Physics*. Anchor, Garden City, N.Y., 1987.

M. Hirvensalo. *Quantum Computing*. Springer, New York, 2001.

M.H. Holzscheiter. Ion-trap quantum computation. *Los Alamos Science*. Available at http://library.lanl.gov/cgi-bin/getfile?27-20.pdf.

R. Jozsa and B. Schumacher. A new proof of the quantum noiseless coding theorem. *Journal of Modern Optics*, 41(12):2343–2349, 1994.

M. Kernaghan. Bell–Kochen–Specker theorem for 20 vectors. *Journal of Physics A*, 27:L829–L830, 1994.

A.Yu. Kitaev, A.H. Shen, and M.N. Vyalyi. *Classical and Quantum Computation (Graduate Studies in Mathematics)*. American Mathematical Society, 2002.

E. Knill. Conventions for quantum pseudocode. *Los Alamos National Laboratory Technical Report*, LAUR-96-2724, 1996.

E. Knill, R. Laflamme, A. Ashikhmin, H. Barnum, L. Viola, and W.H. Zurek. Introduction to quantum error correction. 2002. Available at http://arxiv.org/abs/quant-ph/0207170.

N. Koblitz. *A Course in Number Theory and Cryptography, Second Edition*. Springer, New York, 1994.

D.R. Kuhn. A hybrid authentication protocol using quantum entanglement and symmetric cryptography. 2003. Available at http://arxiv.org/abs/quant-ph/0301150.

R. Landauer. Information is physical. *Physics Today*, 44:23–29, 1991.

S. Lang. *Introduction to Linear Algebra, Second Edition*. Springer, New York, 1986.

S. Lang. *Algebra, Third Edition*. Addison-Wesley, Reading, Mass., 1993.

C.F. Lee and N.F. Johnson. Let the quantum games begin. *Physics World*, 2002. Available at http://physicsworld.com/cws/article/print/9995.

S. Lloyd. Almost any quantum logic gate is universal. *Physical Review Letters*, 75 (2):346–349, 1995.

S.J. Lomonaco. Notes on quantum information theory. 1996. Available at http://www.cs.umbc.edu/ lomonaco/lecturenotes/Qinfo.pdf.

S.J. Lomonaco Jr. A talk on quantum cryptography, or how Alice outwits Eve, 2001. In Quantum Computation: A Grand Mathematical Challenge for the 21st Century Ed by Somuel J. Lomonaco.

J.L. Martin. *Basic Quantum Mechanics (Oxford Physics Series)*. Oxford University Press, New York, 1982.

B. Mazur. *Imagining Numbers (Particularly the Square Root of Minus Fifteen)*. Farrar, Straus and Giroux, New York, 2002.

R. Nagarajan, N. Papanikolaou, and D. Williams. Simulating and compiling code for the sequential quantum random access machine, 2005. Available at http://www.dcs.warwick.ac.uk/ nikos/downloads/newpaper.pdf.

P.J. Nahin. *An Imaginary Tale: The Story of i (The Square Root of Minus One)*. Princeton University Press, Princeton, N.J., 1998.

T. Needham. *Visual Complex Analysis*. Oxford University Press, New York, 1999.

W.K. Nicholson. *Linear Algebra with Applications, Third Edition*. PWS Publishing Company, Boston, 1994.

M.A. Nielsen. Quantum entropy. A PowerPoint presentation available at http://michaelnielsen.org/blog/qicss/entropy.ppt.

M.A. Nielsen and I.L. Chuang. *Quantum Computation and Quantum Information*. Cambridge University Press, Cambridge, UK, 2000.

B Ömer. Quantum programming in qcl. 2000. Available at http://tph.tuwien.ac.at/ oemer/doc/quprog.pdf.

M. O'Nan. *Linear Algebra, Second Edition*. Harcourt Brace Jovanovich, Inc., New York, 1976.

H.R. Pagels. *The Cosmic Code: Quantum Physics as the Language of Nature*. Simon & Schuster, New York, 1982.

C.H. Papadimitriou. *Computational Complexity*. Addison-Wesley, Reading, Mass., 1994.

R.C. Penney. *Linear Algebra, Ideas and Applications*. John Wiley & Sons, New York, 1998.

R. Penrose. *Shadows of the Mind: A Search for the Missing Science of Consciousness*. Oxford University Press, Oxford, UK, 1994.

R. Penrose. *The Emperor's New Mind: Concerning Computers, Minds, and the Laws of Physics (Popular Science)*. Oxford University Press, Oxford, UK, 1999.

R. Penrose. *The Road to Reality: A Complete Guide to the Laws of the Universe*. Knopf, New York, 2005.

I. Pitowsky. George Boole's "conditions of possible experience" and the quantum puzzle. *The British Journal for the Philosophy of Science*, 45(1):95–125, 1994.

T.B. Pittman, B.C. Jacobs, and J.D. Franson. Quantum computing using linear optics. *Johns Hopkins APL Technical Digest*, 25(2), 2004. Available at http://arxiv.org/ftp/quant-ph/papers/0406/0406192.pdf.

J. Polkinghorne. *Quantum Theory, A Very Short Introduction*. Oxford University Press, Oxford, UK, 2002.

R. Raussendorf and H.J. Briegel. A one-way quantum computer. *Physical Review Letters*, 86(22), May 2001, 5188–5191.

R.L. Rivest, A. Shamir, and L. Adleman. A method for obtaining digital signatures and public-key cryptosystems. *Communications of the ACM*, 21(2):120–126, 1978.

P. Rodgers. The double-slit experiment. *Physics World*, 2002. Available at http://physicsworld.com/cws/article/print/9745.

K.H. Rosen. *Discrete Mathematics and Its Applications, Fifth Edition*. McGraw-Hill, Boston, 2003.

K.A. Ross and C.R.B. Wright. *Discrete Mathematics, Fifth Edition*. Prentice-Hall, Upper Saddle River, N.J., 2003.

R. Rüdiger. Quantum programming languages: An introductory overview. *The Computer Journal*, 50(2):134–150, 2007. Available at http://comjnl.oxford-journals.org/cgi/content/abstract/50/2/134.

J.J. Sakurai. *Modern Quantum Mechanics*, Revised edition, Addison-Wesley Publishing Company, Reading, Mass., 1994.

K. Sayood. *Introduction to Data Compression, Third Edition.* Morgan Kaufmann, Amsterdam, 2005.

B. Schneier. *Applied Cryptography: Protocols, Algorithms, and Source Code in C, Second Edition.* John Wiley, & Sons, New York, 1995.

B. Schumacher. Quantum coding. *Physical Review A,* 51(4):2738–2747, 1995.

H. Schwerdtfeger. *Geometry of Complex Numbers.* Dover Publications, Mineola, N.Y., 1980.

P. Selinger. A brief survey of quantum programming languages. In Y. Kameyama and P.J. Stuckey, editors, *Functional and Logic Programming, 7th International Symposium, FLOPS 2004,* Nara, Japan, April 7–9, 2004, volume 2998 of Lecture Notes in Computer Science, pages 1–6. Springer, New York, 2004a.

P. Selinger. Towards a quantum programming language. *Mathematical Structures in Computer Science,* 14(4):527–586, 2004b. Available at http://www.mathstat. dal.ca/ selinger/papers/qpl.pdf.

C.E. Shannon. A mathematical theory of communication. *Bell System Technical Journal,* 27:379–423, 623–656, 1948.

P.W. Shor. Algorithms for quantum computation: Discrete logarithms and factoring. In S. Goldwasser, editor, *Proceedings of the 35th Annual Symposium on the Foundations of Computer Science,* pages 124–134, . IEEE Computer Society, Los Alamitos, Calif., 1994.

P.W. Shor. Scheme for reducing decoherence in quantum computer memory. *Physical Review A,* 52(4):R2493–R2496, 1995.

P.W. Shor. Polynomial-time algorithms for prime factorization and discrete logarithms on a quantum computer. *SIAM Journal Computing,* 26(5):1484–1509, 1997.

P.W. Shor. Introduction to quantum algorithms. In *Quantum Computation: A Grand Mathematical Challenge for the Twenty-First Century and the Millennium,* (Washington, DC, 2000), volume 58 of *Proceedings of the Symposium in Applied Mathematics,* pages 143–159. American Mathematical Society, Providence, R.I., 2002.

P.W. Shor. Why haven't more quantum algorithms been found? *Journal of the ACM,* 50(1):87–90, 2003.

R.A. Silverman. *Introductory Complex Analysis.* Dover Publications, Mineola, N.Y., 1984.

D.R. Simon. On the power of quantum computation. In *Proceedings of the 35th Annual Symposium on Foundations of Computer Science,* pages 116–123, Institute of Electrical and Electronic Engineers Computer Society Press, Los Alamitos, Calif., 1994.

D.R. Simon. On the power of quantum computation. *SIAM Journal Computing,* 26(5):1474–1483, 1997.

M. Sipser. *Introduction to the Theory of Computation, Second Edition*. Thomson Course Technology, Boston, 2005.

A.M. Steane. The ion trap quantum information processor. *Applied Physics B*, 64, 623, 1997.

A. Sudbery. *Quantum Mechanics and the Particles of Nature: An Outline for Mathematicians*. Cambridge University Press, Cambridge, UK, 1986.

D.H. Towne. *Wave Phenomena*. Dover Publications, Mineola, N.Y., 1989.

L.M.K. Vandersypen, G. Breyta, M. Steffen, C.S. Yannoni, M.H. Sherwood, and I.L. Chuang. Experimental realization of Shor's quantum factoring algorithm using nuclear magnetic resonance. *Nature*, 414(6866):883–887, 2001.

U.V. Vazirani. A survey of qunatum complexity theory. In S. Lomonaco, Jr., editor, *Quantum Computation: A Grand Mathematical Challenge for the Twenty-First Century and the Millennium*, pages 193–217, 2002.

J. Watrous. On quantum and classical space-bounded processes with algebraic transition amplitudes. In *IEEE Symposium on Foundations of Computer Science*, pages 341–351, 1999.

R.L. White. *Basic Quantum Mechanics*. McGraw-Hill, New York, 1966.

S. Wiesner. Conjugate coding. *SIGACT News*, 15(1):78–88, 1983.

W.K. Wootters and W.H. Zurek. A single quantum cannot be cloned. *Nature*, 299(5886):802–803, October 1982.

A.C-C. Yao. Quantum circuit complexity. In *Proceedings of 34th IEEE Symposium on Foundations of Computer Science*, pages 352–361, 1993.

S. Zachos. Robustness of probabilistic computational complexity classes under definitional perturbations. *Information and Control*, 54(3):143–154, 1982.

P.A. Zizzi. Emergent consciousness: From the early universe to our mind. Available at http://arxiv.org/abs/gr-qc/0007006.

W.H. Zurek. Decoherence and the transition from quantum to classical – revisited. June 2003. Available at http://arxiv.org/abs/quant-ph/0306072.

Index

Printed in the United States
by Baker & Taylor Publisher Services